Purdah

Purdah

An Anthology

Edited by

EUNICE DE SOUZA

OXFORD
UNIVERSITY PRESS

OXFORD
UNIVERSITY PRESS

YMCA Library Building, Jai Singh Road, New Delhi 110 001

Oxford University Press is a department of the University of Oxford. It furthers the
University's objective of excellence in research, scholarship, and education
by publishing worldwide in

Oxford   New York
Auckland   Bangkok   Buenos Aires   Cape Town   Chennai
Dar es Salaam   Delhi   Hong Kong   Istanbul   Karachi   Kolkata
Kuala Lumpur   Madrid   Melbourne   Mexico City   Mumbai
Nairobi   Sao Paulo   Shanghai   Taipei   Tokyo   Toronto

Oxford is a registered trademark of Oxford University Press
in the UK and in certain other countries

Published in India
by Oxford University Press, New Delhi

ISBN 0 195666615

Typeset in Times New Roman by Jojy Philip, New Delhi 110 020
Printed by Roopak Printers, Delhi 110 032
Published by Manzar Khan, Oxford University Press
YMCA Library Building, Jai Singh Road, New Delhi 110 001

Acknowledgements

The editor and the publisher are happy to acknowledge the following individuals and organizations for their permission to reproduce the essays and articles in this volume: C.M. Naim for 'How Bibi Ashraf Learned To Read and Write'; Sahitya Akademi for Rajender Singh Bedi's 'Lajwanti' and B.P. Sathe's 'Face Showing'; C.W.D.S. for Malavika Karlekar's 'Constructions of Nineteenth-Century Bengal: Readings from *Janaika Grihabadhur Diary*'; Carcanet Press Ltd. for Rashid Jahan's, 'Behind the Veil'; Bhatkal and Sen for S.J. Joshi, chapter 7, *Anandi Gopal* (trans. Asha Damle), Calcutta: Stree, 1992; *Katha* for the extract from 'More from the Autobiography' (trans. Rashmi Govind) in *Ismat: Her Life, Her Times*, Sukrita Paul Kumar and Sadique (eds), Delhi: Katha, 2000.

The editor wishes to thank Gail Minault for sending her Begum Sultan Jahan's 'The Necessity of Purdah' and C.M. Naim's 'How Bibi Ashraf Learned to Read and Write'; Keith Fernandes for sending her Rokeya Sakhawat Hossain's work; S. Anandhi for *Rhetoric and Reform* by Ayesha Khan; Deepak Ananth, Danielle Sargent for material on Louis Rousselet, Dr Ramesh Patkar and Padma Lokur for information about S.J. Joshi, Mr Colin Rowe of Partnership House Mission Studies Library, London, and School of Oriental and African Studies for information about missionaries, the *Economic and Political Weekly* for sending her old issues of the journal, and the library of The University of Mumbai for their endless help.

Contents

Introduction   xi

WESTERN ACCOUNTS   1

MRS MEER HASSAN ALI   3
   Introduction
   Letter XII
      —Observations on the Mussulmans of India
FANNY PARKES   22
      —Wanderings of a Pilgrim in Search of the Picturesque
MRS COLIN (HELEN) MACKENZIE   23
   Funeral Scene in a Zenana
      —Life in the Mission, the Camp and the Zenana
LOUIS ROUSSELET   27
   Bhopal
      —India and Its Native Princes
MARCHIONESS OF DUFFERIN AND AVA   41
   Chapter VIII
      —Our Viceregal Life in India
SIR MONIER MONIER-WILLIAMS   45
      —Modern India and the Indians
SIR LEPEL GRIFFIN   61
   Introduction
      —Woman's Influence in the East
MRS MARCUS FULLER   66
   The Zenana
      —The Wrongs of Indian Womanhood
REV. EDWARD STORROW   78
   Daily Life
      —Our Indian Sisters

J.K.H. DENNY 90

The Beginnings of the Work

Wives and Widows
— *Toward the Sunrising*

ANNIE BESANT 99

The Education of Indian Girls
—*For India's Uplift*

SISTER NIVEDITA (MARGARET NOBLE) 105

The Hindu Woman as Wife

Woman in the National Life
—*The Web of Indian Life*

KATHLEEN OLGA VAUGHAN 113

Osteomalacia in Kashmir
—*The Purdah System and its Effect on Motherhood*

FRIEDA HAUSWIRTH 124

Women in the Zenana

Some 'Helpless' Women of India
—*Purdah: The Status of Indian Women*

CHARLOTTE WISER 139
—*Four Families of Karimpur*

GAIL MINAULT 144
—'Urdu Women's Magazines in The Early Twentieth Century'

DR MEREDITH BORTHWICK 156

Dress Reform and Ideas of Modesty
—'Erosion of Purdah'

INDIAN PERCEPTIONS 167

SIR SYED AHMED KHAN 169
—'The Education of Mohammedan Girls'

CHIRAG ALI 172
—'The Position of Woman'

P.N. BOSE 180

Social Condition
—*A History of Hindu Civilization During British Rule*

MAULANA ASHRAF ALI THANAVI 191
—The First Book of the *Bihishti Zewar*

S. KHUDA BUKHSH 212

Thoughts on the Present Situation
—*Essays Indian and Islamic*

SULTAN JEHAN BEGUM   220
 —*Al Hijab or the Necessity of Purdah*

ROKEYA SAKHAWAT HOSSAIN   240
 —*The Secluded Ones*

AMEERALI SYED   246
 The Status of Women in Islam
 —*The Spirit of Islam*

DR RUKHMABAI   256
 —'Purdah—The Need for its Abolition'

DR KALIKINKAR DATTA   260
 Education of Women
 —*Dawn of Renascent India*

HUSAIN B. TYABJI   275
 Social Reform
 —*Badruddin Tyabji*

MALAVIKA KARLEKAR   285
 —'Constructions of Femininity in Nineteenth Century Bengal'

MAITHILI RAO   306
 —'Screen Image'

FIRST PERSON ACCOUNTS   315

C.M. NAIM   317
 —'How Bibi Ashraf Learned to Read and Write'

SHAH JAHAN BEGUM   336
 Part II
 —*The History of Bhopal*

RASSUNDARI DEVI   361
 The Sixth Composition
 — *Amar Jiban*

NAWAB SULTAN JAHAN BEGUM   365
 Chapter III
 Chapter VI
 — *An Account of My Life*

SUNITY DEVEE MAHARANEE OF COOCH BEHAR   385
 My Childhood
 —*The Autobiography of an Indian Princess*

BIPAN CHANDRA PAL   391
 In the Days of My Youth
 —*Memories of My Life and Times*

x • Contents

MOHAMED ALI   399
—*My Life: A Fragment*
SHAISTA SUHRAWARDY IKRAMULLAH   420
Adjustment
Twilight of an Empire
—*From Purdah to Parliament*
ISMAT CHUGTAI   433
More from the Autobiography
—*Kaghazi hai Pairahan*
SAHIBZADA ATA MUHAMED KHAN   437
—Quoted in *Lives of the Princes*

LITERARY EVOCATIONS   439
ARDERSHIR F.J. CHINOY AND MRS DINBAI A.F. CHINOY   441
—*Pootli: A Story of Life in Bombay*
RABINDRANATH TAGORE   445
Bimala's Story
—*The Home and the World*
ROMESH CHUNDER DUTT   456
What the Women-Folk Said
—*The Lake of Palms*
RASHID JAHAN   462
—'Behind the Veil'
YASHPAL   475
—'The Curtain'
RAJINDER SINGH BEDI   481
—'Lajwanti'
S.J. JOSHI   492
Chapter 7
—*Anandi Gopal*
IQBALUNNISSA HUSSAIN   507
Chapter V
Chapter VI
Chapter VII
—*Purdah and Polygamy*
SAROJINI NAIDU   542
—'The Pardah Nashin'
B.P. SATHE   544
—'Face-Showing'
Bibliography   550

Introduction

For the purposes of this anthology, purdah is understood in its wider sense—not just the burqua of whatever design worn by some Muslim women, or the face covered by the pallav, but the elaborate codes of seclusion and feminine modesty used to protect and control the lives of women. However, despite the fact that a great deal of literature exists on the subject in empirical, theoretical, polemical, and historical terms, it is difficult to arrive at any neat and precise conclusions about the history and evolution of the practice, its regional and class differences. The Khoja Ismaili followers of the Aga Khan, for instance, were told by the Aga Khan to discard purdah.[1] History is used to claim that purdah existed in Hindu society long before the Muslims came, and textual evidence is produced to show that all upper class women were secluded in the Mauryan period (322–183 BC), and that Buddhist and Sanskrit texts refer to seclusion.[2] Other scholars produce other texts to show that there was no seclusion in ancient India.

Broadly, one can say that purdah in Hindu society involved not just the separation of women from male in-laws but also controlled the extent to which a woman could meet with and talk to her husband. The focus in Muslim culture was on the seclusion of girls who had reached puberty, whether they were married or not.[3] These notions of feminine modesty were (and often still are) widely accepted by upper and middle class families, and families that wished to emulate them as a sign of status.

In the widest sense, the attempt to provide a separate space for women can also be seen in railway travel and commuter trains, where separate compartments, and sometimes entire trains, called 'Ladies Specials', are provided for women, and separate seating in buses.

A wide variety of reasons for purdah exists: religious injunction, notions of female behaviour, group solidarity and defensiveness about identity, the control of sexual impulses in men and women, status, family honour and respectability, and, where women have property rights, the fear that misalliances would lead to the depletion of property.

Scholars too numerous to name have agreed that the Prophet improved the status of women. But there has been a great deal of controversy about whether he specified that women should be veiled or not. One of the verses which has been subject to varied interpretations is 24:31 of the Quran which states, 'And say to the believing woman that they lower their gaze and restrain their sexual passions and do not display their adornment except what appears thereof.' According to some commentators, it is the phrase *ma zahara minha* (what appears thereof) that has been disputed.[4] We are told that protocol required the faithful to address the Prophet's wives from behind a screen, but that later this became an excuse to segregate and veil women. It has also been suggested that purdah may have less to do with specifications in the Quran than with customs in the Byzantine and Sassanid territories, conquered about two hundred years after the Prophet's death. Women in these places wore the veil as a sign of rank, and as this was the time Muslim law was being consolidated, it may have led to rules about veiling.[5] Today, actual practice varies in Muslim countries. As for Hindu women, veiling is seen as 'part of a Hindu strategy of maintaining status under Islamic rule'.[6]

In the colonial period, questions were raised relating to reforming the 'excesses' of purdah, its implications for the education and health of secluded women, and the dangers of the erosion of purdah, along with debates on other 'social evils' such as sati, child marriage, the condition of widows and so on. Muslims permitted divorce and remarriage, so the main concerns of the reformers who were Muslim were the superstition, excessiveness, and wastefulness that had crept into religious and social practice. Polygamy was an issue for both Hindus and Muslims. But orthodox elements expressed the fear that the erosion of purdah would mean the 'unleashing of the pent-up sexuality of men and women jettisoning all social controls and notions of correct morality'.[7]

The struggle for reform was both cultural and political, and involved several, sometimes conflicting, elements. Negotiating the colonial critiques of Indian civilization was an important, though not the only, element in the arguments of reformers, revivalists, and the orthodox. James Mill's famous pronouncements about the treatment of women being a marker of civilizations is sometimes regarded as the cornerstone of the colonial critique. His *History of British India* was required reading at Haileybury College, at which administrators coming out to India were trained. Contempt was expressed for the way Indians treated women.

Further, such treatment was regarded as indicating that Indians were low down on the scale of civilizations, that it was important that the British rule, as Indians could certainly not be capable of ruling themselves. However, as consolation, there were the idealizing accounts of the orientalists looking for the harmonies of a pre-industrial state in Aryan and unchanging India.

Mill was wrong about a great many things. His periodization of history according to the religion of the rulers is simplistic. But in hindsight, it is sometimes difficult to say which did more damage—the disparagement or the idealization. The periodization of history, the appeal of a pre-Muslim Golden Age, both proved to be useful fodder for elements which could safely blame the Muslims for everything. But Mill's statement about the treatment of women as a marker of civilization is worth taking seriously (we would now add human rights, the treatment of animals, and the environment). Women in the England of Mill's day were equally though less obviously and less sensationally oppressed, as commentators in the West, both before and after Mill, pointed out. And reaction to unfavourable accounts by Westerners was not the only component of reform. To think so is to ignore centuries of debate about society in India. In various ways, the great religious movements—Buddhist, bhakti, and others—were critiques of prevailing practice, and so were the more than three hundred versions of the Ramayana, some of which foreground women's concerns, while others think of Ravana as the hero of the epic. As Sheldon Pollock has observed: 'Critique, rejection, and reform did not begin in 1800 in India, and their epistemological building blocks, "authentic tradition" and the like are not ideas that spring forth for the first time from the fevered brains of Colebrook, Bentinck, and Rammohan Roy.'[8]

Many Indian intellectuals and reformers were influenced by British and French political philosophers, among others. But there were also reformers such as Vidyasagar (1820–91) who did not have a Western education, and Kandukuri Virasaligam Pantulu (1848–1919), a Brahmin born in Rajahmundry, whose reference point was not the colonial critiques. He conducted his debates in Telugu, the language he championed, and he fought for vernacular education, female education, and widow remarriage. Jotirao Phule (1827–90) and Gopal Hari Deshmukh (1823–92) were non-Brahmins who fought for women, but also attacked Brahmanical power and practice.

It is also useful to be reminded, as Kumari Jayawardena reminds us, that colonialism did not speak with a single voice. Many 'daughters in exile spoke with other voices and shouldered other burdens. They crossed boundaries of accepted race, gender and class positions, proclaiming "sisterhood" and taking stands against colonial rule, thereby problematizing many issues of feminism and nationalism.'[9] Those who wish to subordinate women find it convenient to dismiss feminism as a foreign ideology, she remarked in an earlier book, and 'it should therefore be stressed that feminism, like socialism, has no particular ethnic identity....'[10]

Muslims began to face the challenge of decline after the death of Aurangzeb in 1701, and the decay of the Moghul empire. But the most devastating and humiliating challenge came with the events of 1857 with the virtual extinction of political and social power. Sections of the elite, even those who had been opposed to British rule, began to feel that survival and regeneration depended in some measure on accommodation with the British. The theme of decline haunts the work of many Muslim scholars and writers. Khwaja Altaf Husain Hali (1837–1914) attacked bigoted clerics who had reduced a great religion to a matter of rules about baths and moustaches, in *Mussadas: Madd o Jazr-Islam* (1879). Chirag Ali (1844–95) analyses the verses of the Quran to show that Islam had in fact improved the status of women. The response to the crisis can be divided roughly into the modernist camp of Aligarh, and the orthodox Deoband school, but few of the people involved were in one camp to the exclusion of the other.

In brief, both Hindu and Muslim reformers drew on their own traditions and personal experiences, made their choices from among the options open to them, and determined the direction of change, whether the questions involved were 'social evils' or 'English studies' (regarded in some quarters today as a social evil). Some argued on the basis of religious texts, others such as Vidyasagar were agnostics, while some were liberal humanists. Their lives and work make absorbing reading; so do their struggles to work out 'solutions'. In the process, they often alienated people, as Rammohan Roy alienated his family and orthodox Hindus, and found themselves virtually friendless. If Roy attacked sati as 'murder according to every Shastra',[11] he also attacked missionaries who vilified India. The history of the reformers contains many moving stories, some of which are included in this anthology. Yet one finds them critiqued, in a somewhat judgmental way, for working within the prevailing structure instead of reordering it.

With the re-publication of many of their texts, the women reformers are now better known than they used to be. Rokeya Sakhawat Hossain (1880–1932) has become something of a heroine of the canon for attempting to change the terms of the debate. She argued that the oppression women faced was man-made and not divinely ordained. 'In ancient times whoever had become renowned to others by his own merit made himself known as a god or a god-sent messenger.... So you see that these scriptures are nothing but regulations made by men.'[12] She urged women to find the courage they had lost by seclusion, to go out and work, and not think of marriage and children as the ultimate goal of life. Her utopian fantasy 'Sultana's Dream' (1905) envisages a world in which women take over the administration of a country while men are kept in seclusion. (A similar novel was written by Li Ruzhen in China in 1825, entitled *Flowers in the Mirror.*)[13] 'Sultana's Dream' is a brilliant piece of writing, but perhaps the choice of genre indicates that she was aware of the limits of the possible.

Pandita Ramabai (1858–1922) was a brave and lonely figure. Reviled for becoming a Christian, she was faced with suspicion about her motives even when she opened schools and homes for destitutes. But on doctrinal matters she chose to be independent, as her letters to Sr Geraldine indicate,[14] and this brought her into conflict with her friends.

The nationalist struggle was both good and bad for women. On the one hand, Gandhi, who returned from South Africa in 1915, encouraged women to participate in the civil disobedience movement, and urged them to spin for work and money, and also to recognize the dignity of labour.[15] In fact, his movement of passive resistance has been discussed as a movement eminently suited to women.[16] But many nationalists also expected women to look to the larger struggle and subsume their own interests. The political struggle also gave an extra and often divisive dimension to the women's movements. Muslim women were urged by the Muslim League to form their own organizations, and to work for separate electorates. But blame for this cannot be apportioned only to the Muslim League. Part of the blame most go to the Indian National Congress and to the women's organizations themselves. For instance, Begum Sharifah Hamid Ali, described as a tireless worker for women's rights who rejected all politics that would divide India, was exasperated when she found that 'when she explained Muslim law to her co-workers, they either did not listen or could not understand her point'.[17] Rani Rajwade even told Jawaharlal Nehru that Begum Sharifah was thinking 'along communal lines'.[18] Purdah tended to be regarded as a Muslim problem, and 'worried that condemnation of purdah might be seen as cultural imperialism, the women's organizations adjusted to it as a fact of life and only vaguely condemned it in resolutions'.[19] For Muslim women, more than for most women, coming out of purdah was fraught with the ideological trap of identity, particularly after 1947.

Emergence from purdah has been seen as 'a corollary of female education'.[20] The Government, however, was not particularly interested in either the problems of purdah women or in women's education. Purdah was administratively a nuisance: special arrangements had to be made in court cases as judges refused to hear such cases in chambers, for instance. Where education was concerned, Mary Carpenter, the reformer, repeatedly urged administrators to take interest in the area, as there was a growing interest in female education but many difficulties. Female teachers were hard to come by. Indians did not regard the job favourably, and women who came from abroad would have to respect the government's decision not to interfere in matters of religion, or attempt to make conversions.[21]

Indian reformers themselves were not always interested in women's education. Sir Syed Ahmed Khan (1817–98), described as one of the greatest educationists of the nineteenth century, prioritized the education of men. He founded the Anglo Oriental College at Aligarh, several schools, and a society to propagate and translate modern Western knowledge into Urdu. But he felt that the education women received at home was adequate for domestic happiness. Gail Minault has remarked that 'Sir Sayyid's views on women's education were consistent with his own cultural formation. His mother had been educated at home and showed that it was possible for a woman in purdah to be literate, pious, and an ethical force in her children's lives.'[22] Again, we are told that in 1920, at a meeting convened by non-Brahmins and Brahmin liberals in Poona to demand free compulsory female education, 'Tilak was violently opposed and driven away from the meeting when he argued that there were funds only for male education.'[23]

Formal education gradually replaced home education undertaken by father/husband/brother/teacher, and zenana education offered by missionaries. But setting up schools and keeping them going was no easy task. Parents had to be persuaded that it was worth giving girls formal education, purdah had to be maintained, and special transport arrangements organized. There were also debates about a suitable curriculum for girls.

The Brahmos were in the forefront of reform, and Brahmos, along with Christians, were among the first to send their girls out to school. But they appear to have been ambivalent about purdah. Keshub Chandra Sen (1839–84) believed women should be educated to make better mothers and wives, and that they did not need academic degrees. But he also initiated outings for purdah women to places of interest and arranged that the rest of the public should be kept out at such times. At the same time, while, among Brahmos, the sexes mixed freely at informal occasions, women were separated by a curtain at official religious occasions.[24] Arya Samaj schools with innovative curricula for girls came up notably in the Punjab, though students were required to wear full-length garments that revealed only the face, neck, hands, and feet.[25] Rokeya herself wore purdah to reassure families, though she did not believe in it herself.

Meredith Borthwick tell us: 'By 1886, a Hindu writer defined freedom for a woman in terms of being able to go out with her husband and talk to his friends. Women now talked to their husbands in the presence of others, travelled in open carriages, and attended the theatre and the circus.'[26] Borthwick adds that where visits to the theatre were concerned, it is unlikely that the women were Brahmos, as Brahmos disapproved of the theatre, among other reasons because the actresses were prostitutes, and the plays often ribald.[27]

By and large, women appear to have worked within the prevailing structure, though they worked for as much flexibility as they could within it. They too have been critiqued for this. But as Gail Minault observes, 'Women, once given a voice did not always turn out to be dutiful daughters: although most of them did. Elite women had many reasons to uphold the honour and status of their families, and few reasons to defy them. They too knew about the art of the possible.'[28] Minault is talking about Muslim women, but the statement can be more generally applied.

Significantly, some of the stories appearing is newspapers today could have been written more than a hundred years ago. There is, for instance, the story of Hajra Bi, who has become a role model for the children in her Mumbai slum (*TOI*, November 2000). Forced to drop out of school because the post-seventh standard school was too far away and parents were reluctant to send their girls there, Hajra Bi and her sister pined to go to school. When the Rahat Welfare Trust opened a new school in the neighbourhood, Irfan Merchant went from door to door to persuade parents to enrol their children. Sometimes the problems were financial, but for the most part the community was conservative. 'So we didn't exactly get queues', Mr Merchant observes. Hajra Bi and her sister did well, went on to university, and Hajra Bi was chosen for a stint at Stockholm University where she worked with brain-damaged people. A picture of Hajra Bi with a headscarf accompanies the article. Another photograph (*TOI*, January 2002) shows burqua-clad demonstrators demanding that the wearing of the garment be optional.

I also have a personal story to tell. I was recently invited to a college set up by a Muslim trust. It is a co-educational college, and though it was built primarily to serve the local community, there were students of different faiths there. Many of the girls were in the new-style burquas, though some were not wearing the burqua at all. The atmosphere was relaxed, and the relationship between the girls and boys friendly and companionable. During the session, one of the girls told me that there had been a move among some teachers of other colleges to have certain poems (mine among them) removed from the syllabus as they were 'inappropriate'. From my experience of these matters, it usually means that some male teachers (and a few women) are embarrassed to discuss these poems in class because of references to sexual and bodily functions such as menses and pregnancy. It is rarely the students who have difficulty coping. One of the girls (in burqua) had in fact written a poem about the experience of reading such poems in class, and when invited to do so, read it to the audience. From an Urdu-medium background, she had written the poem in English and in free verse, and had written it well. She captured the voices of her fellow-students, and ended by saying that she wished she had done more to defend the poems. The poems depicted reality, she said, 'But people don't like reality.'

There is a voluminous amount of published material on purdah and female education. There are also several thousand references to purdah on the net, including sites that explain and defend purdah, offer chat rooms to secluded women, and carry news about purdah controversies: threats to force women to wear purdah in Kashmir, the unexplained popularity of purdah in parts of Kerala when, a few years ago, few women wore it. Among the reasons given is the destruction of the Babri Masjid, the high visibility of Hindu symbols, and the effect of the conversion of Kamala Das to Islam and her endorsement of purdah. Shops have now been named after her new name 'Surayya', and an enterpreneur advertises purdah with burqua-clad women driving cars, working at computers and so on. Traditional and modern is the message, while organizations are propagating the 'nice-girls-wear-purdah' attitude.

This anthology is divided into four sections: western accounts, Indian perceptions, first person accounts, and literary evocations. The attempt is to provide a range of attitudes to and experiences of purdah.

The western accounts include accounts by medical and faith missionaries, administrators, travellers, women who married into Indian families or made India and its causes their home, and sociologists who lived in a particular place for a long period of time. Judging by the amount of literature produced by visits to the zenana, such visits were an important part of the Indian experience. This led at least one woman, Eliza Lynn Linton (not included here) to exclaim impatiently against the women who 'swarm over India, knocking at the door of the Zenana, and doing their best to disturb the ancient serenity and seclusion of the Hindu home…. They do not stop to remember the ethnic and ethical differences between the East and West, nor can they believe in happiness where those differences exist.'[29]

Hopefully, the variety of responses to purdah in this section will do something to remedy the simplistic post-colonial reaction to these accounts, which treat them as if they all spoke with one voice. A recent example will illustrate this point: the Marchioness of Dufferin records her visit to a home in which the father-in-law repeatedly urged the Marchioness to lift the veil of his daughter-in-law and look at her. The Marchioness records that she did. But to a publisher's reader this was 'voyeuristic', though it is customary in India to lift the veil to look at the new daughter-in-law.[30]

Similarly, Indian perceptions vary from absolute adherence to purdah, to a belief that the seclusion of women and the general degraded condition of women is responsible for the decay of society. There is a line of critical writing by Muslims of their own community which should be better known. There are biographical pieces about major reformers, quotations from contemporary newspapers in some writings, and a piece on the film image of purdah. First person accounts include the redoubtable Begums of Bhopal who, in or out of purdah, were excellent and enlightened rulers. There are also the ordinary women who taught themselves to read and write clandestinely, accounts by one of the leaders of the Khilafat movement, and by people who lived in rural areas. There is at least one short anecdote about the absurd situations which purdah could create. Literary evocations include material in Bengali, Urdu, Dogri, Hindi, and English, with a range of attitudes to purdah—the failure of an experiment in bringing one's wife out of purdah, tragically depicted by Tagore, concepts of honour and the 'contaminated' woman, key texts of the Progressive Movement, and the writing of a novelist in English who should be better known.

Notes

1. Hanna Papanek, 'Purdah: Separate Worlds and Symbolic Shelter', in Hanna Papanek and Gail Minault (eds), *Separate Worlds*, New Delhi: Chanakya, 1982, p. 16.

2. Doranne Jacobson, 'Purdah and the Hindu Family in Central India', *Separate Worlds*, p. 86.

3. Dagmar Engels, *Beyond Purdah? Women in Bengal 1890–1930*, Delhi: OUP, 1999, p. 19.

4. Asghar Ali Engineer, *The Qur'an, Women and Modern Society*, Delhi: Sterling, 1999, pp. 65–74.

5. Malise Ruthven, *Islam in the World*, UK: Penguin Books, p. 87.

6. Meredith Borthwick, *The Changing Role of Women in Bengal 1849–1905*, Princeton: Princeton University Press, 1984, p. 229.

7. Catherine A. Robinson, *Tradition and Liberation: The Hindu Tradition in the Indian Women's Movement*, UK: Curzon Press, 1999, p. 30, for quotes from Mlll's *The History of British India* and the effect of the book on its readers.

8. Carol Breckenridge and Peter Van der Veer, 'Deep Orientalism? Notes on Sanskrit and Power Beyond the Raj', in *Orientalism and the Postcolonial Predicament: Perspectives on South Asia*, Philadelphia: University of Philadelphia Press, 1993, Delhi: OUP, 1994, p. 100.

9. Kumari Jayawardena quoted by Jasodhara Bagchi in 'Convergence Within Contradictions', *The Book Review*, October 2002, p. 19. Review of *The White Woman's Other Burden: Western Women in South Asia During British Rule*.

10. Kumari Jayawardena, preface to *Feminism and Nationalism in the Third World*, UK: Zed Books, 1986.

11. Bipan Chandra, *India's Struggle for Independence*, Delhi: Penguin Books, 1989.

12. Quoted in Ayesha Khan, *Rhetoric and Reform: Feminism Among Indian Muslims 1900–1940*, p. 33.

13. Kumari Jaywawardena, op. cit., p. 173.

14. A.B. Shah (ed.), *Letters and Correspondence of Pandita Ramabai*, Bombay: Maharashtra State Boards of Literature and Culture, 1977.

15. Amrit Srinivasan, 'Women and Reform of Indian Tradition, Gandhian Alternative', in Leela Kasturi and Vina Mazumdar (eds), *Women and Indian Nationalism*, Delhi: Vikas, 1994, p. 7.

16. Kasturi and Mazumdar, op. cit., Introduction, pp. lii–liii.

17. Geraldine Forbes, *Women in Modern India*, Cambridge: Cambridge University Press, 2000, p. 199.

18. Ibid., p. 200.

19. Ibid., p. 202.

20. Borthwick, op. cit., p. 265.

21. *Report on Female Education in India*, London: House of Commons, 1877.

22. Gail Minault, *Secluded Scholars*, Delhi: OUP, 1998, p. 19.

23. Kumari Jayawardena, op. cit., p. 85.

24. Borthwick, op. cit., pp. 230–1.

25. Madhu Kishwar, 'Arya Samaj and Women's Education', *Economic and Political Weekly*, Vol. XXI, Number 17, 26 April 1986, pp. 9–24.

26. Borthwick, op. cit., p. 268.

27. Ibid., p. 268.

28. Minault, op. cit., p. 307.

29. Quoted in Nancy Fix Anderson, 'Bridging Cross-Cultural Feminisms: Annie Besant and Women's Rights in England and India 1874–1933, *Women's History Review*, Vol. 3, Number 4, 1994, p. 568.

30. The Marchioness of Dufferin and Ava, *Our Vice-Regal Life in India*, Vol. I, London: John Murray, 1889, p. 79.

Western Accounts

Mrs Meer Hassan Ali

The editor of the second edition of Mrs Meer Hassan Ali's book W. Crooke tells us that 'very little is know about the authoress of this interesting book. She is reticent about the affairs of her husband and herself, and inquiries recently made at Lucknow, at the India office, and in other likely quarters in England, have added little to the scanty information we possess about her.'

Mrs Meer Hassan Ali was an English woman who married an aristocrat from Lucknow after she met him in England. The family she married into was said to be of Sayyid origin, descended from the martyrs Hasan and Husain. Mrs Meer Hassan Ali lived in India roughly from 1816 to 1828, much of the time in her father-in-law's house in Lucknow. The editor adds that in the course of her book she gives only one date, 18 September 1825. But she tells us nothing personal about herself or her husband, and nothing about court intrigues in Oudh. Again, almost nothing is known of her life after she left India permanently for England, except that she published her book there. The editor ruefully admits that much that he learnt was only conjecture or 'tradition' or deduction.

Introduction

Very little is known about the authoress of this interesting book. She is reticent about the affairs of her husband and of herself, and inquiries recently made at Lucknow, at the India Office, and in other likely quarters in England, have added little to the scanty information we possess about her.

The family of her husband claimed to be of Sayyid origin, that is to say, to be descended from the martyrs, Hasan and Husain, the sons of

Mrs Meer Hassan Ali, *Observations on the Mussulmans of India*, W. Crooke (ed.), London: Milford, 1917, 1st edn 1832, 3rd edn Karachi: Oxford Asia Historical Reprints, OUP, 1973.

Fātimah, daughter of the Prophet, by her marriage with her cousin-german, 'Alī, the father-in-law of the authoress, Mīr Hājī Shāh, of whom she speaks with affection and respect, was the son of the Qāzī, or Muhammadan law-officer, of Ludhiānā, in the Panjab. During his boy-hood the Panjab was exposed to raids by the Mahrattas and incursions of the Sikhs. He therefore, abandoned his studies, wandered about for a time, and finally took service with a certain Raja—where she does not tell us—who was then raising a force in expectation of an attack by the Sikhs. He served in at least one campaign, and then, while still a young man, made a pilgrimage thrice to Mecca and Kerbela, which gained him the title of Hājī, or pilgrim. While he was in Arabia he fell short of funds, but he succeeded in curing the wife of a rich merchant who had long suffered from a serious disease. She provided him with money to con-tinue his journey. He married under romantic circumstances an Arab girl named Fātimah as his second wife, and then went to Lucknow, which, under the rule of the Nawābs, was the centre in Northern India of the Shī'ah sect, to which he belonged. Here he had an exciting adventure with a tiger during a hunting party, at which the Nawāb, Shujā-ud-daula, was present. He is believed to have held the post of Peshnamāz, or 'leader in prayer', in the household of the eunuch, Almās 'Alī Khān, who is referred to by the authoress.

His son was Mīr Hasan 'Alī, the husband of the authoress. The tradition in Lucknow is that he quarrelled with his father and went to Calcutta, where he taught Arabic to some British officers and gained a knowledge of English. We next hear of him in England, when in May 1810 he was appointed assistant to the well-known oriental scholar, John Shakespear, professor of Hindustani at the Military College, Addiscombe, from 1807 to 1830, author of a dictionary of Hindustani and other educational works. Mention is made of two cadets boarding with Mīr Hasan 'Alī, but it does not appear from the records where he lived. After remaining at the College for six years he resigned his appointment on the ground of ill-health, with the intention of returning to India. He must have been an efficient teacher, because, on his resignation, the East India Company treated him with liberality. He received a gift of £50 as a reward for his translation of the Gospel of St. Matthew, and from the Court minutes it appears that on 17 December 1816, it was resolved to grant him 100 guineas to provide his passage and £100 for equipment. Further, the Bengal government was instructed to furnish him on his arrival with means to reach his native place, and to pay him a pension of Rs 100 *per mensem* for the rest of his life.[1]

A tradition from Lucknow states that he was sent to England on a secret mission, 'to ask the Home authorities to accept a contract of Oudh direct from Nasīr-ud-dīn Haidar, who was quite willing to remit the money of contract direct to England instead of settling the matter with the British Resident at Lucknow'. It is not clear what this exactly means. It may be that the King of Oudh, thinking that annexation was inevitable, may have been inclined to attempt to secure some private arrangement with the East India Company, under which he would remain titular sovereign, paying a tribute direct to the authorities in England, and that he wished to conduct these negotiations without the knowledge of the Resident at Lucknow. There does not seem to be independent evidence of this mission of Mīr Hasan 'Alī, and we are told that it was, as might have been expected, unsuccessful.

No mention is made of his wife in the official records, and I have been unable to trace her family name or the date and place of her marriage. Mīr Hasan 'Alī and his wife sailed for Calcutta, and travelled to Lucknow via Patna. She tells little of her career in India, save that she lived there for twelve years, presumably from 1816 to 1828, and that eleven years of that time were spent in the house of her father-in-law at Lucknow. In the course of her book she gives only one date, 18 September 1825, when her husband held the post of Tahsīldār, or sub-collector of revenue, at Kanauj in the British district of Farrukhābād. No records bearing on his career as a British official are forthcoming. Another Lucknow tradition states that on his arrival at the Court of Oudh from England he was, on the recommendation of the Resident, appointed to a post in the King's service on a salary of Rs 300 per annum. Subsequently he fell into disgrace and was obliged to retire to Farrukhābād with the court eunuch, Nawāb Mu'tamad-ud-daula, Āghā Mīr. With the restoration of Āghā Mīr to power, Hasan 'Alī returned to Lucknow, and was granted a life pension of Rs 100 *per mensem* for his services as Dārogha at the Residency, and in consideration of his negotiations between the King and the British government or the East India Company.

From the information collected at Lucknow it appears that he was known as Mīr Londonī, 'the London gentleman', and that he was appointed Safīr, or Attaché, at the court of King Ghāzī-ud-dīn Haidar, who conferred upon him the title of Maslaha-ud-daula, 'Counsellor of State'. By another account he held the post of Mīr Munshī, head native clerk or secretary to the British Resident.

One of the most influential personages in the court of Oudh during this period was that stormy petrel of politics, Nawāb Hakīm Mehndī. He had been the right-hand man of the Nawāb Sa'ādat Alī, and on the accession of his son Ghāzi-ud-dīn Haidar in 1814 he was dismissed on the ground that he had incited the King to protest against interference in Oudh affairs by the Resident, Colonel Baillie. The King at the last moment became frightened at the prospect of an open rupture with the Resident. Nawāb Hakīm Mehndī was deprived of all his public offices and of much of his property, and he was imprisoned for a time. On his release he retired into British territory, and in 1824 he was living in magnificent style at Fatehgarh. In that year Bishop Heber visited Lucknow and received a courteous letter from the Nawāb inviting him to his house at Fatehgarh. He gave the Bishop an assurance 'that he had an English housekeeper, who knew perfectly well how to do the honours of his establishment to gentlemen of her own nation. (She is, in fact, a singular female, who became the wife of one of the Hindustani professors at Hertford, now the Hukeem's dewan,[2] and bears, I believe, a very respectable character.)' The authoress makes no reference to Hakīm Mehndī, nor to the fact that she and her husband were in his employment.

The cause of her final departure from India is stated by W. Knighton in a highly coloured sketch of court life in the days of King Nasīr-ud-daula, *The Private Life of an Eastern King,* published in 1855. 'Mrs Meer Hassan was an English lady who married a Lucknow noble during a visit to England. She spent twelve years with him in India, and did not allow him to exercise a Moslem's privilege of a plurality of wives. Returning to England afterwards on account of her health, she did not again rejoin him.'[3] The jealousy between rival wives in a polygamous Musalmān household is notorious. 'A rival may be good, but her son never: a rival even if she be made of dough is intolerable: the malice of a rival is known to everybody: wife upon wife and heartburnings'—such are the common proverbs which define the situation. But if her separation from her husband was really due to this cause, it is curious that in her book she notes as a mark of a good wife that she is tolerant of such arrangements. 'She receives him [her husband] with undisguised pleasure, although she has just before learned that another member has been added to his well-peopled harem. The good and forbearing wife, by this line of conduct, secures to herself the confidence of her husband, who, feeling assured that the amiable woman has an interest in his happiness, will consult her and take her advice in the domestic affairs of his children by other wives, and even arrange by her judgement all the settlements for their marriages, & c. He can speak of other wives without restraint—for she knows he has others—and her education has taught her that they deserve her respect in proportion as they contribute to her husband's happiness.'[4]

It is certainly noticeable that she says very little about her husband beyond calling him in a conventional way 'an excellent husband' and 'a dutiful, affectionate son'. There is no indication that her husband accompanied her on her undated visit to Delhi, when she was received in audience by the King, Akbar II, and the Queen, who were then living in a state of semi-poverty. She tells us that they 'both appeared, and expressed themselves, highly gratified with the visit of an English lady, who could explain herself in their language without embarrassment, or the assistance of an interpreter, and who was the more interesting to them from the circumstance of being the wife of a Syaad.'[5]

From inquiries made at Lucknow it has been ascertained that Mīr Hasan 'Alī had no children by his English wife. By one or more native wives he had three children: a daughter, Fātimah Begam, who married a certain Mīr Sher 'Alī, of which marriage one or more descendants are believed to be alive; and two sons, Mīr Sayyid 'Alī or Mīran Sāhib, said to have served the British government as a Tahsīldār, whose grandson is now living at Lucknow, and Mīr Sayyid Husain, who became a Risāldār, or commander of a troop, in one of the Oudh Irregular Cavalry Regiments. One of his descendants, Mīr Aghā 'Alī Sāhib, possesses some landed property which was probably acquired by the Risāldār. After the annexation of Oudh Mīr Hasan 'Alī is said to have been paid a pension of Rs 100 *per mensem* till his death in 1863.

It is also worthy of remark that she carefully avoids any reference to the palace intrigues and maladministration which prevailed in Oudh during the reigns of Ghāzī-ud-dīn Haidar and Nasīr-ud-dīn Haidar, who occupied the throne during her residence at Lucknow. She makes a vague apology for the disorganized state of the country: 'Acts of oppression may sometimes occur in Native States without the knowledge even, and much less by the command of, the Sovereign ruler, since the good order of the government mainly depends on the disposition of the Prime Minister for the time being'[6]—a true remark, but no defence for the conduct of the weak princes who did nothing to suppress corruption and save their subjects from oppression.

Little is known of the history of Mrs Mīr Hasan 'Alī after her arrival in England. It has been stated that she was attached in some capacity to the household of the Princess Augusta, who died unmarried on September 22, 1840.[7] This is probable, because the list of subscribers to her book is headed by Queen Adelaide, the Princess Augusta, and other ladies of the Royal Family. She must have been in good repute among Anglo-Indians, because several well-known names appear in the list: H.T. Colebrooke, G.C. Haughton, Mordaunt Ricketts and his wife, and Colonel J. Tod.

The value of the book rests on the fact that it is a record of the first-hand experiences of an English lady who occupied the exceptional position of membership of a Musalmān family. She tells us nothing of her friends in Lucknow, but she had free access to the houses of respectable Sayyids, and thus gamed ample facilities for the study of the manners and customs of Musalmān families. Much of her information on Islām was obtained from her husband and his father, both learned, travelled gentlemen, and by them she was treated with a degree of toleration unusual in a Shī'ah household, this sect being rigid and often fanatical followers of Islām. She was allowed to retain a firm belief in the Christian religion, and she tells us that Mīr Hāji Shāh delighted in conversing on religious topics, and that his happiest time was spent in the quiet of night when his son translated to him the Bible as she read it.[8]

Her picture of zenana life is obviously coloured by her frank admiration for the people amongst whom she lived, who treated her with respect and consideration. It is thus to some extent idyllic. At the same time, it may be admitted that she was exceptionally fortunate in her friends. Her sketch may be usefully compared with that of Mrs Fanny Parkes in her charming book, *The Wanderings of a Pilgrim in Search of the Picturesque*. Mrs Parkes had the advantage of having acquired a literary knowledge of Hindustani, while Mrs Mīr Hasan 'Alī, to judge from the way in which she transliterates native words, can have been able to speak little more than a broken patois, knew little of grammar, and was probably unable to read or write the Arabic character. Colonel Gardner, who had wide and peculiar experience, said to Mrs Parkes: 'Nothing can exceed the quarrels that go on in the zenana, or the complaints the begams make against each other. A common complaint is "Such a one has been practising witchcraft against me". If the husband make a present to one wife, if it be only a basket of mangoes, he must make the same exactly to all the other wives to keep the peace. A wife, when in a rage with her husband, if on account of jealousy, often says, "I wish I were married to a grasscutter," i.e. because a grasscutter is so poor that he can only afford to have one wife.'[9] Mrs Parkes from her own experience calls the zenana 'a place of intrigue, and those who live within four walls cannot pursue a straight path; how can it be otherwise, when so many conflicting passions are called forth?'[10] She adds that 'Musalmānī ladies generally forget their learning when they grow up, or they neglect it. Everything that passes without the four walls is repeated to them by their spies; never was any place so full of intrigue, scandal, and chit-chat as a zenana.'[11] When she visited the Delhi palace she remarks: 'As for beauty, in a whole zenana there may be two or three handsome women, and all the rest remarkably ugly.'[12] European officers at the present day have no opportunities for acquiring a knowledge of the conditions of zenana life; but from the rumours that reach them they would probably accept the views of Mrs Parkes in preference to those of Mrs Mīr Hasan 'Alī.

Though her opinions on the life of Musalman ladies is to some extent open to criticism, and must be taken to apply only to the exceptional society in which she moved, her account of the religious feasts and fasts, the description of the marriage ceremonies and that of the surroundings of a native household are trustworthy and valuable. Some errors, not of much importance and probably largely due to her imperfect knowledge of the language, have been corrected in the notes of the present edition. It must also be understood that her knowledge of native life was confined to that of the Musalmāns, and she displays no accurate acquaintance with the religion, life or customs of the Hindus. The account in the text displays a bias in favour of the Shīah sect of Musalmāns, as contrasted with that of the Sunnīs. For a more impartial study of the question the reader is referred to Sir W. Muir, *Annals of the Early Caliphate, The Caliphate,* and to Major R. D. Osborn, *Islam under the Khalifs of Baghdad.*

Letter XII

The Zeenahnah.—Its interior described.—Furniture, decorations, &c.—The Purdah (curtains).—Bedstead.—The Musnud (seat of honour).—Mirrors and ornamental furniture disused.—Display on occasions of festivity.—Observations on the Mussulmaun Ladies.—Happiness in their state of seclusion.—Origin of secluding females by Mahumud.—Anecdote.—Tamerlane's command prohibiting females being seen in public.—The Palankeen.—Bearers.—Their general utility and contentedness of disposition.—Habits peculiar to Mussulmaun Ladies.—Domestic arrangements of a Zeenahnah.—Dinner and its accompanying observances.—The Lota and Lugguns.—The Hookha.—Further investigation of the customs adopted in Zeenahnahs.

Before I introduce the ladies of a Mussulmaun zeenahnah to your notice, I propose giving you a description of their apartments.

Imagine to yourself a tolerably sized quadrangle, three sides of which is occupied by habitable buildings, and the fourth by kitchens, offices, lumber rooms, &c.; leaving in the centre an open court-yard. The habitable buildings arc raised a few steps from the court; a line of pillars forms the front of the building, which has no upper rooms; the roof is flat, and the sides and back without windows, or any aperture through which air can be received. The sides and back are merely high walls forming an enclosure, and the only air is admitted from the fronts of the dwelling-place facing the court-yard. The apartments are divided into long halls, the extreme corners having small rooms or dark closets purposely built for the repository of valuables or stores; doors are fixed to these closets, which are the only places I have seen with them in a zeenahnah or mahul[13] (house or palace occupied by females); the floor is either of beaten earth, bricks, or stones; boarded floors are not yet introduced.

As they have neither doors nor windows to the halls, warmth or privacy is secured by means of thick wadded curtains, made to fit each opening between the pillars. Some zeenahnahs have two rows of pillars in the halls with wadded curtains to each, thus forming two distinct halls, as occasion may serve, or greater warmth be required: this is a convenient arrangement where the establishment of servants, slaves, &c., is extensive.

The wadded curtains are called purdahs;[14] these are sometimes made of woollen cloth, but more generally of coarse calico, of two colours, in patchwork style, striped, vandyked, or in some other ingeniously contrived and ornamented way, according to their individual taste.

Besides the purdahs, the openings between the pillars have blinds neatly made of bamboo strips, wove together with coloured cords: these are called jhillmuns or cheeks.[15] Many of them are painted green; others are more gaudy both in colour and variety of patterns. These blinds constitute a real comfort to every one in India, as they admit air when let down, and at the same time shut out flies and other annoying insects; besides which the extreme glare is shaded by them—a desirable object to foreigners in particular.

The floors of the halls are first matted with the coarse dateleaf matting of the country, over which is spread shutteringhies[16] (thick cotton carpets, peculiarly the manufacture of the Upper Provinces of India, wove in stripes of blue and white, or shades of blue); a white calico carpet covers the shutteringhie, on which the females take their seat.

The bedsteads of the family are placed, during the day, in lines at the back of the halls, to be moved at pleasure to any chosen spot for the night's repose; often into the open courtyard, for the benefit of the pure air. They are all formed on one principle, differing only in size and quality; they stand about half-a-yard from the floor, the legs round and broad at bottom, narrowing as they rise towards the frame, which is laced over with a thick cotton tape, made for the purpose, and platted in checquers, and thus rendered soft, or rather elastic, and very pleasant to recline upon. The legs of these bedsteads are in some instances gold, silver gilt, or pure silver; others have enamel paintings on fine wood; the inferior grades have them merely of wood painted plain and varnished;

the servants' bedsteads are of the common mango-wood without ornament, the lacing of these for the sacking being of elastic string manufac-
tured from the fibre of the cocoa-nut.

Such are the bedsteads of every class of people. They seldom have
mattresses; a soojinee[17] (white quilt) is spread on the lacing, over which
a calico sheet, tied at each corner of the bedstead with cords and tassels;
several thin flat pillows of beaten cotton for the head—a muslin sheet for
warm weather, and a well wadded ruzzie[18] (coverlid) for winter, is all
these children of Nature deem essential to their comfort in the way of
sleeping. They have no idea of night dresses; the same suit that adorns a
lady is retained both night and day, until a change be needed. The single
article exchanged at night is the deputtah,[19] and that only when it
happens to be of silver tissue or embroidery, for which a muslin or calico
sheet is substituted.

The very highest circles have the same habits in common with the
meanest, but those who can afford shawls of cashmere prefer them for
sleeping in, when the cold weather renders them bearable. Blankets are
never used except by the poorest peasantry, who wear them in lieu of
better garments night and day in the winter season: they are always
black, the natural colour of the wool. The ruzzies of the higher orders are
generally made of silk of the brightest hues, well wadded, and lined with
dyed muslin of assimilating colour; they are usually bound with broad-
silver ribands, and sometimes bordered with gold brocaded trimmings.
The middling classes have fine chintz ruzzies, and the servants and
slaves coarse ones of the same material; but all are on the same plan,
whether for a queen or the meanest of her slaves, differing only in the
quality of the material.

The mistress of the house is easily distinguished by her seat of honour
in the hall of a zeenahnah; a musnud[20] not being allowed to any other
person but the lady of the mansion.

The musnud carpet is spread on the floor if possible near to a pillar
about the centre of the hall, and is made of many varieties of fabric—
gold cloth, quilted silk, brocaded silk, velvet, fine chintz, or whatever
may suit the lady's taste, circumstances, or convenience. It is about two
yards square, and generally bordered or fringed, on which is placed the
all important musnud. This article may be understood by those who have
seen a lace-maker's pillow in England, excepting only that the musnud
is about twenty times the size of that useful little article in the hands of
our industrious villagers. The musnud is covered with gold cloth, silk,
velvet, or calico, with square pillows to correspond, for the elbows, the
knees, &c. This is the seat of honour, to be invited to share which, with

the lady-owner, is a mark of favour to an equal or inferior: when a superior pays a visit of honour, the prided seat is usually surrendered to her, and the lady of the house takes her place most humbly on the very edge of her own carpet.

Looking-glasses or ornamental furniture are very rarely to be seen in the zeenahnahs, even of the very richest females. Chairs and sofas are produced when English visitors are expected; but the ladies of Hindoostaun prefer the usual mode of sitting and lounging on the carpet; and as for tables, I suppose not one gentlewoman of the whole country has ever been seated at one; and very few, perhaps, have any idea of their useful purposes, all their meals being served on their floor, where dusthakhawns[21] (table-cloths we should call them) are spread, but neither knives, forks, spoons, glasses, or napkins, so essential to the comfortable enjoyment of a meal amongst Europeans. But those who never knew such comforts have no desire for the indulgence, nor taste to appreciate them.

On the several occasions, amongst Native society, of assembling in large parties, as at births and marriages, the halls, although extensive, would be inadequate to accommodate the whole party. They then have awnings of white calico, neatly flounced with muslin, supported on poles fixed in the court yard, and connecting the open space with the great hall, by wooden platforms which are brought to a line with the building, and covered with shutteringhie and white carpets to correspond with the floor-furniture of the hall; and here the ladies sit by day and sleep by night very comfortably, without feeling any great inconvenience from the absence of their bedsteads, which could never be arranged for the accommodation of so large an assemblage—nor is it ever expected.

The usually barren look of these almost unfurnished halls is on such occasions quite changed, when the ladies are assembled in their various dresses; the brilliant display of jewels, the glittering drapery of their dress, the various expressions of countenance, and different figures, the multitude of female attendants and slaves, the children of all ages and sizes in their variously ornamented dresses, are subjects to attract both the eye and the mind of an observing visitor; and the hall, which when empty appeared desolate and comfortless, thus filled, leaves nothing wanting to render the scene attractive.

The buzz of human voices, the happy playfulness of the children, the chaste singing of the domenies fill up the animated picture. I have sometimes passed an hour or two in witnessing their innocent amusements, without any feeling of regret for the brief sacrifice of time I had made. I am free to confess, however, that I have returned to my tranquil home with increased delight after having witnessed the bustle of a zeenahnah assembly. At first I pitied the apparent monotony of their lives; but this feeling has worn away by intimacy with the people, who are thus precluded from mixing generally with the world. They are happy in their confinement; and never having felt the sweets of liberty, would not know how to use the boon if it were to be granted them. As the bird from the nest immured in a cage is both cheerful and contented, so are these females. They have not, it is true, many intellectual resources, but they have naturally good understandings, and having learned their duty they strive to fulfil it. So far as I have had any opportunity of making personal observations on their general character they appear to me obedient wives, dutiful daughters, affectionate mothers, kind mistresses, sincere friends, and liberal benefactresses to the distressed poor. These are their moral qualifications, and in their religious duties they are zealous in performing the several ordinances which they have been instructed by their parents or husbands to observe. If there be any merit in obeying the injunctions of their Lawgiver, those whom I have known most intimately deserve praise, since 'they are faithful in that they profess'.

To ladies accustomed from infancy to confinement this is by no means irksome; they have their employments and their amusements, and though these are not exactly to our taste, nor suited to our mode of education, they are not the less relished by those for whom they were invented. They perhaps wonder equally at some of our modes of dissipating time, and fancy we might spend it more profitably. Be that as it may, the Mussulmaun ladies, with whom I have been long intimate, appear to me always happy, contented, and satisfied with the seclusion to which they were born; they desire no other, and I have ceased to regret they cannot be made partakers of that freedom of intercourse with the world we deem so essential to our happiness, since their health suffers nothing from that confinement, by which they are preserved from a variety of snares and temptations; besides which, they would deem it disgraceful in the highest degree to mix indiscriminately with men who are not relations. They are educated from infancy for retirement, and they can have no wish that the custom should be changed, which keeps them apart from the society of men who are not very nearly related to them. Female society is unlimited, and that they enjoy without restraint.

A lady whose friendship I have enjoyed from my first arrival in India, heard me very often speak of the different places I had visited, and she fancied her happiness very much depended on seeing a river and a bridge. I undertook to gain permission from her husband and father, that the treat might be permitted; they, however, did not approve of the lady being gratified, and I was vexed to be obliged to convey the disappointment to my friend. She very mildly answered me, 'I was much to blame to request what I knew was improper for me to be indulged in; I hope my husband and family will not be displeased with me for my childish wish; pray make them understand how much I repent of my folly. I shall be ashamed to speak on the subject when we meet.'

The habit of strict seclusion, however, originated in Hindoostaun with Tamerlane the conqueror of India.

...

When Tamerlane[22] with his powerful army entered India, he issued a proclamation to all his followers to the following purport, 'As they were now in the land of idolatry and amongst a strange people, the females of their families should be strictly concealed from the view of strangers'; and Tamerlane himself invented the several covered conveyances which are to the present period of the Mussulmaun history in use, suited to each grade of female rank in society. And the better to secure them from all possibility of contamination by their new neighbours, he commanded that they should be confined to their own apartments and behind the purdah, disallowing any intercourse with males of their own persuasion even, who were not related by the nearest ties, and making it a crime in any female who should willingly suffer her person to be seen by men out of the prescribed limits of consanguinity.

Tamerlane, it may be presumed, was then ignorant of the religious principles of the Hindoos. They are strictly forbidden to have intercourse or intermarry with females who are not strictly of their own caste or tribe, under the severe penalty of losing that caste which they value as their life. To this may be attributed, in a great degree, the safety with which female foreigners travel daak[23] (post) in their palankeens, from one point of the Indian continent to another, without the knowledge of five words of the Hindoostaunie tongue, and with no other servant or guardian but the daak-bearers, who carry them at the rate of four miles an hour, travelling day and night successively.

...

Those females who rank above peasants or inferior servants, are disposed from principle to keep themselves strictly from observation; all who have any regard for the character or the honour of their house, seclude themselves from the eye of strangers, carefully instructing their young daughters to a rigid observance of their own prudent example. Little girls, when four years old, are kept strictly behind the purdah, and when they move abroad it is always in covered conveyances, and under the guardianship of a faithful female domestic, who is equally tenacious as the mother to preserve the young lady's reputation unblemished by concealing her from the gaze of men.

The ladies of zeenahnah life are not restricted from the society of their own sex; they are, as I have before remarked, extravagantly fond of company, and equally as hospitable when entertainers. To be alone is a trial to which they are seldom exposed, every lady having companions amongst her dependants; and according to her means the number in her establishment is regulated. Some ladies of rank have from two to ten companions, independent of slaves and domestics; and there are some of the Royal family at Lucknow who entertain in their service two or three hundred female dependants, of all classes. A well-filled zeenahnah is a mark of gentility; and even the poorest lady in the country will retain a number of slaves and domestics, if she cannot afford companions; besides which they are miserable without society, the habit of associating with numbers having grown up with infancy to maturity: 'to be alone' is considered, with women thus situated, a real calamity.

On occasions of assembling in large parties, each lady takes with her a companion besides two or three slaves to attend upon her, no one expecting to be served by the servants of the house at which they are visiting. This swells the numbers to be provided for; and as the visit is always for three days and three nights (except on Eades, when the visit is confined to one day), some forethought must be exercised by the lady of the house, that all may be accommodated in such a manner as may secure to her the reputation of hospitality.

The kitchen and offices to the zeenahnah, I have remarked, occupy one side of the quadrangle; they face the great or centre hall appropriated to the assembly. These kitchens, however, are sufficiently distant to prevent any great annoyance from the smoke—I say smoke, because chimneys have not yet been introduced into the kitchens of the Natives. The fire-places are all on the ground, something resembling stoves, each admitting one saucepan, 'the Asiatic style of cooking requiring no other contrivance. Roast or boiled joints are never seen at the dinner of a Native: a leg of mutton or sirloin of beef would place the hostess under all sorts of difficulties, where knives and forks are not understood to be amongst the useful appendages of a meal. The variety of their dishes are countless, but stews and curries are the chief; all the others are mere varieties. The only thing in the shape of roast meats, are small lean cutlets bruised, seasoned and cemented with pounded poppy-seed, several being fastened together on skewers: they are grilled or roasted over a charcoal fire spread on the ground, and then called keebaab,[24] which word implies, roast meat.

The kitchen of a zeenahnah would be inadequate to the business of cooking for a large assembly; the most choice dishes only (for the highly favoured guests), are cooked by the servants of the establishment; The needed abundance required on entertaining a large party is provided by a regular bazaar cook, several of whom establish themselves in Native cities, or wherever there is a Mussulmaun population. Orders being previously given, the morning and evening dinners are punctually forwarded at the appointed hours in covered trays, each tray having portions of the several good things ordered so that there is no confusion in serving out the feast on its arrival at the mansion. The food thus prepared by the bazaar cook (naunbye,[25] he is called), is plain boiled-rice, sweet-rice, kheer[26] (rice-milk), mautungun[27] (rice sweetened with the addition of preserved fruits, raisins, &c., coloured with saffron), sallons[28] (curries) of many varieties, some cooked with vegetables, others with unripe fruits with or without meat; pillaus of many sorts, keebaabs, preserves, pickles, chatnees, and many other things too tedious to admit of detail.

The bread in general use amongst Natives is chiefly unleavened; nothing in the likeness of English bread is to be seen at their meals; and many object to its being fermented with the intoxicating toddy (extracted from a tree). Most of the Native bread is baked on iron plates over a charcoal fire. They have many varieties, both plain and rich, and some of the latter resembles our pastry, both in quality and flavour.

The dinners, I have said, are brought into the zeenahnah ready dished in the Native earthenware, on trays; and as they neither use spoons or forks, there is no great delay in setting out the meal where nothing is required for display or effect, beyond the excellent quality of the food and its being well cooked. In a large assembly all cannot dine at the dustha-khawn of the lady-hostess, even if privileged by their rank; they are, therefore, accommodated in groups of ten, fifteen, or more, as may be convenient; each lady having her companion at the meal, and her slaves to brush off the intruding flies with a chowrie, to hand water, or to fetch or carry any article of delicacy from or to a neighbouring group. The slaves and servants dine in parties after their ladies have finished, in any retired corner of the court-yard—always avoiding as much as possible the presence of their superiors.

Before any one touches the meal, water is carried round for each lady to wash the hand and rinse the mouth. It is deemed unclean to eat without this form of ablution, and the person neglecting it would be held unholy; this done, the lady turns to her meal, saying, 'Bis ma Allah!'—(In the name or to the praise of God!) and with the right hand conveys the food to her mouth, (the left is never used at meals);[29] and although they partake of every variety of food placed before them with no other aid than their fingers, yet the mechanical habit is so perfect, that they neither drop a grain of rice, soil the dress, nor retain any of the food on their fingers. The custom must always be offensive to a foreign eye, and the habit none would wish to copy; yet every one who witnesses must admire the neat way in which eating is accomplished by these really 'children of Nature'.

The repast concluded, the lota[30] (vessel with water), and the luggun[31] (to receive the water in after rinsing the hands and mouth), are passed round to every person, who having announced by the 'Shuggur Allah!'—All thanks to God!—that she has finished, the attendants present first the powdered peas, called basun[32]—which answers the purpose of soap in removing grease, &c., from the fingers—and then the water in due course. Soap has not even yet been brought into fashion by the Natives, except by the washermen; I have often been surprised that they have not found the use of soap a necessary article in the nursery, where the only substitute I have seen is the powdered pea.

Lotas and lugguns are articles in use with all classes of people; they must be poor indeed who do not boast of one, at least, in their family. They are always of metal, either brass, or copper lacquered over, or zinc; in some cases, as with the nobility, silver and even gold are converted into these useful articles of Native comfort.

China or glass is comparatively but little used; water is their only beverage, and this is preferred, in the absence of metal basins, out of the common red earthen katorah[33] (cup shaped like a vase).

China dishes, bowls, and basins, are used for serving many of the savoury articles of food in; but it is as common in the privacy of the palace, as well as in the huts of the peasantry, to see many choice things introduced at meals served up in the rude red earthen platter; many of the delicacies of Asiatic cookery being esteemed more palatable from the earthen flavour of the new vessel in which it is served.

I very well remember the first few days of my sojourn at Lucknow, feeling something bordering on dissatisfaction, at the rude appearance of the dishes containing choice specimens of Indian cookery, which poured in (as is customary upon fresh arrivals) from the friends of the family I had become a member of. I fancied, in my ignorance, that the Mussulmaun people perpetuated their prejudices even to me, and that they must fear I should contaminate their china dishes; but I was soon satisfied on this point: I found, by experience, that brown earthen platters were used by the nobility from choice; and in some instances, the viand would have wanted its greatest relish if served in China or silver vessels. Custom reconciles every thing: I can drink a draught of pure water now from the earthen katorah of the Natives with as much pleasure as from a glass or a silver cup, and feel as well satisfied with their dainties out of an earthen platter, as when conveyed in silver or China dishes.

China tea sets are very rarely found in the zeenahnah; tea being used by the Natives more as a medicine than a refreshment, except by such gentlemen as have frequent intercourse, with the 'Sahib Logue' (English gentry), among whom they acquire a taste for this delightful beverage. The ladies, however, must have a severe cold to induce them to partake of the beverage even as a remedy, but by no means as a luxury.[34] I imagined that the inhabitants of a zeenahnah were sadly deficient in actual comforts, when I found, upon my first arrival in India, that there were no preparations for breakfast going forward: every one seemed engaged in pawn eating, and smoking the hookha, but no breakfast after the morning Namaaz. I was, however, soon satisfied that they felt no sort of privation, as the early meal so common in Europe has never been introduced in Eastern circles. Their first meal is a good substantial dinner, at ten, eleven, or twelve o'clock, after which follow pawn and the hookha; to this succeeds a sleep of two or three hours, providing it does not impede the duty of prayer—the pious, I ought to remark, would give up every indulgence which would prevent the discharge of this duty. The second meal follows in twelve hours from the first, and consists of the same substantial fare; after which they usually sleep again until the dawn of day is near at hand.

It is the custom amongst Natives to eat fruit after the morning sleep, when dried fruits, confectionery, radishes, carrots, sugar-cane, green peas, and other such delicacies, are likewise considered wholesome luxuries, both with the ladies and the children. A dessert immediately after dinner is considered so unwholesome, that they deem our practice extremely injudicious. Such is the difference of custom; and I am disposed to think their fashion, in this instance, would be worth imitating by Europeans whilst residing in India.

I have been much amused with the curious inquiries of a zeenahnah family when the gardener's dhaullie is introduced A dhaullie,[35] I must first tell you, is a flat basket, on which is arranged, in neat order, whatever fruit, vegetables, or herbs are at the time in season, with a nosegay of flowers placed in the centre. They will often ask with wonder—'How do these things grow?'—'How do they look in the ground?'—and many such child-like remarks have I listened to with pity, whilst I have relieved my heart by explaining the operations of Nature in the vegetable kingdom, a subject on which they are perfectly ignorant, and from the habits of seclusion in which they live, can never properly be made to understand or enjoy.

I have said water is the only beverage in general use amongst the Mussulmaun Natives. They have sherbet, however, as a luxury on occasions of festivals, marriages, &c. This sherbet is simply sugar and water, with a flavour of rose-water, or kurah added to it.

The hookha is almost in general use with females. It is a common practice with the lady of the house to present the hookha she is smoking to her favoured guest. This mark of attention is always to be duly appreciated; but such is the deference paid to parents, that a son can rarely be persuaded by an indulgent father or mother to smoke a hookha in their revered presence—this praiseworthy feeling originates not in fear, but real genuine respect. The parents entertain for their son the most tender regard; and the father makes him both his companion and his friend; yet the most familiar endearments do not lessen the feeling of reverence a good son entertains for his father. This is one among the many samples of patriarchal life, my first Letter alluded to, and which I can never witness in real life, without feeling respect for the persons who follow up the patterns I have been taught to venerate in our Holy Scripture.

The hookha, as an indulgence of a privilege, is a great definer of etiquette. In the presence of the King or reigning Nuwaub, no subject, however high he may rank in blood or royal favour, can presume to smoke. In Native courts, on state occasions, hookhas are presented only to the Governor-General, the Commander-in-Chief, or the Resident at his Court, who are considered equals in rank, and therefore entitled to the privilege of smoking with him; and they cannot consistently resist the intended honour. Should they dislike smoking, a hint is readily understood by the hookha-bahdhaar[36] to bring the hookha, charged with the materials, without the addition of fire. Application of the munall[37] (mouth-piece) to the mouth indicates a sense of the honour conferred.

NOTES

1. Col H.M. Vibart, *Addiscombe*, pp. 39, 41, 42.

2. *Dīwān*, chief agent, manager.

3. William Knighton, *The Private Life of an Eastern King*, London: Hope and Co., 1855, p. 208.

4. Ibid., p. 182.

5. Ibid., p. 290.

6. Ibid., p. 227.

7. *Calcutta Review,* ii. 387.

8. See pp. 80, 422 (see p.3 for publication details).

9. *The Wanderings of a Pilgrim in Search of the Picturesque: During four and twenty years in the East; with Revelations of Life in the Zenana,* London: Pelham Richardson, Vol. i, pp. 230, 453.

10. Ibid., 391.

11. Ibid., 450.

12. Ibid., Vol. ii. 215.

13. *Mahall.*

14. *Parda.*

15. *Jhilmil, chiq,* the Anglo-Indian 'chick'.

16. *Shatranjī.*

17. *Sozanī (sozan,* 'a needle'), an embroidered quilt.

18. *Razāī,* a counterpane padded with cotton.

19. *Dopattā,* a double sheet.

20. Bolster.

21. *Dastarkhwān,* see p. 108.

22. Amīr Taimūr, known as Taimūr Lang, 'the lame', was born AD 1336; ascended the throne at Balkh, 1370; invaded India and captured Delhi, 1398; died 1405, and was buried at Samarkand. There seems to be no evidence that he introduced the practice of the seclusion of women, an ancient Semitic custom, which, however, was probably enforced on the people of India by the brutality of foreign invaders.

23. *Dāk.*

24. *Kabāb,* properly, small pieces of meat roasted on skewers.

25. *Nānbāī,* a baker of bread *(nān).*

26. *Khīr,* milk boiled with rice, sugar, and spices.

27. *Mutanjan,* a corruption of *muttajjan,* 'fried in a pan'; usually in the form *mutanjan pulāo,* meat boiled with rice, sugar, butter, and sometimes pine-apples or nuts.

28. *Sālan,* a curry of meat, fish, or vegetables.

29. The left hand is used for purposes of ablution.

30. The Musalmān *lotā,* properly called *badhnā,* differs from that used by Hindus in having a spout like that of a teapot.

31. *Lagan,* a brass or copper pan in which the hands are washed: also used for kneading dough.

32. *Besan,* flour, properly that of gram *(chanā).* The prejudice against soap is largely due to imitation of Hindus, who believe themselves to be polluted by fat. Arabs, after a meal, wash their hands and mouths with soap (Sir Richard Burton, *Personal Narratives of a Pilgrimage to Al-Madinah and Maccah,* London:

George Bell and Sons, 1898). Sir G. Watt (*A Dictionary of the Economic Products of India*, Calcutta: Government of India, Central Printing Office, 1889) gives a long list of other detergents and substitutes for soap.

33. *Katorā.*

34. The prejudice against the use of tea has much decreased since this book was written, owing to its cultivation in India. Musalmāns and many Hindus now drink it freely.

35. *Dālī,* the 'dolly' of Anglo-Indians.

36. *Huqqahbardār.*

37. Munhnal.

Fanny Parkes

Pat Barr in *The Memsahibs* gives us a particularly lively account of Fanny Parkes (1794–1875): '...Mrs Parkes had the born traveller's habit of popping in and out of people's lives in an unpredictable and unabashed fashion which irritated some. "We are rather oppressed just now by a lady, Mrs Parkes, who insists upon belonging to the camp", wrote Fanny Eden...Fanny Parkes did not see it in the same light. After all, when she had first "made her salaams" to the Misses Eden they had asked her to dine, had been glad to use her services as an interpreter on their visit to a reigning ranee (for she spoke fluent Hindstani in addition to her other accomplishments.'

Fanny Parkes' enthusiasm for everything she saw is contagious. She never tired of travelling in India, and despite every snub or difficulty, she was on her way with her tents, camels, horses, bullock-carts, and her unending zest. Through her friend Colonel Gardner, whose son James had married a niece of the Emperor Akbar Shah, Parkes had access to the Zenana. She has an interesting conversation with Baija Bai, a deposed Maratha queen, and her grand-daughter: she tells them that married women in England were as badly off as women in India. The laws of the land made them virtual slaves of their husbands.

4 February 1837

I spent the day at the Asiatic Society. A model of the foot of a Chinese lady in the collection is a curiosity, and a most disgusting deformity. The toes are crushed up under the foot, so as to render the person perfectly lame: this is a less expensive mode of keeping a woman confined to the house, than having guards and a zenana—the principle is the same.

Fanny Parkes, *The Wanderings of a Pilgrim in Search of the Picturesque: During four and twenty years in the East; with Revelations of Life in the Zenana*, Esther Chawner (ed.), Vol. 2, Karachi: OUP, 1975, 2nd edn.

Mrs Colin (Helen) Mackenzie

Mrs Colin Mackenzie's journal was originally intended for friends and family at home, and not for publication. When she did decide to publish, she omitted passages that could cause offence, and facts of which she was not sure. She also lamented the fact that her husband was so far away that she could not always seek his guidance in the matter of what to publish and what to omit. The two volumes seem to have received a somewhat critical reception in the newspapers. 'Some of the Indian papers', she writes, 'as might have been expected from the character given of them in general, have made unfounded attacks on the Work.' But she does not tell us what these attacks said.

Helen Mackenzie's husband was Brigadier Colin Mackenzie, a veteran of many Indian campaigns. In Ludhiana, Helen helped to attend to wealthy Afghan families living in exile. Brigadier Mackenzie was critical of British policy in Afghanistan, and was highly regarded by the exiles. The Mackenzies met the Henry Lawrences, and visited the school Henry Lawrence had founded in Sanawar in 1847. Helen comments on the deep attachment between Henry and Honoria, and regrets that his work so often keeps them apart.

Helen and Colin Mackenzie toured extensively in North India. She admired the tombs and mosques and other buildings she saw, but felt that their very beauty distracted from the pure worship of God. She felt that her Scottish Presbyterian forbears had been wise to keep places of worship as simple as possible.

She is fairly severe in her journal on English family life in India— apparently not enough church attendance, and far too much wine. Even the ladies drank too much wine. Her religious orientation makes for some insensitivity—she does not, for instance, see the inappropriateness of her companion Mrs Newton using a funeral to preach Christ to the Muslim family in which a death has occurred.

Helen Mackenzie also published a book called *Storms and Sunshine of a Soldier's Life* (1884) and a magnificent companion volume to the present book called *Illustration of Life in the Mission, the Camp and the Zenana.*

Mrs Colin Mackenzie, *Life in the Mission, the Camp and the Zenana or Six Years in India*, London: Richard Bentley, 1854, 2nd edn, 1st edn 1843.

Funeral Scene in a Zenana
MARCH 22

Mr Newton came to ask me to visit one of Shah Zeman's widows who is very ill. Mrs Newton and I accordingly drove thither. All that was to be seen of the house outside was a high mud wall, like that round a large garden: a door in it led into a little court, where a fine cow and calf and a pair of very handsome oxen (intended, I suppose, to draw the Palkigari which stood outside) were eating. Our guide knocked with his stick at a very low door, so that a person outside could see nothing of one within higher than the elbow: it was soon opened, and we found ourselves in a neat little garden full of onions, from whence another door led into a row of very clean, neat apartments, in one of which the poor old lady was sitting up in bed, wrapped in a quilt; two chairs were placed for us. The Shahzadeh, her son, and a row of women were all sitting on the floor, watching the incantations of a strange veiled figure, who turned out to be a native 'wise woman' performing charms for the poor old lady's recovery. She has been ill for more than two months and had hardly any pulse, though she moved wonderfully well. Two elderly unmarried daughters were near her: it is strange how immediately I recognized them as such without being told—there is something quite different in the look of a married woman and an old maid.

Shah Zeman seems, at least in these instances, to have followed the same preposterous system as his brother Shah Shujah, by not suffering his daughters to marry. The old lady must have been very handsome in her youth, and was very courteous and grieved when I stood up to help her. The Shahzadeh was very attentive to her; a handsome man when sitting, though very short and stout, magnificent eyes, eyebrows and beard. Divers of his wives were there; one rather pretty, with a saucy, pert expression, the other very gentle and the mother of two very pretty delicate little boys, dressed in yellow satin, one of whom went to Mrs Newton at once and fell asleep in her arms. I prescribed for the poor old lady, who encouraged us by saying that if she got well we must come again and she would give a Nach! All the ladies were smoking by turns, one chillam being passed round; they offered it to us, and when we declined, one of them, more knowing than the rest, observed, 'Ah they smoke cheroots!'

For the rest of the day I laughed whenever the image which had presented itself to the imagination of these good ladies, crossed my mind, of Mrs Newton and myself with cigars in our mouths! They begged us to come again, which we promised to do. The Shahzadeh stood up and waved his hand like an Italian when we left, but followed us to the door to see us get into the buggy....

MARCH 23

Mrs Newton and I were just going to see the poor old Begum when Muhammad Khan told us that she was dead. She died last night, and was buried today about one o'clock. He had been to the house to join in certain prayers for her soul. On finding, however, that they had sent last night after we had gone out to ask me to come to her, Mrs N. and I agreed it would be better to call and see the family, that they might not think us unkind or neglectful. A respectable grey-bearded man showed us the way to the woman's apartments and garden, the other side of the house being occupied by the men. Prince Teimur's buggy was standing at the door, he having come to pay a visit of condolence. We found the garden full of women of all ranks, so that it was a gay rather than a mournful scene. Some of Shah Shujah's family were seated on a kind of terrace spread with carpets, where they invited us to sit; and after talking to them a little, they asked us to go within to see the nearer relations. Two of these, daughters of the poor old lady seemed in real grief; it is not etiquette for them to speak, but they may be spoken to. One of them seemed as if she had wept until she could weep no more, and she occasionally groaned and rocked herself; we sat down by them and expressed our sympathy, but the other women showed no signs of feeling. The pretty saucy little creature, we had seen the day before talked and smiled close to them, and almost all the other women begged me to feel their pulses, and to prescribe for different aches and pains. One or two gently pulled my skirt to make me look round, that they might see the Feringhi lady properly. In order to introduce the subject on which we most wished to speak, Mrs Newton told them that I was in mourning for my dear father, but that I thought of him with joy as now with God.

When we returned to the Begums, outside, one of the women repeated to them what Mrs Newton had said, which gave her the opportunity of telling that it was only through Jesus, 'Isa Masih', that we could be saved. They seemed to assent, but then began another list of maladies; they were very anxious to know which was Mackenzie Sahib's 'Mem', and said they knew all about him. There were several women there of great beauty, as fair as Europeans, with a very noble style of features and winning manners. There was also the first really beautiful Kashmiri I have seen, rather dark, but such eyes, nose, and mouth! She looked like one of the most beautiful Greek Bacchante. A female servant came with a Persian message to me from the Shahzadeh. As I could not understand her, I bowed and sent many salams, and she seemed quite satisfied. They wanted us to stay to the feast, but this we could not do, as Mrs Newton was anxious to get home. Indeed, the noise and crowd were quite fatiguing; it was more like a fair than a funeral. They wore colours as usual, but no ornaments. It makes one's heart ache to think of the poor old Begum having passed into eternity, and of all these passing away ignorant and heedless of a Saviour. Near relations visit them for three or ten days, and on the fortieth day all their acquaintance go, and there is a feast for them and for the poor.

Louis Rousselet

Louis Rousselet (1845-1929) came to India in 1863 when he was eighteen, to collect information on French influence in the Deccan. He spent a year in Bombay studying modern and ancient languages, and then made a journey in Central India as archaeologist, ethnographer, and photographer. He was one of the first to study the Buddhist monasteries of Sanchi. He also visited several courts, among them Bhopal, and wrote extensively on India. He was associated with one of the major geographical publications of the period, *The New Dictionary of Universal Geography*. Among his other books are *The Snake Charmer* (1878) and *The Tiger's Skin* (1883). The book from which the following extract is taken is *L'Inde des Rajahs*, which contains 317 engraving and maps.

Bhopal

The Begum Secunder.—The Nawabs of Bhopal.—The City, Bazaars, Lakes, and Citadel.—Jehangheerabad.—A Visit to the Doolan Sircar.—Madame Elizabeth de Bourbon.—The Bourbons of Bhopal.—The Fête of Mohurum.—The Fair of Futtehgurh.—The Jogees.—Sehore.

On the day following that of our arrival at Bhopal we were admitted to a private audience of her Highness the Begum Secunder. An equipage from the Court came to fetch us from the Moti Bungalow, and took us to the palace, which is situated at the extreme end of the town, at the foot of the citadel. The grand vizier and the dewan received us at the entrance; and we ascended the great staircase and entered the great hall of the durbar, where the queen awaited us. Rising at our approach, she advanced towards us, and, courteously shaking hands with us, invited us to seat ourslves beside her on the divan.

The Begum is woman of about fifty years of age. Her thin face, lighted

Louis Rousselet, *India and Its Native Princes*, Lt Col Burke (rev. and ed), London: Bickers & Sons, 1882.

up by a pair of intelligent eyes, expresses such a singular amount of energy that one must be aware of it beforehand in order to realise the fact that a woman is before you. The costume itself aids the illusion; tight-fitting pantaloons, an embroidered jacket, and a poniard at the belt, have as a whole, anything but a feminine appearance. Her gestures and manners still less remind one of her sex; on to contrary, they reveal the sovereign and the autocrat accustomed to find everything yield to his all-powerful will; but I must add at once that this majestic haughtiness lasted for only a few moments, and soon gave way to a gracious and winning affability.

It may be said that the Begum Secunder is, in every respect, one of the most remarkable types that India has furnished us with in this century. Daughter of the last Nawab, on attaining her majority, she established her claim to the vacant throne; but the English, interfering, as usual, in all the disputes about sucession, gave their preference to her husband, Jehanghir. At his death she imposed herself as regent, in the name of Shah Jehan, her daughter, who was still a minor; and, rejecting as absurd the Mussulman rules of the Purdah, which condemned her to govern only from behind a curtain, she presented herself to the people with uncovered face, dressed in the costume of the princes, and proudly seated on her horse. From that moment she firmly grasped the reins of the state, and set to work to concentrate in herself alone all the responsibility and all the power which Asiatic customs yield only to the ministers. After having skilfully, and without any rupture, put aside the troublesome intervention of the English, and conciliated the goodwill of her rivals, she undertook the work of reform she had so long meditated. By dint of economy, she succeeded in paying off in ten years a debt of eighty lacs, and raised the revenues of the Crown from twelve to thirty lacs. The country, through her care, soon became covered with roads of communication, and the dykes, to which it owes its fertility, were restored or repaired; she then reorganized her small army, instituted a new judicial system, and created a police. The indifference of her predecessors had allowed the best land to pass by degrees into the hands of the feudal nobility. Using as a pretext the exactions perpetrated by the barons, she constituted herself the defender of the peasant, and resumed her right of high justice; and in a few years her legal confiscations reunited the greater part of the alienated property to the Crown. During the space of ten years she worked twelve hours a day, and displayed an administrative ability which the English themselves termed wonderful. She superintended in person the execution of her orders, travelling over all the provinces of her kingdom on horseback, living in her tent, and going into the midst of her population to seek for the information she required.

The revolt of 1857 interrupted her in the midst of her labours. Her position was full of peril—finding herself, as she did, placed in the heart of the revolted countries, with the most brilliant offers made to her in order to win her over to the cause of the insurrection. Without hesitation, however, she placed herself by the side of England, repressed the seeds of revolt which had begun to manifest themselves in her very palace, and, assembling her little army, marched in person to the aid of the English. This skilful policy gained her a considerable increase of terri-tory, besides numerous marks of esteem which Queen Victoria and the British Government were pleased to lavish upon her; and in 1859 her daughter, having attained her majority, abdicated in her favour, when she became by right, as well as in fact, the true sovereign of Bhopal.

Her work of reorganisation was completed, but she wished to go still further. Attacking the ancient prejudices, she forbade the commerce in slaves and the institution of eunuchs, and established schools and or-phanages in every centre of the population; and, having thus brought her small territory out of its obscurity, she has succeeded in placing it in the first rank among the kingdoms of Rajasthan, by giving it an unusual political importance, and, at the same time, an internal prosperity which even the countries governed by the English might envy.

The States of Bhopal extend over a surface of 6764 square miles, and contain a population of about 670,000 inhabitants. They partly cover the tablelands bordering the northern banks of the Nerbudda, and partly stretch over the beautiful and fertile plains of Eastern Malwa.

...

Our first interview with the Begum lasted several hours, during which she related with much enthusiasm her own history and that of her ancestors, as I have just briefly sketched them. Then, without pausing, she made me undergo a long examination on the Indian States which I had visited, on the customs of their Courts and their policy; plying me with fresh questions almost before I had had time to reply to the last. She next apologised for not being able to introduce us to her daughter, Shah Jehan, whom her husband kept shut up in the harem, and compelled to a strict observance of the rules of the Purdah; which gave the Begum an opportunity for declaring these customs to be absurd and ridiculous. To make amends for this, however, she sent for her granddaughter, Sultana Jehan, a lovely child of eight, who ran forward to embrace and salute us in the European fashion.

The Begum did not allow us to depart until I had explained to her what were my plans for the rainy season; whether I intended wintering at Bhopal as I had done at Jeypore, and in such case how long I thought of staying: and when I declared my intention, should she permit it, of profiting by the bad season to pass some months at her Court, she desired to settle at once what we should do during that period. It was decided that we should reside at the Moti Bungalow, and that during all the time of our stay we should consider ourselves as the Begum's guests. At length the servants brought the ewers; the queen herself sprinkled us with rose-water, and we retired enchanted as well as astonished by our first interview.

The next day Hussein Khan, the queen's secretary, came to instal us definitely at the Moti Bunglow. The apartments were newly furnished, and a numerous establishment of servants and a special guard were placed at our disposal, besides several horses, two carriages, and an elephant.

The same day I sent back to Rewah the escort and the elephant which the Maharajah had given us.

The charming residence allotted to us by the Begum, is situated at the end of the suburb of Jehangheerabad, from which it is separated by beautiful gardens planted with large trees, which encircle it with verdure. To the south and east the view extends over a barren and desolate valley, strewed with stones and brushwood, and a long chain of bare mountain ridges with rounded outlines. The landscape towards the west forms a delicious contrast to this gloomy spectacle; and the blue and limpid waters of a fine lake spread like a splendid mirror, in which the mountains and the long line of forts and gardens which ornament its banks are reflected. This lake entirely covers the eastern front of the city, while only a road passing along the high dyke which confines its waters serves to connect it with the suburb of Jehangheerabad. The city itself is built in the form of an amphitheatre, on the eastern slope of a rocky hill. Thick walls, crowned with battlements and flanked by towers, but without either moats or banks, form an enclosure about two miles in circuit; and access is had to the interior by numerous gates, all having a peculiar stamp, with their elegant pointed arch, their Attic guard-house, and their towers.

The entrace to the city is formally interdicted to strangers, even to Europeans, who can only enter with a permission from the queen; but it is scarcely necessary to add that these orders did not affect us, who were the guests of her Highness. On the contrary, whenever we approached the gate, mounted on our elephant, the guard turned out to render us military honours.

...

The Court of Bhopal

The Monsoon.—Life at Bhopal.—Evenings with the Begum.—Coffee and the Hookah.—The Cathacks.—The Egg-Dance.—The Man with the Iron Skull.—Interview with Shah Jehan.—Death of Oumra Doula.—A Visit of Condolence.—The Tofân.

We were back at Bhopal in the first days of June. Clouds were already beginning to appear on the horizon, and soon the yearly deluge brought us torrents of rain. The sides of the surrounding mountains were furrowed by the impetuous torrents which, spreading themselves over the plains, carried away the roads in many parts, and communication with the city itself became almost impossible during the first fortnight. We were definitely prisoners in Bhopal, and reduced to a state of inaction during three months at least.

It must be confessed that the Begum had done everything to render our prison not only supportable, but even agreeable. The Moti Bungalow had undergone numerous modifications during our absence at Sehore, which had converted it into a charming residence in the European style; the spacious garden which separates it from the lake had been cleared of the exuberant vegetation which encumbered its paths, so as to permit us to take short walks in it during the intervals of respite granted us by the rain; and a numerous establishment of servants, a detachment of soldiers, horses, and elephants, had been placed at our service, and formed round our habitation a singularly animated little colony.

The first rains came in torrential abundance, exceeding everything of the kind that we had yet experienced at Bombay and Baroda; but, on the other hand, they did not bring with them, as at Jeypore, the terrible hot winds. During several days the thunder never ceased rumbling, constantly furrowing the clouds with splendid violet flashes of lightning, and the peals burst forth one after another with a stupendous crash, like a continuous discharge of artillery. Thunderbolts fell several times, but without causing serious damage, and the electricity often played on the surface of the ground, displaying singular phenomena which would have deeply interested a chemist.

At the end of a fortnight, however, during which time it seemed as though we were witnessing one of those cataclysms which must have accompanied the formation of our earth, the grey canopy above us broke in several places, the sky gradually became blue, and we were able to venture as far as the Begum's palace.

One would have thought that, while we had been shut up in our habitation, the country had been touched by some magic wand. The vast bare stony plain was covered with a magnificent carpet of verdure, like the grass of an English park; the trees, but lately grey and withered, now spread out thick pavilions of beautiful foliage; and the mountains, washed by the streams, shone out in the bright tints of their blue granite and rose-coloured sandstone. But the picture was not everywhere equally smiling. The suburb of Jehangheerabad presented a sad aspect of ruins; a great number of houses had fallen, the bridges had disappeared, and the roads were no longer any better than dried beds of torrents.

Our reception at the palace was particularly cordial: the Begum was especially enchanted at our having partly adopted the elegant costume of the nobility of her Court; and she immediately gave orders to the raj-durzi, or royal tailor, to prepare us several costumes.

From that day we became constant guests at the palace. I passed the day talking with the queen on the gravest questions, passing in review the institutions of the different countries of Europe, their productions, their wealth, and the manners and customs of their inhabitants; and I was astonished to see the rapidity with which she seized the slightest details, and compared them with the institutions of her country. Everything relating to the public health, industry, and commerce interested her far more than political questions; which to her were limited to the fact of two powers, England and France, exercising their supremacy over all the countries of the globe, with the exception, however, of Turkey, whose sovereign was the recognised lord of all Islam.

When the weather permitted, the queen rode on horseback, escorted by us; and, attended by the first minister and a small staff, she visited the principal establishments of the capital. The hospitals, schools, and orphanages were the objects of our first visits; and she made me examine all the organisation of these establishments, asking my opinion, which I always gave cautiously, not considering myself sufficiently competent to propose reforms which the queen, with her usual vivacity, would have had executed directly. Often, too, when returning from one of these rounds of inspection, we dismounted from our horses, at the foot of the steps of the great mosque, and took our places in one of the kiosks overlooking the bazaar; whence we commanded a view of all the picturesque tumult of the crowd.

The queen, in fact, never wearied of giving me curious details. She taught me how to recognise the different nationalities, and communicated to me the precise value and commercial importance of this or that product, and the revenues it yielded to the Crown; and other such information.

The moollahs of the mosque generally came and took their places near us in the kiosk, and entered into religious discussions with me. It was curious to see with what ardour these worthy priests argued on the most trivial questions; yet some of them displayed real knowledge, and spoke with tolerable moderation of Christianity, for which indeed it was notorious that the queen entertained a strong sympathy. She often left me alone with the moollahs, and, when we took our departure from the mosque in their company, we continued the learned conversation in the house of our friend Hussein Khan, who always welcomed our arrival with the same demonstrations of satisfaction. As soon as one of his servants announced our approach to him, he ran to his door to bid us welcome, sprinkling our beards and clothes with rose-water; after which he made us sit in the verandah overlooking the garden; coffee and the hookahs were brought to us; and the moollahs resumed the discussion of the disputed points of the Mussulman religion.

The whole day, it will thus be seen, was devoted to serious matters; but the evening was reserved for amusements of every description. We arrived at the palace after our dinner-hour, and found the few intimate friends who composed the usual circle of the Begum assembled in the great saloon on the first floor; all grave men, with white beards and high titles; the first minister a remarkably fine man, of very shrewd intelligence, who possessed great influence over the Begum; an uncle of the queen; some feudal lords, and, finally, our worthy friend Hussein Khan. While awaiting the arrival of the queen, who passed some hours every day in her daughter's harem, we played games of chess and pucheesee.

Towards eight o'clock the sharp sound of the choubdar's silver stick echoing on the pavement of the great gallery notified the approach of the queen, who soon entered the hall in the midst of a bevy of young girls, her attendants, whom she had freed like herself from the rules of the Eastern zenana. The charming little girl, Sultana, glittering with gold and jewels, ran forward to embrace us; the queen then seated herself on the throne of green velvet which occupied the end of the hall; and all took their places on the divan according to the established rules of precedence, my quality as guest entitling me to a place on the queen's right hand.

After they had handed round coffee, the servants brought in the royal hookah, an enormous instrument, three feet in height, ornamented with precious stones; the bowl of which, of vast size, was filled with gooracco, a mixture of tobacco and aromas, upon which were heaped small red-hot coals. On the first evening the arrival of the hookah was the occasion of an incident which made no small noise at the Tittle Court, and even in the city. The hookahburdar came and knelt before the queen, and presented to her the rich amber mouthpiece terminating the tube, which she placed to her mouth, and, after drawing some long puffs of the tobacco, presented it to me. Such was the ceremonial; and without hesitation I took the amber, and in my turn inhaled the odoriferous smoke. The pipe, following the circle, passed from me to Schaumburg, and was afterwards presented to the dewan (first minister); who accepted it hesitatingly, and towards whom all eyes were directed. It is well known that the Mussulmans, looking upon Europeans as infidels, and consequently as impure beings, cannot touch anything that has been polluted by their lips. The poor minister found himself placed in a grievous dilemma. To refuse the pipe would be to insult us, and perhaps displease the queen; to accept it was to disobey the precepts of Mahomet. At last, however, temporal interests seemed to outweigh spiritual scruples; and the dewan, timidly applying the amber to his lips, inhaled a slight puff of smoke; whereupon, following his example, the other Mussulmans accepted the pipe without hesitation. This calumet of peace, indeed, might easily have become a cause of discord: but, as I did not care to see this scene renewed every evening, seeming thus to wound voluntarily the religious scruples of these good people, on the following day I begged the queen to allow us to bring our own hookahs for our use.

As soon as the ceremony of the hookah was over, the choubdars introduced the people who were appointed to amuse us during the evening into the saloon. There were nautchnis, male dancers, acrobats, and performers of tricks of every description.

My readers having already witnessed with me more than one nautch, I shall not return to the subject; but it was the first time I had ever seen men in India execute those dances which are everywhere reserved for women, and are considered degrading to the stronger sex; though this surprised me less in a country where the government has already been for two generations in the hands of women, and is likely to remain so during two more. It was natural that the Begum, wishing to raise the social level of women in her States, should think herself as much at liberty to have a masculine nautch as other rajahs to have a feminine nautch.

The male dancers, who are called cathacks, were fine tall young men, from eighteen to twenty years of age; and, attired in a very rich costume, they executed the very same dance as the nautchnis, with great agility and much grace. Still it was rather a ridiculous spectacle to see those great, powerful young fellows balancing themselves to the sound of little bells, and executing poses plastiques with their scarves. But is it, after all, more ridiculous than the pirouettes of our opera-dancers?

Another dance, infinitely more graceful and interesting, was the egg-dance. This is not, as one might expect from the name, a dance executed upon these fragile articles.

The dancing-girl, dressed in the ordinary female costume of the women of the people, a bodice and very short sarri, carries on her head a wicker wheel of tolerably large diameter, placed in a perfectly horizontal manner on the top of the crown; and round this wheel threads are attached at equal distances, provided at their extremities with a slip-knot, which is kept open by means of a glass bead. The dancing-girl advances towards the spectators, holding a basket filled with eggs, which she hands to us so that we may verify that they are real eggs and not imitation.

The music strikes up a monotonous and jerking measure, and the dancer begins turning herself round with great rapidity. Then, seizing an egg, she inserts it in one of the slip-knots, and with a sharp movement jerks it so as to tighten the knot. By means of the centrifugal force produced by the rapidity of the dancer's circular movement, the thread holding the egg is stretched out so that the egg is placed in a straight line with the prolongation of the corresponding spoke of the wheel. One after the other the eggs are thrown into the slip-knots, and they soon form a horizontal aureola round the head of the dancing-girl. At this point the dance becomes more and more rapid, and the features of the dancer can with difficulty be distinguished. It is a critical moment: the least false step, the slightest stoppage, and the eggs would be smashed one against another.

But, now, how is the dance to be interrupted? How is it to be stopped? There is only one way, and that is by withdrawing the eggs in the same manner in which they have been fixed there: and, in spite of all appearances to the contrary, this last operation is the more delicate of the two. The dancer must with one single clear and precise movement seize the egg and draw it towards her; it is evident that, if the hand were carelessly to place itself within the circle, it would suffice for it to touch one of the threads only for the general harmony to be suddenly broken. At last all the eggs are successfully withdrawn; the dancer stops abruptly; and, without seeming in the least degree dizzy from the constant whirling, she advances with a firm step towards us, and presents us with the eggs contained in the basket, which are broken on the spot into a plate, by way of proving the complete absence of all trickery.

Of the conjurors who thus passed before us in succession on our evenings at the palace, one of the most singular was an individual who juggled in the most extraordinary manner with sharp-edged tools; and let it be remembered that here too it was very difficult to use deception, for the tricks were executed with the poignards or sabres of the company present. This man seemed indeed invulnerable; although almost entirely naked, he pressed the sharp point of a sword against his breast so as to bend the blade into a half circle. At a given moment he placed himself on his back, and laid on his chest once of those thin leaves which form one of the ingredients of the bêtel; his acolyte then approached, armed with a sabre the blade of which had been carefully sharpened, and with a formidably aimed blow cut in half the betel leaf placed on the juggler's breast.

As these tricks had astonished the queen, the juggler engaged, if we would grant him an exhibition by day on the square of the palace, to astonish us still more.

The next day, accordingly, he executed certainly the most prodigious feats of skill, passing over a narrow circle surrounded with sabre points, and walking upon sharp blades. Then asking for some fresh cocoa-nuts, and throwing them into the air, he let them fall upon his skull, whereon they were smashed as upon a rock. Lastly, a waggon was brought, a heavy vehicle which two oxen could scarcely drag; one of the guards' lances was solidly fastened to the shaft, so as to present its point at the extremity, and a certain number of the common people were invited to get into the waggon, which the juggler, placing his naked skull against the point of the lance, pushed forward thus loaded for about ten paces. After this feat, of course, every one wanted to inspect his iron skull. The man complacently showed his head to each of us, and we were able to assure ourselves that he had no other cuirass than the very thick skin which Nature had given him for his share, but which, nevertheless, was stout enough to resist a pressure that would have pierced through the body of an elephant.

It must not, however, be supposed that the evenings at the palace were always devoted entirely to such material amusements. After the solemn ceremony of the hookah and the coffee, we often went to sit on the verandah, or, if the weather permitted it, on the high terrace, whence we commanded the panorama of the valley and the lakes, lighted by the radiance of thousands of stars; when some clever story-teller would relate some of the national legends to us, which he chanted in strophes, interrupted by a series of exclamations, as in our sailors' interminable tales; or else one of the young nobles, accompanying himself on a sort of lute, would sing the Tâza-bi-Tâza, and other poetry of the time of the Great Moguls.

Towards midnight or one o'clock the queen retired; our horses awaited us on the square; and, accompanied by some soldiers of our guard, we galloped through the solitary streets of the sleeping city. These men, armed with lances, riding by our side; the houses with their fantastic outlines; our own costumes even, all glittering with gold—all seemed the effect of some dream which had tranported us back to the Paris of the Middle Ages. Arrived at the gates of the city, we aroused the guards; the heavy doors were half opened, and our little troop proceeded across the country towards our peaceful habitation.

A short time after our return from Sehore, the queen presented us to her daughter, the Begum Shah Jehan. The princess, in obedience to the injunctions of the Mussulman laws, of which her husband, prince Oumra Doula, was a fanatic observer, did not, however, exhibit herself to our eyes. She was separated from us by a blind of fine straw, which permitted her to see us without being seen herself; but at the end of the interview, which was tolerably long, and at which the queen was present, the curtain was lightly raised to give passage to a slender delicate hand with fingers covered with diamonds, which I pressed in mine in Asiatic fashion. This was all we saw that day of the mysterious princess; and the Begum Secunder did not allow the opportunity to pass without again expressing all the aversion which this custom of the purdah, cutting off women so entirely from the society of her fellow-creatures, inspired her with. But a very unexpected event was soon to put an end to this position, so displeasing to the Begum, and permit us to satisfy our curiosity. Some weeks after our interview, one of the nobles arrived on horseback in great haste at the Moti Bungalow, to announce to us from the queen that the Prince Oumra Doula had been found dead in his bed that morning. This news, the sirdar added, had diffused consternation throughout the palace, for the prince was in the prime of life, and seemed to be of a robust constitution. The ladies were confined to their apartments, and received no visits for two days; at the end of which I went to the palace with Schaumburg to pay our visit of condolence to the Begum. Her highness received us with strong demonstrations of grief, exclaiming, 'It was written. Allah had so ordered it. Oumra in dying leaves us only a daughter, and for years to come the kingdom of Bhopal will be governed by the distaff. May the Almighty power come to the aid of two poor inexperienced women!' Then, according to the Indian custom, she sat herself on the ground, and, striking her breast, began reciting a sort of litany in honour of the deceased. 'Aïe! Aïe! how firm was his arm! And how bright his eye! Aïe! Aïe! what wisdom!' We were alone with the Begum, and this grief impressed us greatly. After some moments, I thought I might address some few words of consolation to her. The sound of my voice seemed to rouse her from her state of prostration; she suddenly rose, and, calling an attendant, asked for the dewan. The first minister soon arrived, and received an order from the queen to conduct us himself to the palace of the princess Shah Jehan. 'You will console my daughter', said the queen, on taking leave of us.

Following the dewan, we proceeded towards the palace of Oumra, the façade of which extends along one of the sides of the square of the palace. We were introduced into a large room on the ground floor, which had been transformed by the deceased prince into a sort of museum of European curiosities, and the walls of which were hung with mirrors and pictures of every description, from the engravings of Epinal to the paintings on glass of Parisian manufacture. In the middle of this apartment stood a long table, on which were ranged side by side the most heterogeneous articles—musical boxes, clocks, toys, and articles of hardware.

The minister left us in this room, after having sent to announce our arrival to the princess; and, in a few moments after, one of the doors opened and I saw a young woman enter, dressed in the strange and almost masculine costume which makes the Bhopalese women resemble the young pages who appear on our theatres. Imagining her to be one of the princess's attendants, I advanced indifferently to meet the young girl; but with a gesture full of dignity she stopped me, saying, 'I am Shah Jehan!' I paused a moment in amazement, and bowed profoundly; and my astonishment may be conceived on finding myself suddenly in the presence of the princess whom I imagined to be still strictly confined to her herem. Nevertheless, recovering somewhat from my surprise, I addressed my compliments of condolence to her, telling her how, during the short time I had known Prince Oumra Doula, I had learnt to esteem and even to like him. Without attempting to feign the slightest emotion, the young princess put a stop to my praises saying with a slight shrug of the shoulders this simple word, 'Kismet!' ('It was written'). Then motioning me to seat myself near her on one of the sofas, she said abruptly to me, 'So you come from Paris?' and I was compelled, without taking breath, to give a description of Paris, its monuments and the manners of its inhabitants. I could not get over my bewilderment, and was almost shocked at this utter want of feeling, when the Begum Secunder arrived. She could not help smiling on remarking my astonishment, and, having seated herself beside us, said to me, 'I mourn for Oumra Doula because I lose in him a faithful friend and counseller, but why should my daughter mourn? Does the prisoner regret his gaoler?' Strange words these from the lips of an Asiatic! They are indeed the condemnation of the worn-out custom of the sequestration of women, which Mussulmans persist in keeping up in spite of the constant progress of civilisation among them.

Still from a regard for propriety, the Begums were obliged to exhibit before the people a sorrow which they did not feel at heart; and, during a whole month, every fête and every amusement was to be suspended at the palace, and the princesses were to remain secluded in their harem without receiving any visit from without. At the same time, solemn public prayers had been ordered in all the mosques.

The princess Shah Jehan I should take to have been from five to six and twenty years of age. Her face, which was of great beauty, and of a dull white hue, was lighted by black eyes of a singular expression of pride and determination, indicating that she would be a true daughter of Secunder. One thing alone disfigured her striking countenance, and that was the blackness of the teeth, corroded and roughened by the abuse of bêtel. She wore the singular costume of the Bhopalese ladies of the Court—close-fitting pantaloons of gold brocade, an embroidered jacket, and a light muslin toque; and at her side hung an elegant poignard with jewelled hilt. On taking leave of us, she shook hands with each of us in the English fashion, and appointed to meet us, at the end of a month, at one of the evening receptions of the queen, when she added that she would no longer be compelled to hide herself like a poor slave behind a straw curtain.

On the evening of this singular interview a frightful cyclone burst over the city. As we issued from the palace, typhoons of dust swept the streets, scattering the crowd, which fled uttering the cry of 'Tofan, tofan!' We put our horses to a gallop, but, as soon as we had passed the gates, the wind began blowing with such violence that I expected every instant to be unhorsed. At last we reached the Moti Bungalow, where we found all the servants up and busy solidly barricading all the outlets of the house. It was but just time, for the cyclone approached rapidly, and soon its fearful gusts burst upon our dwelling. The uproar was deafening. To the ceaseless rumblings of the thunder were added the cracking of the falling trees, the howling of the unchained winds, and the roaring of the lake, while every now and then a noise like a distant cannon-shot told us that some house in the city had fallen a victim to the fury of the elements. We expected every moment to see our bungalow share the same fate, for the walls shook frightfully, and the tiles of the roof fell crashing to the ground. At last, about two o'clock in the morning, a profound silence suddenly ensued; and after waiting a few moments, we opened one of the doors; when the sky was bright with stars, and the black mass of the cyclone was disappearing fast in the distance. It would be impossible to conceive a more complete and sudden change, the calm pure atmosphere being scarcely stirred by the faintest breeze.

The next day we were able to realise the effects of these few hours of the cyclone's visit. The greater part of the trees of our garden lay stretched on the ground, and our bungalow had lost half of its roofing. But in the city the disaster had been terrible; a great many houses had fallen, burying some of the unfortunate inhabitants under their ruins.

The newspapers brought us the intelligence some time afterwards that this same cyclone had destroyed a whole suburb in Calcutta.

Marchioness of Dufferin and Ava

Even a quick look at the contents page of these two volumes containing selections from the Marchioness of Dufferin's journal for the years 1848–88 gives us an idea of the almost manic pace at which she and her husband—'D' as she refers to him—led their lives. I quote from the contents of Chapter XV: 'Journey from Calcutta—Lucknow—Tiger shooting at Rewah—Entertainment by the Talukdars of Oude—Cholera in Kashmir upsets our plans—Simla—the Duke of Orleans—the Garden Fete—Sir Frederick Roberts' Eton Dinner—the Simla Races—The Black Mountain Expedition—Masonic Ball...' and so on relentlessly. The Dufferins and their three daughters took their breaks at Barrackpore, which they loved, and at Simla. It was during Lady Dufferin's first season at Simla that she began to work on plans for The Countess of Dufferin's Fund for Supplying Female Medical Aid to the Women of India, partly at the request of Queen Victoria, who had been told of the situation of women in India by the missionary doctors who visited zenanas from around the 1870s. But part of the initiative came from lady Dufferin herself, for she noticed, despite her hectic schedule, the suffering of ordinary people, and understood the plight of zenana women who could not be examined by male doctors. At a time when English women themselves were battling to be allowed to study medicine, Indian women doctors did not exist. In 1886, the foundation stone for the first training hospital was laid at Darbhanga, largely funded by the maharajah of the place.

Chapter VIII

Spring and Summer, 1886

March 9 to October 24

Tuesday, March 9th, to Saturday, 20th—I have not had anything interesting to tell you this week. A. came back with measles, and has been

Marchioness of Dufferin and Ava, *Our Viceregal Life in India,* 2 vols, London: John Murray, 1889.

shut up. He is quite well, and only bored. Mr Tennyson is very slightly better, but has not turned the corner yet.

The Maharajah of Jeypore and the Begum of Bhopal have come to Calcutta to see the Viceroy, and durbars have been held for both, and I have twice met the Begum. The first time I received her here. Mrs Panioty came to translate for me, and at the appointed hour a tiny lady arrived, her face completely covered, a child of ten accompanying her. This was the Begum and her grand-daughter! We sat down in a row and paid compliments to each other, and the Begum uncovered and displayed a little face with big eyes, and then I spoke of my Fund, telling her that I heard she wished to do something in the way of establishing a dispensary and female ward in her own place. Then she asked for Nelly, and we put on the wreaths we had prepared for her, and handed her out again. The child is very self-possessed, and when she came to fetch the Viceroy to pay his return visit to her grandmother she comported herself like a princess and a grown-up person. Her face is still uncovered, and she is a handsome little girl.

I went the next day to pay my visit, Mrs Panioty, Helen, Rachel, and Blanche going with me; and the Begum on this occasion stated that she wished to subscribe 1,000 [lbs], to my Fund, and that she would defray the whole cost of a dispensary at Bhopal. When we were leaving, trays were set down before us, and the Begum proceeded to open some jewel-cases that lay on mine; but I said at once that I could not take anything valuable, but that I should be pleased to accept a hand-screen which was there too, and which she said she had worked herself.

Yesterday we had a garden party, and the child came, and was so pleased with some little two-year-old boys and girls that were with their parents, only unfortunately she always wanted to lift them, and the children objected.

The Maharajah of Jeypore also came to the garden party.

...

Monday, 15th—Lady Reay gave a purdah party for me today, so the drawing-room and part of the large verandah were shut off from the outer world and the native ladies were received there. It was a very pretty sight, and the guests were most of them very cheerful and happy-looking. A few could speak English quite well. There were two Arab ladies with fine faces; and two Persians, wearing short petticoats of brocade, long white stockings, and patent-leather shoes. They had gold-and-white lace shawls over their heads and fastened under their chins. One woman there is rather a celebrity in India just now She is very well educated, speaking English perfectly, but when she was a child she was married, or what we should call betrothed, to a boy, and now that she is grown up she has refused to go to him as his wife, and the case is being tried in Court. It involves a great principle, and is a test case of much interest.

Four little girls arrived so late that I only just saw them, but they were most wonderfully dressed. They had round caps covered with jewels on their heads, some of which were wound up and revolved. Their hair was plaited in a quantity of small tails ending with cord and gold tassels and coins, a very heavy headdress. They had velvet embroidered jackets and very wide short skirts, and they were all very bright and friendly. This tea party was rather hurried over, as we had to go on to another at the house of a Parsee lady. On this occasion it was not a purdah party. The Parsees look particularly pretty when you see them in numbers. They have fine eyes, and they drape themselves in such soft material and such lovely delicate colours. Their garment is generally edged with a band of silver embroidery, and a new pattern has just come out which has the word 'God' in Roman letters repeated over and over again in the same way that the Mahometans have 'Allah'. It is rather startling to our eyes. Our hostess, Mrs Cowasjee Readymoney, has been a good deal in England, and is an exceedingly bright and handsome little woman. She presented me to everyone as 'our Countess'. There were sisters and sisters-in-law, and relations of all kinds assembled in a large room with marble columns and open on to the staircase, with a fine view of the sea from the windows. It was a 'drum', so we went through a number of introductions, had a cup of tea, heard one song, and then tore ourselves away in time to dress for dinner. The society was much amused by the son of the house, a little boy whom I had seen in London. I asked him if he had liked England, and he said, 'Not much', which was a piece of unexpected truth-speaking greatly appreciated by the bystanders. However, as it was the absence of black ants in England he deplored, I could not sympathise with his reasons. These black ants are always crawling about here and make one quite uncomfortable.

Wednesday, 31st—I thought I would like to see what the Zenana Mission in Simla were doing, so I arranged to visit the school in the bazaar and to see as many of the women as could be assembled in one house.

Blanche was with me, and we went down hills and stairs till we reached the room where the school is. There were about twenty of those pretty little Indian girls who always look so attractive in their bright-coloured garments and silver anklets, bracelets, and other jewellery. They sang to me, and read and wrote Bengali. They seem to be extraor-dinarily quick and clever in learning everything, and as their education is such a very short one, generally ending at twelve years of age, it is a good thing that they are.

I next went on to the zenana where the women, to whom Miss James gives lessons in their own houses, were collected together. There were about seventeen or twenty there, and they welcomed me most warmly. The lady of the house was a remarkably pretty woman, and did the honours charmingly. After I had shaken hands with everyone and sat down, they all showered flowers over me, and each one gave me a bouquet. The interpreter was like most interpreters, and would answer my remarks and theirs herself, instead of repeating everything we all said; this makes it so difficult to carry on a friendly conversation. One of the women read English to me, and I was given a cup of tea and a quantity of cakes were spread before me, but as I could not possibly eat them then, we took them away with us in a tray! The house belonged to a Babu in an office here and looked very comfortable, with pictures on the wall, and some special decorations of flowers for me. These women learn reading and work, and Miss James said our hostess was a particularly good accountant. It must be a great comfort to them to have some such occupations. Of course, in every case where these lessons are received, Christianity is taught as well.

The afternoon looked very threatening, nevertheless the Lyalls came over here, and we took them to see the Chadwick waterfall. Such a descent! And such an ascent! I walked down, but came up in a jhampan, and often seemed to be standing on my feet in it.

Wednesday, 24th—I gave the children of the Zenana Schools a treat this afternoon. Thirty little girls arrived in jhampans, arrayed in brilliant clothes, and making music wherever they went with anklets and bracelets and jewels of many kinds. They were not at all shy, and we began the afternoon by showing them the house and taking them through all our rooms. Then we went out of doors, and they played running games, and enjoyed themselves immensely. It was necessary, however, for comfort's sake to take off many of the anklets, they hurt so, and the teacher was soon in charge of a large bundle of these ornaments. I asked a few people who are interested in the mission to come too, and I had tea for them. The children ate nothing; but after distributing their prizes just before they went away I gave each one a bag of sweets and a smart cracker. All the girls got dolls, and those who are about to be married received a picture in addition to a doll, as a piece of furniture for their homes.

Sir Monier Monier-Williams

'The great historian Mill, whose *History of India* is still a standard work, has done infinite harm by his unjustifiable blackening of the Indian character', Sir Monier Monier-Williams (1819–99) wrote; he suggested the idea of an Indian Institute to be based in Oxford to foster and facilitate Indian studies in the University, 'the work of making Englishmen and even Indians themselves appreciate better than they have done before the languages, literature and industries of India'. He came to India in 1875, 1876, and 1883 to further the plan, and the Indian Institute came into being in 1891. He was Professor of Sanskrit, Persian, and Hindustani at Haileybury from 1844–58, and then held the Chair of Sanskrit from 1860–88. He completed his Sanskrit–English dictionary in 1872. He wrote extensively on the religions and thought of India. In 'Camp Life in India' (1850) he took time to describe the birds he saw around him: 'the hoopoo [sic] with its lovely crest hopping about near me, the doves very like those at home, the bright parrots, the jays, the woodpeckers'.

In *Modern India and the Indians* (1891) Monier-Williams describes towns, villages, relief camps, religions, customs, Christianity in India, the progress of the Empire, and ways to promote goodwill between the average Englishman and Indians. He is critical of the 'half sanction' of the British government with regard to sati. He writes, 'Our Government prohibited the burning of any widow except under strict regulations, and except with her own full consent; but in consequence of our half-sanction, the number of widows actually returned as burnt in Bengal rose in one year to 839, while in other years the average was 500' (p. 72). British philanthropy did cause some fresh evils, he says, but 'the suppression of Samadhs, human sacrifices, self-immolations, and self-tortures are among the greatest blessings which India has hitherto received from her English rulers.'

Sir Monier Monier-Williams, *Modern India and the Indians*, London: Kegan Paul, Trench, Trubner & Co., 1891, rpt Routledge, 2000.

Modern India and the Indians

...

I come now to a subject which is perhaps the most momentous of all, in its relation to the progress of India and the promotion of Indian civilization. In England it has been said that the working people are our masters, and that we must educate our masters. There is another saying—equally true in India and England—that

'She who rocks the cradle sways the world.'

In plainer language, it may be said, that if the working men rule the world, the women rule, or at least influence the working men, and so become the world's mistresses. Clearly, then, it is important that the world should take the most direct and decided interest in the education of its own mistresses.

And here I must recall attention to a point to which I have before adverted, that, in all our schemes for educating and elevating the teeming millions of our Eastern Empire, we have to deal with a people who were among the earliest civilized nations of the earth, who in the best periods of their history were active promoters of social and intellectual progress, who have a literature abounding with lofty moral and religious maxims, who still preserve a profound veneration for learning, and who still maintain two lines of educational institutions, suited to the upper and lower classes of the male population, and distinct from the systems introduced by us. Manifestly, therefore, before propounding any scheme of our own for the education of the women or India, we have to ask the question, Is India herself doing anything, or has she ever done anything herself, for the promotion of female education? To answer this question properly, it will be necessary to glance first at the condition of women in ancient times, as depicted in early Indian literature; and, secondly, at their present condition, as shown by the statistics prepared under Government authority.

In regard to the first point, no one can read the Vedic hymns without coming to the conclusion that, when the songs of the Rishis were current in Northern India (fourteen or fifteen centuries BC), women enjoyed considerable independence. Monogamy was probably the rule, though polygamy existed and even polyandry was not unknown. In Rig-veda i.62.II, it is said, 'Our hymns touch thee, O strong god, as loving wives a loving husband.' The Aśvins had only one wife between them (i.119.5). Women were allowed to marry a second time (Atharvaveda ix. 5. 27). Widows might marry their deceased husband's brother (Rig-veda x.40.2).

There were even allusions to a woman's choosing her own husband (*svayamvara*), which was a common practice among the daughters of Kshatriyas in the heroic period. One hymn reveals a low estimate of feminine capacity, declaring that women have minds incapable of instruction (*aśāsya*) and fickle tempers (viii. 33. 17).

The condition of women, as represented in the laws of Manu several centuries later (perhaps about 500 BC), was one of less liberty. But the contradictions in the code show that no settled social organization unfavourable to women prevailed at that epoch. True, a woman is said to owe her condition of inferiority to sins committed in former births. She is declared to be unfit for independence. She belongs to her father first, who gives her away in childhood to a husband, to whom she belongs for ever. Marriage is the final cause of her existence—to bear children the sum of her duty and the great end of her being. Women, says Manu (ix. 96), were created to be mothers. As a mother, he declares, a woman is entitled to more respect than a thousand fathers (ii. 145). And, to this day, marriage and the hope of giving birth to a family of sons form the sole object of ambition—the one all-absorbing subject which engrosses every Indian woman's mind. On the other hand, in one place Manu alludes to circumstances under which a maiden might be allowed to choose her own husband, although he visits her with penalties for doing so (ix. 92). He makes no mention of Satī (*suttee*), and permits—as the Mosaic law did (Deut. xxv. 5, St. Matt. xxii. 24)—a widow, under certain circumstances, to marry a deceased husband's brother.

As time went on, the jealousy of the opposite sex imposed various restraints, restrictions, and prohibitions. A more settled conviction as to some inherent inferiority and weakness in the constitution of women took possession of men's minds. Yet through the whole heroic period of Indian history, and up to the commencement of the Christian era, women had many rights and immunities from which they were subsequently debarred. It cannot, indeed, be said that any Eastern nation has ever been free from a tendency to treat women as inferiors. Even the Greeks and Romans were wanting in that reverence for the female sex which marked the Teutonic races, and was the result of their believing 'inesse feminis sanctum aliquid'. Nevertheless, in India, mothers have always been treated with the greatest reverence. We may note, too, that something of the spirit of chivalry was displayed in the tournaments of Indian warriors, who contended for the possession of the heroine of the Svayamvara. Women were certainly not yet incarcerated. They were not yet shut out from the light of heaven behind the Pardah or within the four walls of the Zanāna. It is even clear from the dramas that the better classes had received some sort of education, or could at least read and write; and it is noteworthy, that although they spoke the provincial dialects, they understood the learned language, Sanskrit. They often appeared unveiled in public. They were not confined to intercourse with their own families. Sītā showed herself to the army. Sakuntalā appeared in the court of King Dushyanta. Damayantī travelled about by herself. The mother of Rāma came to the hermitage of Vālmīki. Rama says in reference to his wife, 'Neither houses, nor vestments, nor enclosing walls are the screen of a woman. Her own virtue alone protects her.' All these characters may be more mythical and ideal than historical, but they are true reflections of social and domestic life in the heroic age of India. Nothing can be more beautiful than the pictures of the devoted wife in the two great Indian epics. Sītā's noble pleadings (in the Rāmāyana) to be allowed to accompany her husband into banishment are well known. Addressing him, she says:

> Thou art my king, my guide, my only refuge, my divinity.
> It is my fixed resolve to follow thee. If thou must wander forth
> Through thorny trackless forests, I will go before thee, treading down
> The prickly brambles to make smooth thy path. Walking before thee, I
> Shall feel no weariness: the forest thorns will seem like silken robes;
> The bed of leaves, a couch of down. To me the shelter of thy presence
> Is better far than stately palaces, and paradise itself.
> Protected by thy arm, gods, demons, men shall have no power to harm me.
> Roaming with thee in desert wastes, a thousand years will be a day;
> Dwelling with thee, e'en hell itself would be to me a heaven or bliss.

Many other examples of noble language expressive of conjugal fidelity might be adduced from Indian literature, and notably that of Sāvitrī, whose story is told in the other great epic (the Mahābhārata). When the god of death appears to summon her husband Satyavān, who was doomed to die a year after his marriage, she pleads passionately for a reprieve: 'Let my husband live! Without him, I desire not happiness, not even heaven itself.'

Yet obviously such sublime devotion to a husband as to a god, was incompatible with independence of character. It is evident that any such useful domestic institution as a sternly critical wife was very unlikely to be common in a nation which made Sītā its paragon of female excellence.

Nor is there any evidence that the women of the heroic period had received much systematic education. They were certainly not thought capable of as high a form of religion as men, and seclusion must have been more or less practiced by the upper classes, as indicated by Pānini's epithet for a king's wife, *asūryam-paśyā,* one who never sees the sun. Marriages were generally arranged without reference to the wishes of either bridegroom or bride. Polygamy prevailed among the richer classes, and polyandry, though a non-Āryan custom, to a certain extent counterbalanced it. Daśaratha had three wives. One of Pāndu's wives became a Satī. Draupadī married five brothers together.

All this shows that woman's downward course of degradation commenced in the earliest times. Step by step the decline went on, and every century added to her debasement. The introduction of Muhammadan customs after the first Muslim invasion of India (about AD 1000) greatly hastened the deteriorating process.

And what has been the condition of women under our own rule?

In Warren Hastings' time a number of the best Pandits were invited to Calcutta from all parts of India. They were directed to draw up an authoritative summary of Hindū law as laid down in their sacred works. A compilation was carefully made by the learned men from the code of Manu, and from all the best legal authorities of later date. A certain Mr Halhed was directed to translate it for Government. The introduction is curiously characteristic of Hindū toleration.

The truly intelligent well know that the differences of created things are a ray of the glorious essence of the Supreme Being. He appointed to each race its own faith, and to every sect its own religion; and having introduced a multiplicity of different customs, he views in each place the mode of worship respectively appointed to it. Sometimes he is with the attendants upon the mosque; sometimes he is in the temple at the adoration of idols—the intimate of the Musalmān, the friend of the Hindū, the companion of the Christian, the confidant of the Jew.

Here are some specimens from the chapter on women:

A man both night and day must keep his wife so much in subjection that she by no means be mistress of her own actions. If the wife have her own free will, she will behave amiss. A woman must never go out of the house without the consent of her husband. She must never hold converse with a strange man. She must not stand at the door. She must never look out at the window. She must not eat till she has served her husband and his guests with food. She may however, take physic before they eat. It is proper for a woman after her husband's death to burn herself in the fire with his corpse.

Warren Hastings wrote a letter to the Court of Directors in 1775, commending this compilation to their attention. We must bear in mind that law, according to Hindu ideas, is part and parcel of divine revelation. It is promulgated by human lawgivers; but they are divinely inspired.

Smṛiti rests on Śruti. These ideas had acquired the greatest intensity when Warren Hastings was laying the foundation of our Empire. All the utterances of Manu and the later lawyers were accepted as echoes of the voice of God. They were held to be infallible guides. They represented women as created inferior to men; as born with evil dispositions; as incapable of education; as made worse by knowledge. Wives were divinely ordained to be the servants of their husbands. Their natures were too weak to stand upright, unsupported by the strongest safeguards. There was no security for their virtue but the absence of temptation. They were the absolute property of their husbands in death as well as life. Hence for a long time our Government felt that it would be dangerous to prohibit the practice of Satī. The Hindūs believed it to be enjoined by inspired authority. Nor was it discovered till quite recently that modern Hindu lawyers, to obtain the highest sanction for their deliverences, had fraudulently substituted the word *agneh,* 'of fire', for *agre,* 'first', at the end of a well-known Rigveda text (x. 18.7. See p. 72). In one year the number of widows burnt in Bengal alone was 839. In other years the average was 500. This after all is no very large number when considered in relation to the density of the population. It proves, at any rate, that the custom was not universal.

And what is the present position of women in India?

A little study of the India Office Statistics reveals a condition of prostration which even the most sanguine might pronounce hopelessly irremediable. One hundred millions of women, supposed to be actual subjects of the British Empire, are, with few exceptions, sunk in absolute ignorance. They are unable to read a syllable of their mother-tongue, they are never taught the rules of life and health, the laws of God, or the most rudimentary truths of science. In fact a feeling exists in most Hindū families that a girl who has learnt to read and write, has committed a sin which is sure to bring down a judgment upon herself and her husband. She will probably have to atone for her crime by early widowhood. And to be a young widow is believed to be the greatest misfortune that can possibly befall her.

Not indeed that an Indian woman's married life can be described as a blissful elysium. The women of India are victims of the worst form of social tyranny. They are allowed no voice in the selection of their own husbands. According to Dr Hunter's Statistics (i. 56), infants are sometimes betrothed when but two or three months old.

As soon as a daughter (of a particular tribe of Brāhmans) is born, the father immediately looks out for a male child belonging to a family equal in rank with himself. When he has succeeded in his search, and obtained the consent of its parents, he returns to his house, summons his relatives and neighbours to a feast, and solemnly affirms before them that his daughter is betrothed to such and such a man's babe. Nothing will induce him to break the oath which he thus takes.

This is exceptional. As a rule, girls are betrothed at three or four (a barber being sometimes the match-maker) and married at six or seven to boys of whom they know nothing. They are taken to their boy-husbands' homes at the age of ten or eleven. From that moment they lose their freedom and even their personality. They merge their individuality in the persons of their husbands. They may be loved, and they are rarely ill-used, as they too frequently are in Christian countries, but they are ignored as separate units in society. They never pronounce their husbands' names, and they are never directly alluded to by their husbands in conversation. For another person to mention their names or inquire after their health would be a gross breach of etiquette. They never appear unveiled before their husbands in the presence of a third person. They often become mothers at eleven or twelve. Their life is then spent in petty household duties, in cooking for their families, in gossiping with female friends, in arranging the marriages of their children, in domestic jealousies and envyings, in a thousand foolish frivolities, in a wearisome round of burdensome religious ceremonies imposed by exacting priests. Add to this that the upper classes are cooped up behind Pardahs or in the stagnant atmosphere of Zanānas. There they are prisoners in apartments set apart for their exclusive occupation. They have no opportunity of listening to the intellectual conversation of educated men. They are shut out from every wholesome influence, and debarred from every healthy occupation likely to conduce to the improvement of their physical condition, or to their social, moral, and intellectual elevation. They become enfeebled in mind and worn out in body at a period of life when European women have barely reached their prime. They are neither fit for independence, nor have they any desire for it.

And what of the young widows? If a young wife has no individuality apart from her husband, a young widow has practically no existence. It is true that our law has prohibited a widow from being burnt with her dead husband. It is true, too, that an old widow is cared for by her children if she has remained a wife long enough to have a large family. She is even more than cared for. Every mother in India is an object of veneration to her offspring. As a wife she may be nothing. But as a mother, even though a widow, she is all in all to her children. It is only a young widow or a childless widow who is regarded as worse than dead.

But nearly every household possesses a widow of this kind. Such a widow belongs for ever to her dead husband. A widower may marry again, but a widow never. She is made a household drudge. She is expected to get up at four a.m. before the servants of the family. No one will supply her with water. She must go to the well and fetch water for herself. It is unlucky to meet her. She is supposed to be in eternal mourning for her deceased lord, though she may never have seen him except at her child-wedding. She must practise a perpetual fast, and only eat one meal a day. If her young husband had acquired property of his own before his death and the household is still undivided, all such property is taken by her brothers-in-law. She retains nothing but her ornaments, which she must on no account wear. She is told that she cannot have food given to her till she has 'eaten her jewels'. In other words, she is expected to sell her ornaments to prevent herself from starving. In short, she suffers a living death, and would often cheerfully give herself up to be burnt, if the law would allow her.

Of course, there are exceptions to all this. In some parts of India—as for instance in the Marātha country—women of all classes are more independent, and assert themselves with more boldness.

There is also a bright side to the picture of female life and character. Hindū women must be allowed full credit for their strict discharge of household duties, for their personal cleanliness, thrift, activity, and practical fidelity to the doctrines and precepts of their religion. They are generally loved by their husbands, and are never brutally treated. A wife-beating drunkard is unknown in India. In return, Indian wives and mothers are devoted to their families. I have often seen wives in the act of circumambulating the sacred Tulsī plant 108 times, with the sole object of bringing down a blessing on their husband and children. In no other country in the world are family affection and reverence for parents so conspicuously operative as in India. In many households the first morning duty of a child on rising from sleep is to lay his head on his mother's feet in token of filial obedience.

Nor could there be a greater mistake than to suppose that Indian women are without influence. If there is any one thing that would lead a thoughtful person to despair of the regeneration of India, it is that female influence is as strong there as in other countries. For it must not be forgotten that, the word family in India means much more than in England. An Indian family does not merely consist of husband, wife, and children. The universal prevalence of early marriages leads to an indefinite enlargement of the family circle. It is said that a Hindū family sometimes consists of a hundred members, including great-grandfather and great-grandchildren. Anarchy is prevented and harmony maintained by vesting supreme authority in the hands of the oldest member, whether male or female. A father often has no voice in the management of his own children. A grandmother or great-grandmother may be omnipotent. Unhappily her influence is generally exerted on the side of ignorance and error. Even in small families the women are powerful for harm. They mould the character of the younger children. They are often adepts in artifice and stratagem. They know how to hide their power over husbands and brothers under the guise of a simulated submission. To them is mainly due the maintenance of superstition and idolatry. The men would willingly emancipate themselves from the tyranny of caste, from the despotism of Brahman priests, and from the bondage of senseless religious forms and absurd religious creeds, but they are prevented by female influence. Many an educated Indian is as bold as Luther in his public character, but sinks to the condition of a timid, priest-ridden, caste-ridden, wife-ridden imbecile in private life. He is a lion out of doors, but a lamb at home. He is cowed and crestfallen in the presence of the women of his family.

In some Native States women secretly pull all the wires of Government with consummate craftiness and ability. Great Britain itself is scarcely so opposed to a Salique *régime* as some Indian Principalities. Women not only reign, they are the real rulers and administrators. Even comparatively young widows have often great authority, if, at least, they have gained much previous influence as mothers. In the same manner ordinary families are often practically subject to feminine jurisdiction. A single old widow will sometimes keep order among a number of sons and daughters-in-law all living together under one roof. Her household is like a magazine filled with the most inflammable materials; yet she knows how to allay outbreaks of jealousy, keep down rivalries, and calm down explosions of temper.

Nor must it be supposed that the women of India are generally unhappy; that they regard themselves as slaves; that they long for independence; that they protest against seclusion; that they hanker after knowledge. They are too feeble-minded and apathetic to be conscious of degradation, too wedded to ancient customs to repine under absence of freedom or want of education. They esteem it an honour to wait on their husbands. The necessity for privacy, and the undesirability of a woman's learning letters, are ideas so intermingled with their earliest feelings—so interwoven with the whole texture of their moral being—that they have become cherished customs with the women themselves. They are more than customs: they are sacred religious obligations. So far from submitting to these restrictions from compulsion, no respectable woman would, as a rule, show herself freely in public, or allow herself to be taught reading and writing or any feminine accomplishment, even if permission were accorded to her. She has no conception of any benefit to be derived from a knowledge of letters, except for the promotion of female intrigue; and she would prefer to be accused of murder than of learning to dance, sing, or play on any musical instrument. She loves ornaments, but she regards ignorance as her truest decoration. She considers herself disgraced by sterility of body, but glories in sterility of mind. Education, music, and dancing are supposed to go together, and are to her badges of a life of infamy. When a sister is observed imitating a brother's first childish attempts at penmanship, she is peremptorily ordered to desist, and that too by the women of the household.

Is there, then, no remedy for this great social evil? Are we Englishmen, who are responsible for the welfare of our Indian Empire, and who derive so much of our own welfare from the purifying and elevating influence of our own home-life, chargeable with indifference to the condition of the women of India? We have made, and are still making, strenuous efforts to bring some sort of education within reach of certain classes of the male population. What are we doing, and what have we already done, to supply India with its gretest need—good wives, good mothers, and well-ordered homes?

All that can be affirmed is that we have been engaged for more than half a century in feeling our way towards the desired end.

In the case of male education the natives themselves have always, as we have seen, been ready to co-operate with us. Nay, they have eagerly seconded our efforts. Their own indigenous institutions have furnished a common standpoint for concerted action. The ground has been prepared and the way smoothed for the introduction of European knowledge. The same men who would have wasted their powers in elaborating ingenious word-puzzles in Sanskrit verse, or in trying to comprehend the incomprehensible abstractions of Sanskrit philosophy, have devoted themselves to the acquisition of scientific truth, through the medium of English. But in the case of female education all the conditions have been reversed. No basis of common action has been found, no ground has been cleared, no open door has invited us to enter. Every avenue of approach has been barred and barricaded. The natives have been more than content to leave their women engulfed in the depths of profound ignorance. They have opposed every attempt at raising or enlightening them as an offence against religion and morality. Without doubt, any scheme of direct Government interference for the education of Indian women would have threatened the people with vast social changes. It would have contravened the sacred usages of the most obstinately conservative nation in the world.

Wisely, then, has our Government proceeded in this matter with caution and circumspection. Something, indeed, has been effected by private efforts, by missionary operations, and even by indirect Government assistance. The first attempt to teach native girls in a regular school was made, I believe, by the worthy Dissenting missionary, Mr May. He was the pioneer of lower female education, as he had already been of male. He opened a girls' school at Chinsurah, shortly before his own death in 1818, but it had so little success that its continuance was discountenanced by our Government. In April, 1819, other Baptist missionaries, wishing to commence an organized scheme of female education, circulated an appeal for help, in which it was stated that 'in the province of Bengal alone, at least ten thousand widows were annually sacrificed; and thirty times a day a deed was repeated, which ought to call forth our tenderest pity.' Such an exaggeration was rather inexcusable, but it had the effect of rousing the sympathies of a number of English ladies, who thereupon founded the Calcutta Female Juvenile Society, for the education of native females. At the end of the first year the number of its scholars amounted to only eight. At the end of five years it reckoned a hundred and sixty pupils in six schools.

In 1818, an institution called the 'School Society' was founded at Calcutta. Its object was male education. But in the course of its preliminary inquiries into the educational status of the people generally, it ascertained that out of forty millions of Hindū females, not four hundred could read or write. When the appalling fact was known in England, the British and Foreign School Society selected Miss Cooke, afterwards Mrs Wilson, and sent her to Calcutta in 1821 to prepare herself for the delicate task of opening a girls' school. She commenced operations under the auspices of the Church Missionary Society in 1822, and on the 28th of January in that year, seven pupils assembled round her in one of the rooms of the School Society. In 1825, the number of scholars in various little day schools had increased to four hundred. But to bring the girls together it was necessary to employ a female messenger, who received a small gratuity from the Society for each child, and a breakfast of rice had to he given to each pupil, which the mother accepted as an equivalent for the loss of her child's services. In 1826, a wealthy Bābū (Rāja Baidanāth Roy) came forward and gave £2,000 to promote female education by the erection of a central school in the heart of the native city, with a residence for the European female superintendent. Mrs Wilson took possession of this building in 1828, and here all her subsequent labours were concentrated. She was a noble-hearted, energetic woman, and her exertions were rewarded for a time with considerable success.

Similar efforts were attended with partial success in other parts of India notably in the Bombay Presidency, and in Bombay itself, where the Pārsīs, who number about fifty thousand, were among the first to set an example of promoting female education. Their schools are to this day a model of good management, and are attended by nearly as many girls as boys, seven hundred and seventy girls being at this moment under instruction in three schools in the town of Bombay.

As a rule, however, female education has not hitherto extended beyond the lowest of the population, while male education has not extended beyond the higher classes. None of the female children of respectable or high-caste natives are permitted to leave their houses. It has not hitherto been possible to reach the Zanānas, or female apartments, of the better classes, except by a system of house to house visitation. This plan has been tried with some success in Bengal, and has been carried on here and there in the Bombay Presidency, and in other parts of India. But competent lady visitors are greatly needed. No lady is fit to undertake the arduous and delicate task, who is not thoroughly conversant, not only with the vernaculars, but with female manners, female habits of thought, female phraseology, and even female 'slang', (zanāna-bolī).

Something, too, has been done in the way of training native school-mistresses, especially under the auspices of the Church Missionary Society at the Sarah Tucker Institution, Palamcottah. I visited this institution in the beginning of 1877, and can testify to the reality of the work effected by its managers, Mr and Mrs Lash. They have successfully trained a large number of native female teachers, and established them at various centres in the Tinnevelly district. They have even succeeded in attracting high-caste girls to some of their best schools.

It is clear, then, that a few energetic missionaries and a few philanthropic private individuals have been the pioneers of female education in India. It is clear, too, that the British Government for a long time purposely abstained from acting towards its female subjects as it acted towards the male. It refrained from any systematic establishment of girls' schools. It doubted the wisdom of direct interference with long-cherished social usages, and deep-seated religious prejudice.

Lord Dalhousie was the first to commit the Government to a more active interest in the instruction of Indian women. In 1849 he ventured to announce that the British Government would encourage female education by its 'frank and cordial support'. And he was not a man of mere words. This great ruler boldly aided existing girls' schools by considerable grants of money from the revenues of India, and took care to bestow honours on all founders of such schools. It was during his administration that the Bethune schools were established for the education of the daughters of the respectable citizens of Calcutta, and when the founder died, Lord Dalhousie himself defrayed the cost of supporting them out of his own pocket.

Sir Charles Wood's great Education Despatch of 1854 only devoted one paragraph out of one hundred to the important subject of female education; but it expressed concurrence in Lord Dalhousie's declaration. Paragraph 83 begins as follows:

The importance of female education in India cannot be over-rated, and we have observed with pleasure the evidence which is now afforded of an increased desire on the part of many of the natives of India to give a good education to their daughters. By this means a far greater proportional impulse is imparted to the educational and moral tone of the people than by the education of men. We have already observed that schools for females are included among those to which grants in aid may be given, and we cannot refrain from expressing our cordial sympathy with the efforts which are being made in this direction.

Here there is a clear promise of sympathy and of indirect support, but no allusion to direct Government action or interposition.

Soon after the mutiny Lord Canning's Government declared that unless female schools were really supported by voluntary aid they had better not be established at all. In 1867 a circular was issued which practically admitted that Government had no desire to take the initiative in the case of girls' schools as it had done in that of boys, but was ready to encourage existing schools by grants in aid.

Nevertheless it cannot be denied that some direct action was taken. In 1870 out of £316,509 of public money spent on education in the whole Bengal Presidency a sum of £1,173 was assigned to government girls' schools, and £4,462 to aided schools, chiefly in the North-west and Panjab. In Bombay out of £198,182 a sum of about £4,000 was allotted to Government female schools. In Madras not a single girls' school was directly maintained by our Government.

In the year 1872 out of about 1,100,000 children in Government and non-Government schools of all kinds, only fifty thousand were girls, and only twenty-two thousand in Government schools. In 1873 there were only one thousand six hundred and forty girls' schools of all kinds in British India; but an American lady had organized a system in

Calcutta by which forty or fifty governesses taught native girls in their own homes. In 1875 there were about one thousand Government female schools, with about thirty-four thousand pupils, in all the eight Provinces under Governors, Lieutenant-Governors, and Commissioners.

In some places and in some years there appears to have been a falling off rather than an increase. Thus, in 1872 the Government female normal school at Calcutta was abandoned as a failure, and the Lieutenant-Governor was inclined to think it 'dangerous to give native women education and a certain freedom of action without the sanction of some religion'.

In short, there is clearly as yet no constantly-increasing demand for either female teachers or female pupils. What demand really exists is generally confined to the low-caste population. Even those girls who are placed at schools are only half instructed, because they are removed to become wives at the age of ten or eleven.

The great question then is: Ought our Government to make direct efforts for female education in the same way as for male? And is this a mere question of supply and demand? And if there is no demand among the people of India, ought its rulers to create a demand? Ought they to force into existence what does not exist voluntarily?

In my opinion the demand ought to be created. But we ought to create it in the right way, and begin at the right end. We require to elevate and enlighten the men of India, before we can hope to elevate and enlighten the women. We require to raise up a whole generation—perhaps two or three generations—of really educated men—men, not only well instructed in scientific truth, but well imbued with moral and religious truth—with the spirit, if not with the letter of Christian teaching—and with European views on all social subjects. And to this end, we have not to denationalize the men of India: we have to strengthen and consolidate their own nationality. We have not to extinguish their own civilization: we have to refine and elevate it. We have not to sweep away their social institutions: we have to shape and mould them according to a higher pattern. We have not to erase every feature of their moral code: we have to expunge the bad and retain the good. We have not even to exterminate their religions: we have only to lay the axe to every root and fibre of error, and, after eradicating the false, to engraft the essential doctrines of Christianity on pre-existing germs of truth.

When we have thus elevated the condition of the men, the elevation of the women will follow as a matter of course. The men will themselves raise their own women. They will throw down the barriers which at present surround their homes. They will tear down their Pardahs, pull down the shutters of their Zanānas, throw open the doors of their inner apartments, invite us to enter in—entreat us to do for their wives and daughters what we have done for themselves.

But how is this previous process of elevating and Christianizing the men to be effected? We must begin with the schools. Our Government has wisely decided to be neutral in religious teaching. We have abstained from imitating the conquering Musalmān—from enforcing our religion by Government influence and authority. It would, indeed, be doubtful morality on our part to take money out of the pockets of native parents, and with it to pay teachers to teach the children of those parents a religion which they believe to be false. Nor under any circumstances could a sufficient number of Christian teachers be found. But our neutrality need not, and should not, imply indifference and inaction in regard to moral teaching; nor even in regard to instruction in certain fundamental truths common to all religions. The principles of true morality, be it remembered, are not confined to Christianity. They are to be found in Hindūism, in Buddhism, in Islām. Nay, I do not hesitate to affirm, that certain lines of rudimentary religion are discoverable in the texture of two of these false systems. I contend that a warp-like basis of truth is traceable in both Hindūism and Islām, though concealed by a thick woof of error and delusion. The fundamental threads of God's attributes and perfections, of His wisdom, goodness, omnipotence, and love for His creatures—of His indwelling as a guide and monitor in the human conscience—of man's duty towards Him as his Maker, and of man's duty towards his fellow-creatures—are all there, and ought to be carefully preserved. Even some essential threads of Christian doctrine (such as the Unity and separate personality of God, man's original corruption, the need of purity of heart, the uselessness of external forms) are there, and ought to be thankfully made use of, while every cross-thread of falsehood, superstition, and fatuous delusion is ruthlessly torn away. Nor are the sacred scriptures of India wholly destitute of true teaching in regard to the principles of domestic economy and social science.

My conviction is that we are bound to search for, and utilize educationally, every true idea in Hindūism, Buddhism, and Islām. And just as we have endeavoured to ground our system of literary instruction on inherent literary tendencies, and inherited literary knowledge already existing among Hindūs and Muslims, so we should ground our moral and religious teaching on their inherent moral and religions tendencies, and such inherited rudimentary truth as their own scriptures contain. We should collect their best moral, social, and religious precepts, separating them from everything false. We should teach them in conjunction with scientific truth in our Government schools. In this way we shall best prepare our Indian school-boys for a voluntary acceptance of Christian truth when their judgments are matured.

And more than this. We should strive to develop our youthful Indian physically as well as mentally, morally, and religiously. We should endeavour to introduce something of our public-school manliness of tone into Indian seminaries. We should aim at educating the whole man in his quadruple constitution of body, mind, soul, and spirit. In a word, we should convert our 'Directors of public instruction', who are generally able and efficient officers, into 'Directors of public education'.

And when we have formed our real man, whether Hindū or Muhammadan, we should admit him to our homes. Having destroyed his caste-feelings, we should give up our own caste-feelings. We should receive our educated Hindū and Muhammadan on terms of social equality. In no other way, and by no other process, can we hope to reach the women of India.

The really educated and enlightened native who has been freely admitted to an English home, will return to his Indian home penetrated by the conviction that, if he would assist in raising his country, he must begin by raising his own household. He will accept the Christian truth that woman was created to be a help-meet for man. He will enter into the meaning of the Christian allegory that, when God formed woman, she was taken out of man's side to be his coadjutor; not out of his lead, to be his intellectual rival; not out of his feet, to be trodden down and kept in subjection. He will educate his daughters, and keep them under education till they are eighteen years of age. He will on no account allow them to become wives and mothers till their bodily and mental powers are matured. He will aim at educating them up to the English poet's standard of an ideal wife—

'A perfect woman, nobly planned,
To warn, to comfort, and command.'

He will permit them to choose their own husbands. He will open his house-doors to every refined and educated guest of whatever caste. He will expose the inner life of his own family to the fresh air of God's day. He will endeavour to mould his household after the fashion of a pure, healthy, well-ordered Christian home, whose influences leven the life of each of its members from the cradle to the grave.

Sir Lepel Griffin

We are told that, in several letters to, and conversations with, the Begum Shah Jahan of Bhopal, Sir Lepel Griffin (d. 1908) tried to persuade the Begum to give up purdah. In a conversation recorded as having taken place in January 1888 he said, 'You are both sensible and intelligent, but you are almost in a prison on account of the purdah.' But she was adamant about remaining in purdah, and his repeated requests were of no avail. Nevertheless, he admired her achievements, and, in his introduction to John Pool's book *Woman's Influence in the East* (1892), hoped that Indian women would never go the way of their Western sisters.

More generally, he held that the Mutiny of 1857 was a 'fortunate occurrence' as it 'swept the Indian sky clean of many clouds. It disbanded a lazy, pampered army...; it replaced an unprogressive, selfish, and commercial system of administration by one liberal and enlightened...'.

Sir Lepel Griffin served in various capacities, among them as Superintendent during the minority of Maharajah Jagajit Singh who became ruler of Kapurthala when he was five; he was chief political officer in Afghanistan for a while, and Lieutenant General of the Punjab.

He also accompanied Raja Deen Dayal on tours to take photographs of colonial life and architecture.

Introduction

This work is a sincere and worthy attempt to assign their fair share of historical interest to the women of India, who, in spite of all popular belief to the contrary, have held in the past, and do hold today, a great and often a dominating influence in the domestic and political life of the country.

A traveller in the East, whether in China, India, Persia or Arabia, who

Sir Lepel Griffin, Introduction in John Pool, *Woman's Influence in the East*, KCSI, London: Elliot Stock, 1892.

sees throughout his wanderings no women save those of the lowest classes who are compelled by the exigencies of labour to appear unveiled, might imagine that feminine influence counted for little in the higher ranks of Oriental society. This would be a mistake. The seclusion of women, with their separation from the outward interests and occupations of men, is, in India, an accident, due to conditions which are now passing away, and chiefly to the constant invasions by Mahommedan armies of the Northern Provinces of India, and the consequent anarchy which prevailed over the whole continent. In ancient days, as we see by the delightful comedies of Kalidása and the epic poems of the Ramáyana and the Mahabhárata, Indian women enjoyed great comparative freedom. They were not married until they had reached womanhood; they were allowed generally a voice in the choice of a husband and always a veto on the selected suitor. They attended, with men, social and religious festivals, and received an equal share of the education of the day, which seems to have been superior in point of accomplishments to that which is provided today in the Government schools. When India fell from its high estate of civilization into comparative barbarism—in the same way as Europe fell from the high ideal of Greece and Rome to the degradation of the Dark Ages—women lost their equality with men, and became, as is the rule amongst barbarians, the prize of the strongest. Wars for the sake of woman's fair face were quite as frequent in Indian as in European history.

In addition to this cause, the example of the Mahommedan conquerors of India, who secluded their women, had a great and lasting effect. The number of Mohommedans in India is very great, and in the Punjab amounts to exactly half the population; while, having been for so many generations the ruling race, whether their monarchs held their court at Delhi or at Kabul, the Mahommedan fashion was naturally followed by all those Hindus who desired to stand well with the rulers of the country, and at the same time to save their women from the too energetic admiration of their charms, which the Mahommedan conquerors were notorious for expressing. The harems of the most powerful of the Delhi emperors were filled with ladies of Hindu families.

The seclusion of women as enjoined by the Prophet Mahommed, and the rules which he prescribed generally for the treatment of the sex, are ignorantly supposed to be degrading and obnoxious to high civilization; but if we consider the state of society at the time of Mahommed and the savage barbarism of the tribes of Arabia amongst whom he preached, it will be found that, although he was unable to abolish polygamy and probably had no wish to do so, yet that he did everything in his power to ameliorate the condition of women, both slave and free, that he gave the wife a higher status than she had ever before held; and it may be fairly asserted that the position of a married Mahommedan woman today is socially and legally more secure and protected against arbitrary violence, either to person or property, than that of an Englishwoman, whose disabilities until the last few years were a reproach to our civilization. Even now, in matters such as divorce, the Englishwoman occupies an ignominious position which it should be the object of all legislators, possessed of chivalry and good sense, to remove as speedily as possible.

In his interesting book, Mr Pool has made an excellent and representative collection of Indian heroines. But there are many others who have filled a considerable space in the romance and history of the country who may well find a place in a future volume. There is the beautiful Rúpmati, whose romantic story is forever associated with the ruined city of Mándu, where her royal lover built for her a palace from the topmost windows of which she might see her beloved Nerbudda, a silver streak of water in the dim distance. The story of Ráni Sahib Kour of Pattiala has been told; but another princess of that house, Ráni Anskour, who ruled the State with great energy and ability from 1811 to 1823, is quite as well worthy of record. Equally remarkable was Ráni Rajindar, who defied the Mahrattas in the fullness of their power, and of whom I wrote in biographies of the Punjab Rajas: 'Ráni Rajindar was one of the most remarkable women of her age. She possessed all the virtues which men pretend are their own—courage, perseverance and sagacity—without any mixture of the weaknesses which men attribute to women; and remembering her history, and that of Ránis Sahib Kour and Anskour, who some years later conducted with so much ability the affairs of the Pattiala State, it would almost appear that the Phulkian chiefs excluded by direct enactment all women from any share of power, from the suspicion that they were able to use it far more wisely than temselves.'

The women who have made the most mark in Indian history have been Sikhs, Mahrattas or Mahommedans; and the reason is probably found in the fact that among these races the marriage of girls is generally deferred to a reasonable age, while among the two former the seclusion of women is much less strict than among ordinary Hindu castes. Even among Mahommedans the rule is relaxed in the case of ruling princesses. The present Begum of Bhopal, Shah Jahán, was, until her second marriage, always accustomed to attend durbar and perform public business and hear petitions in open court, unveiled; and while this practice prevailed, and she was easy of access to ministers and subjects, the State was well administered. It was only when she retired into the strict seclusion of the Zanána that the grave maladministration occurred which called for the interference of the British Government. Her mother, the Sikandar Begum, was a woman of great ability, courage and force of character, and ruled the State quite as skilfully as any man could have done.

The Indore State has produced at least one woman of conspicuous ability, Ráni Ahalya Bai, widow of Kunde Rao Holkar. She ruled Indore for no less than thirty years, from 1765 to 1795, and has left an enduring reputation for wisdom, purity and munificence. The time in which she lived was a stormy one, perhaps the most so in Indian history; but she steered the ship of the State successfully through all the breakers, and procured for her people a lengthened period of prosperity and peace.

Nor should the Rani Durga Batti of Garrah be forgotten, who, to save the estates of her infant son from the rapacity of the Emperor Akbar, called her people to arms, and fought an unsuccessful battle with Asaf Khan, the imperial lieutenant. Scorning to fly, and preferring death to the loss of power and freedom, she killed herself on the field of battle.

By the place of these heroic women who have skilfully administered the State of debauched and imbecile husbands or infant sons, and who have fought in their defence at the head of their troops, some account should be given of other women whose lives have been as romantic and who have as powerfully affected the course of Indian history, but whose influence has been evil, and whose evil passions have brought about their ruin, and that of their States. There are many such, of whom a conspicuous example is the Maharáni Jindan, who rose from the humblest origin to see her son, of nameless parentage, accepted as the Maharaja of the Punjab, and whose unbridled passions and the intrigues of her lovers largely helped to bring about the first Sikh war and the downfall of the monarchy which Ranjit Singh had so laboriously built up.

Whether the time will ever come when Indian women or those of China and Persia and Turkey, will become emancipated in the Western sense, and enjoy the freedom of their English sisters, is more than doubtful; and in spite of some feeble efforts made by Parsis and Bengalis to draw their women into social intercourse with the outside world, the rule of the seclusion of women—once instituted as a protection—is continued as a mark of position and respectability; it becomes more strict each year, while its area enlarges and tends to include every caste or family which rises from a lower to a higher grade. Indian women do not desire to go beyond the privacy of the Zanána, and would consider publicity as a disgrace. It is foolish to judge the customs of other people by our own, or to suppose that the society of London or Paris holds up an ideal which other races must attain or be considered uncivilized. The women of the East are not so much *en evidence* as those of Europe, but their influence within the legitimate circle of their domestic relations is quite as great, their manners are as good and their morality is as high. They do not try to do everything which men do, and conspicuously fail; they do not enjoy the delight of seeing their dresses and their looks recorded in the impertinent columns of society newspapers; they do not rush to the Divorce Court to listen to the unsavoury details of the latest fashionable scandal; and those who know most of the results of this freedom of women in the West, and the history of the richest and most luxurious society which the world has ever seen, may well doubt whether the Occidental or the Oriental method of treating the fair sex is more in accord with practical wisdom.

Mrs Marcus Fuller

Born Jennie Frow, Mrs Marcus Fuller (1851–1900) was a missionary with the Christian and Missionary Alliance (C&MA) in India. She was born in Ohio, and joined Albert and Mary Norton's faith mission work and orphan ministry. Later she worked with her husband to establish a mission in Akola. They were later headquarted in Bombay. In the late 1890s Mrs Fuller wrote a series of articles on the wrongs of Indian womanhood in a weekly Christian newspaper the *Bombay Guardian*. These were later published as a book.

In these articles, Mrs Fuller expressed her concern that people like Annie Besant refused to critique the condition of Indian women. She wrote, 'Being ladies, we should expect they would be deeply distressed at the social condition of women in this country, and the disabilities under which they suffer. We should think that the first question that would confront them, as they see the situation, would be, why has not this beautiful philosophy, which we have come so far to study on its native soil, done more for Hindu women?'

Mrs Fuller died of cholera in India.

The Zenana

As we alighted from the Bombay mail one morning to the platform of the station of one of our northern cities, we saw a Mohammedan gentleman hurrying about the platform. Then there appeared four men bearing a palanquin, who, under his direction, placed it opposite the door of a second-class carriage that had its windows all closed. There was a good deal of bustle, and finally servants held up a cloth on each side of the carriage door, thus making a covered passageway from the carriage to the palanquin. What was it, that had arrived in the train for this man that he so zealously shielded from the gaze of the people crowded on the platform? Had some one sent him a Mysore tiger, and was he afraid it

Mrs Marcus Fuller, *The Wrongs of Indian Womanhood*, London: Oliphant Anderson and Ferier, 1899 would get away? We carefully watched the proceedings, and lo! beneath the cloth, stepping out of the carriage, we beheld the feet—not of a tiger, but of a woman. In a moment the servants dropped the cloth, and the bearers picked up the palanquin on their shoulders and walked off. Its doors were closed we saw no one but the gentleman and the servants that followed it. He had probably come to meet his wife; and their greeting could remain until their home was reached. She, in her seclusion, is what is popularly called in India a *Zenana* or *Purdah* lady.

'The veil, as instituted by Mohammed and prescribed in the *Koran* is', says Sir William Muir, 'obligatory on all who acknowledge the authority of the book. Taken in conjunction with the other restrictions there imposed on domestic life, it has led to the institution of the Harem and Zenana—that is, the private portion of the home in which women are, with more or less stringency in various lands, secluded from the outer world.'

The harem, is an Arabic term meaning anything forbidden or not to be touched. And as we become more fully acquainted with the system, we find how fitting the name is. The seclusion of women has existed among other peoples, 'but it is among the modern Mohammedan peoples that it has attained its most perfect development; and the harems of the Sultan of Turkey and the Shah of Persia, may be taken as the most elaborate and best known specimens of the type'; and to these we might add the Zenanas of the native rulers of Muhammedan states in India.

The word *Zenana*, confined in its use to India, is of Persian origin. *Zan* is the word for women and *Zenana* means pertaining to women. The word Zenana, as popularly used, means the apartments devoted exclusively for the women of the household of an Indian gentleman. When we use the term 'Zenana woman', we mean one who lives in seclusion. The word *purdah* means a veil, and a 'purdah lady' is a term used in the same sense.

The veil or *purdah* as instituted by Mohammed, has the following history. Mohammed was married at the age of twenty-five to a widow of forty by the name of Khadija. But in spite of the disparity of years, it was a happy union. She believed in him, in his visions and in his call; and was a great source of strength and encouragement to him. Two months after her death he married Sauda, another widow, and was betrothed to Ayesha a little girl of six or seven who, till his death, remained his favourite and most beloved wife.

It was after his flight to Medina, that his domestic life, as well as his general character, underwent so great a change. He had married five wives since the death of Khadija. Muir says: 'He was now going on to threescore years; but the weakness for the sex only seemed to grow with his years, and the attractions of his increasing harem were insufficient to prevent his passion from wandering beyond its ample limits. Happening one day to visit the dwelling of his adopted son, Zeid, he found him absent. As he knocked, Zeinab, wife of Zeid, started up to array herself decently for the prophet's reception. But her good looks had already, through the half-open door, unveiled themselves too freely before his admiring gaze, and Mohammed, smitten by the sight, exclaimed: 'Gracious Lord! Good heavens! How thou dost turn the hearts of men!

Zeinab overheard the prophet's words, and proud of her conquest, told her husband. He went at once to Mohammed and offered to divorce his wife for him. "Keep the wife to thyself" he answered "and fear God". But the words fell from unwilling lips. Zeid was ten years younger than Mohammed, and he was short and ill-favoured; and now that his wife seemed to court so distinguished an alliance, he probably did not care to keep her any longer as his wife, so he formally divorced her. The prophet hesitated. Zeid was his adopted son, and to marry the divorced wife of an adopted son was unheard of in Arabia and would create a scandal. But the flame would not be stifled. And so, casting his scruples to the winds, he resolved to have her. The prophetic ecstasy seemed to come upon him. As he recovered he said, "Who will run and tell Zeinab that the Lord hath joined her to me in marriage?" and this was done without delay.'

The marriage caused no small obloquy; and, to save his reputation, Mohammed had recourse to revelation. The Almighty sanctioned it, and the scandal was removed by the revelation, and Zeid was no longer called the 'son of Mohammed', as the revelation had included the admonition that adopted sons were to go by the names of their natural fathers.

'About this time', says Muir, 'the veil was established for the female sex.' The reason for its imposition was said to be that Moslem women were exposed to rude remarks from men of the baser sort as they walked about. *But the prophet's own recent experience in the unwilling sight of Zeinab's charms was perhaps a stronger reason.*' He then promulgated the following command:

Speak unto women that they restrain their eyes and preserve their modesty, and display not their ornaments, excepting that which cannot be hid. And let them cast their veils over their bosoms and not show their ornaments saving to their husbands, their fathers, their sons, nephews, slaves and children.

Muir adds: 'Out of this command of the Koran have grown the stringent usages of the Harem and Zenana, which, with more or less seclusion, prevail throughout the Moslem world. However degrading and barbarous these usages appear, yet, with its loose code of polygamy and divorce, some restraints of the kind seem almost indispensable in Islam, if only for the maintenance of decency and social order.'

Mohammed was even severer with his own wives. 'No one, unless bidden, was to enter their apartments; they were not to be spoken to but from behind a curtain; and, to slake the last embers of jealousy, a divine interdict was declared against their ever marrying again.'

According to Muir, Mohammed had eleven wives, including two slave girls. The number seems uncertain. Abulfeda limits it to fifteen, while other Arabian historians make it as many as twenty-five. He limited his followers, however, to four wives each; but on account of the facility of divorce among them, though a man may never have more than four wives at one time, yet he may be married many times. A traveller once met an Arab, not an old man either, who had been married fifty times. We knew of a family where the first and second wives were permanent, but the changes kept taking place in Nos 3 and 4.

When the Mohammedans invaded India, they brought the custom of the Zenana with them. They often forcibly added a beautiful Hindu woman to their households, even though she had a husband. Hence, to protect themselves from their unscrupulous Mohammedan neighbors, the Hindus began to keep their women indoors, and to veil them carefully. Miss Thoburn says: 'Oriental women have always lived more or less in the background, but Muhammed shut them within four walls and turned the key.' The custom prevails among Mohammedans wherever they are found in India, except the very poor whose wives are forced to labor as well as the husbands; and they often have only one room for all the family to live in. But, here and there, you find a poor man who even in his poverty clings with great pride to the system as tenaciously as his wealthier neighbors.

Among the Hindus the system prevails largely in Bengal, the North, and the Northwest; especially where Mohammedanism is the strongest, and in the old Mohammedan capitals, and in the Mohammedan native states. In the Western and Southern portions of India, it only prevails to a certain extent among the better classes. With the exceptions of the royal families in the Marathi native states, the Zenana does not exist among the Marathi people. That no doubt accounts for the freedom of the women in the city of Bombay. A lady who lived in North India for several years, told us that she had seen more women on the streets in Bombay in one day than she had seen during all her stay in the North. The thing that struck us most on our first visit to the North was the small number of women we met on the streets.

While the Zenana system has not been adopted by the lower castes in the North, and not generally adopted by the Hindus of the West and South, yet it has affected public opinion and thereby restricted the liberty of women to a great extent throughout the country; and when you speak of the women of these sections being free, it must be remembered there are many limitations to their freedom.

We have no idea of the number of women who thus live in seclusion, but it is, we are glad to say, a small proportion of the whole number of more than 140,000,000 of women in India. But this fact does not lessen the wrong of the institution.

1. It deprives them of outdoor liberty and recreation, and must effect not only their own health, but that of their children. It is asserted that a large percentage of Zenana women die of consumption. Where the Zenana is very strictly kept, as at Hyderabad, the women and their young slave-attendants are practically prisoners, servants guard the front entrances to their apartments, and if the ladies make a call, or a take a journey, the greatest precaution is taken to secure their seclusion. In Lucknow we have seen ladies borne past in closed palanquins over which was spread a covering of cloth. How stifling it must have been!

A Mohammedan gentleman in Bombay, accustomed to some laxity in his own household, told us that when he was in Northern India, he saw, on one occasion, a lady put in a closed railway carriage and then over the whole carriage was thrown a tent. 'That', he added, 'was a little too much Zenana for me.' A Hindu gentleman who has lived in Hyderabad for many years, told us that when a wealthy Zenana lady wished to make a call, the street was cleared for her, and she was conveyed to her destination in a palanquin shielded by a cloth on both sides. He also said that once he had some workmen repairing a house, and as they worked on one high corner, they were discovered by the occupants of the Zenana below in the next house. The husband rushed out with a gun and would have fired, had not our friend interfered. They were suspected of climbing to that point so as to look into the Zenana.

2. It makes a woman constantly conscious of her sex. All this is done to shield her from the gaze of man. In ordinary Zenanas, if a water-carrier or other workman has to come into the Zenana court, warning is given so that the lady can flee to her room, or two servants hold up a cloth before her and screen her till the man passes out. The *Koran*, as quoted above, allows her to see her father, brothers and nephews in addition to her husband, and, as one lady added to us, 'and an uncle if he is older than our father.' But in very strict Zenanas this liberty, even, is much limited.

We know of a Mohammedan lady whose husband was absent. Through a lattice or window, she saw her little boy, an only child we think, in physical danger. Mother-love forgot every ban and she rushed into the street to rescue him. On her husband's return that evening, he was told of it and expressed no displeasure but spoke to her 'words of honey'. *But she was never seen after that night.* Another husband, of whom we know, killed his wife because a man by the merest accident saw her back through an open door, though she was unconscious of it. A lady described to us a pilgrimage to Mecca. She was confined to her cabin all through the voyage, while her husband enjoyed the ocean breezes from the deck and had the monotony of the voyage broken by whatever there was to see.

3. The confinement limits their experience of life to a very small horizon and keeps them children. If they cannot read, their knowledge of the outside world depends on hearsay. If a husband is so minded, he can greatly misrepresent events and the world to her. We recently heard of the statement made in a paper conducted in the interests of the Zenana, that the Western world was beginning to adopt the system.

4. The segregation of the sexes is a great evil. It was never the Creator's plan, but, gauging human nature, it was man's plan to save the purity of his wives and the sanctity of his home. But like all man's remedies for man, it is a failure. An author quoted in Dr Murdoch's books says: 'Instead of promoting virtue, it has tended to render the imagination prurient.' Dr Fallon scandalized the Anglo-Indian press with the quotations and proverbs used in his Hindustani–English Dictionary, but in defence he said: 'There is much to be learned from many an otherwise objectionable quotation, if one is willing to learn. It is of the greatest importance, for instance, to know to what depths human nature can sink in the vitiated atmosphere of enforced female seclusion, as contrasted with the purity to which men and women rise as social restraints are withdrawn, and they are permitted to breathe the pure air of liberty and indulge in free social intercourse.'

Miss Hewlett says: 'The idea that because a woman is kept in seclusion she is more modest or womanly, is a sentiment without foundation; in fact, as frequently where purdah is more strictly observed, the greatest impropriety prevails behind the scenes.' 'God meant the home', says Murdoch, 'to be a place of intercourse, where husbands and wives, brothers and sisters, male and female relatives and friends, gather together round the same hearth in loving confidence and mutual dependence.' It is the only safeguard of domestic happiness, and even of national blessing. Says Muir: 'It is impossible for a people who, contrary to nature, exclude from their outer life the whole female sex, materially to rise in the scale of civilization. Men suffer from the loss of the refining influence of woman's society. In such society they cease to talk of what they do not want their wives and daughters to know and hear. We have known the basest man to check his oath or coarse jest, and drop into a reverential, confused silence in the presence of a refined woman. Let the sexes intermingle, and many men will become what they want their women to be.'

A 'Kashmiri Pandit', after residing some time in England, thus gives his experience in the *Indian Magazine:*

'To live for three or four years in a society in which men and women meet, not as *masters* and *slaves*, but as friends and companions—in which feminine culture adds grace and beauty to the lives of men; to live in a society in which the prosaic hours of hard work are relieved by the companionship of a sweet and educated wife, sister, or mother, is the most necessary discipline required by our Indian youths, in order that they may be able to shake off their old notions and to look upon an accomplished womanhood as the salt of human society which preserves it from moral decay. There is a very pernicious notion prevalent in India, that a free intercourse between the sexes leads to immorality. I confess that, before I came to England, I believed there was some truth in this notion. But now I believe no such thing. My own impression is, *that the chief safety-valve of public and private morality is the free intercourse between the sexes.'* This is the sore need of India, and we hope the purdah will soon be rent in twain, and woman be emancipated.

It is often suggested to us that the different denominations among Christians must be a great hinderance and stumbling-block in India. Some of our Indian contemporaries have learned this objection, and occasionally assail the missionaries and the cause of Christ with it, as if sects were unknown in India and unity of mind was a characteristic of the country. The difficulty should not be an incomprehensible one to an Indian mind. India is full of sects, so that in writing an article for the press, it is difficult to make a statement that covers all India, or even one of its divisions.

The Hindus are divided into innumerable sects that vary from one another in customs and even in dress. The Braham community consists of divisions and subdivisions that will not intermarry or eat together. This is also true of the Indian Reformers. We have the Brahmo-Samaj, the Arya-Samaj, the Prarthna-Samaj, and the Adi-Samaj. The *Arya-Messenger* has complained most bitterly of late of divisions in the camp and of the danger of greater splits; but when it was hinted that the Arya and Brahmo-Samaj unite, the thought was most indignantly resented. 'Never!' said the *Messenger*, 'why, the Brahmo-Samaj is only a kind of Christianity!' When we turn to the Mohammedan community we find the same conditions there. True, the pious Moslem cries, 'There is but one God, Allah, and Mohammed is His prophet', but with this general creed and the *Koran* we find them divided and subdivided until it has passed into a proverb that there are seventy-two sects of Mohammedans. Hence it is easy to see that in speaking of the Zenana, it is difficult to make general statements that would cover the whole Mohammedan community.

The customs and practices in North India are often very different from those of Bombay; while a different state of affairs from all other sections of India exists in the Hyderabad State, where perhaps the Zenana in its strictness, severity and style corresponds more with that of other Mohammedan countries. In Bombay the Zenana can be hardly said to have taken root at all. Strictly speaking, it does not exist among the Khojas. The women of other sects move about more or less freely. A glance at the house in Bombay is proof of this. In Lucknow houses are built with reference to the Zenana. The front of a house may look most unpretentious, but if you pass through into the rear, you will find an open court surrounded on its four sides with the women's apartments. In our rows of tall four and five story houses in Bombay, where do we find the court, and the Zenana? The land that makes the square court up north, would represent too much money to a shrewd Parsee, or a speculating Hindu investor; and he would run up a four or five-storied *chawl* on it. It is only in the bungalows with more or less of a compound, that the wealthy Mohammedan, the Arab, and the Persian finds a proper home for his Zenana among us. Perhaps our free Marathi atmosphere of Western India is unfavourable to the Zenana's growth.

In speaking of the Zenana, Sir William Muir suggests that in addition to its being a command of Mohammed, that it may be a necessity to the system. He says: 'With polygamy, concubinage, and arbitrary divorce, some such restraint may be necessary to check the loose matrimonial standard which might otherwise undermine the decencies of social life. But the institution of the veil has nevertheless chilled and checked all civilizing influences, and rendered rude and barbarous the Moslem world. The veil, and the other relations that make it necessary, are bound up together with the *Koran*, and from the *Koran* it is impossible for the loyal and consistent Moslem to turn aside.'

It would be much easier for the Hindus to give up the custom, as it is not commanded by their sacred books and is only custom with them. In speaking to an Indian gentleman of Muir's suggestion that the Zenana holds the social fabric of the Mohammedans together, he said it was not true; that thousands of poor Mohammedans did not keep *purdah*, and that some communities were very lax in its observance, and yet there was no difficulty. 'But', he added, 'Mohammedans are considered the most immoral of nations, and it is the *Zenana* that has made them so.'

The seclusion of women is bad enough, but when intensified by polygamy, it is much worse. A man is allowed by the *Koran*, if he wishes and can support them, to have four wives and as many concubines as he likes. Perhaps the larger number of Mohammedans have only one wife, and an increasing number oppose polygamy; but many still avail themselves of the privilege. It is an expensive luxury. Most of the native princes have been polygamists. It is said that when the last King of Oude was deposed, that there were seven hundred women found in his harem. The majority of this number were no doubt servants and attendants of his wives, for even in some homes of one wife there are from ten to twenty attendants and servants.

If the polygamist has the means, he usually sets up a separate establishment for each wife: i.e. a suite of rooms, a set of attendants, and a separate courtyard, though one large wall may enclose the whole. But where there can be so such arrangement, and the wives live together, it does not require a very great stretch of the imagination to know that there must often be unhappiness, and strife among them: as jealousy must play a part if the husband is more attentive to any one wife than to others.

Mohammed himself had his favourite wife in Ayesha. There is an inherent desire in a woman's heart that, next to God, she shall be first in her husband's affections, and she naturally resents the thought of a rival. The system of polygamy has never been able to eradicate this desire. The fact that some polygamous families may live happily and peaceably under the rule of the head wife, is no proof to the contrary. A Mohammedan government official told us once that he had three wives: that his parents had chosen the first one; that she had no children, and they chose a second, and that he was so dissatisfied that he chose a third himself. 'But', he added, 'between the three, I live a life of it.' The parents of young girls before they are married often take a written promise from the intended husbands that they will not take another wife. One young girl added in telling of this promise they had obtained: 'And my intended husband is a good man and he will never do it.' Said her friend in reply: 'Yes, but a pious Mussalman is allowed four by the *Koran*.' We knew of a wife whom the husband deceived for a long time. She thought she was the only wife, but was almost heart-broken when she discovered that he had another wife living in a little house not far away.

Mrs Isabella Bird Bishop, the celebrated traveller in all lands, speaks even yet more strongly: 'I have lived in Zenanas and can speak from experience, of what the lives of secluded women can be—the intellect so dwarfed that a woman of twenty or thirty is more like a child, while all the worst passions of human nature are developed and stimulated; jealousy, envy, murderous hate, intrigue running to such an extent that in some countries I have hardly ever been in a woman's house, without being asked for drugs to disfigure the favorite wife, or take away her son's life. This request has been made of me nearly one hundred times. This is a natural product of a system that we ought to have subverted long ago.'

Among one sect there is a shameless custom of temporary marriage, which may be contracted for six, nine or twelve months, or for any period that may suit, even for a day. In our astonishment, we asked: 'And are these marriages legal, and does the Kazi unite such couples?' The reply came in the affirmative. It was instituted by Mohammed Jaafel, sixth Iman from Ali. Some writer in referring to it speaks of it as a great blot upon the morals of Mohammedan social life.

In addition to polygamy there is the custom of arbitrary divorce. A man may divorce his wife on any pretext and he need give her no reason if it so please him. In reading through the divorce law of Mohammedans, we were baffled and bewildered by what seemed to us the petty discriminations in the terms used in divorcing a wife. The first chapter opens up with the sentence: 'There are thirteen different kinds of separation of married parties, of which seven require a judicial decree and six do not.' We at last understand this, that when a man had repeated the words of divorce, 'talaq', three times it was irrevocable. And not until the wife had been married to another man and divorced again, could the first husband remarry her. A wife cannot usually divorce her husband, but she can ask him to divorce her; and unless he choose to do it, she cannot be released.

There are many checks to divorce, and one is that the husband is required before marriage to make a settlement upon the bride called 'mahr', and that he cannot divorce her without paying this. In well-to-do communities, it is fixed at from one thousand to fifteen hundred rupees; but to make it impossible to divorce her we have heard of the sum being put at a very fanciful figure. We read of one case where it was set at twenty-six thousand rupees; and the other day we heard of a young clerk on a salary of ten rupees per month signing an agreement to a 'mahr' of three lakhs of rupees. Though Mohammedanism sanctions a loose system of divorce, yet in India it is greatly limited in practice as compared with other Mohammedan countries. There are whole sections of its society in which it is rarely found; and in certain portions of the country this is true even among the better classes. If it did not affect the lot of woman so sorely in making domestic happiness insecure, we would have been glad to have overlooked the subject altogether.

In conclusion we must say that the Zenana, aside from its being a Mohammedan institution, is at present in India largely a custom, a fashion, and a standard of respectability. The majority of women in the Zenanas do not look upon themselves as martyrs to an evil custom; but says a writer, 'It has now become to Indian ladies part and parcel of their creed. Modesty, in a word, is to them as the very breath of their nostrils. To do away with it is a violation of one of the virtues of a woman.'

They even take a great pride in their seclusion. The custom has become a token of great respectability. Dr Murdoch quotes Miss Bielby, as saying: 'A man's social standing in his own class depends, in a great measure, upon whether he can afford to keep his wife and daughters in Zenana or not.' We have known of families who have lost wealth and become very poor; and the women have been forced from behind the purdah by great suffering to seek to earn a livelihood. It has been to them like parting with their respectability to do it. We knew of a Hindu lady who had never left the house but once, and that was to go to her husband's house as a bride. With what pride she must have viewed such intense respectability.

Hindu women have a little more laxity than Mohammedans in going on pilgrimages and to bathing ghauts. The *chadar* well drawn down over the face preserves the purdah for them. It is amusing to know that in Benares the purdah is most strictly kept. A prime-minister of some native state came to Benares and drove about with his wife in a carriage, when he was asked by the Hindus to desist from it. Marathi and Guzerati ladies on going to Benares to live, go into seclusion. We know of one such Guzerati lady who came to Bombay on a visit and went about the city freely. On her return to Benares in the seclusion of her purdah she laughingly told a lady: 'Oh, when I was in Bombay, I went about the streets with a bag in my hands just as you do.' A friend writing from Guzerat, in speaking of the seclusion of Hindu ladies there says: 'Amongst Hindus other than Rajputs and the better class *Kunbis* (cultivators), the Zenana custom is very little in vogue. However there is a tendency among the wealthier families of all classes to affect the Zenana seclusion.

It is coming to be considered fashionable and good form for the ladies in the houses of the rich.'

But it is said that women are contented in their seclusion. This is true. So is the canary, that was born in the cage and never tasted the sweets of the free air. It is also asserted that the women are not clamoring for emancipation. But these statements, though true, do not in any way lessen the evil of the system to women and to society; and we earnestly hope that it will soon be done away.

Rev. Edward Storrow

Rev. Edward Storrow (1818–1907) who came out to India with the London Missionary Society in 1848, served for many years in various capacities, with a break in England because of ill-health. On his final return to England in 1859, he became pastor of the Congregational Church at Rugby. Among his books are *India and Christian Missions* (1859), *Protestant Missions in Pagan Lands* (1888), and *Our Indian Sisters* (1898). Storrow's view is that that the system of seclusion is oppressive, but there are 'some features of Hindu life and character which tend to alleviate and soothe the lot of women....The women...feel their position to be less irksome than we suppose.'

Daily Life

...

Almost every house is the property of the family inhabiting it. They are usually small, with one room, or at the most two. The sides consist of mats, or wickerwork between posts, or of earth formed into low walls, or sun-dried bricks. The roof is very low-pitched, and composed of straw, reeds, palm leaves, or tiles, so small and light that crows often displace them. The interior is bare and gloomy, for there is no window, though there may be a small wooden lattice; and in front, to the south, if practicable, a small raised platform, protected by the overhanging roof from the sun and rain. A mat may be on a part of the mud floor. There are no chairs, drawers, or table, but a box, a few coarse earthen vessels for oil, water, and cooking, and a charpoy, which serves as a bedstead and lounge. The fireplace consists of three or four bricks or stones, but there is no chimney, the smoke finding its way out of the roof as best it can.

Probably nine-tenths of the families in India live in such houses. But there is far less discomfort in them than those unfamiliar with India

Rev. Edward Storrow, *Our Indian Sisters*, London: The Religion Tract Society, 1898.

would suppose. The intense heat causes fires to be unnecessary except for cooking, shoes and stockings to be an encumbrance, body and bed clothing to be of the lightest, and sleeping out in the open air on most nights a pleasure rather than an inconvenience.

But houses of a better class most truly express the Hindu ideal. They, too, stand apart, and usually have a bare, forbidding appearance. The side walls are of coarse brick or bare masonry, with no outlook. The roof is usually flat. On entering the small well-protected door, you pass into a court open to the sky. On either side, perhaps also over the entrance, runs a narrow verandah communicating with small, ill-ventilated, badly lighted rooms. Opposite the door on the fourth side is a raised platform, appropriated to religious uses. Here the images of the gods are placed, and the paraphernalia of worship, and at the great religious festivals, sacrifices and worship are celebrated in the presence of spectators in the courtyard and the surrounding verandahs. At the back of this, communicating with it by a small door, is the women's part of the house, the zenana, constructed somewhat as the front portion, but smaller and with an eye to greater seclusion. At the back of this, again, is often a well-enclosed garden, in which is a tank, so that the ladies and children may bathe and take exercise unseen and undisturbed.

The inhabitants of such houses are usually far more numerous than in any ordinary European family, are more subject to precedent and authority, and live more apart from their neighbours.

It is regarded as a matter of course that sons and daughters are married at a very early age. Equally is it regarded as a matter of course that sons with their wives and children shall live in the family house, not as separate entities, but an integral part of the family or commonwealth. It is a binding obligation on every head of a family to provide for all the distressed, helpless, and unemployed of his kith and kin. The claim is often a wide one, and if the head of the family or even some of its subordinate members, are in fair circumstances, it is surprising what a number of poor relatives may lay claim 'to bed and board'. The claims are generally allowed with the utmost politeness, though made by the idle and worthless, and in many cases sadly weigh on the family resources. But custom sanctions the usage, and nothing must therefore be said. Then, too, since widows in such families do not marry, they and their children help to increase the number of inhabitants in a father or father-in-law's household.

From these various causes it happens that families are often very large, consisting of twenty-five, fifty, one hundred, and even more relatives, including not only parents and children, but brothers and sisters-in-law, uncles and aunts, and cousins of all degrees. Whatever money is gained is put into the common purse, held by the father, or, if he has passed away, by the elder brother. The position of family head is a real, not a nominal one. He is an autocrat whose will is law. So is it on the female side of the house, the two sexes living apart.

It would be regarded as improper, and subject a man to ridicule and contempt, if he were to eat with his wife or any other woman, or converse with them on terms of equality. Nor is there any ordinary occasion when the male and female members of the family come together. There is no dining, drawing, sitting-room, or parlour free to men and women alike. Even on occasions when husbands and wives meet before others, it is considered good form for the husband to refrain from all expressions of affection or partiality for his wife. She too must not sit in his presence, unless requested to do so. It is he, not she, who must introduce conversation; it is her part to listen and obey. She must not directly address him by name; to do so would be to degrade him in the presence of onlookers by too great familiarity. If they have a child, the mother speaks of her husband through the child's name as the father of Gopal or of Sita. If they have no child, she uses a respectful personal pronoun equivalent to 'he,' perhaps adding the expression 'mine' or 'ours.' So the husband never pronounces the wife's name. He speaks of her as the mother of so and so, or uses a yet more vague form of expression, literally meaning 'the people of my family', though generally the allusion is only to the wife. Some ludicrous instances of the former usage occurred when the census was taken, since, in the absence of the husband, wives could not be induced to utter their names, and were too illiterate to write them. The entire demeanour of the wife must be expressive of deference and submission.

The front part of the house, the courtyard, and verandahs are accessible on easy terms to servants and neighbours, but the female side of the house is strictly private, and given over to isolation and monotony. No man must visit there, even though he be an uncle, a brother-in-law, or a cousin. The visits even of female relatives and neighbours are infrequent and formal; no one older than a mere child must penetrate into the men's side of the house, and only for the sleeping-hours may the men retire to that small portion of the zenana which belongs to the wife. If ladies take a journey or visit their own relatives, every precaution is taken that they may not be seen, though some allowance is made that they may see through the lattices of a carriage or palanquin. If a European visits the house, he will be received with marked courtesy, but an introduction into the zenana or to any adult lady of the family is not to be thought of, though he may surmise that feminine eyes observe him by peeping over the balustrades of the roof, or through jalousies or curtains or other coigns of vantage. As few visits are paid, so few are received, excepting in cases where houses are so near to each other that the inmates may pass and repass over some narrow lane without fear of observation.

The apartments in a zenana are usually bare, dreary, and comfortless to an extreme degree. The walls are neither papered nor painted; tables, chairs, sofas, drawers, cabinets are seldom seen. The windows and jalousies are small, and constructed so as to give light only; they look into the courtyard or garden, or toward the open country, never into the street, or if they do, they are placed so high that the sky, not the earth, can be seen.

The difficulty of making word-pictures of a zenana vivid is great. Here is a description from a missionary friend who had felt the difficulty. 'I had often wondered why one had such a dim impression of what a zenana was like, and wished for a minute description. I now wonder no longer. A zenana is simply indescribable, from the fact that no two are alike, and not one seems to have been built on any supposable plan or shape. A collection of dirty courtyards, dark corners, breakneck stair-cases, filthy outhouses and entries, overlaid with rubbish or occupied by half-clad native servants stretched about on charpoys or on the ground; indifferently narrow verandahs, and unfurnished or semi-furnished rooms, and very small; such is a zenana and its surroundings. Very often the approach to the house is so intricate, or rough, or narrow, that it becomes an impossibility for the ghari to approach, and the missionary must go on foot—a perilous proceeding under the scorching rays of a tropical sun. Once inside the zenana, you are struck, as a rule, by the entire absence of all that constitutes to our idea the complement of a room—furniture, tables, and chairs are not to be thought of, *except when brought in from the Babu's apartments*, for the teacher's use for the time being.'

This was written of the Calcutta zenanas. A missionary from Benares writes: 'The homes here are more gloomy, dirty, and devoid of every comfort even than in Calcutta. Even at this cold season the majority of the women wear no other clothing than their thin sarees, and sit on the cold mud or flag floors with their uncovered legs and feet, so that one wonders they are not constantly suffering from rheumatism.' Another writes: 'The women always have the worst part of the house assigned them, and seem to have few comforts given them. Even in the large residences of the rich Babus one can always tell when getting near the rooms allotted to the women by the dirty and miserable appearance of the walls, staircases, and courts. Many of the high-caste natives are very poor, and then they have to live in very small, wretched houses; but some of them are rich enough, and their dwellings are large and airy, and furnished with luxuries, but the ladies do not share in the comforts, though they may be better dressed, and have more servants to wait on them.'

But what of the dwellers in these cheerless, prison-like abodes? In natural endowments, Hindu women will compare favourably with their sisters anywhere. Their features are most regular, and often refined and delicate. They lack expression, as might be expected from their want of intellectual training, but gentleness of disposition and physical beauty commonly belong to them. In form they are elegant and graceful, fit models for any sculptor or painter. They walk with slow and measured step. Their dress is simple and suited to their manner of life, usually it consists of one long piece of light cotton cloth, wrapped in graceful folds round the body, leaving one limb partially free; then from under her arm, gathering it up in front, she draws it across her left shoulder and tucks it in above her waist behind. Usually the upper part rests on her shoulders, but it can easily be lifted on her head and drawn across her face, or the whole upper part be lowered to her waist. This is usually done when she is alone or at work. Thus the one piece of cloth usually serves as skirt, jacket, and bonnet. Sometimes a light bodice with short sleeves is worn.

Next to children, ornaments are the chief joy of women; they not only give pleasure to their minds, untrained to value higher possessions, but are always regarded as the measure of the family position and the affection of the husband. Those of the poor are made of brass, shells, and glass. Those of the rich, of silver, gold, and precious stones. Their number is great; thirty-six distinct kinds may be worn by a Tamil lady, and often several of the same kind, and the number worn by ladies in Northern India is almost as great.

How do they pass their time? The wives of the poor and low castes have far more to interest them than those of higher rank. They go more abroad; they see and hear more. The management of domestic affairs rests with them, and having more freedom, they become more self-reliant and intelligent. They often work hard, have coarse food, few comforts, and are harshly treated. They have daily to bring water from the well, purchase in the market the necessary articles, cook the food, attend to the house and children, and perhaps work in the farm or garden.

Zenana ladies are much more carefully tended, but their lives are intensely dull, monotonous, and trivial—so at least they seem to us. They never leave the house singly or in company for a walk or shopping or visiting. To do so would be not only ruinous to the reputation of any zenana lady, but also regarded as disgraceful to her family.

Visits are rarely paid or received, and then are arranged with much ceremony. There are multitudes of ladies who have never enjoyed a free long walk, or been in any house but their father's and father's-in-law, or travelled a mile from either, or have the least idea of the town or village in which they were born. 'You,' said a young lady in a zenana to an Englishwoman, pointing to a bird on the wing—'you are like that bird soaring to heaven; we are like birds caught, their wings cut, and shut up in cages too narrow for them.'

Cooking is the principal event of the day, and is usually done with great skill and completeness; but, since there is but one cooking for the whole family, and as several members of the family can assist as well as servants, this occupies no great proportion of the time. They clean the cooking utensils; bathe and dress their children; dress and braid their hair; look at their jewels and the jewels of one another; eat, lounge, sleep; hear the gossip brought in on the previous night by each husband to his wife and by the servants—and that is all!

What a dull, cheerless, restricted existence theirs is! Some part of each day many English women are left to themselves, but they ever have the consciousness of freedom: they can go out, they receive visits, read, and toward evening the house is made bright and cheerful by the return of the husband and sons; and the glory and delight of Christian family life is seen in men and women using the same room, sitting around the same table, eating the same food, and conversing freely as equals. Nothing of the kind is seen in India.

This segregation of the sexes in the same family is disastrous alike to men and women, and it is difficult to say which sex is most injuriously affected. What a world of significance is conveyed in the remark that in India there are 'houses, but no homes'! 'We have no homes', said the Dewan Bahadur R. Raghonath Rao. 'There exists', writes Sir M. Monier Williams, 'no word that I know of in any Indian language exactly equivalent to that grand old Saxon monosyllable "home"—that little word which is the key to our national greatness and prosperity. Certainly the word "zenana", meaning in Persian "the place of women", cannot pretend to stand for "home", any more than the Persian "mandana", "the place for men", can mean "home."'

In the zenana itself there are abundant sources of discomfort and trouble. Women's sole companions are near relatives, chiefly nieces, aunts, and sisters-in-law, some married, others unmarried, but all confined within the same restricted intellectual, social, and material horizon.

However patient, gentle, submissive women may be, it is inevitable that many occasions for envy, jealousy, and discord must exist in families so constituted. There is, indeed, an authority whose will is supreme—the grandmother or mother-in-law or sister-in-law, whose Oriental conception of autocratic power is not likely to be softened by previous subordination, and still less by sweet reasonableness, the discipline of education, or the beneficent influence of a pure religion. Usually delighting in the exercise of power over others, and being ignorant and superstitious, and the most conservative where all are so, she is the enemy of all change and reform. Her government is a pure despotism, all the more harsh and overbearing because it is exercised for the most part over the daughters of other women. Report speaks of this as one of the darkest and saddest features of life in the zenanas, and so do such current sayings as the following :

'If the mother-in-law break the pan, it is earthen; if the daughter-in-law, it is golden.'

'Gold answering to the assayer's test and a woman agreeable to her mother-in-law are scarce.'

'Tears come into the eyes of the daughter-in-law six months after the death of the mother-in-law.'

And troubles are sure to be imminent from confining within a narrow space a number of women of different ages and of various forms of relationship, who have little or nothing to do, and nothing whatever to divert their minds from the most commonplace and trivial details. There may be two or more wives of the same husband. Yet more probable is it that there are aunts, sisters, sisters-in-law, daughters, daughters-in-law, nieces, some married, some widows, people of all ages and children of many degrees of relationship. Friction in such families is inevitable. Not only are there no means of escape from the worry, annoyance, and tyranny that are but too possible; there is also no intellectual diversion of mind or thought. What a refuge from trouble have we in thoughts of the love, patience, and pity of God, and in books! They who love books have in them an inexhaustible source of consolation and delight. But a Hindu woman has neither. No one of the numerous gods of whom she has any knowledge is supposed to be loving, kind, and sympathetic.

And she has no books, nor could she read them if she had. Of the 128,467,925 women in British India in 1891, only 543,495 are returned as able to read and write, with 197,662 learning. In the native states female education is yet more backward, and if it be remembered that at least one-third of the readers are native Christians, it will be seen how few have this advantage. Education, no doubt, is spreading, but more slowly than is supposed; and it is a new thing; for hundreds of years not one woman in two thousand has been able to read or write—a well informed writer says 'one in 20,000'—and if they could have read previous to this half of the century, there was little for them to read that was not corrupting. This is proved by the second argument urged against female education—that women, notwithstanding all safeguards, are naturally predisposed to evil; how much more so would they be if they read books! The first being, that if women could read and write, they would be filled with the conceit that they were the equals of men.

Under such conditions of life; assumed to be the inferiors of men, intellectually and morally; to be unfit for freedom; the subordinates of their husbands; subject to the caprice and will of other women, related to them by marriage, not blood; superstitious, ignorant, and without any elevating pursuits or associations, it is inevitable that they should be liable to untold sorrows and humiliations, and that even when they are not, their condition must be lacking in some of the most rational, benignant, and desirable elements of domestic life.

There are, however, some features of Hindu life and character which tend to alleviate and soothe the lot of women. They are much dwelt on by native apologists, and should in all fairness be stated.

Hindus are better than Hinduism, therefore their intelligence and humanity mitigate the tyranny and hardship of some of their customs. The women, for instance, feel their position to be less irksome than we suppose. Society from the top to the bottom has its foundation in despotism. As it rules unquestioned in the state, so does it in the family. Men rule and women submit as a matter of course; unless the subjection can be evaded by favouritism or cajolery, and when the latter have never been taught that they have rights they can assert and claim, or seen or heard of anything but the most abject submission, and where the maxim is unquestioned, 'Whatever is, is best', it is not so surprising that women acquiesce in their lot. They accept custom almost as patiently as they do a law of nature. Even when the knowledge comes to them that the condition of Western women is different from their own, it affects them far less than might be supposed, except as a thing to wonder at rather than to be sought for. 'They are a strange people; they have one set of customs, we have another, and of course it is proper for each to follow its own', expresses their thought, and there the matter ends! Then, by a perverse method of reasoning and some caprice of fashion, that which to an Englishwoman would be intolerable, is regarded by her Hindu sisters as evidence of her husband's regard and of the respectability of her family. A woman who never walks abroad, and whose face is never seen but by women in the zenana, is as proud of being a 'purdah lady' living behind a curtain as an Englishwoman whose husband keeps a carriage; she regards it as a sign of rank, an evidence of her husband's care for her. Then the duties and amusements of such women, though trivial and unintellectual, are sufficient for them, since their minds are never opened to greater and more interesting affairs.

Nor is companionship always lacking. In such large and miscellaneous households, some can usually be found who in age, disposition, and sympathy become friends and helpers. And though the government of the family is despotic, giving a power too great and that may press heavily, even cruelly, on subordinates, it is not often so abused. Submission to authority is far more general than with us, and that disarms severity, and the gentleness and amiability of the Hindu character indisposes those who have power to abuse it, and those who have not power to provoke its exercise.

Nor are husbands usually cruel or unkind. Brutality is not a Hindu characteristic. The husband may be indifferent, contemptuous, even unfaithful to his wife, but he is seldom cruel. Often he is indulgent in a patronizing way. He does not treat her as an equal, but his kindness, sense of honour, and affection induce him to please and humour her in ways he thinks suitable to her weak nature. She has the best food he can afford; he loads her with ornaments, if not of gold and silver, of inferior material; and not seldom she is the actual, though not the acknowledged ruler.

As large a proportion of Hindu women are gifted with great good sense, force of character, energy, grace of manner, charm, and beauty as will be found anywhere else, and these qualities exert their potency in India, as elsewhere. A Hindu gentleman, next to taking care that his caste is kept undefiled, regards it as his highest duty, his point of honour, to protect his female relatives. He thinks of them contemptuously and patronizingly, as weak, helpless, and liable to go astray, and his care degenerates into distrust and suspicion; but in his own way, and according to his sense of propriety, he defends them from evil, pays them due respect, and ministers to their happiness in food, clothing, ornaments, and amusements, as far as his resources will allow; and defends them from insult, dishonour, and danger as sternly as any knight of chivalry or modern gentleman. Indian history illustrates this in many romantic incidents.

Nevertheless, even when these modifying considerations are allowed their utmost weight, the normal condition of women leaves much to be desired. The masculine sentiment has ever been, 'Women are to be protected and cared for, not for their own sake, but because they are the potential or real mothers of men. They are necessary to us, and should for our repute be pleased and indulged as far as prudence will allow, according to their weak natures; but since they are intellectually and morally weak, frivolous, vain, inclined to evil and to lead others astray, and unsteady as the lotus on the running stream, it is never safe to treat them as equals or to entrust them with power. Therefore they should not be left free, for their own sakes as well as ours. A woman is never fit for independence.'

The inevitable results of such sentiments, practically acted on generation after generation, has been to make men tyrants, women far less esteemed than they should be and their houses little better than prisons. At the best, how colourless, dreary, degraded, and unintellectual must be the lives of women who know no more of nature than can be seen from their zenana *jilmills*; who never walk abroad at their own free will; whose own husbands, fathers, brothers, treat them, not as equals, not as companions, but as pretty animals or pleasant toys; whose opinions are never consulted, and whose wishes are usually suspected; who have no inward sources of interest, information, and delight from reading and writing; and who never are trusted without reserve. How 'cabined, cribbed, confined,' are these millions, whose lives might be so bright and fruitful of good and pleasantness!

But how seldom alas! is the highest ideal of any state of society reached, and certainly it is seldom reached in India. Reports, very reliable, speak of extreme ignorance, jealousy, strife, petty tyranny, unhappiness, much unhealthiness and disease, and suicide as far from uncommon. And darker things are said to be—illegitimacy, infanticide, murder. The structure of society, the seclusion of Hindu dwellings, and the jealous privacy of family life lend themselves to the commission of such crimes, without much fear of detection, and the glints of information which come to most who have opportunities of learning what passes in private life justify these statements. Testimony like the following is but too abundant: 'The life of Hindu women is but a career of ignorance, servitude, and superstition.' 'We are prisoners', says a Hindu lady, 'from our birth, and life-long sufferers; and our fathers, brothers, husbands, sons, keep us in this prison. No Hindu brother pauses to think that it is to his own hurt to keep us down in this misery; but it is. We women are shut up in a pit of ignorance. Hearing of our condition, the eyes of strangers fill with tears. But you leave us there. Have you no pity in your hearts?'

Speaking of life in the zenana, another says, 'It is like that of a frog in a well: everywhere there is beauty, but we cannot see it; it is hid from us.' 'Indian women', says Mr Dorabiji E. Gimi, 'are denied the common enjoyments of life, are throughout life behind purdahs, and, to add insult to injury, the excuse for all such unmanly conduct is proclaimed to be, their inborn wickedness.'

The following just and impartial statement is from a zenana missionary, in reply to the inquiry, 'Are Hindu women happy?' The latter part of it, however, takes account of some present-day conditions of life of which previous ages knew nothing.

'We all feel that they are remarkably apathetic under their sufferings. Apathy and a certain childishness are two leading features of their character, which may be accounted for partly by their long-continued state of subjection, and partly by their religion. They are taught to look at everything as ordered by fate, and they have been taught to regard themselves as inferior to men in every way. Their minds are untrained and easily diverted by trifles, and they have been brought up to observe a multitude of small ceremonial particulars, and to regard these as essential. So it is no wonder that they are dull and trifling, and that the heavier sorrows of life seem sometimes hardly to touch them—at least not acutely. It would be untrue to say that they have not in a certain, dull, half-inarticulate way, a feeling of their grievances. Some express it, and others only show it in their careworn and patient faces. But there cannot be much doubt that the childish element in their character, the facility with which they can be diverted from the consideration of their troubles by any little passing amusement, goes a long way to lighten their burden. In the better educated and more thoughtful, this facile disposition tends to disappear, and its place is sometimes taken by a bitter sense of wrong and an inclination to brood over grievances. And so in this case, as in many cases of progress, there must be the inevitable period of increased power to suffer without much increase in the relief of the suffering

'Beside these natural characteristics there is an external influence—the power of custom, perhaps the strongest influence in a Hindu life. What is customary is sacred, and rebellion against it hardly to be thought of; and where rebellion is quite out of the question, resignation of a kind follows, and produces a measure of peace. But there are exceptions among the classes, especially those which are least restricted.

'After saying so much about the dark side of things, it is only fair to say, too, that there are many really happy women among the Hindus and Mahomedans—happy, that is, in their outward circumstances and relationships. I am pretty certain that two-thirds of my present pupils have little or nothing to cause them suffering in the special ways common to the women of this country. They are kindly used, have the opportunity of learning, are not without outside interests, and seem on the whole to enjoy their lives. The things they lack, and which we most pity them for lacking, are things of the want of which they are not sensible.'[1]

NOTES

1. *The Mission World* for 1895, p. 421.

J.K.H. Denny

Toward the Sunrising by J.K.H. Denny is described on the title page as 'a history of work for the women of India done by women from England 1852–1901'. While her views represent one strand of missionary thinking, a simplistic faith missionary view, she gives us information about the work of missionaries in the area of female education, along with her views of the lives of Hindu women.

Chapter I

THE BEGINNINGS OF THE WORK

'Go ye into all the world and preach the Gospel to every creature'
—A.D. 33

'We see not the slightest prospect of success; we see much danger in making the attempt, and we doubt if the conversion of the Hindus would ever be more than nominal.'
—Sydney Smith, A.D. 1808

The Divine Founder of the Church gave the command at the head of this chapter. We see, by the second quotation, how far its authority had been recognised in England after nearly 1800 years, by men not careless or godless—interested indeed in progress at home. For the writer represented the opinions of an age which considered foreign missions absurd, if not even impious, and a mischievous interference with the orderings of God's providence.

In the first half of the 18th century the East India Company had not begun to put any difficulties in the way of missionaries. Ziegenbalg indeed (1705–1719) came out under the patronage of the King of

J.K.H. Denny, *Toward the Sunrising: a history of work for the women of India done by women from England 1852–1901*, London: Marshall Bros & Zemana Bible and Medical Mission, n.d. (c. 1901).

Denmark, and Carey, Marshman, and Ward were settled at Serampur, in Danish territory, but Schwarz (1750–1798) was allowed by it to work at Tanjore, and Keirnander, who came out in 1758, at Calcutta, unhindered. Still from 1793 to 1813 the Company opposed missions in every possible way, though it made grants to temples and mosques. It did not even provide respectable chaplains for the English residents, though it was ready to administer the revenues of heathen temples.

When the new Charter of 1813 removed the opposition to missionary effort, work began at once, and by 1830 there were nine societies in the field and about 27,000 native Christians in India, Ceylon and Burma. The first work amongst women was started in 1819 by the Baptists of Calcutta, under the rather droll title of the 'Calcutta Female Juvenile Society.' After a year's labour, there were only eight pupils, but in six years' time there were six schools and 160 pupils. About the same time the Calcutta School Society, moved by the appalling fact that out of 40 millions of Hindu women not 400 could read or write, applied to the British and Foreign School Society to send out a lady to train native teachers, and Miss Cooke was selected for this work in 1821.

Miss Cooke, finding that the little girls were most anxious to learn, began to teach them herself without waiting to train teachers. 'What a pearl of a woman is this!' the mothers cried, beating their breasts, when they heard that she had left home and friends for their childrens' sakes. Two other schools were quickly established, the Church Missionary Society became interested, and in a wonderfully short time the schools had increased to 22, with from 300 to 400 scholars. In 1824, the Ladies' Society for native female education in Calcutta was founded, under the presidency of Lady Amherst, and by 1828, a large central school was erected, superintended by Miss Cooke, now married and become Mrs Wilson, where about 300 girls could be received.

These girls were all of the poorest class and belonging to inferior castes, for no respectable high-caste children were allowed to attend. 'Dirty, uncouth little girls', an eyewitness calls them; but still they were taught to read and understand the Bible, and here and there, one gave her heart to Christ. Even to bring such low-class children to school, it was necessary to employ women as messengers, who were paid a *pice* (something under a half-penny) daily for escorting the children and providing them with a meal of parched rice.

It was a long and difficult step forward to reach the higher-caste women and teach them. 'Much too saucy are our wives now', said one Hindu gentleman; 'we should not be able to manage them at all if they knew as much as we do.'

'A female child', exclaimed another in amazement, 'she can never learn to read.'

'Why not?' asked Mrs Porter, the English lady he was talking to.

'Oh! females cannot learn.'

'But I have learnt to read and write.'

'Yes, Europe ladies can do so, but not Hindu.'

Mrs Porter sent for some native girls she had been teaching, who read a few sentences in English and in Telegu, answered some questions in geography and sang a hymn.

The three gentlemen lifted up their hands. 'What can we say?'

'You see it is possible', said Mrs Porter promptly. 'Now will you let me teach your little girl?'

'Salaam, ma'am, but my daughter must not leave my house.'

'May I go to her? I will gladly do so.'

'You are very kind, ma'am, but it is not our custom for English ladies to come to our homes.'

So that matter ended, for the time. But in Calcutta the rough little girls were trained and improved; orphan schools and boarding-schools for Christian girls were started, education went on with rapid strides, and once and again a glimpse was caught of the inner recesses of some Hindu gentleman's house.

Some sixty years ago a Hindu boy of wealthy mercantile parentage, named Ganendro, had been educated in a Mission school, where he lost all faith in his own religion. His father was terribly shocked; the next step might be apostasy, and he imprisoned the boy for ten years in his own house. His young wife, Shunduri, daughter of a Kulin Brahmin, had, wonderful to say, been taught to read, and with her and a widowed cousin, Ganendro read many books on English literature and the Bible also. Shunduri became a Christian, and died happily, trusting in Jesus, at the age of seventeen, of consumption. Ganendro had succeeded in bringing a missionary lady to visit her before her death. Mohesuri, the cousin, was banished to Benares, her Bible being burnt in her presence by the family priest, and on her return after a year's absence, she was publicly baptised. She had managed to obtain another Bible and her diligent study of it made her a firm believer. Ganendro had in the meantime confessed Christ and become an outcast from his father's house.

These events, which happened in 1851–2, aroused a great deal of interest in Calcutta. Mrs Mackenzie, the wife of a merchant there, was the prime mover in the effort which resulted to start an institution for training teachers, mostly Eurasians, and in 1851 the Calcutta Normal

School was founded, under the management of the Misses Suter, the passage and outfit money for one of them having been collected by the late Lady Kinnaird. This school was in connection with the old Central School which Miss Cooke had managed, after her marriage to Mr Wilson, since 1828.

Many schools had during this time been begun in different parts of the country. Mrs Stevenson, wife of a Scotch missionary, had opened four in Bombay as early as 1828, and the first Parsee school was begun there in 1849. The Society for the Promotion of Female Education in the East had been founded in 1834, and the Scottish Ladies' Association in 1838, dividing into two branches at the disruption of the Scotch Church in 1843. These gave help to many mission stations.

The idea of educating high-caste Hindu women was also being discussed, and in 1849 took shape in the establishment by the Hon. Drinkwater Bethune, of a Native Female School in Calcutta. He gave the large sum of £6,000 to provide a suitable building, and education was given to many girls belonging to the highest families, but an education from which Christianity was carefully excluded. The Bethune School was much less successful than had been expected, and its defects and exclusion of Christian teaching led Dr Duff to establish a school for high-caste girls in 1857. This went on for many years and did a great deal of good, though it could hardly be called a brilliant success, for Indian opinion and usage change very slowly.

The importance of the Calcutta Normal School lay, not only in its providing teachers, greatly needed, for the increasing numbers of schools, but even more for the facilities it offered for carrying Christian teaching into Hindu homes. Gradually it was seen that Zenana visiting was a most hopeful way of reaching native ladies, and the wish to do this, which Ganendro's story had helped to arouse, was soon in a fair way to be realised, through the personal influence of the Rev. John Fordyce. Indeed, as early as 1855, some of the pupils of the Normal School were received in high-caste houses as teachers.

When the Normal School was founded in Calcutta, an Auxiliary Committee was formed in London to assist it, and from that time Lady (then Hon. Mrs Arthur) Kinnaird took the deepest interest in the work, and by her energy, her untiring efforts and constant sympathy, did more than perhaps any other person to ensure its success. In the trying times after the Indian Mutiny, it was the earnest exertions of the London Auxiliary Committee which tided the School over great difficulties resulting from the loss of funds.

When Miss Cockle and Miss Rutland arrived in Calcutta in 1857, the former as head of the Normal School, the latter as Zenana teacher, the Calcutta Committee gratefully recorded the help they had received from London—in the aggregate, not less than 20,000 rupees—and added that it was 'very satisfactory to find that in all their proceedings and plans during the past year, this Committee enjoyed their entire sanction.'

It was in 1861 that the Auxiliary Committee, being very anxious to extend the benefits of Christian education to other parts of India, formed themselves into a society, subsequently called the INDIAN FEMALE NORMAL SCHOOL AND INSTRUCTION SOCIETY, with which the Calcutta Normal School might remain in connection.

The School was distinctly Church of England, but it was designed from the first that the new society should be undenominational, and in a memorandum drawn up in 1868 by the Rev. Henry Venn, Hon. Sec. of the C.M.S., this principle is affirmed.

'The Female Instruction Society, though originated by the zeal of members of the Church of England, and mainly carried on by their support, and desirous of spreading, through its teachers, the Protestant and Evangelical views of truth contained in her doctrinal articles and formularies—yet, as a society, thankfully accepts the co-operation of members of other churches; and, in its operations abroad, is ready to unite with any of the orthodox Protestant Missionary Societies for the establishment of normal and other schools, where there may be suitable openings for its benevolent intervention.'

These rules were faithfully adhered to, and the wish of the Committee not to infringe them led to their giving up a plan made in 1876 for lightening the labours of their secretaries in India, by affording them the assistance of a corresponding committee of gentlemen belonging to the C.M.S. only. As the desire of the Committee to add members from other denominations did not seem practicable, the plan was dropped.

The work had meanwhile extended to other parts of India— Trevandrum, Lucknow, Benares, Lahore, Amritsar, Madras and Bombay had been taken up in succession. The history of some of these mission stations is given in separate chapters, while others are no longer connected with our Society.

In 1880, some members of the Committee who preferred to work entirely with the Church of England withdrew from the Society, and, forming the Church of England Zenana Missionary Society, appealed to all the associations at home, and obtained the co-operation of a large number. The Female Normal School and Instruction Society was therefore obliged to relinquish its stations at Calcutta, Madras, Amritsar, and Trevandrum, retaining Bombay, the North-West Provinces and Lahore,

In 1888, its title, now no longer specially appropriate, was changed to that by which it is now known—

The Zenana, Bible and Medical Mission

There are now 103 European missionaries, 51 assistant missionaries, and 197 native teachers, nurses, & c., besides 92 Biblewomen, connected with the Society. There are altogether 103 stations, but at two of these only assistant missionaries, and at nine only Biblewomen or native teachers are employed. There are 68 schools and institutions, with 3,739 pupils. 3,084 Zenanas were visited in 1900, and 2,883 pupils taught in them. The Biblewomen visited 1,035 villages and 2,632 houses.

Before proceeding to describe the work carried on by these various agencies, a brief account of the history, religion, and customs of India will be given.

We 'thanked God and took courage.'

Chapter V

Wives and Widows

What is cruel?—The heart of a viper. What is more cruel than that?—The heart of a woman. What is the cruellest of all? —The heart of a soulless widow.'
—Sanskrit Catechism

'Nevertheless, neither is the man without the woman, nor the woman without the man, in the Lord.'

As an infant, a Hindu woman is under the control of her parents; as a wife, under the control of her husband; as an old woman, under the control of her sons. But free—never.

At a very early age, as a mere baby, the Hindu woman is betrothed, and when she is about eight or ten years old she is taken to her husband's home, there to live under the guardianship of his family until she is old enough to undertake a wife's duties. The husband may be a mere boy, perhaps careless and cruel, or he may be an old man of sixty or more. This is no infrequent occurrence among the Kulin Brahmins, whose caste is so high that it ensures immortality to their wives. Some of these old men have a number of wives, indeed they make their living by marrying girls, who continue to reside at their own homes while the husband spends a few days now with one, now with another.

One case was recorded, as late as 1897, where fourteen girls of the same family were married simultaneously, at ages varying from three to twenty-six, to a Kulin Brahman aged sixty-four. It is impossible to speak too strongly against the evil of child marriage in India, and it is something to be very thankful for that public opinion among the natives is slowly wakening to perceive the evil and to take measures against it. The Rajput chiefs bound themselves, as early as 1888, to discourage the marriages of girls under fourteen and boys under eighteen. This indeed seems young enough, but it is a vast improvement on the state of things which permitted children of eleven and twelve to become mothers, thus entailing on them a life-long heritage of disease and misery. A doctor of thirty years' experience says that twenty-five per cent of Indian women die prematurely through early marriage, and twenty-five per cent more are invalided from the same cause.

A secondary evil is the short time allowed for education, for when a girl marries she can no longer leave home to go to school, and any teaching she gets must be given during the necessarily short and occasional visits of the Zenana missionary.

The life of a high-caste Hindu woman is at best, a dreary one. Shut up in small dark rooms, whose only outlook is an enclosed court, only occasionally—*very* occasionally—allowed to go out in a closed vehicle, she has no variety, and little pleasure. She may count over and display her jewels and fine clothes, dress herself and put on her ornaments, quarrel or gossip with the other women in the house, or do her share of the simple cooking, but that is all the amusement she has. One day is like another, dreary, dull, monotonous. She is not naturally stupid, quite the contrary, but long disuse has dulled her faculties, and the utter lack of interest in life has narrowed her mind.

And if it were only the dulness of life which had to be endured—but there is sometimes cruelty and ill-usage too. It is a hard fate for the little child-wife, when she is taken away from the home she knows, and the mother who loves her, to a house where she is strange and perhaps unwelcome, where her husband's family often treat her unkindly and he himself may be brutal, or at least rough and neglectful.

Sad stories are told of the cruelties of mothers-in-law. One girl was so badly treated that she would run away to her own home whenever she could, so, to cure her of this habit, the husband and his mother tied her to a pole and mercilessly branded her foot with a hot iron, the scar of which covered the sole of one foot entirely. The husband got three years' imprisonment, but at the end of the time the poor wife would not dare to go back to him, and what future lay before her but one of darkness and disgrace?

Another girl was brought to a native Christian lady doctor suffering from a bad fever, but her mother-in-law would give her no medicine and only stale food to eat and kept her grinding all day. A child, only eleven years old, had her arm broken by her mother-in-law's blows, and twenty-seven marks of burns on her body where she had been pinched with red-hot tongs to make her do more grinding than she could possibly get through.

These may be exceptional cases, noticed because an excess of ill-usage has brought them to the front. But on the other hand, who can tell what may go on in these secluded houses day by day, where there is no public opinion and no redress? It is not denied that there are happy homes, kind husbands, affectionate mothers-in-law to be found. All we can say is that irresponsible power does not tend to produce them.

Things are changed for the young wife when she becomes the mother of a son. Then her husband is probably indulgent towards her and treats her with some respect. She has the management of the household in her hands, and he may even consult her as to his own affairs. This is the one happy time in a Hindu woman's life, and well is it for her when she does not outlive her husband and become that most miserable creature in the world, a Hindu widow.

A poor man's wife is in some ways more fortunately circumstanced than her richer sister. She has more freedom to go about, though, if she is a village-women, she has hard and exhausting work to do in the fields, and is often wearied out with her labours. Besides, a poor man cannot generally afford to take another wife, so the evils and heart-burnings of polygamy are avoided.

Even though the Hindu woman's status is improved when a son is born to her, her position is still a most humiliating one. She may not eat with her husband, nor mention his name, nor speak to him in other people's presence, and no amount of insult or outrage to which she may be subjected by him, warrant her in any resentment or estrangement. She cannot worship with him, for though she must be present during some of the ceremonies he performs, she cannot take any part in them. She can, however, go through a humble sort of *puja* by herself, with little uncon-secrated images.

It is said by some that the good deeds of husband and wife are transferable after death, but there seems to be equally good authority for saying that while the woman's good deeds can benefit her husband, nothing that he does can have any effect on her. She stands and falls by her own merits alone. The chief way in which the wife can help her husband is by ascending the funeral pile with him and being burnt alive, but this the British Government does not permit.

Though, indeed, it would be happier for many of these poor women to die, than to live the life they do.

...

Annie Besant

One of the most 'notorious' women of her day, Annie Besant (1847–1933), sometimes referred to as 'Red Annie', championed a number of radical causes in England: women's rights, birth control, secularism, trade unionism, socialism, and anti-imperialism. She converted to Theosophy in 1889, among other reasons because it recognized the equality of men and women, had a woman leader, and involved mystic and occult practices associated with 'feminine' nature. In 1893 she came to India to lecture for the Theosophical Society, felt India was her true home, and even felt she had been Indian in an earlier life.

Reformists were critical of her because when she first arrived she did not want to be critical of the condition of Indian women as she felt she did not know enough. Later, in a British paper she said she did not think Indian women were suppressed, and insisted that people respect cultural difference. Missionaries too were irritated by Besant's refusal to be critical. The orthodox and nationalists were annoyed by what they considered her patronising defense of Hinduism.

But later she began to carefully espouse the cause of education for girls, and founded the Hindu College Girls' School in 1904.

Though she felt that it was Indians who should decide the kind of education girls should receive, she set out her ideas in a pamphlet published in 1904. Still later, Besant's main focus was the nationalist movement.

Referring to James Mill's remarks about the treatment of women being a marker of civilization, she said that 'the position of the child even more marks the state of the community'. She fought for the protection of children both in England and in India, and for the protection of animals.

The Education of Indian Girls*

One of the first things done by Countess Wachtmeister and myself, when we came to India in 1893, was to concern ourselves with the question of

Annie Besant, *For India's Uplift*, Madras: G.A. Natesan & Co., n.d.

* A pamphlet published in 1904.

the education of girls. But many thoughtful Indians begged us to wait until we had secured the confidence of the Hindu community, so that no suspicion could arise with regard to our objects. The unhappy perversion of an Indian lady had shaken the confidence of the Hindu public with respect to girls' education, and they feared Christian proselytising under the garb of interest in education. The advice seemed sound and we accepted it.

Ten years have passed since then, and we may truly say that the confidence of the Hindu public in the purity of our aims and the straight-forwardness of our actions has been won. The appeals to me to take up the education of girls have been many and urgent, and unqualified approval of the scheme I have submitted in writing and speech has been expressed. It seems time, therefore, to give this scheme a wider public-ity, and, if it be acceptable, as it seems to be, to a large number of Hindus, then to let it serve as the basis of a national movement for the education of girls. It is already being followed in a few small girls' schools, carried on by Lodges of the Theosophical Society, and may henceforth take fuller shape.

The national movement for girls' education must be on national lines; it must accept the general Hindu conceptions of woman's place in the national life, not the dwarfed modern view but the ancient ideal. It must see in the woman the mother and the wife, or, as in some cases, the learned and pious ascetic, the Brahmavadini of older days. It cannot see in her the rival and competitor of man in all forms of outside and public employment, as woman, under different economic conditions, is coming to be, more and more, in the West. The West must work out in its own way the artificial problem which has been created there as to the relation of the sexes. The East has not to face that problem, and the lines of western female education are not suitable for the education of eastern girls. There may be exceptional cases and when parents wish their daughters to follow the same course of education as their sons, they can readily secure for them that which they desire. But the *national* move-ment for the education of girls must be one which meets the national needs, and India needs nobly trained wives and mothers, wise and tender rulers of the household, educated teachers of the young, helpful counsellors of their husbands, skilled nurses of the sick, rather than girl graduates, educated for the learned professions.

Let us, then, put down in order the essentials of the education which is desirable for Indian girls.

I. Religious and Moral Education

Every girl must be taught the fundamental doctrines for her religion, in a clear, simple and rational method. The Sanatana Dharma Series I and II, in the Vernaculars, will suit Hindu girls as well as Hindu boys, and girls thoroughly grounded in these will be able to study the Advanced Text Book after leaving school, as they are not likely to remain there to an age fit for such study. The *Mahabharata* and the *Ramayana*, in the Vernaculars, should be largely drawn on for moral instruction, as well as *Manuṣmriti*; and Tulsi Das' *Ramayana* should be read by all Hindi-knowing girls. To this should be added the teaching of hymns in the Vernacular and stotras in Samskrit, as well as the committal to memory of many beautiful passages from the *Bhagavad Gita,* the *Hamsa Gita,* the *Anugita,* and other suitable works. They should be taught to worship, and simple plain explanations of the worship followed should be given, and, while the devotion so natural to an Indian woman should be nurtured, an intelligent understanding should be added to it, and a pure and enlightened faith, their natural heritage, should be encouraged in them. Where any girl shows capacity for deeper thought, philosophical studies and explanations should not be withheld from her, so that opportunity may be afforded for the re-appearance of the type of which Maitreyi and Gargi and the woman singers of the Vedas were shining examples. Girls belonging to the Islamic and Zoroastrian faiths should be similarly instructed, the books of their respective religions taking the place of the Hindu works named above. There is an abundant wealth of beautiful devotional verse in Persian, to culture and elevate the mind of the Muslim girl, to whom also should be opened the stores of Arabic learning. The Zoroastrian has also ample sacred treasures for the instruction of his girls, and can utilise selections from the Avesta, Pahlavi and Persian. I do not know if there is much available vernacular literature in these faiths in Southern India, but in Northern India Urdu literature for the girls of Islam is not lacking.

II. Literary Education

A sound literary knowledge of the Vernacular should be given, both in reading and writing. Vernacular literature, in Hindi, Urdu, Bengali, Marathi, Gujerati, Telugu and Tamil, is sufficiently rich in original works and translations to give full scope for study, and to offer a store of enjoyment for the leisure hours of later life. A colloquial knowledge of some vernacular other than her own would be useful to a girl, if time would allow of the learning. A classical language, Sanskrit or Arabic or

Persian, according to the girl's religion, should be learned sufficiently to read with pleasure the noble literature contained therein, and the quick Indian girl will readily master sufficient of one of these tongues to prove a never-failing delight to her in her womanhood, and to listen with intelligent pleasure to the reading of her husband as he enjoys the masterpieces of the great writers. Indian history and Indian geography should be thoroughly taught, and reading-books should be provided consisting of stories of all the sweetest and strongest women in Indian story, so that the girls may feel inspired by these noblest types of womanhood as compelling ideals, and may have before them these glorious proofs of the heights to which Indian women have climbed. The very narrowness of their present lives, their triviality and frivolity, render the more necessary the presentation to them of a broad and splendid type as a model for their uplifting, and while their minds will be thus widened and their ideas enlarged, at the same time they will be led along lines purely national and in consonance with immemoral ideas. If the westernising, in a bad sense, of Indian men be undesirable, still more undesirable is such westernising of Indian women; the world cannot afford to lose the pure, lofty, tender and yet strong type of Indian womanhood. It is desirable, also, seeing how much English thought is dominating the minds of the men, and how many sympathetic English-women seek to know their Indian sisters, that the girls should learn English, and have thus opened to them the world of thought outside India; in later life they may make many a pleasant excursion into that world in the company of their husbands, and the larger horizons will interest without injuring.

III. SCIENTIFIC EDUCATION

Nothing is more necessary to the Indian wife and mother, ruler often of a household that is a little village, than a knowledge of sanitary laws, of the value of food-stuffs, of nursing the sick, of simple medicines, of 'first aid' in accidents, of cookery of the more delicate kind, of household management, and the keeping of accounts. The hygiene of the household should be thoroughly taught, the value of fresh air, sunlight, and scrupulous cleanliness; these were, indeed, thoroughly understood and practised by the elder generation, and must still, if learned in the school-room, find their field of practice in the home; but the latest generation seems to be in all this far behind its grandmothers. Essential again is a knowledge of the value of foodstuffs, and of their effects on the body in the building of muscular, nervous and fatty tissues, of their stimulative or nutrient qualities. Some knowledge of simple medicines is needed by every mother, that she may not be incessantly calling in a doctor; she should also be able to deal with accidental injuries, completely with slight ones, and sufficiently with serious ones to prevent loss of life while awaiting the surgeon's coming; simple nursing every girl should learn, and the importance of accuracy in observing directions, keeping fixed hours for food and medicine, etc. Sufficient arithmetic should be learned for all household purposes, for quick and accurate calculation of quantities and prices, and the keeping of accounts. A knowledge of cookery has always been part of the education of the Indian housewife, and this should still have its place in education, or there will be little comfort in the house for husband and children.

The Indian cook—like cooks in other countries—does his work all the better if the house-mother is able to supervise and correct.

IV. ARTISTIC EDUCATION

Instruction in some art should form part of education for a girl, so that leisure in later life may be pleasantly and adequately filled, instead of being wasted in gossip and frivolity. South India is leading the way in musical education, and the prejudice against it is disappearing. The singing of stotras, to an accompaniment on the *vina,* or other instrument, is a refining and delightful art in which the girls take the greatest pleasure, and one which enables them to add greatly to the charm of home. Drawing and painting are arts in which some find delight, and their deft fingers readily learn exquisite artistic embroidery and needle-work of all kinds. Needless to say that all should learn sewing, darning and the cutting-out of such made garments as are used in their districts. In all of these, the natural taste of the pupil should be the guide to the selection of the art, though almost all, probably, will take part in singing.

V. PHYSICAL EDUCATION

The training and strengthening of the bodies of the future mothers must not be left out of sight, and, to this end, physical exercises of a suitable kind should form part of the school curriculum. In Southern India, the girls are very fond of exercises in which they move to the sound of their own songs, performing often complicated exercises, in some of which patterns are woven and unwoven in coloured threads attached to a centre high overhead, the ends of the threads being held by the girls, whose evolutions make and unmake the pattern. Other exercises somewhat resemble the well-known 'Swedish exercises', and all these are good, and there are games which give exercise of a pleasant and active kind.

These conduce to the health of young bodies, and give grace of movement, removing all awkwardness. Nothing is prettier than to see a group of girls moving gracefully to the sound of their own young voices, in and out, in mazy evolutions, with clapping of soft palms or clash of light playing-sticks. The lack of physical exercise leads to many chronic ailments in womanhood and to premature old age.

Such is an outline of the education which would, it seems to me, prove adequate to the needs of the young daughters of India, and would train them up into useful and cultured women, heads of happy households, 'lights of the home'.

There will always be some exceptional girls who need for the due evolution of their faculties a more profound and a wider education, and these must be helped to what they need as individuals, each on her own line. Such girls may be born into India in order to restore to her the learned women of the past, and to place again in her diadem the long lost pearl of lofty female intelligence. It is not for any to thwart them in their upward climbing, or to place unnecessary obstacles in their path.

Of this we may be sure, that Indian greatness will not return until Indian womanhood obtains a larger, a freer, and a fuller life, for largely in the hands of Indian women must lie the redemption of India. The wife inspires or retards the husband; the mother makes or mars the child. The power of woman to uplift or debase man is practically unlimited, and man and woman must walk forward hand-in-hand to the raising of India, else will she never be raised at all. The battle for the religious and moral education of boys is won, although the victory has still to be made effective all over India, The battle for the education of girls is just beginning, and may Ishvara bless those who are the vanguard, and all beneficent Powers enlighten their minds and make strong their hearts!

Sister Nivedita (Margaret Noble)

In his introduction to one of the later editions of *Web of Indian Life* (1904) by Sister Nivedita (1867–1911), Rabindranath Tagore writes, 'Indians, like all other peoples of the world, are naturally susceptible to flattery. But they have been deprived of it....' So he is 'deeply grateful' to 'Nivedita, that great-hearted Western woman' for her understanding, sympathy, and love of India. Certainly, her account of the lives and status of women in India is lyrical, if not rhapsodic.

Born in Ireland of a Scots Methodist family that had lived in Ireland for generations, and been involved in the struggle for Irish Home Rule, she grew up in England. She met Swami Vivekanand in London in 1895 and was gradually won over by his ideas and his personality. She came to Calcutta in 1898, threw herself into social work and plague relief, opened two schools, joined the Ramkrishna order, and, after Vivekanand's death in 1902, joined India's freedom struggle. Her special educational interest in India was in purdah women and child widows.

The Hindu Woman as Wife
...

The good breeding of the Hindu woman is so perfect that it is not noticed till one comes across the exception—some spoilt child, perhaps, who, as heiress or beauty has been too much indulged; and her self-assertiveness and want of restraint, though the same behaviour might seem decorous enough in an English girl of her age, will serve as some measure for the real value of the common standard.

It is not merely in her quietness and modesty, however, that the daughter-in-law betrays good training. She has what remains with her throughout life—a *savoir faire* that nothing can disturb. I have never known this broken; and I saw an extraordinary instance of it when a

Sister Nivedita, *The Web of Indian Life*, Bombay: Longmans, Green, 1918.

friend, the shyest of orthodox women, consented to have her photograph taken for one who begged it with urgency. She stipulated, naturally, that it should be done by a woman. But this was found to be impossible. 'Then let it be an Englishman', she said with a sigh, evidently shrinking painfully from the idea of a man, yet feeling that the greater the race-distance the less would be the impropriety. The morning came, and the Englishman arrived, but in the Indian gentlewoman who faced him there was no trace of self-consciousness or fear. A superb indifference carried her through the ordeal, and would have been a sufficient protection in some real difficulty.

All the sons of a Hindu household bring their wives home to their mother's care, and she, having married her own daughters into other women's families, takes these in their place. There is thus a constant bubbling of young life about the elderly woman, and her own position becomes a mixture of the mother-*suzeraine* and lady abbess. She is well aware of the gossip and laughter of the girls amongst themselves, though they become so demure at her entrance. Whispering goes on in corners and merriment waxes high even in her presence, but she ignores it discreetly, and devotes her attention to persons of her own age. In the early summer mornings she smiles indulgently to find that one and another slipped away last night from her proper sleeping-place and betook herself to the roof, half for the coolness and half for the mysterious joys of girls' midnight gossip.

The relationship, however, is as far from familiarity as that of any kind and trusted prioress with her novices. The element of banter and freedom has another outlet, in the grandmother or whatever aged woman may take that place in the community house. Just as at home the little one had coaxed and appealed against the decisions of father or mother to the ever-ready granddam, so, now that she is a bride, she finds some old woman in her husband's home who has given up her cares into younger hands and is ready to forego all responsibility in the sweetness of becoming a *confidante*. One can imagine the rest. There must be many a difficulty, many a perplexity, in the new surroundings, but to them all old age can find some parallel. Looking back into her own memories, the grandmother tells of the questions that troubled her when she also was a bride, of the mistakes that she made, and the solutions that offered. Young and old take counsel together, and there is even the possibility that when a mother-in-law is unsympathetic, her own mother-in-law may intervene on behalf of a grandson's wife. Before the grandmother, therefore, there is none of that weight of reverence which can never be lightened in the mother's presence. Even the veil need not be dropped.

The familiar 'thou' takes the place of the stately 'you', and there is no respect shown by frigid reserve.

...

With all the shyness of the religious novice comes the girl to her new home. Its very form, with its pillared courtyards, is that of a cloister. The constant dropping of the veil in the presence of a man, or before a senior, is the token of a real retirement, the sacrament of an actual seclusion, within which all the voices of the world lose distinctness and individuality, becoming but faint echoes of that which alone can call the soul and compel the eager feet. For India has no fear of too much worship. To her, all that exists is but a mighty curtain of appearances, tremulous now and again with breaths from the unseen that it conceals. At any point, a pinprick may pierce the great illusion, and the seeker become aware of the Infinite Reality beyond. And who so fitted to be the window of the Eternal Presence as that husband, who is at once most adored and loved of all created beings?

For there is a deep and general understanding of the fact that only in its own illumination, or its own feeling, can the soul find its highest individuation. To learn how she can offer most becomes thus the aim of the young wife's striving. All her dreams are of the saints—women mighty in renunciation: Sita, whose love found its richest expression in the lifelong farewell that made her husband the ideal king; Sati, who died rather than hear a word against Siva, even from her own father; and Uma, realising that her love was given in vain, yet pursuing the more eagerly the chosen path. 'Be like Savitri', was her father's blessing, as he bade her the bridal farewell, and Savitri—the Alcestris of Indian story—was that maiden who followed even Death till she won back her husband's life. Thus wifehood is thought great in proportion to its giving, not to its receiving. It would never occur to anyone, in writing fiction, or delineating actual character, to praise a woman's charms, as we praise Sarah Jennings', on the score that she retained her husband's affection during her whole life.

...

It is evident then that the laws of Manu are rather the unconscious expression of the spirit of the people than a declaration of the ideals towards which they strive. And for this reason they would afford the most reliable foundation for a healthy criticism of Indian custom. The conception of domestic happiness which they reveal is very complete, and no one who has seen the light on an Indian woman's face when it turns to her husband—as I have seen it in all parts of the country—can doubt that that conception is often realised in life. For if the characteristic emotion of the wife may be described as passionate reverence, that of the Hindu husband is certainly a measureless protection. If we may presume to analyse things so sacred as the great mutual trusts of life, it would seem that tenderness is the ruling note of the man's relation. Turning as he does to the memory of his own mother for the ideal perfection, there is again something of motherhood in what he brings to his wife. As a child might do, she cooks for him, and serves him, sitting before him as he eats to fan away the flies. As a disciple might, she prostrates herself before him, touching his feet with her head before receiving his blessing. It is not equality. No. But who talks of a vulgar equality, asks the Hindu wife, when she may have instead the unspeakable blessedness of offering worship?

And on the man's side, how is this received? Entirely without personal vanity. The idea that adoration is the soul's opportunity has sunk deep into the life of the people. And the husband can recognise his wife's right to realise her highest through him without ever forgetting that it is her power to love, not his worthiness of love, that is being displayed. Indeed, is not life everywhere of one tint in this regard? Does anything stir our reverence like an affection that we feel beyond our merit?

It is often glibly said that this habit of being served spoils the Indian man and renders him careless of the comfort of others. I have never found this to be so. It is true that Indian men do not rise when a woman enters, and remain standing till she is seated. Nor do they hasten to open the door through which she is about to pass. But then it is not according to the etiquette of their country to do these things.

Woman in the National Life

...

There is doubtless some truth in the idea that society in a military state tends always to seclude its women. The fact that in the aristocratic strictness of retreat the Mussulmannin ranks first, the Rajputni second, and the Bengali woman only third, in India, goes far to support this conclusion. But the case of the Rani of Jhansi is sufficient indication that the custom is by no means so universal as is often stated. The lower classes move freely in all countries, for household work and the earning of their livelihood compel; and the screen is always more easily lifted for the Hindu than for the Mohammedan. A thousand considerations intervene to mitigate its severity in the case of the former, while in the South and West, where Moslem rule was brief, and Moslem fashions had little force, it is actually non-existent.

By this it is not to be understood that any Hindu women meet men outside their kindred with the freedom and frankness of their Western sisters. Very old adaptations of the Ramayana show us the brother-in-law who has never looked higher than the heroine's feet, and the wife who blushes rather than mention her husband's name. But the power of the individual to isolate himself in the midst of apparently unrestrained social intercourse is necessary in all communities, and has its correspondence in Western society itself. Freedom is granted only to the self-disciplined. It might be added that a good wife has as little occasion to realise the possible jealousy of her husband in the East as in the West, and that an unreasonable fit of suspicion would be considered the same weakness and insult by the one society as by the other.

The liberty of Madras and Bombay is, however, a reality for all its limitations. And in certain parts of the province of Malabar woman is actually in the ascendancy. This curious country, of women learned in Sanskrit, and kings who rule as the regents of their sisters, will have many disclosures to make to the world when India shall have produced a sufficient number of competent sociologists of her own blood. It is commonly said to be characteristically polyandrous; but it is not so, in the same sense as Tibet and some of the Himalayan tribes, for no woman regards herself as the wife of two men at once. The term *matriarchal* is more accurate, inasmuch as the husband visits the wife in her own home, and the right of inheritance is through the mother. Thus, far from India's being the land of the uniform oppression of woman by a uniform method, it represents the whole cycle of feminist institutions. There is literally no theory of feminine rights and position that does not find illustration somewhere within her boundaries.

With regard to the seclusion of women by Hindus, the statement that it arose as a protection against the violence of a ruling race is thoughtless and untrue. The custom in its present rigour dates undoubtedly from the period of Moslem rule. Where that rule was firm and long established, it has sunk deep into Hindu habit, and in Bombay and Madras, under opposite conditions, has been almost passed by. In the plays of Kalidas, and in old Sanskrit literature generally, there is abundant evidence that it was not practised in its modern form in the Vedic, Buddhistic, or Puranic periods.

But although it dates from the era of Ghazni or Ghor—except where the Rajput made an independent introduction of the purdah—there is nothing to show that the cloistering of women was spread in Hindostan by other means than by the force of fashion and imperial prestige. Indeed, sooner or later we have to face the question: What induced the Mohammedan to screen his women? Islam derives the religious sanction of its social institutions from Arabia, and the Arab woman is said to enjoy considerable freedom and power. Hence it is sometimes claimed that the Mussulman himself adopted the practice from Persia, from China, or from Greece. Such explanations are little more than recrimination. What are we to regard as the root of a convention which in certain parts of the Orient appears to be almost instinctive? Climate, inducing scantiness of clothing, cannot be the whole secret, for in that case Madras would be more deeply permeated by the custom than Bengal, whereas the very opposite is the fact.

Might we not as well reverse the inquiry, and try to assign some reason for the Western assumption of equality between man and woman? The first point that strikes us is the very uneven distribution of the theory in Europe itself. It is by no means so strong in Latin as in Teutonic countries, nor so clearly formulated amongst the Germanic peoples as in the Norse Sagas. This fact lends colour to the theory of modern sociologists that fisher-life is the source of all equality between the sexes. For the man, pursuing the conquest of the sea, must leave his wife regnant over the affairs of field and farm. It is supposed by some that the very use of the wedding-ring originated in the investiture of woman at marriage, by means of the signet-ring, with a fulness of authority similar to the husband's outside, over all that lay within the house. Surely it is clear that land and sea are not the only possible antitheses, but that wherever a race is employed in a sustained and arduous conquest of Nature there it will tend towards fulness of co-operation, similarity of manners, and equality of rights as between men and women; and that, other things being equal, under long-settled conditions, from which anxiety is largely eliminated, there is a progressive inclination towards divergence of their lines of activity, accompanied by the more complete surrender of woman to the protection of man, and the seeking of her individuality in the sphere of morals and emotion.

The tendency to divergence of function would be accelerated in Asia by the nature of the climate, which makes stillness and passivity the highest luxury. This fact would combine again with military prepossessions, to make the custom of seclusion especially characteristic of royal households, and having once achieved such social prestige it would speedily extend over wide areas. Thus it becomes characteristic of conquering races, and among Hindus is imitated with marked energy by Bengal, which is not only the most idealistic of all the Indian provinces, but also—owing to the existence of the zemindar class—the most persistently feudal, after Rajputana.

If this theory be correct, the freedom of the Indian woman of the first

Aryan period is to be explained as an outcome of the struggle with earth and forest. The early immigrations of agricultural races across the Himalayas from Central Asia must have meant a combat with Nature of the severest kind. It was a combat in which the wife was the helpmeet of the husband. If he cleared the jungle and hunted the game, she had to give aid in field and garden. The Aryan population was scanty, and she would often be required to take his place. Vicissitudes were many. At a moment's notice she must be prepared to meet an emergency, brave, cheerful, and self-helpful. In such a life woman must move as easily as man.

It began to be otherwise, however, when the country was cleared, agriculture established on the Aryan scale, and the energy of the race concentrated on the higher problem of conserving and extending its culture of mind and spirit. It is doubtful whether Indian philosophy could ever have been completed on other terms than on those of some measure of seclusion for woman. 'This world is all a dream: God alone is real', such an ultimatum could hardly have been reached in a society like that of Judaism, where love and beauty were held as the seal of divine approval on a successful life. Not that India would decry these happy gifts. But they are secular joys in her eyes, not spiritual. 'The religion of the wife lies in serving her husband: the religion of the widow lies in serving God', say the women; and there is no doubt in their minds that the widow's call is the higher of the two.

While we talk of the seclusion of woman, however, as if it were a fact, we must be careful to guard against misconception. In society and in the streets of Indian cities, it is practically true that we see men alone. This fact makes it a possibility for the religious to pass his life without looking on the face of any woman, save such as he may call 'Mother.' Inside the house, if we penetrate so far, we shall probably meet with none but women. But if we live there day after day, we shall find that every woman has familiar intercourse with some man or men in the family. The relation between brothers and sisters-in-law is all gaiety and sweetness. Scarcely any children are so near to a woman as the sons of her husband's sisters. It is the proud prerogative of these, whatever be their age, to regard her as their slave. There is a special delicacy of affection and respect between the husband's father and his daughter-in-law. Cousins count as brothers and sisters. And from the fact that every woman has her rightful place in some family it follows that there is more healthy human intercourse with men in almost every Hindu woman's life than in those of thousands of single women, living alone, or following professional careers, in the suburbs of London and other Western cities.

It is an intercourse, too, that is full of a refined and delicate sense of humour. Indian men who have been to Europe always declare that the zenana woman stands unrivalled in her power of repartee. English fun is apt to strike the Eastern ear as a little loud. How charming is the Bengali version of 'the bad penny that always turns up', in 'I am the broken cowrie that has been to seven markets'! That is to say, 'I may be worthless, but I am knowing.'

We are too apt to define the ideal as that towards which we aspire, thinking but rarely of those assimilated ideals which reveal themselves as custom. If we analyse the conventions that dominate an Indian woman's life we cannot fail to come upon an exceedingly stern canon of self-control. The closeness and intimacy of the family life, and the number of the interests that have to be considered, make strict discipline necessary, doubtless, for the sake of peace. Hence a husband and wife may not address each other in the presence of others. A wife may not name her husband, much less praise him, and so on. Only little children are perfectly untrammelled, and may bestow their affection when and where they will. All these things are for the protection of the community, lest it be outraged by the parading of a relationship of intimacy, or victimised by an enthusiasm which it could not be expected to share.

This constant and happy subordination of oneself to others does not strike the observer, only because it is so complete. It is not the characteristic of the specially developed individual alone, for it is recognised and required, in all degrees of delicacy, by society at large. Unselfishness and the thirst for service stand out in the Western personality against a background of individualistic conventions, and convey an impression of the eagerness and struggle of pity, without which the world would certainly be the poorer. But the Eastern woman is unaware of any defiance of institutions. She is the product of an ethical civilisation. Her charities are required of her. Her vows and penances are unknown even to her husband; but were they told, they would scarcely excite remark in a community where all make similar sacrifices.

This is only to say that she is more deeply self-effacing and more effectively altruistic than any Western. The duty of tending the sick is so much a matter of course to her that she does not dream of it as a special function, for which one might erect hospitals or learn nursing. Here, no doubt, she misses a great deal, for the modern organisation of skill has produced a concentration of attention on method that avails to save much suffering. Still, we must not too carelessly assume that our own habit of massing together all the hungry, sick, and insane, and isolating them in worlds visited throughout with like afflictions to their own, is the product of a higher benevolence on our part.

Kathleen Olga Vaughan

Several writers on purdah make passing remarks on the health of purdah women. Kathleen Olga Vaughan was a doctor and medical superintendent of the Maharajah's Zenana Hospital in Srinagar, and commented extensively on the effect of osteomalacia on women deprived of sunlight in her book *The Purdah System and its Effect on Motherhood* published in 1928. She contrasts the health of boatwomen who do not suffer from osteomalacia because they work in the open with the purdah women who have no access to sunlight.

Osteomalacia in Kashmir

(a) THE DISEASE ITSELF
(b) WATER AND DIET
(c) SOCIAL CUSTOMS
(d) HEREDITY
(e) CLIMATE
(f) WANT OF LIGHT
(g) TREATMENT

Osteomalacia is extremely common in Kashmir. During a period of nearly three years I was medical superintendent of the Maharajah's Zenana Hospital in Srinagar—the capital—and out of 29 Caesarian sections performed by me during my first year there, at least 25 were due to pelvic deformity caused by osteomalacia. There were 120 midwifery cases admitted to hospital that year, and of these none came until they had had all possible advice at home, and with the exception of two, *after* rupture of the membranes.

Many of them still die at home, in some cases undelivered. Almost all

Kathleen Olga Vaughan, *The Purdah System and its Effect on Motherhood: Osteomalacia caused by absence of light in India*, Cambridge: W. Heffer & Sons Ltd, 1928.

Kashmiri women who live in the towns and have borne children, are affected in some degree, with the exception of the manji (boatman) class. I have never seen a case among them.

In Kashmir the disease is unknown among men or boys.

The ordinary Kashmiri women who live on land, especially the city dwellers, have the disease—sometimes slightly, when there is tenderness of the pelvic bones and the antero-posterior curve of the sacrum is exaggerated, or so acutely that the sufferers can only crawl by means of their arms and legs, the legs being flexed at the knees and the knees drawn up to the shoulders. The worst cases are seen in the houses of the wealthy, who keep their women in seclusion, and among those of the poorer classes who do the same because it is considered respectable.

There is a marked seasonal incidence; the disease is worse in winter and early spring, during and after confinement to the house in the cold weather, and improves markedly during summer and autumn. A common history is that of confinement to the house at 8 or 9 years of age, marriage at 10 or 11, menstruation at 12 or 13, and close confinement in the husband's house until after the first child is born; in the very high-class families the women hardly leave the house till they die. Some women have more freedom, and when they have borne two or three children, they go out with other women.

The height is diminished partly due to lordosis, and the head also is sunk between the shoulders, while the chest is flattened laterally, and the sternum comes forward like a keel. The forearms are twisted and the legs bent antero-posteriorly, differing from the outward bowing of rickets.

The following are sample measurements:

Saro, Mohammedan, aged 30. Purdah, married two years before menstruation began:

Interspinous	16 cm.	Normal	26 cm.
Intercristal	19 cm.	Normal	29 cm.
Intertrochanteric	18 cm.	Normal	32 cm.
External conjugate	15 cm.	Normal	21 cm.
Bi-ischial	5 cm.	Over	8 cm.

(Whitridge Williams)

Hajra, aged 28. Never went out of the house after 8 years old; was married two years before menstruation began. Her mother also suffered from osteomalacia.

Interspinous	17 ½ cm.
Intercristal	22 cm.

Intertrochanteric	23 ½ cm.
External conjugate	17 cm.
Bi-ischial	4 cm.

Mohammedan, aged 30. Purdah. Married two years before menstruation began.

Interspinous	16 cm.
Intercristal	19 cm.
Intertrochanteric	18 cm.
External conjugate	15 cm.
Bi-ischial	5 cm.

A Woman, aged 28. Purdah. Married two years before menstruation began. Her mother also suffered from osteomalacia.

Interspinous	17 ½ cm.
Intercristal	22 cm.
Intertrochanteric	23 ½ cm.
External conjugate	17 cm.
Bi-ischial	4 cm.

In a few of our cases it was difficult, if not impossible, to reach the os or rupture the membranes; in others the pubic rami were so close together that a finger could with difficulty be inserted sideways. Tetany is a common accompaniment of osteomalacia; women are brought to the hospital with their thumbs flexed in the palms of their hands, and the whole hand flexed at the wrist. It is not a hysterical manifestation, as experience shows its close connexion with osteomalacia, and probably with thyroid and parathyroid deficiency. In many of these cases the thyroid is smaller than normal, and the neck seems wasted on inspection.

Toothache is a common complaint, and pyorrhoea is often present; but the most obvious symptoms are the pains in the bones, in the ribs, pelvis, and the shafts of the long bones, especially the tibia and ulna, which are tender on pressure about the centre. No tenderness or change is to be observed *at the joints*. The epiphyseal lines seem to me quite unaffected, thus differentiating the condition from rickets.

There may be improvement after confinement, and when lactation ceases. Lactation only ceases when the child dies, otherwise it is continued for from two to four years, and the osteomalacia becomes more acute when the woman again becomes pregnant. Many when pregnant are suckling one or two previous children.

The acute pains are usually better after delivery, but recur in the second and later pregnancies. The third confinement results in more crippling, and by the fifth month the patient cannot sit or stand or walk without severe pain. She gets up from the ground or from a chair with difficulty and much pain, placing her hands on her thighs, and raising them alternately higher as she straightens her back—in fact, climbs up them as one sees in pseudo-hypertrophic muscular paresis. The feet are turned in to keep the balance. This is the earliest symptom noticeable in the street in walking behind such a woman, who looks as if she was going to fall over her big toes, and the gait has a well-marked waddling character, most marked in mounting steps. Many suffer from phthisis and tuberculous glands, and many of the men of the families in which there is osteomalacia suffer from tuberculosis. It is too constant a relationship to be mere chance.

Anaemia is always present, and unfortunately is admired, as a fair complexion is considered a sign of being well-bred. The Kashmiri of pure Aryan parentage is fair, and many of the men carry umbrellas to guard their complexions from the sun. The pale hue so much sought after is increased by the seclusion of the women, not only from the outside world, but from sun and air. The better-class women when they go out wear, from the age of 10, a 'burka'—a cloak covering the head and body, with two lattice-work holes for the eyes.

Palpitation and breathlessness, the usual accompaniments of anaemia, are present, and a dilated heart is not uncommon. In a well-marked case the pulse is always rapid, and may rise to 120 or 140 on the least exertion. The temperature is not raised. Oral sepsis, indigestion, and intestinal worms are common.

Some apparently impossible midwifery cases terminate spontaneously after several days in labour—provided, of course, the deformity is not such as to prevent the head engaging in the superior strait of the pelvis; the pressure of the head may be sufficient to make the softened bones yield, but as the woman gets older, the bones ossify in faulty positions, and the crumpled pelvis becomes unyielding.

Many deaths take place in childbirth, owing to conditions consequent upon osteomalacia, and as skilled assistance is not available, mother and child are often lost. The native midwife, according to custom, holds the labia apart with her big toes, pressing on the perineum with her heels—gangrene of the vulva is not an uncommon result. She has had no training but tradition (the trade is hereditary), and so performs a rough craniotomy with the sharp end of a spindle, removes the infant's brains, places a loop of string round the neck, and extracts. In a difficult case she may pierce the mother's uterus, who frequently dies of septicaemia, if she survive the first few days after delivery by these crude methods. A native midwife will 'clean' her hands before making an examination by rubbing them on the mud floor. She completes her attentions to the patient by rubbing salt or mustard oil into the lacerated vagina. Atresia of the vagina caused by such measures is very common. The placenta is buried, often in the mud floor of the patient's room.

A natural cure of the pains and softness of the bones occurs at the menopause.

One of the most remarkable things where Caesarian section is done for these women is the size and healthiness of the child. The women are thin, anaemic, and deformed, but their offspring at birth are often extremely fine, healthy, heavy specimens, and later show no sign of rickets. All the mothers suckle their infants and rickets is not common in Kashmir. The few cases I have seen were in female children who had lost their mothers in infancy, they belonged to wealthy Kashmiri families, and had been kept indoors with the women. Usually even infants go out, and male infants are taken out by the men and boys to show to their friends when very young. A girl child is never made so much of, no one wants to see her, so she stays indoors.

Another point noted at a Caesarian is the extreme thinness and wasted appearance of the abdominal walls. They resemble paper, and the various layers are barely distinguishable. The omentum too is noticeably devoid of fat in nearly all the cases I have operated upon.

DIET AND WATER SUPPLY

The richer classes cook all their food. The milk is boiled and re-boiled. The city dwellers, who keep their own cows have them in dark stables or in the courtyard, and send them out daily to graze. In some cases they are fed on dry food and rarely go out. Sheep and goat's milk is used too, generally when prescribed as medicine by the Kashmiri practitioner. Vegetable oil, either mustard or sesamum, is used for cooking. The oil is heated to boiling point first. They think anything uncooked must be unwholesome, as in a place decimated by cholera every few years, it probably is. The rich eat rice husked by machinery, which removes the pink pericarp and the germ. The bran which is thus produced is given to the cattle, and is of course, rich in phosphates. The women eat after the men, and therefore get less meat and milk, as both are considered luxuries, but otherwise their diet is the same as that of their menfolk.

The drinking water in the city comes from two sources—the river Jhelum and the tap water. The tap supply is often contaminated by the breaking of the lids of the wooden troughs which convey it to the city from a valley three or four miles away. When broken, the nearest inhabitants drink and wash themselves at the break, so that last year warning had to be given to consumers that the water should be boiled before use, as it was probably infected with cholera. Both rich and poor drink water, but tea is the favourite beverage for all. The better kinds come from Tibet in bricks, from which shavings are made and these are boiled up with salt and spices.

The natural supply from the river is preferred by the most religious, as the water of the Jhelum is sacred. The river is also the natural sewer of the town. One encounters corpses in it—from those of rats and fowls to those of drowned sheep and cattle, bodies of unwanted babies, and of persons drowned by accident. In addition to this, the Hindus attend to the calls of Nature, wash themselves, and drink of its waters at the steps leading to it, and the Mohammedans have boxes in the stream for washing and sanitary needs. Persons may thus be seen drinking water from the river a yard or two lower down from those passing their urine and faeces into the same stream. The water of the river is considered so sacred that it cannot be defiled. It can hardly be matter for surprise that everyone suffers from intestinal worms. Large round white ones are the commonest.

Social Customs

I have mentioned the absolute freedom from the disease enjoyed by the 'manji' or boatwomen. The one boatman's wife I found with it turned out to be a town-dweller married to a boatman. Dr Neve also says in 25 years' experience he never remembers to have seen a case in a boatwoman. These women live in the open air on the large boats used for carrying rice, wood, etc., on the great Kashmir highway, the Jhelum river; and besides the men, women, and children, fowls, goats, and sometimes a cow with her calf, are on board. These women work hard, and feed with the men. They are too poor to cook their food much, and eat raw cucumber, tomatoes, etc., with their rice, which they husk by hand. They pole and paddle the boats like the men, and are out in all weathers. They wear but one garment, a kind of loose shirt reaching to the middle of the calf of the leg. Their milk supply is provided by their goat or cow, and one may be fairly certain it is not boiled, but consumed as soon as drawn.

Purdah, which means a curtain, is used of the system which ensures the seclusion of the woman from all men except her husband and her brothers. It varies in strictness, and is much less strict in Kashmir than in India. In Kashmir it really only affects the women of marriageable and child-bearing age. Among the better classes they are more or less confined to the house, often in rooms where they cannot look out.

Girls of 8 are not allowed out alone, and if brought to hospital are often closely veiled. The Hindus, who in *theory* do not observe this custom, do so in practice. The young girls from 8 or 10 to 15 rarely go out until married, and then not till after the birth of one or two children. Marriage takes place before puberty in many cases, because in order to ensure early marriage, the younger the bride, the less are the fees to the priests. One of the greatest sins a father can commit is not to have married his daughter at puberty. After marriage she is confined to her husband's house, and her food and happiness depend entirely upon her mother-in-law, who often keeps her short of food, from an idea that she will have an easier confinement if the foetus is kept small by spare diet, and also short commons make her more obedient to her mother-in-law. It has been pointed out by other observers that much tuberculosis originates in these girls during the first year of married life, owing to these miserable conditions.

At childbirth the woman is confined in a dark unventilated room, often with no window at all, and no fireplace, but a charcoal brazier or the fire basket. Forty days is not an uncommon time for the young mother to be in this unventilated place, and she emerges weak and ill. Osteomalacia usually begins with the first pregnancy, or soon after marriage.

Heredity

Mothers with old osteomalacia will bring daughters or daughters-in-law to hospital, and are anxious to say that the disease is *not* in their family, but is hereditary in some other family with whom marriages have been made. One finds the truth of the matter is that as they must marry within their own caste, the ones affected all belong to the same social caste whose rules require the seclusion of girls from 8 or 10 years of age, until after marriage, when they have borne several children.

CLIMATIC CONDITIONS

Kashmir lies between 32 and 36° latitude, and is roughly at the same distance from the equator as Southern Spain or Morocco. The city of Srinagar lies in the valley through which the River Jhelum flows, and the town is built on each side of the river. The valley lies at an altitude of 5000 feet. The hills round this valley are 7000 or 8000 feet in height; further away are hills of 12,000 to 13,000 feet, and still higher peaks overtop these in the distance.

All English flowers and fruit grow well. The temperature may rise to 90° or over in the hottest days of July and August; and again in winter the thermometer may fall 10° and more below zero; yet on the whole it is a temperate and equable climate for eight months of the year. In the winter months osteomalacia becomes much worse. Wood is the fuel burnt, and during the four winter months a thick pall of fog and smoke hangs over the city in the early morning and evening. One notices the extreme cold and how the sun rises late and sets early, and is obviously much lower in the sky, never being directly overhead as in summer. The rays are thus more oblique even at noon, and courtyards and streets with high walls facing north receive no sunshine at all.

The streets leading from the river are narrow and tortuous, and the houses, which are of wood, are high and built round small courtyards, where in the winter the sun never shines. Nor does it reach the ground of many of the streets where the aspect faces north. Icicles ten feet and more in length hang for weeks in such places from the roof, and snow to a depth of four or five feet lies in the streets. The roofs have to be cleared of snow, or they would give way under the weight; men shovel it off, and it lies in the streets until spring. Owing to reflection there is some slight improvement in the light in the dwellings when the snow comes.

The women wear but one garment, and go out in the winter as little as possible. They live in the lowest rooms of the high wooden houses in the winter, so as to be on the same floor as the water supply and the fire. The ground floor is the warmest. The windows are sometimes less than half-a-yard square, and protected against thieves by being near the ceiling and closed by wooden lattice-work. All windows are so made, but on the upper floors they are larger. In winter they are covered with oiled paper to keep out the cold. The minimum of available light is thus admitted, and some rooms, especially liked for warmth, have no windows at all. There is very little wind throughout the valley.

That the available light supply is sufficient for health in ordinary life is proved by the rarity of rickets and the healthiness of the boatwomen, and the country women working in the fields, but a degree of seclusion which would have little effect on the plains of India produces osteomalacia in Kashmir. A photographer who lived for many years in Kashmir said that he always gave twice the exposure he would in India to get a good result in Kashmir, which looks as if the actinic rays might be deficient. Most of the oblique rays of the sun in midwinter are cut off by the mountains encircling the valley.

The seasonal incidence above described points to the same cause— absence of sunlight. In spring and summer the women go out and improve in health. The disease only occurs in those deprived of sunlight, and one meets women walking about who have evidently had the disease, and who will tell you they were shut up as *young women* but on the death of the husband were free to go out and recovered their health. One woman told me she only began to suffer in her later confinements when her husband had moved from a house facing an open space to the crowded quarters of the city. The fact that the men of the families where the women have osteomalacia are so often tuberculous points to the same cause—want of sunlight.

At Islamabad, higher up the valley than Srinagar, the doctor tells me that wherever she goes she sees cases, especially among the wives of priests, shopkeepers, and butchers—all men having some means and so able to keep their young wives in seclusion during their early married life. At Ladakh, 11,000 feet, with long cold winters, it is unknown, except for one case in a Kashmiri woman who was taken up there by her husband. The women there go out freely. At Peshawar among the Afghan women, who go out freely and live an open-air life, osteomalacia is unknown, the only cases reported from there were in Hindu shopkeepers' wives, who married young and were kept in purdah. In Lahore the disease is not very common; the worst cases occur among those who seclude their women and are rich enough to have glass windows, sometimes fixed in the wall so that they cannot be opened.

The most instructive notes come from Bombay, where the Parsee women are completely free from it. A Parsee doctor tells me that out of 25,000 deliveries he did not encounter one case of osteomalacia among Parsees. These people have great freedom, and often do not marry until 20 or 22. The women of the weaver class, on the other hand, living in the same town, are almost all affected, and were they not constantly replaced by women from the country villages round Bombay, they would die out in a generation. The Superintendent of the Cama Hospital tells me they suspect osteomalacia in every weaver woman coming for her confinement, and take careful pelvic measurements. These miserable women live in buildings which are eight stories high. The loom is on the ground floor in the room facing the street, because all available light is needed for the work, and the women live in dark rooms behind that; the mortality rate is 678 per 1000 among infants under 1 year.

In Chamba, in the Himalayas, the village women do not suffer, but in the hill town there is 'hardly any sunlight' in their houses, and consequently those in purdah, the richer women, suffer badly. In Hyderabad the disease is very rare, but cases are known in Hindu women, who eat some kind of earth to cure it.

TREATMENT

Our first acquaintance with the osteomalacia patient was usually at the time of confinement, when in labour and after failure to be delivered at home. The women are only beginning to come for advice before labour begins, and only exceptional cases would come in to hospital to be treated for osteomalacia prior to confinement.

There are three indigenous Kashmiri cures for 'trouble in the bones':

(1) A special clay called Baramulla earth;
(2) Pills made of fish liver;
(3) Rubbing with mustard oil and exposing to sunlight.

1. Baramulla earth is a greyish-white fire-clay used for making fire-places in wooden boats, and for portable fire-pots on which to cook food. A lump of this earth taken from a patient with osteomalacia, who ate pieces of it, was analysed for me by the Clinical Research Association, who reported that it was a ferruginous clay containing a fairly high percentage of calcium phosphate (calcium phosphate 16.2 per cent, ferric oxide 11.8 per cent, hydrated aluminium silicate (in clay) 71.2 per cent, and undetermined residue 0.8 per cent). Sulphates were present to a very small extent. The radio-activity of the sample was not more than is usually found in any natural earth; arsenic and similar metals were not detected.

2. The fish-liver pills are sold by a Panditani (Hindu woman) living at the city fish market. She makes them herself. The analogy with cod-liver oil is interesting.

3. The mustard-oil and sunlight cure is chiefly used by the men for their rheumatic pains, as a woman could not sit unclothed in the sun, unless she belonged to one of the religious mendicant orders.

At the Zenana Hospital we prescribed cod-liver oil and phosphorus oil, and considered it did good. Calcium lactate seemed to slow the heart and relieve the pains in acute cases. Hypodermic injections of sodium morrhuate seemed to give good results, but we found that the one patient really cured had been sitting in the sun all day in order to get tea from the kitchen. I am inclined to think the same of all cases said to improve when admitted to hospital, as the light in the wards is better than anything they have at home. We also tried bone marrow, as it was easily obtained, and cheap; but we found that so long as patients remained in their old surroundings at home, there was very little improvement, even when cod-liver oil was being given, and we could never be sure they took it, unless we saw it administered.

In the East a physician is expected not only to prescribe medicines, but to lay down rules of life for the patient, who must not eat and drink certain articles of diet or must go on a pilgrimage or the medicine or charm will not work. Knowing the need for fresh air I frequently said, 'My medicine will do her more good if you take the patient out to the gardens across the lake in a boat twice a week.' This ensured sunshine—and these patients improved at once.

Frieda Hauswirth

Frieda Hauswirth tells us in her introduction that she was born and brought up in Switzerland, studied at Leland Stanford University in California, then attended the California Institute of Art, and later went to India as the wife of a Hindu graduate student in agricultural industries at the University of California. She tells us that her friends urged her to write about India as she had eight years in 'intimate contact with Indian family life of different classes' and in different parts of the country. Her friends felt she was in a position to be 'comparatively free from the racial, national, or imperial bias' to which most ordinary white sojourners in India are prone.

Purdah: The Status of Indian Women discusses the status of Indian women from Vedic times to the time she is writing. She claims that it was because Muslim conquerors were not permitted by religion to carry off married women as slaves or concubines that Hindus started the practice of child marriage. She also says that while Moghul or Muslim influence was extensive, particularly in the North, 'Hindu men adopted the worst and rejected the best among the customs affecting women.' She reminds us that there were several laws in Islam to protect the status of women in Islam, such as widow remarriage which was permitted, the right to divorce, the right to inheritance and money given to her at the time of her marriage. Hindu women could have been liberated by these customs, but Hindu men chose polygamy and seclusion instead. Long after any threat of Muslim conquest and its implications disappeared, purdah continues to be observed among Hindus.

It is possible that an earlier book by Frieda Hauswirth called *A Marriage to India* contains personal details. As it stands, her dates are not available.

Women in the Zenana

In the previous chapters we have indicated the cause, extent, and reasons for stricter imposition of purdah. No doubt it would have been abolished

Frieda Hauswirth, *Purdah: The Status of Indian Women*, London: Kegan Paul, Trench, and Trubner Co., 1932.

as soon as the Mohammedan aggression and with it the protective value of purdah ceased, were it not that it found powerful support in the general age-long Hindu belief in the advisability of restricting women's freedom. Classical and later Hindu literature gives further proof of this attitude, it teems with slighting references to woman's character. 'One may trust deadly poison, a river, a hurricane, the beautiful, large and fierce elephant, the tiger roaming for prey, the angel of death, a thief, a savage, a murderer; but if a man trust a woman, he will surely be reduced to wander through the streets in desolation.'

The fact that purdah turned the zenana into the exclusive dwelling-place of women had far-reaching effects. It soon inculcated in their minds the deep conviction that freedom of movement outside the house would lower their standing and place them on a common level with low-castes. Not only this, but even within the house itself it made for a sharp division of family life into two sections, zenana and men's quarters. The outer rooms and verandahs became closed territory for the women. They never visited them except on rare and furtive excursions, and when fully assured that no men were about. Servants only took care of these quarters. This had the unfortunate result of withdrawing all housewifely interest and pride from these rooms, though it was in them that the family's guests were received. Verandahs, gardens, the outsides of houses and the adjoining portions of the street consequently and inevitably assumed a neglected appearance—spotted walls, dust in every cranny, rubbish-heaps and litter of all sorts in courtyards and by the side of the doors became the common order of the day. Servants did not hesitate to fling out garbage and refuse into the street as the easiest method of disposal. The joy in beautiful surroundings insensibly disappeared from the daily world in which men lived. Nor did the women preserve a practical sense of beauty within their own quarters. Zenanas were usually overcrowded, poorly lit and ventilated, and swarmed with small children—still more difficult conditions under which to renew and cherish the beauty of outer things, of walls, furniture, or the joy of colour. Moreover, the fact that these rooms were never the home of social cheer, in which men took part, inevitably made for neglect. In consequence the women's rooms soon became the barest and ugliest in the whole house, with rolled-up bedding tucked into any odd corner, and clothing hung over racks in full view. Under such crowded segregation, shut away from all cultural life, with no stimulation from outside, how could women have retained that sense of beauty which certainly had been keenly alive in former ages? It disappeared so wholly from the home environment that women grew insensible to all ugliness or untidiness of surroundings. Only on the rare occasions of great religious festivals did the ancient custom of drawing of geometrical designs in coloured powders before door-sills still persist to add an unusual touch of transient beauty. Otherwise the sense of beauty survived in only one form in the lives of women. A particular factor conditioned this. The segregation of sexes both within and without the home inevitably brought about an over-emphasis on sex interest both in children and adult women within the zenana; it made for prurience among adolescents and over-stimulation in wives. Taught from earliest days that to please their husbands was their main aim in life, women under these conditions transferred what would have been a normal interest in home decoration entirely upon bodily adornment. The possession of beautiful saris, and more particularly of jewellery, became and still is, a veritable obsession with Indian women. Their quantity, value, and workmanship was estimated very closely and compared with much secret and open jealousy and heart-burning. A little bride's main consolation was to find that the jewellery she brought compared favourably with that possessed by the women of her new household; or if, to her shame, it fell below their standard, she attempted restlessly to increase and better her treasures. It has been estimated that the interest on capital unproductively invested in women's ornaments covers the full amount which the peasants have to pay in land taxes. I have had an endless amount of pity showered on me by Indian women for my lack of ornaments, and the idea that I could treasure some ornament purely for the sake of its beauty of form and colour, apart from its money value, has been received with scorn. Only the lifting of purdah and the release of women will restore to them a sense of balance in this matter, renew their interest in home beauty, and awaken in them a desire to adorn their mind at least as much as their body.

The drawbacks of the zenana went further. Purdah abolished all possibility of high-caste women's participating in the social life of the community. Visits, feasts, discussions, musical parties, all these took place in the men's quarters. Only the houses of the very great were so constructed that a screened or latticed gallery enabled women to observe unseen the festivities in the central hall. By far the greater number of them never participated in such social events in any other way than by retaining the 'privilege' of working behind the scenes for endless hours, sometimes for days, to prepare the innumerable delicious dishes and dainties to be served to the feasting men—dishes which custom forbade them even to taste until the men had had their fill. This exclusion from stimulating discussions and diversions completed the evil effects of the prohibition to study the scriptures. At the discussions of men, women could have kept in touch with the life of the community; the scriptures— which contained not only religious and philosophical matter, but also poetry, arithmetic and rhetoric—would have given training to their minds. Deprived of both, their mental life became inevitably stultified. Men succeeded so amazingly in their efforts that they were able to inculcate deeply into the minds of women the conviction that to desire knowledge was not dignified nor virtuous. They became incapable of aspiring even to learn to read and write. Most women would have been heartily ashamed of an accusation that they were hankering after these very elementals of knowledge, and hotly resented it. This went to the extent of making many Brahmin women honestly believe that their knowing how to read would bring evil and sickness upon the heads of their husbands, most dreaded of possibilities. For long ages, religion taught that absolute self-abnegation alone could bring women near to the ideal type of womanhood.

There is no doubt that such teaching at its best succeeded in producing an exquisitely selfless, softly gracious, tender type of womanhood, but a type fearfully inhibited and negative on the whole. At its worst, such unquestioning contentment and limitation led not only to mental, but to moral stagnation as well. The lives of women were filled by monotonous routine, by sensual and frivolous preoccupations. Where women of all ages were compelled to live daily in inescapable and uninterrupted intimacy, under at least an outer show of absolute obedience to husband and mother-in-law, it was inevitable that dislikes, pettiness, jealousies, and endless squabbles should germinate and mature. The extent to which even high-caste women could not escape degeneration of thought and feelings is clearly indicated by the form of expression their quarrels tended to take. Whenever they dared to vent their emotions against their equals or inferiors, their shrill scolding was full of vile language and obscene abuse. Still more amazing and revealing was the coarse ribaldry in which these delicate creatures delighted. Little children who grew up in the midst of such stifling, warping conditions, witnessed these scenes, drank in their meaning, and in turn lustily handed on their spirit. No doubt all zenana generations have heard, as I have, twelve-year-old boys in a transport of rage scream at an old servant the ultimate insult, 'I'll sleep with your wife!' and be rewarded by appreciative smiles all around—a terrible revelation of knowledge harmfully acquired by ob- serving children forced into the too close intimacy of adult ant-heap life.

Children were bound to suffer in other ways from the mental starvation of their mothers. In a desire to quiet the babel within the zenana, what more natural than to soothe infants with opium, or frighten them into obedience by harrowing tales of monsters and demons lurking to grab them around the corner? And what of the indiscriminate praise and scolding meted out in an endless stream?

So imprisoned and restricted within the zenana, it is not surprising that the vital urge towards expression in women had to pour itself out through such twisted and warped channels; the marvel is that despite all the ugliness and frustration, great beauty of aspiration and tenderness of feeling sprang up ever anew within the Hindu home. To complete the concise picture of the home background against which Indian women lived and moved, it is essential to realize that from the earliest days the joint family system has prevailed in most parts of India, though chiefly among the upper castes, where possession of property and of a large family house enabled this custom to retain its hold. Among the lower castes the trend towards more and more minute division of land, the need to disperse in search of work long ago led to the virtual disappearance of the joint family; another reason for the much greater amount of liberty always enjoyed by low-caste women. Its persistence among the only classes whose men were in possession of knowledge and culture is significant; the mentality induced, fostered, and perpetuated by life within the joint family system makes for inordinate regard for authority and submission to power, and is the chief factor in the continuance of the slave mentality (a term first applied by Indians themselves in self-criticism) which had taken its primary hold on the Hindu mind with the advent of the Moghul conqueror.

....

Some 'Helpless' Women of India

Even the briefest account of the women who, in India, have done remarkable work in reform and education, would of itself fill a great book. But to mention a few may serve to let the West appreciate to what extent women of the future promise to have the power to further development in India. Such women will take from Western systems and apply in India whatever may be genuinely helpful, while continuing to treasure and guard the valuable content of their own traditions. No outsider, no matter how understanding and sympathetic, will ever be able to equal these Indian women in insight into the real needs of the growing generation, or in wisdom of choice when trying to find what will answer such needs.

Let me start with one with whose work and life I have been privileged to come into close contact, Lady Abala Bose. She is the daughter of a reformer, a member of the Brahmo Samaj, and not only has never been in Purdah, but had the rare privilege of being given regular physical exercise in childhood—no doubt the source of her unflagging physical energy.

She took a four-year course in medicine in Madras, being the first wom[a]n of her section to take up such studies. At twenty-two she married a young Bengali Professor of Physics of Calcutta University, a man who had voluntarily taken it upon his shoulders to liquidate a debt of his father's of Rs. 40,000, though under no legal obligation to do so. For years they both sacrificed many a comfort until this load was off their shoulders. But even afterwards, Abala Bose continued to supervise personally every detail of the expanding household, taking that intimate, motherly, unobtrusive interest in the welfare of every creature under her roof which is so characteristic of Indian housewives. Every morning by seven she had already bathed and breakfasted. Breakfast-time was also the visiting hour for friends and relatives, and as often as not for people who came to consult with her on outside matters. Breakfast cleared away, Abala Base sat on talking with these visitors, but her hands were not idle—she herself prepared every bit of the vegetables and fruits needed for that day. She pared them, cut them into cubes and slices, washed each ready pile once, and then let the pieces drop into shining brass bowls full of clear water, so that the cook had nothing more to do than make them into delicious curries or other dishes. Thus, even in this modernized household, the absolute purity of food was as rigidly controlled and ensured as it is in orthodox families where the housewife, no matter how high her rank, first bathes, and then dons a special clean linen sari to prepare and cook the food with care as scrupulous as if performing a religious ceremony. Not only that, but Abala Bose herself makes all the purchases for the household, driving to the New Market for that purpose, closely examining all she buys, and driving good bargains, for no one better than she knows the value of money and what great things even a little of it can accomplish in impoverished India. For her house and family she purchases and uses largely Indian materials, and is fully alive to their beauty. She keeps the accounts, writes out the laundry list for the dhobie, engages and supervises the *durzi* (tailor) in his mending and making of new clothes, sees that the entire house is kept spotless despite listless servants, bandages cut fingers, entertains guests, arranges the usual dinner for about six people or a special feast for sixty, with the same unruffled, unhurried, competent ease and despatch. At each and every turn she looks to the minutest details of her absent minded husband's comforts, his clothes, his food, his appointments. Nothing is ever forgotten, nothing only half done. At every meal she sees to it that he has only just what is good for him; knowing his impatience and carelessness, every little thing is made ready for him as if for a baby. None of these personal details are left to servants. The orange pulp on the plate before him has not a trace of skin or seed, the shelter of the mosquito curtain not a single imprisoned tormentor, as a result of her care. Every evening at dusk, no matter how absorbed or unwilling he may be, she persuades, cajoles, or purloins her husband from his preoccupations, to take the ride in the open air so necessary to his health and work. Before or after their return and dinner, there are endless letters to write, more visitors to talk to, and the family to settle to sleep.

This sounds a daily programme sufficient to fill a woman's whole time. But it is cited merely to illustrate one phase of a Hindu housewife's attitude toward life. Be it under compulsion or free from it—at no stage, no matter how high her station or how Westernized her training and education, will she neglect, or relegate to other hands or brains, the care and welfare of her home.

But this scrupulous and quiet fulfilment of endless domestic duties is but one half of Abala Bose's life. The other half is smoothly woven into the web of her daily occupations, so that no friction results between the two.

She is profoundly interested in the bettering of woman's status all along the line, and sets a thousand wheels in motion through her dynamic energy, starting with her nearest relatives and reaching outward thence. Her nephew was induced to sponsor the first bill for Woman's Suffrage in the 1921 Legislative Council of Bengal; she herself was one of the signatories to the All India Woman's Delegation to the Hon. E. S. Montagu, Secretary of State for India, in 1917, which demanded woman suffrage and education. Abala Bose has also travelled extensively in Europe and America, and has had full opportunity of comparing and selecting. She has come out of this as intense a patriot as she started out to be in early life. But her patriotism and interest in education are not theoretical; they are pre-eminently practical—as practical as is her housekeeping.

She is the founder of the *Nari Siksha Samiti*, or Women's Education League, an organization intended to further women's education in every possible way; the consultations, meetings, and work involved by it are endless, and start while Abala Bose sits preparing her vegetables in the coolness of seven o'clock. One of her objects was to bring education to purdah women, instead of waiting till they should break free and come out to seek information of their own accord. She knew that the mother-in-law behind the purdah is the most formidable obstacle to progress, and has power to keep all women under her within the purdah, all girls away from school. Win her over, and half the battle is won, the younger generation is liberated; so through Abala Bose's efforts a whole chain of purdah schools has been started, not only in Calcutta, but extending wider and wider through dozens of villages. Then came another realization, the need of relieving widows, and their value as teaching material. One of India's greatest difficulties, arising naturally out of the old conditions, was that so few women teachers were, or still are, available. It was most desirable, for the satisfactory training of girls, to displace the old-time Brahmin pundit by women teachers. Abala Bose, after endless effort, started her Widows' Home, in which two objects might simultaneously be achieved—women could be taught industrial handicrafts to free them from their dependence and to fill their lives with interest; they could also be trained as teachers to carry on the work of the purdah schools, both in the towns and villages. This Widows' Home has for years received daily care and direction, encouragement and supervision from Abala Bose herself, in whose heart and brain deeper and greater plans and hopes are continually blossoming. One widow had come to the Home, quite unlettered, but showing from the first all the marks of an unusual intellect. In next to no time she could read and write, and soon was even able to be sent out as a pioneer for village work, for the purpose of establishing adult centres and juvenile schools. The intention was to impart the rudiments of literacy, but above all, through talks, illustrations, and examples, to teach the elements of hygiene, sanitation, food values, child care, and handicrafts. To ensure the successful establishment and progress of such village centres, it was important to win over the local bigwigs, above all the pundits. Abala Bose's Brahmin widow, only a short time ago, not uncultured, but illiterate and without hope in life, dared to face these village elders in meetings to argue matters out. She bore herself with quiet dignity in her widow's austere garb, and repeatedly won in the battle of wits against the village pundits. Abala Bose is ever on the lookout for such unusually promising women, and if once they are discovered, she brings all her influence to bear to get them trained, abroad if necessary, for ever wider and more responsible work.

But this is not all. Abala Bose's family helped to found the great Brahmo Girls' School, and her own share of property has gone towards its upkeep. In this school an effort is made to evolve a practical blend of Western and Eastern educational methods and aims. Particular stress is laid on inducing girls to take physical exercise, and to eradicate the traditional and home-ingrained dislike of high-caste people for manual work. There is not a day on which Abala Bose, when in Calcutta, does not attend to some of the affairs of this school herself; she is the unfailing supporter of its new experiments, and adviser of its teachers. No wonder that her day, too busy for the usual noonday rest of the tropics, rarely ends before eleven o'clock. Yet never, in all the years I have known her, do I remember having seen her flustered.

Abala Bose has no child, but her unremitting care for a scientist husband, curiously dependent and absent-minded in small things, and for a drove of nephews and nieces has given her that same training in extraversion which we find to be so marked a characteristic of Indian head-of-the-household women. I have cited her case at length (without her permission, but knowing she will forgive me) as an embodiment of that quiet reserve of strength which exists still untapped in millions of Indian women, and bears within itself such untold promise when once it shall be released for social service, as hers has been.

It is because of this intimate beholding, this actual experiencing, that I hold the deep conviction that the education of India's girlhood and womanhood is safest in, and will be most fruitfully directed by, Indian hands.

To illustrate how effective can be such Indian-initiated and managed reform, let me cite the case of another enthusiastic Bengali worker. Saroj Nalini Dutt was one of the women who came under the influence of Abala Bose's purdah school and village-reform ideas. She also was a high caste, married, had travelled, and had received a thorough education in Calcutta. She also realized that the mother-in-law of joint families, if orthodox, is the real obstacle to progress, and that reform must be brought to bear intimately on the home life of secluded women. The few schools established by Government are not attended by, and therefore of no use to, orthodox Indian girls.

Saroj Nalini Dutt, wife of a Government official, went with her husband for a few years' stay at a time—for Government officials are shifted frequently—to various places in Bengal. Wherever she went, she used all the effects of her high enthusiasm and winsome personality to establish community centres calculated to quicken the entire life of each village. In these centres, both children and adults were taught the elements of reading and writing, classes were held for women, to train them in industrial handicrafts; first aid courses were given, midwives trained, simple hygiene and food values taught. Women were urged to take an interest in hospital work, and given all the rudiments of civic training. A special effort was made, and that successfully, to reach purdah women. These centres definitely refused to discriminate between caste, class, or religion; not only so, but a valuable attempt was made to draw the various groups together on a common social basis, and the social arts, such as music, singing and the drama—so long despised as practically the monopoly of prostitutes—were once more encouraged. As almost all the workers in these village centres were from high castes, many of them Brahmins, they had the power to make these despised arts once more acceptable. While missionaries, because of their very foreignness, and their converts, because mostly drawn from low castes, were always met with guarded reserve or even veiled antagonism, and their innovations with uneasy suspicion, these high-caste women on the other hand, were met with a respect and confidence which greatly facilitated the acceptance of reform. While Hindus are always wary of the missionaries because they know and distrust their proselytizing motives, they knew that in this case these high-caste workers came to them with no selfish intention. This is another of the many reasons why indigenous reform promises infinitely more, and why Government funds turned over to such groups, accomplish infinitely more than Western efforts. What two or three highly paid Westerners would absorb, while giving less effective service, will keep going a hundred Indian workers who can reach the people as can no one else.

With what gratifying rapidity such reforms can spread is best seen from the figures of *The Central Association*, formed to correlate the work of all those *Mahila Samitis*, or centres, which Saroj Nalini Dutt had established throughout Bengal. In one year these *Mahilas* had increased from 7 to 50, in the second year to 100, in the third to 158, and in the fourth to 240, all organized and managed exclusively by women, though male lecturers are called in, whenever funds permit, to give talks and lantern lectures on special subjects. This organization has established an Industrial Training School at Calcutta which already has 500 students, and has sent out over 400 trained women for village work. How earnest and radical are the devotees to this new crusade for social reform can best be gauged by the fact that some effort has been made to succour even prostitutes. In one instance at least, a Brahmin woman has set a glorious example by actually being trained for midwifery, that most despised of professions. Especially satisfying is the fact that widows, once so hopelessly cut off from active interests, are finding in all these forms of work the marvellous release and satisfaction which valued and useful social service can give. During this transition period we must almost be glad that the prejudice against remarriage is still strong, for it ensures the availability of social workers from this source for a long time to come.

Speaking of widows, we will cite one special case to show how much high courage and selfless striving lies hidden in this field. One of these women, trained in the *Poona Widows' Home*, was inspired by the idea of helping to build it up into a great institution. Though its founder was already working for the establishment of the Women's University, this Poona centre was still a very humble thing and incredibly hampered both by lack of funds and trained teachers. This particular widow, though knowing hardly a word of English, decided to visit the United States for a double purpose, to acquire a working knowledge of Western educational methods, and to collect funds. Quite without money, she landed in San Francisco about twenty years ago, having earned her passage as travelling aid to an Indian and his family. She overcame her mighty difficulties, accomplished her object, and has long been a valuable worker back in her own group.

A most interesting, many-faceted figure was the famous Pandita Ramabai, particularly significant once more as being the daughter of one of our Brahmin square pegs. Despite popular disapproval and even ostracism, her father, a Sanskrit scholar profound enough to have pierced through the sham of his own priestly caste, himself instructed Ramabai in Sanskrit lore. She became the very image of Gargi, that woman scholar who had successfully argued with Yajnavalkya, one of the greatest sages of antiquity. Together with her father, Ramabai visited many of the most sacred temple sites, saw through their corruption, but profited by the learning stored there. She met the greatest pundits and became famous for the profundity of her knowledge and the powers of her dialectic. She could repeat nearly 20,000 stanzas of the *Puranas* by heart, and often replied in arguments in the form of poems composed on the spot. In Calcutta, she came in touch with the important early reformers of the Brahmo Samaj, such as Keshup Chandra Sen, who were congenial to her views. But though she interested such liberal groups intensely, it was a very small group which really appreciated her, and pointed to such a woman with pride. The vast mass of the orthodox bitterly opposed her activities, the more so because she repeatedly worsted in public arguments the local shining lights, those pundits who had set out to humiliate her, for to every objection they could raise in favour of old customs, she could quote a stanza from some still more ancient and more sacred scripture to refute them.

After the death of her parents she was without family ties. As she had remained unmarried beyond the age laid down for Brahmin girls and was at war with all the customs of her caste, marriage offered a special problem. No Brahmin within the pale would have her, few others were her equals. Of her own choice she at last married a Sudra, a member of the lowest and still despised caste, but a man who had obtained a good education. This congenial marriage was cut short by the husband's death, but served still further to embitter the orthodox against her and make her feel more than ever at war with society.

At last she found her way back to the Bombay Presidency and came in touch with men of such eminence and power as Tilak and Judge Ranade. In the latter's house, she was surrounded by congenial spirits, and started her world by organizing the *Arya Mahila Samaj*, a society opposed to child-marriage and seeking to raise the status of women through education. Here both men and women sat at her feet in weekly meetings, at which she put forward her radical views in inspiring talks. She, who knew the Sanskrit scriptures as did few, pointed to the state of freedom existing for women in ancient days, and denounced the later degeneration. India will perish unless women are raised again, she shouted from the housetops, for 'ignorant, unpatriotic, selfish and uncultivated, they drag men down with them'. She pointed out how deplorable was the existing state of things. By 1881, out of 99,700,000 women and girls directly under British rule, after more than a century of that rule, only 200,000 had yet been taught to read or write, and these could 'not all be reckoned as educated, for the school-going period of a girl is generally between 7 and 9 years of age'.

Her influence and personality soon began to tell, so that it was she who, as the chosen representative of the women's cause, gave evidence before the Education Commission of S. W. Hunter, and uttered the bitter indictment that 'in 99 cases out of 100 the educated men of this country are opposed to female education'.

The continuous opposition she had encountered throughout her life, and her realization of the seeming hopelessness of women's position, aroused in her bitter resentment against the Hindu priest class. She despaired of all possibility of women's escaping from its fetters. When in addition she had occasion to contrast the callous indifference and exploitation of the Brahmin priesthood in the case of widow-pilgrims to sacred shrines, with the work of mercy and loving-kindness of the Sisters of St. Mary the Virgin among prostitutes in London, she fled from her perplexities and sense of frustration into the escape of conversion to Christianity. This gave her at last a sense of personal release and peace, but it broke the strength of her power for reform in India. For when she returned, she had to contend against not only the orthodox, but even the radical Hindu group. From then on, they met her efforts with the guarded suspicion which is always shown to white missionaries. Her work aroused opposition because of her continued proselytizing tendencies.

At Bombay she started the *Sarada Sadan* (Home of Wisdom) for training girls and women, especially widows, but, because of this religious opposition, what might otherwise have grown under her hand into a wonderful institution, failed to flourish. Then her work with widows and her former experiences at sacred temples drew this remarkable woman to a new experiment. She disguised herself in the garb of a religious ascetic and visited the sacred cities of Northern India for a closer investigation into the fate of pilgrim widows. She saw 'hundreds...I might say thousands of widows, young and old, come to these places every year and fall into the snares of the priests...when the poor women get a little older...they are turned out to take care of themselves as best they can...oh, the sin and misery and heartless cruelty of men to women!'

Pandita Ramabai's last experiment was in the Central Provinces and Central India, ravaged by famine in 1896. She opened a rescue home at Mukti, and took in girls who were famine victims, cut off from their families. At one time she had nearly 2,000 such starvelings under her care, ranging from babies to women of 30 years of age. All were without the elements of education; she organized a school in which, as soon as possible, the pupils of the higher classes became teachers of the lower. Often hardly knowing where the next day's food for her charges would come from, she struggled on with undaunted courage till the day of her death. The Ramabai Mukti Mission still continues to shelter hundreds of deserted widows.

But though Pandita Ramabai's work had been limited because of the antagonism aroused by her conversion, yet her influence upon other personalities had been telling. Judge Ranade's wife, in whose house Pandita Ramabai had begun her social activity, was one of those who had been fired by her enthusiasm. Mrs Ranade's case is again of particular interest, for while Ramabai's Brahmin father had educated his daughter despite caste injunction to the contrary, here was a girl who, married at eleven to a man of thirty-two, was fully taught by her husband despite bitter opposition from the rest of the household, especially the women. These women of the family-in-law made her suffer intensely. But hers was a marriage embodying all the beauty of ancient Hindu tradition in a lifelong unbroken companionship between husband and wife. Judge Ranade steadily encouraged his young wife, sustained her step by step till she found the strength to defy all conventions and start work of her own. Fifty years ago this woman stood up to read in public an address to the Governor of Bombay, petitioning for a girls' high school for Poona. It was an act so unusual in those days that it required splendid courage. Once launched on the path of reform, Mrs Ranade was indefatigable. She started to teach illiterate women and widows, and later expanded her work into the *Seva Sadan*, a society devoted to 'education, mutual helpfulness and national service'. This organization, wholly Indian as it was, met with less prejudice than Pandita Ramabai's, expanded rapidly, and soon had over a thousand married women attending classes for primary instruction. The society had an ever-increasing influence, and took active steps to promote maternity and infant welfare, while its founder continued to lead in all agitation for compulsory education, women's suffrage, and other reforms. To Mrs Ranade is due to a large extent the credit for winning, as early as 1922, women's suffrage in Bombay Presidency.

A very different type of woman is Sarojini Naidu, India's poetess. In her live again not only the ancient Vedic singers, but the inspiring, women leaders of heroic days. At the call of her country she turned from her singing to the public platform, and has since then swayed millions through the emotional power of her speech. She has headed many deputations of Indian women, such as that to the Hon. F.E. Montagu, then Secretary of State for India, to plead for women's rights. She was at one time President of the Madras Provincial Congress, and had the greatest unofficial honour of India bestowed upon her by being made President of the Indian National Congress.She served for long periods on its organizing and subject committees, took part in the Conference of the International Women's Suffrage Alliance at Geneva, has been the valued adviser of the greatest men of India such as Gandhi, has suffered imprisonment for the national cause, has lectured on India to thousands of eager listeners in the United States, and last but not least, was one of India's representatives at the Round Table Conference in London, following this up, by way of relaxation, with a strenuous trip to Africa on behalf of her troubled countrymen there. She has gone like a meteor in flaming splendour from success to success, and knows the West and all its faults and merits as intimately as she knows her India. She shrugs her shoulders with a sardonic smile when she hears the modern legend that Indians do not know what is good for them, and are not fit to govern themselves. She has told the men of her own race just what she thinks of the ancient outwork trash of customs, she has told the foreign Government just what she knows it can never hope to achieve for her people, and has (bless her heart!) told the present writer how absurdly futile and tiresome it is for Westerners to persist in writing about India!

If we marvels, the proud hundred per cent literate women of the West, could keep pace with this downtrodden woman of India, our unemployed would not equal the untouchables of India in numbers, nor our prostitutes exceed in proportion the *devadasis*. Had we retained our missionaries for work at home, we might perhaps be able to point to-day to 15 per cent of real Christians in the West, instead of having, after more than two centuries of proselytizing, converted merely 1½ per cent of Indians.

We might go on endlessly to multiply examples of the blossoming into power and promise of the forces that lie dormant in Indian womanhood, mention women rulers such as her of Travancore, who has appointed a woman Health Minister, has abolished the *devadasi* evil, and whose state has anticipated British India in educational progress; mention individual work such as that of Dr Muthulakshmi Reddi, a successful physician, whose active life and service has been crowned by her election as Deputy President of the Madras Legislative Council and latest President of the All-India Women's Conference; or that of a woman Municipal Commissioner of Indore; or the director of the Baroda Women's Hospital, the first Indian woman doctor to be head of a hospital; or that heroine of steely persistence, Mrs Hansa Mehta, boycott leader; or the soft-voiced determination of Begum Shah Nawaz, who declared to the world at the Round Table Conference that, whatever the men might do, India's women stood united; or such a woman as Kamala Devi, the powerful organizer of women's associations.

Every passing year will see a twofold increase in the number of Indian women to arise and draw after them an enthusiastic following, women whose greatest pride is always that they are rooted in the high traditions of their ancient land.

Charlotte Wiser

William and Charlotte Wiser came to Karimpur, India in 1925, and Charlotte Wiser (1892–1981) continued to live there after William's death in the US where he went for surgery. Their first account *Behind Mud Walls*, first published in 1930, has been reprinted numerous times, and in new editions with chapters added by other scholars working in Karimpur and observing changes over a period of time. William and Charlotte's books are considered classics, and widely prescribed in the US.

Later Charlotte published *Four Families of Karimpur* (1978), a detailed, sympathetic study, from which the following extracts have been taken. India awarded Charlotte the Kaiser-i-Hind Medal, the highest honour that can be given to a non-citizen, and the Peace Corps awarded her with a plaque commemorating fifty years of service in India. Charlotte and William are credited with setting up a community-oriented village which served as a model used by the Indian Government in its Block Development programme. Despite a lifetime spent in the village, Charlotte wrote, 'In these larger families it is almost impossible to distinguish real from fictitious fear of husbands until one knows the individuals, and hears the reactions of the women when there are no men about.' She also added that the women of the village could hardly be expected to be interested in instruction which was just one way, from the visitor to themselves. 'The visitor's contribution may come from extensive study. Their's comes from intensive experience.'

Four Families of Karimpur

...

Gopi proved to be a good mechanic as well as driver. He was strong and ready to learn and undertake any task assigned to him. His wages rose from barely enough to cover his room and food to more than Bhalai was

Charlotte Wiser, *Four Families of Karimpur*, Susan S. Wadley (ed.), Syracuse: Maxwell School of Citizenship and Public Affairs, Syracuse University, 1978.

getting. During his second year of service, he was selected to go to other stations where an experienced driver was needed. It gave him an opportunity to visit many parts of India while the generous travel allowance added considerably to his income. He seldom came home, having just one month's vacation each year. If he wanted to make the trip between annual leaves, it had to be when a special holiday covered more than one day.

Although the visits home were short, Gopi managed to tell a good deal about his travels. Every young neighbor who could, came to listen. On one visit he flourished a watch, regarded in the village as the first sign of success. He did not call attention to it but consulted it frequently. On a later visit he walked about the village with a camera slung over his shoulder. This was an even greater sensation. Anyone who owned a camera must have a great deal of money to spend. Obviously, Gopi was enjoying his popularity. He was now self-confident, established, and secure.

Following Bhalai's example, he made a trip home at the end of two years' service to take his wife to Delhi to cook for him and his cousin. He assured his parents that his quarters were as good as Bhalai's had been in the Red Ford. They were smaller, only two small rooms plus a tiny kitchen and courtyard, but sufficient for three persons and were protected by a high brick wall. There were friendly neighbors on each side, and the older women would be glad to act as chaperones for his wife while he was away at work. She need not go out because he, like all the men he knew, did the shopping. After all, he was twenty-one and she was seventeen—old enough to take care of themselves. By this time Parbat and Shanti were so accustomed to gossip that they allowed her to go without demanding that another woman of the family accompany her.

In Delhi, she was a success both as cook and as companion. Gopi knew just what sights Bhalai had taken the other women of the family to see, and he took his wife by motorcycle rickshaw to visit them all. On their first excursion, she saw little. She was so afraid that some man might have a glimpse of her face that she kept it well covered. Also she was still unaccustomed to sitting beside her husband in public, and was uncomfortable and self-conscious. She was just beginning to enjoy her emancipation in Delhi when Gopi was obliged to take her back home. He explained to his village friends that he might be sent to some distant place and could not leave her alone. Actually, food prices in Delhi had become so exorbitant that his pay was not sufficient to provide for two. In his father's house, one more person to be fed made little difference. Also at home she could do more than cook two meals a day which was all that she found to do in Delhi. Her help in caring for raw products from the fields would more than compensate for the food she ate.

Less than a month after Gopi had brought his wife home, he was sent to the Punjab just before the conflict between India and Pakistan broke out. He was working in an area where there was no actual fighting; but after bombs had been dropped several times on neighbouring fields, it seemed wise to abandon the project until later so he was transferred back to his regular job near Delhi. He was now listed as a 'permanent' employee. Had he been in regular government service, this would have meant that no one could displace him; but he was employed by a private agency cooperating with the government, therefore it simply indicated that he was considered a good workman and that as long as his services proved satisfactory, he was secure. It also indicated that his supervisor approved of his work and that he would not be lightly dismissed.

The Family of Devi and Balram, Carpenters

I had often visited the small Carpenter houses across the lane. Knowing that their husbands worked with Devi, I asked about his wife as I had never seen her and wondered why. In answer they simply shrugged. She had no place in their lives. Was she confined to her courtyard, because men might see her if she were to cross the lane to visit them, or had Devi forbidden her to leave? She never went, like the others, to the well. Instead one of the boys of her family filled the water jars and brought them home to her. Much as I wanted to know her as head of Devi's courtyard, I was unwilling to walk in without some friendly gesture from her or from him. Then, without warning, we met, not in her house but at the door of my tent. There she stood, just outside the bamboo screen serving as our door, a baby on her hip and two small bundles tied in cloth dangling from her free hand. Her face was covered and I had no inkling as to who she was. Other women who came were accompanied by relatives and were ready to explain their own ailments or those of their companions. A woman would introduce herself as 'mother of Ramesh' or of Sundar, or one of the other boys we knew. This woman simply stood, mute, until one of the children playing nearby came up and explained that she was his aunt. But which aunt? Why, Devi's wife, of course. I was dumbfounded. I asked what I could do for her. She partially uncovered her face and announced bluntly that it was her intention to go into Mainpuri with us that noon. We were surprised that she had come this far from home and was prepared to go farther, without her husband. Village women do not walk out like this, especially one as secluded as she. Only desperation could have driven her to it. The child, about a year old, was in a state of collapse. He had had violent dysentery for several days. Her husband had told her earlier about our simple remedies and about the patients we had taken to doctors in town. She had tried everything that the local *hakim* had advised and had called on the spirit exorcisor, but the child had grown steadily worse.

Taking a mother to town with her child is not simple. We could find a place for her to sleep, but what about food? She would not touch ours. In answer to our query she held up her bundles. One contained food enough for herself for three days and the other contained whatever covering she and the baby might need. It was warm weather so this was very little. She was wearing what was obviously her best full skirt and blouse and cotton shawl. I knew that if she were like other village women she would not own another such outfit to carry to town. Apparently she was going without a change of clothing. We sent someone to her house to make sure that she had Devi's permission. He came himself to assure us that he had agreed to her going. They would do anything that we or the doctor advised, in the hope of saving their child.

Later, when she uncovered her face, I found her one of the least prepossessing women I had seen in the village. Her features were large and uneven. Her front teeth were gone. Her hair, straggling out from under the edge of her shawl, was unwashed and stringy. There seemed nothing to relieve her plainness. I would have guessed her age to be fifty. But with so small a child she must have been younger. If I had met her in her own courtyard I would have thought her uninteresting, but a woman with enough spirit to travel to a strange town with strangers, alone, on short notice, must be far from dull. We could not refuse her nor would she have accepted refusal.

The next few days became an ordeal, both for her and for me. The doctor give strict orders that the baby should have only water and the prescribed medicines, given at regular intervals day and night. No milk. The mother was prepared to give the baby the medicines but to deny her child her own milk? Never. So we struggled, both of us trying to save the baby's life by methods that clashed. When a village baby cries, feeding him is the first step in pacifying him. If that fails, jouncing and making loud noises to distract him are resorted to. What else is there for the women to do? The child was too weak to cry, but his wailing was even more pitiful.

Keeping him in a room apart from his mother, as the doctor advised, would have simplified the treatment, but she flatly refused to do this. He had slept with her at night ever since he was born, and during the day he had always been in her arms or in the arms of an older child in the family or on a charpai near her while she worked. The only food he had ever had was her milk. She became too frantic to listen to reason. After all, I was a stranger, as was the doctor. On the morning of the fourth day, when she threatened to carry the child home on foot and I would have been relieved to have her do so, he opened his eyes. The strain was over and, slowly, we both relaxed. From that point on there was no question of her cooperation. The child was not going to die.

She refused to go near our coal-burning range. Instead she set up a makeshift *chulha* in our small yard, and over the wood fire she toasted *chapatis* from whole-wheat flour, and cooked the pulses or vegetables brought from the bazaar. To our surprise she settled down in her routine without demur. By the time we returned to the village she was prepared to carry out all of the doctor's final instructions as to feeding and care, and the baby became healthier than he had been before the bout of dysentery. Our return would have been quite different had he died—which was what the doctor had feared on the first night. As it was, we were warmly welcomed by Devi and his relatives.

Gail Minault

Described as one of the foremost post-orientalist historians, Dr Gail Minault is Professor of History at the University of Texas, Austin. She is the author of *The Khilafat Movement: Religious Symbolism and Political Motivation in India* (1982), *Secluded Scholars: Women's Education and Muslim Social Reform in Colonial India* (1998), and numerous articles on social reformers, women's language, and purdah. She has also edited *The Extended Family: Women and Political Participation in India and Pakistan*, and co-edited with Hanna Papanek *Separate Worlds: Studies of Purdah in South Asia*. She has translated Altaf Husain Hali's *Majalis un-Nissa* and *Chup ki Dad* as *Voices of Silence*.

Urdu Women's Magazines in The Early Twentieth Century

Readers of *Manushi* know that it not only describes the realities of women's lives but also seeks to change those realities. It advocates women's rights and permits women to communicate with each other about their problems. *Manushi*'s format and spirit are new, but it represents a long and distinguished tradition in Indian journalism that goes back into the nineteenth century

Early Indian women's magazines, in a number of languages, championed women's education, condemned social customs that kept women subservient, and encouraged women's self expression. As champions of women's rights, however these publications have a mixed legacy. They portrayed the ideal woman as skilful wife and nurturing mother, educated but wholly domestic, the helpmate to the educated, middle class man. Education for women was seen as contributing to that ideal, not as preparing women for careers outside the home (except for teaching), nor

Gail Minault, 'Urdu Women's Magazines in the Early Twentieth Century', *Manushi*, Number 48, 1988.

an independent existence. From a contemporary viewpoint, it is easy to see in this ideal of womanhood the basis for women's continued subordination within the patriarchal family. Examined in their historical context, however, these women's magazines were brave pioneers, expanding the frontiers of women's roles and consciousness at a time when those frontiers were severely limited.

I propose to examine this mixed legacy in the cases of several women's magazines in Urdu, publications that I read in the course of doing historical research on Muslim women in India in the late nineteenth and early twentieth centuries. *Tahzib un-Niswan* of Lahore, founded in 1898, *Khatun* of Aligarh, which ran from 1904 to 1914, and *Ismat* of Delhi, founded in 1908, raised important social issues and helped enlighten and alleviate the isolation of women in *parda* while promoting an ideal of competent domesticity. In so doing these magazines were not very different from women's magazines founded by Hindu social reformers in Hindi, Bengali, and other languages. Patriarchy, and social reform were symbiotic, regardless of religious community.

TAHZIB UN-NISWAN

Sayyid Mumtaz Ali and his wife, Muhammadi Begam, launched the Urdu weekly newspaper for women, *Tahzib un-Niswan,* in 1898. *Tahzib* was not the first Urdu periodical for women, but it was the first to survive. The success of the newspaper was surprising, for when the couple began publishing it, they mailed it out free of cost to names on the civil list, hoping to enlist subscriptions. Many of their prospective subscribers responded by returning the paper to sender, often with obscenities scribbled on the label. It was not an auspicious beginning. After a few months, *Tahzib* had only 60 or 70 subscribers, but the couple persisted, and gradually the number of subscriptions increased to some 300 or 400 after four years. Publishing a women's periodical was a difficult and certainly not lucrative enterprise, and the fact the *Tahzib* survived into the 1950s is due largely to the talents and energies of its founders.

Mumtaz Ali (1860–1935) was from a family with a tradition of religious learning; his father was in government service in Punjab. As a youth, he had one year of schooling at the Deoband *madarsa* before going to Lahore for an English education. In Lahore, he became involved in religious controversy, at first simply listening to the debates among Christian missionaries, Muslims, and Arya Samajis that took place in public squares, but later joining in the debates himself. As an adult, he used his skill in debate to address his fellow Muslims on the subject of women's rights in Islamic law.

His work, *Huquq un-Niswan* ('Women's Rights'), emphasised that the position of women in Islamic law was theoretically much higher than their contemporary status was in fact. The cause of this discrepancy, he felt, was adherence to false customs that had been given the force of religion. The key to the reform and advancement of the Muslim community, therefore, was to combat women's adherence to superstitious customs, but also to challenge men's views concerning women's rights. Women are equal souls before god. Thus, keeping women in ignorance and isolation is not a requirement of Islam, and to think that it is betrays a lack of understanding of religion as well as a fundamental mistrust of women, which is destructive of family life, of human love, and of all that the prophet's message stood for in a dynamic, just society. To support his point, Mumtaz Ali argued in the clear and logical style for which he became known: 'The question is: Does the ability to do things [requiring physical strength] give men true superiority or nobility or give the male sex exclusive claim to those qualities? Our reply to that question should be quire clear....Both sexes have nobility, excellence, and both are needed in complete the other....A donkey can carry more on its back than a man, but that does not mean that the donkey is superior to the man. By the same token, man cannot establish his superiority [over women] on the basis of this argument.' (*Huquq un-Niswan*, Lahore, 1898: 7–8).

But how could he best bring about the kind of change in attitude that he advocated? Writing a learned treatise such as *Haquq un-Niswan* would reach only a few, well educated Muslims. The answer, Mumtaz Ali decided, was to reach women with an enlightened message. They needed to know what rights they had in the *shariat*. They could inherit property, and therefore needed enough education to be able to manage it. Further, they needed to be aware of contemporary ideas concerning child rearing, health, nutrition, budgeting, etiquette, and so on.

Respectable Muslim women in the 1890s did not usually go out to school, but a number of *parda* observing families had a tradition of home instruction. What was missing was useful reading material. A woman who had nothing appropriate to read might relapse into illiteracy. A newspaper written in simple Urdu, designed with women's needs in mind, would help make women better wives, mothers, homemakers, and more devout Muslims. Educated men whose desire for educated wives was emerging at that time, would also respond positively to a more enlightened home life, and their attitudes, too, might change.

Mumtaz Ali was aided in founding his women's newspaper by his wife, Muhammadi Begam. This remarkable woman is usually viewed simply as her husband's helpmate, but she was a strong personality in her own right. She was educated at home, together with her numerous brothers, and when they went off to school, she continued to learn somewhat haphazardly from their textbooks. She learned to write letters in order to stay in touch with her sister when the latter married and moved away. She managed her father's household and cared for the younger children when her stepmother was away visiting relatives. When she married, she continued her education under Mumtaz Ali's tutelage, even as they founded their journal. She mothered his two children from a previous marriage, managed his household, and eventually bore their own son. Muhammadi Begam also served as editor of *Tahzib un-Niswan* and was, in addition, the author of several novels, a cookbook, a manual of housekeeping, and books of etiquette. She died prematurely in 1908.

During its first decade, under Muhammadi Begam's editorship, *Tahzib* aimed at reaching the *parda* observing woman at home and meeting her need for useful reading matter and broadened hoizons. Articles discussed education, household management, gave good advice to the daughter-in-law on how to get along with her mother-in-law, and so on. A constant theme was the reform and simplification of custom, the need to eliminate wasteful expenditure on rituals, dowry, ornaments. Mumtaz Ali's views on women's rights in Islamic law were also serialised in the paper.

Tahzib classified itself as a newspaper, so it carried a lot of news items, notices of women's meetings, of fundraising drives for schools, and summaries of speeches by women to women's organisations. The weekly format made possible a lot of give-and-take between the journal and its readers, in the letters to the editor section. One letter, for example, discussed the reasons why girls should learn English: 'Nowadays, many girls are keen to learn English, but their parents are displeased by this. They feel that girls have no reason to learn English, since they are not going out to work in an office. They don't realise that boys who learn English also would like wives who know English. It is my opinion that this is the reason why so many unfortunate women sit home alone.... Also, if they knew English, they could contact the men in their offices in event of an emergency....' (*Tahzib un-Niswan*, 4 April 1907: 170).

The style of this, and of the paper in general was straightforward and conversational. *Tahzib* struck a balance between popular format and reformist substance. It maintained a clarity of style with a content that was both practical and edifying.

Later volumes of *Tahzib* reflected women's increased level of education and variety of activities outside their homes. The style become somewhat more complex; the vocabulary expanded. Reports of women's organisations and speeches proliferated. In one such report, Mumtaz Ali commented: 'Ever since the founding of the Muslim Ladies' Conference four years ago, we have been interested in it, and always hoped that it would be able to do something for reform in the community. I always thought, however, that it was premature...and a number of people thought I was against the conference for that reason. But I am its well-wisher....What do I mean when I say the conference is premature? I mean that a great deal of unusual and hard work will be necessary or it will not be successful.' (*TN*, 6 April 1918: 221–22).

Other articles revealed that women were indeed receiving education in English as well as Urdu, and the paper printed the names of women passing their BAs, MAs, and medical degrees, with warm congratulations and exhortations to other readers to go and do likewise.

Articles began to appear on the contemporary political scene, the events of World War I, noncooperation, and *swadeshi*. Women started collecting funds for political purposes: the Khilafat movement and Turkish relief. In one appeal that combined these causes, Nazar Sajjad Hyder, wife of Syed Sajjad Hyder, herself an Urdu novelist and short story writer and the mother of the contemporary Urdu woman novelist, Qurratulain Hyder urged: ' I am not asking you to give rupees but...give up foreign cloth and wear only *swadeshi*....The day is coming when we will be ashamed to go out without wearing *khaddar*. Instead of burning your foreign cloth, send it to the Smyrna [Turkish Relief] Fund to be given to Turkish women 'who need warm clothes for winter'. (*TN*, 29 October 1921: 689–94).

Readers also sent in travel accounts and descriptions of the *haj* pilgrimage. Literary criticism appeared. And a number of younger women contributors began to take issue with the strictures of *parda*, with polygamy, and with unilateral divorce. By the 1930s, the readers of *Tahzib* had come a long way.

Tahzib overcame initial opposition and succeeded because it met a felt social need. Mumtaz Ali, after all, was not the only educated Indian Muslim male of his time who desired a more enlightened home life. Nor was Muhammadi Begam the only literate Muslim woman of her time who lacked a source of news and an outlet for self expression. *Tahzib* articulated an impulse for reform of custom, of religious observance, and of household practice that was essentially patriarchal. The desires and opinions of men were behind the effort, and the institution of *parda* and

the subordinate position of women in the family were in no way challenged. Further, the emphasis on the reform of custom in favour of
scriptural religion challenged a cultural realm in which women were
relatively autonomous.

Still, Mumtaz Ali's attitudes, based on his published interpretation of
Islamic law, were remarkably egalitarian, and his partnership with
Muhammadi Begam was a close and creative one. *Tahzib*'s ideal of
domesticity may now seem dated, but in the first decades of this century,
its advocacy of women's education and of broader imaginative horizons
for women in *parda* were in advance of the times.

KHATUN

Another husband and wife who were active in the movement for women's
education and who started a magazine for women were Shaikh Abdullah
of Aligarh (1874–1965) and Waheed Jahan Begam (1886–1939). Shaikh
Abdullah was a convert to Islam who attended Aligarh College, established a law practice in that town, and married the educated sister of one
of his classmates. In 1904, they started the Urdu monthly *Khatun* as the
journal of the Women's Education Section of the All-India Muslim
Educational Conference. Shaikh Abdullah was the secretary of the
Women's Education Section, and the main purpose of the journal was
thus to advocate schools for girls, especially the Abdullahs' project to
found a girls' school in Aligarh.

The Abdullahs established Aligarh Girls' School in 1906, and by
1914 had raised money and built a hostel to transform their local school
into a boarding school, with clientele coming from a wider area. Waheed
Jahan Begam devoted her energies to running the school and supervising
the hostel. The school, which struggled to survive at first, later expanded
to become the Women's College of Aligarh Muslim University.

Khatun provides important documentation for the history of Muslim
women's education. The Shaikh exhorted his readers to found local
associations to raise funds and start girls' schools. He recorded fundraising
drives and his own speeches and reports to the annual meetings of the
Muslim Educational Conference. In one particularly interesting editorial, cast in the form of a dialogue between himself (Editor) and a
supporter of education (*Hami*), the Shaikh asked:

Editor: From your words, am I to understand that you are a firm supporter of
women's education?
Hami: Why not? Anyone who opposes women's education in this day and age is
either illiterate (*jahil*) or mad (*diwana*).

Editor: But not being opposed to women's education is quite a different matter from supporting it...I simply wanted to ask if you were truly a supporter of women's education, or whether your were simply among those who refrain from opposing it.

Hami: (frowning) Please repeat your question. I am not sure I understand.

Editor: *Janab*! I merely said that anyone who is a genuine supporter of women's education would want to support it by his actions, words writing, and so on. And if he had money, he would also support that effort with a donation.' (*Khatun*, August 1912: 46–7)

Waheed Jahan too gave an occasional speech or wrote about management of the school. In one speech at a meeting of Muslim women gathered to voice support for girls' education, she mentioned that women in Turkey and Egypt were being educated and could hold meetings, and this had been beneficial to their societies: 'When women meet among themselves, there will be more solidarity....Now there is division between educated and uneducated women. Uneducated women, who do not go out, think that respectability is confined to the four walls of their houses. They think that people who live beyond those walls are not respectable and not worthy of meeting. But God has ordained education for both men and women, so that such useless ideas can be gotten rid of.' (*Khatun*, January 1906: 7–8)

The journal also contained much discussion of educational matters, curricula, the pros and cons of teaching English to women, the need for improved textbooks, the students' need for fresh air and exercise (behind high walls so that *parda* could be maintained), reports of meetings of women's associations and school committees, and speeches by women, including the Begam of Bhopal, the chief patron of Aligarh Girls' School. Reporting on the Begam's speech before the inaugural function of the hostel building in 1914, *Khatun* noted that the doors of the hall had stuck when she tried to open them, prompting her to quip that this symbolised the obstacles still facing Muslim girls' education (*Khatun* February–March 1914: 35, 44–54)

Women's views on education appeared in its pages, but *Khatun* was chiefly addressed to the members and patrons of the Muslim Educational Conference, that is the educated elite of the Muslim community, largely men. Shaikh Adbullah wrote clearly and persuasively in Urdu, but without many concessions to the need for a simplified style to reach a newly literate female readership. One exception to this observation simply proves the rule, for a wonderfully idiomatic article by one A.W.J. Begam from Delhi was in striking contrast to most of the journal. 'I have heard a lot of noise about the fact that the quest for knowledge has not reached Muslim women, and that they are not interested in education in any way. People make speeches at meetings and write articles in newspapers....But if you ask them what they have done to spread knowledge among women...the answer is simply nothing. Everyone says that our *gari* [train/cart—the double meaning is intended] will reach its destination, but no one seems to be willing to hitch it to an engine, or a horse, or even a bullock and then everyone regrets that the cart is sitting in one place. If this keeps up, we will never get anywhere.' (*Khatun*, August 1904: 41–4).

Khatun's purpose was to promote women's education. Providing women with useful household information, tips on childrearing and embroidery patterns was left to publications closer to the style of *Tahzib*. *Khatun* fulfilled its purpose, but in 1914, with the opening of the hostel, the Abdullahs had a great deal to do to run the boarding school, and so *Khatun* ceased publication.

ISMAT

The third in this trio of early women's magazines in Urdu is *Ismat* of Delhi, founded in 1908 by Rashidul Khairi (1868–1936), whose chief claim to fame was as an Urdu novelist. He was the nephew of another famous Urdu novelist 'Deputy' Nazir Ahmad (1830–1912). Rashidul Khairi, during his prolific career as a novelist, earned the nickname *musavvir-e-gham* ('portrayer of sorrow') for his melodramatic and extremely popular stories about the tragic lives of oppressed women. His earnings from his novels helped him to finance *Ismat*, a monthly which was founded primarily as a literary journal, to encourage creative writing by women. It also contained a substantial amount of writing by Rashidul Khairi and other men, articles designed to promote women's education and the respectable domesticity so favored by social reformers of the day, whether Hindu or Muslim.

Reading Rashidul Khairi's novels gives one a clue to his attitudes toward women, their education and enlightenment. An early work, *Hayat-e-Saleha* or *Salehat* is the story of the beloved and well educated daughter of an elderly man who, having lost his wife, remarries. The ignorant stepmother decides to marry off this daughter to her wastrel younger brother. Since her father agrees to the plan, the daughter also accepts it. She makes an exemplary wife and mother, but is unappreciated by her worthless husband. Her father eventually dies, and so does she. The heroine, Saleha, even though educated, is ill used by her father and husband, but she remains dutiful and uncomplaining. Many of Rashidul Khairi's heroines die, often of consumption. They are then honoured in death, unlike in life. One begins to see why he was dubbed 'the painter of sorrow', and one suspects that the ghost of Rashidul Khairi lurks among today's Bombay film writers.

The first issue of *Ismat* contained stories, poems, several articles on education, one on housekeeping, a description of the Taj Mahal, and several letters of welcome. One of those letters was from Waheed Jahan Begam Abdullah; one of the poems was by Muhammadi Begam Mumtaz Ali. The issue also contained a statement of purpose: *Ismat* was a journal in Urdu for 'respectable Indian women', which would contain edifying articles dealing with scientific and educational subjects, literature, and useful knowledge, but no political articles. It also aimed to 'make the sanctuary sanctified' (*haram ki harmat qaim rakhna*) or 'as the English saying goes, to make the home a castle', to 'bring progress to the world of women', and to 'advance the cause of women's literature'. (*Ismat*, June 1908, appendix.)

If one couples the name of the journal (*Ismat* means purity or chastity) with its statement of aims, and compares these with the plots of Khairi's novels, one senses a unity of purpose in his literary endeavours. *Ismat* assumed the modesty, honour, and respectability, but also passivity, of its readers. It viewed women as the objects of a programme of ameliora- tion. The home was to become a 'sanctuary' (the double meaning of the word *haram* is significant); progress and enlightenment were to be brought to women.

Such a view of women is highly conventional. It coincides with the vision of women in Khairi's novels. No matter how well educated and competent his heroines may be, they are always dutiful, even to the men who oppress them. They are victims, incapable of defending themselves because they are devoted to the overriding ideals of obedience and fidelity. Some women criticised Khairi for this aspect of his writings. In an example of the early literary criticism that appeared in *Tahzib un-Niswan*, a woman noted: 'He captures women's idiom better than anyone....But his books, whose subjects deal with happenings that we see every day are not very realistic....[He shows] women's weakness and inferiority, but this portrayal gives us nothing to build on or be proud of. It shows what should be changed without giving us any notion of how to get out of the situation....He doesn't really help anyone [by showing] women in a state of crying day and night.' (*TN*, 9 July 1921: 433–5)

To end the oppression of women, according to Rashidul Khairi, men had to undergo a change of heart. Consequently, in the early years of

Ismat, unlike in *Tahzib un-Niswan*, there was little, if any, discussion of women's rights in Islam. Rather, the journal contained articles and stories designed to inform women about how to make their husbands' lives more comfortable, what sorts of difficulties they would encounter (and have to bear patiently) when they married and went to live with their in-laws, and so on.

In one article, entitled 'Have Our Women Made Progress?', Radhidul Khairi outlined what he thought were important indicators of change: 'Let us simply look at what are the differences between formerly and now in daughters and daughters-in-law. Nowdays, women realise that their duty is not simply to populate the world, but actually to bring about some betterment....There is no denying the fact that today's wives are trying to improve the condition of their homes. This is significant. They also recognise better the tenets of their religion, and that one of its most important commandments is to seek knowledge.' (*Ismat*, October 1912: 2–6.)

The didactic purpose of *Ismat* was as clear as that of Rashidul Khairi's novels, and neither challenged traditional female roles or male authority. There was an important reason for the journal's emphasis on respectability: *Ismat* hoped to avoid the kinds of moral objections and attacks that other women's journals such as *Tahzib,* had met. In this, it was successful. *Ismat's* circulation by 1912 had reached 900, much better than *Tahzib's* during its fourth year of life.

To be fair to Rashidul Khairi, however, his concern for purity, honour, and respectability was not a façade. His morality was highly conventional, but to champion the cause of women's education, to urge women to express themselves in print, and to urge men to undergo a change of heart required a good deal of courage at that time.

An example of his writing, addressed to men, urging them to end their injustice to women is the following passage from *Tamaddun*, another one of his journals. The tone is typically lachrymose: 'The story of women's rights is heartrending. Women are oppressed day and night and find no relief from their fate. Blessed will be that time when a spirit of sympathy [for women] will spread [among men] upon the earth. Torment will change into paradise and sorrows will change into happiness. Even when going to their graves, husbands do not recognise the oppression they have visited upon their wives. Nor has news of the rights which Islam has given them reached women's ears.' (*Tamaddun*, March 1913, cited in Rashidul Khairi, *Ismat Ki Kahani*, Delhi 1936: 12.)

Rashidul Khairi would have been horrified, however, if women had started demanding their own rights. Confirmation of this point came in

1918, when the Anjuman-e-Khawatin-e Islam, otherwise known as the All-India Muslim Ladies Conference, meeting in Lahore, passed a resolution condemning polygamy. The resolution stated that '...the kind of polygamy practised by certain sections of the Muslims is against the spirit of the Quran and of Islam, and that it is inimical to our progress as a community', and called upon women to exercise their influence to end the practice.

Rashidul Khairi, much to the shock of many loyal readers of *Ismat*, attacked the resolution: 'We regret greatly that wives and daughters of respectable Muslims could agree to such a thing....I am not myself a supporter of polygamy, but for a Muslim meeting to make such a declaration, in the presence of non-Muslims [some Englishwomen were present] only brings hatred upon Islam and has a detrimental effect on the minds of young Muslim girls. It also goes against the meaning of the *shariat*.' (*Ismat*, March 1918: 8.)

The women were astonished, because Rashidul Khairi had exposed the evils of polygamy in several of his novels and had made clear his own position that no man could do justice to more than one woman, in the spirit of the Quranic injunction. Yet, when women themselves addressed the problem and invoked the spirit of the Quran, as opposed to its letter, Rashidul Khairi fell back upon the letter, saying that since Islam permitted polygamy, it would not do for Muslim women to seek its abolition. A number of women criticised him for his inconsistency, and yet his stance is quite consistent with his position that men must be the reformers of society and the improvers of women, not women themselves. His position is thus internally consistent, whether or not one agrees with it.

Rashidul Khairi's writings overflow with sympathy for the oppressed women of the Indian Muslim community. He regarded himself as a champion of women's rights within the Islamic tradition, and for his time, he certainly was. It took courage to expose the social evils that he described in his works, such as polygamy and unilateral divorce. It took talent to do so and simultaneously to be one of the biggest bestsellers in the history of the Urdu novel.

The modern reader may find his characters stereotypical, his plots maudlin and repetitive, and his view of women condescending and patriarchal. But Rashidul Khairi was a pioneer. He founded his journal to encourage women writers, and it did so, giving rise to many who went on to write openly about subjects that he surely would have disapproved. *Ismat* moved to Karachi in 1947 and continued to appear from there until recently. Its pages contained the writings of many of the great Urdu women writers of the twentieth century.

CONCLUSIONS

The three Urdu women's magazines discussed here are only a few examples of the genre, though *Tahzib un-Niswan* and *Ismat* both had very long careers and hence provide the historian with a guage of social and attitudinal changes over time. All three were started by men, two with the close collaboration of their wives. All three championed women's education and defined greater enlightenment for women in terms of competent domesticity rather than in terms of individual autonomy. When they addressed religious questions, they supported a scriptural standard rather than folk or customary practice, meaning that they played down women's rituals or condemned them as superstitious.

In setting up social norms for women, these journals defined those standards in terms that men could recognise. Women accepted such norms as well, but in the process may have surrendered some control over their own sphere. The legacy of these socially reforming journals is thus ambiguous. As women became educated and as they read these journals and became more aware of the external world and its values, their definition of what was acceptable, or respectable, was more closely controlled by what men thought. It took several generations before a newer standard could evolve, but these early women's magazines at least gave women a place where their voices could be heard.

Dr Meredith Borthwick

Dr Meredith Borthwick (d. 1995) was a noted Australian scholar and diplomat who specialized in work on Bengal. She also translated Thai literature. In her book, excerpted here, Dr Borthwick explores the changing role of women in Bengal. In the specific extract used here, she examines the bebates on what women would wear once they came out of purdah.

Dress Reform and Ideas of Modesty

The purdah system of the early nineteenth century allowed some freedoms that seem to have been essential outlets in an otherwise rigid system. Ironically, it was these areas of freedom that proved most shocking to opponents or purdah. Most *bhadramahilā* were able to appear at public places such as religious shrines or bathing *ghāts* without self-consciousness. Although most of the bathing *ghāts* in Calcutta were designated for one sex or the other, some were mixed.[1] Kasi Mitra's *ghāt* was one such place, where modest Hindu women who would insist on covering their faces in the presence of men 'shamelessly' bathed in public.[2] In the *mofussil* all women bathed at mixed *ghāts*.[3] The Dacca magistrate issued an order forbidding anyone to bathe in certain *ghāts* at certain hours, because of the 'shameless way which some women used to go through the process'.[4] What was interpreted by nineteenth-century puritans as lasciviousness is more likely to have betokened a straightforward lack of inhibition about normal bodily functions. An article on mixed bathing in the *Bāmābodhinī Patrikā* revealed the author's own obsessions in describing how 'obscenely' women rubbed their bodies and washed the saris they were wearing. It noted that these women would not dare go into mixed society when their clothes were dry, but would unbashedly expose themselves to the public gaze when they were

Dr Meredith Borthwick, 'Erosion of Purdah', in *The Changing Role of Women in Bengal, 1849–1905*, Princeton, NJ. Princeton University Press, 1984 wet and practically naked.[5] In a composition 'Modesty' in the *Bāmā-bodhinī Patrikā,* a young Brahmo girl was very censorious of the 'immodesty' of women who wore thin saris, even in front of the servants, and who bathed publicly. She recommended that servants should not be allowed to enter the house without permission and that baths should be taken secretly.[6]

Another aspect of purdah that presented itself as an affront to those outside the system was women's clothing. An upper-caste woman would habitually wear a sari of fine transparent muslin.[7] It was a single piece of cloth, draped around the body. No undergarments were worn.[8] The only other component of a woman's dress was her ornaments.[9] This clothing seemed well suited to the hot climate of Bengal, yet the wearing of such a revealing form of dress, even if only in front of male relatives, appears incongruous in a strict purdah system. However, it may have served to reinforce pardah by exposing female sexuality and then demarcating sharply the boundaries within which it could be expressed. Women themselves probably preferred their traditional dress for reasons of comfort, but Bengali men were also reputed to have a 'jealous repugnance' to 'any alteration in female attire'.[10] Once women came to symbolize tradition and continuity, any changes in their condition were forcefully resisted by men. As 'reforms' in female dress would have enabled a lessening of purdah restrictions, the retention of traditional dress may have served to buttress the existing system.

The preoccupation with women's dress in the nineteenth century was a result of taking a fresh look at traditional clothing through the puritanical perspective of Calvinist Christianity and Victorian England. Compared with the thick gowns worn by English women, the type of sari worn by Bengali women appeared to leave them practically unclad. The Reverend Krishna Mohan Banerjea declared in 1841 that to wear such a garment in public would be a breach of decency.[11] Shib Chunder Bose expressed the view that 'it would be a very desirable improvement in the way of decency to introduce among the Hindoo females of Bengal a stouter fabric for their garment in place of the present thin, flimsy, loose *sari,* without any other covering over it'.[12] Another writer ventured to suggest that women could at least wear silk saris when they appeared in public. They were as beautiful as muslin, yet less transparent and more modest.[13]

A puritanical concern for decency was frequently expressed by the British in Bengal. In 1850 J.E.D. Bethune wrote to Lord Dalhousie that he made 'occasional presents of dresses, when any of the little girls appeared in rather too primitive a state to correspond with my notions of decency'.[14] To Annette Akroyd, even when women were well covered, 'the very bundling of themselves up in swathes of muslin suggests immodesty'.[15]

Traditional dress was seen by the *bhadralok* as a stumbling block in the way of reforming the condition of women. They wished to promote female education and female participation in public social events. Traditional dress had evolved within a purdah society and was unsuitable for appearing in front of men outside the intimate family circle. Women would need to feel their dress provided protective covering if purdah were to be discarded. Koilasbasini Debi, one of the first Hindu female authors, thought it necessary for women to dress differently if they wanted to benefit fully from public education.[16]

The progressive *bhadralok,* especially the Brahmos, actively sought a solution to the problem. In 1865 the Brahmo young men's group, the Sangat Sabha, met to discuss a suitable form of dress for modern women. The problem was of immediate importance to them because they wanted to bring their wives into public society, but at that stage they were not able to form any definite conclusions.[17] In 1871, the Brahmo women's auxiliary group the Bama Hitaisini Sabha discussed the same topic. Some of the views presented by members were published in the *Bāmābodhinī Patrikā.*[18] One member, Saudamini Khastagir, said of traditional dress that

if the kind of thin clothing customary here at present is worn the whole body can be seen clearly. This kind of shameless dress cannot be worn in polite society. If a person was preaching or lecturing in a place, it would be possible that if we wore this dress there we would not hear any of the fine talk. Considering this, the extent to which progressives object to this dress will be understood.

She considered the adoption of English dress, but dismissed the idea as too costly and impractical. Saudamini favored the costumes of Bombay and northwest India, but felt that direct adoption of their dress would confuse regional identity. Rajlaksmi Sen, another member of the Bama Hitaisini Sabha, expressed similar views. She noted that women dressing in the reformed style had to avoid not only 'denationalization,' but also the danger of being mistaken for prostitutes, some of whom wore chemises, jackets, and shoes with their saris. Her idea was for a *bhadramahilā* to be distinguished from them by wearing an additional *cādar,* or wrap, covering her from head to foot. The editor made the final recommendation for the reformed dress:

At home: *ijār* (short trousers) *pirān* (blouse) and sari; or long *pirān* and sari

Outside: *ijār, pirān* and sari, *cādar, pyjāma* and shoes
(optional)

Two months later, a woman from Bombay wrote to the editor of the *Bāmābodhinī Patrikā* giving her views on dress reform. The anonymous correspondent was clearly identifiable as Jnanadanandini Debi, one of the first Bengali women to act as official hostess at public functions hosted by her husband. The dress question was therefore of direct practical relevance for her. Her suggestion was to improvise a new form of dress that drew inspiration from diverse groups, including the English, Muslims, and Bengalis, which would take on a distinct Bengali identity if all Bengali women started wearing it. She said that many Calcutta women, when visiting each other, had already adopted a dress very similar to that suggested in the *Bāmābodhinī Patrikā*. For herself, she wore shoes, stockings, bodice *(āngiyā kācali),* blouse *(jāmā)* and a short skirt *(ghāghara)* or *ijar* with a sari over the top at home, and a *cādar* covering her head in addition when she went out. As women may have had difficulty envisaging all the garments she described and may have felt uncertain as to how to wear them, she offered to make a set for anyone who was interested, or to send them a picture of how the clothes should be worn.[19] The style she invented became known as the 'Brahmika sari.'[20]

Increasingly women adapted their clothing along the lines suggested, although the quest for a definitive style continued throughout the century. An advertisement in the *New Dispensation* in 1881 under the heading 'Woman's Dress' asked readers, 'Have you any idea as to what the reformed Hindu woman's dress ought to be? Put it upon paper; if possible, draw and paint the design and let us see it. Decent not costly.'[21]

The direct adoption of European dress, favored by some, was seen to have numerous drawbacks. It was too costly, as well as being too bulky for the average Bengali home.[22] Some men objected to it on the grounds of immodesty, with reference to the amount of bare flesh exposed by a low-cut evening gown.[23] Others noted its unhealthy aspect, including the fact that tight lacing was coming under attack from doctors in England.[24] Bengali Christian women were the only group who wholeheartedly adopted English dress.[25] Even Annette Akroyd, a staunch opponent of the traditional sari, said that she had no temptation to put her girls into English dress because it made them look 'irretrievably common'.[26]

The model for a reformed dress was derived from other parts of India rather than from England, and was a result of the wide exposure to other Indian regional cultures gained through travel. As early as 1865, it was noted in a news item in the *Bāmābodhinī Patrikā* that women in western India were able to move around with greater freedom because they had suitable clothes.[27] A lady writing from Bombay in 1904 described in detail the different modes of dress she saw there. Women draped their saris differently, and wore a jacket called a *celi* underneath. They wore brighter colors than Bengalis, and rich women always wore silk saris. Parsi women wore trousers and a long shirt underneath, with a silk sari and jacket on top, and shoes. On their heads they wore a white cloth or handkerchief.[28] The Parsi woman's dress inspired Jnanadanandini's 'Brahmika sari'.[29] Her design and its popularity transcended regional boundaries. It could even be said to have fostered a sense of national awareness by creating a fashion for Bengal that drew its inspiration from western India, and that eventually came into vogue all over the country.[30]

As the first group to take up the reformed dress, Brahmo women would initially have been clearly distinguishable from the Hindu *bhadramahilā* by their clothing. In his autobiography, Brahmo Gurucharan Mahalanabis recalled his quest for a reformed mode of dress for his wife. As it used to cost him two rupees or so to send her to weekly meetings of the Brahmika Samaj, even though it was within walking distance of their home, it struck him as unfair that his wife was not free to walk there. After discussing the matter with a group of friends, he concluded that the chief obstacle to her mobility was her dress. He decided to get her to wear a chemise, jacket, and full-length *cādar* over her sari, as well as shoes. Wearing 'pantaloons' himself, he then walked with her to the Brahmika Samaj, where they were greeted with surprise by all the women present. Still uncertain, he later got her to wear gown, boots, and veil in the manner of a Bengali Christian friend. This caught on among other Brahmos, and Bijoy Krishna Goswami made his wife follow suit. He sold a gold amulet of hers to buy her a gown, which she wore back to her home in Santipur. Being only eleven or twelve years old at the time, she was too young to be embarrassed by the stir she caused among her relatives, who mistook her for a *memsaheb*. Even Keshub Chunder Sen's mother was surprised by this kind of Anglicized garb, and once asked Gurucharan's wife if that was the dress of her region in East Bengal.[31]

After a visit to Bombay, Keshub Chunder Sen introduced a new form of dress to the Bharat Ashram. He proposed that women wear sari, chemise, and jacket at home, with the addition of a petticoat and piece of net over the hair for going out. Harasundari Datta, who was living in the Bharat Ashram at the time, felt that petticoats were an inessential extra expense for middle-class families.[32] Many women must have shared her objection to the additional cost of the new items of clothing, which would have made a considerable difference to the family budget.

Annette Akroyd objected to the reformed mode of dress because she sensed that women's normal aesthetic judgments foundered when dealing with an unfamiliar form, and her puritanism remained unsatisfied with the level of decency attained. She remarked that 'the prevalent fashion among those who are emancipated at all, of placing a wreath of flowers over the veil, looks very tawdry and is most unbecoming. There must be a decided change too in at any rate the lower garments.'[33] She, too, urged the adoption of petticoats, and tried to devise a new kind of undergarment that would be 'from the shoulders, all in one piece'. She also cut squares of Brussels net for girls to cover their heads with when going out, and made them wear boots. Despite her awareness of the dangers of 'denationalization', her reforms were not generally well received because they were too Anglicized. Her concept of modesty was an alien imposition for many women. For instance, a new pupil at the Banga Mahila Bidyalaya was depressed by the thought that emancipation seemed to consist in always wearing a petticoat. The girls' resistance to her reforms, and the realization that her own views of the subject were not shared by many, shook Miss Akroyd's customary confidence and complacency. In 1873 she visited the wife of Ananda Mohan Bose, who was sick at home. She found her dressed in muslin 'swathing' with no shoes or stockings, her hair down, and surrounded by young men. Afterwards she wrote to her sister with genuine puzzlement that 'I am thrown back on radical questions of modesty and delicacy often, and have to ask myself why are such sights so shocking to me?' However, she felt that she had made some progress. She had become 'so accustomed to dhutie that when properly worn I do not notice it'.[34]

Non-Brahmo women did not begin to change their dress habits on a large scale until the end of the century. The chemise was worn mainly by city women, and by a few in the *mofussil,* but was not regarded as essential.[35] Older women, especially, resisted the imposition of a less comfortable form of dress. Enthusiasm among promoters of dress reform sometimes reached absurd proportions. At one stage progressive young men were said to have taken bodices and chemises home to their old mothers and grandmothers in the villages to wear while doing their daily round of domestic duties.[36]

There was some discussion on the wearing of jewelry as a part of dress reform. Apparently rich ladies would sometimes wear six or seven pounds of gold ornaments as an indication of their wealth and status. Shib Chunder Bose noted, however, that by 1881 the spread of English education had 'improved' their taste, creating a preference for elegance over weight.[37] Newspapers were filled with advertisements for the new type of jewelry. Hamilton's, the most famous jewelers in Calcutta, had illustrated advertisements of the latest fashions, including dangling gold earrings from 20 to 40 rupees, broad gold band bracelets from 120 to 200, and engraved gold lockets from 16 to 50 rupees.[38]

Brahmos, with their puritanical and thrifty habits, disapproved of the traditional practice of investing in ornaments and ostentatiously wearing them as a visible proof of wealth.[39] An article in the *Bāmābodhinī Patrikā* in 1865 suggested alternative forms of investment—in shares, banknotes, railway holdings, or land. It added that the wearing of so many ornaments was not only unsafe but also unhealthy, because it stopped the blood circulation.[40] The editor of *Somprakās* concurred with this disapproval, and called on managers of girls' schools to desist from giving jewelry to school girls as prizes.[41] It was said that women preferred the 'immodesty' of traditional dress because of a desire to display their ornaments, and they were reminded that with English dress they still had their necks, ears, feet, and even possibly parts of their arms exposed as areas for display.[42] Swarnamayi Gupta attempted a much deeper analysis of the reasons behind women's partiality for ornaments. She contended that in the present state of society husbands soon lost interest in their less educated wives, and women felt that they could only retain their husbands' affections by enhancing their own physical attractions with the help of ornaments. In addition, she pointed out that ornaments were often a woman's sole source of support after the death of her husband, and therefore meant far more to her than a mere item of adornment.[43]

Another debated aspect of dress reform was the wearing of shoes. Orthodox women never wore shoes. Apart from the practical consideration that in a hot climate wearing shoes and stockings inside the house was unnecessary, shoes were associated with immoral women.[44] Shoes would also have been a further costly addition to the family budget. In 1881, ladies' plain elastic-sided boots were advertised for four to six rupees, and kid leather or glove-kid boots sold for ten to fifteen rupees.[45]

However, most dress reformers, with their Anglicized perspective, insisted that women be taught to wear shoes and stockings. To middle-class Victorians such as Annette Akroyd, bare feet were a sign of barbarism. The first time she saw Jaganmohini Sen, dressed in the style of a well-to-do Hindu *bhadramahilā*, she remarked that she was 'dressed like a poor wife of some uncultivated Hindoo—in red silk wrapper, no shoes and stockings, and a barbaric display of jewels, necklaces, chains, great earrings etc.[46]

Jnanadanandini Debi wrote in the *Bāmābodhinī Patrikā* that from the point of hygiene shoes might be necessary, but not stockings. The editor added that the wearing of shoes was optional. He said that if women did not have to do much walking outside, then stockings covered with a strong 'preserver' would be sufficient to keep the feet clean.[47] Another writer noted that Hindu ladies outside Bengal had adopted the practice of evening walks, for which shoes and stockings were essential for beauty and comfort.[48] Others were of the opinion that shoes and stockings were unnecessary.[49] It was said in praise of Sarojini Ghose that she had never worn shoes in her life, a proof of her simplicity and orthodoxy.[50]

During the nineteenth century, wearing shoes was a distinctive trait of the Brahmo *bhadramahilā*. Punyalata Cakrabarti recounted that when her mother, a Brahmo, went to her in-laws' house as a young bride, they expected her to wear shoes. They told her she was free to follow her own customs but she eventually convinced them that she was used to going barefoot and happy to do so.[51] Nalinibala Chaudhuri, a Brahmo living in Assam at the turn of the century, was criticized for being a *memsaheb* because she wore shoes. She must have been an imposing sight—she had to wear men's boots because ladies' shoes were only available in Calcutta.[52]

Dress reform was initiated by Bengali men, under the influence of alien concepts of modesty, but was soon taken up by women themselves as they perceived that it was a necessary prelude to greater freedom from the restrictions of purdah. Although initially limited to a small group, the new form of dress was gradually adopted by all middle-class women.

...

NOTES

1. Radharaman Mitra, 'Gangār ghāt', *Oitihāsik*, 4, January 1977, 50.

2. Ambujasundari Dasi [Dasgupta], 'Kalikatār Gangasnān', *Bāmābodhinī Patrikā* (henceforth *BP*), 8.1, 495, November 1994. See also 'Abagunthan', *BP*, 2:2, 42, February 1867.

3. 'Strīlokdiger snān pranālī', *BP*, 5, 72, August 1869. See Chapter One for discussion of the greater freedom of women in the *mofussil*.

4. *Dāccā Darpan*, 27 April 1864 in *Report on Native Newspapers, Bengal* (henceforth *RNNB*), 4 May 1864, *Dāccā Prakās*, 28 April 1864 in *RNNB*, 11 May 1864 indignantly called for a repeal of the order, which was only for the benefit of English ladies whose modesty was shocked at seeing nude bodies of natives in the water.

5. 'Strīlokdiger snān pranālī', *BP*, 72.

6. Kumari Saudamini, 'Lajja', Bamabodhini Sabha, *Bāmāracanābalī, Prathom bhāg*, Calcutta, 1872, pp. 22–4.

7. Priscilla Chapman, *Hindoo Female Education*, London: R.B. Sealy and W. Burnside, 1839, p. 18.

8. In the seventeenth century women wore a *kanchali* or bodice under the sari. Rich women also wore *ijar* as underwear. T. Raychaudhuri, *Bengal under Akbar and Jahangir*, Calcutta: A. Mukherjee, 1953, p. 221. The women standing on the verandas of the *antahpur* in Plate 3 were wearing the 'traditional' sari.

9. S.C. Bose, *The Hindoos as they Are: A Description of the Manners, Customs and Inner Life of Hindoo Society in Bengal*, Calcutta, 1881, pp. 298–9.

10. K.M. Banerjea, *Native Female Education*, 2nd edn, Calcutta, 1858 (1841), p. 80.

11. Ibid.

12. S.C. Bose, *The Hindoos*, op. cit., p. 194.

13. Jogendranarayan Ray, *Banga-mahilā*, Chinsurah, 1881, p. 35.

14. He was referring to pupils at the Bethune School. Letter of 29 March 1850, in J.A. Richey (ed.), *Selections*, Part II, p. 53.

15. A. Akroyd, *Diary and Notebook in India 1872–1878*, 26 December 1872, Akroyd-Beveridge Papers, India Office Library.

16. Koilasbasini Debi, *Hindu mahilāganer bīnābasthā*, Calcutta, 1865, p. 66.

17. *BP*, 1:2, 17, January 1865.

18. Letters from Saudamini Khastagir and Rajlaksmi Sen, and editorial comment, in 'Bangānganāganer paricchad', *BP*, 8, 97, September 1871.

19. 'Bangānganāganer paricchad', Bāmāracanā, *BP*, 8, 99, November 1871.

20. Sarala Debi, *Jībaner jharāpātā*, Calcutta, 1975, pp. 53–4. Plates 6, 8 and 9 all show women wearing the 'Brahmika sari'.

21. *New Dispensation*, 31 March 1881.

22. 'Bangānganāganer paricchad', *BP*, op. cit., 97.

23. See *Sanjībanī*, 20 January 1894 in *RNNB*, 27 January 1894; and P.C. Mozoomdar, 'The Emancipation of Women in Bengal', *CR*, 118, 236, April 1904.

24. 'Mahilār paricchad', *Antahpur*, 4, 6, July 1901. See also P.H. Chavasse, *Counsel to a Mother*, p. 135, on the ill effects of tight lacing. He said that it caused diseases of the lungs, fainting, indigestion, offensive breath, purple complexion, red noses, impurities of the blood, and constipation.

25. A few Anglicized Hindu and Brahmo *bhadramahilā* also wore gowns. Monomohan Ghose's wife was one of these. Sarala Debi, op. cit., p. 53.

26. Akroyd-Beveridge Papers, op. cit.: letter to Fanny Mowatt, 10 February 1874.

27. *BP*, 1:2, 17, January 1865.

28. 'Patra', *BP*, 8:1, 495, November 1904.

29. 'Mahilār paricchad,' *Antahpur*, 4, 6; Gurucharan Mahalanabis, *Ātmakathā*, Calcutta, 1974, pp. 101–2.

30. Sarala Debi noted this; op. cit., p. 54.

31. Gurucharan Mahalanabis, op. cit., pp. 100–4.

32. Harasundari Datta, *Swargīya Srīnāth Datter Jiban-katha*, Calcutta, 1922, pp. 158–60.

33. Akroyd-Beveridge papers, *Diary and Notebook*, op. cit., entries for 26 December, 27 December, 28 December 1872.

34. Ibid., letters to Fanny Mowatt: 20 March 1873, 20 October 1873, 10 February 1874.

35. S.C. Bose, op. cit., p. 194; Jogendranarayan Ray, *Bang-Mahīlā*, Calcutta, 1922, p. 37; *Paricārikā*, 1, 7, December 1878.

36. *Sandhyā*, 9 May 1905 in *RNNB*, 13 May 1905.

37. The new taste showed a preference for ornaments of 'delicate diamond cut workmanship' set with pearls and precious stones rather than for old-fashioned solid gold ornaments. S.C. Bose, op. cit., pp. 298–9.

38. Advertisements in *Liberal and New Dispensation*, 1882, 1884. See the chain and locket worn by Nirmala Deb in Plate 7. For the rich, there were far more expensive items. Sarala Debi was given a diamond and ruby necklace with a matching pair of bracelets worth 1000 rupees, from the shop next door to Hamilton's. Sarala Debi, op. cit., p. 80.

39. P.C. Mozoomdar, *Strīcaritra*, 3rd edn, Calcutta 1936 (1890), p. 87.

40. 'Alangkār paridhan', *BP*, 2:1, 23, July 1865.

41. *Somprakās*, 25 March 1867 in *RNNB*, 30 March 1867.

42. Jogendranarayan Ray, op. cit., p. 37; the editor of *Somprakās*, ibid., said that the wish to exhibit their jewels led women to wear such flimsy clothes.

43. Swarnamayi Gupta, *Ūsā-cintā arthath adhunik arjya mahilaganer abastha samandha kayekti katha*, Calcutta, 1888, pp. 86–8.

44. The distinction was made in ancient literature and sculpture, where shoes were interpreted as a sign that women did not keep to the home. See M.M. Urquhart, *Women of Bengal*, Calcutta: Associated Press (YMCA), 1925, pp. 96–9.

45. *Indian Mirror*, 18 August 1881.

46. Akroyd-Beveridge Papers, *Diary and Notebook*, op. cit., 27 December 1871. At a later date her reaction was more mellow. Keshub Chunder Sen and his wife dined with her on 6 March 1873, and she commented that Jaganmohini 'looked very pretty in her saree, but not wearing shoes or stockings'.

47. 'Bangānganāganer paricchad', *BP*, 99.

48. 'Bangīya Hindumahilār paricchad', *BP*, 712, 443, December 1901.

49. Jogendranarayan Ray, op. cit., p. 38.

50. Renuka Ghose, *Sarojinī-carit*, Calcutta, 1975 (1958), p. 34.

51. Punyalata Cakrabarti, *Chele belār din guli*, Calcutta, 1975 (1958), p. 123.

52. Interview with her daughter, Manika Ray, Calcutta, 14 February 1978.

Indian Perceptions

Sir Syed Ahmed Khan

Interesting parallels have been drawn between Sir Syed Ahmed Khan (or Sayyid Ahmad Khan, 1817–98) and the reformer Rammohun Roy. Both came from high-ranking families, were educated in Persian an Arabic, made a study of Christian scriptures, and sought to purify their religious traditions, and both travelled to England. But Raja Rammohun Roy fought for women's rights, particularly for the banning of sati. Sir Syed made education for Muslim men his priority and felt Muslim women did not need any education beyond that provided in the home. Concerned that the British were blaming Muslims for 1857, he tried to persuade the government of Muslim loyalty, and also tried to teach his own community to take what was worthwhile in the West. In 1877 he opened the Mohammed Anglo-Oriental College in Aligarh. In 1886 he founded the annual Muhammadan Educational Conference and in 1888 the United India Patriotic Association. He was against the Indian National Congress, fearing that anti-government sentiments would spill over into education, turning away Muslims from the education they needed. Sir Syed is regarded as the greatest educationist of the late nineteenth century.

Major General Graham's biography of Sir Syed was originally published in 1885 by Blackwoods in Edinburgh, and subsequently reprinted. A new edition, with an introduction by Zaituna Umer of St Anthony's College, Oxford, was published by OUP, Karachi in 1974. Umer describes Graham as 'one of the half-dozen Englishmen of the period seriously drawn to Muslim culture who did much to form an indulgent attitude towards Muslims among the British'. Graham and Sir Syed met in Ghazipore where they were both posted, in 1864. He was a fervent admirer and friend of Sir Syed's, whose circle included a number of westerners. Umer says that the importance of such a biography, written in praise of a 'native', cannot be overestimated, as it was instrumental in creating the reputation and legend of Sir Syed, though Sir Syed was well-known and important in his own right.

Sir Syed Ahmed Khan, quoted in G.F.I. Graham, *Sir Syed Ahmed Khan*, Edinburgh: Blackwoods, 1885.

The Education of Mohammedan Girls

...

Before proceeding to answer the question, I beg leave to say that the general idea that Mohammedan ladies of respectable families are quite ignorant is an entire mistake. A sort of indigenous education of a moderate degree prevails among them, and they study religious and moral books in Urdu and Persian, and in some instances Arabic. In families of the better classes, there have been ladies in comparatively recent times who possessed a high degree of ability. The poverty of the Mohammedans has been the chief cause of the decline of female education among them. It is still a custom among the well-to-do and respectable families of Mohammedans to employ tutoresses (*Ustanis or Mullanis*) to get their girls instructed in the Holy Koran, and in elementary theological books in the Urdu language. Sometimes a father or a brother, or some other near kinsman, teaches them to write letters in Urdu, and occasionally imparts to them instruction in Persian books. To qualify them to read and write telegraphic messages, some boys have taught English to their sisters sufficient for the purpose; and I know of two girls who can even write letters in English. I admit, however, that the general state of female education among Mohammedans is at present far from satisfactory. I cannot blame the Mohammedans for their disinclination towards Government girls' schools, and I believe that even the greatest admirer of female education among European gentlemen will not impute blame to the Mohammedans if he is only acquainted with the state of those schools in this country. I have also seen a few of the girls' schools in England. Were these institutions for a moment supposed to be just like those in India in every respect, would any English gentleman like to send his daughters for education to them? Certainly not. The question of female education much resembles the question of the oriental philosopher who asked whether the egg or the hen was first created. Those who hold that women should be educated and civilised prior to men are greatly mistaken. The fact is, that no satisfactory education can be provided for Mohammedan females until a large number of Mohammedan males receive a sound education. The present state of education among Mohammedan females is, in my opinion, enough for domestic happiness, considering the present social and economical condition of the life of the Mohammedans in India. What the Government at present ought to do, is to concentrate its efforts in adopting measures for the education and enlightenment of Mohammedan boys. When the present generation of Mohammedan men is well educated and enlightened, the circumstance will necessarily have a powerful though indirect effect on the enlightenment of Mohammedan women, for enlightened fathers, brothers, and husbands will naturally be most anxious to educate their female relations. Any endeavours on the part of Government to introduce female education among Mohammedans will, under the present social circumstances, prove a complete failure so far as respectable families are concerned, and, in my humble opinion, will probably produce mischievous results, and be a waste of money and energy.

In May 1882, Sir Salar Jang paid Syed Ahmed a visit, and inspected the college, of which he was one of the visitors. He was received with every honour, and was very much pleased with what he saw. He made Syed Ahmed promise to pay him a visit at Hyderabad, and in September of the same year Syed Ahmed fulfilled his promise, staying with the minister for a month. During this time he had many long and important conversations with Sir Salar Jang, visited Bolarum with him, and had a big dinner given him by his host. Many of the nobles wished to entertain him at dinner, but he invariably begged them to give him the money that the dinners would cost, as donations to his college fund. They did so, and he carried off with him to Allygurh Rs 30,000! He is now (February 1885) meditating another visit to Hyderabad.

Chirag Ali

Chirag Ali (1844–95) has been described as 'a scholar of rare caliber', who learnt Hebrew, Greek, and Latin in order to study the Bible in relation to the Quran. He was associated with the Aligarh movement, though his connection was 'purely intellectual'. He spent most of his life in Hyderabad state, and became finance secretary in the state government. 'The Position of Woman' is part of a book published by Chirag Ali in 1883, *The Proposed Political, Constitutional, and Legal Reforms in the Ottoman Empire and Other Mohammedan States.* The book is concerned with the interpretation of the basic sources of Muslim law, the Quran and the Hadith, and the section on women is an attempt to develop a theory of the rights of women based on the Quran. While Sir Syed Ahmed Khan, the founder of the Aligarh movement, prioritized the education of men, Chirag Ali's book can be regarded as a feminist contribution to the movement.

Sayyid Ahmad Khān's associate Chirāgh 'Alī was also concerned primarily with the question of the reinterpretation of the two basic sources of Muslim law, the Koran and the hadīth. Writing in both English and Urdu, he views the Koran as neither a civil nor political code and holds, therefore, that it cannot form the basis of law in modern Muslim society. He regards the six classical collections of hadīth as not based on critical investigation of the text in the modem sense and as containing much more apocryphal material than the Muslims are generally ready to concede.

Another result of the modernist self-view of the school of Sayyid Ahmad Khān was a feminist movement. It is represented chiefly in the writings of Mumtāz 'Alī and Chirāgh 'Alī. The selection 'The Position of Woman' shows his apologetic effort to construct a theory of the rights of women on the basis of his interpretation of certain Koranic verses.

Chirag Ali, 'The Position of Woman', in Aziz Ahmad, G.E. von Grunebaum (eds), *Muslim Self-Statement in India and Pakistan, 1857–1968*, Wiesbaden: Otto Harvassowitz, under the auspices of Near Eastern Center, UCLA, 1970.

...

The Position of Woman[1]

The position of woman was ameliorated to a greater degree by the mission of Muhammad than it might have been expected by the dispensations of all reformers and prophets prior to him. Before the social amendments introduced by Muhammad throughout Arabia, an unlimited license of polygamy and capricious divorces together with a revolting system of concubinage had been prevalent. Some tribes had the nefarious practice of murdering their infant daughters to avoid the disgrace of being fathers-in-law, and those girls who escaped the horrible doom of their fathers never received any inheritance from them at their death. There were also some other tribes whose people were allowed by custom to marry their fathers' widows, as well as two sisters at one and the same time. The wives of a deceased father were in the eye of his surviving sons a sort of goods and chattels or personal possession void of life and humanity. They had no respect for the gentle sex, nor showed them any reverence while addressing them; and some, the most savage of them all, went the length of slandering virtuous women with an unbridled and licentious tongue. The dress and demeanour of the females themselves stood in need of improvement. Female orphans, when young, were maltreated by their guardians, who used to marry a great number of them in order to obtain their property, and then to forsake them in an impoverished state, forlorn and friendless. The Koran gradually improved and elevated the degraded condition of women by curtailing in the first place the unlimited plurality of wives to four, and even this latitude was made strictly conditional on the husband feeling confident that he could deal justly—equitably by them all; and, in the second place, declaring it impossible to deal *equitably* with more than one wife even if men 'would fain do so' and thus virtually abolishing polygamy.

The new connubial laws imposed by the Prophet of Islam on his followers suppressed the facility of divorce by certain wise, judicious, and discouraging restrictions, reasonable and consonant to the interests of the parties concerned. The Koran advised and exhorted the Arabs to refrain from their evil practices regarding their wives. Muhammad abolished the institution of concubinage by doing away with slavery,[2] and countenancing marriage with the then existing female slaves otherwise destined to be concubines.[3] But against the murder of infant daughters his invectives were trenchant in the highest degree. He abrogated it by reprimanding this unnatural vice in the Koran; and threatening its perpetrators with the future punishment awaiting their crime.[4] Thus was infanticide exterminated out of Arabia and all parts of the Mohammadan world. The law of inheritance was established for the first time in the Koran in the interest of females throughout Arabia.[5] Marrying father's widows, and two sisters at one and the same time, were terribly denounced by Mohammad as heinous offences,[6] and widows were no more to be disposed of as part of their deceased husband's possessions.[7]

Men were enjoined to treat the sex with deference[8]; and perfect reverence was prescribed to be observed in speaking to them. The suppression of slander was the next subject that engaged the Prophet's attention, and he ordained corporeal punishment on those who calumniated virtuous women.[9] Reforms were also introduced in the dress and general deportment of women.[10] Persons entrusted with female orphans during their minority were inhibited from marrying their ward.[11]

All these beneficial measures were fraught with incalculable advantage to the debased condition of women who, by these innovations in their social sphere of life, were greatly relieved from the miseries and insults they had hitherto suffered at the hands of males.

Some verses of the Koran bearing on the subjects above treated are given below:

O Men! fear your Lord, who hath created you of one soul, and of him created his wife, and from these twain hath spread abroad so many men and women. And fear ye God, in whose (name) ye ask mutual favours, and respect women. Verily is God watching you! (4:1).

And if ye are apprehensive that ye shall not deal fairly with orphans, then, of other women who seem good in your eyes, marry (but) two, or three, or four; and if ye still fear that ye shall not act equitably, then one only: or the slaves whom ye have acquired: this will make justice on your part easier. And give women their dowry as a free gift, but if of their own free will they kindly give up aught thereof to you, then enjoy it as convenient, and profitable (4:3).

Men ought to have a part of what their parents and kindred leave, and women a part of what their parents and kindred leave: whether it be little or much, let them have a stated portion (4:8).

O Believers! it is not allowed you to be heirs of your wives against their will; nor to hinder them from marrying in order to take from them part of the dowry you had given them, unless they have been guilty of undoubted lewdness; but deal kindly with them; for if ye are estranged from them haply ye are estranged from that in which God hath placed abundant good (4:23).

And if ye be desirous to exchange one wife for another, and have given one of them a talent, make no deduction from it. Would ye take it by slandering her, and with manifest wrong? (4:24).

How, moreover, could ye take it, when one of you hath gone in unto the other, and they have received from you a strict bond of union? (4:25).

And marry not women whom your fathers have married:—for this is a shame and hateful, and an evil way:—though what is past may be allowed (4:26).

And whoever of you is not rich enough to marry free believing women, then let him marry such of your believing maidens as have fallen into your hands as slaves; God well knoweth your faith. Ye are sprung the one from the other. Marry them then, with the leave of their masters, and give them a fair dower: but let them be chaste and free from fornication, and not entertainers of lovers (4:29).

Men are superior to women on account of the qualities with which God bath gifted the one above the other, and on account of the outlay (they make) from their substance (for them). Virtuous women are obedient, careful during the (husband's absence), because God hath of them been careful. But chide those for whose refractorines ye have cause to fear; remove them into sleeping-chambers apart, and scourge[12] them: but if they are obedient to you, then seek not occasion against them: Verily God is High, Great! (4:38).

And if ye fear a breach between *man and wife,* then send a judge *chosen* from his family, and a judge *chosen* from her family; if they are desirous of agreement, God will effect a reconciliation between them: Verily, God is knowing, apprised of all! (4:39).

Moreover, they will consult thee in regard to women: Say: God hath instructed you about them; and His will is rehearsed to you, in the Book, concerning female orphans to whom ye give not their legal due, and whom you refuse to marry; also with regard to weak children: and that ye deal with fairness towards orphans. Ye cannot do a good action, but verily God knoweth it (4:126).

And if a wife fear ill usage or aversion on the part of her husband, then shall it be no fault in them, if they can agree with mutual agreement, for agreement is best. *Men's* souls are prone to avarice, but if ye act kindly and piously, then verily your actions are not unnoticed by God! (4:127).

And ye may not have it at all in your power to treat your wives with equal justice, even though ye fain would do so: but yield not wholly to disinclination, so that ye leave one of them as it were in suspense: if ye come to an understanding, and act in the fear of God, then verily God is Forgiving, Merciful (4:128).

But if they separate, God can compensate both out of His abundance; for God is Vast, Wise (4:129).

Say: Come, I will rehearse what your Lord hath made binding on you—that ye assign not aught to Him as sharers of His divine honour, and that ye be good to your parents; (and) that ye slay not your children because of poverty—for them and for you will We provide: and that ye come not near to pollutions outward and inward: and that ye slay not anyone whom God hath forbidden you, unless for a just cause. This hath He enjoined on you: haply ye will understand (6:152).

Moreover, kill not your children for fear of want: for them and for you will We provide. Verily, the killing them is a great wickedness (17:33).

They who defame virtuous women, and bring not four witnesses, scourge them with eighty stripes, and receive ye not their testimony for ever, for these are impious persons (24:4).

Verily, they who throw out charges against virtuous (but) careless women, (who yet are) believers, are cursed in this world and in the world to come, and a terrible punishment doth await them (24:23).

And speak to the believing women that they refrain their looks, and observe continence; and that they display not their ornaments, except those which are external; and that they draw their kerchiefs over their bosoms, and display not their ornaments, except to their husbands or their fathers, or their husbands' fathers, or their sons or their husbands' sons, or their brothers, or their brothers' sons, or their sisters' sons, or their women, or their slaves, or male domestics who have no natural force, or to children who note not women's nakedness. And let them not strike their feet together, so as to discover their hidden ornaments. And be ye wholly turned to God, O ye Believers! haply it shall be well with you (24:31).

O Prophet! Speak to thy wives and to thy daughters, and to the wives of the faithful, that they let their wrappers fall low. Thus will they more easily be known, and they will not be affronted. God is Indulgent, Merciful! (33:59).

And...the damsel that bath been buried alive shall be asked (81 :8).

For what crime she was put to death (81:9).

The general tenor of the Koran is to establish a perfect equality between the male and female sex, in their legal, social and spiritual positions, except in physical strength, and possession of wealth.

The same is due to women as it is due from them, but men have precedence over them (2:228).

The men shall have a portion according to their deserts, and the women a portion according to their deserts (4:36).

Men are superior to women on account of the (qualities) with which God hath gifted the one above the other, and on account of the outlay (they make) from their substance (for them) (4:38).

Truly the men who resign themselves to God, and the women who resign themselves, and the believing men and the believing women and the devout men and the devout women, and the men of truth and the women of truth, and the patient men and the patient women, and the humble men and the humble women, and the men who give alms and the women who give alms, and the men who fast and the women who fast, and the chaste men and the chaste women, and the men and the women who oft remember God: for them hath God prepared forgiveness and a rich recompense (33:35).

Even these passages do not exhaust what Muhammad did to better the low (status) of females, for besides his promulgating stringent laws at first against polygamy, and putting restrictions upon the shameful levity of divorce, he stirred up in the minds of his followers the laudable sentiments of love and affection towards women, and incalculated in his Revelations the respect due to them, as well as precepts to secure the mutual comfort and happiness of husband and wife.

And one of his signs it is, that He hath created wives for you of your own species, that ye may dwell with them, and hath put love and tenderness between you. Herein truly are signs for those who reflect (3:20).

The social equality of both sexes is implied fully in the simile, 'husbands are garments to their wives, and wives are garments to their husbands'; and the very word (Zaujain), (couple) or (twain), indicates the propriety of monogamy, and emphasizes the indissolubility of the marriage tie.

Compared with Paganism, Judaism, and even Christianity, Islam sanctioned for women a greater stride in civilizarion and liberty than they had enjoyed prior to the mission of Muhammad. The Mosaic Law fell short of accomplishing any great good for the moral and social elevation of the Hebrew females, and the New Testament did comparatively nothing towards their worldly preferment.

It is only the influence of the codes of the Roman Law, and the innate respect felt by the Teutonic nation for the female sex, and centuries of civilisation, which have raised woman to her proper position in European countries.[13] The condition of Christian women in Eastern Turkey, Syria, and Palestine is as intellectually depressed as that of their Muhammadan and semi-Pagan sisters in the East, or Asiatic countries.

The subordination, subjection, inferiority and degradation of women were generally believed in, and taught by the Jewish and early Christian fathers in conformity with the laws of the Bible. As the introduction of sin into the word was believed to have proceeded through the instrumentality of woman, the blame of human vices lay at her door. Therefore she was considered to have brought on her own degradation by her own hands, and her condition of subordination was turned into subjection. It was also said to her of her husband, 'he shall rule over thee' (Gen. 3:16), a sentence which regarded as a prediction has been strikingly fulfilled in the position assigned to women in oriental countries.

Shortly before the Christian era an important change took place in the views entertained on the question of marriage as affecting the spiritual and intellectual part of man's nature....In the interval that elapsed between the Old and New

Testament periods, a spirit of asceticism had been evolved....The Essenes were the first to propound any doubts as to the propriety of marriage: some of them avoided it altogether, others availed themselves of it under restrictions (Josephus, *De Bello Judaico,* II. 8, 2, 13). Similar views were adopted by Therapeutae and at a later period by the Gnostics (Burton's *Lectures,* I. 214); thence they passed into the Christian Church, forming one of the distinctive tenets of Encratites (Burton II. 161), and finally developing into the system of monachism.[14]

Another injurious consequence, resulting, in a great measure, from asceticism, was a tendency to depreciate extremely the character and the position of women. In this tendency we may detect in part the influence of the earlier Jewish writings, in which an impartial observer may find evident traces of the common Oriental depreciation of woman. The custom of purchase-money to the father of the bride was admitted.[15] Polygamy was authorised and practised by the wisest man on an enormous scale. A woman was regarded as the origin of human ills. A period of purification was appointed after the birth of every child; but, by a very significant provision, it was twice as long in the case of a female as of a male child. 'The badness of men', a Jewish writer emphatically declared, 'is better than the goodness of women'. The types of female excellence exhibited in the early period of Jewish history are in general of a low order, and certainly far inferior to those of Roman history or Greek poetry; and the warmest eulogy of a woman in the Old Testament is probably that which was bestowed upon her who, with circumstances of the most aggravated treachery, had murdered the sleeping fugitive who had taken refuge under her roof.

The combined influence of the Jewish writings, and of that ascetic feeling which treated woman as the chief source of temptation to man, was shown in those fierce invectives, which form so conspicuous and so grotesque a portion of the writings of the Fathers, and which contrast so curiously with the adulation bestowed upon the particular members of the sex. Woman was represented as the door of hell, as the mother of all human ills. She should be ashamed at the very thought that she is a woman. She should live in continual penance, on account of the curses she has brought upon the world.

NOTES

1. Chirāgh 'Alī, op. cit., pp. 111–19. [Ed.]. See p. 172 here, for details
2. Sura, 47:5.
3. Sura 4:29; 70:29, 30; 13:5,6.
4. Sura 6:152; 17:33; 81:8,9.
5. Sura 4:8.
6. Sura 4:26.
7. Sura 4:23.
8. Sura 4:1.
9. Sura 24:4, 6, 23.

10. Sura 33:59; 24:31.

11. Sura 4:3 and 126.

12. See Chirāgh 'Alī, op. cit., para. 99.

13. R. Bosworth Smith, *Mohammed and Mohammedanism*, London: Elder and Co., 1876, p. 243.

14. Smith's *Dictionary of the Bible,* Vol. ii Vide Art. Marriage, pp. 242–3, London: John Murray, 1863.

15. The Koran abolished this custom.—C.A.

P.N. Bose

P.N. Bose was Officiating Superintendent of the Geological Survey of India, and the author of *The Centenary Review of the Researches of the Asiatic Society of Bengal in Natural Science*, and a four-volume *History of Hindu Civilization During British Rule*. Vol. II, from which the following extract has been taken, is concerned with socio-religious and industrial conditions. Bose writes that seclusion was unknown in ancient India, and cites examples to prove his point.

Social Condition

The Social Position of Women

Greater Freedom in Ancient Times

The Aryan ladies of ancient India did not lead a secluded life like that of their descendants at the present day. Several of the hymns of the Rigveda were composed by female Rishis. At a meeting of theologians convened by Janaka, king of Mithila, a learned lady named Gárgi carried on discussions with the sage Yájnavalkya. Young ladies of the Vedic period appear to have had a voice in their marriage. 'But the woman who is of gentle nature and of graceful form', runs a verse of the Rigveda, 'selects among many her loved one as her husband.'

Instances of Svayamvará

Numerous cases of Svayamvará,[1] that is, of ladies selecting their own husbands, are mentioned in the Mahábhárata and other works of a later period. Kuntí, Draupadí, Sítá, and Damayantí chose their own husbands.

P.N. Bose, *A History of Hindu Civilization During British Rule*, Vol. II, Calcutta: W. Newar & Co., 1894, London: Kegan Paul, Trench and Trubner, 1894.

Devayání, daughter of a priest, offered her hand to king Yayáti. The Rájá hesitated as she belonged to a superior caste. Her father, however seeing that her resolution was inflexible overruled the question of caste and gave her in marriage to the king.

Sávitrí

Sávitrí is a household word amongst the Hindus. When she became marriageable her father told her that as he had received no proposals, she must make her own selection. She drove with her companions to a forest where she met a young man named Satyaván who though of royal lineage was reduced to poverty and living in a hermitage. Sávitrí fell in love with him, and after due inquiries resolved to wed him. Returning home she expressed her wishes to her father. He however, being informed by the sage Nárada that Satyaván would die after one year, interceded with her to change her mind. But Sávitrí had given her heart away and could not think of marrying anyone else. After her marriage she came to live with her husband in the forest, cast off her ornaments and other fineries, and endeared herself to everyone in her husband's family by her excellent qualities.

A Sea-Side Picnic

In a picnic at a seaside place given by Krishna and most graphically described in the Harivamsa, we find, that ladies and gentlemen ate, drank, and danced together without even the reserve observed in modern European society. While bathing, 'Krishna and Nárada, with all those who were on their side began to pelt water on Bala and his party, and they in their turn did the same on the party of Krishna. The wives of Bala and Krishna, excited by libations of arrack, followed their example, squirted water in great glee with syringes in their hands. Some of the Bhaima ladies, overweighted by the load both of love and wine, with crimson eyes and masculine garbs, entertained themselves before the other ladies squirting water.' Refreshed by the bath, the party began to eat and drink. 'Surrounded by their loved ones, they drank of Marieya, Mádhvika, Surá, and Aśava, helping them on with roasted birds, seasoned with pungent condiments, ghi, acids, sochel salt, and oil…. After their feast the gallant Bhima chiefs, along with their ladies, joyfully commenced again to sing such choice delightful songs, as were agreeable to the ladies.'[2]

When Ráma returned home from exile, the ladies of his family came out to receive him. Sítá was present at his installation in the Court Hall.

On the occasion of the coronation of Yudhishthira, Draupadí sat on the throne by his side; and Kuntí and Gándharí were present in the Hall.

RESTRICTIONS UPON FEMALE FREEDOM IN THE MANUSAMHITÁ

About the time of the Manusamhitá, restrictions which, as we have just seen, were unknown in more ancient times, began to be placed upon the freedom of ladies. 'In childhood', declares Manu, 'a female must be subject to her father; in youth to her husband; when her lord is dead to her sons; a woman must never be independent. She must not seek to separate herself from her father, husband, or sons. By leaving them she would make both her own and her husband's family contemptible.'[3]

'Though destitute of virtue, or seeking pleasure, or devoid of good qualities, yet a husband must be constantly worshipped as a god by a faithful wife.'

'No sacrifice, no vow, no fast, must be performed by women apart from their husbands; if a wife obeys her husband, she will for that reason alone be exalted in heaven.'[4]

While the husband can divorce his wife if she only speaks unkindly to him, she is to cling to him with blind devotion and implicit obedience. Manu cautions the learned not to take undue delight in the company of the fair sex, and enjoins the youthful pupil not to show his respect towards the wife of his instructor by bowing to her feet.[5]

On the other hand, however, it is enjoined, that 'women must be honored and adorned by their fathers, brothers, husbands, and brothers-in-law, who desire their own welfare.

'Where women are honored, there the gods are pleased; but where they are not honored, no sacred rite yields reward.

'Where female relations live in grief, the family soon wholly perishes; but that family where they are not unhappy, ever prospers.'[6]

Strict Seclusion Unknown in Budhist-Hindu Period

There are passages in the Manusamhitá which clearly shew that the ladies were not yet immured in the zenana. In one place we are distinctly told that the husband should feed his class fellows and other intimate friends with his wife.[7] The absolute seclusion of women was unknown even in much later times. In the dramas and other works composed in the earlier centuries of the Christian era, the parts played by women show that they exercised a very important influence upon men, and that they were treated with tenderness and respect. 'In no nation of antiquity' says H.H. Wilson 'were women held in so much esteem as among the

Hindus.' In the *Kathásaritságara,* composed towards the close of the eleventh century, it is stated of a young bride, that she persuaded her husband 'to throw open the doors of the inner apartment and allow free access to his friends and associates observing that 'the honour of women is protected by their own principles; and when they are corrupt all precautions are vain.' In *Mrichhakati,* Chárudatta's wife converses freely with his friend; and we find ladies in the enjoyment of similar freedom in several other works.

In the *Samkaravijaya,* it is stated that Lílávatí, wife of Mandana Misra, acted as arbitress in a controversy which that scholar had with Samkara. 'Contemporaneous with Samkara were the four Tamil sisters, Avyar, Uppay, Valhe, and Uravay. The first sister died a virgin, much admired for "her talents in poetry and science". She knew chemistry; and wrote on ethics, on which subject the second sister also wrote. The two other sisters employed their pens on various subjects.'[8]

One of the latest authentic cases of Svayamvará was that of the daughter of Jaychánd, the last Hindu King of Kanauj. Owing to a long-standing feud between Jaychánd and Prithvírája, the last king of Delhi, the latter was not invited at the Svayamvará festival, but his effigy was kept at the gate as a doorkeeper. The princess passed by the assembled princes and placed her garland upon the neck of the effigy at the door. Prithvírája hearing of this came with an armed band and carried her away. She proved a most devoted wife. When the bad news of her husband's death on the field of Panipat reached her, she ordered a funeral pyre to be prepared and entered it.

Mahomedan Influence

That the Mahomedan occupation tended to make the seclusion of ladies more stringent than ever is evidenced by the fact, that ladies in parts such as Maháráshtra, where Mahomedan influence was never very strong, enjoy comparatively greater freedom than in other parts of India. The strictness of the Mahomedan zenana must to some extent have served as an example in Upper India. Besides, the standard of chastity among the male members of the Mahomedan nobility was never very high[9]; and the best protection against their lascivious proclivities was considered to be in the strictest seclusion.

Present Zenana

It need scarcely be observed, that amongst the lower classes, the women do not lead a secluded life. They have to help their male relations in agricultural and other out-door occupations. Their seclusion however, invariably follows the elevation of their social status. The zenana is most stringent in large towns. In villages, ladies enjoy opportunities of walking about which are denied to their sisters in cities. Here they cannot stir out of the zenana, usually not over-commodious, and situated in narrow and not over-clean lanes at least from the Western point of view, except in palanquins and carriages with closed doors. It must not be supposed, that the zenana is felt as a hardship by the ladies themselves. They live in a world of their own and find as much happiness in it as falls to the lot of average humanity. The joint family system, presently to be described, while favouring dissentions also favours companionship.

It must not be supposed that Hindu ladies though living in the zenana do not exert any influence on the sterner sex. 'Some of the rich and highly respected members of Hindu society have confessed', writes the Rev. W.J. Wilkins, 'that they owed their success in life to the sympathy, encouragement, and carefulness of their wives. As the women are most religious, their influence over sons and husband in religious matters is very great indeed!'[10]

Some Distinguished Hindu Ladies during British Rule:

Ahalyá Bái

Notwithstanding the restricted opportunities enjoyed by the Hindu ladies for the development of their minds, they have not unoften distinguished themselves by their business and even administrative capacity. Ahalyá Bái is a conspicuous instance. She administered the affairs of a large territory in Central India:

She assumed the Government, and sat in *open durbár* at the age of thirty. She was remarkable for her patience and unwearied attention, in the consideration of all measures affecting the welfare of the country. She respected private rights sacredly, listened to every complaint personally, and studying the interests of all classes, she was a great advocate for *moderate assessment,* and rejoiced at the prosperity of her subjects. In the morning she was engaged in prayer, hearing *sacred works* read, performing ceremonies and giving alms. She lived on vegetable food. After breakfast clad in white clothes as a widow, and having no ornaments except a small necklace, she sat in open durbár from about 2 to 6 P.M.: after which she devoted two or three hours to religious discipline. The books she was fond of reading were the *Puránas,* from which she drew chiefly food for her mind. The life of self-abnegation she led, imparted to her thoughts and acts a *deep tinge of religion:* In the performance of her daily duties, as the highest authority of the land, she deemed herself answerable to God for every exercise of power; and whenever any severe measure was proposed, she said, 'Let us mortals beware how we destroy the works of the Almighty.' She considered herself 'a weak, sinful woman'. She loved truth and hated adulation. When a Brahmán submitted to her a work written by him and full of her praises, she ordered it to be thrown into the Narbadá.' She was judicious in the selection of her agents. She was not only successful in the internal administration, but possessed great diplomatic powers by which the country enjoyed tranquillity as long as she governed; and she reigned for thirty years. She built numerous temples, holy edifices, dharm sálás, forts, wells, and a road over the Vindhya Range. She was not only humane to *man*, but also to the brute creation. The oxen ploughing the fields were refreshed with water, the birds and fish also partook of her compassion.'[11] Malcolm says: 'In the most sober view that can be taken of her character, she certainly appears within her limited sphere to have been one of the purest and most exemplary rulers that ever existed; and she affords a striking example of the practical benefit a mind may receive from performing worldly duties under a deep sense of responsibility to its Creator.'[12]

Ráni Bhaváni

Maháráni Bhavani ruled the Natore State with conspicuous success towards the end of the last century. She was 'endowed with a large capacity for business. She thoroughly understood Zamindari affairs, and the tact and judgment with which she managed the Ráj were most admirable....She enhanced the profits of several estates and arrested the ruin of others. She was a gifted genius—with the talent of governing and managing men, and her *regime* was the culminating period of the influence and wealth of the Natore family. She was a strong-willed and large brained woman, but she was amenable to the advice of those whom she trusted. She was a proud woman, but her pride was defensive and not aggressive. It was pride of a princess who could condescend to be familiar with her Amla and officers, but could when necessary keep them at arm's length.' Ráni Krishnamani was a worthy successor of Ráni Bhavani. She was a very capable lady. 'Her efforts to rescue the residue of the estate from being swallowed up by litigation and rival claims were unceasing and at last crowned with success.' Her daughter-in-law, Ráni Sibeshwari, also evinced great capacity for business. A writer in the Calcutta Review notices as 'the great peculiarity of the Nátore family, that the women have been immeasurably superior to the men. While the male members have been mediocrities, the female members have been celebrities.'[13]

English Influence

The influence of the Western environment has been to considerably slacken the rigidity of the female seclusion. Long journeys are now usually accomplished not, as in former times, in palanquins with closed doors, but in railway carriages and steamers which are not favourable for the maintenance of strict seclusion. Then, again, in cities like Calcutta, such places of amusement as Museums and Zoological Gardens are largely resorted to by ladies whose curiosity considerably shortens the conventional length of veils. 'During the Calcutta Exhibition' says the Rev. W.J. Wilkins 'a great mark of progress was to be seen in the thousands of Hindu ladies who were permitted to come forth from their homes to witness the great show. Ladies in bands of four to twenty were to be seen under the guidance of their young brothers-in-law, or the Zenana teachers of the various missions, most busily engaged in examining all the wonders that were collected together. The prospect and retrospect of their visit to the outside world must have given immense delight to multitudes who for years had not been permitted to see or be seen by the outside world. Some Hindu gentlemen went so far as to say that in their opinion, had the Exhibition, continued open for a year, the doors of the zenana-khanahs would not have been again closed; that the ladies, having once tasted the sweets of liberty, would not have been content to remain immured.'[14]

The ladies of the Bráhma Samáj of India (the Church of the New Dispensation) lead a some-what more secluded life than their sisters of the Sádháran Bráhma Samáj. In the Church, the former sit behind screens, while a good number of the latter dispense with the necessity of such protection.

Advanced Hindu ladies in Calcutta have for sometime past been getting up Fancy Fairs and Theatricals from which however, the male sex is at present wisely excluded. They may be occasionally met with riding or driving, or at the dinner-table in hotels and refreshment rooms, at public meetings, millinery and other shops, and even at levees at the Government House. In Bengal, there are now many Hindu ladies who have graduated at the Calcutta University, and a few who are practising medicine as a profession. There are also Hindu authoresses of distinction.

There is, however, still a strong body of conservative Hindus who look upon progress such as we have just indicated with disfavour. The following extracts from a Madras paper[15] very fairly represent their views on the subject. We are aware of but few cases of educated ladies in Bengal to whom the charges made in them would at all apply. We do not know the exact state of matters in Madras, but are inclined to think, the writer has given undue prominence to exceptional facts.

Before giving out our views on the subject of education for our women, let us see what sort of education is given to them. The matrons of the house give lessons to young women about the duties they owe to their relations and neighbours and the good examples they place before them, teach them better than the lessons they give. The daily avocations of a Hindu woman are—to rise early from bed, saying the name of God, to wash herself, to clean the house, to worship her deity after bathing, and then to cook food for the inmates of the house. In the midst of these avocations, she ministers to the wants of her children, and gives alms to the poor. In the event of a stranger making his appearance, be he a mendicant or a recluse, she ministers to his wants and feeds him sumptuously. After feeding the inmates of the house, she takes her meal. If a stranger comes at this time, she cheerfully cooks food for him, and considers herself happy in satiating his hunger. Young women assist matrons in these works, and thereby learn practically the duties incumbent on them. In the afternoon our women get some leisure, and they pass it profitably. There are some matrons who have read the Ramayana, the Mahabharata and other religious works: and they either peruse portions of the same or narrate the incidents described in them for the edification of the females of the neighbourhood who meet together to hear them. The accounts of the noble lives, led by Síta, Sávitri and other celebrated women of ancient times, tend not a little to imbue the minds of our women with noble ideas. This is supplemented by the edifying lessons, given by Kathaks or Puranics, from time to time.

The works of our women are not confined to their own domiciles. They cheerfully help their neignbours when necessary. They cook food for their neighbours, attend on sick persons day and night. These are the good results coming out of the training which our women receive from the matrons. The object of education is to form the mind and to make the recipients of it useful members of society. It does not matter whether education is received in a public school or in the midst of a family, so long as the wished-for object is attained. It is true that several of the matrons are without letters: but when we see that the training they give leads to good results, we cannot but give them the meed of praise they deserve. In certain parts of India, notably in Bengal, Hindu women are seen making free use of some proverbs, when they find anything amiss on the part of the inmates of the house. These proverbs are replete with wholesome lessons and they are addressed by matrons to the juvenile members, male as well as female, in the way of admonition or advice. This also is a good method of educating our young women.

Let us now take a review of the method, adopted by educated young men, in imparting education to our women. Schools for girls are being established, and the Government are lending them their helping hands. The girls remain in these schools up to the 8th or 9th year of their age, when they are withdrawn on account of their marriage. The education that is given during this short period is necessarily of an elementary nature, and the smattering of knowledge they receive is very soon forgotten. It is not too much to expect that the husbands of these girls should supplement the education their wives received before marriage, by giving them salutary lessons, but we are disappointed to notice a different state of things. And it is not a wonder.

The education our young men receive, feeds their minds with facts and figures, but fails to elevate their character, morally and religiously. These young men become themselves devotees of fashions and frivolities: and they educate their wives in a manner that would make them their suitable companions. They read with them the novels and the dramas that depict in glowing colours love scenes of a debasing nature, and thereby vitiate the tastes of the innocent girls. This is not all. They embellish them with all the decorations and fineries of European ladies, and instances are not wanting of their partaking with them foreign food. Some of our so-called advanced young men give undue indulgence to their reformed wives: and the latter, as a matter of course, look upon other members of the family with disdain. They consider it a drudgery to cook and to attend to other domestic work. They pass their time in the drawing-room with a few lady companions, decorating themselves with all the embellishments that fashion has at its command. Here they pass their time, sometimes in playing and sometimes in reading love-tales: and if they do aught that is useful, they sew woollen caps or comforters, and that is done as a diversion rather than as a work of utility. These articles are seldom used in the family. They are generally given to friends as presents.[16]

The doings of the so-called enlightened ladies disgust the matrons of the house, and bring in dissensions in the family. The other juvenile members, who are not of the enlightened type, perform only their share of the work. So that the work, left undone by the fashionable ladies, devolves on the matrons. The state of things cannot last long. The household work will be performed as long as the matrons are living, but it is hard to conceive the pitiable plight in which our young men will be placed after the demise of these good women. There are only a few among us who have means to employ cooks and maid-servants: so that, matters will come to such a pass that our reformed young men will find themselves in the painful necessity of cooking their food and performing other work. For, they will scarcely have the audacity to request their fashionable wives to perform the work of menials. Fortunately, the number of young men of this type is limited. We have made a prominent mention of their doings with a view to warn our young men generally.

There is another agency at work to give education to our women. Some of the Christian Missions are sending to the zenana, ladies brought from Europe and America to impart to Hindu females secular instructions interspersed with the doctrines of Christianity. These Christian ladies teach needle work, and this has induced our young men to open the doors of the zenana to them. The injury they are doing to the Hindu community is very great. Their teaching is secretly sapping the very foundations of our nationality. Outlandish manners are gradually permeating through the system, and the evil effects of the same are distinctly visible. The virtues for which Hindu women are famous, are, one after another, disappearing from among them. Their sympathy towards their relations and neighbours is giving place to selfishness, their regard towards their superiors is giving place to hauteur, and their remarkably religious habits are giving place to the fineries of the European ladies. It cannot be said that our women derive no benefits from the lessons they receive, but the little good that comes out of them is smothered under the crushing weight of the injurious effects that are engendered.

Some of our reformers allow their daughters to attend school after their marriage. This may be taken to be a move in the right direction: but as there is a Christian element in the tutorial staff of the schools, established for females, good results cannot be expected. We do not deny the sincerity of purpose which actuates the Christian school mistress: but the infusion of foreign ideas among students mars the object of education. Our family system is quite different from that in vogue in Europe: so that, what is considered beneficial in that continent may not be so to this country.'

NOTES

1. At the Svayamvará, the lady chooses her own husband from among the assembled guests by placing a garland upon his neck.

2. 'Indo-Aryans' Vol. I. pp. 440–1. The poet, in this description has no doubt, largely drawn on his imagination. He must be presumed however, to represent the manners of the time he depicts with some approach to faithfulness.

3. Manu. V., 148–9.

4. Manu. V., 154–5.

5. Manu. II., 213–16.

6. Manu. III., 55–7.

7. Manu. III., 113.

8. The *Calcutta Review*, Vol. LV, p. 53.

9. They were sometimes debauched to a degree. Akbar tried some peculiar remedial measures, but with what success is not known. He appointed a Daroga and a clerk to register the names of such as visited women of the town, or wanted to take them to their houses. If any body wanted to have a virgin, he was required to first apply to His Majesty and get his permission. It is said that His Majesty called some of the principal women of the town and asked them who had deprived them of their virginity. After hearing their replies, some of the principal and must renowned grandees were censured, or punished, several to long terms of imprisonment. (Abul Fazal Allami, *Ain-i-Akbari*, trans. H. Blochmann, Vol. I, Calcutta: Royal Asiatic Society of Bengal, 1939, p. 192).

10. Rev. W.J. Wilkins, 'Modern Hinduism', Calcutta 1887, p. 361.

11. The *Calcutta Review*, Vol. LV, 1872, p. 56.

12. John Malcolm, *Memoir of Central India*, Vol. 1, 1823, pp. 194–5.

13. The *Calcutta Review*, Vol. LVI, pp. 10–27.

14. Wilkins, op. cit., p. 375.

15. The *Madura Mail* quoted in the *Indian Mirror*, 14 December 1893.

16. As we have said in the text, the charges made above are greatly exaggerated, at least as regards Bengal.

Maulana Ashraf Ali Thanavi

Sickened, as he says, by the irrelevancies, superstitions, and improprieties that had crept into 'religion', Maulana Ashraf Ali Thanavi (1864–1943) decided the best way to attempt to cure these ills was by writing a book, aimed primarily at women, but equally relevant to men. He aimed to teach women basic literacy, letter-writing with the proper forms of address, household management, and of course all that he could in relation to religious practice. The education of women he saw as essential for the improvement of family life and society as a whole.

A product of the Deoband school, Thanavi was both a scholar and a mystic, but not a mystic who paid no concern to practical matters, as the book indicates. He has obviously paid detailed attention to the kind of rituals he feels are foolish and wasteful, or 'nonsensical'. He remarks, for instance, that people have decided that a child should begin schooling at the age of four years, four months, and four days. 'This precision', he says sharply, 'is simply unfounded and nonsensical....Illiterate people consider this a matter of the shariat....' Women appear to have a long list of faults, but they are intelligent and can be 'managed' if properly instructed. The lack of intelligence displayed is not inherent but acquired through the adoption of stupid customs.

Thanavi was one of several scholars who wrote 'guide books' for women. There were also novelists such as Nazir Ahmad (1833?–1912) who wrote didactic tales with model women as the main characters.

The First Book of the *Bihishti Zewar*

I. [INTRODUCTORY COMMENTS]

> All praise to God, who declared in his Book: 'O believers, save yourselves and the people of your households from the fire whose fuel is people and stones.'

Perfecting Women: Maulana Ashraf Ali Thanavi's Bihishti Zewar: *A partial translation with commentary*, Barbara Daly Metcalf, Delhi: OUP, 1992. First pub. Lahore: Shaikh Ghulam Ali and Sons,1905.

And Almighty God declared: 'Remember what is read in your houses of God's verses and wise teachings; and praise and blessings on your messenger Muhammad, God's blessings and peace upon him.'

He is the elect of the prophets who declared: 'Every one from among you is guardian of my words, and every one is liable to be questioned about that guardianship.'

And the Messenger, God's blessings and peace upon him, also declared: 'It is a duty incumbent on every Muslim man and every Muslim woman to acquire knowledge.'

And praise descend on his family and his Companions who learned and taught his virtues and his ways.

Here I, Ashraf 'Ali Thanawi Hanafi, contemptible and worthless as I am, declare my purpose in writing this work.

For many years, I watched the ruination of the religion of the women of Hindustan and was heartsick because of it. I struggled to find a cure, worried because that ruin was not limited to religion but had spread beyond to everyday matters as well. It went beyond the women to their children and in many respects even had its effects on their husbands. To judge from the speed with which it progressed, it seemed that if reform did not come soon, the disease would be nearly incurable. Thus I was ever more concerned.

Thanks to divinely granted insight, experience, logic, and learning, I realized that the cause of this ruination is nothing other than women's ignorance of the religious sciences. This lack corrupts their beliefs, their deeds, their dealings with other people, their character, and the whole manner of their social life. Their faith is barely spared, for they speak many words and commit many deeds that verge on infidelity. Beyond that, their words, their thoughts, and their style of behavior take root in the hearts of the children whom they nurture in their very laps. So the children's religion is ruined, and their daily life grows vapid and tasteless. The reason is that faulty belief leads to faulty character, faulty character to faulty action, and faulty action to faulty dealings that are the root of the disquietude of society.

As for the husband, if he is like his wife, the two together grow even more corrupt. They can expect a desolate afterlife, and desolation is likely in this life, too, for the end of such corruption is mutual contention. If instead there is some rectitude in the husband, the hapless fellow is subjected to life imprisonment. For him, his wife's every act is a source of distress; for her, his every counsel is annoying and offensive. If he cannot put up with her behavior, the result is dissension and distance between them; if, on the contrary, he is resigned to her, his prison is bound to be bitter. It is this ignorance of the religious sciences that brings his daily life to ruin. Look at some examples:

If his wife engages in backbiting, she makes enemies. Inevitably, someone is hurt.

If she spends money on wasteful ceremonies in order to get attention and status, she changes wealth into poverty.

If she makes her husband angry, he either expels her or deliberately neglects her.

If she puts up with everything from her children, they wind up ill trained and ill bred. Watching them, a person could pass a whole lifetime in grinding sorrow.

If she wants riches and jewelry, she cannot get enough to keep up with her desires. She spends her whole life in frustration.

Thanks to this ignorance, many such causes of corruption inevitably spring up. Because the cure of each thing is its opposite, the cure for all this is clear: sure knowledge of the science of religion.

I have for some time, therefore, realized that in order to manage women, it is absolutely necessary to teach them the science of religion— even if it must be through the medium of Urdu. With this in mind, I looked over the existing Urdu books and pamphlets and found them insufficient to alleviate the need. Many books were simply unreliable and wrong. The style of several others, which were reliable, was not sufficiently simple to be intelligible to women. Moreover, they covered subjects that were irrelevant. In contrast, I found other books, written for women, that were so thin that they fell short in covering the requisite rules and points of law. I therefore came up with the idea of writing a book, particularly for women, whose style would be very simple; it would be composed of the sum of all necessities of religion and would exclude those injunctions that are necessary only for men. It would be just the right length, so that reading only this volume would obviate the need for other reading on everyday religious obligations. Obviously, the whole scope of the religious sciences cannot be contained in one book. It is absurd to think that Muslims can dispense with *'ulama.*

For many years, this idea ripened in my heart, but because of various considerations, particularly a lack of time resulting from other pressing tasks, there was no chance to begin. Finally, in A.H, 1320 [1902–3], taking God's name, I did begin as best I could. And, with God's grace, there appeared at the same time the first contributions to support the publication of the book. Almighty God provided the cooperation of the director of the Surati Women's Madrasa in Rangoon, Seth Sahib, as well as help from the late daughter of Janab Maulana 'Abdu'l-Ghafar Sahib Lakhnawi, *God's mercy on her*, who was married to Hakim 'Abdu's-Salam Sahib Danapuri. With their contributions, this promising undertaking began. May Almighty God accept it. Let us see who will take part in the future. The book has been attributed to this worthless person, but in truth its 'finest flower' is my beloved relative Maulawi Saiyid Ahmad 'Ali Fatahpuri, *may the peace of Almighty God be upon him with instructions and benefactions. May the reward of Almighty God be upon him, and the best of rewards on me and on all Muslim men and Muslim women.*

Now, *what God has willed*, this book—may it be protected from an evil eye—includes not only most of the obligations but even the niceties of religion; and, beyond that, it deals with many obligations of everyday life as well. If anyone reads it with understanding from start to finish, she should be the equal of a middling *'alim*. Moreover, its style is so simple that greater simplicity is clearly beyond our power. Those matters that are not usually necessary for women, such as the rules relating to the Friday prayer, to 'Id, and to leadership of prayer, are excluded. Only two kinds of injunctions are set out: first, those that are necessary for both men and women; and second, those that are specifically for women. In the latter cases, however, the rules for men are given in marginal notes so that they might also profit and avoid error. With a view to making it unnecessary to search out another book, the alphabet is provided here at the beginning. It is based on the pamphlet 'Tarkibu'l-haruf' (The shape of letters), written by my revered maternal uncle Makhdumi Janab Mamun Munshi Shaukat 'Ali Sahib, *may his life be protracted*. As soon as a girl has finished the Glorious Qur'an, she can begin this book.

The name of the work is meant to appeal to women. It is called *Bihishti Zewar* (Heavenly ornaments) because real ornaments are none other than those perfections of religion thanks to which one shall receive ornaments to wear in heaven. In the words of Almighty God: *'Gardens of Eternity will they enter; therein will they be adorned with bracelets of gold and pearls.'* And in the words of the Messenger of God, God's blessings and peace upon him: *'The jewels of the believer will reach as far as the water of ablution reaches.'*

Because it is impossible at this point to make a correct estimate of the length of this work, and because waiting to finish it would delay a worthwhile endeavor, it seems appropriate to divide the work into several separate books. This both facilitates publication and gives the reader heart; so that she will be able to say, 'Now I have read one book; now I have read two books'; and so forth. Moreover, it gives scope for writing as much as seems necessary. Also, if a girl is already familiar with the subject matter of some of the books from reading other works, those books can be de-emphasized in instructing her. Similarly, if for some reason there is a pressing need to teach a particular subject, it is easy to give it precedence.

Book One is in your hands. Pray to Almighty God that you may master it quickly and well. By the proofs of Qur'anic verses and *hadis* cited above, it is required of men that they set their wives and daughters to study this work; and it is required of women that they learn it and direct the attention of their progeny, especially their daughters, to it as well. My heart will be joyous when those matters that are in my mind are assembled and printed and when I may see with my own eyes that this book is generally included in the instruction of girls and talked of in house after house. The future is in the power of the grace of the Truth, eminent is his glory and majesty.

At the time I was to write this introduction, I caught sight, in the paper *Nūrun 'Ala Nur*, of a poem with the same name as this work and making the same point. To my heart, this seemed auspicious, and I fancied ending my introduction with the poem for the delight of my readers, especially young girls, who would then be more favorably inclined toward the subject of the work. If this poem were at the beginning of every section of the work, it would offer the sweet delight of successive lumps of sugar. Here it is:

The True Jewelry of Humanity

A little girl asked this of her mother dear:
'Tell me about all jewelry; since I am unclear

Which pieces are good, this make known to me;
And which of them are bad, that too explain to me

So that of good and bad I can the difference tell;
With your blessing, then, to me the secret tell.'

The mother then replied, with love, 'O Daughter mine,
To this word on jewelry an attentive heart incline.

Jewelry of silver, gold—people may call it fine.
In it put not your trust—never, Sweetheart mine.

The glint of silver, gold, is only a thing to see.
Four days of silvery light, and then dark night will be.

It is required of you the kind of jewelry to want
From which good faith and life, my dear, may never want.

Good sense, dear, always be the *head fringe* you put on;
Sense is the means by which your work gets done.

If you *earrings* wear, ears of attentiveness, dear,
And your earrings' little *bells*: good counsel [*nasihat*] for you to hear.

And the *pendants* that hang down tell the heart to bow down too.
If act on them you will, good fortune swift to you.

Earrings of the upper ear always cause you pain,
Put in your ears the Book, good counsel yet again.

And if some jewelry you need to put upon your neck,
Good deeds, my beloved, be the *chain* upon your neck.

The yield of the strength of your arm, the *bracelet* of your arm be,
With your success in that, you will merry and joyful be.

All of the *jewelry of the arm*, none of it serves an end;
The ability of the arm, O Daughter, that does serve an end.

More than *jewelry of the hand*, cherished is handiwork fine;
Handiwork is the skill toward which everyone does incline.

What will you do, O my dear, with *anklets* that ring away?
O Daughter, a nuisance like that just simply throw away!

The best *jewelry for the feet* is surely the light of insight
That on the path of good you remain, sure-footed, aright.

If gold and silver jewelry be not on the feet—no fear—
If from the path of right your feet never slip, O my dear.'

II. [LEARNING TO READ]

[The Alphabet]

[The next seven pages of the text, omitted here, present the Urdu alphabet as well as examples of joining letters. (Urdu letters, like the Arabic from which they are derived, change shape depending on their position—initial, medial, final—in a word.)]

The Names of the Days

[In the text, the Persian names are given in larger script and the Hindi names are in smaller script below them (here in parentheses), suggesting that the latter would be more familiar, although the former would have been used by the more educated. The first day is Saturday.]

Shamba (Sanicar)	Chahar-shamba (Budh)
Yak-shamba (Itwar)	Panj-shamba (Jum'arat)
Du-shamba (Pir)	Jum'a
Sih-shamba (Mangal)	

The Names of the Months

[Only the names of the Muslim lunar months are given here and are thus presumably preferred; later, in Book Ten, other local calendrical systems are also presented.]

Muharram	Rajab
Safar	Sha'ban
Rabi'u'l-awwal	Ramazan
Rabi'u's-sani	Shawwal
Jumada'l-awwal	Zi-qa'd
Jumada'l-ukhra	Zi'l-hij

Practice Sentences

[These are meant to be used for practice in reading, but their content is also of interest. Many of the injunctions derive from traditions of the exemplary sayings and behavior of the Prophet—sometimes amended, as when the more common 'Heaven is at the feet of your mother' is expanded to include the father, too. The first four imperatives are in the direct (*tu*) form; the rest are in the familiar (*tum*).]

Fear God.
Do not sin.
Perform the ablution and pray.
The person who performs the canonical prayer is beloved of God.
The person who does not perform the prayer is far from mercy
Oppress no one.
The supplication of the oppressed is readily accepted.
It is very bad to tease any animal or bird for no reason or to beat
    a dog or cat.
Obey the word of your mother and father.
Consider a beating from them to be an honor.
Serve them with your heart.
Heaven is at the feet of your father and mother.
Never answer them back with an argument.
Listen quietly to whatever they may say in anger.
Annoy them in nothing.

Act respectfully before your elders.

Treat those younger than you with love and affection.

Consider no one contemptible.

Regard yourself as less than everyone else. To consider yourself
great is very bad

It is a great sin to make fun of other people, to call attention to them,
or to pick out their faults.

Eat with your right hand,

Drink with your right hand. The devil eats and drinks with his left
hand.

Drink water in three gulps.

Cool your food before eating it. There is no blessing in hot food.

Whatever you say, say the truth.

To lie is a great sin.

Always greet your elders when you arise in the morning.

Read the Noble Qur'an after performing the prayer.

Memorize your lesson carefully.

Do not always want to be playing and jumping.

Do not take an oath on every matter. To take an oath frequently
is very bad.

Put away your book carefully.

Do not ridicule someone because her appearance is bad. To God,
beauty and ugliness are the same.

Do not be naughty, and you will not be beaten.

Clean your nose with your left hand.

Clean yourself with your left hand after defecation.

When entering a toilet, put your left foot inside first.

When leaving, put your right foot outside first.

Place your shoe first on your right foot, then the other on your
left foot.

[The next two sections, 'Special Rules for Certain Letters of the Alphabet' and 'The Use of Certain Pronunciation Signs Called Motions and Rests' are omitted here. They cover the nasal, aspiration, vowels, elision, glottal stops, and so forth.]

III. On Letter Writing

If you plan to write a letter, first ascertain whether the person addressed is older than you, younger than you, or your equal. The words used in a letter should match the rank of the person. A letter from an elder is called *wala nama* (an eminent letter), *sarfaraz nama* (a letter conferring distinction; literally, a 'head-raising' letter), *iftikhar nama* (an honoring letter), *karamat nama* (a letter of generosity), *e'zaz nama* (an honoring letter), *sahifa-yi 'ali* (a lofty epistle), *sahifa-yi garami* (a precious epistle).

Do not use *ap* [the respectful second-person plural] for a person who is extremely superior to you; instead, use *anjanab* (sir, 'that place of refuge'), *janab-i 'ali* (exalted sir), *janab-i wala* (eminent sir), *hazrat-i wala* (your eminence, eminent sir, 'the eminent presence'), *hazrat-i 'ali* (your highness, lofty sir). For example, if you intend to write 'Your letter came', write *janab wala ka sarfaraz nama aya* (the honor-bearing letter of your eminence came). And instead of 'came', write *sadir hu'a* (was issued) or *musharraf farmaya* (conferred honor, nobility).

Letters from younger people are *masarrat nama* (a joy-bringing letter) or *rahat nama* (a comfort-bringing letter).

The letters of equals are *wala nama* or *karamnama* (a letter of generosity or kindness).

As an example, if you write a letter to your father, write thus: 'Respected father, sir, the *qibla* and *ka'ba* of your offspring, *may your lofty shadow never vanish*. After salutation with endless respect and veneration, I beg to submit to you that your eminent letter arrived. I derived great satisfaction from ascertaining the well-being of your blessed constitution.' After that, write whatever you want.

The section up to '*may your lofty shadow never vanish*' is called 'titles' (*alqab*). The section of greetings and supplications is called 'respects' (*adab*). The section after that, in which you write whatever you wish, is called the 'content' (*mazmun*) of the letter.

Titles and Respects for Elders

For a Father

1. Respected father, sir, the *qibla* and *ka'ba* of your descendents, the object of service from your dependents, *may your lofty shadow never vanish*. After salutation with endless respects and exaltation, I beg to submit...

2. Respected father, sir, the *qibla* of both terrains and the *ka'ba* of both domains, *may your lofty shadow never vanish*. After respects and salutation with endless veneration and exaltation...

3. Respected father, sir, revered and honored by your offspring, *may your lofty shadow never vanish*. After salutation with endless veneration, I beg to represent that...

4. Respected father, sir, my *qibla* and *ka'ba*, *may your lofty shadow never vanish*. After respects and salutations, I beg to submit that...

5. My *qibla* and *ka'ba, may your lofty shadow never vanish.* After salutation, I beg to submit that...

For a Paternal Uncle

1. The *qibla* and *ka'ba* of your scions, the object of service by your minions, *may your lofty shadow never vanish.* After salutation and endless veneration, I beg to submit...

For a Maternal Uncle

1. Respected uncle, sir, venerated and honored by the lesser, *may your lofty shadow never vanish...*
2. Respected uncle, sir, served and exalted by the humble, *may your lofty shadow never vanish...*

For a Mother

1. Respected mother, madam, served and venerated, *may her shadow never vanish...*
2. Respected mother, madam, venerated and exalted, *may her shadow never vanish...*
3. Respected mother, madam, venerated and honored, *may her shadow never vanish...*

To an Elder Sister

1. Venerated and honored sister...
2. Venerated and exalted, *may her shadow never vanish...*

To an Elder Brother

1. Respected brother, sir, venerated and honored, served and exalted, *may your lofty shadow never vanish...*

The titles used for the father are also used for a paternal grandfather, maternal grandfather, father's elder brother, mother's brother, and father-in-law.

The titles used for the mother are also used for a mother's sister, mother's brother's wife, maternal grandmother, father's brother's wife, and such elder relatives. In place of 'mother, madam,' write 'aunt, madam.'

As far as possible, do not engage in correspondence with your husband's younger or elder brothers. Do not cultivate familiarity with them. If some necessity should befall, then write and address them as 'Respected brother, sir'.

The 'respects' for all elder relatives are the same.

Titles and Respects for Younger Relatives

For a Son, Grandson, Nephew, and So On

1. Most prosperous, light of the eye, comfort to my life, settler of joy and fortune, *on him the peace of Almighty God.* After supplication for prolongation of life and advance in rank, may it be set out...
2. Light of my life, piece of my liver, may his life be prolonged. After supplication for length of life and obtainment of joy in both worlds, may my happy opinion be set out...
3. Child tied to my heart, of my liver a part, may his life be prolonged. After copious supplications, may it be set out that...

For a Younger Brother

1. Brother dearer than life, *may the peace of Almighty God be upon him.* After supplication, may it be set out...
2. Brother equal to life, *may the peace of Almighty God be upon him.* After supplication of felicity and good ways, may it be set out...

For a Younger Sister

1. Dear sister, light of the eye, most virtuous, *may the peace of Almighty God be upon her.*
2. Auspicious sister, may her life be prolonged.

Respects for all are the same. Then write whatever you like.

Titles and Respects for a Husband

1. My lord, may you prosper! After greeting and desire for meeting, I beg to submit...
2. Confidant of secrets, companion, my consoler of sorrows, may you prosper! After longing greetings, it is humbly represented...
3. Knower of secrets; breath-sharer, play-sharer; may you prosper! After greetings and desire for meeting, I beg to submit...

Titles and Respects for a Wife

1. Confidante of secrets; breath-sharer, play-sharer; may you prosper!

After expression of my longing and desire for our meeting, may it be set out...

2. Light of the dwelling and adornment of the lodging, may you prosper! After expression of longing for our meeting, may it be set out...

3. Companion of my afflicted life, mitigator of the sorrows of my dejected heart, may you prosper! After longing for meeting, may it be set out...

[Examples of Letters]

A Letter to a Father

Venerated and honored by his offspring, *may his shadow never vanish.* After salutation with endless veneration, I beg to submit that for some time no ennobling epistle has issued from your eminence. Thus everyone here is anxious and worried. We hope that you will honor us by quickly communicating to us that your blessed constitution is well.

My dear sister, entitled Zubaida Khatun, through the grace and generosity of God, is well. Yesterday she completed her reading of the Glorious Word. Now would you kindly send some Urdu book for her that she can set to reading? The book *Ta'limu'd-din* (Instruction in religion), which you sent me, is excellent. All the ladies are looking for it. So please send four or five more copies.

For the rest, all is well. Please let us know soon that you are well, so that we shall no longer be anxious but may rest content. My obeisance. End.

The petition of respect of Hamida Khatun from Allahabad, 13 Muharram, Monday.

A Letter to a Daughter

O piece of my liver, my good omen, light of my eye, comfort to my life, Mistress Khadija, *may the peace of Almighty God be upon her.* After praying for thy long life and progress in learning and skill, may it be set out that for some time no letter of thine has come, so that my heart has been anxious. But the day before yesterday, the joy-bringing letter of your elder brother arrived. I was content when I ascertained that you were well.

From this letter I also learned that you have no enthusiasm for reading and writing and that you are scarcely putting your heart into your lessons. I also learned that several women talk about your reading and writing, saying, 'What is the point of teaching girls to read and write? They should be taught sewing, cooking, *chikan* embroidery, things like that. Do you want to teach them to read and write to turn them into *maulawis*, like men?' It seems that the chatter of these people has made you discouraged, and you have done little work. O my daughter, do not be caught up in the talk of these foolish women. You must realize that no one could want your best interests more than I do. Hold fast to what I tell you. Their talk is completely foolish.

Every woman should at least be able to read and write Urdu. There are great benefits in this; and in ignorance of reading and writing there is great harm.

The first great benefit is that educated women speak clearly. I have heard many illiterate women say *sabab* for *sawab*; *surwa* for *shurba*; *qabutar* for *kabutar; dahez* for *jahez, jukham* for *zukam*, or even *zukham*. Women who are literate laugh at them and mimic them. With reading and writing, this flaw completely disappears.

Second, educated women perform the prayer and fast correctly; their religion and faith are put in order. Illiterate women, in their ignorance, do many things so that their faith is lost, and they do not even realize it. If, God forbid, death should come when they are in such a state, they will have to burn in hell like the infidels; salvation is impossible. With reading and writing, this dread possibility disappears, and faith grows strong.

Third, educated women manage their homes well. This is the special responsibility of women. They personally keep their eyes on books and household accounts at every moment.

Fourth, they raise their children well. Little children stay mostly with women; and girls stay only with their mothers. The habits and conversation of a literate woman will be good. Her offspring will learn from her example. From their earliest age, the children will be of good character and well behaved, because every minute their mother is teaching and reproving them. Look how valuable this is.

The fifth benefit is that when a woman has learning, she knows every minute the proper status of her mother, father, husband, and other relations; and she will fulfill her obligations (*huquq*) to them, so that both her worldly life and her afterlife will be in order.

Finally, a serious disadvantage of not knowing how to read and write is that an illiterate woman must reveal household matters to outsiders— or else keep them to herself, with resultant harm. Women's matters are often ones that affect the women's honor, but at times must be revealed to a mother or sister who may not be nearby. In this case, a woman must either be immodest and have a letter written by someone else or, alternatively, say nothing at all and cause great harm.

There are, in addition, thousands more benefits from learning and many more disadvantages in not learning. How much longer must I go on? Just remember my advice; do not in any way shirk your reading and writing. With many prayers for you. End.

The writer: 'Abdu'llah, from Banaras, 25 Ramazan. Friday.

An Answer to This Letter, Sent by the Daughter

O *qibla* and *ka'ba* of your offspring, *may your lofty shadow never cease*. After salutations and respects, I beg to submit that the issuing of your lofty epistle bestowed felicity. Your welfare being ascertained, everyone was content. May Almighty God always keep your auspicious self fixed over our heads.

What your eminence wrote in relation to the reading and writing of this servant was very beneficial. It is certainly true that I had become disheartened on account of people's talk. Now, since the day your epistle arrived, I have put my heart into my reading, and I have even begun to write a little. What you said is absolutely right, and there *are* countless benefits in this. Those women who do not know how to read and write lament continually and ask themselves why they never learned.

The day before yesterday, the wife of the *peshkar* who lives in our neighborhood got a letter from her maternal uncle. Nowadays, there is no man in her house. The poor creature wandered around imploring everyone to read the letter or have it read, saying, 'How is my aunt? I know that she is doing poorly.' So she was truly in a state. The letter came in the forenoon; it lay all day with no one to read it. After sunset, she came to me, and I read her the news. Only then she settled down. Since then, the point has stuck with me that the skill of reading and writing is wealth indeed and that ignorance is often the source of great trouble.

I also realized that there are five women among our kinfolk (*biradari*) who are well educated. Everyone honors them wherever they go. Whenever someone commits something that is against the *shari'at* or observes some false custom at a wedding, they interrupt it, insist that it stop, explain what is wrong, and give advice. All the ladies keep quiet and set their ears to listen. The ladies consult them if they have some question. All the ladies ask them first, and everyone praises them on and on.

I will surely put my heart into learning to read and write. I have become very enthusiastic on my own. You pray to Almighty God, too, that he may grant me this wealth.

For the rest, all here is well.

With great respect. End.

Your maidservant Khadija, *may she be forgiven*, from Saharanpur, 28 Ramazan, Tuesday.

A Letter to a Brother's Daughter

Light of my eye, comfort of my life, Mistress Sadiqa, *on her be the peace of Almighty God*. After supplication for you, may it be set out that your joy-bringing letter arrived. I was content when informed of your state.

It made me very happy to learn about your reading. May Almighty God give abundance to your age and quickly grant you the fruit of your work. On the day when you write me a letter with your own hand, I shall dispatch five rupees for sweets.

I give you one more bit of advice. I have heard that you are somewhat saucy and do not have regard for the respect due anyone. I felt grieved at hearing this, because a person's honor does not derive only from being able to read and write. Until you learn to have regard for *adab* (civility), people will not love and cherish you. Along with reading and writing, it is necessary, above all, for boys and girls to learn civility, for with civility a person is dear to the heart of everyone and everyone seeks to please that person. A person of civility is a person of good fortune. As someone once said: *Ba adab ba nasib; be adab be nasib* (With civility, good fortune; without civility, bad fortune). Now I shall tell you what civility is and why you must behave in accordance with it.

You should greet anyone superior to you in age and relationship with great veneration. Never let an indecent word come out of your mouth in front of such a person.

Do not play or joke around with your equals in front of an elder.

If an elder calls you, answer in a very soft voice; and when given something, respond with a salutation.

Listen with close attention to whatever advice an elder gives. When she speaks, do not interrupt her.

Never sit in a place higher than where she happens to be sitting.

Never call an elder by name, but rather call him or her by the relationship to you. Indeed, use a long form of that title, as: *khalu jan* (auntie dear); *phuphi aman* (auntie mama); *nanaji* (dear grandfather); *appa jan* (dear big sister).

If your elders speak sharply to you in anger, you must never answer back. Disappear and say nothing.

The name of all this is civility, and it is of great importance for all people. End.

Muhammad Wajid Husain, from Faizabad.

Titles for an Equal

If you are to write to an equal, first include the titles for equal rank: O most bounteous to me, may you prosper...; My kindred kindly friend, may you prosper...; My gracious friend, may you prosper...

Then offer your respects: After grateful salutation and desire for meeting, I beg to submit...

Then write the content of the letter, keeping in mind not to be too expansive, as when you write to elders, and not to be too brief, as when you write to younger relatives. On every point, keep equality in mind.

Two Examples of Addresses

1. Place: City of Lucknow, Quarter Aminabad. Near the house of Hakim 'Abu'l-Ghani Sahib, Assistant Tahsildar, To the service of him of eminent rank, the respected *darogha*, my *qibla* and *ka'ba*, Wahidu'z-Zaman Sahib, *may his lofty shadow never vanish.*
2. Place: Faizabad, the market. By the shop of Liyaqat Husain Sahib, Goldsmith. To the attention of him prosperous in joy and good ways, Munshi Muhammad Sa'idu'd-Din, *may the peace of Almighty God come upon him.*

IV. NUMERALS

[The next two pages, omitted here, provide a chart of the cardinal numbers from one to one hundred.]

V. TRUE STORIES FROM THE *HADIS*

The First Story

Hazrat Messenger of God, *God's blessings and peace upon him*, recounted this story:

Once, a man came to a deserted place where he suddenly heard a voice in a cloud, telling the cloud to water the garden of a certain person. The cloud moved and rained down heavily on barren ground.

The man then followed the water, which had gathered into a channel, until he came upon someone standing in a garden, directing the water with a spade. He inquired of this person: 'O Servant of God, what is your name?'

The person answered with the name spoken in the cloud and asked in turn: 'O Servant of God, why do you inquire about my name?'

He answered, 'I heard a voice in that cloud say your name and tell the cloud to water your garden. What do you do that deserves this?'

He said, 'I shall tell you only because you have asked. When my crop is ripe, I give one-third of the harvest in charity, put aside one-third for myself and my children, and invest one-third in the garden.'

Moral: Praise be to God. Such is God's mercy that help from the unknown furthers the work of those who obey him, even without their knowing it. Surely it is true that if a person belongs to God, God in turn belongs to that person.

The Second Story

Hazrat Messenger of God, *God's blessings and peace upon him*, once recounted this story:

Among the Bani Isra'il, there were three men: one was a leper, one was afflicted with scalp disease, and one was blind. Almighty God wished to test them, and, to do so, he sent an angel.

First, the angel went to the leper and asked, 'What is your greatest wish?'

He replied, 'I wish that I might have a good complexion and beautiful skin and that this evil that makes people shun me and refuse to let me sit near them might disappear.'

The angel passed his hand over the leper's body, and, lo, his skin was clear and his complexion beautiful.

Then the angel asked, 'What sort of goods would you most like to have?'

He answered, 'A camel.'

So the angel gave him a pregnant she-camel and said, 'May Almighty God give you increase of it.'

Then the angel went to the man with scalp disease and asked, 'What is your greatest wish?'

He replied, 'I wish that my hair would grow in and that this evil that makes people shun me would disappear.'

The angel passed his hand over his head, and, lo, his scalp was healed and grew good hair.

Then the angel asked, 'What sort of goods would you most like to have?'

He answered, 'A cow.'

So the angel gave him a pregnant cow and said, 'May Almighty God grant you increase of it.'

Then the angel went to the blind man and asked, 'What do you need?' He answered, 'I need Almighty God to restore my sight so that I might again see other people.'

The angel passed his hand over the blind man's eyes, and Almighty God restored his sight. Then the angel asked, 'What sort of goods would you most like to have?'

He answered, 'A goat.'

The angel gave him a pregnant goat.

The animals of all three men bore young, and in a short time the area was filled with the camels of the first, the cows of the second, and the goats of the third.

Then the angel, at the order of God, came in the same fashion to the leper and said, 'I am a poor man; all the goods I needed for my journey have been used up. Today I have no recourse for my return travel other than God and then you. In the name of that God who bestowed on you a clear complexion and fine skin, I ask of you one camel that I may ride on it and reach home.'

The man answered, 'Be gone! Get away from me! I have other people to take care of and nothing left for you.'

The angel then said, 'I think I recognize you. Weren't you that leper whom people shunned? Weren't you very poor until God gave you so much?'

He replied, 'Ha! Very good. Well, in fact, this wealth goes back several generations in my family.'

The angel said, 'If you lie, may God make you as you were before.'

The angel then went in the same way to the man who had had scalp disease and asked him the same question and got the same kind of answer. The angel again said, 'If you lie, may God make you as you were before.'

Then the angel went in the same way to the blind man and said, 'I am a traveler and have ended up with no goods. Today, except for God and then you, I have no recourse. In the name of him who restored your sight, I ask for one goat that I might use it to complete my journey.'

The man replied, 'Of course. I was blind, and Almighty God, through his mercy alone, granted me sight. Take whatever you like and leave whatever you like. Upon God, I deny you nothing.'

The angel said to him, 'Keep your goods. I need nothing. I was sent to test you, as I have. God is pleased with you and displeased with the others.'

Moral: You must reflect on the cost suffered by the first two men for their ingratitude. They lost all their blessings, and they became as they had been. God was displeased with them, and they were deprived of salvation in this world and the next. The third man, however, because he was grateful, won great reward. He kept his blessings; God was happy with him; he reaped satisfaction and joy in both this world and the next.

The Third Story

Once Hazrat Umm Salama, *may God be pleased with her*, was given some meat. God's Messenger liked meat very much; and Hazrat Umm Salama therefore told her servant to keep the meat on a shelf in case he wanted it. Meanwhile, a beggar came and stood at the door and called out, 'Send something out to me, in the name of God. God will bless you.'

From within the house, she answered, 'May he bless you also.'

This reply meant that she had nothing to give him. The beggar left.

Then God's Messenger arrived and asked Umm Salama if she had anything for him to eat. She replied that she did, and she instructed her servant to fetch the meat for him. The servant went and saw that there was not even the name of meat—only a stone.

The Prophets declared, 'The meat turned into stone because you gave nothing to the beggar.'

Moral: Reflect on the fact that this misfortune of the meat turning into stone happened because of a refusal to give in the name of God. Any persons who make excuses to beggars but themselves eat will be eating a stone whose effect is a stony heart that is increasingly hard. Because of God's great mercy and generosity to the people in the household of the Prophet, he physically changed the appearance of the meat so that they would be saved from the ill effects of using it.

The Fourth Story

It was the excellent custom of God's Messenger to read the prayer at daybreak and then to attend to his friends and companions, asking if any among them had had some dream in the night. If they had, he would offer an interpretation of the dream. Once, following his custom, he asked if anyone had had a dream, and all replied that they had not. He then declared:

I had a dream last night in which two men came to me and clutched my hand. They led me toward a sacred place, where I saw two men, one seated and one standing. The man who was standing had iron tongs in his hand with which he was tearing the other man's cheek off completely to the nape of his neck; then he did the same thing to the other cheek. The first cheek was then restored, and the man began again. I asked the two men who were leading me what was happening, but they told me to move on.

We moved on until we came to a man who was lying down. At his head stood another man with a huge, heavy rock in his hand. He dashed the rock on the head of the man who was lying there. The rock rebounded and fell far away. While he went to retrieve it, the head of the first man was restored to its previous state, and the second man began again. I again asked the two men who were leading me what was happening, but again they told me to move on.

We moved on until we reached a cave shaped like an oven, wide at the bottom and narrow at the top, with fire burning inside. It was filled with naked men and women. When the fire rose to the top, they all rose with it and almost came out. Then, when it settled, they too went to the bottom. I again asked the two men who were leading me what was happening, but again they told me to move on.

We moved on until we reached a river of blood. One man stood in the middle; another stood on the bank, surrounded by rocks. Whenever the man in the river came toward the bank and tried to get out, the man on the bank hit him in the face with a rock with such force that he fell back to his original place. This happened again and again. I again asked the two men who were leading me what was happening, but again they told me to move on.

We moved on until we reached a green and verdant garden. An old man, surrounded by children, sat under a big tree. Another man sat near the tree, fanning a fire. The two men took me up into the tree, where a very fine house had been built in its midst. They led me inside. I had never seen such a house. It was filled with men, old and young, and women and children. They then took me farther up, where there was a house even finer than the first. They led me inside it also, and again it was filled with young and old.

I finally said to the two men, 'You have led me about the whole night. Tell me at last what all this has meant.'

They answered, 'The man whose cheek was being torn was a liar who told lies that spread throughout the whole world. They will keep doing this to him until the Day of Judgment.'

'The man whose head was being crushed was a man to whom Almighty God gave knowledge of the Qur'an. In the night, he slept, oblivious: in the day, he failed to act on what he knew. He will continue thus until the Day of Judgment.

'The persons in the cave of fire were adulterers.

'The person in the river of blood was a usurer.

'The old man under the tree is Hazrat Ibrahim, *peace be upon him.* The children around him are children who died young. The man blowing the fire is the guardian of hell. The first house you entered is the house of ordinary Muslims; the second house, the house of martyrs.'

They then revealed that they were Jibra'il and Mika'il and instructed me to look up. I lifted up my head and saw a white cloud. They told me that was my house. I asked them to leave me so that I could enter it.

They said, 'Your life remains unfinished; it is not completed. Only if it had been completed could you have entered your house.'

Moral: You must know that the dreams of the prophets are divine revelation. All these events are true. In this *hadis* many points are clear: first, the harshness of the punishment for lies; second, the fate of a learned man who does not act on what he knows; third, the punishment for adultery; fourth, the punishment for usury. May God keep all Muslims safe from these deeds!

S. Khuda Bukhsh

A Patna lawyer, later Chief Justice of Hyderabad State Court, S. Khuda Bukhsh (1842–1908) in his *Essays Indian and Islamic*, lists the many criticisms made against contemporary Muslim society—fanaticism, ignorance, oppression of women—admits they are true, and adds many of his own. He refers with admiration to Hali's poem on the decline of Islam, the *Musaddas*, and regrets that there are no longer sincere leaders such as Sir Sayyid Ahmed and Nawab-ul-Mulk, or saints like Kabir who sought to unite Islam and Hinduism, who can lead Muslims out of the morass. He feels that the main causes of decline are blind acquiescence to the rules that have come down from the past, want of progressive standards, and the neglect of Oriental studies. He helped to repair this last by founding the Oriental Public Library in Patna, a treasure house of books and manuscripts that belonged to his father and to him. But while faulting his fellow-men, he also faults the Hindus who, though ahead of the Muslim community in wealth and learning, are not particularly sympathetic to them.

Khuda Bukhsh recalls his years at Oxford with deep pleasure, says that he admires much in Western civilization, regrets that Indians pick up the worst Western habits rather than the best, but continues to hope that while Indians open themselves to the culture of the West it should not be done at the cost of 'our Eastern individuality'.

𝖐

Thoughts on the Present Situation

POLITICAL

'For each tree is known by its own fruit. For of thorns men do not gather figs, nor of a bramble bush gather they grapes.'—St. Luke vi. 44.

Rightly or wrongly, I have always kept aloof from modern Indian politics, and I have always held that we should devote more attention to social problems and intellectual advancement and less to politics, which,

S. Khuda Bukhsh, *Essays Indian and Islamic*, Delhi: Idarah-i-Adabiyat, 1912, 1977.

in our present condition, is an unmixed evil. I am firmly persuaded that we would consult our interest better by leaving politics severely alone. I am aware that no progress is made in one march or even series of marches, but we must set about it in a proper, practical manner. It is not a handful of men, armed with the learning and culture of the West, but it is the masses that must feel, understand, and take an intelligent interest in their own affairs. The infinitesimal educated minority do not constitute the population of India. It is the masses, therefore, that must be trained, educated, brought to the level of unassailable uprightness and devotion to their country. This goal is yet far beyond measurable reach, but until we attain it, our hopes will be a chimera, and our efforts futile and illusory. Even the educated community have scarcely yet cast off their swaddling clothes of political infancy, or have risen above the illusions of power and the ambitions of fortune. We have yet to learn austerity of principle and rectitude of conduct. Nor can we hope to raise the standard of private and public morality so long as we continue to subordinate the interest of our community and country to our own. India must needs be washed clean of her stains of racial warfare, religious bigotry, narrow prejudices, and must come out fresh-robed in the wedding garment of purity before she can aspire to have fixed, effective politics of her own. There can be no freedom without the spirit of union. But irresponsible political pedlars have filled the country, from one end to the other, with wild, insane speeches which have corrupted the youths of the country, drawing them away from their legitimate occupation to the paths of sedition and anarchy. This false and ignominious system has borne fruit in producing mistrust and disaffection, in exacerbating racial warfare, in destroying personal security, in paralyzing the efforts of commerce and industry. Nothing is more needed than our whole-hearted co-operation with the Government in stamping out, root and branch, this seditious propaganda which, like a network, has overspread the whole country. I do not believe in lip-sympathy or word-coining or phrase-making; nor do I set much value on lengthy speeches consisting of splendid periods and elegant perorations. We must actively support the Government in destroying sedition and anarchy.

Our immediate field of work lies in spheres social, religious, and educational. We must, for the present, banish politics from the programme of our activity. To the problems affecting us most vitally we must turn, with single-minded devotion, and upon these must we concentrate our attention if we are intent upon the advancement of the interest of our community.

Let us, to begin with, make a solemn effort to heal the breach in our own camp; to unite, in loving brotherhood, the two sects—the *Shiahs* and *Sunnis*—divided, as they now are, by envy, malice, hatred, and all uncharitableness. We talk of unity, but we have the barrenness of death and division at home. The fabric of Islam is torn by dissensions, fierce and bitter to a degree; and we sit in our arm-chairs, comfortably and complacently speculating over franchise, self-government, membership of councils, etc.

Long speeches are delivered at educational conferences and Muslim leagues, but not a voice is raised for the restoration of peace, concord, and harmony among our own people, bound by the ties of religion, and linked by the ties of kinship. What a noble sight it is to see the police officers interfere at Moharrum between the followers of the Prophet to prevent a breach of the peace! Does this redound to the credit of our community? I trow not.

Look at the state of affairs a little deeper! What must we say of a society which transforms licentiousness into elegant frailty, and treachery and falsehood into pardonable finesse? Should we not combat, with all our might, these social evils which are sapping the very life and vitality out of our community? Are these not problems calling for attention and solution? I am drawing up (I am only too keenly aware of it) a severe indictment against my own community, but we need have no delicacy any longer if we are to proceed onward. We want no palliatives, but the surgeon's knife to cut the cancer—social cancer—away.

Education may not be the cure for all social evils, but it undoubtedly goes a long way towards regenerating a community. But it is just that which we neglect. It is perfectly painful to consider the number of students—*bona fide* students—who, for sheer want of means, are unable to pursue their studies. I have personally known a number of men in Calcutta who had to discontinue their studies because no one would come forward to help them. If a tithe of the money which the rich wickedly and wantonly waste over their sordid pleasures and marriage festivities were applied to the education of the members of the community, a great number of students would be relieved of their embarrassing position. But there is no society to plead for them; no organized charity to bring relief to them.

The education of women, the elevation of their status, is a question which yields to none in weight and importance. By a kind of tacit prescription they are relegated to the four walls of the *zenana*, steeped in ignorance and superstition. Can a society reach its real stature of progress and development if divested of those soft, refining influences; those heart-subduing graces; those unfailing springs of encouragement and compassion, the exclusive privilege and prerogative of women, and which constitutes life's deepest, holiest joys?

But for *Khadijah's* encouraging counsels, Mohamed would scarcely have been the prophet and law-giver of the Islamic world! But for his mother, Abdullah Ibn Zubair would have died the death of a coward and renegade! Instances might be indefinitely multiplied, but it is a proposition which none would dispute. Bertrand Barere's noble tribute to womanhood will not be out of place here: 'The wives and mothers are the priests of the family. They give their children their first education; they teach them religion and charity; they preserve their purity of heart while stimulating and directing their intelligence. Happy are those whose education has been directed by mothers, who combine the virtues of their sex with studies fit for them. A good mother is the basis of the family; she devotes to it her care and tenderness equally. No one can better know and apply what is necessary to the first stage of life, the physical and moral influence of which is so great on our after-existence....A mother gives her child the first teachings of that Divine religion which emancipated woman, and assigned such a pure, useful, noble, and necessary part in family life to her.'

A great deal of our social evils is due to the condition of our womankind, and so long as we keep them in ignorance we cannot hope to impart to our children those lofty virtues which adorn a civilized and free people.

It is at home that we learn the sense of duty, the sense of unity, the feeling of sympathy and compassion for the poor and suffering, honesty, uprightness, fidelity, and dignity.

We must deserve before we demand. Let us prove ourselves worthy, and everything will come to us. But let us not mistake the twilight for the dawn. Let us proceed, but with slow, cautious steps, improving our social conditions, enlarging our intellectual horizon.

ALLEIN

'Der Frauen Zustand ist beklagenswerth.'—Goethe.

In that supreme masterpiece, 'Iphigenia in Tauris', Goethe makes Iphigenia say: 'Yet truly deserving of lament is woman's lot.' This pathetic, tragic utterance, drawn, as it were, from the deepest depth of despair, Iphigenia supports with a logic at once forcible, trenchant, and convincing. At home an imperious lord to obey and to serve; abroad, a life of utter forlornness to face. Such is the destiny which fate has woven for women; very unlike man, indeed, who

'Rules alike at home and in the field,
Nor is in foreign climes without resource:
Him conquest crowneth, him possession gladdens,
And him an honourable death awaits.
How circumscrib'd is woman's destiny!
Obedience to a harsh, imperious Lord,
Her duty and her comfort, sad her fate,
Whom hostile fortune drives to lands remote.'

From the earliest dawn of history man has asserted a right and dominion over woman, enjoyed advantages and privileges which have been denied to her. This, undoubtedly, has been due to his physical superiority rather than his intellectual eminence. It is only within recent times that women have awakened to their claims and to the assertion of their rights, and this, indeed, all the world over. In England the forward march has been more apparent than elsewhere; but even in the pacific and conservative East women have raised their heads, and have called for their due.

Pierre Loti, in his 'Les Desenchantees', has very truly remarked that among the Turkish women there is a decided spirit of revolt against the severe regime of the harem. But this is as true of India as it is of Turkey. Muslim women are getting educated day by day, and now assert their rights. Though the *purdah* system still prevails, it is no longer that severe, stringent, and unreasonable seclusion of woman which existed fifty years ago. It is gradually relaxing, and women are getting, step by step, rights and liberties which must in course of time end in the complete emancipation of Eastern womanhood.

Forty years ago women meekly submitted to neglect, indifference, and even harsh treatment from their husbands, but such is the case no longer. They claim and, indeed, have succeeded in securing, a decided position in their household (no longer the position of a housekeeper), and cases are not rare of women completely controlling the movements of their husbands, and holding the strings of the purse. Eastern women are by no means now those poor, suffering, patient, and unfortunate creatures whom the missionaries fondly delight in describing as the women of the East. Education, though very imperfect still, is daily gaining ground, and with education new hopes have dawned upon them; and, possibly, the sex question may, in the remote future, become as acute here as it is in the West. The more educated families have done away with the *purdah* altogether, such as the family of Tyyabji in Bombay and that of Mr Syed Ali Belgrami in Hyderabad Deccan. It is not Islam which enjoined the *purdah* system, but as Mr Ameer Ali, in his

'History of the Saracens', points out (p. 199): 'The custom of female seclusion, which was in vogue among the Persians from very early times, made its appearance among the Muslim communities in the reign of Walid II. And the character and habits of the sovereign favoured the growth and development of a practice which pride and imitation had transplanted to the congenial soil of Syria. His utter disregard of social conventionalities, and the daring and coolness with which he entered the privacy of families, compelled the adoption of safeguards against outside intrusion, which once introduced, became sanctified into a custom. *To the uncultured minds, walls and warders appear to afford more effective protection than nobility of sentiment and purity of heart.*' It is incontestible that the improvement in the social status of women, here as elsewhere, is due to a large extent to European influence, which is predominant throughout the East. In the East women have always been regarded as child-bearing machines, and hence they have never risen to that position and eminence in which we find them to-day all over Europe. It is true that the East has produced women of high culture and political insight, but these are exceptions and not the rule; the average woman has always been what we have described, 'a child-bearing machine', devoted solely to domestic affairs. When Haji Baba tells us how he showed himself a true Muslim by his contempt for womankind, he expressed a universal truth openly accepted and publicly avowed in Eastern countries. What is the cause of this low estimate in which women are held? True, European influence has largely alleviated their lot, has considerably widened their outlook on life, has invested them with rights and rescued them from oppression; but to our mind the true emancipation of womankind must indefinitely be put off so long as the system of polygamy flourishes, drawing its sanction from religion.

The author of 'Reforms under Muslim Rule' seeks to make out that polygamy is an institution which Islam does not sanction, but I am not quite sure that he is right. At all events, the unanimity and consensus of opinion is the other way. It may, with growth of education and freedom of women, die out, but the question which we must decide, and that once for all, is whether it is an institution compatible with present-day notions. The question, then, resolves itself into this: Is this institution to be retained or done away with? Is it conducive to the interests of society or otherwise? If the general sense of the Mohamedan world condemns it as pernicious to the stability, happiness, comfort and peace of the family, let it be expunged from our law. If it approves it, retain it by all means. I do not believe in the argument constantly put forward that the conditions which the Qur'an imposes upon its practice are too difficult of realization, and, as such, according to the strict letter of the law, the practice cannot be supported or sustained. But this is no answer to the question raised here. Is the institution *per se* good or bad? Is it beneficial to the interest or subversive of the well-being of society? There can be no two opinions on this point. To our mind the social corruption behind the *zenana* is, to a large extent, due to this system. It is a fruitful source of discord, strife, harassing litigations, the ruin of many wealthy families. Nor can we ignore the fact that it is this system which is responsible, in no small degree, for the degraded view of womanhood current in the East. It is impossible to expect among a polygamous people that exalted idea of wedded life which we would expect, and which we do, as a matter of fact, find among those that are monogamous. Take a European and an Indian home and see the contrast. The wife in the West is a friend, a companion who is never in that mortal terror of a rival to contest or to supplant the affection of her husband in which a wife in the East is. The Eastern wife may at any moment be dislodged by another, and relegated to everlasting sorrow and perpetual gloom. This idea colours the whole life of our women. They are meek and submissive, humble and accommodating, patient and painstaking; but this, in most instances, not by choice, but by compulsion. There is not that relation which is founded upon the equality of rights; that feeling of oneness which the ceremony at the altar at once creates, strengthens and perpetuates. There is not that feeling of fellowship and partnership of two human beings linked together to toil through life's journey, in weather foul or fair, and to remain one unto death in the eye of the law without the darkening shadow of a rival, or a co-wife or a concubine. Hence the supreme difference between a Mohamedan and a Christian marriage. While the former is merely a contractual relation liable to termination at the will and caprice of one of the contracting parties, the other is a deeply religious function, sanctified and consecrated by the Church, and to be severed only by death.

Polygamy and divorce generally go hand in hand. In Eastern Bengal divorce is the order of the day, and wives are put away as we cast off our old clothes. And so also in Egypt and Arabia. No judicial inquiry, no positive proof, not a tittle of evidence of any sort is needed. The lord of creation is invested with the power of divorce, and he makes full and free use of it. Is a high regard and reverence for womankind conceivable under a system such as this? Marriage becomes only one remove from promiscuous intercourse. Its significance, sanctity, importance in domestic life is destroyed, and women become mere instruments to satisfy passion and gratify lust.

Whatever may have been the origin of the *purdah* system, it is clear enough that it is founded in the belief, though not openly confessed yet clear enough, that women cannot be trusted to themselves; that the female sense of virtue, piety arid chastity is too frail and feeble to withstand the temptations of free social intercourse. In no other light is the existence of this system to be explained or justified. I may be charged with drawing a picture of our society in colours far worse than it is; but I am confident that no thoughtful man will disagree with me that these are defects, most vital defects, which we must seriously attempt to remove and set right. The barbarous and wanton waste of money on wedding festivities, the perverse prejudice against widow-marriage, and the equally perverse system of early marriages, are evils too patent to be passed over in silence. Nor shall we omit to point out that iniquitous system, obtaining very largely in Behar, the system of keeping good-looking female servants and a retinue of female slaves who usually give to the children their earliest lessons in vice and immorality.

True, within the last quarter of a century there has been a distinct and pronounced tendency to check these evils, but there is not yet a deliberate, strenuous. persistent effort to destroy them, root and branch. Occasional voices, indeed, do we hear protesting against them, but they fall on unwilling ears. The Muslim societies, in our opinion, should take it upon themselves to grapple with these problems, to arouse an interest in them, to bring home to our people the necessity of united and concerted effort to purify the stream of domestic life and social system.

Sultan Jehan Begum

The first of the Bhopal Begums, Qudsiya Begum (b. 1801), was seventeen when she became the ruler of Bhopal. Though she had grown up in purdah, she discarded it, with the permission of her brothers, who are said to have quoted the example of ancient ruling families to support their approval. The British Political Agent who visited Bhopal in 1854 recorded his astonishment at meeting Qudsiya, her daughter Sikander and grandaughter Shah Jahan, all out of purdah, though Shah Jahan was seventeen, and unmarried. After she was married, however, Shah Jahan's husband insisted on purdah for her, much to the annoyance of Sikander Begum. Sultan Jehan Begum (1858–1930) had been critical of her mother for remaining in purdah, at the insistence, Sultan Jehan thought, of her mother's second husband. But she herself became a strong advocate of purdah, as her book on the subject indicates. She felt that Indian women should not go the way of Western women who were far too free. She herself sat behind a screen while giving orders to or listening to her ministers. While on tour she wore a burqua.

Nevertheless, she made various kinds of provisions for purdah women, such as special clubs and gardens, and in the matter of education for women was particularly enlightened.

Introduction

The problem of the seclusion of women is one of the most important and serious questions that have been engaging the thought and attention of the Islamic world for the last thirty or forty years. It has been discussed and debated much more vehemently in countries which have, to a large extent, come under the influence of western civilization than anywhere else. Among such countries, Turkey, Egypt, and India deserve special mention where, with the dawn of the new era and the spread of new

Sultan Jehan Begum, *Al Hijab or the Necessity of Purdah*, Calcutta: Thacker Spink and Co., 1922.

learning, the education of women has also received considerable attention, along with other national reform movements; and, as a part of the
greater question affecting their rights, education and position in society,
the question of their seclusion has also come under discussion, and
divided the people into three distinct groups:

(1) Those who are totally opposed to the seclusion of women;
(2) those who wish to lessen the hardships of Purdah by modifying it
    according to *their* interpretation of the religious injunctions; and
(3) those who want to retain the Purdah System in its entirety and
    consider any modification in the system as dangerous for national
    honour and repugnant to the spirit of the Islamic Law.

There is a very sharp difference of opinion among men belonging to
these groups, which is frequently expressed in newspapers, magazines,
periodicals and books. Each group tries to bring round the other to its
own way of thinking by defeating the arguments of its opponent; and this
has now gone on for a long time past in the Islamic world.

India, too, is in the throes of this controversy. Its influence has
penetrated even the seclusion of Muslim homes. Certain families seem
to be inclined towards breaking with the Purdah System. Many educated
Muslim ladies have begun to regard their seclusion as an imprisonment.
While among those women who do not think so themselves, the authority of their liberty-loving husbands is being brought to bear upon them to
discard Purdah. The evil has not yet become common even in the
sections of society affected by these ideas; still, certain families have
given up the veil in favour of modern show and fashion, and I wish these
emancipated ladies had utilized to some good purpose their newly
adopted freedom and, like their western sisters, worked for the material
welfare of their people. They should have opened and worked schools;
or studied medicine and served their less enlightened sisters. If they had
diverted their energies to some such work of public good, the evil would
have possessed at least some redeeming feature: but I do not find a single
instance of this among the 'progressive' section of our society to-day. So
I look upon this change with great concern and anxiety; and consider it
as the harbinger of our national downfall and religious degradation. I do
not hold this view because it is a part of my religious belief but I have
come to this conclusion as the result of much anxious thought and deep
meditation, and after an elaborate study of the subject from books and a
careful observation of the conditions I witnessed during my travels
abroad.

A great portion of my life has been spent in thinking over the important and grave problems touching the welfare of my own sex; and the most interesting and important among them are the education and seclusion of women. I have expressed my views on education publicly, on more than one occasion, and have tried, to the best of my ability, to encourage the same in my sex. But I had few occasions to speak about the Purdah system. On my return from Europe, in 1911, I delivered a speech, at the local Ladies' Club, in which while narrating the story of my travels and speaking in very high terms of the civilization and culture of Europe and the advancement of its women, I also happened to say:

'In spite of their education I am not in favour of the freedom enjoyed by women of the West where it has passed certain well-defined lines. Our uneducated and even educated sisters in the Purdah cannot even imagine such a freedom. It is possible that the liberty enjoyed by the women of Europe is suited to the conditions prevailing there; or that it is permitted by the teachings of the Christian Faith, but for Indian and especially Muslim ladies, I think such freedom can, under no circumstances, and at no time, be proper. We must, therefore, always act upon the old adage, *'Khuz ma safa wa da ma kadir'*, i.e. 'take the good and discard the evil'. Musalman women should never hanker after greater freedom than has been granted them by their religion; a freedom, which, while permitting them the fullest enjoyments of their rights, also shields them against all manner of evil.'

Since then I made up my mind to write a book on the Purdah System; and began collecting materials for it. I also felt that a study of the works of the divines of Islam alone would not answer my purpose, so, I decided to consult the publications of Western writers also who have come to some definite conclusion after thinking about the freedom of the women of their countries and published the results of their thoughts for the careful consideration of their countrymen.

I have met many missionary ladies, of great fame and virtue, who have consecrated their lives to the service of their religion. A cursory glance on their mode of life shows how very near, in certain aspects of life, they approach the saintly ladies of Islam. They dress themselves in a manner which does not expose any part of their body; and then, how simple is their dress! Embellishment and adornment are foreign to them. Especially, the Roman Catholic nuns, living in convents, or nunneries, are constrained by the rules of their community from mixing with the members of the male sex, nor are they permitted to marry. Although from the Muslim view-point, celibacy is as objectionable as mixing freely of the two sexes, still their manner of living clearly shows that the commandments of Christianity are opposed to too promiscuous intercourse of men and women; and that Christian tradition and conscience look with disfavour on the free exhibition of beauty and adornment in women. The religious bodies have kept themselves always aloof from the false freedom prevailing at present among the women of Europe. I have also had opportunities of conversing with many self-respecting Europeans belonging to higher walks of life and have invariably found them dissatisfied with, and complaining against, the unchecked freedom prevailing in their community and whose pious prayer is to see the institution of Purdah introduced in their countries.

Having collected all books and other materials bearing on the point I went through the whole subject carefully. Some matters in these books are discussed with such frankness and directness, and evils of freedom of women exposed in such a manner, that no woman who possesses an iota of Islamic virtue and modesty would condescend to peruse them, much less republish them as extracts, in her work. But since the toleration of a small evil for a greater good is an accepted human principle, I deemed it my solemn duty to leave such a book behind me, for the guidance of my sisters-in-faith, who out of their profound regard for me, hold me up as a model for others, in the hope that when they think of freedom, they my be warned in time, from its perusal.

I, therefore, ordered the translators in my office to put before me only such reviews and articles as were of comparatively less offensive nature; so that I may carefully go through them. In spite of all these precautions a good many of these had to be rejected as unfit for publication. I have, however, selected some typical passages and given extracts from these, in the succeeding chapters, as samples of [the] social condition obtaining in the West.

I have also, whenever suitable, drawn on excellent books written in Arabic, on this subject, by the *savants* of our own day, in Egypt, in which they have given expression to their views quite freely and openly.

I should like to mention here that the facts given in this volume are not intended to disparage or lower the reputation and honour of any country, or to deny the high qualities of the Western people, which have raised the standard of their material civilization so high, and are the main cause of their worldly superiority and greatness to-day. Neither is it intended to run down any particular civilization, organization or society. My sole object is to establish the superiority of Islamic injunctions regarding the retention of Purdah among women, as compared with the evil effects of the non-existence of this wholesome institution, and the license enjoyed by women, in other societies. I readily admit that in countries where women observe Purdah the evil consequences of their uncontrolled freedom are [not] entirely absent. But we are here concerned with the question of the excessive and the scarce, the normal and the abnormal. There are greater chances of evil in freedom than in seclusion. Doctor Le Bon also admits this, when he says:

'What is abnormal in the East is normal in the West'.

For fear of robbers and thieves men keep their precious things in underground cellars and secure their hoardings in strong-rooms. Yet robberies and thefts do occur. Yet it does not follow that we should become careless about our valuables; and give up all precaution.

It is clear that the Commandment of God regarding Purdah that, 'O! Thou Prophet! Speak to thy wives and to thy daughters, and to the women of the faithful, that they draw their wrappers over them. That is nearer for them to be known, and they will not be affronted. And God is Forgiving and Compassionate,' (Sura xxxiii, Ayat 59)[1] was revealed to our Prophet because we women used to be insulted and molested by men. But similar conditions prevail even to-day, and shall endure, so long as the two sexes co-exist in this world. It is sometimes contended that the present is not the age in which man would do deliberate injury to women. But harm can be done in several ways. Injury may be inflicted by means of deceit, fraud, or seduction and, what injury can be more heinous than the complete and total ruin of the entire future of a woman?

The former type of crime, i.e., injury by force, can perhaps be checked by the laws of the realm, but the latter kind can only stopped by the moral and unwritten code of society. When the laws of the realm are silent on this point, what other remedy is better suited to the purpose than the seclusion of the weaker sex; a seclusion so perfect in its way as was practised by the 'Mothers of the Faithful', the wives of the holy Prophet, the following of whose example is incumbent on every daughter of Islam.

I concede, that after the glorious days of the Prophet the injunctions about the seclusion of women became rather strict; but it was never intended to lower the status of women. As the circle of Islam grew wider and wider, it came increasingly in contact with different civilizations, creeds, thoughts and convictions; wealth and prosperity increased in Muslim countries. Islamic culture advanced and became complex, with the result that the possibilities of social evil and disintegration also multiplied. Greater strictness therefore became necessary, in order to guard against the dangers that threatened Muslim society.

There is such a thing as 'piety' recognized in Islam as well as by all human beings. 'Piety' means restraint from every such thought and deed as is likely to do some material or spiritual harm to anybody. When society reaches a stage where all manner of sin and evil are found in it; when the difference between lawful and unlawful perilously reaches a vanishing point; 'when the distinction between acts allowed and forbidden almost disappears; when music and dancing and free intercourse between men and women in public places is openly tolerated; when men and women, boys and girls sit shoulder to shoulder and side by side in theatres and cinemas where scenes violating the sense of decency and modesty are exhibited on the screen and the stage; when fashion and the demands of high life are on the increase daily; when social temptations multiply and 'wants create more wants' almost every day, and the law of the realm be so mild that in the infringement of certain extreme cases (where Islam inflicts 100 lashes, in the case of an unmarried person, and, orders stoning to death, in that of a married one)—if it punishes the particular offence with only two years' imprisonment at most, and that also, in the latter case, when the husband institutes proceedings; and when a husband goes to court for the restitution of his conjugal rights, the Highest Court of the realm lays down that:

'In these days of progress and civilization no woman should be compelled to live with a husband she does not like.' At times like this, I ask, what will be the predicament of the women following a religion in which chastity and modesty are held in the highest esteem, and in which, even to look at the faces of men, and to talk to them in private or to expose their charms is strictly forbidden, and in which according to the saying of the saintly Ali, the very modesty of women should be secluded? Is it possible I ask, for those women who have discarded *Purdah* to act according to the Commandment as laid down in ('La yubdina zinatahunna') 'do not show your beauty and grace'; and would it be possible for them not to adorn and embellish themselves when they go out on business, or for their drives and joy-rides? And how can men be compelled not to look at them?

It should also be borne in mind at this stage that punitive laws alone, however hard they may be, can never be an effective safeguard for the chastity of women.

Ancient Rome too has passed through such a period when the punishment for social sins of this nature was that both the culprits were bound together and thrown into the fire, and yet this was the very period when immorality had reached its highest point in Rome. The Pentateuch has laid down stoning as the punishment for this crime. Christianity too adopted this law and did not repeal it: 'He that is without sin among you let him first cast a stone at her.' (Dr Moffat's Translation.)

At the present day in Canada the crime is punishable with stripes and imprisonment, with hard labour for five years; and, in some special cases, with penal servitude for life. But as the country also permits absolute freedom to both sexes, the object of this law is not attained. Since Islam is the most perfect of all religions, it kept intact the punishment enjoined in the code of Moses on the one hand, and provided against the recurrence of causes of such immorality on the other; and it must be admitted that there cannot be a better method of reaching the goal in view. If men and women do not get opportunities of free social intercourse and their places of enjoyment and recreation are kept apart, if women are stopped from going to theatres and public shows, and if evil-minded men get no chance whatsoever to tease them; also if adultery be recognized in the criminal law of the country, as one of the capital offences punishable with death, like murder, then and then only, can women be permitted to content themselves with mere veils. But so long as other conditions prevail, our ladies should strictly adhere to the injunction: 'Abide in your own homes.'

The following extract from a book: 'Hamari Mushkilat', written by a *Hindoo lady, Chand Rani* deserves out serious attention:

'Many of our brethren regard the Purdah System as an evil, and are making attempts to abolish it. But the existence of the Purdah System shall remain a necessity so long as our men do not purify their hearts.'

It is possible that such a time may come; but it can come only when men and women are as pure as angels, and then this world is changed into a paradise.

In truth, seclusion of women is fundamentally connected with that modesty and self-respect which are the means of guarding honour and good fame of a family. Modesty is the chief and distinctive attribute of human beings, and for a man, it is the essence of all that is brave and chivalrous in him. A portion of this quality has been bestowed by Providence upon certain animals also with the result that a male never tolerates separation from its mate or the presence of another of his own sex, in his domain! Man is the last word in the evolution of God's creation and consequently his share of modesty should be commensurate with his exalted position. Where Islam has ordered women to live within the four walls of their homes, not to mix freely with the other sex; it has, on the other hand, given them such legal rights and privileges as are not enjoyed by the women of even the most civilized and advanced countries, in spite of their having attained to the highest pinnacles of social and political glory, and which are envied by the leaders and reformers of other communities. It is a fact worth noting that the women of the West, notwithstanding the recommendations and support of great commissions and the persistent demand of their societies, have not yet won those rights which Islam accorded to its women-folk, more than thirteen centuries ago. Let us grant, for the sake of argument, that Purdah is only another name for imprisonment, even then these rights so far outweigh this restriction, that liberty itself might very well feel jealous of it. If these rights are fully granted then women could never have cause to complain of any physical or spiritual privation, and her mind would ever remain fresh and happy as the beautiful flowers of spring. Such conditions do generally obtain in all good families, and where they do not exist, the reasons for it are either violent disagreement in the temperaments of the husband and wife or the ill-temper of one of them.[2] Hundreds of incidents bear testimony to the fact that the peaceful and calm life spent by a Muslim lady, inside her home, is never the share of her sister in the civilized West. The domestic happiness and peace of mind which a Muslim lady generally derives in her own home are seldom found in those countries where outwardly total freedom is granted to women. Here, in the East, the husband or other male members of the family are the bread-winners; while there, in the West, a large portion of the female world has to suffer unmentionable hardships for the sake of earning a livelihood, the very idea of which is painful.

It is said that women here, in Purdah, suffer in health but there, in the bracing climate and open air, conditions are still worse. The real fact is that in both hemispheres the real causes of bad health are the same, and they are generally neglect of the first principles of sanitation and insufficient and unwholesome food. With all her freedom, woman, in the West, has fallen so low that she is described as the root cause of all immorality and crime, and men hurl imprecations and anathemas on her head. In the East, on the contrary, she is an innocent spirit in the seclusion of her home. To quote a Western lady:[3]

The seclusion of Moslem women, instead of being, as is generally assumed, a result of their 'degraded position', is on the contrary, the outcome of the great respect and regard entertained for them by the men of their own nation.

She is the personification of honour and virtue. The more we study history and the deeper we investigate the causes of the existing conditions of to-day, the more we shall be forced to the conclusion that all moral evils can be traced to the free and unnecessary intercourse of the two sexes. The ordinary sort of education imparted to her now-a-days generally does not, and cannot, stop these evils; on the contrary it lends a helping hand to them. Facts and figures conclusively prove that in the countries where, along with the freedom of women, education is comparatively general, cases of immorality are, as a rule, greater. That is to say, this excessive liberty has changed even the antidote into poison.

It is sometimes vehemently asserted that Purdah is a great obstacle to all progress and advancement of women; but we have first to determine the object and the standard of advancement of women, and to fix the stage at which they become entitled to be called 'advanced' and 'civilized'.

In western thought, we find that[4]:

'The whole idea of women's position in social life, and their ability to take their place, independently of any question of sex, in the work of the world, was radically changed in the English-speaking countries, and also in the more progressive nations beyond their bounds, during the nineteenth century. This is due primarily to the movement for women's higher education and its results. To deal in detail with this movement in various countries would here be too intricate a matter; but in the English-speaking countries at all events the change is so complete that the only curious thing now is, not what spheres women may not [sic] enter, more or less equally with men, but the few from which they are still excluded....

The temperate, calm, earnest demeanour of women, both in the schools and in university life, awakened admiration and respect from all; and the movement brought into existence a vast number of women, as well educated as men, hardworking, persevering and capable who invaded many professions, and could hold their ground where a sound education was the foundation of success....

In the literary field they soon invaded journalism, and took an important place on the staffs of libraries and museums....They form an important section of the teaching profession in the state schools....Women have long practised law in the United States. In France an Act was passed enabling women to practise as barristers. In Finland and Norway women have long practised as barristers and in Denmark they have been admitted as assistants to lawyers. By the law of the Netherlands they are admitted as notaries....It is not possible for every woman to be a scholar, a doctor, a lawyer, or possibly to attain the highest position in professions where competition with men is keen, but the development of women's work has opened many other outlets for their energies. As members of school-boards, factory inspectors, poor law guardians, sanitary inspectors, they have had ample scope for gratifying their ambition and energy. The progress made in philanthropy and religious activity is largely due to their devotion, under the auspices of countless new societies. And increasing provision has been made, in the arts and crafts, for the furtherance of their careers. There are successful women architects; a large number of women travel for business firms; in decorative work, as silversmiths, dentists, law copyists, proof readers, and in plan tracing, women work with success; wood carving has become almost as recognised a career for them as that of typewriting and shorthand, in which an increasing number are finding employment. Agriculture and gardening have opened up a new field of work, and, with it, kindred occupations. Women have always found a peculiarly fitting sphere as nurses, but their admission to the medical profession itself was one of the earliest triumphs of the nineteenth century movement.'

The above refers to the social and economic progress woman has made. Her political status has been thus described[5]:

'Women in England may fill some of the highest positions in the State. Among the public offices a woman may hold, are those of county, borough, parish and rural or urban district councillor, overseer, guardian of the poor, churchwarden and sexton. She can vote in county council, municipal, poor law and other local elections. The granting of the parliamentary franchise to women was, however, still withheld in 1910.'

But now, as all the world knows, Women's Suffrage movement has obliged the Government to do away with that restriction also.

Commission after Commission has sat to investigate her position and status and Bill after Bill has been brought forward to improve her condition. Some of these efforts have succeeded while others have failed and certain measures are still under consideration.

But the backward progress that has followed this material advancement can be gauged only after a perusal of the painful revelations which have created such a great sensation in the civilised world of the West and which are engaging the deep and serious attention of the thinkers and reformers of those countries. They are now lamenting over the position given to the members of the weaker sex in the political and social life of the country, in consequence of which woman takes her share in every department of human activity and works shoulder to shoulder with man, in the most unrestrained manner.

Dr. Le Bon says:

According to this creed, woman demands equal rights and treatment similar to man, and she forgets the difference which exists in the mental capacities of the two sexes. But if she succeeds in her object, there will remain neither home nor family for men in Europe.

As opposed to this, the meaning and object of the progress of woman in Islam, is that she should perform the duties natural to her, as has been explained by the Holy Qur'an—'And one of His signs is that He created mates for you from yourselves that you may find quiet of mind in them, and He put between you love and compassion; most surely there are signs in this for a people who reflect' (Sura Rum). She should be the means of comfort to her husband. She should bring up and train the children. She should make her home an abode of peace and rest for her husband, and the male members of the family; and she should be always ready in time of need, to undergo hardships and suffer privations. She should be a bright example of chastity, courtesy and piety, and above all she should be a living personification of righteousness, adorned with modesty and bashfulness.

Now, I ask, can a woman, taking active part in the bustle of social and political life of the present day, attain to this ideal? Is it possible for her to become an advocate, a solicitor, a clerk, an inspectress, or to work in the many departments of active service now open to her, and still be what has been said about her? Is it within the bounds of possibility for her to enter into electioneering campaigns and discharge her domestic duties also, or to have free intercourse with members of the other sex and guard herself against its evil consequences, by overcoming her natural weakness?

It should also be kept in mind that no intelligent human being will ever tolerate such restrictions and limitations as retard human progress, whether they affect only one sex or both of them. Islam claims to have revealed to the world the hopeful message of human progress, material and spiritual, and to have granted the two sexes the rights which open for each the paths to liberty and advancement. How could it, therefore, be possible that any of its commandments should come in the way of progress? Islam would have remained imperfect had it not paid due regard to human nature. But, because Islam is Nature itself, all its commandments and injunctions are based on the Laws of Nature. It is an admitted fact that the natures of the two sexes, male and female, are quite distinct from each other; therefore, their natural duties and functions in this life are poles apart. Consequently, the laws and rules for each sex are based on this divergence of natures. And finally, with the existence of this natural difference in the sexes, it is but obvious that the meaning and import of the word 'progress' and 'advancement', when used with reference to men and women, cannot be identical.

It is self-evident that when God has divided humanity into two sections, the very division is proof positive that He must have marked out different fields of activity for each sex. For the physically stronger of the two, the field is larger and wider, and for the weaker it is proportionally smaller, and more restricted. It is incumbent on the weaker sex that it should not step beyond the limits of its own sphere of activity in order that the discharge of its primary and natural duties in life may not be interfered with, and that it may be kept guarded against evil influences, fraught with misery, to domestic life. This is the *raison d'etre* of the Purdah System; and this is what the reformers of Europe and America have been yearning for.

...

The Opinions of Muslim Jurists and Divines Regarding Purdah

If to-day we wish to explain how it first occurred to man to cover his body with some kind of dress, and to what extent such covering was thought necessary for the male and the female, we shall not be able to assign any sufficient reason for it. Similarly, we cannot account for other distinctive features to be observed between man and woman. Consequently, it is futile for us to try to fix the exact date when these prehistoric distinctions arose; and to trace their causes and reasons. On the other hand, to investigate what took place during historic times would not be improper and out of place. Purdah can be divided into two kinds:

(1) Covering of the face and all the limbs of the body.
(2) Not joining the assemblies and society of men.

Purdah of the former type already used to be observed in Arabia before the advent of Islam; and the system was adopted a mostly owing to natural needs. At the time when this kind of Purdah began to be observed it was not peculiar to women alone, but was observed by men as well. Perhaps, this custom first came into vogue in the tribe of Himyar, which had its home in Yaman, and ruled over the country. A branch of this tribe established a small principality in Spain, called the *'Mulassameen'*. This family ruled the country with great vigour, and showed much prowess on battlefields by winning many a hard-fought battle. Now, men of this tribe used to keep their faces veiled, and that is why they were called *'Mulassameen'*. A member of this family, Yusuf bin Tashqeen, became a very powerful and renowned monarch. The great scholar, Ibne-Khallakan, explaining the philology of this term says that:

The reason of this is, that the people of the tribe of Himyar used to cover their faces with veils, both in winter and summer, to protect them from the inclemency of weather. At first the custom was confined to the nobles only, but gradually the whole tribe adopted it.

The learned scholar also assigns a further reason for the adoption of this custom. Whenever the men of the tribe Himyar used to leave their houses on some business, an unfriendly tribe used to attack their homes and carry away their womenfolk. When they got tired of this, the Himyarites planned a ruse. On a certain day their women put on men's clothes and went out, and the men remained inside the houses, with veils on. The enemy, as usual, made the attack. These veiled men then rushed out and fought very gallantly and killed their enemy. The victors began to veil their faces in memory of the success which they obtained over their enemies on that day, with the help of the veil. Even after the advent of Islam the men and women of this tribe kept their faces veiled. In his description of this custom a poet of the period uses the following words:

When these people had gathered together all the good qualities unto themselves, modesty got the mastery over them, so they covered their faces with veils.

Certain other accidental reasons have also been the cause of the establishment of this custom. For example, the handsome and the good-looking among men, in order to protect themselves from the malignant consequences of an evil eye, used to go out with veils drawn over their faces. This custom was not confined to Pre-Islamic times; we find instances in the Islamic period also. For this very reason *Maqna Kindi*, the famous Poet of the Umaiyaid period, used to put on a veil whenever he went out of his house. The custom spread gradually and people began to go to large gatherings with veiled faces. Men, as a rule, used to go with covered faces to the great market at Ūkāz where, for their feats of minstrelesy, the Poets of Arabia usually received encouragement from the applause of the people.

Allama Ahmad Ibn-e-Abee-Yaqoob, a very old historian, writes in his book that:

The people of Arabia used to assemble in the fair of Ūkāz; and veils covered their faces. It is reported that the first Arab who discontinued the practice was Zareef, the son of Ghanam; thereafter others followed his example.

There must have existed special reasons for the adoption of Purdah at particular periods, but it was based mainly on two causes:

(1) Self-protection, such as has been described in the incident of the tribe of Himyar where the rich and the poor alike had begun to use the veil. But, in other tribes, the custom was confided to the chiefs and elders only because such love of ease and fashion are peculiar to the rich alone.

By and by reasons of necessity disappeared and people began to use the veil, with or without reason, merely because it was the special and distinquishing piece of apparel of the nobility.

(2) The idea of superiority and distinction.

It took sometime to work out this idea in the earlier period of the *history* of Arabia. At first the Arabs used to live quite a simple and democratic life, in uniform style; but soon, with the advance of civilisation, differences and distinctions began to appear in Arabian society. The foremost among these distinctions was the adoption of a system of Diwan-i-Khas so that the assemblies of the chiefs and the elders should not become the general meeting place of the whole tribe. Thus we find that even in Pre-Islamic days the offices of doorkeepers and guards had been created, and free access had begun to be denied to the common people at the gates of kings and chiefs of the tribes. By and by this custom took such deep root that even when the king held a public Durbar his person was kept veiled from the public gaze, and so some of the Arabian kings are known to have used veils over their faces with this very idea.

And, finally, we find the person of the king being entirely veiled from the sight of the people. For a long time during the Abbaside period the rule obtained that the Khalifa used to sit behind a screen and all royal decrees were issued from behind this Purdah; and this custom seems to be derived from Arabian kings using veils over their faces.

Thus it will be seen that at the time of its origin the custom of Purdah was not peculiar to women alone. But men could not keep it up for long. So when Zareef bin Ghanam threw off the veil at Ūkāz, the men of Arabia gladly followed his example. Thereafter if any one used a veil over his face for pleasure or pride, it was considered as opposed to prevailing custom. Veils were, however, used by women till the advent of Islam; Islam elaborated rules and regulations for, and appointed the degrees of observance of Purdah, and made the system compulsory for women.

No one who has studied with care the Pre-Islamic history or Arabia can deny these facts, but as the common belief prevails that the custom of observing Purdah among women began with Islam, we shall now produce copious and conclusive evidence to prove that it did obtain even before the advent of Islam.

The best and most approved means of getting at the authentic facts about the observance of Purdah during Pre-Islamic days are the poems of the Arabian poets of that period. We now proceed to give numerous extracts from these poems in support of our contention.

Rabee-bin-Ziad-I'sa, a famous poet of the Pre-Islamic days, in an elegy on *Malik-ibn-e-Zubair* says:

May he who has felt happy at the assassination of *Malik*, see the faces of our women in day time. He will see them lamenting Malik's tragic end with their heads uncovered, and beating their faces with both their hands in the morning.

Our women always used to cover their faces with a veil, because of their modesty; but to-day, contrary to their custom, they appear before the people unveiled.

In his commentaries on the Chapter on *'Habiliments'*, Allámá Tabrizi writes that they used to hide their faces for reasons of chastity and bashfulness.

Amr-Ma'd-i-Karab in describing a hard contested battle says:

When the face of Lemais became uncovered it seemed as if the full moon had appeared on the horizon.

It should be noted that *Amr-Ma'd-i-Karab* was a *'Mukhazrami'* poet, that is to say, he lived to the days of Islam also, but the above couplet was written before the spread of Islam.

Another poet of the same time, *Seerat-bin-Umar-Faqáll,* in a satire on his enemies, says:

The faces of your women-folk became uncovered during the battle; hence they appeared as slave-girls although they were ladies.

Naabigha Zubyani, a renowned poet of the Days of Ignorance, was a courtier and a great favourite of *Nu'maan bin Munzir*. Once the poet went on a visit to *Nu'maan*. The queen *Mutajarreda*, was sitting by the side of the king. On *Naabigha's* sudden appearance, Mutajarreda hurriedly got up and let fall the covering of her head, in her confusion. At once she hid her face with her hands. This action of *Mutajarreda* greatly pleased Naabigha; and he has eulogised this event in a 'Qaseeda', where he depicts the incident in the following couplets:

Scarf fell down, but she did not let it fall intentionally. She bravely tried to retain the long veil on her head and face, and she delicately hid her face with her hands.

Another poet, by name *Auf,* in describing how, owing to the intensity of hunger, the women came out and sat in the open air near the ovens, where the food was being cooked, says:

They were sitting near the fire keeping watch, and the girls of the tribe were feeding it. Their faces were uncovered, there was no veil on them. and whenever the fire went out they rekindled it.

The fact is that the people of Arabia had made much progress in the matter of dress even in the Days of Ignorance. It is true that refinement was to be noticed only among the wealthier classes and the elders of the tribes; still, in whatever circle it was found, it showed considerable taste and choice, in the domain of dress. Even in those days, a lady's wardrobe contained several sorts of clothing designed for dress and general wear which were quite sufficient to cover every part of the body. A proper sense of Dignity and Pride of position in life were mainly responsible for the various styles of dress worn by the nobility; and that was why common people were denied the use of such distinctive dress. So far as our researches go in the matter, we find that the Ummaiyyads and the Abbasides could not improve appreciably upon the cut and style of the dress worn by the Pre-Islamic women. In other words, no further style of dress was added to those already in existence for the use of women of by-gone-days. This establishes the fact that even in Pre-Islamic days the idea of keeping their womenkind in Purdah, and seeing them decently and elegantly dressed, had laid hold of the minds of men in Arabia.
...

Religious Exception to the Rule of Purdah

As it is my wish to place before the reader all I know about Purdah, that as far as possible, nothing be left out from what has to be said in this connection, I deem it necessary here to mention the fact that there are also certain exceptions to the rule of observing Purdah, which is allowed by our holy religion, which having taken into consideration the needs and requirements of our daily life, has laid down definite directions that in certain unavoidable and urgent cases, a woman may lawfully expose certain parts of her body, to the view of a stranger. I do not wish to make any authoritative pronouncement of my own on this point. I shall merely content myself with quoting the summary of the observations made by the renowned Imam Razi in this matter in his famous 'Tafseer-e-Kabeer':

'In case of any real and lawful necessity, it is quite permissible for a man to see a woman, provided there be no danger of disturbance or any sort of evil thereupon. He can do so under the following conditions:

Firstly, if a man wishes to marry a woman, it is lawful for him to have a look at the woman's face; and also he can see that palms of her hands. It is reported through Hazrat Aboo Huraira that a companion wanted to marry an Ansar woman, whereupon the Prophet bade him, "see her once, since they generally had some defect in their eyes". The Prophet is also reported to have once observed as follows:

(1) Whoever among you makes a proposal of marriage, it is not sinful for him to see the face of the girl, provided it is done with the intention of getting engaged to her. Mugheera-ibn-e-Shuba has reported that when he got engaged to a woman the Prophet inquired whether he had seen her. On receiving the answer in the negative the Prophet said: "See her, so that mutual affection be created in your hearts."

(2) If a person wishes to buy a slave-girl he can see those portions of her body only, which she can legally uncover before strangers.

(3) It is permitted to look at the face of a woman carefully, only when a man is bargaining for her or entering into any business transaction with her, so that he may recognise her in case of necessity.

(4) It is lawful to look at a woman when she is giving evidence, but only at her face; because identification is possible by means of the face alone.

(5) A medical man, of pure heart, is permitted to look at a woman, if it is necessary for him to do so.

(6) In courts of law, if it is required to see any portion of the body of a woman, it is allowed by law to do so.

(7) If a woman's life is in danger either by fire or water, it is allowed to look at her in trying to save her.'

(Tafseer-e-Imam Razi, Vol. VI, Egyptian Edition, pp. 375–6.)

RESULTS OF NON-OBSERVANCE OF PURDAH

The laws and restrictions laid down by Islam, for Muslim women, in connection with Purdah, and the modern desire to break with the Purdah System in the minds of some men, compel us to investigate, with the utmost care and attention, the causes and effects of this movement; so that the supporters, as well as the opposers of the system, may know which party is in the right, so far as the results are concerned. Really speaking the opposition to Purdah does not spring from any desire to secure the much talked of educational and moral advantages of the community. The real cause lies in the desire to imitate European manners and customs. Man naturally loves to imitate in every way those whom he finds in a higher and more exalted position that himself.

...

In Egypt 10 million out of the 12 million inhabitants are followers of the Prophet Mohommad, and to understand at all the Eastern woman one must learn something of the religion that dominates the entire life of the

Mohommedan. The actions of the Moslem woman, whether in India, Arabia, Egypt, Persia, or Algiers, are controlled and forced to comply with the laws made by the Arabian Prophet of the seventh century, and even to-day his word practically governs each act of the domestic life as well as the world outside the home.

An Egyptian woman, from the time when she is seven or eight years old, never shows her face unveiled to any man except her father, her brother, or her husband. No chance is given the followers of the Arabian Prophet to have the little flirtations that are so dear to the heart of many of her Western sisters.

This seclusion does not rest heavily upon the Mohommadan woman, as she considers it the desire of her husband to protect her and she would be the first to resent the breaking of her seclusion as showing that she had lost value in his eyes.

Women are not prisoners in any sense of the word, nor are they pining behind their latticed windows, as we are sometimes led to believe by writers of fiction. They visit freely amongst each other, and their visits are not confined to the passing of a few senseless platitudes that generally mark conversation of Western women making afternoon calls upon each other. They do not 'call', they go for a visit of several hours or even days.

'The Eastern woman loves perfumes and prefers them much stronger than we of the Western world think agreeable.'

In Ceylon, Mrs. Abdul Hamid Le Mesurier says:

The custom of keeping wives indoors is to protect them from insult and not, as is popularly supposed, to make them servile....I think the lot of the Muhammadan woman is far happier than her sister in England, because she can obtain divorce, if ill-treated. (H. Cyclo. Page 939.)

The American Cyclopedia, discussing the life of women in Persia, although adversely criticizing some of the aspects of life, admits that:

Among the great mass of the people, a man has rarely more than one wife, and the condition of the women seems to be easy and comfortable. The ladies of the upper class lead an idle, luxurious, monotonous life. Contrary to the common opinion of Christendom, they enjoy abundant liberty, more, perhaps, than the same class in Europe....Women of the higher class frequently acquire a knowledge of reading and writing, and become familiar with the works of the chief Persian Poets. These, however, are the best aspects of female life in Persia.

Gustav le Bon, author of the '*Civilization des Arabies*', writes:

Great misconceptions exist in the minds of Europeans generally about the harems of the East. They think of the harem as an abode of luxury and voluptuousness, where oppressed and imprisoned women lead lives of indolence; and lament over their fates. It has been fully demonstrated how far this is from the truth. European women, who have had opportunities of visiting these harems, have been greatly surprized at seeing the love shown by the women inside these harems towards their husbands; and the attention paid by them to the training of their children and the management of their households. They are happy and contented in their secluded state; and would resent to exchange it with that of their European sisters. They sincerely sympathise with, and regret the lot of, their sisters in Europe who have to suffer physical hardships and the miseries of life. On the other hand, the women of the East have no other occupation, but the management of their households; and in their own eyes and those of their husband's, this occupation is the only suitable one for women. Eastern people look upon the people of Europe, who force their women to enter into trade and industries, and to take part in active life, with the same feelings with which we would look upon the person who yoked a race horse to a plough or a mill. To them the main function of a woman is to make the life of her husband happy and to educate her children. They can never believe that it is possible for women, engaged in other occupations, to discharge this function satisfactorily. Men are generally influenced by the nation whose civilization they have seen with their own eyes; and for this very reason in this matter my own ideas are unquestionably in full agreement with the Eastern nations.

The Observer of Lahore published in 1906 a series of articles on the questions of the education of women. During the course of this series the writer produced extracts from the writings of a Musalman and an American, on domestic life. It would be interesting to reproduce them here for comparison. The picture drawn from the viewpoint of the Musalman was as follows:

Let us now compare the life at present passed by Western Muhammadan women when they are not endowed with Western civilization with that of their Western sisters. In the words of a member of this advanced body, the domestic life of a Muslim woman is thus related: 'She is the mistress of her home, quite free and happy in her limited surroundings. Her little children are the bright angels and joys of her existence. She takes a heavenly delight in attending them, often sings them songs, and finds time fly quickly in their society. Her daughters rise early, offer their prayers to God, and read a Chapter of the Qur'an, before they take up the round of their domestic duties. Indian women excel their European sisters at needlework. Their household duties done, they pay or receive calls from their friends. The evenings they spend in the society of their husbands, to whom after the day's toil the calm of home is delightful. To the Muslim woman, her husband is everything; her soul and life are wedded to his. She does her best to cheer him up after his day's hard work. If the surest symptom of a healthy mind is rest of heart and pleasure at home, that symptom is not wanting in an Indian home. A woman always strives hard to study household good, and good works in her husband to promote, and so passes the day's drama with an its blended tints. It might not be *a variegated or an ideal life, the dissipations of theatre or dancing parties may be wanting*; but the pleasure she takes in her husband and children is a sufficient reward for all she does and ho[p]es for.

As opposed to this the American writer thus depicts the conjugal and domestic life of a Western woman:

Turning our attention to the West, we find the following account of the treatment of husbands by ladies in advanced Europe and America: 'Intent upon her own affairs, she will be oblivious of her husband's interests and anxieties. When tired and weary from his daily toil, he returns home, he will look in vain for any comfort from his natural help-mate, and he will be fortunate if he is not plagued by petty grievances and household annoyances, which without tact or forbearance she will pour into his patient ear. Demands for more money will be made just at a time when the whole expenditure may have to be seriously curtailed; and whilst her attention should be given to the consideration of some matter of vital importance, her whole mind is set upon the discussion of some paltry triviality. But never will be the lack of sympathy be more grievously felt than when the husband is sick; then the naked selfishness of the unsympathetic wife will be laid bare. Forgetful of all his care and love for her, she will grudge him a single day's solicitude. If he hides his complaint, she will never question him; and if he tells her of his pain, she will receive the information with chilling indifference or absolute silence. She will never smooth his pillow, stroke his forehead, or hold his hand; but she will contentedly pursue her own affairs and leave him to bear his lonely sickness as best he may. He is in fact much more lonely than when he was a bachelor, since he looks in vain for comfort to one who regards him with indifference. She will, even against his entreaty, accept invitations to dinners or evening parties, and enter with gusto into these diversions.

(Article on Female Education in the *Observer*, Lahore, 2 June 1906, pp. 2 and 3).

Notes

1. As translated by Abul Fazal. See page 826 of the Translation of the Quoran published by G. A. Asghar.

2. Note: On this subject I have written a pamphlet entitled the 'Hadyat-uz-Zaujain', in which I have described the rights and privileges of the married couple in great detail.

3. Lucy Mary Jane Garnett, *The Women of Turkey and their Folklore*, London: D. Nutt, 1893.

4. *Encyclopedia Britannica*, Vol. XXVIII, pp. 785 and 786.

5. *Encyclopedia Britannica*, Vol. XXVIII, p. 786.

Rokeya Sakhawat Hossain

Roushan Jahan, who has edited and translated the work of Rokeya Sakhawat Hossain (1880–1932), says that, in relation to purdah 'Rokeya did not pretend to be impartial. She selected incidents that exposed the ridiculous, the absurd, the horrible, and the tragic aspects of purdah observance.' She adds that these incidents belong to the time Rokeya wrote and do not represent present reality. *The Secluded Ones*, from which the following episodes have been selected, was a collection of forty-seven anecdotes written in Bengali, and serialized in the journal *Monthly Mohammadi* in 1929. The utopian fantasy 'Sultana's Dream' was published in 1905. It was written in English and translated by Rokeya herself into Bengali.

Rokeya is perhaps one of the best known feminists of the reform movement, and has been extensively written about. While her highly-educated father did not encourage education for women, her husband was supportive and encouraged her to write and work for the education of women. She opened a school for girls which had to close down because of property disputes with her son-in-law, but, undaunted, she began again in Calcutta. She wore purdah to reassure the families of the children who came to school, though she did not believe in it herself.

REPORT EIGHT

Once, a house caught fire. The mistress of the house had the presence of mind to collect her jewelry in a handbag and hurry out of the bedroom. But at the door, she found the courtyard full of strangers fighting the fire. She could not come out in front of them. So she went back to her bedroom with the bag and hid under her bed. She burned to death but did not come out. Long live purdah!

Rokeya Sakhawat Hossain, Sultana's Dream *and Selections from* The Secluded Ones, Roshan Jahan (ed. and trans.), New York: The Feminist Press, 1988.

REPORT ELEVEN

I went to Ara [a small town in Behar] in 1926. Two of my granddaughters (actually the daughters of my stepdaughter) were getting married. I went to attend their weddings. The pet names of the two girls were Mangu and Sabu. At that time they were confined in the *Maiya Khana*.[1] In Calcutta the bride-to-be usually stays only four or five days in such confinement. But in Behar the girls are kept in such solitary confinement for six or seven months.

I could not stay in Mangu's 'cell' for long—I felt suffocated in that close room. I opened the window but within a couple of minutes a haughty Begum walked over and closed the window, remarking curtly, 'The bride is in the draught.' I had to leave the room. I failed to stay in Sabu's cell even for a minute. Those poor girls, at that time, had already stayed in those rooms for six months. Ultimately, Sabu had a spell of acute hysteria. This is how we are trained to endure seclusion.

REPORT FOURTEEN

The following incident happened about twenty-two years ago. An aunt twice removed, of my husband, was going to Patna from Bhagalpor; she was accompanied by her maid only. At Kiul railway junction, they had to change trains. While boarding the train, my aunt-in-law stumbled against her voluminous burqa and fell on the railway track. Except her maid, there was no woman at the station. The railway porters rushed to help her up but the maid immediately stopped them by imploring in God's name not to touch her mistress. She tried to drag her mistress up by herself but was unable to do so. The train waited for only half an hour but no more.

The Begum's body was smashed—her burqa torn. A whole stationful of men witnessed this horrible accident—yet none of them was permitted to assist her. Finally her mangled body was taken to a luggage shed. Her maid wailed piteously. After eleven hours of unspeakable agony she died. What a gruesome way to die!

REPORT SEVENTEEN

About fourteen years ago, we had a teacher from Lucknow [capital of old Oudh, an important city in modern Uttar Pradesh in India] in our school. Her name was Akhtar Jahan. At that time, her three daughters were studying in our school. One day she was commenting on the immodesty of modern girls, laying regretful emphasis on the shameless conduct of her own daughters.

Then she started to talk about her own youth and remembered an extraordinary thing that had happened shortly after her marriage. She related that she was married when she was only eleven. When she went to her father-in-law's house, a corner room was allotted to her. It was rather lonely and farther away from the rest of the house. A younger sister of her husband would come to her room three or four times a day to look after her needs, especially to accompany her to the toilet. One day, for some reason, the sister-in-law did not come for a long time. The poor bride needed to go to the toilet badly but could not. [A new bride does not wander about the house by herself; it is deemed highly improper.]

Now, the brides of Lucknow used to get *pan-dan*s [betel-leaf containers] from their parents as part of their dowry and bridegift.[2] One of her huge containers was in her bedroom. She emptied the container of all the betel nuts and spices; she tied all these in a handkerchief. What she then filled the container with is not fit to be written about. In the evening, when a maid from her father's house came to prepare the bed, the bride tearfully told the maid how she had abused the container. The maid took it from under the bed and consoled her, 'Please don't take on so. I'll see to it that this is tinned again. Let the betel nuts stay in the handkerchief for now.'

REPORT EIGHTEEN

A doctor from Lahore has thus described his experience of purdah—
Whenever he went to visit a patient in a purdah house, he would find two maidservants holding a thick blanket in front of the bed. He would put his hand below the blanket and extend it to the other side of the blanket. The patient would then put her wrist in his hand to enable him to take her pulse. (A certain non-purdah lady asked me once, 'If there was no woman doctor available, how would you let a male doctor examine your tongue? You could not possibly make a hole in the blanket and protrude your tongue through that hole?' I am presenting [this] question to my sisters with one of my own in the hope of finding an answer. How would they let doctors examine their eyes, teeth, and ears?)

[The doctor told me:] 'A certain Begum was down with pneumonia. I said, 'the condition of the lungs will have to be examined. I could examine it from the back.' The nawab [head of the family] ordered, 'Ask the maid to put the stethoscope wherever necessary.' Of course, it is common knowledge that the stethoscope has to be shifted in various positions before any diagnosis is possible. Yet I had to comply with the nawab's commands. The maid took the end of the stethoscope inside the blanket and put it in place. After a few minutes I was getting really worried at not hearing any sound. For once, I decided to be audacious and lifted the corner of the blanket nearest me. To my consternation and disgust, I found the stethoscope resting on the Begum's waist. I was so irritated that I left the room immediately. The nawab Sahib had the gall to ask me what I made of the case! What the—, did he expect me to be ominiscient?'

...

REPORT THIRTY-SEVEN

A train was coming from the western provinces of India to Calcutta. In the station of Bali, three burqa-clad women boarded the 'female' compartment. There were a lot of Muslim women in that compartment. They thought it curious that even after the train left the station, these three women did not raise their *nekab* [the detachable front part of the burqa covering the face]. Suddenly they became rather suspicious. Also, the height of these newcomers was rather awe-inspiring. After they had prayed silently for a few moments, the train stopped at Lilua station. A women ticket-collector got into their compartment. Immediately one woman complained about those three women. Before the ticket-collector could advance toward them, the one next to the door on the opposite platform jumped down and ran away. The ticket-collector shouted, 'police, police,' and caught hold of one. When the *nekab* was raised, a face full of mustache and beard was revealed. The ticket-collector, stunned, could only mutter—'What, beard and mustache in a burqa?'

REPORT THIRTY-EIGHT

A certain lady doctor, Miss Sharat Kumari Mitra [Hindu], whom I know rather well, was telling me the other day, 'If you only knew the trouble some of you Muslim women cause me. Even the smallest timely assistance is out of the question. No matter what it is—a clean bandage or hot water—one has to wait so long for it.'

Once a servant from a distant village came to ask her to go and see the younger Begum of the house. She had a severe toothache, the servant informed the doctor. The doctor took the medicine and instruments necessary for extraction of teeth. After she reached there she found that the younger Begum was actually suffering labor pain—not toothache! What was the doctor to do? She was now in Jamgaon, which is eight miles away from Bhagalpur where she lived. She could not possibly take the same pair of horses back to Bhagalpur because the pair was already exhausted. But Jamgaon was like a village. Horse-drawn carriages or palanquins were rarely to be found.

Somehow she managed to get back to Bhagalpur and procure the medicines and instruments necessary for delivering a child. By the time she returned to Jamgaon, the poor patient was in a critical condition. When Dr Mitra asked for an explanation from the mistress of the house as to why she was so misinformed about the problem, the senior Begum answered, 'I had to send a man to you; what could I talk about but toothache? How could I have told a man about the real situation? Wouldn't that have been too embarrassing for both of us? What sort of a lady doctor are you if you don't have the sense to realize that?'

REPORT FORTY-SEVEN

In the words of a poet:

> Not fiction, not poetry, this is life.
> No theatre this, but my real house.

Only three years ago, we had our school bus. The day before the bus came, one of our teachers, an English woman, had gone to the auto depot to inspect the bus. Her comment was, 'This bus is horribly dark inside. Oh, no! I'll never ride that bus!'

When the bus arrived, it was found that there was a narrow lattice on top of the back door and the front door. Excepting these two pieces of latticework, three inches wide and eighteen inches long, the bus could be called completely 'airtight'!

The bus took the girls to their homes that first afternoon. The maid, accompanying the girls, reported after she came back that it was terribly hot inside the bus. The girls were very uncomfortable. Some of them vomited. Some of the little girls were whimpering in the dark.

Before the bus went to fetch the girls on the next day, the English woman who taught in our school opened the shutter of the back door. She hung colored curtains on the open shutters. Even then it was found that a few of the girls fainted away, a few of them vomited on the way, and most of them had headaches, etc. In the afternoon, the aforementioned teacher opened the shutters on the side of the bus and hung curtains there also.

That evening, a Hindu friend, Mrs Mukherjee, came to see me. She was glad to know about the progress the school was making. Suddenly she said, 'Incidentally, what a fine bus you have! The first time I saw it,

I thought a huge chest was being drawn on wheels. My nephew ran out and said, 'Oh, aunty! Look! The moving black hole of Calcutta is passing by! Really! How can the girls possibly ride that bus?'

On the afternoon of the third day, several of the mothers came to complain. They said, 'Your bus is certainly God's punishment. You are burying the girls alive! I said, helplessly, 'What can I do? If the bus was not such, you would have been the ones to criticize the bus as 'purdahless'. They said angrily, 'What? Do you want to maintain purdah at the expense of our children's lives? We are not going to send our daughters to your school anymore!' That evening the maid reported that every guardian complained about the bus and warned that the girls would not ride this sort of bus.

The next evening, I had four letters. The writer of the letter written in English had signed himself, 'Brother-in-Islam'. The other three were in Urdu. Two of these letters were anonymous.

The third one had five signatures. The import of all four letters was the same—all of them were from well-wishers. For the continuing welfare of my school they were informing me that the two curtains hanging by the side of the bus moved in the breeze and made the bus purdahless. If something better was not arranged by tomorrow, they would be compelled, for the benefit of the school, to write in the various Urdu newspapers about the purdahlessness and would stop the girls from riding in such a purdahless bus.

What a dilemma I was in—

If I don't catch the cobra
The King will have my head—
If caught carelessly
Surely the cobra'd bite me!

I do not think anyone else had tried to catch such a cobra [the irate critics] to satisfy the whims of such a king [the equally irate guardians]. On behalf of the women imprisoned in seclusion, I wish to say—

Oh, why did I come to this miserable world,
Why was I born in a purdah country!

NOTES TO SELECTIONS FROM *THE SECLUDED ONES*

1. The bride-to-be used to be confined in a close room after the turmeric-paste ceremony which followed the formal engagement. The groom's family sent new clothes and turmeric paste which was smeared on the face and hands of the bride. This seems to be more strictly followed outside Bengal.

2. Pan-dans were made of various metals and came in various sizes.

Ameerali Syed

Ameerali Syed's *The Spirit of Islâm* is a history of the evolution of Islam, its spread, its philosophical, literary, and scientific spirit. It was written with Western readers in mind, and he hopes that it may be 'of help to wanderers in quest of a constructive faith to steady the human mind after the strain of the recent cataclysm.' He also hopes that it will help fellow-Islamists to understand their faith better.

In a long chapter on 'The Status of Women in Islâm', Ameerali Syed (1849–1928) traces the origins of polygamy, an institution wrongly associated only with Islam. He says that among all ancient Eastern civilizations, including Hindu civilisation polygamy was a recognized institution. Referring presumably to kulin Brahmins he says they can marry as many wives as they wish. Polygamy existed among the Israelites before Moses, among Athenians, and even among the cultured Athenians a woman was mere chattel. St Augustine apparently said it was not a crime where it was the legal institution of the country. Christianity tried to cure the problem but without much success. Ancient Arabs and Jews even entered into temporary and conditional marriages. Western authorities have said that in many cases it is force of circumstances that drives people to polygamy in the East—such circumstances as the decimation of the menfolk in a war.

At the time of writing, Syed says, ninety five Muslim men in India out of a hundred are, either by conviction or necessity, monogamous. And in Persia, only a small fraction 'enjoy the questionable luxury of a plurality of wives'.

Ameerali Syed's work is regarded as the high point of the modernist Calcutta school which developed parallel to the Aligarh movement. Certainly Muslim scholars consider *The Spirit of Islâm* a classic.

Educated at Calcutta and England, Syed was a judge in the Bengal High Court. He was appointed to the Viceroy's Council in 1883, and in 1909 to the Judicial Committee of the Privy Council in London, the first Indian to hold such an appointment. He wrote exclusively in English.

Ameerali Syed, *The Spirit of Islâm*, London: Christophers, 1922.

The Status of Women in Islâm

It cannot be denied that several institutions which the Musulmans borrowed from the pre-Islâmic period, 'the Days of Ignorance', and which exist simply as so many survivals of an older growth, have had the tendency to retard the advancement of Mohammedan nations. Among them the system of the seclusion of women is one. It had been in practice among most of the nations of antiquity from the earliest times. The *gynaikonitis* was a familiar institution among the Athenians; and the inmates of an Athenian harem were as jealously guarded from the public gaze as the members of a Persian household then, or of an Indian household now. The *gynaikonomoi*, like their Oriental counterpart, were the faithful warders of female privacy, and rigorously watched over the ladies of Athens. The seclusion of women naturally gave birth to the caste of *Hetairai*, various members of whom played such an important part in Athenian history. Were it not for the extraordinary and almost inexplicable spectacle presented by the Byzantine empire and modern Europe and America, we should have said that in every society, at all advanced in the arts of civilised life, the growth of the unhappy class of beings whose existence is alike a reproach to humanity and a disgrace to civilisation, was due to the withdrawal of women from the legitimate exercise of their ennobling, purifying, and humanising influence over the minds of men. The human mind, when it does not perceive the pure, hankers after the impure. The Babylonians, the Etruscans, the Athenians and the pre-Islâmite Meccans furnish the best exemplification of this view in ancient times. The enormity of the social canker eating into the heart and poisoning the life-blood of nations in modern times is due, however, to the spread of a godless materialism covered with a thin veneer of religion, be it Christianity, be it Mohammedanism, or any other form of creed. Mohammed had, in early life, observed with pain and sorrow the depravity prevailing among the Meccans, and he took the most effective step suited to the age and the people to stamp out the evil. 'By his severe laws at first', to use the expressive language of Mr Bosworth Smith, 'and by the strong moral sentiment aroused by these laws afterwards, he has succeeded, down to this very day, and to a greater extent than has ever been the case elsewhere, in freeing all Mohammedan countries—where they are not overgrown by foreign excrescences—from those professional outcasts who live by their own misery, and, by their existence as a recognised class, are a standing reproach to every member of the society of which they form a part.'

The system of female seclusion undoubtedly possesses many

advantages in the social well-being of unsettled and uncultured communities; and even in countries, where the diversity of culture and moral conceptions is great, a modified form of seclusion is not absolutely to be deprecated. It prevails at the present moment, in forms more or less strict, among nations far removed from Moslem influences, to which is ascribed the existence of the custom in India and other Oriental countries. In Corea, female seclusion is carried to the height of absurdity. In China and among the Spanish colonies of South America, which are not within the immediate ambit of the European social code, the *Purdah* is still observed. The Prophet of Islâm found it existing among the Persians and other Oriental communities; he perceived its advantages, and it is possible that, in view of the widespread laxity of morals among all classes of people, he recommended to the women-folk observance of privacy. But to suppose that he ever intended his recommendation should assume its present inelastic form, or that he ever allowed or enjoined the *seclusion* of women, is wholly opposed to the spirit of his reforms. The Koran itself affords no warrant for holding that the seclusion of women is a part of the new gospel.

'O Prophet! speak to thy wives and to thy daughters, and to the wives of the Faithful, that they let their wrappers fall low. Thus will they more easily be known, and they will not be affronted. God is indulgent, merciful.'[1]

'And speak to the believing women, that they refrain their looks and observe continence; and that they display not their ornaments except those which are external, and that they draw their kerchiefs over their bosoms.'[2]

Directions easy to understand[3] in the midst of the social and moral chaos from which he was endeavouring, under God's Guidance, to evolve order—wise and beneficent injunctions having for their object the promotion of decency among women, the improvement of their dress and demeanour, and their protection from insult.[4] It is a mistake, therefore, to suppose there is anything in the law which tends to the perpetuation of the custom. Considerable light is thrown on the Lawgiver's recommendation for female privacy, by the remarkable immunity from restraint or seclusion which the members of his family always enjoyed. 'Âyesha, the daughter of Abû Bakr, who was married to Mohammed on Khadîja's death, personally conducted the insurrectionary movement against Ali. She commanded her own troops at the famous 'Battle of the Camel'. Fâtima, the daughter of the Prophet, often took part in the discussions regarding the succession to the Caliphate. The grand-daughter of Mohammed, Zainab the sister of Husain, shielded her youthful nephew from the Ommeyyades after the butchery of Kerbela. Her indomitable spirit awed equally the ferocious Obaidullah ibn Ziyâd and the pitiless Yezîd.

The depravity of morals, which had sapped the foundations of society among the pre-Islâmic Arabs, as well as among the Jews and the Christians, urgently needed some correction. The Prophet's counsel regarding the privacy of women served undoubtedly to stem the tide of immorality, and to prevent the diffusion among his followers of the custom of disguised polyandry, which had evidently, until then, existed among the pagan Arabs.

According to von Hammer, 'the *harem* is a sanctuary: it is prohibited to strangers, not because women are considered unworthy of confidence, but on account of the sacredness with which custom and manners invest them. The degree of reverence which is accorded to women throughout higher Asia and Europe (among Mohammedan communities) is a matter capable of the clearest demonstration.'

The idealisation of womanhood is a natural characteristic of all the highest natures. But national pride and religious bigotry have given rise to two divergent theories regarding the social exaltation of women among the cultured classes in modern Christendom. The one attributes it to Mariolatry, the other to Mediaeval chivalry, alleged to be the offspring of Teutonic institutions. Of Christianity, in its relation to womankind, the less said the better. In the early ages, when the religion of the people, high and low, the ignorant and educated, consisted only of the adoration of the mother of Jesus, the Church of Christ had placed the sex under a ban. Father after father had written upon the enormities of women, their evil tendencies, their inconceivable malignity. Tertullian represented the general feeling in a book in which he described women as 'the devil's gateway, the unsealer of the forbidden tree, the deserter of the divine law, the destroyer of God's image—man'. Another authority declared with a revolting cynicism, 'among women he sought for chastity but found none'. Chrysostom, who is recognised as a saint of high merit, 'interpreted the general opinion of the Fathers', says Lecky, 'when he pronounced women to be a necessary evil, a natural temptation, a desirable calamity, a domestic peril, a deadly fascination, a painted ill'. The orthodox Church excluded women from the exercise of all religious functions excepting the lowliest. They were excluded absolutely from society; they were prohibited from appearing in public, from going to feasts or banquets. They were directed to *remain in seclusion,* to observe silence, to obey their husbands, and to apply themselves to weaving and spinning and cooking. If they ever went out they were to be clothed from head to foot. Such was the position of women in Christianity when Mariolatry was recognised and practised by all classes. In later times, and in the gloomy interval which elapsed between the overthrow of the Western empire and the rise of modern society in Europe, a period which has been described as one of 'rapine, falsehood, tyranny, lust, and violence', Christianity, by introducing convents and nunneries, served, in some respects, to improve the lot of women. This questionable amelioration, however was only suited for an age when the abduction of women was an everyday occurrence, and the dissoluteness of morals was such as to defy description. But the convents were not always the haunts of virtue, nor the inculcation of celibacy the surest safeguard of chastity. The *Registrum Visitationem,* or the diary of the pastoral visits of Archbishop Rigaud, throws a peculiar light upon the state of morality and the position of the sex during the most glorious epoch of the Age of Faith. The rise of Protestantism made no difference in the social conditions or in the conception of lawyers regarding the status of women. Jesus had treated woman with humanity; his followers excluded her from justice.

The other theory to which we have adverted is in vogue among the *romanceurs* of Europe. They have represented each historical figure in the Middle Ages to be a Bayard or a Crichton. The age of chivalry is generally supposed to extend from the beginning of the eighth to the close of the fourteenth century—a period, be it noted, almost synchronous with the Saracenic domination in Spain. But, during this period, in spite of the halo which poetry and romance have cast around the condition of society, women were the frequent subjects of violence. Force and fraud were the distinguishing characteristics of the golden age of Christian chivalry. Roland and Arthur were myths until the West came in contact with the civilisation and culture of the East. Chivalry was not the product of the wilds of Scandinavia or of the gloomy forests of Germany; prophecy and chivalry alike were the children of the desert. From the desert issued Moses, Jesus, and Mohammed; from the desert issued 'Antar, Hamza, and Ali.

The condition of women among the Arabs settled in the cities and villages, who had adopted the loose notions of morality prevalent among the Syrians, Persians, and Romans, was, as we have already stated, degraded in the extreme. Among some of the nomads, however, they enjoyed great freedom, and exercised much influence over the fortunes of their tribes. 'They were not, as among the Greeks,' says Perron, 'the creatures of misery'. They accompanied the warriors to battle, and inspired them to heroism; the cavaliers rushed into the fights singing the praises of sister, wife, or lady-love. The guerdon of their loves was the highest prize of their prowess. Valour and generosity were the greatest virtues of the men, and chastity that of the women. An insult offered to a woman of a tribe would set in flame the desert tribes from end to end of the peninsula. The 'Sacrilegious Wars', which lasted for forty years, and were put an end to by the Prophet, had their origin in an insult offered to a young girl at one of the fairs of Okâz.

Mohammed rendered a fitful custom into a permanent creed, and embodied respect for women in his revelations. With many directions, which reflect the rude and patriarchal simplicity of the age, his regulations breathe a more chivalrous spirit towards the sex than is to be found in the teachings of the older masters. Islâm, like Christianity, is different with different individuals and in different ages, but on the whole, true chivalry is more intimately associated with true Islâm than with any other form of positive faith or social institution.

The hero of Islâm, the true disciple of the founder of the *Hilf-ul-Fuzûl*, was as ready with lance and sword to do battle with God's enemies as to redress the wrongs of the weak and oppressed. Whether on the plains of Irâk or nearer home, the cry of distress never failed to bring the mailed knight to the succour of the helpless and suffering. His deeds translated to legends, and carried from the tent to the palace, have served to influence the prowess of succeeding ages. The caliph in his banqueting-hall puts down the half-tasted bowl on being told that an Arab maiden, carried into captivity by the Romans, had cried out, 'Why does not Abd ul-Malik come to my help?'—he vows that no wine or water shall wet his lips until he has released the maiden from bondage. Forthwith he marches his troops upon the Roman caitiffs, and only when the maiden has attained her liberty is he freed from his vow. A Mogul emperor,[3] sore pressed by relentless foes, is marching towards the frontiers when he receives the bracelet of an alien queen—the token of brotherhood and call for succour. He abandons his own necessities, retraces his steps, defeats her foes, and then resumes his march.

Oelsner calls Antar 'the father of chivalry'. Ali was its beau-ideal— an impersonation of gallantry, of bravery, of generosity; pure, gentle, and learned, 'without fear and without reproach', he set the world the noblest example of chivalrous grandeur of character. His spirit, a pure reflection of that of the Master, overshadowed the Islâmic world, and formed the animating genius of succeeding ages. The wars of the Crusades brought barbarian Europe into contact with the civilisation of the Islâmic East, and opened its eyes to the magnificence and refinement of the Moslems; but it was especially the influences of Mohammedan

Andalusia on the neighbouring Christian provinces which led to the introduction of chivalry into Europe. The troubadours, the trouveurs of Southern France, and the minnesingers of Germany, who sang of love and honour in war, were the immediate disciples of the *romanceurs* of Cordova, Granada, and Malaga. Petrarch and Boccaccio, even Tasso and Chaucer, derived their inspiration from the Islamic fountain-head. But the coarse habits and thoughts of the barbarian hordes of Europe communicated a character of grossness to pure chivalry.

In the early centuries of Islâm, almost until the extinction of the Saracenic empire in the East, women continued to occupy as exalted a position as in modern society. Zubaida, the wife of Hârûn, plays a conspicuous part in the history of the age, and by her virtues, as well as by her accomplishments, leaves an honoured name to posterity. Humaida, the wife of Fârûk, a Medinite citizen, left for many years the sole guardian of her minor son, educates him to become one of the most distinguished jurisconsults of the day.[6] Sukaina, or Sakîna, the daughter of Husain,[7] and the grand-daughter of Ali, was the most brilliant, most accomplished, and most virtuous woman of her time—'la dame des dames de son temps, la plus belle, la plus gracieuse, la plus brillante de qualités', as Perron calls her. Herself no mean scholar, she prized the converse of learned and pious people. The ladies of the Prophet's family were noted for their learning, their virtues, and their strength of character. Bûrân, the wife of the Caliph Mâmûn, Umm-ul-Fazl, Mâmûn's sister, married to the eighth Imam of the house of Ali, Umm-ul-Habîb, Mâmûn's daughter, were all famous for their scholarship. In the fifth century of the Hegira, the Sheikha Shuhda, designated *Fakhr un-nisa* ('the glory of women'), lectured publicly, at the Cathedral Mosque of Bagdad, to large audiences on literature, rhetoric, and poetry. She occupies in the annals of Islâm a position of equality with the most distinguished *'ulama*. What would have befallen this lady had she flourished among the fellow-religionists of St Cyril can be judged by the fate of Hypatia. Possibly she would not have been torn to pieces by enthusiastic Christians, but she would, to a certainty, have been burnt as a witch. Zât ul-Hemma, corrupted into Zemma, 'the lion-heart', the heroine of many battles, fought side by side with the bravest knights.[8]

The improvement effected in the position of women by the Prophet of Arabia has been acknowledged by all unprejudiced writers, though it is still the fashion with bigoted controversialists to say the Islâmic system lowered the status of women. No falser calumny has been levelled at the great Prophet. Nineteen centuries of progressive development working with the legacy of a prior civilization, under the most favourable racial and climatic conditions, have tended to place women, in most countries of Christendom, on a higher social level than the men—have given birth to a code of etiquette which, at least ostensibly, recognises the right of women to that higher social respect. But what is their legal position even in the most advanced communities of Christendom? Until very recently, even in England, a married woman possessed no rights independently of her husband. If the Moslem woman does not attain in another hundred years, the social position of her European sister, there will be time enough to declaim against Islâm as a system and a dispensation. But the Teacher who in an age when no country, no system, no community gave any right to woman, maiden or married, mother or wife, who, in a country where the birth of a daughter was considered a calamity, secured to the sex rights which are only unwillingly and under pressure being conceded to them by the civilised nations in the twentieth century, deserves the gratitude of humanity. If Mohammed had done nothing more, his claim to be a benefactor of mankind would have been indisputable. Even under the laws as they stand at present in the pages of the legists, the legal position of Moslem females may be said to compare favourably with that of European women. We have dealt in another place at length with this subject. We shall do no more here than glance at the provisions of the Moslem code relating to women. As long as she is unmarried she remains under the parental roof, and until she attains her majority she is, to some extent, under the control of the father or his representative. As soon, however, as she is of age, the law vests in her all the rights which belong to her as an independent human being. She is entitled to share in the inheritance of her parents along with her brothers, and though the proportion is different, the distinction is founded on the relative position of brother and sister. A woman who is *sui juris* can under no circumstances be married without her own express consent, 'not even by the sultan'.[9] On her marriage she does not lose her individuality. She does not cease to be a separate member of society.

An ante-nuptial settlement by the husband in favour of the wife is a necessary condition, and on his failure to make a settlement the law presumes one in accordance with the social position of the wife. A Moslem marriage is a civil act, needing no priest, requiring no ceremonial. The contract of marriage gives the man no power over the woman's person, beyond what the law defines, and none whatever upon her goods and property. Her rights as a mother do not depend for their recognition upon the idiosyncrasies of individual judges. Her earnings acquired by her own exertions cannot be wasted by a prodigal husband, nor can she be ill-treated with impunity by one who is brutal. She acts, if *sui juris*, in all matters which relate to herself and her property in her own individual right, without the intervention of husband or father. She can sue her debtors in the open courts, without the necessity of joining a next friend, or under cover of her husband's name. She continues to exercise, after she has passed from her father's house into her husband's home, all the rights which the law gives to men. All the privileges which belong to her as a woman and a wife are secured to her, not by the courtesies which 'come and go', but by the actual text in the book of law. Taken as a whole, her status is not more unfavourable than that of many European women, whilst in many respects she occupies a decidedly better position. Her comparatively backward condition is the result of a want of culture among the community generally, rather than of any special feature in the laws of the fathers.

NOTES

1. Sura xxxiii. 59.

2. Sura xxiv. 31.

3. Those who have travelled in Europeanised Egypt and in the Levant will understand how necessary these directions must have been in those times.

4. Hamilton, the translator of the *Hedâya*, in his preliminary discourse dealing with the *Book of Abominations*, has the following: 'A subject which involves a vast variety of frivolous matter, and must be considered chiefly in the light of a treatise upon *propriety* and *decorum*. In it is particularly exhibited the scrupulous attention paid to female modesty, and the avoidance of every act which may tend to violate it, even in thought. It is remarkable, however, that this does not amount to that *absolute seclusion* of women supposed by some writers. In fact, this seclusion is a result of *jealousy* or *pride*, and not of any *legal injunction*, as appears in this and several other parts of the *Hedâya*. Neither is it a custom universally prevalent in Mohammedan countries.' Marsden, in his *Travels*, says: 'The Arab settlers in Java never observed the custom, and the Javanese Mussulman women enjoy the same amount of freedom as their Dutch sisters.'

5. The Emperor Humâyûn, pursued by the Afghans, received, on his march to Cabul, the bracelet from the Jodhpur queen, and at once came to her help. I have mentioned two instances of Moslem chivalry, which might be multiplied by hundreds.

6. Fârûk was away for twenty-seven years engaged in wars in Khorâsân. His son's name is Râbya-ar-Ray.

7. Husain was married to one of the daughters of Yezdjard, the last Sasanian king of Persia.

8. For a full account of the distinguished women who have flourished in

Islâm, see the article in the May number of the *Nineteenth Century* for 1899 and Syed Ameer Ali, *A Short History of the Saracens*, London: Macmillan, New York: St. Martin's Press, 1955.

9. Centuries after the principle was laid down by the Moslem jurists, the sovereigns and chiefs of Christendom were in the habit of forcibly marrying women to their subjects.

Dr Rukhmabai

Dr Rukhmabai (1864–1955) studied at the Royal School of Medicine for Women and at the Royal Free Hospital. She was the Medical Officer for Women for twenty-two years and Zenana Medical Officer for the Women's Hospital in Rajkot for twelve years. She retired from active service in 1930.

Rukhmabai became a cause celebre in 1887 when she refused to go to the home of the man she had been married to as a child, because she disliked him. Sudhir Chandra studies this case in his book *Enslaved Daughters* (1998).

Purdah—The Need for its Abolition

It is an extraordinary thing what unnatural cruelties can be perpetuated all over the world under the crushing weight of long-established custom and superstition. Open air and sunlight may not be denied to plants and animals if healthy growth is to be secured and yet, under strict Purdah conditions, they are denied to women young and old all through their lives. From the time they attain puberty numbers of young girls, Hindu and Mahomedan, often just children in instinct and feeling, retire into seclusion. They see no men except those of their own household; they go out veiled or in closed and curtained conveyances when they do go out at all; and even this degree of liberty is denied them under the stricter Purdah conditions.

Purdah, the seclusion of girls who have attained puberty, is a Mahomedan institution more rigidly enforced in north India. In that part of the country, it has been frequently adopted by the Hindus, especially in Rajputana. It does not prevail at all among south Indian Hindus; or among the people of Maharashtra and a large section of Gujarat, or in the Madras and Bombay Presidencies. As a result of this, it is less rigid

Dr Rukhmabai, 'Purdah—The Need for its Abolition', in Evelyn Gedge and Mithan Choksi (eds), *Women in Modern India*, Bombay: D.B. Taraporewala Sons & Co., 1929.

among the poor Mahomedans of South India. Unfortunately there is a tendency, even at the present day, for communities that have not originally adopted Purdah to do so as a mark of growing social status and prosperity. The Kathiawaris, for instance, have adopted it only in the past fifty years; and doctors working among them have already felt the deplorable physical results of this adoption, the increase of tuberculosis and of early maternal mortality.

Purdah differs very much in the degree of seclusion practised in various parts of the country. At its best and especially among the poor classes, women can move about on the public road and go about their outdoor work with a veil over their faces. If rich they can use curtained conveyances, and social intercourse of a restricted kind is not denied them. Even under such conditions the system is an infliction on the natural dignity of womanhood, and, on the purely physical side, results still in a deplorable lack of air and exercise that will lead to the physical deterioration of the race. On the other hand Purdah may be so rigid that a woman may, among the poor, be confined to a small house, practically windowless or with openings high up in the walls, and she may not leave the house even to fetch water for household purposes. However poor the household, she can take no share in the work, except for the cooking which she can do indoors. It has been said that a Rajputani may not leave her house to fetch water though the house may be in a jungle and the well in front of it. The experience of doctors working among these *Purdah nashin* women is a tragic revelation of numberless cases of tuberculosis, stunted growth, disease, both among the women themselves and their children.

Purdah has pressed least hard on the very poor and the rich. For the rich there could be alleviations, air and light were not denied them, in the physical or in the cultural sense. There have been in Indian history, many very cultured Moghul and Rajput princesses. They had spacious gardens, they painted and read. For the poor the demands of hard necessity often raised the veil, though less so in India than in other Moslem countries and much less so in North than in South India. The conditions of modern town life have also intensified the worst physical evils of Purdah.

If in the richer houses, especially the household of those princes and zamindars who have adopted Purdah, there is less suffering from lack of the elementary essentials such as air and sunlight, the mental effect is still often disastrous. Because of the restrictions on education, companionship, and the development of outside interests, women are thrown for companionship on the society of female servants, and the atmosphere is often clouded with domestic gossip, jealousy, intrigue. Undoubtedly numerous instances may be quoted of Moghul and Rajput ladies, cultured in the arts and music, living within Zenana walls a free and liberal life. But these instances are not numerous enough to be considered any real alleviation of the system and assuredly they are not a justification of it.

Women of the wealthier classes and of the aristocracy have in other countries contributed considerably to social and philanthropic work. Purdah has been a restriction on the activities of a considerable body of women similarly situated in India, and the country has suffered thereby. Voluntary social enterprise has lagged behind in India as compared with other countries and in India itself those provinces where Purdah prevails are far behind those where women have been able to do organized social work.

Progress is being made, though with painful slowness in the attempt, to increase the spread of education within Purdah. Even as this paper is being written one reads of a Girl Guide Rally held at Secundrabad under Purdah, of a Women's Conference on Educational Reform to be held at Ajmere-Merwera in Rajputana, the stronghold of Hindu Purdah, the conference in its agenda laying considerable stress on the need for physical training. One reads of Purdah Clubs with facilities for games and social intercourse. In all these cases, 'under Purdah' implies the absence of men from the proceedings. The Women's Political Conference recently held at Meerut was more militant in spirit! There the Purdah arrangements provided for the ladies were strongly resented by them, and it was not until all the screens and curtains were removed that they would enter the pandal!

The attempt to educate girls while still maintaining Purdah conditions has led to many comic anomalies. An Urdu primary teacher may often have to take her normal examination in the practice of teaching under a male Inspector of Schools. In that case both the teacher and the class may be in Purdah, while the Inspector sits outside behind a screen, with the guidance of a senior lady teacher inside who affords assistance by remarking, 'Now the teacher is writing on the black-board', 'Now the class is doing an exercise.' The unfortunate man on his part has been known to complain of being stifled, as the windows of his side are firmly closed, so that no chink of light may assist him to glimpse behind the curtains.

A sweeping change through legislation would finally be a simpler matter than cautious attempts at compromise. Turkey has completely abolished Purdah by such legislation.

A very slow and laborious method has often been suggested and occasionally followed of attacking this institution by education, by a method of house-to-house visiting in order to teach Moslem girls, and by holding classes under secluded conditions and at times when it is possible for these girls to leave their domestic work. But the method is slow, laborious and very costly in proportion to the results attained. These attempts, though praiseworthy, are an ineffective means of dealing with the strongly conservative influence of the older women of the house. And this influence is often a very strong factor in the Moslem Purdah household. Such women have no outside interests, and have often a dominating personality. With adult natures and no general interests or education, this personality is a considerable reactionary force in all domestic affairs, against which the invasion of the house-to-house visitor is ineffectual. If schools are provided, it is practically impossible to enforce regular attendance. In fact it has been stated ironically by an educational authority that, 'It would be as easy and far more profitable for a provincial Government to legislate against child-marriage as to enforce the regular school attendance of girls and prolongation of such attendance after puberty.' This applies to Purdah as to child marriage. Under such conditions, the adoption of compulsory primary education for Moslem girls becomes almost impossible.[1]

Surely the work lies in the hands of the younger women who have energy and enthusiasm to work decisively for the immediate abolition of this deplorable custom, which by causing unhealthy conditions for mothers drains the national vigour, and which degrades India in the eyes of the world.

Notes

1. A beginning in compulsory education for Moslem girls had however just been made in some Municipal Schools in Bombay City—*Editor*.

Dr Kalikinkar Datta

The extract included here from *Dawn of Renascent India* was inititally part of a series of lectures, the Mahadeo Hari Wathodkar Lectures of the Nagpur University in 1949. It was later published as a book in 1950 by Nagpur University. At the time of the lectures, Dr Datta was professor and Head of the history department at Patna College. The special interest of this piece is the frequent quotation from contemporary newspapers and journals on the issues of reform.

A New Era of Social Reform

EDUCATION OF WOMEN

When human minds are stirred by new ideas, society can not remain static. So, as a logical sequel to the various stimulating forces, we have already tried to survey, there dawned during the first half of the 19th century a new era of social reform in India. The essence of social renovation is uplift of women, which has been indeed one of the most valuable contributions of modern Indian renaissance, and has been furthered by significant changes in the outlook and education of women themselves.

Cultured womanhood in India is not a gift of modern civilization. We have a brilliant tradition of female education in the old annals of our country. The writer of the article on *Native Female Education* in the *Calcutta Review* of 1855 justly believed that the 'practices of close seclusion, and of non-education, are an innovation upon the proper Hindu system.'[1] The Auxiliary Committee of the Indian Statutory Commission admitted in September 1929 that there is nothing 'inherent either in the Hindu or in the Muslim religion which militates against the education of women. In fact there were in India even in early days many

Dr Kalikinkar Datta, *Dawn of Renascent India*, Nagpur: Nagpur University, 1950.

examples of women possessing wide knowledge, particularly of sacred and classical literature.' Notwithstanding the long march of time and successive changes in politics and society, this tradition survived till late in the 18th century and the beginning of the 19th century. The women in India were not then universally steeped in the darkness of ignorance; in the distant corners of the cities and the villages there flourished female poets and writers, who can be regarded as worthy predecessors of their more educated sisters of the later generations.

Study of religious literature was considered to be a pious recreation by the ladies in respectable families. Further, many women amongst the followers of Vaishnavism[2] in Bengal were well conversant with literary works relating to their cult; some of them had knowledge of Sanskrit too and were able to work as public preachers.

Secular considerations, chiefly for management of estates, prompted some members of rather aristocratic families to educate their daughters. Rani Bhavani of Natore and Sri Devi Ahalya Bai of Indore are striking instances of this practice which was prevalent also in such families as that of Raja Radhakanta Dev of Calcutta and some others. William Adam, in a report referring to Bengal, notes that the Zamindars 'in general instruct their daughters in the elements of knowledge....They hope to marry their daughters into families of wealth and property, and they perceive that, without a knowledge of writing and accounts, their daughter will, in the event of widowhood, be incompetent to the management of their deceased husband's estates....' [3] A Bengali newspaper of 1822 states as follows: 'At the present time there are many educated ladies in different places; in this famous city of Calcutta, there are many fortunate men having educated wives....Even to-day many educated ladies are to be found in Karnat, Maharastra, Dravida, Tailanga and other places; some women transact affairs of their estates, and at Benares there are many of them who can talk in Sanskrit[4]....It is clearly observed that among the girls who are reading in the Pathsala (school) established through the efforts of (a few) English ladies, some have learnt reading and writing in one year, some again in one and a half years and they can easily read the books written in a language of which they had never any knowledge before. It appears from this that the women can be very learned if they devote themselves to reading and writing. So they should be given education during their early days just as they are taught to discharge their household duties[5].... We read in an account of 1849: 'There are not a few Hindu ladies among the upper classes in this city (Calcutta), that can read and that do read. In such cases, when they are children they attend the instructions of a *Guru-mahasai*, either in their own house, or at the house of some near neighbour....By the time this is finished, they are married....They are now removed from school, and, for want of practice, soon forget to write. But they do not lose their knowledge of reading. Some of the matrons in the family—it may be an aunt—continue the study of the Bengali with the little girl, and she soon learns to read fluently. The books, with which the young women's minds are chiefly engaged, are the following; *Ramayan, Mahahharat, Annada Mangal Chundi,* and a few other works, especially such as treat of the incarnation of Krishna, and the attributes of Shakti or Durga. The vernacular newspapers, especially the *Bhaskur* and *Probakhur,* are in great demand with them. In one of the divisions of this city, called Bartollah, there are a great many printing presses, employed in printing books, of which many are bought by respectable Hindu ladies. The other day we learned with great pleasure and surprise that a young married lady, being obliged to visit her mother, who was very ill, and who lived at the distance of six days' journey from Calcutta, took with her in her palkee (palanquin) a number of books for her travelling companions, to relieve the *ennui* of her journey'.[6]

The East India Company's Government remained absolutely indifferent[7] to female education in India during the early period of empire-building. But the Christian missionaries had included it in the programme of their work in this country since the early years of the 19th century, and made earnest efforts to bring girls under their own system of instruction. Mr May, a Dissenting missionary, who may be regarded as the pioneer of 'lower female education' in India, started a girls' school at Chinsurah. But, as he died shortly in 1818, his efforts did not produce much success and this institution was discountenanced by the company's Government.[8] In the month of April, 1819, some Baptist missionaries, intending to commence 'an organised scheme of female education' issued an appeal for help. This elicited a favourable response from several English ladies who founded (before 1820) the Calcutta Female Juvenile Society, under the presidentship of Rev. W. H. Pearce, for the education of Indian girls.[9] The Society had eight students at the end of the first year of its existence.[10] At the Annual Meeting of the School Society, held on the 2nd May, 1821, Reverend Mr Keith 'made some remarks on the importance of female education, when the Chief Justice stated that he had the gratification to know that some natives were to be found of the highest respectability, who were giving their attention to the subject; and in some instances privately endeavouring in their circles to give effect to these designs for the instruction of their females'.[11] In a public examination arranged by the School Society in 1822, about forty poor Bengali girls belonging to the Female Juvenile Society, were examined.[12] Raja Radhakanta Dev writes in his Report of this examination that 'several native girls educated by the Female Society were also examined, whose proficiency in reading and spelling gave great pleasure'.[13] At the end of six years of its existence, the Calcutta Juvenile Society maintained one hundred and sixty female pupils in six schools.[14] About this time Raja Radhakanta Dev handed over to this Society the publication of a Bengali book, on the subject of female education, entitled *Strisiksavidhayaka*,[15] written by Pandit Gourmohan Vidyalankar of Calcutta School Society in 1824.[16]

The name of Miss Coke (afterwards Mrs Wilson, wife of Rev. Isaac Wilson, a missionary of the Church Missionary Society, residing at Mirzapur, Calcutta) deserves special mention in the history of female education during the period under review. In 1821 the British and Foreign School Society of London, in consultation with the Calcutta School Society's agent, Mr Harrington, and with Mr Ward of the Serampore Mission, both then being in England, decided to depute Miss Coke for this work. Starting from England in May, 1821, she reached India in November of the same year.[17] The funds of the Calcutta School Society being inadequate to finance her work, she commenced it under the auspices of the Church Missionary Society. By 1822 eight 'little schools for girls' were formed[18] under her supervision. Their number rose to 22 by 1822 and of scholars to 400. These schools enjoyed the patronage of the Marchioness of Hastings.[19]

In the year 1824 the Corresponding Committee of the Christian Missionary Society, under the auspices of which Miss Coke had so long been working, transferred the management of their female schools to a Society formed in March of that year under the designation of the 'Ladies Society for Native Female Education', with the Right Hon'ble Lady Amherst as its patroness.[20] David Hare became a subscriber to it and 'encouraged native female education by his presence at the periodical examinations which were held.'[21] Under the guidance of Miss Coke, then Mrs Wilson, this Society soon came to manage 30 girls schools with about 600 students in Calcutta and its neighbourhood.[22]

At the suggestion of Rev. Carey, it was then decided to concentrate efforts and activities, and a Central School was established accordingly in the eastern corner of the Cornwallis Square, Calcutta.[23] The Right Hon'ble Lady Amherst laid the foundation stone of this on the 18th of May, 1826, and Raja Baidyanath Roy of Calcutta gave two liberal donations, amounting to 20,000 rupees.[24] On the 1st of April, 1828, Mr and Mrs Wilson took charge of the Central School with fifty-eight girls.

The first examination of the Central School was held on the 17th December, 1828. We find in the report of Miss Ward (December, 1829), who had been placed in charge of the Central School during Mrs Wilson's temporary absence in the Upper Provinces, that in 1828 the daily attendance of the girls was 'from one hundred and fifty to two hundred, divided into twenty classes.' The Central School in Calcutta flourished gradually, and Mr W. Adam noted in 1834: 'An allowance is made of a pice a head to women under the name of hurkarees, for collecting the children daily and bringing them to school, as no respectable Hindu will allow his daughters to go into the street except under proper protection. The School numbers 320 day-scholars, besides 70 Christian girls who live on the premises. The latter are orphans, and most of them have been collected from the districts south of Calcutta that have recently suffered from inundation and famine. Together with these, 40 poor women have been admitted by Mrs Wilson to a temporary asylum, who are all learning to read and receive daily Christian instruction, and are at the same time employed in various ways to earn in whole or in part their own living. In connection with the Ladies' Society, there is also a girls school on the premises belonging to the Church Missionary Society in Calcutta. The number of pupils fluctuates between 50 and 70. Spelling, reading, writing, needle-work and religion are the subjects in which instruction is given. Many of the scholars have become teachers. Native ladies of the most respectable castes in society have both sent their daughters, and in some instances have themselves expressed anxiety to obtain instruction....There are three schools connected with the London Missionary Society in Calcutta. In a school situated in the Thunthuniya Road there are 45 scholars, in the Greek Row School about 25; and in the Mende Bagan School 28; in all (about) 108. In these schools the girls are taught reading, writing and arithmetic, besides plain needle-work and marking.... [25] *The Samachar Chandrika* of 13th Sravana 1234 B.S. (28th July, 1827) noted that the Bengalees had begun to send their daughters to schools for education up to an advanced age and that in Burdwan particularly girls aged 14 or 15 years came to schools.[26]

There were three agencies then used by the Christian missionaries for female education, viz., (1) girls' day schools, (2) orphans' boarding establishments, (3) domestic teaching arranged in the families of the middle and higher classes. They tried hard for extension of domestic education through governesses in the families of the Indians. Mrs Wilson and Rev. Krishna Mohan Banerjea, baptised into Christianity on the 17th October, 1832, when questioned about this scheme of the domestic instruction gave favourable replies.[27]

Rev. Krishna Mohan Banerjea was of opinion that 'many would instruct the female sex if their reputation and perhaps caste were not at stake'.[28] He was a staunch advocate of the cause of female education. In 1840 he wrote an essay on Indian Female Education in competition for a prize of Rs 20 offered by Captain Jameson of Baroda for the 'best English essay by a native of India on the subject of Native Female Education'.[29] In the second chapter of this essay he discussed what should be the duties of women in different spheres of life. He expected that 'Hindu females ought to be what the first mother of the human species undoubtedly was, and what Providence intended all her daughters to be—helpmates to their husbands, bone of their bone and flesh of their flesh. They are not to remain unconcerned in the affairs of the family nor only to bear the drudgery of the household, as if the recesses the Hindu's dwelling were a mere menagerie; but on the contrary to advise and counsel their consorts to the utmost of their power....There is a charm in the rational sympathy of an intelligent wife which operates almost with talismanic power upon the mind which is agitated and disturbed by temporal crosses and disappointments.' He pointed out that the minds of the women 'should in the first place be cultivated', and in the third chapter suggested what he considered to be the suitable means for their education. He recommended 'private tuition' instead of a 'system of public schools', as he felt that 'if instruction could be offered under the auspices of a well-organised European Native Society without demanding a sudden and violent revolution, as it were, in the domestic economics of the Hindus, the cause of female improvement would gradually prosper, in Calcutta at least.' Referring to the fact that Babu Prasanna Kumar Tagore of the distinguished Tagore family had engaged a European tutoress for the education of her [sic] daughter, he noted that the employment of European female teachers and the 'establishment of infant schools in different parts of the country for the instruction of both male and female children, would also greatly help the cause of female Education'. In a public meeting of the citizens of Calcutta held in the Calcutta Town Hall on 24th December, 1847, he expressed 'a strong opinion that respectable Hindu girls should be allowed to attend classes in Christian schools'. In 1851 he joined the Bethune Society, being thus one of its original members along with Pandit Iswar Chandra Vidyasagar, Babu Ram Gopal Ghose, Debendra Nath Tagore and others.

As regards the efforts of the Christian Missionaries for female education in other parts of India, it may be noted that in Madras, they opened a school for this purpose on the 17th October, 1821.[30] On the 10th of March, 1826, Sir Thomas Munro remarked[31] that the 'number of schools and of what are called colleges in the territories under the Presidency amount to 12,498, and the population to 12,850,941, so that there is one school to every 1,000 of the population, but as usually a few females are taught in schools, we may reckon one school to every 500 of the population.' But the number of Christian schools for girls gradually increased. In 1845 the first girls' school under partial native management was opened.[32] It was reported before the Education Commission of 1882 by the Madras Provincial Committee that the following were the earliest schools for the education of girls in Madras: The Church Mission Boarding Schools in Tinnevelly from 1837; the Free Church Day School, Madras from 1841; the Free Church and Boarding School from 1842; the S.P.G. Boarding Schools in Tinnevelly from 1842; the Free Church Day Schools at Chingleput and Conjeveram from 1845; the Native Female Education Society Central School, Black Town, Madras, from 1845; the Wesleyan Mission Boarding School, Royapettah, Madras from 1849.

In Bombay, among the missionaries, the American Mission Society were the pioneers of female education. That Society opened there a girls' school in 1824[33] and 'two years later they reported an increase of nine girls' schools with an aggregate attendance of 340 pupils.' In 1829 the 'number of pupils rose to 400 of whom 122 were able to read, write and cipher and to do plain needle-work'. Two girls' schools were opened by the same Mission in 1831 at Ahmednagar which was followed by the starting of a boarding school for girls in that city.[34] Dr and Mrs Wilson established six girls' schools in Bombay during the year 1829–30 and the number of pupils in them were about 200.[35] The Church Missionary Society started girls' schools for the first time in 1826 and 'in the course of the next ten years the Society opened separate elementary schools for boys and girls at Thana, Bassein and Nasik.'[36]

At the close of 1850, the missionary 'efforts for female education in India embraced three hundred and fifty-four day schools with eleven thousand five hundred girls; and ninety-one boarding schools with two thousand four hundred and fifty girls taught almost exclusively in the vernacular languages.'[37] Then the Missionary Girls' Schools were thus[38] distributed as shown in the following table.

But, with all their efforts, the Christian missionaries could not attract to their institutions girl students from the upper stratum of the Indian society, the bulk of those drawn therein being from the lower ranks. Rev. K.M. Banerjea observed in 1840. 'The lower classes that is, those who are not much under the bonds which society imposes, and whose poverty and degradation render them invulnerable so far as literacy is concerned, are in the habit even now of sending girls to schools upon the prosecution

	Day Schools		Boarding Schools	
	Schools	Girls	Schools	Girls
Bengal	26	690	28	836
N.W Provinces	8	213	11	208
Madras Presidency	222	6,929	41	1,101
Bombay Presidency	28	1,087	6	129
Ceylon	70	2,630	5	72
	354	11,549	91	2,416

of sufficient motives, such as a few pice or other Bakhshish being occasionally given to the children.'[39] Sometimes they received ornaments.[40] A Brahmin of Chinsura wrote to the Editor of the *Samachar Darpan* on the 25th of February, 1838, that though a few European ladies and gentlemen had been making efforts for the education of the women by establishing schools, only some girls belonging to low classes attended their schools under the temptation of getting cloths and other presents and the missionaries were unsuccessful in other quarters. Mr Adam saw 175 girls in 4 female schools in the Burdwan district in 1838; of these one was Muhammadan, 36 were either daughters of Christian parents or orphans supported by the missionaries, and 138 Hindus; but of the Hindu girls 58 were Bagdis, 18 Muchis, 17 Domes, 12 Haries, 6 Vaishnavas, 6 Tantis, 2 Chandals, 1 Kurmi and 1 Bate.[41] In a girls' school visited by him in the city of Murshidabad all the students were Hindus, 17 of them being Bagdis, 6 Malas, 3 Kaivartas and 2 Vaishnavas.[42] An account of 1851 recorded as follows: 'Female Education has occupied much of the attention and anxieties of missionaries; but such hindrances lie in its way, as to have greatly crippled the efforts, which they were desirous of making. Boarding Schools for orphans and the daughters of native Christians have been most successful; many of the most intelligent and best behaved of the native Christian women have received their education....But female day-schools have in most parts of India, met with little encouragement....In Bengal there are very few of these schools now; though at one time they were most numerous, especially in Calcutta. In Madras, however, and in Bombay, they flourish much better.[43]

The chief reason for this was that the instruction which the Christian missionaries provided for was mostly of religious character, which did not appeal to Indian sentiments. In the words of Rev. K. M. Bannerjea, 'In those schools little had been done in an educational though much attempted in the catechising way.'[44] Adam too noticed this defect.

Referring to the Christian Boarding Houses for girls' education, he observed: 'These institutions are exclusively under Christian management and the instruction is chiefly religious but not to the exclusion of general knowledge and the arts of domestic industry. It must be evident that they give the teachers and superintendents an absolute control over the minds of the pupils, and this is the object of their establishment. They also tend to break the ties between parents and children in those cases in which the former are alive, especially if they are not Christians.' As for the day schools he wrote as follows: 'The children are the offspring of the poorest classes of native society. They are paid for attendance, and elderly females are employed to conduct them to and from school....It is opposed to native prejudices, as it requires that the scholars should have to leave home to attend school and it involves unproductive expenditure, as the matrons are paid only to secure attendance at school, not attention to study; and yet the reports of such institutions are filled with expressions of regret on account of irregular attendance, slow progress, withdrawals from school after marriage, etc.'[45]

An enlightened public opinion in favour of girls' education was gradually gathering momentum, though there was a sort of opposition to it from the side of some orthodox members of the Hindu community.[46] The local journals of that time tell us that some virulently opposed it, while others warmly advocated its expansion. The editor of the *Samachar Darpan* published a note in his journal on 25th June, 1831, attacking female education and its advocates; but the editor of the *Bangaduta* gave a very strong reply to that note on 20th August, 1831, by emphasising the need of female education in our country and citing instances of educated ladies among the Marathas.[47] The editor of another local paper named *Gananeswana* published a note on 29th April, 1834, encouraging the determination of some respectable Indians, like Babu Moti Lal Seal and Babu Haladhar Mallik, to convene a meeting with the object of devising plans for the improvement of female education and for introducing other social reforms.[48] It is interesting to note that a particular Brahmin of Chinsura wrote to the editor of the *Samachar Darpan* on 28th February, 1838, expressing a clear support for the spread of female education with the argument that all-round improvement of the country would never be possible unless the girls were educated. He further urged respectable gentlemen of Calcutta, Baranagar, Chinsura, Santipur and some other important places to make organised efforts for opening a girls' school in each village so that the girls might keep pace with the growth of education and new ideas among the youths of the country.[49] By the year 1835 some women of Santipur had begun to express discontent with their lot and demanded arrangements for their education and other reforms. Some women of Chinsura also wrote to the editor of the *Samachar Darpan* on the 15th of March, 1835, strongly supporting the efforts of their sisters of Santipur.[50] It is noted in the *Bengal Spectator* of December 1,1842, that a Hindu gentleman had then offered through the Council of Education, 'a gold and a silver medal to the students attached to 1st class of the Hindu College for the best and the second best essays on Native Female Education.'

Thus there was a growing recognition of the need of female education in Bengal before the establishment of the first separate school for the instruction of the girls of high class Hindus under the name of the Hindu Valika Vidyalaya, in the month of May, 1849 through the efforts of Hon'ble J.E. Drinkwater Bethune, Legal Member of the Governor General's Council and President of the Council of Education, and of Pandit Iswarchandra Vidyasagar, one of the great educationists and social reformers of modern India. The Hon'ble J.E.D. Bethune thus stated his viewpoint to Lord Dalhousie through his letter to him, dated the 29th of March 1849: 'The failure of every attempt to induce respectable Natives to send their daughters to Missionary Schools and the conviction which I have that the system of the Government schools is best calculated for producing a rapid and salutary effect in the country induced me to establish my school on the same principle of excluding from it all religious teaching, though I was well aware of the additional difficulty which this restriction would cause to me for procuring efficient female teachers.'[51]

The Hindu Valika Vidyalaya was started with eleven pupils, and 'it was vehemently opposed by many of the most influential natives of Calcutta, chiefly however', as Mr Bethune believed, 'on the ground of mortified vanity because they had not been consulted in the matter.'[52] But he received considerable encouragement and help from some other educated citizens. Babu Ram Gopal Ghose, the well-known merchant of Calcutta and the first Indian public man to deliver orations in English of literary merit, was his 'principal adviser in the first instance'[53] and procured him his 'first pupils'.[54] Babu Dakshina Ranjan Mukherjee, a Zamindar who did not previously know Mr Bethune, offered the free gift of a site for the school, or five bighas of land valued at 10,000 rupees in the native quarter of the town,[55] as soon as his desire was published.[56] Pandit Madan Mohan Tarkalankar of the Calcutta Sanskrit College not only sent his two daughters, named Bhuvanmala and Kundamala, to Mr Bethune's School, but 'continued to attend it daily, to give gratuitous instruction to the children in Bengali and...employed his leisure time in the compilation of a series of elementary Bengali books for their use'.[57] The Hon'ble Justice Sambhunath Pandit (the first Indian Judge of the High Court of Judicature in Calcutta) also helped Mr Bethune's enterprises considerably.[58]

A girls' school had already been started at Barasat (about 20 miles from Calcutta) by some respectable gentlemen like Peary Chand Sarkar, Headmaster of the local Government School, Nabin Chandra Mitra, an assistant in the Calcutta Excise Commissioner's office and another, a graduate of the Medical College.[59] That School was then (1849) 'attended by more than 20 girls, chiefly of Brahminical caste...two of them being already married'.[60] In August, 1849, Babu Jaykrishna Mukherjee and Babu Rajkrishna Mukherjee, Zamindars in the Hugli District, sent before the Council of Education a communication relating to the establishment of a female school at Uttarpara near Howrah.[61] They noted therein: 'Many respectable people of this neighbourhood concur with us in thinking that if an experimental school for the education of female children should be established here under the patronage of Government, it may, if successful, eventually lead to the establishment of others all over the country. We, therefore, beg to propose to place in the hands of Government landed property yielding a clear monthly income of 60 rupees, provided the Government will pay a like sum for the furtherance of the object—the cost of the building will be about 3,000 rupees which shall be equally borne by the Government and ourselves.'[62] The Council of Education regretted 'that the existing state of the education funds would not permit them to entertain the proposal submitted',[63] and that 'they preferred awaiting the result of that (Mr Bethune's) experiment, to taking any steps in the matter of female education themselves at that time'.[64] Babu Jaykrishna Mukherjee, however, 'proposed to open the school at once without any further application to Government'. Girls' schools had been started also near Jessore. at Nebudhia and at Sooksagar, and Mr Bethune, on visiting the Government Vernacular School at Chota Jagooleah in the Barasat district, found that the Indian managers of that school had 'given, among other prizes, a silver Medal for the best Bengali Essay on the benefits to be expected from Female education'.[65]

Thus, in spite of hostile opinions against female education in certain quarters, faith in its importance for general improvement of society was gradually increasing throughout the country. In an address on 'Native Female Education' delivered at a meeting of respectable Indians (several of whom belonged to the orthodox class), held at Maniktola Street, Calcutta, on 25th July, 1855,[66] Babu Hurchunder Dutt strongly advocated it. He made a very stirring appeal in the following terms: (a) 'The education of our Females is a duty which we owe to ourselves, and the more speedily it is fulfilled the better'; (b) 'Immediately to set about the work of Female Education is a duty we owe to our country'; (c) 'Immediately to set about the work of Female education is a duty we owe to God.' He concluded his speech with the following striking passage: 'And now, when the highest personages in the realm have condescended to take an active interest in the cause of Native Female Education— when the cry of our women has not only reached their ears, but has crossed intervening oceans and reached the ears of our gracious Sovereign—let us cordially co-operate—let us encourage the poor to send their daughters to school, and let those that have the means educate their wives and daughters at home. Let us also encourage the plan of training up Female Teachers who shall knock at every door with food for the soul. Then, in the process of time, would be realised the most glorious of results.' There were several others sincerely desiring this reform. Mr Kristodas Pal expressed on 1st June, 1856: 'A new race has risen on the land which had ere long no name or local habitation. The worthies of their newly sprung up class are a glory to the nation...they have discovered that women like them are made of flesh and blood, are governed by similar motives, influenced by similar affections, watched over by the same Providence, have equal rights, are entitled to similar treatment. Accordingly they find it no breach of morality or religion to dispel from their minds the gloom of ignorance, and open to them the Pardiseal region of Literature and Science.'[67]

In Bombay too Indian society had begun to show interest in extending education to girls. In 1851, a sum of rupees 20,000 was endowed by Maganbhai Karamchand of Ahmadabad for the establishment of two girls' schools in that city. In the same year one gentleman of Poona, named Joti Govindrao Phule, started a private school at Poona for girls' education. Professor Patton of the Elphinstone College promoted the formation of a 'Students' Literary and Scientific Society', which supported some vernacular free schools for girls in the city of Bombay.[68]

The attitude of the Company's Government towards female education in India was one of apathy for many years. Even the school established by Mr Bethune was maintained for some time by him, and after his death in 1851, Lord Dalhousie, who was in favour of extending a frank and cordial Government support to female education in India, paid for its maintenance for nearly five years Rs 8,000 a year out of his personal purse.[69] Sir Charles Wood's Despatch of 1854 observed: 'The importance of female education in India cannot be over-rated, and we have observed with pleasure the evidence which is now afforded of an increased desire on the part of the natives of India to give a good education to their daughters. By this means a far greater proportional impulse is imparted to the educational and moral tone of the people than by the education of men. We have already observed that schools for females are included among those to which grant-in-aid may be given and we cannot refrain from expressing our cordial sympathy with the efforts which are being made in the direction.' Soon Rs 5,000 were assigned by the Government as grant for girls' schools in Bengal and about 40 such schools were started by the Inspector of Schools in the districts of Burdwan, Hugli and the 24-Parganas.[70] But after the movement of 1857–9, the grant was withdrawn.[71] Within a few years, however, there was a change in the attitude of the Government in this respect.

NOTES

1. *Calcutta Review,* July–December 1855, p. 64.

2. W. Adam, *Reports on the State of Education in Bengal,* (1835, 1836, and 1838), ed. A.M. Basu, Calcutta, 1941, p. 189.

3. Ibid., p. 188.

4. Compare *Hati Vidyalankar,* Ward, *A View of the History, Literature and Religion of the Hindoos,* Vol. I, Serampore, 1818, p. 399.

5. B. N. Banerjee, *Sambad Patre Sekaler Katha,* Pt I, 3rd edn, Calcutta: Bangiya Sahitya Parishad, n.d., p. 8.

6. *Calcutta Review,* January–June, 1849.

7. J.A. Richey, *Selections from Educational Records,* Vol. II, 1840–59, Calcutta: Superintendent, Government Printing, 1920, p. 32.

8. Monier Monier-Williams, *Modern India and the Indians,* 3rd edn, London, 1879, p. 322.

9. Richey, op. cit., p. 35.

10. Monier-Williams, op. cit., p. 322.

11. *A Biographical Sketch of David Hare* by Peary Chand Mitra, pp. 52–3.

12. Ibid.

13. Quoted in ibid.

14. Monier-Williams, op. cit., p. 322.

15. Richey, op. cit., p. 36.

16. B.N. Banerjee, op. cit., Part I.

17. Priscilla Chapman, *Hindoo Female Education,* London: R.B. Sealy and W. Burnside, 1839, p. 75.

18. Ibid., p. 79.

19. Ibid., P. 81.

20. Ibid., p. 86.

21. Mitra, op. cit., p. 56.

22. W. Adam, *First Report*, 1835, pp. 47–8. See note 2.

23. Richey, op. cit., p. 36.

24. Ibid., B.N. Banerjee, op. cit., p. 10.

25. W. Adam, *First Report*, op. cit., pp. 48–9. See note 2.

26. B.N. Banerjee, op. cit., p. 11.

27. *Calcutta Review*, 1850.

28. Ibid.

29. *Englishman*, June 8, 1840.

30. Extract from '*A Memoir of the First Centenary of the Earlier Protestant Mission at Madras* by Rev. W. Taylor', quoted in Richey, Part II, op. cit., p. 49.

31. As gathered from information furnished by collectors; vide a table given in *Fisher's 'Memoir on Education of Indians'*, in *Bengal: Past and Present*, 1919, Vol. 18, Calcutta Historical Society.

32. *Report of the Education Commission of 1882.* p. 522.

33. Ibid, p. 14.

34. Ibid.

35. Ibid.

36. Ibid.

37 *Calcutta Review*, 1851, p. 242.

38. Ibid., p. 249.

39. K. M. Banerjea, *Native Female Education*, 2nd edn, Calcutta, 1858 (1841), pp. 102–3.

40. B. N. Banerjee, op. cit., Part II, p. 72.

41. *Third Report*, 1838, p. 305. See note 2.

42. Ibid. p. 300.

43. *Calcutta Review*, 1851, pp. 248–9.

44. K. M. Banerjea, op. cit., p. 105.

45. *Third Report*, op. cit., p. 453. See note 2.

46. B. N. Banerjee, op. cit., Part II, p. 67.

47. Ibid., pp. 61–70.

48. Ibid., p. 71.

49. Ibid., pp. 72–3.

50. Ibid., p. 187.

51. Richey, op. cit., p. 52.

52. Ibid.

53. Ibid.

54. Ibid.

55. Ibid.

56. Ibid.

57. Ibid.

58. Sitanath, op. cit., p. 44; Chandicharan, *Life of Vidyasagar* (in Bengali), p. 195.

59. *Calcutta Review,* July–December, 1855, p. 77.

60. Richey, op. cit., p. 54.

61. Ibid., pp. 47–9.

62. Ibid.

63. Ibid., p.49.

64. Ibid.

65. Ibid., p. 54.

66. *East India Pamphlets,* (National Library, Calcutta.)

67. Kristodas Pal, *Young Bengal Vindicated,* a discourse read at the Hare Anniversary Meeting held on 1st June, 1856.

68. *Report of the Education Commission of 1882,* p. 14.

69. Ibid., p. 525.

70. Ibid.

71. Ibid.

Husain B. Tyabji

Writing his father's biography some forty years after his death, Husain observes, quite rightly, that he was 'one of the greatest Indians of our time'. Along with his brothers, Badruddin Tyabji (1844–1906) became a leading force in the formation of Anjuman-i-Islam, he supported the Indian National Congress, played an active part in social reform and education, and was the first Indian Muslim to become a London-trained barrister.

Husain Tyabji undertook the writing of his father's biography when he was seventy. He writes, 'His life is naturally inextricably connected with the history of social reform among the Muslims, the education of their women and the gradual emancipation from the injurious restraints which custom had imposed upon them. His broad and progressive outlook necessarily brought him into conflict with the reactionary Muslim political forces....

Social Reform

When conversation turned upon life in England and English education, everybody knew that Badruddin prayed and fasted, abstained from pork, led a most moral life, never touched wine and never smoked, and there could not but be a certain feeling of respect and admiration for him. For how many young men before and after him had abandoned their traditions, married in England, adopted English dress and ways, and aping Europeans become alienated from their own people? Badruddin was a striking example for them which proved that an English education and even a long stay in England for acquiring it did not necessarily lead to denationalisation or to other undesirable results, and if a young Indian was well-grounded and fit, he could go to England and return with much benefit to himself and his people, and with greater love for his country. Badruddin believed that association with a people like the English was most edifying.

Husain B. Tyabji, *Badruddin Tyabji*, Bombay: Thacker and Co., 1952.

There was a charge of immorality levelled against the English people, because they drank wine and observed no *purdah* among their women. Badruddin admitted there were immoral men and women in England as there were everywhere else in the world. England was no exception, but while we objected to respectable English men and women dancing together, we had a worse institution of entertaining dancing women of loose character in our homes for *nautch* parties. The English were a high class people whose character was built up by education. Women were allowed great freedom and from childhood they were disciplined and had opportunities to know the world, learn to be on guard against its temptations and protect themselves. Some few did go wrong but he thought the general morality was probably far higher in England than in India because of their education, and because the open ways and free-dom which they enjoyed, were the best school for virtue. It was natural that prisoners should ever be on the look-out for outlets of escape, and that free men should learn to be on guard themselves. To go about among men with faces uncovered was not in itself immodesty. Queen Victoria and all the great ladies of the Court and the women of respectable families of England were highly modest and moral. Both peoples, Indian and English, sought the same virtue—one, by imposing bars and exter-nal restraint, the other, by cultivation of discipline and self-control through freedom and a sense of responsibility.

People wished to know whether his stay in England was dull by reason of being among an unsympathetic people whom they believed to be cold, proud and arrogant, with contempt for the Indians. Badruddin said that on the contrary, he had found them most interested in the affairs of their great dominion, and most hospitable to the Indians. They were not a demonstrative people, but were genuine and true. They were a people of great character. They were sincere friends of the Indians, and except when their interests clashed, they did what they believed to be best for India, though no doubt they were often misled by their country-men who were biased against the Indians or were hostile to them. Personally he had received the utmost kindness from them and could count many genuine friends among them. He certainly had the greatest admiration for them.

There was a common feeling that drinking wine was a wicked thing and that because it was permitted among the English people and they drank, they could not be virtuous. Badruddin spoke strongly against this prejudice, for he thought such prejudice as existed against other people, because of their different habits and customs, caused alienation and enmity, and therefore was most injurious to the country. There was no doubt that drunkeness was a great evil. But no one in England approved of drunkenness. What was permissible among them was moderate drinking, and this they believed was desirable in a cold climate. This was what their scientists also believed, and the people were so disciplined from their childhood that it was a rare thing in respectable families for anyone to be found drinking to excess or getting drunk. He himself never drank but he felt there was no justification whatever to condemn other people for drinking who thought it beneficial, at least harmless and therefore resorted to it. If a nation or people despised or hated another for differences in their religious notions or habits, religions would only produce hatred and enmity among men, instead of love and brotherhood, and frustrate the very object of their founders. Religion was merely a training school for virtue. By prohibition, Islam sought to protect the health of the people and keep them away from drunkenness. The Christians sought to achieve the same end by cultivation of self-control and discipline. It was most essential to root out racial prejudices for the creation of the feelings of brotherhood among men and this was the most cherished object of Islam. It was with that object that it preached toleration. Of course, the question came up whether Islam was not the best and truest religion. That was readily admitted, but then it was only a course of training for the purpose of acquiring the true virtues common to all mankind. And therefore if a man of another religion as a fact acquired more virtue than another, even though that other be a Muslim, he must necessarily be better. Prayer was only a path to attain merit and mere recitation was of no avail if merit was as a fact not sought and acquired. Nature ruled by law which it was the first to honour and obey and it never committed a breach of the law it made, by what are called miracles. Those were deceptions doing incalculable harm, misleading and diverting people from the right path. People spent thousands and took no end of trouble to visit the tombs of *Pirs* and to pray for intercession, for recovery from illness, wasting their energies contrary to the dictates of the *Koran* itself, whereas their energies would be far better directed to seek proper medical treatment.

On the question whether English customs were all better than Indian, Badruddin considered many Indian customs far better than English. For instance cleansing with flowing water was in his opinion a superior way of cleaning than in a basin or tub using the same water over and over again, and water was a better mode of personal toilet than paper.

But wherever judgment and experience pointed to a better custom among them, it would be unfortunate and unwise to be prejudiced against it and deprive ourselves of its benefit. On the other hand it was a slavish mentality to adopt anything European simply because it was European, as unfortunately there was a tendency among the people to do. Then, there was the subject of the recognition of European advancement, and Badruddin said that pride in the glorious past of the Muslims often led them to claim that all inventions and discoveries of modern Europe were, as a matter of fact, known to Muslims in the past, that it was only necessary to turn over their old books and there was no need to seek knowledge from the West. Badruddin argued that it may well be contended that Muslim classical literature was equal or even superior to European and that Islam had produced men as great or greater than Christian Europe, but the fact was that man had continued to progress by stages, and each generation built and climbed higher on the ladder than its predecessor. It had thus the advantage of all the fruits acquired by past labours, and it was only natural therefore that man's knowledge should continually increase. It would be a mistake not to recognise this. For example it would be unfortunate and unwise not to learn and benefit from the knowledge Europe had acquired in medicine and surgery during the past 200 or 250 years, or not to consult qualified European physicians and surgeons and to rely only upon *hakeems* and *vaids*, especially those whose qualifications were untested and unascertained, and not as high as they certainly had been in the past. It was foolish to resort to quacks who might prove dangerous and so on. Conversations like these could not fail to broaden the outlook of the community, bring about better understanding and toleration of the customs and manners of other people, and even produce a desire to learn and acquire Western knowledge.

Badruddin deplored the hostility which existed between the different Muslim communities which made them oppose and disparage each other. He pointed out how it weakened the Mussalmans, and pleaded for unity. He contemplated with favour not only intermarriages between the different sects of Mussalmans but also between good and broad-minded Hindus and Mussalmans with a view to cement and unite the people.

With the same end in view he was largely instrumental in the founding and deeply interested in the success, of the Islam Club as a meeting ground of Muslims of all communities. He was president of this club from its commencement in about 1890 to the end of his life, and did his best to promote social union among them, and was a constant visitor.

He attached the greatest importance to the physical development of the people through exercise and games. So devoted was he to the cause of physical fitness that he never missed his three games of badminton every morning or his walk in the evening in sun and rain with his carriage following him. He took the keenest interest in the Islam Gymkhana which owed its birth to the initiative of the members of his own family, and of which afterwards he became the president. There he never failed to impress on the young the importance of games, and always presided at the Annual Matheran sports in which his family took an active part and gave a good account of itself often carrying off a large number, sometimes the entire bulk, of prizes every year.

In those days the management of the funds of his community as of other Muslim communities was practically in the hands of the religious heads and the doctrine was that they had the right to manage all affairs. Religion pervaded everything. All worldly affairs must be under the supreme control of the *mullas*. Badruddin advocated the separation of the purely worldly and financial questions from religious ones, and pleaded that in their own interest, the religious heads should keep themselves aloof from all purely financial and mundane matters. He believed that religious authority in worldly affairs stifled criticism leading to irresponsible and corrupt practices. It resulted in the sacrifice of spiritual values for selfish ends, and ultimately ended in the contempt and destruction of their authority. He himself established *waqfs* (trusts) for the benefit of his community, the first of their kind in which the entire management was vested in persons free of all control of the religious heads.

Purdah had through the ages assumed an aspect so severe that it was intolerable, crushing and stifling. Of course Badruddin was devoted to the cause of liberalising it so as to give life and freedom to women. Some were anxious that he should take rapid strides. Badruddin's method of reform was a cautious advance, step by step. He wished to take the community with him as far as possible. He deprecated sudden and violent methods. If the women themselves were not accustomed and prepared for the company of men, nor men fit for their society, a forced step would result in discrediting the movement instead of advancing it. He therefore advised and himself adopted a cautious advance along the line of least resistance. He set the example himself and drew with him such people as were prepared to follow him. He guarded against a break in his community. When the first girls' school was opened in Bombay at Mazagaon under the auspices of the Zenana Bible Medical Mission in 1876, and soon after began to take day scholars, Badruddin sent his three daughters—the first among Muslim girls, to this school, and they continued their schooling till they were fifteen or sixteen. They rode horses in the outskirts of the city, avoiding the thickly populated parts, and on the Hill of Matheran. The ladies drove in closed carriages in Bombay with curtains up, pulling them down in the crowded parts of the city. They had their cloaks covering them from head to foot partially covering the face, which they discarded outside the busy localities. The circle of those before whom they appeared was constantly enlarged till it included practically all relatives and friends. In 1894 one of his nieces (Mrs Ali Akbar) and his daughter (Mrs Abbas S Tyabji) went to England where of course they had to cast off the *purdah* altogether. In 1898, another niece (Mrs afterwards Lady Hydari) cast off the *purdah,* in Bombay, attending a large mixed evening party at Jamsetji Tatas and in 1904 Badruddin sent two of his daughters to a boarding school in England (Haslemere) for their education. The family had thus the distinction of being the first to discard the *purdah*.[1] For, it was not till 1919 that Madame Zaghlul cast off her veil in Egypt at the bidding of her great husband and she was the first Egyptian woman of high family to do so.[2]

In promoting and effecting the reforms, Badruddin had often to go directly in opposition to the religious feelings of his community and even the personal interests of the religious heads. The purity of his domestic life, the reputation of his personal character, his wisdom and largely his prudent policy shielded him, and warded off or weakened the opposition of the *mullas.* He never allowed a breach of his relations with them, and throughout his life he was held in the highest respect by the *nyodnas* of his own community the MullaJl Saheb of the Dawoodi Bohras, and the Aga Khan of the Khojas. One reason for this perhaps was his recognition that in the state of the social development of the Mussalmans at the time, it was necessary that respect for their religious heads should be maintained, and he himself rendered it to them.

...

THE MAHOMEDAN ANGLO-ORIENTAL CONFERENCE

Badruddin deprecated the introduction into the Conference of anything likely to hurt the feelings of their other fellow subjects, and expressed the hope that the Congress and the Conference would work together harmoniously. He attributed the backwardness of the condition of the Mussalmans largely to the religious and literary prejudices and the absence of female education. He strongly urged, that while cherishing the love of their religion and literature, they should turn their attention to Western Arts and Sciences which had made Europe what it was. And he strongly urged likewise, that the education of Muslim girls should be taken in hand. Mussalmans had lagged behind because of the restrictions of the *purdah* which had been extended far beyond the demands of the *shariat.*

'There are' he said 'no doubt, plenty of passages in the *Koran* and in the traditions of the prophet which lay down the highest principles of morality and modesty, which inculcate modesty and decorum, which prohibit the ostentatious display of beauty and ornaments, which upbraid impropriety of conduct, but I have not been able to discover anything in the *Koran* which either directs or even sanctions the system of *purdah* in all its strictness as it obtains amongst us at the present day.'

His treatment of the whole subject of education was exhaustive and the above are the most notable features. He excluded from the scope of the Conference the original aim and purpose of the Aligarh School of thought led by Syed Ahmad Khan, of opposition to the Congress, and preached its support. Again, from that platform where its founder would have limited the education of women within the restrictions of the prevalent custom, and regarded all agitation against them as harmful,[3] he declared that the restrictions were unwarranted by the dictates of the *shariat*, and should be done away with. Thus he justified both the tribute paid to him by H.H. The Aga Khan, as 'a leader, such as they had not', and the hopes and expectations of the reformers. His bearing and attitude abundantly indicated perfect self-confidence. His words were pregnant with the weight of consummate leadership and authority. But there was of course intense commotion over his address among the more conservative and orthodox. There was even fear of violence.

Reformers rejoiced but the opponents were bitter. The very next day after the inaugural address of the President which declared that there was nothing in the *Koran* justifying the severe restrictions of the *purdah* as were then in vogue, a light-complexioned, tall *moulvie* from the North, of stentorian voice, rose from the midst of the assemblage and challenged the President's statement. Excitement was intense, and a single match could set the whole on fire and put an end to the Conference. With that quick perception, tact, and judgment, with which he was gifted, Badruddin rose, cut short the *moulvie's* argument and said: 'You need not read the passage, write it down and send it over.' Some little time passed in finding paper, writing the passage, and bringing it over to the Chair. Badruddin then closely read and scanned the passage, and said: 'This is nothing new and different, and it only forms part of the passages I read.' The *moulvie* disappointed and angry, disputed the ruling, and attempted to argue. One moment more and ten others would have risen to support him. But Badruddin allowed not a moment for the conflagration to flare up, and his voice pealed like thunder: 'Sit down sir, Sit down!' Speechless, the *moulvie* staggered to his seat, the opposition collapsed and the fire was extinguished. The quick and decisive handling of the situation so fraught with danger is an example of Badruddin's leadership, courage and power.

After the above incident, a new role was unfolded for the Conference—not of mere speeches but of influential committees carefully to think out plans for improvement of Muslim education, and their social, moral, and physical advancement. Badruddin did not attend their meetings but two of his nominees represented him, and an exhaustive programme was thought out. In accordance with the observation of the President 'that the absence of any well defined constitution must always tend to make the duties and functions of the Conference somewhat vague and uncertain', his nephew Mr Mohammad Akbar (afterwards Sir Akbar Hydari) moved the resolution 'that it was necessary to change the rules and regulations of the Conference to make it popular, and create an interest among Mussalmuns'. In spite of some strong opposition, that since Syed Ahmad Khan did not think it necessary in his days, it was not necessary now, the resolution was carried, and a strong and influential committee was appointed to draft the constitution. This was followed by a carefully drafted resolution providing for the establishment of schools for Muslim girls: 'with complete regard to the modes and customs of respectable Muslim families'. It might be imagined that such a resolution would not have created any serious opposition. But it was otherwise. For the scent of danger to purdah had filled the air. The more bigoted and fanatic Muslims believed that it was an attack on the *purdah*, others, that it was only the thin end of the wedge. The speeches were heated and wild. They wandered away from the resolution and became irrelevant. There was such a storm that Nowab Mohsin-ul-Mulk earnestly requested the President not to retain in his address his remarks about the *purdah*. His own opinion was that the *purdah* was a religious question, and it should be maintained as it might be proved to be in accordance with the dictates of religion.[4] He was 'afraid that on account of the discussion the Aligarh party would be discredited'. 'I am sorry', he said 'that people think that it is the opinion of the Aligarh College people and of the Conference that *purdah* should be abolished. I say it is the opinion neither of the college people nor of the Conference. As to the founder, Syed Ahmad Khan, he excelled the ignorant of ignorants, and the fanatic of fanatics among Mussalmans. The ladies of Judges and Collectors desired to see his daughter-in-law Mahmood Begum, but he did not hold even that as permissible, or to meet the ladies of his own friends or of Syed Mahmood.[5] Ninety per cent of the Aligarh party and Aligarh College are of the opinion that the *purdah* as it exists should be maintained.' Mohsin-ul-Mulk expressed great anxiety that if the observations made in the inaugural speech about the *purdah* were not removed they would cause excitement among the Mussalmans and bring about disruption of the Conference. He therefore appealed to the President not to allow any discussion on the question of *purdah* as that was a religious question, outside the limits of the Conference, but Badruddin did not accept the plea. His reply was characteristic: 'It is neither my intention nor the intention of anybody else that a religious question be provoked. But those who do not regard *purdah* as a question of religion have a right to bring forward the question as to what was *purdah*, just as those who hold a different view have a right to discuss it.' Ghulam-us-Saklain, a member of the standing committee, feared that if the discussion was not severely restricted 'such a storm would arise that it would be more terrible than the flood of a river, and with a single wave would carry off the whole Conference'. Badruddin was not heedless to these appeals and entreaties, and he listened to them and sympathised with them for the fears they entertained. It was not his policy, nor did he desire or approve of forcing reforms, but a beginning had to be made and although changing any part of his inaugural speech was unthinkable and uncalled for, nevertheless, he desired to pacify their fears and reconcile them. He therefore intervened in the heated discussion and inserted in the resolution the words 'according to the *Sharai purdah*', and addressing the Conference, he pointed out the significance of those words, and to bear them in mind in further discussion. When some speakers thought that the words would be explained away on the ground that there was no *purdah* according to the *shariat*, and demanded that there should be a clear declaration in the resolution relating to the schools for girls that there was to be no alteration in the existing *purdah*, Badruddin quieted them. 'Who would be so foolish', he said, 'to establish schools for girls if proper provision for their *purdah* as you wish is not made? Would they be so foolish as to have schools without girls? Walls standing with no pupils inside?' The resolution was then carried, the faces of the reformers beaming with happiness at their success and admiration for the strong and tactful chairmanship and the management of a dangerous and stormy session. After the resolution was passed, Badruddin took the opportunity of again explaining his views and advocating the cause of *purdah*. At a lecture by Miss Nasiruddin, who belonged to the Timur family, and who suggested that arrangements should be made for Muslim ladies to attend meetings of the Mussalmans, he strongly supported her. He mentioned that Moulana Shah Sulaiman had acknowledged that the customary *purdah* had far exceeded the *sharai purdah*. Badruddin declared that it was the duty of the *Ulemas* to point out and explain to their followers the proper limits of the *sharai purdah* and called upon them to discharge that duty. He expressed his anxiety to know and asked who were willing to undertake that task.[6] After the resolution for the establishment of schools for girls, which in some way was believed to involve the grave question of *purdah* was disposed of, many other resolutions were passed for the betterment of Muslim education, for the establishment of boarding houses for non-resident students, for the introduction of the kindergarten system, for the creation of a fund out of small gifts on occasions of marriages and *eids*, for the eradication of pernicious customs, such as extravagance on occasions of death and marriage, for prevention of early marriages, for discouragement of gifts to able-bodied beggars, prevention of marriages against the wishes of the parties, for the prevention of idle living, for the establishment of a Mahomedan University, for the establishment of schools for arts and crafts, for the establishment of a national paper in English, and for the right guidance and proper utilisation of Mussalman *waqfs*, involving their diversion for the benefit of education when the original objects had proved useless. Many of these resolutions were so well-meaning and beneficial as to inspire hope of much real good if put into effect, and gave Badruddin great satisfaction. He expressed this by saying: 'Truly if we regard the Conference as a body, these resolutions are its very life, because the whole of its proceeding is bound up and dependant upon those resolution, and not merely the Conference, but in truth, all our present and future hopes are also bound up with those resolutions, and are dependant upon them. Gentlemen, all the resolutions which you have passed are here before me ready written up on this paper. When I see these resolutions, I feel delighted in my heart, and it is not only I who feel delighted, but I saw that whenever any of these resolutions was passed, there was evidence of joy and happiness on the faces of the whole audience. But gentlemen, this is only a temporary, sentimental joy, of no substance, merely imaginary, because the genuine joy of the soul is only possible when everyone who had exerted himself that it should be passed, should also try that effect be given to it and consider that as his duty.'

NOTES

1. *Daily Graphic* (London), 23 August, 1906.
2. Paul Tabari, *Bombay Chronicle*, 21 November, 1945.
3. Mohsin-ul-Mulk Report, p. 345.
4. Report, p. 124.
5. Report, pp. 124 and 344.
6. Report, p. 273.

Malavika Karlekar

Malavika Karlekar is the editor of *Indian Journal of Gender Studies* and Project Director, Photo Archives on Women, Centre for Women's Development Studies, New Delhi. Since 1975, she has been a researcher and university teacher in education, gender and equality issues. From the 1990s she has focused on (a) project conceptualization, and related research and administration; (b) editorial and management functions and (c) monitoring and evaluation.

She is the author of *Poverty and Women's Work: A Study of Sweeper Women in Delhi* and *Voices from Within: Early Personal Narratives of Bengali Women*. Malavika is Co-Editor of *Women's Studies Women's Lives: Theory and Practice in South and Southeast Asia* and *Breaking the Silence: Violence against Women in Asia.*

In 2001, she curated *Re-presenting Indian Women 1875–1947: A Visual Documentary*, based on over 200 archival photographs, in December 14–23, 2001, for the Centre for Women' s Development Studies. Supported by the confederation of Indian Industry and in collaboration with India International Centre, the event was held at the Art Gallery of the IIC. Karlekar is now coordinating a companion publication based on the visual documentary.

𝄞

Constructions of Femininity in Nineteenth Century Bengal: Readings from *Janaika Grihabadhur Diary**

Contemporary trends in the understanding and writing of history and society have emphasized a search for new sources. There is a growing

* I am grateful to Andre Beteille, Vina Mazumdar, Hanna Papanek and Esha Beteille for comments on earlier versions of this paper.

Malavika Karlekar, 'Constructions of Femininity in Nineteenth Century Bengal: Readings from *Janaika Grihabadhur Diary*', *Samya Shakti*, Vols IV & V, 1989–90, pp. 11–29.

belief that knowledge and information available through government documents and reports, manuscripts, the occasional autobiography, journals and newspapers are no longer sufficient. Apart from untapped written material, there is an increasing stress on oral history and on life histories. If we restrict ourselves to the written word as available in the latter half of 19th century Bengal, we find that the social reform movement and subsequent debates on the woman's position led to a proliferation of ideological viewpoints, some of which were put forth in the print media. By the second half of the century, a handful of women began writing fiction as well as exhortatory tracts on the need to adjust to changing times; a few also wrote about their own lives. However, so far such writings have hardly attracted the attention of historians or literary critics. Yet, a reading of these texts provides valuable information on little-known aspects of how families were affected during a process of rapid social change. They also give insights into women's perceptions of their lives. The fact that these women were able to express themselves in writing was a result of the extension of facilities for learning and literacy.

How one writes and how these writings are then interpreted is part of a growing area of theoretical discourse. I have looked at some aspects of these theories elsewhere;[1] here I shall describe why I chose to study selection of women's writings. Apart from providing in brief, information on some of the selected texts, I also discuss how my reading of these has led to construction of a femininity which was distinctly different from contemporary accounts. Such a construction is based more on women's self-perceptions than on societal ideas of what women were like or should have been like. Finally, to illustrate my point, I have analyzed Kailashbashini Mitter's *Janaika Grihabadhur Diary*.

In recent years, the need to understand Indian history from the viewpoint of the 'subaltern', in 'terms of class, caste, gender and office' has resulted in several case studies of peasant consciousness, *adivasi* uprisings, trade union organizations and agrarian tensions.[2] Historians have provided insights into how non-elitist, underprivileged groups perceived their reality. Though the upper middle class educated *bhadramahila* or gentlewoman was, in absolute terms privileged, she was clearly underprivileged *vis-a-vis* the *bhadralok* or men of that society. As we read some of their writings we become aware of a well-articulated dismay at an unfair social order. Such quiet protests are to be seen in the context of an overall acceptance of their family situation: nonetheless, given the times in which they lived and the forces against which they had to express themselves, women's questioning of established traditions and of new values is of considerable significance. When Western education came to India at the beginning of the last century, early recipients were boys and men. Particularly in the urban areas, school and college-going became increasingly popular and white collar jobs the preferred goal. Introduction to an entire literary tradition encouraged the growth of a reading public which also soon took to writing and public speaking. Fiction, poetry, moral and didactic discourses in both English and Bengali found expression in journals and magazines as well as in separate books. Social matters were actively discussed. As learning for girls involved a completely different set of responses than education for boys, and necessitated special arrangements, the issue became an area of considerable debate in the print media, discussion groups and in homes. A wide and varied cross-section of opinion expressed its views on the subject. Put very simply, questions related to the function of this education and how it could adapt to other predominant requirements such as feminine seclusion, division of labour within the home and a belief in the different natures of men and of women. At the same time, alienation from social practices such as *sati* or widow immolation, child marriage and polygamy among those who were later to be broadly categorized as social reformers[3] brought with it an appreciation of the need to improve the status of women. Ostensibly the issue was the woman's position though in actual fact it went far beyond: it was not only a question of granting women access to a privilege or abolishing rituals derogatory to them, but involved thinking anew on the entire ideological foundations of upper caste, middle class Bengali Hindu society. Education appeared to be an obvious answer to the woman's lowly position though clearly it had to be tailored to prevailing social conditions and expectations.

Women authors of exhortatory texts clearly accepted the need to bring about change in life styles and all that this would entail; what is not so clear is how other women reacted to a re-fashioning of their lives. In this context, writing about oneself becomes particularly important as it provides many important insights into attitudes, perceptions as well as anxieties and fears. Did women see sexual difference only as a celebration of male superiority, and view themselves as victims of an unfair social order? Could they find ways of overcoming their disadvantages, in however limited a manner? Would it be appropriate to speak of an emerging feminine consciousness? By this I do not mean a consciousness culminating in a demand for separatism or militant activism but of varying perceptions, of how women experience the world. Often private or personal writings became the medium through which this emergent consciousness expressed itself. In fact, studies in the present century show that the autobiography, journal, and diary have an important role to play in the lives of a range of individuals[4] as they not only document events but also feelings and attitudes in great detail. A close reading of many of the texts mentioned here helps in a reconstruction of femininity as seen from the point of view of the object, who now becomes a mediating subject. Before going into methodological and theoretical implications, it is necessary to briefly look at the historical setting in which these issues became relevant.

Nineteenth century Bengal witnessed a substantial degree of change, conflict and accommodation among the *bhadralok*[5] as well as between them and the British rulers. *Bhadra samaj,* or the society of the civilized, was the society of men, of the *bhadralok.* Literally translated to mean 'gentleman', the same word encompassing both the singular as well as the plural, this term as also *bhadra samaj,* symbolized an entire way of life; urbanization, proliferating white collar jobs in the professions and in the many offices suited the rulers as much as it did the newly emergent middle class. Competition, both for a limited number of jobs and over the emulation of the right style of life, also brought with it factionalism. It would be more apt to envisage the *bhadralok* as a conglomeration of several sub-groups rather than as one homogeneous category. Occupational mobility was aided by a fast-expanding educational system and the opening up of new professions. Education and literacy for boys had a handstart of about three decades over that of girls, and it is only around the 1840s that schooling for girls gained acceptability among middle class Hindus. Earlier, the system of *zenana* or home education had become popular; introducing girls to the rudiments of learning and etiquette, it effectively combined the principle of feminine seclusion with the growing need for education. From the early part of the century, home instruction for boys had become established; this facility, when extended to girls took its name from the Persian word *zenana* which meant both women and women's apartments.

The introduction of learning through Western institutions implied not only the adoption of new teaching methods and content but also of an underlying ideology. Put simply, this meant an acceptance of structured teaching based on syllabi which stressed Western scientific and literary knowledge, discovery and training. Ideologically, it was premised on the superiority of Western education and of the roles and obligations it created. At a more personal level, individual encounters were characterized by a certain measure of give and take,[6] though the balance of advantage was weighted distinctly in favour of the ruler. In turn, men internalized Victorian attitudes towards women, vital for the development of the right kind of *bhadramahila* or Bengali gentlewoman. Such a woman was to be a 'helpmate' and an intelligent companion to her husband, caught up in the stormy days of social and occupational change. The first teachers of many women, confined to the *antahpur,* were fathers, brothers and husbands. Literally translated to mean 'inner house', the *antahpur* consisted of the rooms, courtyard and kitchen in which women lived and worked. Only children and a few men had access to these areas. The principle of seclusion normally resulted in the women's quarters being less exposed and open. In practical terms this meant that they were often ill-ventilated, dark and humid. Equally important in the present context is the physical and emotional experiences of which the *antahpur* was symbolic. It was the world of the *aturghar* or lying-in room, rituals or *bratas,* an endless repertoire of food items prepared according to specific rules on how to cut and cook fish, meat and vegetables. An in-marrying woman's identity was shaped and organized by the norms of the *antahpur* dictated usually by senior female affines.[7]

It is tempting to liken the attitude of men to the *antahpur* as one of enlightened despotism towards the Other, what Edward Said has characterized as the 'surrogate or underground self'. Often, according to Said, when the European observer wrote and thought about 'a distant barely intelligible civilization or cultural movement'[8] he did so as a superior, distanced outsider; economic hegemony in the colonies was buttressed by notions of cultural superiority and the pre-eminence of Western manners and customs. Again, the relationship between the colonizer and the colonized has been described as being similar to that of a parent's attitude to an unknowing child.[9] The primary emotion of the colonial rulers, and, analogically of Western-educated men was that of a superiority committed to bringing about change. The modes adopted were many and varied. However, any encounter implies a mutuality, a degree of absorption, much of which may be unconsciously internalized. Nor is it always easy to either document or analyze this complex interplay of cultural streams. Some of its impact, however, does come through in letters, journals and other personal writings.

By the second half of the last century Bengali women started writing about themselves as well as noting down their responses to the changing environment. Often, their point of view was quite different from that of men, or of the ideas put forth of them by men as well as by some women. As my main interest was with the constructions of femininity during a particular historical phase, that is, the 1860s to the beginning of the present century, I felt it was necessary to be flexible in the choice of texts and when they were written. Thus, I studied memoirs written in the middle of the present century because they relate to the lives and experiences of women towards the end of the colonial period. There appears to be a broad ideological continuity (with of course some variations) during the period on notions of femininity. Two factors which substantially influenced these constructions were formal education, and later, the national movement. I am mainly concerned with the former, and accordingly the narratives and texts I examined relate to the pre-Gandhian period in Indian politics. These writings were affected by politics and political mobilization only to the extent that fathers, brothers or husbands were involved in the British Indian Association, the Brahmo Samaj, the early Indian National Congress and so on. Though Kadambini Ganguly, for instance, addressed the Indian National Congress, she was not involved directly in the waves of *swadeshi* and *ahimsa*. Sarala Debi Chaudhurani (nee Ghoshal) (1982) and Rani Chanda (1972) were two notable exceptions though their writings deal with their early lives. While Sarala Debi did become intensely involved with terrorist groups even during the period covered by her autobiography, her sustained contribution to the national movement was after her marriage; this is a phase with which her book does not concern itself.

Between 1856 and 1910 almost 400 works by Bengali women were estimated to have been written. These ranged from short poems to full-length novels and autobiographies. During the same period, to cater to a growing readership, over 20 periodicals which dealt primarily with women's issues were being published. Interestingly, women were associated in various editorial capacities with these publications.[10] More specifically, over the last century, there is a record of at least 50 autobiographies and autobiographical sketches having been written by Bengali women.[11] Here these are referred to as personal narratives, a term which encompasses the more formal, structured autobiography as well as the musings of a daughter at the death of her father. My study concentrated primarily on the personal narratives of 11 upper middle class, upper caste Bengali Hindu women, two dictated biographies, and a selection of didactic writings and two collections of short stories for neo-literates, which dealt with incidents about 'good' and 'bad' girls. In addition a few personal writings and moral discourses by some men have also been used. While young women by and large accepted their guardians' decisions, instances of questioning of roles and expectations, of wanting to know why boys should have access to science and mathematics were not unknown. These and many other observations have been documented in essays, journals, diaries and in random jottings and letters. In Bengal, the women who wrote formed a tiny percentage of an elite section of society,[12] their access to writing was in most cases, a result of sustained efforts by men to make women literate. Literacy was part of a larger design to enable *bhadramahilas* from the *antahpur* to have access at least through reading and writing, to the outer world as well. In an important sense then, literacy (and the use to which some women put it) mediated between the private world of the *antahpur* and the public world of men.

In Bengal, by the middle of the last century, the writing of tracts on social relations, the correct demeanour and modes of behaviour for young men and women as well as on how an educated girl should behave became increasingly popular. Most had strong moral overtones, exhorting leaders to follow a specific path, avoid others, and stand firm by their values. For girls and for women, it was essential that education, changes in dress and other Western influences were not to distract from their basic goals: it was important to be reminded that femininity implied chastity, obedience, docility and acquiescence. In the present context, the study of these texts becomes important as they put forth the 'official' construction of femininity. When these are juxtaposed with the personal narratives of women, more than one image of femininity becomes available. Such constructions also help in an understanding of a society viewed now from the point of view of women. Among other things, their writings urge us to look afresh at the ideology of hierarchy and its ramifications. Some of the questions which Rassundari, Kailashbashini Mitter and Kamini Ray raised in however a tentative manner, brought to light differing points of view on gender relations in an unequal, stratified society.

Though specific information on the social background, age and marital status of women authors referred to here was not available, clearly all had been married, and about half were widows at the time of writing. Most were above 50 years of age and came from Brahmo families or those associated with the reform movement. Notable exceptions were Rassundari Debi, Rani Chanda and Shudha Mazumdar whose families were staunchly Hindu. With widowhood and age came the right to some leisure time and a period of reflection as younger women took on the responsibilities of the household. Writing was an act of catharsis in an unequal society and helped women reflect on gender roles and on the specificities of their lives. Education, in whichever form, was instrumental in facilitating self-expression. Almost half had been to school, and a third to college. Only Sarala Debi had been employed in a job while others like Bamasundari, Kailashbashini Gupta, and later, Saratkumari Chaudhurani, Punyalata Chakravarti and Rani Chanda were recognized as authors. All except Shudha Mazumdar's dictated biography are in Bengali. It is interesting to note variations in the language of earlier writings; thus Rassundari Debi and Kailashbashini Mitter wrote in a colloquial Bengali, occasionally using words and phrases familiar only to the *antahpur*. Around the same time, the well-instructed Bamasundari and Kailashbashini Gupta wrote in Sanskritized Bengali. Chaste language became more the norm in the present century.

The texts analyzed were written between 1868 and 1967 and range from full length books to essays in journals and pamphlets of a few pages put together for a father's *shraddha* or death rites. Not only do they vary in length, but also in levels of sophistication, use of language, internal logic and so on. Some reflect much more the private anxieties of their authors while others deal with changing times, social and political events and so on. Sarala Debi Chaudhurani (1872–1945) in her *Jibaner Jhara Pata* deals at length with an early childhood anguish over her mother Swarna Kumari's rejection of her. Almost half-way through the 243 page book her writing becomes more impersonal and matter of fact as events of several years are crammed into a few pages. Thus descriptions of her roles as choreographer of some of her uncle Rabindranath Tagore's songs, editor of the family magazine *Bharati* and organizer of a group of young men committed to a free India, give us a picture of a spirited woman who was determined to overcome her early deprivations. This book as well as Punyalata Chakravarty's writings (1956, 1964) provide valuable insights into the growth and development of institutions such as the modern family, the educational system and early professions as well as of nationalism and a nationalistic view point. On the other hand, Rassundari's (1981) *Amar Jiban* (My Life)[13] and Kailashbashini Mitter's (1981) *Janaika Grihabadhur Diary* (A Certain Housewife's Diary), two of the earliest texts, are also among the most candid and self-critical, deeply evocative of personal dilemmas.

The earliest personal narrative to be written by a Bengali woman is *Amar Jiban;* Rassundari's work is in many ways a most outstanding articulation in this genre. In his undated 'Bhoomika' (Introduction), Rabindranath Tagore's younger brother Jyotirindranath was greatly impressed by the author's 'thirst for religion which inspired her to learn how to read and write' (Rassundari Debi, 1981:3). Unlike many who wrote later, the self-taught Rassundari received little encouragement from her family. The wife of a prosperous East Bengal *zamindar* recounted how she used to hide pages removed from her son's books within the folds of her sari. She felt strongly about being denied education and reflected that 'women were indeed unfortunate and could be counted as being animals'. But 'my mind would not accept this, and was always restless with the urge to learn' (Rassundari Debi, 1981:28). The quest for God led her to specific activities prohibited to women, namely reading and writing. In the early years it was not unusual for illiterate or semi-literate women to talk about their lives to scribes and Keshub Chunder Sen's mother dictated her life to her grandson-in-law; several decades later, Shudha Mazumdar's (1977) early life was put together by an American historian. Written in the first person, these memoirs reconstruct Shudha's early life, marriage and involvement in social work.

As already pointed out, it was important to use texts which more or less covered the historical period under study; I chose these writings on the basis of their availability and overall relevance to a central concern which was how women viewed change at both the personal and social levels. One may well ask, why did women choose to write about themselves and about their lives? Were there important differences between the writings of men and of women? The second question is less easy to answer primarily because my information on men's personal writings is scanty if not negligible. Writing about oneself is a conscious act[14] as it represents the subject's desire to express—and thus record—feelings and emotions, as well as events. Though an individual diarist may start writing initially at random, the fact that the momentum is sustained over a period of time implies that the act of writing is performing a certain role. It helps in the formation of a distinct identity and of a sense of self; as the writer is able to physically view on palm leaves or paper what she feels about herself, a period of reflection, observation and even recantation can follow. Out of all this, a being emerges, a creation often of fractured, disjointed accounts of life which do not always follow a chronological pattern. Sometimes, this self expression comes at a specific time of life when, due to a number of reasons, opportunities coincide with the desire to write.[15]

Literacy provided 19th century women and many more men with a unique tool for self-expression, and self-discovery. In fact, it is possible that diary-keeping was part of the socialization process of some of those introduced to writing. Providing as it did the format for noting down dates, events and activities a diary helped in organizing its writer's thinking and reflective processes. All the autobiographical writings I studied are in the nature of reflections on past events. None of them was written as a diary, though Kailashbashini Mitter's 30-odd page text was titled *Janaika Grihabadhur Diary*. There are gaps of many years, and the final version appears to be written on the basis of detailed notes. Many of the personal narratives are rich in dates, and incidents long past are described with amazing clarity. It is also possible that in the present context women wrote about themselves rather than fiction, poetry or essays because this form not only satisfied a basic urge but also because it came more easily; there was no need to think about plot, theme or structure, literary niceties in which they had no training.

Again, encouragement for Bamasundari and Kailashbashini Gupta indicates that many men actively supported a concrete outcome to their efforts at educating wives and daughters. Clearly, access to writing led to a range of responses: Kailashbashini Mitter's self-confessional *Janaika Grihabadhur Diary* and Kamini Ray's (1906) comments on her father tell us of their resentment towards the existing situation as much as they provide insights into changing social conditions. Debates on various social practices, treatises on education for women, criticism of the *antahpur* were all apart of the formal moral discourse of the times. Men were its usual exponents, and in time some women also internalized the need to speak and write of all that was happening to their lives. A few had their reservations, and the personal narrative became the medium through which they expressed themselves.

Analyzing Virginia Woolf's six volumes of letters Catharine Stimpson (1984:68) has pointed out that these exemplified 'a particular women's text, one that is neither wholly private nor wholly public'. Letters occupy a 'middle space' between writings written for oneself (a diary, journal) and fiction; in this context a few of the journals and autobiographies discussed here too occupy a middle space, thereby reaching out to the outer, public world whilst expressing some extremely personal thoughts; interestingly it is the two earliest texts which appear to straddle domains. There is of course a school of thought which believes that nobody writes without an audience in mind, though the definitions of audience may vary. While pointing out that the dichotomy between private and public audiences is false, psychoanalyst Sudhir Kakar[16] stresses that an individual always writes for the Other, which may be one's split or divided self, the mother-in-law one hates, or for a specific public audience. Here whether the audience actually reads a text is not of consequence; what is relevant is that an individual writes for, against or to another. An outside agent provides the impetus for the act of writing, and the sense of audience 'whether defined or indeterminate'[17] is always present. In the present context some texts were specifically written for an audience; others appeared to be more in the nature of highly personal thoughts. Absence of adequate information on who first put together and published some of these writings further complicates the issue of why and for whom these women wrote.

Clearly, the common-sense notion of audience is easier to comprehend in the context of some forms of personal writings than in others. Nonetheless, it is not always easy to establish distinctions within the genre. Broadly speaking, an autobiography is presumably written to be read by an actual audience, and concentrates more on major events and incidents rather than on the daily routine documented in the diary or journal. The former can also tend to be more impersonal, with lengthy arguments or discussions focused around an issue. On the other hand, the diary or the journal usually consists of random here-and-now jottings, which may or may not be edited and sharpened later on. While all forms of writing in this genre record events in time, diaries and journals convey a sense of contemporariness, of immediacy which is not always present in the autobiography; they provide 'raw data' rather than 'synthesized memory' (Cooper 1987:95). The everyday usage of the terms diary and journal would indicate that the former records events while the latter catalogues these as well as reactions and responses. However, those who have worked extensively in the area feel that though formats may differ, content may not. By and large, both provide commentaries 'on life as it was lived, that is on process rather than as product'. (Bunker 1987:9).

Accordingly, these texts, written over a period of more than a century, incorporate a range of reflections on changing lifestyles, expectations and aspirations. A few also give expression to a certain sense of loss, of resentment, if not anger. In part, this resentment arose primarily out of a questioning of some of the assumed implications of the differences between men and between women; all the authors apparently complied with what was expected of them as women. Yet that they did so was often a function of deeply ingrained socialization, of years of training and apprenticeship in being good wives and daughters. A distinction needs to be made between dutiful behaviour and an inherent belief in the validity of the existing system. Bamasundari (1861) and Kailashbashini Gupta (1862, 1864) clearly wrote out of a deep commitment to a society where men decided on how women should lead their lives. On the other hand, among the earlier writings Rassundari, Kailashbashini Mitter and Sharadasundari (1981) were amazingly candid in appraisals of their own situation as well as of male attitudes towards them. Kamini's fear of her father's judgmental censure and Punyalata's regret at not having been allowed to study further are indicative of a conviction of their ability to define limits—which in some spheres may not have been very different from those of men.

This conviction arose, as mentioned earlier, out of an ambivalence towards supposed differences between men and women, which tilted the balance in favour of the former. Rassundari's agonized question on whether it was right for her to be treated as a caged bird or Kailashbashini Mitter's rational arguments with her weak-willed husband were the voices of women asking to be taken seriously as individuals and not merely as victims of an unequal society. That they were in part success-ful was a tribute to their strong convictions and their tenacity. This construction of women as victims, as patients[18] in need of immediate treatment, has, over the past decades, grown deep roots both in common discourse as well as in social science analysis. It is only when women's own voices are heard can one begin to question these stereotypes; the reconstruction of women's lives through a reading of personal narratives and recording of life histories and oral histories help not only in creating alternative models but also in understanding better analytical categories such as gender,[19] woman and femininity.

In this context, a reading of Kailashbashini's *Diary*[20] is useful in constructing an image of an unusual *bhadramahila*. She apparently started maintaining her diary a few years after her marriage at the age of about eleven to Kishory Chand Mitter, who was in the service of the East India Company, and younger brother of the reputed novelist and social commentator, Peary Chand Mitter. Both brothers were well-known for their commitment to an improvement in the lives of women, and for their strong stand against polygamy. The women of the Mitter household were educated through the *zenana* system, and Kailashbashini was tutored by her husband and later by an English woman. In a society where it was the established tradition for a man to leave his wife with his family while he was posted in the districts, Kishory Chand chose to take Kailashbashini with him. For her part, Kailashbashini maintained strict *purdah,* and made sure that she did not overlook any requirement expected of a *bhadramahila*.

Kailashbashini had a great eye for detail, dates and names; the de-scription of each incident or occasion is accompanied by meticulous information on the day, month and year as well as of the persons encountered. Her ability to enjoy the countryside and the experience of travelling for days on end along the waterways of East Bengal are evocatively described. Her visit to Plassey—'where the British and the nawabs first fought'—was an exciting event: she writes, 'even though at that time I felt the loss of my son acutely, I experienced a deep sense of satisfaction when I came home'. After the birth of her daughter in 1847 she writes: 'My mother-in-law was very sad. She said, 'I've lost gold and got glass instead'. Kailashbashini did not dwell on her mother-in-law's feelings much but went on to describe Kishory Chand's responses, and the discomforts of her confinement. Her husband wrote to say that he was very happy and that 'you should feel no sorrow. All are the same in the eyes of the *Jagatpita* (father of the world, or God). We should also treat all equally. I am awaiting the time when you will be able to write to me' (Kailashbashini, 1981:10). But it was long before Kailashbashini could reply, confined as she was to a room which she likened to 'a kind of jail room'. For over a month, the upper caste post-partum woman was not to touch anything nor communicate with others except functionaries assigned specific tasks. She wrote,

But my husband did not know my situation. In every letter he wrote, 'you are so cruel, you are so heartless; I didn't know that you'd be so happy at my suffering. In every letter I ask you to write one line but you don't write. I won't write to you anymore'. I was greatly concerned; if he did not write for two or three days, I would die (Kailashbashini, 1981:11).

Soon, the determined Kailashbashini found pen and paper to write to her lonely husband.

With their young daughter Kumudini, the couple soon started touring together, often spending long days on the river 'when we played cards and chatted'. Kailashbashini kept track of her husband's work and proudly reported the establishment of a hospital or a school. Wherever possible, she made friends with other Bengali women. About her life in Natore, where she was fortunate in having a number of women to befriend, she wrote 'we were happy. The reason for this was that as women our demands were few, our minds slight; hence, we were satisfied with little; that independence was enough'. Obviously Kailashbashini was referring to the freedom to interact with other women and occasionally bathe with them in the river at dawn. When

Babu (her husband) went out in the sun or to the *mofussil* (provincial) areas, those days all of us used to wander in the garden. There was no restriction on that. You (referring to her husband) also used to walk with me in the garden, but then they (her women friends) could not join: they did not come out before my husband, nor did I appear before their husbands (Kailashbashini, 1981:18).

Nonetheless, the world of *purdah* had its consolations for Kailashbashini: once when she was ill, and her female attendant was not available, her husband took care of all her needs. While family members used to visit the districts occasionally, the young couple spent most of the time on their own. On her visits to either her parents or her in-laws, Kailashbashini recounted how she used to be counting the days for her return to her husband. Kishory Chand used to teach her English, and in 1852 when he was posted to Calcutta, he engaged an English woman, Miss Tugod, as tutor for his wife. This lady used to teach two other *bhadramahilas* also, and was paid Rs. 25 by each family. Kailashbashini commented 'and there was tuition from the home *guru* as well. In this way a certain amount of knowledge was acquired' (Kailashbashini, 1981:30). In Jahanabad there were not many women with whom Kailashbashini could spend time. Thus,

My daughter and my husband were my only support. I did not see the faces of any other living being. Not that this caused me much discomfort. When he used to go to the *mofussil*, I used to live like Robinson Crusoe. I ate, slept, read and did needle-work. I also taught my daughter and wrote this book. And I used to count the days for his return. When my husband came back, I was greatly relieved (Kailashbashini, 1981:21).

Life changed for Kailashbashini when her husband became a Junior Magistrate in Calcutta; the last few pages of her brief *Diary* make frequent mention of her husband's growing attraction for the more Westernized, liberal Bengalis, many of whom were Brahmos. Kishory Chand obviously enjoyed the ideas of his new friends, where no doubt discussions were carried out over a glass of port or wine. When Kailashbashini objected, her husband chided her affectionately, but did not give much attention to her protestations. As her husband's interaction with social reformers increased, Kailashbashini too started mixing with their wives. At the homes of eminent Brahmos Ramtanu Lahiri and Ramgopal Ghosh, she ate food prepared by a cook and served by a Muslim bearer. Though she clearly found the situation somewhat unusual, strong conviction of the validity of her own way of life left her unaffected. She reported,

I told Babu about Ramtanu Babu's wife, Babu asked, 'where did she eat?' I replied, 'why, with everyone else. After all who am I or who is she or who is anyone for that matter?' Babu replied 'that indeed is true and it is only Bengalis who make an unnecessary fuss'. I don't believe in Hindu rituals, but nonetheless I observe them. The reason for this is that if I slacken even a bit, my husband will cease being a Hindu. The Hindus are my closest relatives. I cannot give them up and hence I observe all the rituals....My husband can do what he likes, there is no problem in that. Bengalis observe this religion, and hence those who have brains, do not observe the Bengali religion. I don't believe in it but I will never tell my husband this. If Babu heard this from my lips I cannot describe how happy he would be (Kailashbashini, 1981:32).

While it is not evident from the *Diary* whether Kishory Chand had in fact become a Brahmo, he clearly was greatly impressed by their views, many of which he supported. While Kailashbashini was not actively hostile to the Brahmo faith, she was reluctant to give up what she had been brought up to believe in. In a particularly dramatic passage she describes her discussion with Kishory Chand regarding their differing beliefs: She told her husband that as from childhood he had been teaching her as one would teach a pet bird to speak, 'I cannot have any views that are basically different from yours. But I will not leave Hinduism and I have given you the reasons why.' Her husband retorted, 'Do you have so little belief in me?' To which Kailashbashini replied, 'No, that can never be; but I do not believe in your style of life.' She concluded that 'Babu understood and did not say anything more' (Kailashbashini, 1981:32).

The year that the rule of the East India Company ended, 'there was a comet sighted in the sky and in the month of *Aswin,* there was a terrible earthquake'. It also brought to an end Kishory Chand's employment with the British and he was unceremoniously stripped of his title of Rai Bahadur. In the days that followed, Kailashbashini consoled him and even suggested that she could contribute to the family income by selling her needle-work. Her husband was apparently appreciative of her support and understanding:

Babu said, 'I have gained great courage from your words....From your words I realise that you are as brave as I am, that you are as intelligent as I am and in fact that your staying power is greater than mine. In knowing this all my pain has gone' (Kailashbashini, 1981:34–5).

The pages of Kailashbashini's *Diary* are alive with descriptions of her relationship with her husband, which among other things was characterized by a strong sense of companionship and mutual respect. They not only played cards with each other, read together but also argued on matters of considerable social and religious significance. Kailashbashini's writings give the distinct impression that not only were the discussions frank and forthright, but also that Kishory Chand often accepted his wife's point of view and reasoning. Despite her maintenance of strict *purdah* travels in the districts of Bengal gave Kailashbashini the opportunity to observe different ways of life. The fact that Kishory Chand ha[d] chosen to keep his wife and child with him provided for the development of a strong family bond where both partners looked upon the home as a refuge from the fast changing world outside. Judging by the narration of events, neither Kailashbashini's family nor her conjugal home had much of a role to play in their lives. Though as a dutiful daughter-in-law she attended every important family function,

Kailashbashini never failed to recount how both she and her husband were counting the days for her return.

Janaika Grihabadhur Diary describes in some detail the life of an Indian working for the East India Company through the eyes of a woman who was educated enough not only to teach her child, be familiar with the scriptures of other religions but also to write lucidly on moral issues. At the end of the *Diary,* the editors have included a page of monthly accounts and details of jewellery; both had been meticulously maintained by Kailashbashini. Her *Diary* described life in a nuclear family, unusual for its times, and the commitment of both husband and wife to its survival. Without the all-encompassing purview of older family members and in-laws, Kailashbashini developed a strong sense of personal identity and was quite clear on her role in preserving domestic harmony: though she did make occasional statements about the limitations of a woman's mind, her well-reasoned response to Hinduism at the level of ritual and behaviour convey the impression of a balanced, independent-minded woman.

Kailashbashini's *Diary* began in the year her son died and ended with the death of Kishory Chand in 1874.

Oh reader, here my book ends. Today my life is finished....I came back a widow. When this name (widow) comes to my ears, it is like a thunderbolt. Alas! What a frightening name (word)—hearing it is like having a heart attack! (Kailashbashini, 1982:45).

It is possible that Kailashbashini's apprehensions of widowhood were based on an awareness of the singularly oppressive and limited life of a Hindu widow. What is more possible however is that her agonized words lamented the end of a life of companionship and mutual trust. This evolution of a husband-wife bond with limited interference from the larger family collectivity was not usual in nineteenth century Bengal. To characterize it as a marriage based on the 'romantic love' notion which was growing in the West would also perhaps not be correct. It would be more appropriate to liken Kailashbashini's attitude to one of *bhakti* or devotion: Despite her independence of spirit, Kailashbashini was very much a creation of her husband's commitment to women's emancipation. He had moulded and influenced her from an early age by exposing her to a whole range of experiences; Kailashbashini remained ever grateful to her liberator. Again, through this very process of education emerged a well-articulated cynicism of existing traditions.

Janaika Grihabadhur Diary is the story of a strong-minded woman whose commitment to traditional beliefs was tempered by pragmatism.

Education equipped Kailashbashini to argue cogently with her husband on literary texts as well as on the meaning of social reform. It also helped in the opening-up of a questioning mind. Kailashbashini knew well that the correctly trained and supportive *bhadramahila* was essential for the maintenance of the family in a process of change. At the same time she had to be intellectually convinced of what was expected of her. Her *Diary* became a confidant, an escape clause at a time when her family life was under considerable strain. It also provides a record of a woman who did not mutely accept the emergent modes of femininity and patterns of social life. The fact that 'the text was organized and re-arranged later obviously indicated an interest in its dissemination: however we do not know though whether this was at Kailashbashini's instance.

This paper has attempted to focus on two points: first, that women's writings throw light on a hitherto unknown, or, at any rate invisible, aspect of family life. The personal narrative, when juxtaposed with exhortatory writings, provides a convincing picture of the ideal and of reality. This is not to say that Rassundari or Kailashbashini Mitter were negligent wives and mothers. Rather, it is only to highlight their response to social change, and concomitantly to their roles. Second, a reading of these texts makes clear that despite women's vital role in the family and indeed indirectly in facilitating meaningful participation of fathers and husbands in the public sphere, they were not merely helpless dependents performing subordinate service roles. Education, which ostensibly brought women within the arena of male control, also provided them with the tools of self-expression. Analysis of these writings indicates a degree of strength, self-assurance and even resentment of the existing social order. In broad terms *bhadra samaj* or civilized society may have been divided and segregated on the basis of sexual difference; when judged as individuals, the lives and experiences of many questioned the typification of women as victims. Thus the search for new sources can yield substantial information for a re-examination of persistent stereotypes, and for alternate constructions of femininity.

The entire process of literacy and learning was in theory liberating: it exposed women to a new world of which they had only heard whispers so far. At the same time new demands on time and emotions had now to be fitted into an already busy schedule: the relatively autonomous, integrated *bhadramahila,* a familiar figure of the *antahpur* had now to become a student, a neophte in a world organized and controlled by men and male-dominated systems of knowledge. Again, loss of a sense of integrated existence in the *antahpur* was in no way matched by the promise of a full life elsewhere. Some accepted eagerly what was being offered; others were less enthusiastic, if not dismayed at the prospect of what they had to give up. A few found other ways out: Kailashbashini's *Diary* is an example of how an intelligent, thoughtful *bhadramahila* mediated between conflicting pressures. Without compromising too much she ensured that her fundamental values remained intact.

NOTES

1. Some of these are discussed in a forthcoming book on *bhadramahilas* and the construction of femininity to be published by Oxford University Press in 1990.

2. To date, six volumes of essays (and a single volume of selections from them) entitled *Subaltern Studies* have been published by Oxford University Press, New Delhi. This quotation is from page 1 of Ranajit Guha's article (1982) in Vol. 1.

3. By and large, the impact of the social reform movement (I am using the term to encompass changes not only in social customs but also to the introduction of education and a new style of life) has been viewed as beneficial and liberating for those concerned. Till a decade ago there was little attempt to look at the point of view of those affected more closely. Thus, for a conventional discussion of the social reform movement, see Charles H. Heimsath, *Indian Nationalism and Hindu Social Reform*, Princeton: Princeton University Press, 1964 and S. Natarajan, *A Century of Social Reform in India*, Bombay: Allied, 1959. Edward Said, *Orientalism*, London: Routledge and Kegan Paul, 1978 marked a break with this tradition. In the Indian context, see the six volumes of *Subaltern Studies* edited by Ranajit Guha, op. cit.

4. For instance, apart from providing an extensive bibliography, Brian Finney, *The Inner Eye: British Literary Autobiography in the Twentieth Century*, London: Faber and Faber, 1985, deals with the role of autobiographies in the lives of men. Here, for purpose of convenience, I use the term 'private or personal narratives' to cover anything from letters to structured full-length autobiographies.

5. See J.H. Broomfield, *Elite Conflict in a Plural Society*, Bombay: OUP, 1968, 13 ff, for a discussion of the term *bhadralok*. While Broomfield envisaged the *bhadralok* as a distinct category, Rajat Kanta Ray, *Social Conflict and Political Unrest in Bengal 1875–1927*, New Delhi: OUP, 1984, is more inclined to view the *bhadralok* as comprising 'respectable society' rather than a homogenous group. Here, I have used the term 'middle class' to include mainly the newly emergent white collar salariat as well as sections of the landed gentry, some of whom had moved to the urban areas in search of alternate forms of employment.

6. Tapan Raychaudhuri, *Europe Reconsidered*, New Delhi: OUP, 1988, writes on the mutuality of the colonial encounter as evidenced in the writings of

three major nineteenth century Bengali figures, Bhudev Mukhopadhyay, Bankim Chandra and Vivekananda. Partha Chatterjee, *Nationalist Thought and the Colonial World*, New Delhi: OUP, 1986, also analyses the nationalist response to colonialism as articulated by Bankim Chandra, M.K. Gandhi and J. Nehru.

7. The Bangladeshi historian Ghulam Murshid, *Reluctant Debutante: Response of Bengali Women to Modernisation 1849–1905*, Rajshahi: Rajshahi University Press, 1982, and Meredith Borthwick, *The Changing Role of Women in Bengal: 1849–1905*, Princeton: Princeton University Press, 1984, provide considerable material on attitudes to and of women during this period. Borthwick categorizes the *bhadramahilas* as women from *bhadralok* homes and deals at length with their attitudes to education, the family, marriage and so on. Here, I have dealt only with upper middle class Hindu women from the Brahmin, Baidya and Kayastha upper castes as well as those who belonged to the Brahmo Samaj (which eschewed caste affiliations).

8. Said's neo-classic has greatly influenced a generation of scholars committed to an understanding of the colonial experience from the point of view of the colonized. Between 1800 and 1950, Said estimates that at least 60,000 books were written on the Near Orient. The relationship between the Orient and the Orientalist was basically hermeneutical, interpretive. Yet the images which emerged often had little relationship with existing Eastern religion, custom and tradition. Cultural domination and belief in the innate superiority of the white man or white woman lay at the basis of such conceptualizations. Nonetheless, the East had an inexorable attraction at a time when the work ethic, Puritanism, industrialization and later, the strait-jacket of Victorian morality, governed the middle class Briton's way of life.

The main thrust of Said's argument then is that what was sought to be presented as objective truths were in fact reflections of a distinct and well-defined superior-subordinate relationship. In short, the Orientalists, be they creative writers, administrators or adventurers, interpreted the East within the framework of Western superiority. Among those who have applied his theory to India is anthropologist Ronald Inden, 'Orientalist Constructions of India', *Modern Asian Studies* 20, part 3, July 1986, and Indian social scientists and teachers of English Literature in the special issue on Orientalism of the *Social Scientist,* June 1986. Gauri Viswanathan looks at the discourse which led to the establishment of certain English institutions in India (see Viswanathan, 'British Indian Educational History: A Methodological Critique', mimeo., 1986, and idem., 'The Beginnings of English Literary Study in British India', *Oxford Literary Review*, 9 (142), 1987). Of related interest are Benita Parry's competent overview ('Problems in Current Theories of Colonial Discourse', *Oxford Literary Review*, 9 (142), 1987), and Homi K. Bhabha's paper ('Signs Taken for Wonder: Questions of Ambivalence and Authority under a Tree Outside Delhi, May 1817', *Critical Inquiry,* Autumn 1985), where he puts forth the idea of hybridization of cultures which results out of the colonial encounter.

9. Ashis Nandy developed this theme in Chapter One of *The Intimate Enemy,*

Delhi: OUP, 1983. See also his *Tao of Cricket*, New Delhi: Viking, 1989, in which he sees 'the game of cricket as a 'truer' projection of cultures and of encounters of cultures than many other forms of self expression' (xi).

10. Usha Chakrabarty in *Condition of Bengali Women around the Second Half of the Nineteenth Century*. Calcutta,1963, 143ff. discusses women's writings.

11. See Chitra Deb, *Antahpurer Atmakatha* (The Autobiography of the Inner Home), Calcutta: Ananda Publications, 1984, for a list of these writings as well as brief notes on several authors, pp. 133–58.

12. If it is accepted that the *bhadralok* comprised mainly the Brahmin, Baidya and Kayastha castes, then according to the Census of 1881, not more than 10 per cent of the Bengali population came from these three. At the same time, students from the three constituted over 70 per cent of the college-going population. For relevant definitions of elite and intelligentsia, see Sabyasachi Bhattacharya, 'Notes on the Role of the Intelligentsia in Colonial Society: India from Mid-Nineteenth Century', mimeo., 1979. Anil Seal provides much useful information and analysis of what he calls the political arithmetic of the Presidencies (*The Emergence of Indian Nationalism*, Cambridge: Cambridge University Press, 1971). Then, if women comprised approximately half the total population, only a tiny fraction were literate, and an even smaller number wrote and commented on their lives, and on the changing environment.

Chitra Deb gives a comprehensive account of some of these women's responses based on quotations and descriptions from various personal writings (Deb, op. cit.). In addition, 'Daimalir Karagar Bhangar Gaan' (Daimali's Song of Prison Destruction) by Srabashi Ghosh published in the *Sharadiya Anushtup* (1985) analyzes some trends in Bengali women's autobiographies. (See also her 'Birds in a Cage, Changes in Bengali Social Life as recorded in Autobiographies by Women', *Economic and Political Weekly*, 21 (43), 25 October, 1986).

13. Rassundari's *Amar Jiban* was published in two parts, the first in 1868 when she was 58 years old and the second part in 1897. Both parts have been reprinted in *Atmakatha* by Naresh Chandra Jana et. al.

14. At a seminar entitled 'The Individual and Society', organized by the India International Centre and Max Mueller Bhavan, New Delhi, in December 1988, political scientist Sudipta Kaviraj asked whether it would not be in order to characterize women's conscious act of writing as a political statement in a changing environment. This was particularly so as often the women were daughters or wives of men involved in or closely associated with the forces bringing about socio-political changes in the Bengal of the last century. While agreeing in part with Kaviraj, I nonetheless felt that it was important that the definition of 'political' should be widened to include education as the most important political event in women's lives; not only did it expose them to a wide range of ideas, and views, but also provided access to the means of expression.

15. See Donna Stanton, *The Female Autograph*, Chicago: The University of

Chicago Press, 1984, for a useful collection of essays on women's letters, journals and memoirs.

16. Kakar made this point at the December seminar (footnote 14). He was intervening in the discussion following the presentation of my paper 'The Autobiography as Women's Response to Society: *Janaika Grihabadhur Diary*'.

17. From Suzanne L. Bunker ('"Faithful Friend": Nineteenth Century Midwestern, American Women's Unpublished Diaries', *Women's Studies International Forum* 10 (1), 1987: 8). This article provides many interesting insights into why women wrote and continue to write for themselves.

18. Amartya Sen, in 'Gender and Cooperative Conflicts', Discussion Paper No. 1342, Harvard Institute of Economic Research, 1987: 45, draws attention to the consistent tendency of viewing women as patients rather than as agents within the family and in society as a whole. Reiterating his well-known position that bargaining relations in the family which result in cooperation does not overrule the existence of conflict over entitlements, Sen shows that it is important to understand the role of 'perception and agency' in determining women's general well-being. Gerda Lerner discusses the trend in American history of 'contribution' history which, while documenting the roles of important women, nonetheless ends up 'treating women as victims of oppression which again places them in a male defined conceptual framework' (*The Majority Finds its Past: Placing Women in History*, New York: OUP, 1979: 148).

19. It is now generally accepted that while 'sex' refers to physiological distinctions gender is a 'cultural construct, a set of learned behaviour patterns' (Pat Caplan, 'Introduction', in Caplan (ed.), *The Cultural Construction of Sexuality*, London: Tavistock, 1987). Caplan goes into differences between sex and gender and historical as well as anthropological understandings of these terms. More recently, Val Plumwood, in 'Do We Need a Sex/Gender Distinction?', *Radical Philosophy* 51, Spring 1989, critically analyzed this distinction.

20. *Janaika Grihabadhur Diary* was serialized in the Bengali monthly *Basumati* in 1953 and in *Ekshan,* annual number of 1981, pp. 9–48. Present references are from the latter version.

Maithili Rao

Bombay-based film and media critic Maithili Rao examines the portrayal of purdah in Bollywood films. She has written extensively on cinema, and her essay 'Heart of the Movie' is included in *Bollywood* (2001), edited by Lalit Mohan Joshi.

Screen Image

Popular cinema is the distorted, and distorting, mirror of our times. Its brainwashing potential, despite all the jeering at its melodramatic excess, burrows away at the subliminal level. It creates new myths, reworking the old ones, which infiltrate the unconscious world of a collective psyche, its historically inherited fantasies. This is an insidious osmotic process as cinema draws upon and reinforces the moral and cultural status quo upholding patriarchal society.

The status quo is a presiding deity of the box-office the world over. Only the Don Quixotes of offbeat cinema tilt at the windmills. In the West (which we often perceive as the liberated promised land) wellmade, serious commercial films like *Kramer Vs. Kramer* or *Ordinary People* (two Academy Award winning examples) reflect the backlash against feminism. They portray women as home wreckers when they set out to find themselves. Hindi cinema which looks Hollywoodwards for technological gimmickry and the new formula for success is not immune. So we have the disturbing phenomenon of deeply entrenched ideas of female servitude and subservience given gloss and the dubious sanction of updated psychology. It is this seeming liberalism, coupled with a spurious concern for the oppression of women, which is more dangerous than the endless repetition of the atrophied *Sati Savitri* image. Even the unsophisticated filmgoer, however much he instinctively and consciously

Maithili Rao, 'Screen Image', *Manushi*, Number 48, 1988.

identifies with and approves of the timeworn sanctity of *Sati Savitri*, is lured by the 'bright new image' of the emerging Hindi film heroine. New in the superficial sense of being a working girl or a victim of hidebound society. The new woman is so hazy, so hedged by safe bets that she is still caged in the ghetto of purdah.

Elsewhere in this issue, the term purdah culture is explored in all its connotations. It would be singling out the 'Muslim Social' to tar with the regressive brush if we apply the term purdah mentality only to this hothouse genre. What is undeniable is that the 'Muslim Social', with its elaborate courtesies and courtly elegance, incantatory poetry and mellifluous music, romanticises the concept of the beauty behind the veil with far-reaching effects. *Chaudhvin Ka Chand, Palki, Mere Mehboob* et al exploit a beleaguered minority's collective nostalgia for bygone grandeur and etherealise the aristocratic women till they almost vaporise into impossible dreams. A woman is a melting glance, a musical voice, a seductress shrouded in mysterious silk and glittering in sequinned unreality. So unearthly that smitten men have to offer love as worship and sigh in adoration. In short, a *Mehbooba* (Beloved) is treasured for her fragility, innocence and compliance.

The 'Muslim Social' did not come out of its dreamworld to tackle contemporary problems until *Nikah* and *Bazaar*. *Bazaar* was unbearably moving in its expose of the genteel flesh trade through marriage with the grooms flaunting petro dollars. The whiplash documentary footage proved too uncomfortable to a community's conscience. It certainly soft peddled the identity of the bride buyers through diplomatic evasion. But *Bazaar's* sincerity is an exception to the general romantic myth. *Nikah* goes halfway and retreats in alarm. At first, it is unbelievably daring for tackling the threat of unilateral divorce which hangs like the sword of Damocles over the Muslim wife, specially when you take into account that Muslims form a big segment of faithful, repeat audience for a specifically Muslim subject.

At the very outset, B.R. Chopra is careful not to be too revolutionary, defining the parameters of woman only in relationship to man as wife, mother and beloved. The kitsch paintings of woman in quite a few titillating poses are the visuals for the background commentary which laments the dishonoring of the wife/mother ideal. Not her selfhood as such. Salma Agha is the educated girl, dabbling with writing, whose world is shattered when her cousin/husband pronounces the dreaded talaq, talaq, talaq in a fit of temper. The issue of maintenance or the return of mehr is evaded while Salma turns a freelancer to make a living.

She does not go back to the parental home for fear of humiliation. Her knight in a crumpled sherwani is the pan-chewing, good humoured college mate who has all along been in love with her. His middle class heart is liberal enough to offer her marriage. The point of the film is the inquitious right of divorce given to men.

The director picks his way artfully through a potential minefield of outraged Muslim opinion and ensures that his heroine is ensconced in middle class comfort even after the nawabi first husband divorces her arbitrarily. More than an educated and self-respecting woman's own resources, it is the faithful lover's decency which gives her happiness. As long as there are decent men around, a divorced woman can be happy again, the film says in effect. A safe retreat into the purdah syndrome— the Cinderella factor in fact—despite the heroine's climactic indictment of both men for making her a plaything of their emotional quirks. What the film pleads for is a moderation in the exercise of male rights, not redressing the inequality itself.

The other perennial theme of 'Muslim Socials' is the wronged *tawaif* longing for true love and respectability. The distinction between respectable wife material and the erotically accomplished *tawaif* schooled in the art of pleasing men, was drawn because the seclusion of women behind purdah denied them access to the outer world. Respectable women were virtuous but dull. The *tawaifs* to whose salons men flocked for not only song, dance and sex but also poetry and intellectual stimulation, long to escape the *Kotha* and seek the sanctuary of the veil. According to knowledgeable scholars, the *tawaif* is a uniquely Indo-Islamic institution which does not exist in the puritanical cultures of the fundamentalist Middle East. The contribution of ancient Hindu India, the courtesan celebrated for her erotic skills and intellectual accomplishments (in Sanskrit drama and sex manuals) made the cross cultural pollination possible in the self-indulgent decadence prevailing when Mughal power was crumbling.

Pakeeza remains the apotheosis of the romance shrouding the un-sullied *tawaif*. Great care is exercised to preserve her virginity till the right man comes along to rescue her. She has to survive lecherous men, pan-chewing harridans (the madames) and run the gauntlet of outraged respectability for daring to cross the indelible line which sets her apart. Meena Kumari's self-flagellation takes the form of dancing on shards of broken glass before she is accepted as the *bahu* of the hero's family. The bleeding soles of dancing feet continues to be a visual metaphor for films of this genre. B.R. Chopra's latest success, *Tawaif* takes the woman out of the nawabi ethos and plants her in the lower middle-class chawl of Bombay. Rati Agnihotri gives up her beedi smoking and provocative postures in next to no time (after providing the initial titillation) because she really longs to be the demure begum of Rishi Kapoor, as the inquisitive neighbours assume. She has not yet been deflowered (the price is being negotiated) and being pitchforked into a risque situation, she turns acceptably saucy and selflessly devoted as the situation demands.

The film also has Poonam Dhillon as the aspiring novelist whose first novel happens to be about the tragedy of a *tawaif*. The budding writer voices some near incendiary statements, that women are forced to sell themselves, either for the security of marriage or accept the flesh deals of the *Kotha*. The director does not care to develop the idea any further for it would disturb an audience charmed by the old fashioned comedy and general goodness of all people in the film. At one point Rati Agnihotri claims that the *burqa* is the mantle of protection cast by the decency of a good man, something that is dearer than life itself. The truth is out. A *tawaif* can turn respectable provided she is a virgin and submits to the dictates of purdah.

A much publicised film, claiming to be based on a legendary poetess, was *Umrao Jan*. The authenticity was in the opulent period detail, the nawabi ethos and intonations of a culture under assault. And of course, Rekha's sultry beauty. The Urdu classic by Sadat Hassan Manto is reputed for the conscious exercise of Umrao Jan Ada's power over men. Muzaffar Ali downgrades Umrao's status by not using her original poetry and in the final account, reduces a remarkable woman to a pretty plaything of fate and lustful men.

The purdah mentality when it operates in the majority of films dealing with Hindu characters takes on the sanctimonious hypocrisy and hyperbole of revivalist ideas. The emotional purdah of dependency is as stifling as the *burqa*. 'Na stree swatantram ayrhati' (a women does not deserve freedom), the dictum of Manu, is invoked and given new interpretations to calcify into immutability. She may not ecstatically take off her husband's shoes and trill 'Mera chotasa dekho ye sansar hai' (Nirupa Roy in the '50s hit *Bhai Bhai*). The heroine is usually in form-hugging western clothes (easier to disco in) in most of the young love or action films oozing machismo. But as in the superhit of the '80s, *Betaab*, the arrogant girl has to be schooled to submission by the brawny hero. As the sartorial line between the erstwhile vamp and new heroine disappears, the veneration for the self-sacrificing mother doubles.

Hindi cinema has flirted with tight mini saris and churidar outfits before settling for slit skirts and cleavage-showing dresses for its superficially modern misses. The voyeuristic camera degrades the actress and prepares for her humiliation as a rape victim. The zoom lens has been the libidinous aid for rousing collective male lust. The underlying doctrine seems to be that the woman who does not threaten male superiority is to be chivalrously protected; the one who challenges traditional mores, even dress wise, is to be punished. This is inextricably mixed up with the dangers of illustration. Illustrating female victimisation itself becomes a new form of exploitation.

The test case is the resounding success of B.R. Chopra's *Insaf Ka Tarazu*. The film was granted the coveted entertainment tax exemption and won some second rate awards for its daring theme. The heroine, symbolically named Bharathi, takes her rapist to court, loses and when her young sister is raped by the same man, kills him, and is let off after farcical courtroom histrionics. She is even accepted as the *bahu* by the self-righteous parents of her fiance who had once spurned her. This film is a classic case of a superficially progressive stance undermined by the emotional subtext. First of all, the casting makes a perfect fusion of off-screen reputation and the screen persona. Zeenat Aman, entering films via modelling and beauty contests, plays the heroine who is a model and unconventionally, lives only with a younger sister. She poses in a variety of revealing clothes (brazenly, the film implies), and is constantly in the public eye. The rapist is a personable, suave and rich young man smitten by her and the film generates sympathy for him as the rejected suitor. The act of rape is from his point of view, inviting the male audience to vicarious participation. The audience is expected to nod in approval when Bharathi draws back from marriage with the steadfast fiance saying, 'My body is a temple which has been defiled'.

Her humiliation in court by the cleverly manipulative defense lawyer (for the rapist) rouses all the latent prejudices of the courtroom audience (and the wider one in the theatre) against the woman who exhibits her violation. Instead of slinking away in masochistic shame. 'Such women do not deserve to live', he declaims and at this point, the male audience in the theatre clapped. No further comment is required. In contrast, the prosecuting lawyer is an overwrought emotional woman (Simi) who cannot argue with coherence or rationality but has to face snide remarks about the learned '*Saheba*'. An appreciative snigger follows. *Insaf Ka Tarazu* also had the dubious distinction of making the rapist (Raj Babbar) hypnotically attractive, the easier to make voyeurs of the audience. Such is the clever dialectic of the 'progressive' film. It is no surprise that Raj

Babbar continued to play the rapist in a few more films and a cigarette advertisement capitalised on the rampaging macho image.

More recently, *Be-Abroo* proved to be the most objectionable example of how unscrupulous film makers exploit the theme of exploitation. The film would normally be considered a B or C grader but turned out to be a hit. For showing with crude details how women are lured by pimps and the flesh trade operators. The heroine, a victim of the flesh trade, is a crusading journalist. Not content with exposures in the press, she turns into a female Jack the Ripper and goes about killing off pimps one by one, and commits suicide in the end. Similarly, the topic of bringing bride burners to book seeks the sensationalist route. In *Bahu Ki Awaaz,* Supriya Pathak marries her spineless sweetheart who had mutely watched his family finish off his first wife, who also happened to be Supriya's best friend. As the resourceful girl who collects damaging evidence of the murder (she is a lawyer's daughter), what does the heroine do? Mad glitter in her eye and hair flowing loose, she becomes an avenging Kali despatching the murderers one by one.

What is evasive, even subversive, is precisely this invoking of religious symbolism. Kali is more distant, her retribution is in the realm of the might be. Here and now, a woman who uses her intelligence and courage to bring the criminals to court is more threatening to the pillars of patriarchy. Whipping up the tired old myth of the avenging Kali puts a safe distance between crime and punishment. Only the filmmaker can bask in the self-congratulatory glow of having used our ancient mythology to cinematic purpose. The purdah mentality pushes women into irrational hysteria when they are not docile.

Another absurdity for its tall cinematic claims, is the misuse of mythology in Johnny Bakshi's *Raavan*. The twist is in making the hero a bestial Raavan and not a virtuous Rama. The heroine is a naive village girl who worships the supremely egoistic Raavan for rescuing her from abject poverty. Played by Smita Patil, she is named Ganga with an obvious lack of imagination, her task is to sit like another patience on a monument, reviled as a mad woman and finally immolate herself on an effigy of Raavan instead of the pyre of a sati. She is supposed to make a human being out of the beast. A woman has enough trouble to be a woman without burdening her with the onerous archetype of the redeeming angel.

Of late, there have been a spate of films professing concern for the wife caught in an oppressive marriage. The very first film which let a woman walk out of marriage was *Ek Bar Phir*. But only after making the husband sufficiently caddish and blatantly unfaithful. And also set in the anesthetising distance of permissive London. Even when Dipti Naval has an extramarital relationship and decides to walk out on her selfish husband, there are plenty of weak and vacillating moments. And, bowed down by the burden of guilt. Guilt is inevitable when women have shame bred into their bones. The director, Vinod Pande, makes more concessions to conventional morality in his next film *Ye Nazdeekiyan*. A decade old happy marriage between Shabana Azmi and Marc Zuber fails when the husband falls in love with the stunningly seductive Parveen Babi. Naturally she is model to his ad-filmmaker. The wife has the dignity to release him with no tantrums, makes a career for herself and rejects his offer of financial help, and takes him back without a question when the model's charms pall.

A woman with a broken marriage is hardly ever shown happy or fulfilled in a career. She pines for her two-timing husband in her heart of hearts. Shabana did so once again in *Kamla*. For an intelligent woman, ten years were not enough to tell her what kind of selfish, egoistic cad her husband was. The thrust of the Tendulkar script is to expose the hollowness of investigative journalism but his portrait of marriage, and the woman's subservient role, is tainted by intolerance; and the old resurrection of a wife not abandoning her man when he is down and out, however disillusioned she is. Another, a less successful film perhaps, but of the same ilk was *Dil Aakher Dil Hai*. Rakhee played the untouched, older wife to sexually inhibited Nasseruddin Shah who meets his dream girl, Parveen Babi again. Sexual fulfilment follows but the seductress is a bad housekeeper and inconsiderate wife. So, it is back to Rakhee again who, despite having become a successful career woman meanwhile, takes the chastened husband back.

The film which was being praised skyhigh for being truly revolutionary, in the sense that the wife rejects the repentant husband, was Mahesh Bhat's portentiously titled *Arth*. India's own unmarried woman had Shabana Azmi picking up her shattered life again after the trauma of divorce. She not only rejects the husband, absolves the neurotic homewrecker (other woman Smita Patil) of guilt but gently (yet firmly) says no to the purely fantasy figure of the understanding ghazal singer who falls in love with her. Not only is the film supremely unfair to the other woman, making her an insecure schizophrenic in search of a father substitute. The heart of the film is the male chauvinism of making two attractive women go mad with desire to possess and keep a man who looks like a shoddy, spineless egoist. Putting most of the blame on the other woman reiterates the purity of the stay-at-home wife.

Urban marriages caught in the professional flux face far more stresses and cannot be defined in the black and white terms of *Arth*. For all Shabana's bid for independence, she needs the clutch of surrogate motherhood to the young daughter of her jailed maidservant. Only Jabbar Patel's *Subah* had the honesty and courage to show the strength of a woman's commitment to her vocation and leave a home which had anyway become hollow and emptied of emotional bonds. But such disturbing films don't get a wide viewing. Very often, a career is only a consolation prize when the heroine does not get her man due to the conspiracy of circumstances. Think of Rekha's dedicated doctor in *Mehendi Rang Layegi*. Or the crusading lawyer in *Mujhe Insaaf Chahiye*.

The fashion has set. A woman setting out to find herself has such a hardened purveyor of porn in the guise of sex education (of the infamous *Gupt Gyan* series), B.K. Adarsh that is, jumping on the Ibsen bandwagon. *Aurat Pair ki Juti Nahin Hai* is the proud proclamation as he mutilates the classic *A Doll's House* beyond all recognition except in the bare story line. For all but the last fifteen minutes, Dipti Naval plays the cowering, fearful wife with such abject servitude that you wonder how she had the gumption to marry Marc Zuber, the specialist in caddish husband roles. Her rich father had opposed the marriage to the hard, priggish lawyer with not an iota of feeling or concern for anything but his honour, spotless reputation and a positive mania for truth. The husband's constant putdowns, calculated snubs and intemperate outbursts have crushed the spirit out of her. Funnily enough, the way she is made to behave with the husband's dying best friend, can be construed not only by the jealous Marc Zuber but by a majority of the audience, as perfectly reprehensible for a respectably married woman. So, part of the husband's boorish temper is justified. What makes the husband villainous beyond redemption is his throwing out the idols which his wife has installed in a fit of piety. And he shows the door to his widowed, penitent and helpless mother-in-law.

Nineteenth century morality is what operates in most Indian homes but a splendid opportunity for transcreating a literary classic into our conditions has been lost. The cardinal sins of the man's filial ingratitude and impiety are invoked to justify Dipti Naval's slamming of the door in the final scene. Only, it may not reverberate through the subcontinent as Nora's firm slamming of the door of her doll's house did through a shocked Europe. Our filmmakers have to make veritable monsters of the husbands before a wife can assert her selfhood. That she is equally or more subtly oppressed in a seemingly happy marriage is too subversive an idea to the pillars of the status quo. Only Benegal did it in *Bhumika*. The shining exceptions are rare and getting rarer still. The protesting woman is ossifying into a new box-office stereotype. Unless discriminating women audiences themselves see and recognise the con games and cop outs of such 'progressive' filmmakers, a gullible public is mesmerised into clutching at these straws as meaningful explorations of womens' status.

First Person Accounts

C.M. Naim

C.M. Naim is Professor Emeritus, South Asian Languages and Civilizations, University of Chicago. He is co-founder and former editor of the *Journal of South Asian Literature*, and also edited until recently the *Annual of Urdu Studies*. He has written extensively on Urdu literature, and his most recent work is an annotated translation of *Zikr-e Mir*, the Persian autobiography of Mir, one of the greatest Urdu poets.

The article included here contains, in translation, the full text of Ashraf Bibi's account of her attempts to teach herself to read and write. Ashrafunnisa Begum (1840–1903) was called Bibi Ashraf by her students. The account was first published in 1899 in *Tahzib un-Niswan*. Ashrafunnisa came from a family that, as Gail Minault notes, had traditionally taught its women to read, though not to write. Her story is a moving one, that parallels the efforts of other women in her situation who faced enormous difficulties in their attempts to educate themselves, and faced these difficulties with extraordinary determination.

ʔ

How Bibi Ashraf Learned to Read and Write

There are very few documents—particularly of an autobiographical nature—that throw light on the life of the common people of South Asia prior to the twentieth century. Rarer still is an autobiography by a woman. That is, however, only one reason why the story of Bibi Ashraf's education as told by her is so valuable to us. For even otherwise her simple tale would have gripped our attention due to its poignant, yet matter-of-fact narration of the tremendous odds against which this young Muslim girl of remarkable determination struggled to educate herself in mid-nineteenth century North India. In what follows we shall first present a biographical sketch of Bibi Ashraf, then a translation of her

C.M. Naim, 'How Bibi Ashraf Learned to Read and Write', *Annual of Urdu Studies*, 6, 1987, pp. 99–115.

autobiographical account, and lastly some discussion of two relevant issues suggested by her story.

WHO WAS BIBI ASHRAF?[1]

Bibi Ashraf's full name was Ashrafunnisa Begum—in calling her Bibi Ashraf we merely follow the example of her biographer, Muhammadi Begum,[2] and show her both affection and respect. She was born on 28 September 1840 in a family of Shi'ah Sayyids in Bahnera, a small rural community in Bijnor, Uttar Pradesh. Bahnera must have been a very small place: even in 1901, according to the Gazetteer, its total population was 2,582, of which the Muslims accounted for 1,561; its main feature was a weekly market.[3]

Bibi Ashraf's ancestors were said to have come from Bukhara in Central Asia to serve under various Mughal kings. Her grandfather owned land in Bahnera and the family lived comfortably on the income from it. Bibi Ashraf's father, Sayyid Fateh Husain, nevertheless left Bahnera and moved to Agra and then to Gwalior—some 250 miles away—where he took up the profession of a lawyer. This development was much to the disgust of Fateh Husain's father, who couldn't understand why his son wanted to 'work' when he, the father, already had, 'thanks to God's kindness, enough to feed ten servants of his own'.

When Fateh Husain went to Gwalior, he did not take his family with him—which was more or less the rule at that time—but left them in Bahnera with his father. Bibi Ashraf was only eight years old when her mother died, and she and her baby brother were brought up by their loving grandmother and a not-so-loving aunt and uncle.

Soon after her birth, Bibi Ashraf was engaged to be married to a second cousin, Sayyid Alamdar Husain, who was nine years older to her. They were married in 1859. Alamdar Husain had been educated in Arabic and Persian at the famous Delhi College in Delhi and, before his marriage, had been a deputy inspector of schools in Jullundur District in the Punjab. When that job was curtailed for some reason, he returned to Bahnera, but after his marriage he took his wife to Lahore where he began to teach Arabic in a school. In 1865, Alamdar Husain was hired as the Assistant Professor of Arabic and Persian at Government College, Lahore, which had been established only the previous year. They had four children, two of whom—a boy and a girl—died very young. Alamdar Husain himself was consumptive and succumbed to the disease in 1870,[4] leaving the surviving two daughters and Bibi Ashraf to fend for themselves in Lahore. By that time Bibi Ashraf's grandparents were already dead; then, just a few months later, her father also passed away.

Alamdar Husain had been well regarded by his superiors as well as by the gentry of Lahore, and they tried to help the bereft family. The Director of Public Instruction in the Punjab—Captain W. R. M. Holroyd—offered Bibi Ashraf a small teaching job, and the two girls scholarships of five rupees per month. Bibi Ashraf declined the job, preferring to support her family on whatever she could earn from sewing clothes and making lace. She did, however, accept the scholarships and had her daughters admitted to a local school for girls. But there were too many mouths to feed, for Bibi Ashraf always had several children of relatives staying with her while getting education in Lahore. Eight years later, when she was again offered a teaching job, she agreed and became a teacher at Victoria Girls School, a semi-official primary school. She worked hard and eventually became its head teacher; she also strove to improve the school's reputation—which had not been too good—and finally saw it raised to the level of a middle school. She continued to work until she died—after only a short illness—on 7 May 1903.

Bibi Ashraf was a woman of great fortitude and determination. By the time she was thirty years old she had lost her mother, her grandmother, two of her children, her husband and her father. Even the two remaining daughters predeceased her, both dying as young women, one unmarried, the other married with a baby boy who too did not survive long. Muhammadi Begum reports that a student of Bibi Ashraf's later told her:

When I entered school, the two daughters of *Ustani Sahiba* [Bibi Ashraf] were already dead. She was, however, still grievously affected and constantly wept remembering them. She would put a piece of cloth over her face below the eyes, and as she taught tears would soak into the cloth. When it would become too wet she would squeeze the cloth dry, then put it back on her face.[5]

Bibi Ashraf was a gentle and caring person, generous to friends and strangers alike. She adored her students and fretted over them. At the same time she cherished her independence. Though she observed strict purdah, she never sought to put the burden of her needs on anyone else, preferring to live frugally and independently. She was also a deeply religious person, devoted to her Shi'ah faith which sustained her through her grief-ridden life. Every year during the month of Muharram, she mourned the martyrdom of Imam Husain by holding *majālis*[6] at her house and distributing food among the poor—as is wont among pious Shi'ahs. Muhammadi Begum tells us of a most touching incident:

Once during Muharram she was distributing *tabarruk* [in this case, breads that had been blessed in the *majlis*] to a small crowd of poor women gathered around her. Some of the women felt they had not received their proper share and knocked her down with the basket of breads. Some women even started hitting her. When part of her body began to feel numb, she merely said to them, 'Please, ladies, don't keep hitting at the same place.'[7]

She was, however, free of religious prejudice. She adored Muhammadi Begum—a Sunni Muslim—because of the latter's pioneering efforts to spread education and new ideas among Muslim women. Muhammadi Begum recounts many instances of this love, including the following:

[Bibi Ashraf] told one of her relatives: 'When I learned to read and write, my uncle got very angry with me. I asked him to forgive me and made a promise before him never to write to any man or to any married woman who was not also a relative. I kept that promise for a very long time, and broke it only in the case of the editor of *Tahzīb-e NiswāN* [i.e., Muhammadi Begum]. Otherwise I had never written to any married woman, and if ever such a need arose I had either one of my students or someone else write for me.[8]

When Muhammadi Begum started her weekly magazine for women, Bibi Ashraf contributed several poems and essays, including the following, most moving account of how she taught herself to read and write. The original Urdu essay appeared in two installments, in the issues dated March 23 and 30, 1899.

How I Learned to Read and Write[9]

It had long been customary in my family to teach the girls how to read—but to teach them how to write, that was strictly forbidden. The girls were taught only to vocalize the Arabic of the Qur'an and to read a bit of Urdu so that they could gain some knowledge of their faith and learn the rules of prayer and fasting.

We were six girls altogether—big and little—in our family. Our grandfather, may God grant him paradise, hired a lady teacher [*ustānī*] for us; she lived with us and received ten rupees per month as well as food and clothes. The three older girls and the daughter of a maidservant had already finished the Qur'an, while I was reading the seventh section [*sipāra*] and the other two girls the eighth. A score or so of other girls who were our kinfolks [*birādarī*] also joined us. In this way, you may say, a little school got started. Our teacher—may God grant her paradise—did not know Urdu,[10] though she belonged by race [*qaum*] to a high-born [*šarīf*] Pathan family. The elders of my family tried hard to find a lady teacher who could teach us Urdu, but none could be found.

Our teacher used to give us a holiday on Fridays. I well remember how every Friday all the girls would bring her a little flour, some rice, and a few pennies from their homes. Then they would jointly cook whatever she asked them to. She would tell them to make *rōtī, qōrma* and *kabāb,* adding to that list sometimes *pulāo* other times *zarda,* sometimes *fīrni* other times some savory snack. She would often ask them to cook other dishes too. She also taught them needlecraft. I was then quite young, so the teacher would ask me to do only the easier chores. But even at that tender age I was most eager to do every kind of work. I avidly watched whatever was done and put in work beyond my capacity.

For several years our teacher taught us with much affection and care, never even taking a day off. Then, suddenly one day, her mother came to our house and said, 'You would do me a great favor if you would allow my daughter to come home with me for a fortnight. There is some important business to take care of.'

She took her home and there she married her off to a Sayyid. I have heard it said that our teacher had been eleven at the time of her first marriage, and fifteen when she became a widow. Twelve years passed before she was married again. And all during that time she had lived with extreme modesty and propriety. May God bless her soul! She was full of virtue and piety, and remained devoted to prayers and fasts till her dying day. This second marriage, which was clearly her privilege under religion [*haqq-e šar*], was in fact not something she had wanted—she merely gave in to the pressure mounted by her mother.

Be that as it may, my grandfather was terribly shocked when he heard the news. Out of his sense of shame, he did not stir out of the house for a whole month. Everyone reasoned with him: 'Why must you feel so bad about it? She was only a hired teacher in your household: she was not, God forbid, a kin.' My grandfather always replied, 'She was, nevertheless, the tutor to my girls. It shames me greatly if my girls' tutor should marry a second time. When I think of it I want to hide my face from the world.'

He sent word to our teacher never to cross his threshold again. He also would not allow the Sayyid who had married her to come before him, and kept that vow as long as he lived. When we girls learned of these developments, we were all very grieved. Much worse, however, was the condition of our teacher, for she loved us girls very much—just as we loved her. There was, however, nothing that we could do except resign ourselves to the situation.

Then several members of the family suggested that another woman should be hired who could teach us Urdu as well as the Qur'an, but my grandfather did not agree. He said, 'No, I can't even bear the thought of having an outsider [ǧair] in the house teaching my girls. I absolutely forbid it. Compared to such education, it would be better if the girls remain illiterate.'

Modesty was a value so integral for my grandfather that he would rather have the girls not speak even to their fathers and brothers. He used to say, 'Talking to her male relatives makes a girl disrespectful.' What chance was there then to have some male relative teach us? There were, no doubt, several poor and widowed women among the Sayyids, but none dared ask them to teach us. Thus, in short, stopped all formal instruction of the girls.

Eventually, as time went by, all the girls except for me began to study with their mothers; my mother, as my ill luck would have it, fell ill. I was at the time about seven or eight and my brother, may God preserve him, was just six months old. My mother was not so much worried about her illness as she was concerning my lack of education, but there was nothing she could do. She was, however, the daughter of a marsiya-xwān and herself knew how to recite a marsiya.[11] Even as she lay sick she taught me from memory a number of religious, benedictory poems [mujrē salām]. Woe, a thousand times woe, that life failed her and she died while we were still very young.

May God never deprive any child of her parents. My mother was sick for one whole year before she bade farewell to this life. That was the first calamity to scar my heart. Later so many terrible things happened to me, both at home and elsewhere, and so many of my dear ones passed away, that neither my tongue has the strength nor my pen the power, to narrate them. Mankind has no choice but to accept whatever happens and be always grateful to God. What happened was for the best. What pleases my Creator also pleases me.

I cannot describe the pain and grief I felt when my mother died. I thought of her night and day. I would wander through the house and break into tears at all the places where my mother used to sit or sleep or say her prayers. If a majlis was held I would cry all day long, for I would remember how my late mother used to participate. I was then too young to shed tears over the misfortunes of the martyred Imam and his blessed household. I did not think that anyone could be more afflicted with adversity than I was.

Just to show you how ignorant I was: for several years after my mother's death I kept praying in my daily ritual prayers [namāz] for her to come back to life. I would recite the sacred names of God, feeling convinced that the blessed effect [barakat] of those names and my prayers would make her alive again. Not only that, I taught my little brother the same thing. He had been only eighteen months old when our mother left us and passed away. I told him: 'Raise your arms and repeat, "May God bring Mother back".' After that day you could see him all the time raising his tiny arms in supplication and saying, 'May God bring Mother back. May God bring Mother back.' And if he sat down in someone's lap he would press that person to repeat the same words. If that person didn't respond, my brother would persist and soon begin to cry. But if that person repeated the words with him, he would become very happy. Those words of his used to make even strangers break into tears. Even now, at this moment, that image has come back to me and I am unable to calm my heart.

Anyway, it was simply amazing the way I used to cry. My days were distracted and my nights were without sleep. After the fortieth day observance [cālīswān] of my mother's death the traffic of female relatives and other guests stopped, but I still continued to cry. Then my grandmother told me what was right and what was wrong according to religion. 'Daughter,' she said, 'when girls shed tears over the martyrdom of Imam Husain, may peace be upon him, they doubtless get much spiritual reward [ṣawāb], but it is a great sin for them to cry over the loss of their parents or brothers or sisters or other relatives. Then God gets angry with them, and the deceased is also much discomforted. Now you must stop your endless weeping. For if you don't, your mother will greatly suffer and be angry with you. On the other hand, if you wish to please your mother, there is nothing better for you than to read something in her name and offer her the reward for that reading.'

'What should I read?' I asked her. 'And how should I offer her its reward.'

'Those seven sections of the Qur'an,' she replied, 'you should read them every day. Then raise your arms to God and say, "I give their reward to my mother's soul." That will please her very much.'

From then on, I made it a daily habit to read those seven sections. In fact, I would read each section several times and offer its reward to the soul of my mother. The constant repetition greatly improved my reading skills. I could now decipher new material, and began to read ahead on my own. In this fashion—through God's favor and my own efforts—I finished the Qur'an in just one year, and had a *majlis* to celebrate the event.

I was, however, still dying to learn to read Urdu, but I could not find any woman who would teach me. Why was I so eager to read Urdu? In our house, during the forty day observance of Muharram, separate *majālis* for men and women used to be held every day. In addition, a *majlis* was held every Thursday in fulfillment of someone or other's vow. That was the reason I was so keen to read Urdu. All the ladies in my family knew Urdu quite well. When they visited other homes—on some happy or sad occasion—or when other ladies came similarly to visit us, my female relatives would read aloud from books on matters of faith and religious observances. Listening to them I came to know by heart a lot about such matters, just as one does with stories, but that did not at all lessen my keenness to be myself blessed with the gift of reading.

Once I went to each and every lady in the family and begged her to teach me just one or two words every day. I said, 'Teach me and I would be your slave for life.' But not one of them was the slightest moved by my pleading. Each gave the same reply: 'Girl, have you gone crazy? You better find some cure for this madness. First of all, what will you do with it even if you learned to read? Secondly, why do you think it is all that easy to teach someone to read? It's not an easy task. It demands much hard work. I don't have so much energy to waste on you.'

I lost all hope when I heard that response, and began to cry. In fact, I felt so hurt I screamed. That only made them more angry.

They said: 'That's just wonderful! Now you're trying to scare us with your tears. Well, your silly tears don't scare anyone. It's terrible the way you go around whining and wailing just because you wish to read. We never saw a girl like you. Most girls run and hide if someone even mentions books. Children your age have to be scolded and spanked to make them read. You, on the contrary, weep and wail wanting to read. Your inauspicious, constant crying has already lost you your mother, who knows what your tears will bring about next. Don't come near us. Go, cry somewhere else. You only make us fear for the future.'

These remarks totally crushed me. My tears just poured out. Then the ladies said: 'For God's sake, girl, go away. If your grandmother sees you crying she would just assume that we must have said something nasty to her darling granddaughter.'

Only my God knows how I felt when I heard those words. My parents had brought me up with much love. They had always used gentle language in my presence, never saying a harsh word to anyone. That is why I was not accustomed to hearing such cruel remarks. The words of those ladies were like salt to my wounded heart. I wiped my tears and walked away. When I was by myself, I prayed to God: 'Most Benevolent God, show me mercy and guide me across this dreadful chasm to my goal. If ever I get to learn how to read I shall, God willing, teach that skill to anyone who desires it, and even forcibly to those who may not want to learn, for I shall never forget so long as I live the anguish I feel at this moment.'

Later one night, as I was engrossed in similar thoughts, it occurred to me that if I had a *salām* or a *mujrā* I could myself figure out the words and begin to read. What was so difficult about that! After all, I already knew the letters of the alphabet. What did I care if no one wanted to teach me! That idea so much raised my courage and hope that the very next morning I sent a maid to all my friends with this message: 'I need some *salām* and some *mujrē*. Please let me borrow some from you. I shall have them copied and returned.' May God ever keep them happy, for all of them sent me some.

But who was there to copy them for me? That had been merely an excuse. I used the same excuse again and said to my grandmother. 'Please get me some paper. I shall ask Uncle to copy these poems for me.' She immediately sent someone to the market and got me some paper. Now the question was, how should I make copies and where should I hide myself to do that? For it would have been disastrous for me if anyone was even to suspect me of writing. I had no mother to cover up for me, and writing was strictly forbidden to girls. How was then I to reach my goal and also keep it secret? My aunt was already furious with me. She used to call me nasty names for reading the Qur'an so much; she would say, 'Thank God, this girl hasn't learned anything else, otherwise she would have time for nothing at all.' God knows what she would have said if she were to see me writing.

After thinking about these matters at length I decided that at noon, when everyone was resting, I would make some ink with the blacking from the griddle [*tawā*] and start copying. Believe me, that is exactly what I did. I got hold of some blacking from the kitchen, the clay lid of one of the water pots, and a fistful of twigs from the broom. Thus equipped I went up on the roof, pretending that I was going to rest there, and excitedly began to copy out words. I cannot tell you how I happy I felt at that moment. Childhood is so innocent! No sooner had I copied a few words than I felt I had already won the battle. Before returning downstairs, I broke the ink-stained lid and threw away the pieces. That was the routine I followed for many days, using a fresh lid to make the ink in. The ladies would find the water pot lidless and grumble: 'Who's the wretch who steals the lid every day? May God break his arms for doing this.'

I felt so ashamed, and also so scared. I was afraid someone would find out how bad I had been and scold me. I feared people, not having the sense to consider my misplaced boldness a sin and so fear God. My intense desire made me blind. I did not give up my improper ways, and continued to blacken sheets after sheets of paper. However, I could not understand what I was writing. I didn't have the sense to know that one cannot learn to read without a teacher. I believed that just as other skills could be learned merely by watching and imitating others so would be the case with reading. As a result, I spent a great deal of time and effort for nothing. When no headway was made my crying spells started again. Then God gave me a teacher.

One morning as I was reading the Qur'an the son of my grandmother's sister came by. He saw what I was doing and asked, 'Sister, can you read the Qur'an?'

'Yes,' I replied.

He said, 'I would be so grateful if you can help me learn my lessons. I have trouble memorizing the daily assignment and get thrashed by the teacher. You will be doing me a big favor.'

'Don't call it a favor', I replied. 'I will be happy to teach you every day.'

This made him so happy he pulled up his shirt and showed me his back. It was covered with welts. My heart welled up for him, and from that day onward I would not only go through his daily assignment with him but also help him prepare the text ahead. He never got a thrashing again.

That boy's coming to me for help was how God took pity on my despair and my fortune took a turn for better. It happened this way: one day a book fell out of his bag. I picked it up and began to flip the pages. The writing had no diacritical marks to indicate correct pronunciation. I asked him, 'What book is this? Its script looks like that of a *marsiya*. Here, read me some of it.' The boy did. I liked the contents and my hope was revived. I said to him, 'I would cherish your kindness all my life if you would teach me to read this book.'

He flatly refused. 'I don't have the time', he said. 'Also, the book is very difficult—you will never learn it.'

I replied, 'I will work very hard to memorize the lessons. You need only agree to teach me.'

'No', said he, 'I can't promise that. I don't think I can teach you this book.'

I was very hurt when I heard him say that. 'If you won't teach me this book', I retorted, 'I won't help you with your lessons either.' Then I started to weep.

My remark made him remember the beatings. 'Don't get angry', he quickly said. 'Here, read!'

How relieved I felt! Wiping my tears, I recited, '*Bismillah*', and began to study with him every day. But I had not completed even three pages when his father sent him away to study at Delhi. I was so depressed when he left. He was just a child, what could he teach? He never showed me how to syllabify words, neither did he explain the text—but even the very little that he did was a lot for me.

Once again I was in despair. I went around begging everyone to teach me. No one did. Finally I started reading that book on my own. I would look at new words, and if I recognized any familiar letters I would put them together. Slowly, in this piecemeal manner, I would figure out whole words and read on—half right, half wrong. I also memorized whatever I read. In this way I read through the entire book. I then used the same method on other books and eventually began to read Urdu fairly well. Then I turned to all those several *mujrē* and *salām* that I had earlier copied down without understanding a word. You can't imagine how happy I was the day I read those copies: I don't think there has been a happier day since. As I read my own handwriting I felt doubly encouraged and that much more confident. I told myself, 'Whatever man gets, he gets it through his own efforts. By God's grace, I now possess what I had so keenly sought—if not in its perfect form, then at least poorly.' Then I returned to those broom twigs and that kitchen blacking and, regarding them as my teachers, began to copy from different books. After only a few days' practice I could write from memory. No one yet, however, came to know my secret.

At that time my father [did not live at home but] worked as a lawyer in [a distant city,] Gwalior. After my blessed aunt passed away, my father had my uncle come and live with him. My father had two children, my brother and I, and my uncle had two sons. For the sake of the children, my father did not marry again, neither did he allow his brother to remarry. A great many proposals came from among our own relatives, but my father turned them all down. His reply was always the same: 'Men marry a second time because they desire children. We already have children of our own. It would, therefore, be improper for us to remarry and bring home a possible enemy to these innocent children. We don't live at home; we live away in another city. God knows what trouble could develop in our absence.'

After my uncle left [Bahnera] and joined my father in Gwalior, the fact that I could write came to be known by the ladies at home. How long could I hide it? In any case, it was my uncle I had mainly been scared of, for he strongly disapproved of women's learning to write. When he was gone, I began to practice writing openly. No one objected. On the contrary, my skill at writing was viewed as a novelty by my relatives, and also by others. Whenever any woman had the need to send a letter, she would come to me to get it written. On my part, I gladly transcribed—any which way I could—whatever was dictated to me. During that process, women would disclose to me their innermost secrets; they would tell me things that they would never speak of in front of anyone. And their letters brought replies. I could, however, understand only a tenth part of what I was told.

Another thing. I knew only [one] way to address someone [*alqāb*] and used that form all the time, regardless of the age and relationship of the addressee. One lady had me write letters to her husband. This was the way I addressed her husband on her behalf: 'Dear young man, light of my eyes, comfort of my life, pupil of my eye, may your life be long!'[12] I used these same words in all her letters. Finally the husband wrote back: 'I can fully understand your letters, for their language is just like your own speech. But tell me this, where did you find this strange scribe who knows only one way to address people? Do tell him kindly not to use these words to address me.' From that day onward, whenever that lady asked me to write a letter she would say, 'Write only this at the beginning: "May the father of Muhammad Husain know..."'.

When the mutiny in Delhi occurred it put an end to all exchanges of letters. Consequently, for nearly eighteen months, we received no letter from my father, neither could we write to him. All of us were greatly anxious about each other. Finally when some peace returned, my father sent a man to get our news. When that man was ready to return to Gwalior, my grandmother gave him a letter that she had her brother write for her. I gave him a letter too, a letter that I had written myself, containing all that I had seen or heard of the mutiny. Yes, even in that letter to my father and my uncle I had used those words: 'Dear young man; light of my eyes, comfort of my life....'

My father was absolutely delighted when he read my letter. He wrote to my grandmother: 'The letter written by Uncle gave me the news of only the immediate members of the family. He didn't write about the other relatives. Nor did he write about the events of the mutiny. The letter from the girl, however, made me very happy. She wrote what she had herself heard or seen. Her letter gave me the pleasure I get from a newspaper or a book of history. I read her letter every day. But do tell me, who taught her to write?'

My grandmother wrote back: 'Even to this day no one has ever taught her. She has learned through her own efforts and out of her own desire.'

Then I wrote my father the whole story—how I had learned to write on account of my own intense desire. He rewarded me by sending me an expensive comforter and several suits of clothes, having had them sewn for me in Gwalior. But my uncle, may God grant him peace, was very angry to learn that I could write. He wrote me a chiding letter and never quite forgave me so long as he lived.

This is the story of how I learned to read and write, and now it is finished. With much toil and struggle I managed to obtain some little skill. I rest content with it and thank God for His kindness.

COMMENTS

As I read Bibi Ashraf's narrative I couldn't help being reminded of the fiction heroines created by some of her male contemporaries, men like Nazir Ahmad (1830–1912) and Altaf Husain Hali (1837–1914), who were in the forefront of the reform movement among Indian Muslims during the second half of the nineteenth century and also particularly concerned with the plight of the women.[13] Both Nazir Ahmad and Hali built some of their writings around female characters possessing remarkable strength and intelligence, and also dealt with issues that find mention in Bibi Ashraf's story. It may be instructive to examine some such issues in the light of the lives of Bibi Ashraf and the fictional heroines. I shall attempt to do so in what follows, restricting myself to two issues: female literacy and widow remarriage.

*

We learn from Bibi Ashraf's account that several women in her family knew how to read the Qur'an without, of course, understanding the Arabic; they could all read religious writings in Urdu, and were well-informed concerning the regulations and conventions that governed their lives as women. We are told that the ladies the house did not normally teach their daughters themselves; the girls were taught by a woman teacher—usually some poor widow—who lived with the family. But, if it ever became necessary, the girls could study with their mothers. The male members of her family never offered to play the role of a teacher. Some of them, in fact, opposed female education.

When we turn to our fictional heroines—Zubaida Khatun of Hali's *Majālis-al-Nissa* (1874)[14] and Asghari Khanam of Nazir Ahmad's *Mirāt-al-'Arūs* (1869) and *Banatal-Na'š* (1873),[15] we find that neither was educated by her mother. Zubaida we taught by a woman teacher and by her father—it was the latter, in fact, who taught her how to write. About Asghari's education we know nothing except that her father wrote her edifying letters which she could answer on her own, and that her mother was not terribly smart even in the traditional sense. (Asghari, of course, is overbearingly smart.) The two male writers/reformists create fictional fathers who take strong interest in the education of their daughters. In the patriarchal society for which they were writing all initiative for reform had to come from the fathers to make any effect. As for Bibi Ashraf, her father—somewhat of a rebel himself—could have helped her if he had been at home, though perhaps only after the death of the domineering grandfather. She did receive much encouragement from him, whereas her uncle—and aunt—only made her life miserable.

What is most curious, if not astonishing, is that even as late as the 1850s it was not considered proper for women to learn to write. This matter of there being a stricter prohibition against writing, as against reading, is not brought out in the reformist fiction—at least not overtly. But Hali's heroine, Zubaida, was taught writing not by her *ustānī* but by her father, which he did only after Zubaida was eight and had already spent three years learning the Qur'an. Nazir Ahmad tells us nothing about Asghari's own education, but he makes writing an integral part of the curriculum of instruction at the girls school started by Asghari, without referring to any special prohibition. It may have been because both Hali and Nazir Ahmad were not concerned with literacy alone; they wanted to emphasize education in general and the practical benefits that could accrue to women from it.[16]

It was not as if Muslim women never learned to write, a few always did, but it is true that for centuries writing was not considered a suitable thing for women to learn. If we go by our sources on the education of the elite in the past—and it is among the elite that we find the women who wrote—we come across quite strong strictures against women being taught writing. The *Qābūs Nāma* of Kaika'us ibn Iskandar written in 1082 A.D. is a book of edifying instructions that a nobleman wrote for the benefit of his son;[17] it belongs to what is referred to as the literature of *adab,* and was fairly widely read. In the chapter on the upbringing of sons, its author has a few brief remarks concerning daughters, including the following: 'Do not teach her writing, for therein lies great danger.'[18] Approximately one hundred and fifty years later, Nasiruddin Tusi in his much more famous book, *Axlāq-e Nāsirī,* is much more strict: 'Teach the girls neither reading nor writing.'[19] Tusi's book was widely read for centuries and its influence on the thinking of South Asia's Muslim elite cannot be overestimated. Prior to the introduction of English education in South Asia, practically every educated Muslim had to read Tusi's book at some stage in his education.

Coming to more recent times, we may note some comments of Maulana Ashraf Ali Thanawi (1863–1943), one of the most influential religious teachers of this century in South Asia. He was also the author of countless books including *Bihištī Zēwar,* a book of *adab* exclusively for women, which was for two decades as much a part of an educated Muslim girl's dowry as a copy of the Qur'an.[20] Maulana Thanawi was not averse to teaching women how to write—he included a chapter on writing in the book—but he had certain reservations. In an essay on women's education that he wrote in 1913 and then reprinted in a later edition of the book, the Maulana concluded his seven-page long argument as follows:

The preceding discussion was concerned with the matter of teaching women to read. As for teaching them to write, there is nothing wrong with it except in the case where you get the impression that the girl might be somewhat brazen by nature. Writing is needful for domestic life. But if there is any fear of impropriety [on the part of the girl], it is more important to protect yourself from iniquity than to seek a thing that may be useful but is not in fact obligatory. Under such circumstances, do not let the girl be instructed in the art of writing, and do not let her write on her own either. This is the conclusion to which wise men have come concerning the question: how is writing for women?[21]

Later day readers of Hali and Nazir Ahmad—like myself—can get any sense of the hardships education-seeking women had to face only when they come across first-person accounts such as Bibi Ashraf's. It may, incidentally, be pointed out that Bibi Ashraf's family seems to have been 'progressive'—given the times—in that her father left home and developed a career for himself, and that her husband, first cousin of her father, went to Delhi to be educated, as did the young boy who helped her with her first Urdu book. Apparently, by the 1850s, institutional education and professional careers were acceptable goals for the sons in Bibi Ashraf's family; the education of the daughters, however, was still too controversial an issue. It is indeed remarkable that Bibi Ashraf, by no stretch of imagination a 'brazen' person, actively sought to educate herself and, when circumstances required it, did not hesitate to take up a career.

Bibi Ashraf might have been just a few hours old when she was engaged to be married to a second cousin—such engagements were at the time more the rule than exceptions. She was nineteen when the marriage itself took place. Eleven years later, at the age of thirty, she became a widow, and had to take care of herself and her two surviving daughters. She stayed on in Lahore, quite far from her village in Bijnor, and eventually became a school teacher. Apparently there never arose the possibility of a second marriage for her. We remember, of course, the fierce reaction of Bibi Ashraf's Sayyid grandfather to the remarriage of her Pathan teacher:

perhaps we should also recall that it was a Sayyid youth who had married the Pathan widow.

Widow remarriage was a major issue for the Muslims of South Asia during the nineteenth century. Islam allows remarriage of widows—in fact encourages it—but among the Muslim elite of South Asia widow remarriage occurred extremely rarely and usually when dictated by some worldly gain. The first person to take up this issue and work for the removal of this pernicious custom was Sayyid Ahmad Shahid (1786–1831), who belonged to the tradition of Shah Waliullah and led a *jihād* against the Sikhs. He married the widow of his older brother, Sayyid Ishaq, in 1819, and declared the prevailing custom un-Islamic.[22] A charismatic person, he had an extensive following among the Muslims of North India. His example was emulated by those who followed the Waliullahi tradition. In particular, his influence was very strong among the Pathans of North India. It is possible that the family of Bibi Ashraf's female teacher had come under the influence of Sayyid Ahmad Shahid and his followers.

Nazir Ahmad and Hali were also concerned with the issue of widow remarriage: the former wrote a novel, *Ayāmā,* devoted to this subject, while the latter wrote a long poem, *'Munājāt-e Bēwa.'* Hali's poem, written in 1884, contains 448 rhyming couplets; a work of great pathos, it is in the form of a widow's prayer to God.[23] The widow, though resigned to her fate, is yet bold or desperate enough to question God as to why such a fate was assigned to her as a woman. In other words, she complains on behalf of herself and also on behalf of the entire womankind. 'What profit lay in my existence', she asks. 'Why did you create me?' Then later: 'If peace and comfort had been our share//You wouldn't have created womankind.' The poem refers to the fact that girls were often married away at a tender age and became widows likewise. 'When the transient [admirer] came to the garden//the flowers had not yet come to bloom.//But when the flowers finally bloomed,//the transient [admirer] was resting in dust.' Near the end of the poem, the widow says: 'God, You should summon the woman first,//or summon the man and the woman together;//or else, God, erase this custom from the earth//which has caused all love to die here.' Hali, however, was a peace-loving man; he concluded his poem with the widow asking God to fill her heart with His love alone, for her restless heart has suffered enough.

Nazir Ahmad was different: he made the emotional and sexual life of the young widow very much a concern of his novel, *Ayāmā,* which was first published in the 1890s. He also pointed out how men exploited young widows in order to satisfy their own appetites. Nazir Ahmad's heroine dies at the end, but before her death she gathers around her all her relatives and gives them a long sermon. She describes the evil of the custom that prohibited the remarriage of widows, using her own life and the lives of other widows as examples. She also questions the logic of those who looked down upon a widow who remarried, when in fact widows sought marriage chiefly to protect their honor.

Maulana Thanawi also denounced the prevailing custom, but couched his plea exclusively in religious terms. He too accused women of being contemptuous toward the widows who got remarried. He told his female readers: 'Your faith would not be correct unless you regard first and second marriages as co-equal. [The Prophet has declared,] "Those who revive some practice of mine will receive reward equal to the reward of one hundred martyrs." Consequently, anyone who strives to get widows remarried as well as any widow who will remarry in order to gain the Prophet's approval, will get the blessings and rewards that accrue to one hundred martyrs.'[24]

Bibi Ashraf never remarried, for that was something quite beyond her own powers. But in those areas of life where only her own determination and effort mattered, she was exemplary. Though surrounded by hostile people, she taught herself to read and write. Later, when she became a widow with two young daughters, she preferred to live away from her village for the sake of her daughters' education, and chose to support herself through her own hard work, first as seamstress then as a school teacher. Bibi Ashraf was not born rich like Hali's Zubaida Khatun, neither did she become rich like Asghari Khanam, the super woman of Nazir Ahmad's novels. She was born in modest circumstances and lived a life governed by modesty, piety, charity and service. We are charmed by her innocence just as much as we feel admiration for her 'true grit', and we are grateful to Muhammadi Begum for preserving her memory for us.

NOTES

1. This biographical note is based on *Ḥayāt-e Ašraf,* the only detailed account of Bibi Ashraf, written by Muhammadi Begum (Lahore: Imambara Sayyida Mubarak Begum, n.d.). The original edition must have come out in the first decade of this century. We have used the recent photo-reprint published by Sayyid Babar Ali as a public service (Lahore, n.d.).

2. Muhammadi Begum, another remarkable person, was the first woman to edit an Urdu magazine devoted to the welfare of Muslim women; she was also one of the first to write novels in Urdu for women. She edited *Tahẓīb-e Niswān,* a weekly magazine for women which was published by her husband, Sayyid

Mumtaz Ali (1860–1935); this magazine lasted from 1898 to 1949. For a discussion of Muhammadi Begum's novels, see Shaista Akhtar Banu Suhrawardy, *A Critical Survey of the Development of the Urdu Novel and Short Story*, London: Longmans, Green and Co., 1945, pp. 123–30.

3. *District Gazetteers of the United Provinces of Agra and Oudh, Vol. XIV, Bijnor*, Allahabad: Government Press, 1928, p. 304.

4. Alamdar Husain became seriously ill in August 1869 and died on 14 May 1870. There is an interesting sidelight to this event. When Alamdar Husain went on sick leave, his temporary replacement was no other than Maulvi Muhammad Husain Azad—the author of *Āb-e Ḥayāt*—who, after the former's death, was made permanent at a salary of Rs 150 per month. Aslam Farrukhi, *Muḥammad Ḥusain Āzād: Ḥayāt aur Taṣānīf*, Karachi: Anjuman Taraqqi-e-Urdu, 1965, pp. 212–13.

5. *Ḥayāt-e Ašraf*, p. 32.

6. *Majālis*, pl. of *majlis* (lit., a gathering), refers in the Shi'ah culture of South Asia to religious gatherings organized to commemorate the martyrs of Karbala. Elegies and sermons, recalling the sufferings of the martyrs, are read, people openly weep and cry, then at the end some food is bless and distributed. Among the pious these gatherings are held daily during the month of Muharram and forty days afterward; they are also held weekly during the rest of the year. Frequently people vow hold a *majlis* in return for some boon from God.

7. *Ḥayāt-e Ašraf*, pp. 64–5.

0. *Ḥayāt-e Ašraf*, p. 6.

9. *Ḥayāt-e Ašraf*, pp. 5–20. I have tried to keep the translation as close to the original as possible without becoming overly literal.

10. I take this to mean that she probably spoke some local dialect, not Standard Urdu, and knew only to vocalize the Arabic of the Qur'an by a sort of rote.

11. *Marṣiya*, lit., elegy, generally refers in Urdu to the elegies that commemorate the martyrdom of Imam Husain, the grandson of the Prophet Muhammad, at Karbala in 680 A.D. Apparently, Bibi Ashraf's mother was the daughter of a man who recited such elegies professionally. *Mujrā* and *salām* are shorter poems that honor the Prophet and his family and are often more celebratory in nature. For more on Urdu *marṣiya*, see my article, 'The Art of the Urdu *Marṣiya*,' in Milton Israel and N. K. Wagle (eds), *Islamic Society and Culture*, New Delhi: Manohar, 1983, pp. 101–16.

12. *'Barxurdār, nūr-cašm, rāḥat-e jān, qurrat-al-'ain ṭūla' umrahu.'* A nice, proper way to begin a letter to a son, for example.

13. For more on Nazir Ahmad and Altaf Husain Hali, see Muhammad Sadiq, *A History of Literature*, London: Oxford University Press, 1964, pp. 263–74 and 316–25; M. Tahir Jamil, *Hali's Poetry: A Study*, Bombay: Taraporevala, 1938; and S.A.B. Suhrawardy's book mentioned above.

14. Professor Gail Minault of the University of Texas has prepared an English

translation of his book: *Voices of Silence*, Delhi: Chanakya Publications, 1986. Also see her article, 'Hali's *Majlis Un-Nissa:* Purdah and Woman Power in Nineteenth Century India', in Milton Israel and N.K.Wagle (eds), *Islamic Society and Culture*, New Delhi: Manohar, 1983, pp. 39–49.

15. An English translation of Nazir Ahmad's *Mirāt-al-'Arūs* exists: G. E. Ward (trans.), *The Bride's Mirror*, London: Henry Frowde, 1903. For more on these two novels, see my article, 'Prize-Winning *Adab*: A Study of Five Urdu Books Written in Response to the Allahabad Government Gazette Notification', in Barbara Daly Metcalf (ed.), *Moral Conduct and Authority: The Place of Adab in South Asian Islam*, Berkeley: University of California Press, 1984, pp. 290–314.

16. In their devotion to the cause of female education, Hali and Nazir Ahmad were mavericks among their more prominent contemporaries. Sayyid Ahmad Khan, for example, did not consider it a critical issue; on the contrary, he felt it might detract from his main concern, the education of Muslim boys. Similar was the case with Maulvi Zakaullah. When the latter wrote an *adab* book, *Makārim al-Axlāq* (1891), he devoted nearly one-fifth of the book to the instruction of boys but not one line to the education of girls.

17. Kaika'us ibn Iskandar ibn Qabus, *Qābus Nāma*, edited by Amin 'Abd al-Majid Badavi (Tehran: Ibn Sina, 1963). A popular book during the medieval period, it was a great favorite of Akbar, who had it read to him several times.

18. *Qābus Nāma*, p. 116. The English translation by Reuben Levy, *A Mirror for Princes*, London: The Crescent Press, 1951, is based on a different manuscript which has: '…do not teach [the daughter] to read and write', p. 125.

19. Khwaja Nasiruddin Tusi, *Axlāq-e Nāṣiri*, edited by Mujtaba Minawi and Ali Raza Haidari (The Khwarizmi, 1977), pp. 229–30.

20. The book first came out in sections at the beginning of this century. As a book it went through number of revisions and innumerable printings. See the articles by Barbara Daly Metcalf: 'The Making of a Muslim Lady: *Maulana Thanawi's Bihishti Zewar*', in Milton Israel and N.K. Wagle (eds), '*Islamic Society and Culture*, New Delhi: Manohar, 1983, pp. 17–38; 'Islamic Reform and Islamic World: Maulana Thanawi's *Jewelry of Paradise*', in Barbara Daly Metcalf (ed.), *Moral Conduct and Authority: The Place of Adab in South Asian Islam*, Berkeley: University of California Press, 1984, pp. 184–195. Dr Metcalf is also preparing a new and complete English translation. Two somewhat partial English translations already exist, one (by Rahm Ali Al-Hashimi) published from India, the other (by M. Masroor Khan) from Pakistan.

21. Ashraf Ali Thanawi, *Bihištī Zēwar* (*'Aksī*), Delhi: New Taj Office. n.d., p. 85.

22. Ghulam Rasul Mihr, *Sayyad Aḥmad Šahīd*, Lahore: Kitab Manzil, 1953?, pp. 143–8.

23. I have used the text published in *Maṣnawiyāt-e Ḥālī* edited by Murtaza Husain Fazil, Lahore: Sh. Mubarak Ali, 1966, pp. 154–74, where it is titled '*Bēwa Kī Munājāt*'.

24. *Bihištī Zēwar*, p. 433.

Shah Jahan Begum

The extract included begins with a summary of a diary Shah Jahan's mother Begum Secunder kept of her pilgrimage to Mecca. She then goes on to describe her administrative work in various provinces of her kingdom, her second marriage, and the problems it caused. Unlike her mother and grandmother, Shah Jahan Begum (1868–1901) remained in purdah, which presumably meant, in her case, using the veil, as she travelled extensively and met visitors: Her second marriage, after the death of her first husband, created a rift with her mother, who felt that widows should not remarry, and that the husband's status was not good enough for her daughter; Shah Jahan's daughter suspected him of dynastic ambitions, especially when he tried to marry her to one of his sons.

Nevertheless, Shah Jahan Begum and her second husband Siddiq Hasan Khan, both writers, created a lively literary atmosphere in Bhopal: they invited numerous writers to the court, in addition to men with scientific interests, and founded a second printing press. Urdu poetry was the court language instead of Persian; Hindi was also encouraged. Shah Jahan Begum herself composed poetry, and compiled two dictionaries. In addition she built mosques and public buildings, widened roads, improved sanitation, established about thirty schools, some of which taught the children handicrafts such as carpet-making, tent-making and so on. She also introduced judicial reforms.

Part II

Chapter VII

Journey to Mecca

As soon as my revered mother had put in order the affairs of the State, and obtained some rest, she determined upon visiting Holy Mecca. Her

Shah Jahan Begum, *Taj ul-Ikbal Tarikh Bhopal* or *The History of Bhopal*, H.C. Barstow (trans.), Calcutta: Thacker, Spink and Co., 1876.

mother, the Nawab Kudsia Begam, and uncle Mian Faujdar Muhammad Khan also accompanied her. On the 22nd Jamadi-ul-awal 1280 A.H., corresponding with the 5th November 1863 A.D., on a Thursday, she left Bhopal, and spent three days in the 'Farhat Afza' Bagh, outside the city, and having sent on her train of attendants of both sexes to the number of nearly a thousand on the road to Bombay, she herself, with her private servants, her mother and uncle, set out on the 24th of the same month, and marched, stage by stage, as far as Mahargam, near the town of Búrhanpúr, the furthest point to which the railway was then open; where they took the train for Bombay, which place they reached in safety on the 2nd of Rajab. Here three ships were engaged, two being sailing vessels, on which all her attendants and baggage were embarked, while she herself, accompanied by her mother, her uncle, the Minister of Bhopal, and her more immediate attendants, were accommodated on a steamer. They sailed on the 25th of Rajab 1280 A.H., corresponding with the 6th January 1864 A.D., and by. God's blessing had a prosperous voyage to Jeddah, which was reached on the 13th of Shábán 1280 A.H., corresponding with the 23rd January 1864 A.D.; and on the 17th of the same month, at the time of *vespers,* they arrived in Holy Mecca and performed the prescribed observances; and on the 9th of Zilhij completed the rites of the Hajjul-Islam. Their proposed visit to the illustrious Medina was postponed on account of the road being infested by Bedouins. On the 14th of Zilhij of the same year, corresponding with the 21st of May, the port of Jeddah was reached, and sailing thence in the steamer, accompanied by her mother, uncle, and immediate attendants she arrived at Bombay on the 5th Muharram 1281 A.H., corresponding with Friday, the 10th of June 1864. Here she interchanged visits with the Governor and leading gentlemen of the place, and on the 16th of Safar 1281 A.H., corresponding with the 21st July 1864, she look rail for Mohiabad[1] (Poona). After staying there a few days she departed on Saturday, the lst Rabi-ul-Akhir 1281, corresponding with the 3rd September 1864 A.D., and on Wednesday, the 3rd of Jamadi-ul-awal 1281 A.H., corresponding with the 5th October 1864, she entered Bhopal. She was officially escorted in, from as far as Sikandrabad.

We are not informed by any History that any Emperor of Hindustan, or Muhammadan Chief, has ever before performed the Hajj; now, any Chief who may do so, will only follow in the Sikandar Begam's lead. In this journey, besides the cost of cloth and jewels of great price, which were presented to the Sherif of Mecca and the attendants at the shrine and to beggars and the poor in charity, Rs. 1,99,882-8 were spent, and the Kudsia Begam also spent a like amount.

My sainted mother has kept a diary of this pilgrimage bound in quarto, which was translated into English and published by Mrs Osborne, wife of Lieutenant-Colonel J. W. Willoughby Osborne, C. B., Political Agent of Bhopal; the following is a summary of her diary.

Jeddah is situated on the sea shore, and the houses rise to the height of seven storeys, which gives the town a striking appearance from a distance. The walls and foundations are brick and mortar, but the roofs are of mud. Masonry bathrooms[2] and kitchens form part of the houses themselves. The town contains a mixed population of Arabs, Turks, Abyssinians, and a few Hindustanis principally engaged in trade. The Arab costume is adopted, and Arabic is the language in common use. The better classes are well fed and well clothed. The water in the town is brackish, which necessitates the storage of rain water in huge reservoirs outside the town, whence the drinking water of the whole population is drawn throughout the year. There are British, French and Persian Consuls resident here. Outside the town is the shrine of the Holy Eve. This shrine is enclosed by parallel walls, about 300 yards long, and breast high; at the head end there is a small cupola and a similar cupola at the feet; while in the middle, where the waist would be, is a large dome. The shrine is srrounded by a large enclosure filled with graves. Syud Abdálla, Sherif of Mecca, and Izat Ahmad Pasha, Governor of Mecca, heard the news of my coming, and wrote to me. After leaving Jeddah, and before we had proceeded far, Suleman Beg, son of the Pasha, and the Oherif's younger brother, each with a retinue of fifty Turkish cavalry, met us and performed the ceremony of istikbal.

On the 17th Shaban, about *vespers,* the Holy Mecca was reached. We found 100 infantry in full uniform, with some cavalry, who had been sent by the Sherif of Mecca, drawn up for our reception. These men presented arms to us, while our ears were saluted by the voice of the Muezzin calling to vespers. We passed through the Báb-ul-Salám to the Ham Sherifa, and performed the observance of the Toáf-i-qudoom, then the ceremony of 'Sai,' and were on our way to the buildings reserved for the accommodation of the Hajjis, when the Sherif's slaves came up and said that the Sherif had found us separate apartments in his own house, to which we were to repair. We were received on our arrival by the Sherif's brother, who, after the first formal greetings, conducted us into a spacious house; all the verandahs of which were covered with gold embroidered carpets of blue velvet. Some Abyssinian slaves, who stood respectfully at the edge of the carpet, requested us to partake of refreshments, but I hesitated to do so, on which Jafir Effendi, our interpreter, informed us, that to do so was in accordance with the customs of the place, on which we sat down to dinner. Every variety of food in 500 dishes was set before us; and when dinner was over, we retired to our sleeping apartments. Next day the Sherif sent us trays of food, both morning and evening; on the third day I took a house near the Amar-bin-Akil. Mighty Mecca is a very large city, and contains many large seven storeyed houses; the products of every quarter of the globe are procurable there, and many of the inhabitants are rich, but far the richest of all is the Sherif. The city is surrounded by hills devoid of trees, grass and water, which accounts for the intense heat during the day time, when the wind blows fierce and hot; the nights are somewhat cooler, and the moon is very clear and bright, Notwithstanding the frequent presence of clouds accompanied by thunder and lightning, it seldom rains. Singing and dancing are never mentioned; and if there be any, it is held to be very disreputable. The Turkish soldiers resemble English soldiers except in their drill and dress, which is different. The chief food of the place is camel's flesh and mutton; coffee, tea and the hukah are fashionable. The Arabs are very industrious and strong, and although as dark and spare as Indians, I have seen porters lift on their shoulders a load of two maunds[3] weight, and carry it upstairs with ease. The voice and the hair of the inhabitants are not pleasing. The women are bigger than the men. No other religion besides that of Islam is professed there. The language spoken is an impure dialect of Arabic; in fact, with the exception of the household of the Shebi, who is the custodian of the holy shrine, and that of the Sherif, and perhaps one or two other families, there are no pure Arabs in the place. The population is composed of Indians, Bokhariots, Afghans, & c., who have become like Arabs in appearance from their long residence, and having been settled there for one or two generations. Besides there is an annual influx of pilgrims of various countries speaking different languages which accounts for the impurity of the language spoken. The country folks are still pure Arabs, and their language is purer. The custom of taking service and receiving wages does not prevail there, but slaves of both sexes, Abyssinians, Georgians and Circassians, are sold in open market; these persons are made to do domestic service, and can be sold again at pleasure. Each ward of the town contains large and beautifully built hot baths with separate accommodation for the two sexes. The Zabída Khátun canal affords good and sweet water for drinking purposes. Figs, pomegranates, water melons and cucumbers are imported from Taíf, and most excellent they are. The horses of Arabia, the saddlery and harness, both Persian and Turkish, require no remark; they should be seen to be properly appreciated. At all times of the night and day every kind of food can be procured in the bazars, but there is no salt in the stews and roasts, because it is the custom of the Turks to keep salt ground fine by them, and to add it when they take their meals according to taste.

In the Masjid Al Harám are the five calls to prayer: and after midnight the call to 'tahejd', and in the morning the tahrim, and at the time of afternoon prayers the takbir—all of which services are read in a loud voice. The tahrim is as follows: A man ascends to the top of a lofty tower in the early morning and chants in a loud voice some verses of the Koran, containing allusions to the majesty and powers of God and the unity of the Divinity, and His grace, mercy and forgiveness, and he asks blessings on the Prophet; his descendants and companions. This tahrim is a very inspiring and beautiful service.

The buildings around the tomb of the Prophet are called colleges, and the chambers are called 'khalwat', and in them the pilgrims are housed.

On the 16th Ramzan 1280 A. H., I visited the Sherif at his house, and after the 'istikbal' reached the palace, where three eunuchs conducted us to the first floor, and then withdrew to be succeeded by Georgian slave girls in clean dresses, who, in like manner, escorted us to the second floor and made way for the Egyptian women, who were drawn up in a row to receive us. They took us by the arm and carefully led us up the stairs to the third storey, where we were received by two wives of the Sherif, and conducted into the hall of audience. The Sherif's mother rose on seeing me, and advanced to the edge of the carpet to meet us; then his two wives shook hands with us, and kissed us on both sides of the neck, on both cheeks and on our lips and chin, and, with the greatest politeness, led us to the centre seat in the room. The whole house was furnished with glass lamps and beautiful carpets. The Sherif's wives were young and very beautiful, and from their heads to their waists were quite smothered in diamonds. They had silk kerchiefs, called in Arabic 'asabah', tied on their heads; and on their kerchiefs were set circlets of diamonds in clusters like a coronet; their elegance and beauty was beyond description. The sprays of diamonds shook with the least motion when they spoke or moved. After an hour had elapsed, the Sherif asked leave to be introduced; so he came and conversed with the greatest courtesy. Coffee, pomegranate sherbet, rosewater, and incense burning in a censer were set before us, and, according to Arab custom, I drank coffee and sherbet, and after fumigating my skirts and sleeves with the fragrant censer, took leave, the wives accompanying us to the door.

Suleman Beg, son of the Pasha, is our authority for the statement that the monthly pay of each Turkish soldier is twenty karash, which amounts to Rs. 3–8 in British rupees, besides which his clothes, food three times a day, tea, coffee and uniform, are found for him by the State, so that the total cost of each man to the State is about Rs. 21. Muhammad Husain, our interpreter, told us that gentlemen visiting the Sherif had to kiss the back of his hand before taking their seats, and that Bedouins and common people kiss the skirts of his coat, and attendants and slaves kiss the corner of his Divan, although this custom is not sanctioned by the divine law, but is disapproved and even condemned.

Arafát[4] is nine coss (18 miles) from the abode of God (Mecca), and there, on the 8th Zilhij, the clothing of abstinence is put on; the 9th is the day of the Haj. Clothed with the outward signs of abstinence, but with head bare, and continually repeating the prayer, beginning Labek-alla-ham,[5] the pilgrims collect in this place which is covered with their tents. There is no prohibition against eating or drinking; every man may cook and eat whatever he pleases, only he may not pass out of the bounds of Arafát. The priest arrives on a camel at the time of afternoon prayers, and ascends to the summit of Jabal Rahmat, where there is a pulpit, whence he reads the service (khutba) till vespers. 'Wakuf' is the name given to this space of time; this wakuf is strictly enjoined, but there is no divine sanction for ascending the hill; every one may stand where he pleases. Towards evening, one section of pilgrims, after sunset on that day leave Arafát and pass the night at Mazdulfah. Salutes are fired from the Turkish cannon, dragged to the place by Egyptian mules. In this procession the guns are loaded and fired without being halted for the purpose. This part of the ceremony is, according to the law, an innovation and an error. On the 10th Zilhij, Mazdulfah is left in the early morning for Maná, whence the pilgrims go to Holy Mecca, and perform the ceremony of walking round the tomb (Toaf) after which they return to Maná the same day and stay there for three days, performing the Rami-Jumar. These three days go by the name of tashrik; after their accomplishment on the 12th or 13th of Zilhij, the pilgrims come to Mecca, perform their farewell procession round the shrine, and then join their respective Kafilas, and start for their own countries.

The day of the Haj presents a most marvellous spectacle. Thousands and tens of thousands of men and women, young and old, ignorant and learned, nobles and beggars, from far and near, clad in one dress, the outward sign of abstinence, are collected together, practice humility, confess their sins, and send up prayers for forgiveness. Tents of every colour are to be seen for miles, and all sorts of curiosities are to be met with in the bazar; countless numbers of camels and sheep are slaughtered. Every year the Sultan of Turkey sends a covering of black silk for the Kaaba. This is brought by the Egyptian Kafila on a pack camel, with great ceremony, honoured by an escort of Turkish soldiers. The animal selected is of great beauty, and is caparisoned with green velvet embroidered with gold. It is also accompanied by several other camels, also beautifully caparisoned and ready to carry the sacred pack, should any accident befall the camel originally selected. On the day of the Haj, this pack is halted at the foot of Jabal Ráhmat, and after the Haj, is taken to Holy Mecca, when the covering of the previous year is removed, and this one for the ensuing year is put on in its place. Of the old covering half is the perquisite of the Shebi or Porter of the Kaaba, and the other half is divided among the attendants and ministers of the shrine, and by them sold in little pieces to the pilgrims as relics. The curtain over the door and the gold-embroidered 'waist-band' are the shares of the Sherif Sahib. The internal covering of the tomb is of red silk, but is not changed every year; it is only when a new Sultan of Turkey ascends the throne that a new covering is sent. Jaláluddín Syútí states in his book that the pack in which the covering of the Kaaba is carried, is returned to Egypt for good luck, and the day of its return is celebrated with rejoicing like the Ede. This unauthorised custom dates from the year 675 A.H. Originally the Kaaba was draped with a white cloth till the Abbasi Kalifah Nasruddín gave it a coloured covering, since which time the custom has continued.

On the 8th, 10th, and 14th Zilhij, a State procession is made by the Sherif. In front are led twenty-two Arab horses with trappings and housings of gold and silver, studded with gems; then swift she-camels with gold embroidered coverings, two of which are for the Sherif Sahib's special use, and have their necks adorned with strings of pearls, the value of which cannot be less than four lakhs of rupees (£40,000); behind them come 200 or 300 horsemen in Turkish costume; next a regiment of Turkish infantry; next 400 slaves of the Sherif's all well-armed and well-dressed, then the Sherif's sons and kinsmen mounted on horses with saddles of gold, followed by Elders, Arab Shaikhs, Turkish officers, and Abyssinian and Georgian slaves; next come the various Arab clans and hermits, all on camels, to the number of nearly a thousand; and finally the Sherif Sahib himself, mounted on a horse, with jewelled furniture. The procession is accompanied by music. After the Haj, for three days the table of the Sherif is kept ready spread, and all visitors are entertained with food.

Yelmalam is the name of a hill, before which, on the seashore, the pilgrims from India and Arabia don the garb of abstinence. This dress is as follows: The pilgrims first bathe and then gird a white cloth round their loins, and throw a white scarf over one shoulder. Women are not required to change their dress, but it is incumbent on them to wear no silk, nor to cover the face with their skirts when awake, nor to use either scent or antimony, nor to wear jewellery, nor to mingle with the other sex. The dressing of the hair with scented oil, and the use of combs, are forbidden, and the slaughter of any animal is prohibited until after the ceremonies of the Toáf round the Holy Kaaba and the Sai, or race between Safá and Marwah, and the performance of the 'Korbani' and 'Halk' be completed. Halk is the name given to the complete shaving of the head; and cutting a portion of the hair off with scissors is known as 'Kasar', or the shortcoming. It is the practice for women to cut off a hand-breadth with scissors. 'Korbani' is the name given to the sacrifice of some animal, either camel, goat or sheep, the clothing of which is given away in charity, and the meat may be eaten by all comers.

Six miles from Mecca in the mountains is a place called Tunáim, from whence a pilgrimage is made; after dressing as above, and reciting two extra prayers, the pilgrims come to Mecca calling out Labék by the way, and after observing the Toáf they recite two extra prayers at the house of Abraham, run the race between Safa and Marwah, shave their heads, or cut their hair, and then divest themselves of their pilgrim's dress.

Bérzdí Tuí is the name of a well outside the city of Mecca but within the sacred precincts, where the Hajjis bathe before entering Holy Mecca. This bath is indispensable; there is now a mosque near the spot.

The Masjid Járánah is eighteen miles from Mecca, and is also a starting place for the Hajjis, and this is called the long pilgrimage.

The Jabal Nur,[6] Ghar-hara (the hill of light and the cave Hará) is within the holy precincts, but outside the town of Mecca. Here it was that the revelation of God first descended upon the Prophet. This mountain is nearly two miles high; there is an arched doorway over the mouth of the cave Hará, and the pilgrims have to recite two extra prayers. There is a mosque also on the Koh i-núr.

The Jabal Súr is also included in the limits of the Haram but outside the town of Mecca, and is celebrated as the place where the Prophet of God offered prayers. The Hajjis offer up two extra prayers in this place also, but it is not obligatory to visit this mountain.

Jinnát al Máalla is the name of the cemetery of Holy Mecca; it contains many tombs of the elders of Islam, and is reverently visited by the Hajjis. Veneration of the departed is enjoined by the sacred writings, especially of such holy men and saints as are buried here.

The mosque of the Jinns is situated without the city of Mecca. It was on this spot that the Jinns came and professed their belief in the Prophet. Musalmans also offer up two extra prayers in the Shajra mosque.

The hill Bukbís is near the sacred precincts; there the Prophet of God was in the habit of worshipping; this hill is now covered with houses.

Safa and Marwah are two hills between which there is now a bazar; near one corner of the Kaaba there is an arched doorway, the name of which is Safá; opposite to it and at a distance of 250 paces is another hill, named Marwah, the space between has to be traversed seven times, prayers being offered up the while. Between them are two pillars, which are called miles; men have to run, but women are allowed to walk at their own pace. This running is called the 'Sai' (Race).

The precincts of the Holy Kaaba contain twenty-two gates, with one, two and three doors. The following is a list of them: On the western side, the Gate of Pilgrimage (Bab-i-Umra); (2) the Gate of Abraham; (3) The Báb-al-bida (the gate Farewell); and on the south side, (4) Bab-a-Maháni; (5) Bab Hakim-ul-Jadid; (6) Bab Sherif; (7) Bab-al-Akd; (8) Bab-al Safá; (9) Bab-al-Bagla; (10) Báb-al-Rab, also called the Bab-al-Naush; on the east side, (11) Bab Ali; (12) Bab Abbas; (13) Bab-al-Natr; (14) Bab-ul-Salams; and on the north side, (15) The Bab Dareba; (16) Bab Madrasa Sulemani; (17) Bab-al-Mahakma; (18) Bab-al-Ziyada; (19) Bab Kutbi; (20) Bab Basti; (21) Bab Madrasa Zamaniah; (22) Bab-Atik.

The well of Zam-Zam is inside the sacred precincts, and the water of it is brackish; although thousands of buckets of water, both night and day, are drawn out of it, the supply never diminishes in any season. This water is carried far way on account of its being holy; people drink it standing; its use for pouring over the body and for washing the hands and face is allowable, but for meaner purposes it is prohibited.

In the four quarters of the blessed Mecca, the prayers of the four doctrines are used. There are four pulpits: the Hanafi, Shafai, Malik, and Janbali pulpits were built in the time of the Abbaside Caliphs. Originally there used to be but one doctrine. The present building over the Kaaba was built by Amad Hajjaj bin Yusuf Shakfi. The Makam of Abraham is opposite to the chamber of the Kaaba, and extra prayers are recited there after the Toaf. The pulpit is ascended every Friday and on the Ede-ul-Fitr by the priest, and the Khutba[7] is recited therefrom.

The Library contains many thousand volumes on every subject arranged on bookshelves. It is frequently visited by learned men, who sit and study there, but are not allowed to remove the books.

The clock-house contains a collection of beautiful clocks and watches of every description of Turkish and European manufacture, and those skilled therein sit there and find out the exact time for prayers, this is a heresey which has sprung up in these later times. There are 152 gilt minarets surmounting the walls of the Haram.

The to'af, the blackstone, which stands in the corner of the chamber of the Kaaba, is kissed by the pilgrim, who then walks seven times round the building. This makes one Toaf, each separate circum-ambulation is called a Shawat. Rakan Yamani is a corner of the chamber of the Kaaba, which the pilgrims touch with their hands, which they then kiss,

Round the Hatim is an enclosing wall of marble shaped like a bow; this used to be part of the Kaabah, but is now separate. Here extra prayers are read, and certain people here put on the pilgrim's garb and go hence to the Hajj at Arafát. Mizah Rahmat is the name of a spout through which rain-water from the roof of the mausoleum is carried, and falls into the Hatim, the mouth of the spout is of gold. Every year on the 10th Muharram all the male population, and on the 11th Ramzan all the women, congregate in the chamber of the tomb from early morning till 9 A.M. On the 12th Rabi-ul-awal and the first Friday in the month Rajab and on the 27th Rajab and on the 15th Shaban and the first Friday in Ramzan and on the 27th and 15th of Zikat only men are allowed to enter the Kaaba, and separate dates are appointed for women. Every year three times, on the 20th Rabi-ul-awal, 20th Zikat, 12th Muharram, the Sherif and Pasha in person and the Shebi who keeps the keys of the Kaaba with two or three attendants wash the Kaaba twice with water, and a third time with rose water, and rub the walls and doors with sandal wood powder and attar of roses. This is not enjoined by the sacred writings but is done for the sake of cleanliness. Every year on the 25th Zikat the covering of God's seat is lifted from the ground to the height of a man and a white cloth is tied to it, and the common people call this the Ahram of the Kaaba. The total number of servants of the sacred precincts is 260, and there are 22 gateways, 12 large domes, 172 gold minarets, and the expenses of the Kaaba amount to 30 lakhs of Turkish rupees annually.

CHAPTER VIII

The Second Journey to Akbarabad, a Tour to Various Cities, and the Demise of my Sainted Mother, Now in Heaven

Colonel Richard John Meade, Agent to the Governor-General for Central India, addressed my revered mother from Indore by letter, dated the 14th August 1866, to the effect that the Viceroy and Governor-General, the Grand Master of the Most Exalted Order of the Star of India, had informed him of his intention of holding a Durbar at Agra on the 10th of November, and that the investiture of certain Knights of the above Order would take place at the same time; that Her Highness was also invited to attend, and that to meet the Viceroy in such a Durbar was an honour;

further that for Her Highness to take part in the Durbar in her character of Grand Commander of the Order, with the Grand Master of the Order was most appropriate and befitting. A reply to this was sent, that she would with pleasure attend the Durbar, and then, according to custom, in concert with Major Osborne, C.B., Political Agent at Sehore, she made preparations for going to Agra. On the 19th of Jamadi-ul-awal 1283 A.H., her advanced tents were despatched, and she herself followed on the 21st attended by the officers of State and her relatives.

Agra was reached on the 21st of Jamadi-ul-Akhir. On the 2nd Rajab, corresponding with the 10th of November, on Saturday evening, the Governor-General arrived by rail from Calcutta, and on the 12th he met each Chief separately in private Durbar, and invited all the Chiefs to a public Durbar on the 19th of November. When all the Chiefs had assembled, the Governor-General himself entered, and, addressing himself to all the Chiefs, spoke as follows:[8]—'Maharajas, Rajas and Sirdars— It is with great satisfaction that I see you all assembled before me this day. I bid you all a hearty welcome to this famous city renowned for its splendid Taj; and, above all, as having been in former days the seat of Government of the Great Emperor from whom it derives its name Akbarábád.

It is good for us thus to meet together: it is advantageous for me, as the Viceroy of the Illustrious Queen of England and India to see and become acquainted with so many Chiefs of rank and reputation: and for you all, it is right that you should be able to speak face to face with me, and hear my views and wishes regarding the management of your respective territories.

The art of governing wisely and well is a difficult one, which is only to be attained by much thought, and care and labour. Few Kings and Chiefs in Hindustan have possessed the necessary qualifications because they have not taken the precaution, in their youth, to learn, to study, and to act for themselves; nor did they care to have their sons, those who were to succeed them, well instructed and carefully trained. Hence it has so often happened that after a Chief has passed away, he has not been remembered as a good and wise Ruler. Great men, when living, often receive praise from their friends and adherents for virtues which they do not possess; but it is only after this life is ended, that the real truth is told. Of all fame that such men can acquire, that alone is worth having which is accorded to a just and beneficent Ruler. The names of conquerors and heroes are forgotten, but those of virtuous and wise Chiefs live for ever.

The days of war and rapine, it is to be hoped, have passed away from Hindustan, never to return. But perhaps some of the Chiefs now present can recollect the time in India, and all must have heard of the times, when neither the Palace of the Ruler nor the cottage of the peasant, nor the most sacred edifices of Hindu and Muhammadan, were safe from the hands of the plunderer and destroyer. In those days whole provinces were one scene of devastation and misery; and in vast tracts of country scarcely the light of a lamp was to be seen in a single village. English rule in India has put all this down. No longer is the country a waste and a wilderness, the abode of savage animals. Now it is to a great extent covered with populous villages, and rich with cultivation, and all the inhabitants are living in comparative safety under the shade of English power.

But while such no doubt, to a great extent, is a true picture of the state of India, still when we enquire closely into the condition of different parts of the country, we cannot but perceive that much tyranny and oppression are still practised; that much individual suffering still exists: and that much crime escapes unpunished. That peace and security from outward violence which the British Government confers on your territories, you must extend to your people. None but the Rulers of their own lands can accomplish this; and they only can do it by constant care and supervision. They have plenty of time to do all that is necessary, if they have only the will. Chiefs have abundant time for their own pleasure and amusement, indeed many of them have more leisure than they can employ; and are often weary from want of something to interest them. Others again waste their time in disputes with their neighbours, in quarrels with their feudatories, and even in still less satisfactory ways.

If a Chief will neglect his own proper duty, the care of his State, how can he expect that a deputy will perform it properly for him? Good laws and well selected officials, carefully supervised, are necessary to insure good government. All efficient Police and a well-managed revenue are equally desirable, so that people may live in safety and enjoy the fruits of their industry. Schools for the education of the young, and hospitals for the care of the sick, should also be established. Some Chiefs are perhaps in debt, and would find it difficult to do much in the way I have sketched. But other Chiefs have abundant revenues; and all I ask is that every Ruler should act according to his means. Some among you vie with each other for precedence and feel aggrieved at the position you occupy. How much to the purpose it would be, if all would try who can govern his country in the wisest manner: in this way there is abundance of scope for all.

The British Government will honour that Chief most who excels in the good management of his people; who does most to put down crime and improve the condition of his country. There are Chiefs in this Durbar who have acquired a reputation in this way. I may mention Maharajah Scindia and the Begam of Bhopal. The death of the late Nawab Ghaus Khan of Jowrah was a cause of grief to me, for I have heard that he was a wise and beneficent Ruler. The Rajah of Seetamow in Malwa is now ninety years old, and yet it is said that he manages his country very well. The Rajah of Khetri in Jaipur has been publicly honoured for the wise arrangements he has made in his lands. It is to me a very great pleasure, when I hear of the meritorious conduct of any Chief, and try and make this known so as to encourage other Rulers to follow his example.

Kings and Chiefs in former times had no idea of opening out their countries. They often lived in difficult and almost inaccessible positions, surrounding their palaces with all kinds of fortifications, out of which they seldom ventured to any distance, and then only when attended by as many soldiers and armed followers as they could muster. As to travelling to see the wonders of other countries such an idea never entered their minds, or if it did, it was dismissed as utterly impracticable. Now the Princes of Hindustan have little hesitation in moving from one place to another at a distance from their own territories, and some Chiefs have become so enlightened and far-seeing as to be willing to have roads made through the length and breadth of their lands and some have contributed annually considerable sums for this purpose. I hope that others will follow their example, and do all they can to construct roads, canals, and wells in their country, thus enriching themselves and their people.

I will now conclude by wishing you all again a welcome to Agra, and trust that what you will have seen and heard, and the general reception you have received, may make you long remember this Durbar. I have but one object, namely, that you should try and govern your people well and thus conduce to your own good name and their happiness.'

The Durbar then broke up and on Thursday, the 22nd of November 1866, the Governor-General left Akbarabad for Gwalior, and the Chiefs all left for their respective States. On the 15th Rajab, corresponding with the 23rd of November, my sainted mother went by rail to see the city of Shahjahanabad and on the 23rd (Rajab) returned to Agra; and on the 26th visited Fatehpuri Sikri which she left on the 30th for Bhartpúr; and after spending the 2nd Shaban at Deeg, the 4th at Goberdhan, the 7th at Muttra, returned to Agra on the 10th Shaban, whence she marched on the 17th reaching Dholpur on the 19th and Gwalior on the 23rd, Duttia on the 29th, and the city of Jhansi on the 2nd Ramzan, the town of Sewans in Bhopal territory on the 20th, and on the 3rd Shawal, corresponding with the 9th of February 1867 safely returned to Bhopal.

In this journey the expenses were more than ordinarily heavy; the nazar to the Governor-General cost Rs 27,135-0-9 and the travelling expenses amounted, to Rs 75,070-0-3, making a total of Rs 1,02,205-1-0.

Fatehpur is 12 coss (24 miles) from Agra and 25 (50 miles) from Deeg which is 6 coss (12 miles) from Goberdhan. The following is a short account of these places. The buildings of Fatehpur Sikri which are of stone and very fine, are the work of the Emperor Akbar. Within the Fort there is a stone mosque, in the courtyard of which is the tomb of Salim Chishti containing a lattice work screen in marble of great delicacy and beauty; inside the mausoleum there are mosaics in mother-of-pearl. In the courtyard there is a reservoir for water; and on the south of the courtyard a large and lofty gateway from the top of which the Taj at Agra can be seen. There is also another reservoir of water outside the gate. There are also many other buildings of Akbar's Court besides the above, for instance, the house of Rajah Birbal and others, which are now uncared for and in ruins; there are many runnels for water and many reservoirs. The following lines are carved on the mosque and tomb: 'In the reign of the Emperor Akbar who brought his dominions to prosperity, Shaikh-ul-Islam built this mosque which for beauty rivals the Kaabah, the year of the completion of this lofty building saw arise a second Majid-ul-haram.'

'Advocate of the faith and Holy Guide Shaikh Salím whose goodness and holiness is Janed and Taifur, he illuminates as a shining light the family of Chisht, he is the most dearly beloved son of Farídganj Shakar, Let not thine eyes be double. Think not of thyself, but be steadfast to God, so the year of his passing away will be known throughout all ages.'[9]

Deeg is in the country of the Rajah of Bhartpur, its buildings of stone and gay flower gardens are very picturesque. There is one building of white marble to which hundreds of fountains are attached, the reservoir to feed the fountains is a large tank with wells at each of the four corners, from which the water is drawn to fill the reservoir. When all the fountains are at play, the sun's rays shining through the water make an arch like a rainbow. The buildings of this place are worth seeing but are in the Hindu style. The roofs are low and the rooms gloomy

Goberdhan is the name of a hill to accomplish the circuit of which is an act of great piety according to the Hindu religion. There is a road round the hill, some Hindus perform the circuit at a foot's pace, others measure their length on the ground round it; others with their hands clasped in devotion. There is a small masonry tank on this hill, on the banks of which is an upright stone fixed in the earth about the height of man, which is considered to be the top[10] knot of the hill, and is an object of worship.

After her return from this journey and tour, the health of my revered mother began to fail; she was attacked by disease of the kidneys, and notwithstanding that she was put under the care of both 'Yunani'[11] practitioners and English doctors she got no better, but the disease gained on her. She suffered from great weakness, her vital heat failed and at length she passed away from this transitory world after Vespers on the 13th of the month Rajab 1285 A.H., at the age of 51 years 8 months and 15 days, and next morning at 8 o'clock she was buried in the Farhat Afzá garden, which she herself had laid out. In pursuance of the provisions of her will that her burial should be strictly in accordance with the true faith, no dome was built over her grave, which was enclosed by a screen of white marble. Her Majesty the Queen sent her condolences, and congratulations on my accession were also received by me from England, and I felt much honoured thereby.

My revered mother upheld in perfect good faith the nobles of the State in possession of their estates, she promoted the loyal with dignities and titles and treated all the members of our family with great affection. With great foresight she introduced the practice of entering the words 'for life only' into her grants instead of the words 'from generation to generation' which had hitherto been entered in all such documents. It is a happy coincidence that the year in which my revered mother departed this life witnessed the demise of many celebrated men of learning such as Asadallah Khan 'Ghalib' (poet) of Delhi, who recalled the times of Arfi and Naziri, he died on the second of Zikat of this year, also Afzal ud Daulah, Thaniyat Ali Khan, Nawab of Haidrabad in the Decean, who in the flower of his youth on the 14th of the same month and year departed this transitory life for eternity.

Part III

CHAPTER I

The History of this Suppliant at the Threshold of God, from the Day of Her Birth to Her Accession, and a Narrative of the Administration of the State up to the End of Her Tour in the Southern Division of the State of Bhopal

I was born on the 6th of the month Jamadi-al-awali 1254 A.H., and 1245 Fasli, corresponding with the 20th of July 1838 A.D., in the Fort of Islamnagar, and was set upon the throne of the State of Bhopal on the

15th of Muharram 1263 A.H., and 1254 Fasli, corresponding with the 4th of January 1847 A.D. On the 9th of Jamadi-ul-awali of this year corresponding with the 25th of April, Sunday, my mother celebrated the occasion of my ears being pierced with great rejoicings. On the 15th of Rajab 1266 A.H., and 1256 Fasli, corresponding with the 24th May 1850, the day being Friday, magnificent festivities were held at a vast expense in honour of my having read the Koran through to the end. I read the usual Persian reading books and acquired a knowledge of reading, writing, accounts and the conduct of State affairs.

On the 11th of Zikat 1271 A.H., and 1262 Fasli corresponding with the 26th of July 1855 A.D., my marriage took place as has been related in the second chapter of the second part, and on the 27th Zikat 1274 A.H. and 1265 Fasli, corresponding with the 9th July 1858, I gave birth to the Nawab Sultan Jahan Begam, and on the 9th Shawal 1276 A.H., answering to the 1st of May 1860, I voluntarily resigned the title of Ruler to my mother and became her heir-apparent as has been related in the second chapter of Part Second. On the 12th Jamadi-al-awali 1277 A.H., I gave birth to my second daughter the Suleman Jahan Begam who died on the 13th Muhanam 1282 A.H., her tomb is in the Nur Bagh, and the Sulemani school and mosque called after her name will be mementos of her in this State.

On the 21st Safar 1284 A.H., occurred the death of Nawáb Báki Muhammad Khan, my husband. He fell ill while at Mecca, and returned to Bhopal in the height of his illness; notwithstanding his treatment under the Yunani and English system of medicine he obtained no relief; after his death he was buried in his own garden. On the 13th Rajab 1285 A.H., my revered mother passed away, as has been related in the 8th Chapter of Part II. After her departure to Paradise, all the business of the State was suspended for three days, according to custom, and the pre-scribed lamentations were performed. Great regret was expressed by the British officers. In the towns of Sehore the seat of the Political Agency, and of Indore, of the Agency to the Governor-General, all the forms of public mourning observed by European nations were gone through, such as closing the shops and offices, &c. Inasmuch as this day must at some time be undergone by every living being, and resignation to the will of God is our refuge, therefore after waiting the above interval, on the 17th Rajab of the same year, the ordinary administration of the affairs of the State was undertaken by me.

On Tuesday the 1st of Shaban 1285 A.H., corresponding with the 16th November 1868 A.D., Colonel Osborne C.B., Political Agent of Bhopal, and Colonel Meade, Agent to the Governor-General for Central India, honoured Bhopal with their presence, and at 7 o'clock in the morning proceeded to invest me as Ruler, delivering to me on behalf of His Lordship the Governor-General a letter acknowledging me as Chief, and my daughter the Nawab Sultan Jahan Begam as Heir-apparent. The artillery fired a salute; the officers of State and members of my family presented me with 'Nazars' and I and the Heir-apparent both delivered speeches in Durbar. The English gentlemen offered me many kind and gracious congratulations on the occasion. They published in Bhopal a proclamation announcing my accession, after which they took leave and departed for Sehore and Indore respectively. The following is the speech delivered in Durbar by me: 'First and foremost I render thanks to my God, that I am the daughter of the Nawab Sikandar Begam, Ruler of Bhopal, who was proved by the English Government faithful, staunch, far-seeing and of great capacity for administration. Secondly I return thanks to my Sovereign the Great Queen Victoria, Queen of Hindustan and England and to her Ministers for the great favours shown to my mother the Sikandar Begam, first in placing her on the throne of her father Nazir-ud-daula Nawab Nazar Muhammad Khan and making her Ruler; secondly in increasing her dignity, when her loyalty and fidelity had stood the test of trial, by granting her the Pargana of Bairesia, conferring upon her the Star of India and raising her to a first class feudatory Chief. Thirdly in the complimentary notice by the Viceroy of the merits of her administration and the active part she herself took in promoting the welfare of her subjects. In the Durbar at Agra in the presence of the most renowned Chiefs of India there assembled, the Viceroy called attention to her administration as an example to be followed, and honoured her more than the other Chiefs. Now after her death the Viceroy has appointed me to succeed her.

'I thank Colonel Meade, Agent to the Governor-General for Central India, for acceding to my request by honouring Bhopal with his presence and for investing me as Ruler, and acknowledging my daughter as Heir-apparent in the same manner that Sir Richmond Shakespear invested my mother as Ruler and me as Heir-apparent. I also thank Colonel Osborne, Political Agent in Bhopal, for the unremitting attention which he paid to the Nawab Sikandar Begam during her illness in obtaining the best advice for her, also because after her death he lost no time in reporting the occurrence to the Supreme Government according to precedent, and I thank him for continuing to me the support and countenance which he always showed to the Sikandar Begam, and for maintaining at my accession the same ceremonies which were observed at that of my late mother. I shall be mindful of the great kindness shown by my Sovereign and these her servants to the end of my days, and I now pray to the merciful God that my whole life may be spent like my mother's in loyalty to the English Government, in improving the administration of the state of Bhopal and ameliorating the condition of my subjects.'

The following is the speech of the Light of my Eyes, the Sultan Jahan Begam favoured of fortune, may her days be long! 'Thanks be to God who of his exceeding great kindness has advanced me this dignity, and I thank His Lordship the Governor-General and the Agent to the Governor-General for Central India, and the Political Agent of Bhopal who have appointed me Heir-apparent and my mother Ruler of Bhopal: I trust that the merciful God will keep me loyal to the British Government during the whole of my life.'

This is a copy of the Proclamation which was promulgated by Colonel R. J. Meade, C.S.I., Agent to the Governor-General for Central India, to all subjects and nobles of the State of Bhopal:

To all whom it may concern, be it known, that the Nawab Shahjahan Begam, after the death of her beloved father, the Nawab Jahangir Muhammad Khan, was, on the 4th December 1846 A.D., with the sanction of the Government of India, proclaimed Ruler of the State of Bhopal, and her mother, the Nawab Sikandar Begam, was appointed Regent during her minority; and when the Nawab Shahjahan Begam attained her majority on the 20th July 1859, Major Hutchinson, the Political Agent of Bhopal at that time, was instructed to enquire of her whether she wished to take the direction of affairs into her own hands or no, to which she replied that she surrendered of her own free will the supreme authority to the Nawab Sikandar Begam for her life; subsequently she addressed a letter *pro formâ* on the 13th of December 1859, to Sir Richmond Shakespear, Agent to the Governor-General for Central India, that it was proper for the British Government to grant the Nawab Sikandar Begam two boons, *viz.*, the dignity of Regent and the authority of Ruler. Accordingly the purport of this letter was communicated to Government, and His Excellency the Governor-General instructed his Agent for Central India to publish to the people, officers, and nobles of Bhopal, that the Nawab Sikandar Begam was recognized as Ruler during her lifetime, and the Nawab Shahjahan Begam as her Heir-apparent and the succession was confirmed to her issue, and the English Government pledged itself to uphold this arrangement, therefore a proclamation to this effect was issued from the office of the Agent to the Governor-General for Central India on the 17th December 1859 A.D., and the Nawab Sikandar Begam according to the written agreement of the Nawab Shahjahan Begam, with the sanction of Government, was made Ruler of the State of Bhopal on the 1st of May 1860, and remained Ruler with a high character for justice and administration up to the day of her death. Now, whereas on the 30th October of this year, the Nawab Sikandar Begam departed from this transitory life to eternity as had been reported to Government, and Government has a second time sanctioned the appointment of the Nawab Shahjahan Begam as the rightful Ruler of Bhopal, and her daughter the Sultan Jahan Begam as her Heir-apparent, with succession to her issue, therefore the Nawab Shahjahan Begam has this day, in a public Durbar of her officers, chiefs, nobles, relatives and officers of State, in the presence of the Agent to the Governor-General for Central India, the Political Agent in Bhopal, and other gentlemen of rank, taken her seat upon the 'Masnad' of the State of Bhopal, and the Nawab Sultan Jahan Begam has been appointed Heir-apparent thereto; and by means of this Proclamation all the subjects, nobles, relatives, jaghirdars and officers of the State of Bhopal are informed hereof and all people are warned to acknowledge the Nawab Shahjahan Begam as their constituted Ruler, and to render her a true and hearty obedience with all readiness, loyalty, and zeal.'

After the ceremonies attending my accession were over, I took upon myself all the daily administrative and executive functions of Government. In the month of Ramzan I performed the customary fast and prayers. In the month of Shawal, I entertained the English visitors and the nobles my friends and relations in the State in honour of my accession. It is superfluous to enter into a detailed description of the festivities.

I next looked over the treasury, and counted the jewels and robes of my revered mother's 'Toshakhana'.[12] Set jewels to the value of Rs. 72,95‎ 5-9, which my mother had selected and caused to be put away in her wardrobe, but the price of which had not been agreed upon owing to her failing health, were returned by me, as their purchase did not appear to me to be necessary, and with regard to the debt on my mother's private estate amounting to Rs. 1,25,688-9-3, and state debt of Rs. 5,52,752-11-3, making a total of Rs. 6,78,471-4-6, arrangements were made for paying off the amount by instalments. In the present year, 1289 A.H., by God's blessing, the debt has been paid off.

Petitions, letters, and reports in revenue, civil, criminal cases, and reports from the Vakil's office, Commissioners of Divisions and District offices, and the Customs offices of Bhopal had accumulated to the number of 4,086 in the fourteen years preceding the late Begam's death, consequent on Her Highness' inability to attend to them from want of time, through her travels in Hindustan, her pilgrimages to Mecca, and from ill-health. Suitors in consequence were clamorous for justice. I therefore heard each petition one by one, and by God's help passed final orders on them, besides disposing of the cases which had been referred to the Councils in the late Begam's reign.

Whereas there were many complaints that cases of long standing were lying undecided in the various courts, I caused lists to be prepared of pending cases in the courts of the first and second Ministers and the Commissioners of the three Divisions, and the Customs and Judicial officers, from which it was ascertained that 16,631 cases remained undisposed of. These longstanding cases were referred for enquiry and decision to the Heads of the respective Offices to which they belonged, and a suitable term was fixed within which the incomplete cases were to be finished, and if within the competence of the Head of the Office he was to decide them; but if they exceeded his jurisdiction they were to be sent to my Court for disposal, and subsequently in consideration of the great number of cases of long standing in some of the Offices, an extra establishment was entertained for their disposal.

The poorer inhabitants of the city of Bhopal had long complained of the dearness of corn; the cause of which appeared to be that, although in former times and up to the early days of the Sikandar Begam's reign, plenty of corn used to be brought into Bhopal and sold there by the zemindars, yet on the establishment of the rule that a remission of half the tax should be made on all corn puchased for the use of British cantonments, &c., while no remission was made on corn brought to Bhopal for sale, a much smaller quantity was imported into the city on account of the full tax being enforced, and corn was always dear in the city. I thought this unfair to my subjects and unjust that foreigners should be allowed to profit by the reduction of the tax, while my own subjects of Bhopal were burdened with the full impost; accordingly on the 10th February 1869, corresponding with the 27th of Shawal 1285 A.H., orders were issued to the chief customs officer, that whereas the inhabitants of Bhopal were more worthy of consideration than foreigners, therefore, with the view of ameliorating the condition of the people, the tax on grain, gram, &c., 'imported from other parts of Bhopal into the city, should cease to be levied from the 1st Muharram 1286 A.H., corresponding with the 14th of April 1869.

The Cavalry and Infantry whose uniforms are red, and the troops of black-coated cavalry attached to the offices of the First Minister and the Vakil, had long complained that their duties, and expenses in maintaining their horses and uniforms, were heavier than those of the forces employed in the country, though they received the same pay, accordingly, from the 1st Muharram 1286 A.H., their pay was raised by the sum of Rs. 18,780 distributed proportionately over the different ranks.

From one cause or another, the late Begam had not visited her provinces for eighteen years, and the peasantry and other inhabitants of the interior were loud in their complaints of the oppression of the tax-collectors; charges of their corruption and extortion were repeatedly coming to our ears, it was necessary to relieve our oppressed subjects and to inflict a well-merited punishment on unjust officials, therefore notwithstanding that the cold weather had come to an end and the season for travelling had passed, I left Bhopal on Saturday the last day of Shawal, corresponding with the 18th February 1869, for a progress through my southern provinces, which comprise eight sub-divisions, of which Chipanir was the first visited.

A narrative of my tour in the Southern division—On our arrival at the above town on the 4th of Zikat 1285 A.H., corresponding with the 18th February, the village headmen, notaries, feoffees and grantees, bankers and village watchmen being collected, a proclamation, as follows, was read to the crowd assembled—It is seventeen years since this province was visited by the Ruler, although every year the Commissioner, and every third year the Deputy of the First Minister comes here. I have now determined that any wrong and oppression suffered by you during this time at the hands of any official of this State, whether high or low, shall, after enquiry made, be redressed, and the wrong-doers be adequately punished for their corruption and bribery; therefore whoever has been aggrieved in any way by Tahsildars or thanadars, past or present, or their subordinates, or by the Commissioners and their officials, or by the First Minister's Deputies and their underlings, or by the Customs officers of all grades and their subordinates, let him come forward without fear and lodge his complaint, the allegations of tyranny and oppression on the part of the servants of the State shall be fully enquired into in our own presence, and if you are still so afraid of these officials as not to make a true disclosure, which should subsequently be brought to light, then, on proof being forthcoming, both the corrupt official and you who have screened his guilt shall alike receive punishment.

And the second proclamation was as follows—Let all persons from whom demands unauthorized by the State, such as fees[13] on marriages, &c., have been exacted by collectors past or present, and by former or present Thanadars, come forward and declare them that the exactors may be punished and restitution may be made.

And the third proclamation was to this effect, that should any servant or official of the State of Bhopal take a bribe, and information of this be given to the ruler, then, on the bribe being proved, adequate punishment shall be meted out to the offender, and even if the offence be not proved, the informer shall not be punished.

After this a general examination was made of all the subordinates in the Tahsils, thanas, and rural police outposts, and my custom's Departments; and such as were incompetent or physically unfit, or had been detected in any crime, were discharged, and others appointed in their places; such sepoys and clerks whose descriptive rolls had been omitted

by the negligence of the collectors; but who had performed their prescribed duties, were enrolled up to the prescribed numbers; the subordinates in the land Revenue, Police and Customs Department in Chipanir
were required to take the oath of allegiance in the same way as the clerks
and writers of the city of Bhopal. The Revenue, Police and Customs
offices of Chipanir were examined, and written directions were drawn
up to remedy such defects as were observed.

Next, enquiries were made in my own presence into the petition of
those applicants in the district who had brought charges of bribery on the
part of officials, or embezzlement of Government revenue or extortion
on the part of the farmers, and orders for punishment were passed on
some during my tour, but those which required a more prolonged investigation were postponed till my return to Bhopal. The petitions relating
to Civil, Criminial, and Revenue cases were referred, according to the
ordinary procedure, to the Collectors, Police Officers, Commissioners,
Customs officers and to the First Minister; and all monies extorted by
collectors and farmers were restored to the cultivators.

The weights used for weighing corn and other goods were tested and
reduced to a uniform standard.

Orders were given for building and repairing courts, thanas, revenue
and customs offices where necessary, also for planting encamping grounds
with trees for shade and shelter to travellers.

The Parganas of Baironda, Murdanpur, Chechli, Bari, Bareli and
Udepura were next visited, and in the latter district the excess which had
been extorted by the lumbardars over and above the rents which had
been fixed by the State, were refunded to the tillers of the soil, besides
which fines were inflicted. After visiting Chandpura and the Fort of
Chokigarh, we went to the town of Kaliakhcri, the head-quarters of the
southern Division, and in every district visited, the procedure adopted at
Chipanir was followed, and on the 27th Muharram we returned in safety
to Bhopal.

In this tour, through eight districts of the southern division, 4360
complaints were gone into, orders passed, and a complete report of the
tour drawn up, a copy of which, according to the established practice,
was forwarded for the information of the Political Agent of Bhopal.

On the 27th Jamadi-ul-akhir 1286 A.H., corresponding with the 4th of
October 1869, Colonel Edward Thompson, Officiating Political Agent
of Bhopal, sent me a kharita to the following effects—'A report of your
good management and ability, your excellent administration of the State,
with the zeal and energy shown in your braving the extreme heat of
summer and the noxious hot winds, to improve your administration and

to promote the comfort of your subjects, was forwarded by me, together with a translation of the narrative of your tour in the South, and your proceedings for bettering the condition of your people, through the Agent to the Governor-General for Central India to the Supreme Government. In reply to this a letter has been received from the Secretary to the Government of India, of the date of September 21st, addressed to the Agent to the Governor-General for Central India, to the effect that His Excellency the Viceroy and Governor-General of India has perused with great satisfaction and interest the report, in which has been described the wise zeal and energy of Her Highness the Begam of Bhopal in extirpating the corruption &c., of ill-disposed collectors and carrying out new and beneficial reforms. The details show conclusively that Her Highness is determined to emulate her mother to govern her State in a liberal and enlightened spirit, to discountenance fraud and oppression, and to adopt measures which shall aim at the welfare and prosperity of all classes of her subjects. The course taken by Her Highness, in this view, would, in the opinion of His Excellency in Council, reflect credit on the administration of old and experienced Rulers of States. His Excellency in Council will have much pleasure in giving publicity to Her Highness' memorandum, and in transmitting copies thereof at an early date for the perusal of the Secretary of State.'

'It is with great pleasure and satisfaction that I send you a copy and translation of the above letter, which is the strongest proof of your appreciation by the Government of India and the best evidence of your worth and ability, and I beg to add, that the approbation of His Excellency the Governor-General of India and the widespread reputation of your Highness for good administrative ability, is a direct reward of those hearty labours undergone by your Highness for the welfare of your State. I feel assured that the praises and commendation of the British Government for your enlightened measures, will afford a pleasing incitement to you to continue in the same paths of progress and loyalty to the English Government, and that the Almighty God will increase your virtue and wisdom already known throughout the world.'

Subsequently on the 6th Zikat 1286, or 7th February 1870, A.D., Colonel Ousely, Officiating Political Agent of Bhopal, informed me of a despatch received by His Excellency the Governor-General from His Grace the Duke of Argyll, Secretary of State for India to this effect: 'It is gratifying to learn that Her Highness Shahjahan has already given proof of her desire to conduct the affairs of her State in the liberal and enlightened spirit which distinguished the late Sikandar Begam during a long course of years with such signal benefit to all classes of her subjects, and Her Majesty's Government concur in the sentiments of approval you requested to be conveyed to Her Highness Shahjahan at the salutary reforms she has effected in the Bhopal State.'

CHAPTER II

Contains a Notice of The Receipt of a Firman from Her Gracious Majesty, and the Narration of My Journey to Calcutta, and the Report of my Tour in the Western Division of My Bhopal Dominions, Together with a Notice of the Reforms Introduced

On the 2nd of September 1869 A.D., Colonel Edward Thompson, Officiating Political Agent in Bhopal, sent me a kharita,[14] in which was enclosed an English letter from the Duke of Argyll, Secretary of State for India, to my address. The letter is annexed—

To Her Highness the Nawab Shahjahan Begam of Bhopal

My Esteemed Friend—I have received the commands of the Queen to communicate to your Highness the sincere regret with which Her Majesty has learnt the death of your mother, Her Highness the late Nawab Sikandar Begam of Bhopal, and to offer to you her affectionate condolence on this much lamented event. And I am at the same time to express to you Her Majesty's gracious assurance that she feels every confidence that your Highness will administer the country under your charge with the wisdom and benevolence which characterized the government of the illustrious Princess whom you have succeeded.

That your Highness may enjoy length of days and continued prosperity is the heartfelt desire of your Highness' sincere friend and well-wisher

ARGYLL

NOTES

1. Mohiabad, probably named from Mohi-uddin-Aurungzeb Emperor.

2. In India the kitchens, at any rate, are in a separate building.

3. Two maunds would be nearly 200 lbs English.

4. Arafát, a sacred hill.

5. Labék—The following is a translation of this Prayer: I am present, O God, in Thy service I am present; I am present, Thou art God alone, I am present in Thy service. Of a truth all praise, glory and power is Thine, and Thine alone. I am

present in Thy service, O cherisher of the world, I am present. O Thou w ho forgivest sins, I am present in Thy service. I give Thee help in Thy work: all good is in Thy hands and all things incline to Thee.

6. Jabal Nur and Koh-i-nur appears to be the same place—The Hill of Light

7. Kutba, an oration in praise of Muhammad, his successors and the reigning sovereign. Vide Forbes' *Hindustani Dictionary*.

8. Note—Vide *Gazette of India Extraordinary*, 29 November 1866.

9. In the Persian, the date is given by one of the words, the letters of which, combined as numerals, give the year of his death by the Hijra era.

10. Chutia is the lock of hair on the crown of the head which all Hindus allow to grow to its full length.

11. Yunan—Persian name of Greece.

12. 'Toshakhana' is an untranslatable word familiar to all persons in India. Each native State and the Foreign Office of the Government of India has a toshakhana, where stores of costly robes, jewellery, trappings, and housings are kept. It is from such stores that 'Khilats' are given, and State processions are provided by Native States.

13. Fees on second marriage of Hindu women are still levied in some of the Hindu principalities. This tax appears to be of great antiquity, and mention of it is found in Malcolm's Central India.

14. The despatches of Native Princes are enclosed in a kincob bag the mouth of which is closed by a string, to which the State seal is attached. These despatches are called *Kharitas* which is the Hindustani for the bag, the older and more correct form is 'khat kharita' the letter with the bag.

Rassundari Devi

Rassundari Devi's *Amar Jiban* (My Life) published in 1876 is now one of the best-known autobiographies by women (the first to be written in Bangla), in which she is unexpectedly frank about her feelings. A commentator writes, 'A persistent, almost tenacious sense of her individual identity, one that she struggles to hold on to in the most adverse of circumstances, is a striking feature of the narrative.' The extract included here, one of a set of sixteen published in 1876 (the next fifteen were published in 1906) talks about her attempts to teach herself to read and write, skills generally forbidden to women.

The Sixth Composition

I was so immersed in the sea of housework that I was not conscious of what I was going through day and night. After some time the desire to learn how to read properly grew very strong in me. I was angry with myself for wanting to read books. Girls did not read. How could I? What a peculiar situation I had placed myself in. What was I to do? This was one of the bad aspects of the old system. The other aspects were not so bad. People used to despise women of learning. How unfortunate those women were, they said. They were no better than animals. But it is no use blaming others. Our fate is our own. In fact older women used to show a great deal of displeasure if they saw a piece of paper in the hands of a woman. So that ruled out my chances of getting any education. But somehow I could not accept this. I was very keen to learn the alphabet. When I was a child I used to sit in the schoolroom and listen to the chanting of the students. Could I remember any of that? By and by I recalled the thirty letters with all their vowel combinations. I could recognize the letters, but was still not able to write them. What was I to do? Actually one cannot learn without a teacher. Besides, I was a

Rassundari Devi, *Amar Jiban*, Enakshi Chatterjee (trans.), 1876.

woman, and a married one at that, and was not supposed to talk to anyone. If anyone spoke a harsh word to me I would die of shame. That was the fear that kept me from talking to anyone. My only hope was God and my constant prayer was, 'Dear God, I can only learn to read and write if you teach me. Who else is there to be my teacher?' Days passed in this manner.

One day I dreamt that I was reading the *Chaitanya Bhagavata.* When I woke up I felt enthralled. I closed my eyes to go over the scene. It seemed that I was already in possession of something precious. My body and my mind swelled with satisfaction. It was so strange! I had never seen the book yet I had been reading it in my dream. For an illiterate person like me, it would have been absolutely impossible to read such a difficult book. Anyhow I was pleased that I was able to perform this impossible feat at least in a dream. My life was blessed! God had at last listened to my constant appeals and had given me the ability to read in my dream. Thank you, dear God. You have made me so happy. He had given me what I had wanted so much, and I was happy.

Our home contained several books. Perhaps the *Chaitanya Bhagavata* is one of them, I thought to myself. But what did it matter to me after all? An illiterate woman like me wouldn't even recognize the book. So I prayed to God again, saying, 'You are the friend of the poor; allow me to recognize the book. You must let me have that book. You are the only one whom I can approach.' That was how I prayed to God silently.

How strange are the ways of God and the effects of his kindness! He heard my prayers and set out to grant me my wish. My eldest son was then eight. I was working in the kitchen one day when my husband came in and said to him, 'Bipin, I am leaving my *Chaitanya Bhagavata* here. Please bring it over when I ask you to.' Saying that he put the book down there and went back to the outer house.

I listened from the kitchen. No words can express the delight I felt when I heard his words. I was filled with happiness and rushed to the spot to find the book there. Pleased with myself, I said to God, 'You have granted my wish', and I picked the book up. In those days books were made differently. There were illustrated wooden frames to hold the sheets. Since I did not know how to read, I tried to remember the illustrations.

When the book was brought into the room I detached one sheet and hid it. But I was afraid lest it were found. That would be a disgrace. I might even be rebuked. It was not easy to face criticism or rebuke. I was very sensitive about those things. Those days were not like present ones. We were completely under the control of men. And I was particularly

nervous. I was at a loss with that sheet. Where should I keep it so that
nobody would find it? But if they did, what would they say? Finally I
decided to put it in some place where I would be present most of the time
and nobody else was likely to go. The *khori*[1] in the kitchen was the only
hiding place I could think of. Housework kept me busy the whole day.
There was no time even to look at it. In the evening the cooking
continued until it was very late. By the time I was free, the children had
awakened. Some demanded to be taken to the toilet, some were hungry,
some wanted to be picked up, some started crying, so I had to attend to
their demands. Then I felt sleepy myself—so where was the time for my
education? I did not see any way out. No one could learn without the help
of a teacher. There were some letters that could recognize but I wasn't
able to write them. How can one be literate without being able to write?
So how was I to read that sheet? I thought and thought about it but could
not find a way out. Besides, the danger of being seen was very much
there.

Gradually I began to lose hope, but I prayed to God constantly,
'Please, God, teach me how to read. If you don't, who else will?' That
was my constant prayer. Sometimes I used to think that I would never
succeed. Even if I tried hard and somebody was willing to teach me,
where was the time? It was useless. I'd never learn. The very next
moment I thought, Of course I will. God has given me hope. He can
never disappoint me. Encouraged, I kept that sheet to myself. But I had
no time to look at it. I kept the sheet in my left hand while I did the
cooking and glanced at it through the sari, which was drawn over my
face. But a mere glance was not enough, because I could not identify the
letters.

I decided to steal one of the palm leaves on which my eldest son used
to practice his handwriting. One look at the leaf, another at the sheet, a
comparison with the letters I already knew, and, finally, a verification
with the speech of others—that was the process I adopted for some time.
Furtively I would take out the sheet and put it back promptly before
anybody could see it.

Wasn't it a matter to be regretted, that I had to go through all this
humiliation just because I was a woman? Shut up like a thief, even trying
to learn was considered an offense. It is such pleasure to see the women
today enjoying so much freedom. These days parents of a single girl
child take so much care to educate her. But we had to struggle so much
just for that. The little that I have learned is only because God did me the
favor.

Actually the man who was my master happened to be a likable person.

But it is difficult to ignore or reject accepted customs and practices. That was why I had to undergo all that misery. Anyway it is no use crying over spilled milk. In those days people considered the education of women to be wrong. Even now we come across some who are enemies of education. The very word excites their displeasure. Actually they were not really to blame; it was a time that was very precious. If you compare that period with the present you find many changes—beyond count. If the people of the earlier generation were here to witness all these changes, they would have died of disgust and shame. But whatever God directs seems to be for the good. The heavy dress of the women in those days, the heavy jewelry, the conch-shell bangles, and large vermilion dots used to look very nice. Of course not all clothes were like that.

But I have no reason to complain. God has looked after me well and I spent my time with a happy heart. Suffice it to say that whatever he does is for the best. As a child I used to sit with the other children in the primary school. This proved to be useful when I compared the letters of the palm-leaf and sheet of the book with the memory of the alphabet I had. All through the day I went on doing this in my mind. After a great deal of time and with great effort I somehow managed to stumble through the *Chaitanya Bhagavata.* Books were not printed in those days. The handwriting was difficult to decipher. Oh, the trouble I had to take to read. In spite of all that, I did not learn to write. One needs a lot of things if one is to write: paper, pen, ink, ink pot, and so on. You have to set everything before you. And I was a woman, the daughter-in-law of the family. I was not supposed to read or write. It was generally accepted as a grave offense. And if they saw me with all the writing paraphernalia, what would they say? I was always afraid of criticism. So I gave up the idea of writing and concentrated on reading. I never thought I would be able to read. It seemed an impossible task in my situation. The little that I have learned was possible because God guided me. I was deeply engrossed in whatever I could read and the idea of writing did not cross my mind.

Notes

1. The *khori* is an elevated bamboo platform, used as a storage space in East Bengali (now Bangladeshi) village kitchens.

Nawab Sultan Jahan Begum

1858 was the year of Sultan Jahan Begum's birth; as she points out in her autobiography, it was a memorable one in the annals of India because Queen Victoria was declared Empress of India and ushered in an era of peace and prosperity.

The fourth and last of the great line of women rulers of Bhopal, Sultan Jahan Begum (1858–1930) was, like her mother and grandmother, particularly interested in female education, both academic and practical. She introduced new classes which, in addition to the teaching of the Quran also taught Urdu, arithmetic, domestic economy, geography, and, in other schools, nursing. She opened schools for both Muslim and Hindu girls, widows and poor women, and the aristocracy. She herself was the only woman ever to be Chancellor of Aligarh Muslim University.

Sultan Jahan Begum believed in purdah and wrote a book to defend the institution. At the same time, she built clubs and created gardens for the exclusive use of purdah women. She travelled extensively in India and in Europe.

Like her forbears she went to Mecca, had several impressive buildings erected in Bhopal, and patronised literature and the arts. She was also a prolific writer, and published about fifty books.

Her husband died a few months after she became ruler. When in 1924 she lost two of her sons, she was so stricken that she decided to abdicate in favour of her youngest son, Habibullah Khan. He was proclaimed heir apparent in 1926, and crowned ruler in June of the same year.

Chapter III

My Childhood

The description of my early life contained in the *Táj-ul-Ikbál* is so brief and void of detail, that it seems to me better that I should myself give

Nawab Sultan Jahan Begum, *An Account of My Life*, London: John Murray, 1910.

some account of my education and general training, and the way in which the days of my childhood were passed.

I was born in the year 1274 A.H. (1858 A.D.), and I cannot help recording this fact with feelings of pride, for it was a year rich in memorable events, and the forerunner of a prosperous and happy era. Before the year 1857, as my readers know, the English, although masters of India, left the administration of its affairs in the hands of a Company, and many parts of the country were still in a disturbed and lawless state. Railways and the telegraph had scarcely been introduced: trunk-roads and district highways were few and ill-maintained: higher education was scarcely thought of, and schools existed only in a few of the large cities. Backwardness was visible on every side; and, if the country was advancing at all, its progress was too slow to be apparent. But it pleased God that this state of affairs should come to an end. The Mutiny of '57 was not a mere chance event. It may be wiser to draw a veil over its dark tragedies; but let us not forget that it was a touchstone on which, if the loyalty of some turned to dross, that of many others showed bright and clear; and that, if its darkness was black, it was the darkness that came before the dawn.

The year 1858 is a memorable one in the annals of India. It witnessed the restoration of peace, the abolition of the Company, and the assumption by Her Majesty Queen Victoria of the reins of government. It witnessed the arrival of her Majesty's Dispatch, the Magna Carta of India, which, like a sun rising in the West, brought life and vigour to the fainting East, and dispersing the clouds of ignorance, insecurity, and distrust, spread in their stead the light of peace, progress, and knowledge. And it witnessed the beginning of that rule which, though ushered in by the sword, has won, by its beneficence and justice, the willing obedience of a loyal people. The year 1858 was, in fact, the standard-bearer, behind whom marched the armies of civilization and progress, led onward by Western thought and Western enterprise, to do battle against the darkness of this land. If my birth at this time is not a thing on which I have a right to pride myself, I must at least regard it as a high privilege, and one for which I shall never cease to thank Almighty God.

Before my birth even my own country was not free from the troubles of revolt. In the district of Gadhi Ambapáni a rising had taken place, set on foot by Fázil Muhammad Khán. Nawáb Sikandar Begam was greatly distressed at the prolongation of these disturbances, and was much concerned on account of the hardships which they entailed on her troops; for scarcely had they had time to draw breath after their services during the Mutiny, when this second revolt broke out, and threw the whole district once more into the wildest confusion. This happened about six months before my birth, and, as the Begam was one day meditating upon the difficulties of her surroundings, she made a vow that if, by the grace of God, the revolt could be put down ere these six months were past, the district of Ambapani should become her grandchild's *jágír*. She prayed that it might happen according to her wish, and her prayer was granted. For it is written in His Holy Word, 'Whatsoever ye shall ask in faith, ye shall receive.' The insurrection was quelled: and when, on the 27th of the month Zil Kádah, in the year 1274 A.H. (July 10th, 1858), my birth took place, the above-mentioned district became my *jágír*.[1]

Both the Kudsia Begam and Nawáb Sikandar Begam had looked forward to the birth of a son, for it was a matter of sorrow to them that for fifty-eight years no male child had been born in the family. When, contrary to these hopes, I made my entrance into the world, the Begam showed none of the regret which the birth of a girl might naturally have been expected to cause; and as soon as she saw me, animated by I know not what thoughts and emotions, she clasped me in her arms and said, 'Thank God I am not one of those about whom it is written:

And when any of them is told of the birth of a female, his face becometh black, and he is deeply afflicted.[2]

This child is dearer to me than seven sons.' Indeed, had a son been born, she could not have rejoiced more.

The news of my birth was proclaimed by a salute of guns, and entertainments and feasts were provided for all the servants of the State, as well as for the general public both in the city and in the districts, while presents of clothes were distributed among the poor. For six months these rejoicings continued, shared by nobles and commons alike. My birth, coinciding as it did with the advent of the new era, gave a double signification to the occasion, and on every side the air resounded with the music of peace and happiness.

Before I had reached the age of two years, Nawáb Sikandar Begam had been confirmed as the ruler of the State, and the law of succession had been established. At the Jabbalpúr durbar the district of Bairasía had been formerly made over to the State, thus increasing both its area and population: and the Begam had had the honour of receiving a *Khilát,* and of being invested with the Most Exalted Order of the Star of India. It is no wonder, then, that she regarded my birth as an auspicious event. Day by day she treated me with more and more kindness. Indeed, her love for me outweighed that of my parents and of all the other members of my family combined. I was the main object of her life, around which all her hopes and pleasures centred. Whenever she went on tour, she used to leave me in the care of my Mother, lest the difficulties of travelling through hilly regions and over rough roads might prove too much for me; but she never failed to arrange that news of my welfare should reach her daily. And although I was so young that I could neither read nor understand what was read to me, yet she continually wrote letters to me full of expressions of love and affection. After my marriage, these letters were given to me by my Mother, and, although I neither remember receiving them nor hearing them read, I never look upon them now without pleasure.

For the first five years of my life I experienced only my Grandmother's fostering care, play being the only matter to which I gave any serious attention. At the close of this period the foundation of my education was laid, with the customary invocation of the divine blessing. A regular course of study was prescribed for me, and my daily routine was as follows :

Before Noon

From 5 o'clock to 6	Open-air exercise.
From 6 o'clock to 7	Morning meal.
From 8 o'clock to 10	Reading of the Korán.
From 10 o'clock to 11	Breakfast with Nawáb Sikandar Begam.
From 11 o'clock to 12	Recreation.

After Noon

From 12 o'clock to 1	Handwriting lesson.
From 1 o'clock to 3	English lesson.
From 3 o'clock to 4	Persian lesson.
From 4 o'clock to 5	Arithmetic.
From 5 o'clock to 5.30	Pashtu lessons and fencing practice alternately.
From 5.30 o'clock to 6	Riding lesson.
From 6 o'clock to 7	Evening meal.
And so at 8 o'clock to bed.	

The following were my teachers:

Reading the Korán	Háfiz Syad Muhammad Surati.
Translation and *tafais* of the Korán.	Maulavi Jamál-ud-dín.

Handwriting	Razá Ali Shírín Rakam.
English	Munshi Husein Khán.
Persian	Maulavi Bukhári.
Arithmetic	Guru Jí Pandit Ganpat Rai.
Fencing	Syad Amír Ali.
Riding	Ustád Hakdad Khán.
Pashtu	Akhúnd Sáhib.

All the arrangements connected with my education, health, and guardianship were in the hands of my Grandmother, and I remained by her side day and night, three evenings only in each week being spent with my Mother. In 1280 A.H. Grandmother performed the *haj*. Distressed at the idea of being separated from me, she had desired to take me with her on her pilgrimage, together with my Mother and my Father, Nawáb Umrao Dula. The Nawáb Sáhib was quite willing to go, but my mother was so terrified at the idea of a journey by sea, and made so many stipulations, that the idea of taking her had to be abandoned; and, consequently, the Nawáb Sáhib also was obliged to remain behind. The Begam set out from Bhopál on the 24th of Jamádi-ul-awwal, 1280 A.H. (November 5th, 1863), and the moment when she took her farewell of me is still fresh in my mind. There is no doubt that the parting was a great trial to her, and nothing but her desire to show her gratitude to God, and the knowledge that she was performing a religious duty, would have reconciled her to it. Every post brought letters from her, containing injunctions in regard to my education, besides numerous other instructions for my Mother, which clearly manifest the anxiety she was in on my account. The following are but a few out of the many that I received:

ADEN, *7th Shábán,* 1280

I thank God that to-day, Saturday, the 7th of Shábán, 1280 A.H., at 2 p.m., our good ship *Indore* reached Aden in safety, and all of us are well. Whenever you think of me, make ablutions, and perform *namáz* on the prayer-mat which was sewn for you by Zafran, and pray for your grandmother, and ask God to bring her back safe and well from the *haj*.

ADEN, *8th Shábán,* 1280

I have bought for you, on board the ship, a box with a small space to hold an inkpot, and another to keep your letters in; also a small tooth-powder casket, a tea-kettle, a cup, a sweetmeat basket, and a bouquet of real sea flowers that grow in the sea; and I am sending them, together with similar presents for Sulaiman Jahán Begam, with this letter. Give your sister's share to her, and keep your own.

The coloured ruler which I am sending is for you only, and not for Sulaiman Jahán Begam.

Mecca, 17th Shawwál, 1280

I have received your two letters of the 2nd Ramazán, and I heartily thank God to hear that you are quite well. But the letters are not signed by you. I understand that Nawáb Shah Jahán Begam Sáhiba has asked Kanwál Sen to write answers to my letters addressed to you; but he has neglected to make you sign them. In future, whenever you receive a letter from me, you should go to Rája Sáhib Bahádur, and dictate an answer to it with your own lips. Your seal that was with Injir Nána I am now sending you through Háji Husein, the Agent of Háji Ismail, and, God willing, you will soon receive it. I learn from the letter of Munshi Husein Khán, Superintendent of Post Offices, that you still cry whilst reading the Korán, and that you have to be punished. You must remember that you are almost grown up, and that it is, therefore, a great shame for you to cry while you are reading, and to have to be punished. It is quite time that you gave up this bad habit. Whenever you are tired of reading, and you want to do something else, you should tell your teacher so, but do not cry. When you have finished reading you can go to Alík-ullah and practise handwriting. Always tell me about Sulaiman Jahán Begam in your letters.

Mecca, 28th Shawwál, 1280

To the fruit of the tree of my heart, the star of my prosperity and good luck, Sultán Jahán Begam. May God enhance her happiness and prolong her life.

I learn from the letter of Munshi Husein Khán that you very often think of me, and grieve very much over our separation. Now, therefore, I write to tell you that when children are parted from their parents they should pray to God for reunion, and He will grant their prayer, and bring back their parents to them. I told you before I left Bhopál that, God willing, I should return after a year. Now there are 12 months in a year, and 30 days in a month; and if you go to the Rája Sáhib he will help you to find out how many days there are in a year, and then you will know when I am coming back. I should like to know what words you are learning to write now; so send me some of your copy-books. When you dictate your letters to me, say everything that comes into your mind: but, dear child, do not grieve for me at all. God willing, I will return as soon as I have performed my *haj*. Your Injir Nána performs the *tawáf*[s] oftener than anyone else. He prays continually for your health, prosperity, and long life. He hopes you will finish the Korán before we return, and that you no longer cry whilst reading it, for it is our Sacred Book, and it is our duty to study it cheerfully.

These letters I read with the most eager joy; but how much greater was my pleasure when, after the expiration of a year, came the news of her approaching return.

On the day of her arrival, my Father, Nawáb Umrao Dula, together with all the nobles and chief officials of the State, assembled at Sikand-arábád, three miles outside Bhopál, to bid her welcome; and, to my great joy, I was taken with them. As soon as her cavalcade came in sight, she saw me, though she was yet a long way off, for we were both mounted on elephants. Instinctively she stretched out her arms to me, and I remember how I wished that I had wings that I might fly to her. In a short time our elephants were side-by-side, and the next moment I was in her lap. Until the appointed halting-place was reached she continued to shower bless-ings and caresses upon me, while tears of joy and thankfulness fell from her eyes. Those, indeed, are pleasant days to recall, the days when I was absolute monarch in childhood's happy kingdom, with trouble, sorrow, and care banished from my dominions.

One of the first things Nawáb Sikandar Begam did after her return was to put me through an examination, to find out what progress my edu-cation had made during her absence. Since I had taken care to follow to the letter the injunctions she had given me, I passed this test with credit, and became a greater favourite with her than ever. My studies went regularly on, and whenever the Political Agent, or any other English gentleman, came to Bhopál, the Begam used to ask them to examine me in English, and to write me a certificate as to the result of the examina-tion. The object of this expedient was two-fold; it was meant to stimulate my own zeal for study, and to enable my Grandmother, who was not acquainted with English, to form a correct idea of the progress I was making. These certificates, of which the following will serve as ex-amples, I have carefully preserved to this day.

BOMBAY CASTLE, *May 8th,* 1866

To HER HIGHNESS SULTAN JAHAN BEGAM OF BHOPAL

Your Highness,

I have received your kind letter written in Persian and English, and was gratified to observe the progress you are making in your studies.

Accept my best wishes for your welfare and happiness, in which Lady Frere joins me, and believe me,

Your sincere friend,

(Signed) W. E. FRERE,

GWALIOR AGENCY, *New Year's Day*, 1867

I am greatly pleased to have had an opportunity of hearing the Princess Sultán Jahán repeat her lessons. Her Highness can read English in the First Reader fluently and correctly, has been well and carefully grounded in the first rules of Grammar, and altogether possesses a knowledge of the language which, considering her tender years, gives great promise for the future, and is very creditable to her instructor.

I hope some day to have an opportunity of certifying to still higher attainments on the part of the Princess, who, having so early made such remarkable progress on the ladder of learning, requires only continued diligence and attention to surmount every step, and thus to qualify herself for the exalted position she will occupy.

(Signed) A.W. HUTCHINSON,
Political Agent, Gwálior.

In the year 1284 A.H., my renowned and honoured father Nawáb Umrao Dula died. My love for my Grandmother, combined with my tender age, did much to mitigate my grief, but my Grandmother herself felt the blow very keenly. Indeed, her heart never entirely recovered from this sorrow, and she never ceased to deplore the loss of one who had proved himself a loyal and obedient son-in-law, as well as a kind and loving husband. Who could have believed that, ere the expiration of sixteen months, she herself would have passed away from this world! My age at the time of her death, which, as I have already mentioned, took place in 1285 A.H., was 10 years and 7 months, but I can feel as plainly as if it were yesterday the grief which fell upon me. Her kindly deeds are ever in my mind, her wise counsels come daily to my aid, and I never cease to offer up prayers for the welfare of her soul.

I now commenced to live permanently with my mother, Nawáb Shah Jahán Begam, but my mind was constantly depressed with sad thoughts. My Mother sincerely sympathized with me, and gave me all the consolation in her power. I was now her only child, for her younger daughter, Sulaiman Jahán Begam,[4] died of small-pox at the age of five, in the year 1277 A.H. In these altered circumstances the arrangements for my education were entirely changed. The handwriting exercises were given up altogether, and my usual hours of study dwindled down to four a day. In my Mother's eyes it was much more important that I should acquire experience in domestic and official duties, than that I should progress in scholarly knowledge. The Korán I had read through before I was eleven years old; but I was now made to study it a second time, and for an hour daily Maulavi Jamál-ud-dín was employed in explaining to me the Holy Book and its commentaries. I read English for two hours a day, and Persian for one hour. These were the only actual lessons I had, but in addition to them I was made to read, and write orders upon various official papers which it was now Her Highness's practice to send me daily. The following *parwánahs*[5] which I received from time to time will give some idea of the system under which I was educated after my Grandmother's death:

(1) It has been brought to my notice that at the present time your studies are not being pursued with regularity, and it is not clear in what manner you employ your time from morning till evening. These are the hours which your should devote to study. You are, therefore, to draw up a time-table of the work that you are doing. On receiving this, I will myself send you a revised time-table for your daily guidance.

(2) You are to study the Holy Korán, with translation, from 7 a.m, till 9 a.m. with the Madár-ul-muhám Sáhib. You may then take your morning meal and rest. Between 2 and 4 p.m., you are to read the official papers which I shall send to you, and write on them any orders that you consider necessary. After 4 o'clock, your time is at your own disposal. You may go for a walk, or attend to household matters, or employ yourself in any way that you like.

(3) I am pleased to send you two certificates in English: one from Major Hutchinson, Political Agent in Gwalior, and the other from Major Wood. These certificates you should regard as a *sanad*. I hope that you will so persevere with your English studies that you may gain many more such certificates.

(4) I have received your letter in which you say that you would like to send your files of official papers to me, so that I may see the orders that you have passed upon them. I am very glad to grant your request. Let all the papers, along with drafts of your orders, be sent to me. It will be still better if you yourself come to me, so that you may the better understand the corrections that have to be made in them.

(5) You are to sign all urgent papers every day, and those that are not marked urgent twice a week, just as I myself am accustomed to do. I hope that you will strictly observe these instructions, so that the people concerned may not complain of delay.

On the first day of Shábán, in the year 1285 A.H. (November 16th, 1868), Nawáb Shah Jahán Begam ascended the throne, and I, at the same time, was proclaimed heir-apparent and received a *khilát*. At a durbar held on this occasion, at which Colonel Meade, Agent to the Governor-General in Central India, and Colonel Osborne, C.B., Political Agent in Bhopál, were present, I made the first speech of my life. It was as follows:

I thank God who of His great goodness has advanced me to this dignity, and I thank the Agent to the Governor-General for Central India, and the Political Agent in Bhopál, who have appointed me heir-apparent, and my Mother ruler of Bhopál: I pray that the merciful God will keep me loyal to the British Government during the whole of my life.

All those who were present were delighted with my speech, and marvelled that one so young could speak with such clearness and confidence.

When a Muhammadan child has completed the reading of the Holy Korán it is customary to mark the occasion with great rejoicings, and for this purpose the ceremony of *nashrah* takes place. In the case of both my Mother and my Grandmother the *nashrah* had been performed with great splendour. So in 1288 A.H., my Mother decided that my own *nashrah* should be celebrated; and since this was the first occasion on which she had ever arranged a ceremony for me, it was performed on a grand and liberal scale. Invitations were sent to the European officers at the Residency and the Agency, and to the neighbouring Chiefs, and entertainments were also provided for the servants of the State and the citizens of Bhopál. Every night the streets were illuminated, and brilliant displays of fireworks took place. Festivities of various kinds were continued throughout a whole month, the entire cost amounting to Rs. 2,96,419. 9. 6.

In the same year Nawáb Shah Jahán Begam married her second husband Sidik Hasan Khán, an event which marked the commencement of one of the unhappiest periods of my life. Intrigue became rife in the palace, and every kind of attempt was made to undermine my Mother's affection for me, which in truth began to lessen day by day. The story of these days is best left untold, and I shall now pass on to the only event of interest which took place during the time that I remained in my Mother's charge, namely, my marriage, an account of which will form a fitting conclusion to the history of my early life.

Chapter VI

A ROYAL VISIT—BIRTH OF BILKIS JAHAN BEGAM AND OF NAWAB NASRULLAH KHAN

Towards the end of the year 1875, it was known that His Royal Highness the Prince of Wales was about to visit India. It would be difficult to convey an adequate idea of the pleasure with which this intelligence was received in all parts of the country. More than a century had elapsed since the English had laid the foundations of their Eastern Empire, and during that period neither the king nor the heir-apparent to the throne had set foot on Indian soil. But the name of Queen Victoria had long been a household word amongst all sections of the people, and the prospects of welcoming to their own land the eldest son of their beloved ruler filled them with unbounded joy. From time immemorial Eastern races have been accustomed to see authority vested in the hands of a single individual, and to regard the person of a king as the incarnation of power and dignity, an attitude which is both sanctified by tradition and enjoyed as a religious belief. This is particularly true of the peoples of India; for although British rule has resulted in the growth of Western modes of thought, yet the worship of 'the hero as king' is as natural to them now as it was in the days of Akbar the Great. They love their Emperor with a deep and sincere love, and whatever democratic principles have found their way into the administration of India they look upon as subordinate parts of a whole which he alone has fashioned, and which he alone controls.

To no part of India did the tidings of the royal visit bring greater joy and satisfaction than to Bhopál; for from the very first days of its existence the relations of the State with the dominant Power have been of the closest and most cordial nature. Nawáb Shah Jahán Begam at once instructed the state Vakíl to write to the Political Agent for official confirmation of the report, so that a *kharíta* of welcome might be dispatched to the Governor-General. On June 26th, 1875, the Political Agent wrote in reply that the report was true, but that he was not yet in possession of any details. On August 4th of the same year, Sir Henry Daly, C.B., Agent to the Governor-General for Central India, sent a letter to Her Highness, informing her that the Prince would arrive in India at the end of December, and that His Excellency the Viceroy, by order of Her Majesty the Queen, would hold a Chapter of the Order of the Star of India in Calcutta, and that His Excellency invited Her Highness, as a Knight Grand Commander of the Order, to be present on the occasion. Nawáb Shah Jahán Begam's reply to this communication was dated August 5th, and was to the following effect:

Before the receipt of your letter I sent, through you, two *kharítas* to His Excellency the Governor-General; one to express my joy at the news of the approaching visit of the Prince, and the other to say that I would very gladly attend the Durbar in question, should nothing occur to prevent my doing so.

On August 16th Sir Henry Daly sent the following reply:

Since writing your *kharíta* of 28th ultimo to the Viceroy, my note, announcing that the Prince of Wales will hold a Chapter of the Star of India in Calcutta, will have reached you. You will remember that on such occasions the members of the

Order only take part in the Ceremony, and that this is not a Durbar or assembly for any other purpose.

Should Your Highness be prevented from attending in Calcutta at the Investiture, I am sure your unavoidable absence will be regretted. There will, however, be other opportunities during the visit of H.R.H. the Prince of Wales of Chiefs meeting him. I will write distinctly on this matter directly the programme is settled, but it is the intention of the Viceroy to fix several places at which Chiefs and Nobles may pay their duty to the Queen's Heir. But the assembly in Calcutta will be, I believe, confined to the members of the Order of the Star of India.

Under these circumstances probably you will prefer that I should not forward your *kharíta* of the 28th ultimo. I will keep it till I hear from Your Highness.

In the course of her reply Nawáb Shah Jahán Begam wrote:

I did not decline to be present at the Durbar, for I am most desirous to meet His Royal Highness on that occasion, and, God willing, I shall do so. But I stated that in case the confinement of my daughter Sultán Jahán Begam should prevent me from leaving Bhopál, I would send my husband to Calcutta to represent me. Since, however, you, as my friend, advise me to go, it will be better to return the *kharíta* to me, so that the necessary emendations may be made. That portion in which I ask for information regarding the Prince's visit may stand as it is, for the preparations which I may have to make depend on the answer I receive to these inquiries. There is no one who at this time does not wish to have evidence of his loyalty to the heir-apparent to the throne, and this must be specially true of one who is bound, as I am, by the strongest ties of affection to the British Government.

After a few days, the following *kharíta*, dated August 16th, was received from His Excellency, Lord Northbrook, Governor-General of India:

Your letter of friendship, dated July 12th, 1875, in which you express your joy and pleasure at the forthcoming visit of His Royal Highness the Prince of Wales to India, and in which you desire me to convey to His Royal Highness your warm and loyal greetings, has reached me through my Agent in Central India. These renewed assurances of your fealty, and of your desire for the increase of the honour and prosperity of the British Throne and the Empire, are a source of great gratification to me. It will give me much pleasure to convey your greetings and felicitations to His Royal Highness on the first opportunity. A letter from you is always welcome to me. I hope I may often have the happiness of hearing from you of your welfare and prosperity, for which, be assured, I am deeply solicitous.

Shortly after the receipt of this *kharíta,* a copy of a communication, addressed to the Agent to the Governor-General for Central India, by the Secretary to the Government of India, was sent to Nawáb Shah Jahán Begam. In this it was stated that ruling chiefs might, when visiting the Prince of Wales, present to him any articles of manufacture peculiar to their own States, provided that they were not of great value. In forwarding this communication,[6] the Political Agent requested the Begam, in the event of her wishing to take advantage of this privilege, to furnish, as soon as possible, a list of the articles which she proposed to present, with their approximate values.

The Political Agent in Bhopál, in a memorandum dated August 30th, informed Her Highness that all Knights attending the Chapter of the Order of the Star of India should wear the robes and insignia of the Order, and that these could be renewed if necessary. He also recommended the dispatch of a trustworthy agent to Calcutta to make arrangements for Her Highness's lodgings. A *kharíta* was also received from Lord Northbrook stating that the Chapter would take place on January 1st, 1876. The official invitation to the same was sent by the Secretary to the Order of the Star of India.

In her second *kharíta* to His Excellency the Viceroy, the Begam had made inquiries about the arrangements that would be made for her lodging in Calcutta. As a considerable time elapsed without any reply being received to these inquiries, a reminder was sent to the Political Agent. On September 20th, however, a letter was received from that officer, stating that a house would be engaged for Her Highness in Calcutta, the rent of which would not be charged to the State, and that Her Highness's private apartments would be supplied with furniture by Government. But if, in addition to these, a public reception-room was required, arrangements for its decoration and furniture would have to be made by the officials of the State; who, however, would be helped with supplies from the government *tosha-khána*.[7]

A second letter from the Political Agent stated that the Prince of Wales would hold no Durbar in Calcutta, but only a Chapter as above stated, at which only those persons who were Knights of the Order were qualified to take a prominent part; and that it was, therefore, all the more necessary that the Begam of Bhopál should be present. The Secretary to the Order also wrote a second time, saying that if anything should prevent Her Highness leaving Bhopál, she would have other opportunities, either at Jabbalpúr or at Akbarábád, of meeting the Prince of Wales. But he hoped that she would, according to her original intention, and according to the strong desire expressed in her letter of September 18th, come to Calcutta in time to attend the Chapter, at which, he felt sure, Her Highness would consider it an honour to be present.

These matters having been so far settled, the Begam wrote to inform the Political Agent that she proposed to send the state Vakíl to Calcutta to superintend the arrangements for her lodging. She requested the

Political Agent to provide him with a letter of introduction to the Foreign Secretary, stating that accommodation would be required for about two hundred and fifty people, besides horses and carriages. The Vakil, accompanied by the Darogha of the *kár-khána* proceeded, on the 1st of Ramazán, to Calcutta, with instructions to inspect and report fully upon the house which should be selected, as well as to take measures for its adornment. Accordingly the Vakíl, on arrival in Calcutta, with the assistance of the Foreign Secretary and the Superintendent of the *tosha-khána*, was enabled to see the house and the manner in which it had been arranged, a detailed account of which, together with a plan of the building, he sent to the Begam. This house occupied one of the best sites in the Matia Burj.

On October 23rd, 1875, the State Vakíl asked the Political Agent if he could ascertain the opinion of His Excellency the Viceroy in regard to the propriety of the Begam's remaining *purdah* during her stay in Calcutta, and in regard to her paying and receiving visits, as no answer had been received to the *kharíta* in which information on these points was requested. The Political Agent happened to come to Bhopál at this time to inspect the robes and insignia of the Order of the Star of India, which Her Highness was proposing to wear at the Chapter, and in the evening of the same day he had a private audience with her, at which only Nawáb Sidik Hasan Khán and the First Minister of the State were present, and the *purdah* question was discussed. The Begam, anxious for more reasons than one to conform to the requirements of Oriental etiquette, quoted the examples of many Ránees and Begams to support her view of the question. But the Political Agent pointed out that that if she remained *purdah* at the time of the visits of the Prince of Wales and the Viceroy, these visits would be deprived to a large extent of their official significance. For some time the matter was warmly debated, but at last my Mother decided to bow to the necessity of the occasion, and consented to appear at the Chapter and at other functions wearing a *burkha*. It must not be supposed that Nawáb Shah Jahán Begam in any way lacked the loyal sentiments which have always distinguished the Begams of Bhopál, or that she underrated the honour of being received by the Prince of Wales and the Viceroy. Her sole motive in raising the *purdah* question was to promote the honour and dignity of Sidik Hasan Khán by appointing him her representative; so that, in fact, he might occupy a position similar to that of former Nawábs who were actual rulers of the State. With this object alone she wished, first of all, to send Sidik Hasan Khán to welcome the Prince, on her behalf, in Bombay, and afterwards to make him her representative on public occasions in Calcutta.

for which latter the *purdah* difficulty was to be the excuse. As a matter of fact, her plans for the advancement of Sidik Hasan Khán were impossible of fulfillment, nor was the fact of her being *purdah* a legitimate excuse, for the laws of Islam do not prohibit a Musalmán lady from appearing at public assemblies in a *burkha,* nor is there any reason why the ruler of a State should not go abroad clad in this fashion if she wishes to do so. Her Highness had, however, been induced to believe that allowing Sidik Hasan Khán to represent her and act for her, in the manner proposed, could in no way detract from her own dignity, while it would very materially add to that of her husband, and, in her anxiety that he should receive all the honours that Government could bestow upon him, she was willing to put herself in the background, and to forgo her own share of the advantages and honours which this unique occasion would afford. That this was so can be easily seen from the following communication, which at this time was sent to the Madár-ul-mohám:

LETTER ADDRESSED TO THE MADAR-UL-MOHAM, BY NAWAB SHAH JAHAN BEGAM

The *kharíta* received from His Excellency the Governor-General states that His Royal Highness the Prince of Wales will disembark at Bombay. As many Indian Chiefs will be present there to bid His Royal Highness welcome, I am anxious that my own greetings and good wishes should not be wanting at such a time. Owing to the approaching confinement of my daughter Nawáb Sultán Jahán Begam, it will be difficult for me to go to Bombay myself, and I therefore desire to send the Nawáb Sáhib in my stead. But should the Agent to the Governor-General for Central India sanction this arrangement, it is necessary that the Government should show to the Nawáb Sáhib, in Bombay, the same marks of distinction as would be shown to myself, so that the dignity of the State may be upheld in the presence of the other Chiefs.

A great deal more correspondence on the same subject took place between Her Highness and the Political Agent, which it is not necessary to reproduce. From what I have already said, and from what follows, my readers can easily perceive my Mother's design, and the methods by which she endeavoured to accomplish it.

Although there was no real necessity for the ruler of a State to be accompanied by the heir-apparent when attending public durbars, and although only twenty days had elapsed since the birth of my daughter, so that I was in too weak a state to bear the fatigues of a long journey, my Mother decided that I was to go with her to Calcutta, for it was neither practicable, nor in accordance with her wishes, that I should remain alone in Bhopál. She also told me that the same arrangements would be made for me as had been made for herself by Nawáb Sikandar Begam on a like occasion, and that there would be no necessity for me to appear in public in a *burkha*. As it had always been my habit to act according to the orders of my parents, I signified my readiness to comply with her desire. This conversation took place in the morning, and on the evening of the very same day my Mother again came to me and said that, as she herself was going to appear in a *burkha*, it was fitting that I, too, should adopt the same course. I had no choice but to agree, and at once set about making the necessary preparations for the journey.

The secret of these contradictory orders was this. Sidik Hasan Khán, finding that his plans for making himself the Begam's representative had come to nought, determined that, if he could not occupy the highest place, he would at any rate try to occupy the next highest, and the possibility of my being unwilling to go to Calcutta, or of my refusing to appear in public in a *burkha*, seemed to offer the chance he was looking for. It was, therefore, at his instigation that the order for the *burkha* was given.

These controversies being settled, I prepared for my departure, and dispatched to Calcutta all such necessaries as were not likely to be available there. On the 1st of Zil Kádah, 1292 A.H. (November 30th, 1875) Ghulám Mahbub Khán, Mohtamim of the State hár khána, was sent on in advance with the heavy luggage, tents, and carriages along with seventy-eight men. He reached Itársi on the 5th of Zil Kádah, and, proceeding thence by rail, arrived at Calcutta on the 10th, and took up his quarters in a bungalow close to that which the Government had selected for ourselves.

On Monday, the 7th of Zil Kádah, Her Highness, myself, Nawáb Ihtishám-ul-mulk, and Nawáb Sidik Hasan Khán, with about a hundred retainers and servants, set out from Bhopál. We reached Itársi in three days, and met the Political Agent there. From Itársi we went by rail to Calcutta, where we arrived on Wednesday, December 16th. We were met at the station by Captain Medif, A.D.C., and Mr. Keary, Under-Secretary to Government, who made kind inquiries after our welfare, and then Her Highness, myself, and Sidik Hasan Khán drove in a closed carriage to our lodging. As we were the guests of His Excellency the Viceroy all the arrangements for our meals were in the hands of the Government, and during our month's stay in Calcutta we were enter-tained in a most sumptuous fashion.

On the 23rd of Zil Kádah (December 23rd), the Begam paid a State visit to the Viceroy, accompanied by the following nobles and officials

of the State: Nawáb Sidik Hasan Khán; Nawáb Ihtishám-ul-mulk; Mián
Nazír Muhammad Khán; Munshi Jamál-ud-dín Khán Sahib, late Prime
Minister; Mián Núr-ul-hasan Khán; and Mián Alamgír Muhammad
Khán. In the afternoon of the same day His Excellency returned the visit
at our lodging, Sidik Hasan Khán escorting him from the house of Sir
Sálár Jang. Owing to my ill-health I was not present on this occasion, but
I took part in all the other receptions. December 23rd was the happy day
on which His Royal Highness the Prince of Wales arrived in Calcutta.
All the ruling Chiefs present in Calcutta assembled at the landing-place
to bid him welcome. By the special favour of His Excellency the
Viceroy, the Begam and I, instead of being at the landing-place, were
permitted to await His Royal Highness at Government House, in company with His Excellency's daughters, where we had the privilege of
paying our loyal respects.

On December 24th, Her Highness and I, attended by a few of the
nobles of the State, paid a state visit to His Royal Highness at Government House. A guard of honour was stationed at the entrance and
presented arms as we drove up, and the Foreign Secretary and the Under
Secretary received us at the door of our carriage, while guns were fired
by the saluting battery. We were then conducted to the audience hall,
which was about fifty yards from the carriage. This chamber was furnished partly in European and partly in Eastern fashion. It contained
many costly and beautiful ornaments, and the roof was hung with glass
chandeliers of great beauty and fine workmanship. The entire floor was
covered with rich carpets; and down the centre a pathway was formed of
scarlet cloth along which we walked, and on either side of which
chobdárs, in liveries of red and gold, stood at intervals. His Excellency,
wearing full durbar dress, was seated in the chair of state. When Her
Highness had approached to within forty paces, His Excellency advanced to meet her, and shaking her by the hand inquired after her health.
The Political Agent acted as interpreter, and Her Highness inquired after
the health of His Excellency. The latter then shook hands with me, and
said that he hoped I had not suffered from the fatigues of my long
journey to Calcutta. I replied to his inquiries with befitting modesty; and,
since I was able to converse somewhat in English, my answers did not
require to be translated. After His Excellency had spoken to Nawáb
Sidik Hasan Khán, Nawáb Ihtishám-ul-mulk, and others of our party, we
all took our seats, my Mother on the Viceroy's right, myself next, and the
others in the order of their rank, the chairs on the left being occupied by
the members of the staff. We were all greatly delighted at the courteous
and affable manner in which Lord Northbrook entertained us. He talked

to my Mother for nearly ten minutes, making many inquiries about Bhopál and our journey to Calcutta. We were then conducted by the two Secretaries and the Political Agent to another chamber, and ushered into the presence of the Prince of Wales. As we entered, His Royal Highness rose from his chair and bowed to us with princely dignity. He then shook hands with my Mother, and expressed a hope that she had recovered from the fatigues of her journey; then, extending his right hand to her, and his left to me, he led us to our seats. After conversing for some minutes with Her Highness the Prince turned to me, and said, with great good-humour, 'You and I are in similar positions, for you are the Crown-Princess of the State of Bhopál, and I am the Crown-Prince of England.' When I recall these words I cannot but regard it as a strange coincidence that the death of Her Majesty Queen Victoria took place in the same year as that of my own Mother, and that His Royal Highness the Prince of Wales became the ruler of the British Empire in the same year that I became the Begam of Bhopál. The visit was brought to a conclusion by the distribution of *'itr* and *pán*.

On December 29th, His Royal Highness honoured us by returning our visit. He was met by Sidik Hasan Khán at the house of the Mahárája of Gwálior, and conducted thence to our residence. The Prince talked with my Mother in a most friendly manner, and clearly manifested his royal favour. At the close of the visit, the following gifts were exchanged:

From His Royal Highness the Prince of Wales to Her Highness Nawáb Shah Jahán Begam:

A gold medal bearing the image of His Royal Highness.
A diamond ring.
A portrait of Her Majesty Queen Victoria.
A gold chain.
A portrait of H.R.H. the Princess of Wales.
A portrait of His Royal Highness.
A gold seal.

From Her Highness Nawáb Shah Jahán Begam to His Royal Highness the Prince of Wales:

A gun of Bhopál manufacture.
An Indian scimitar.
A shield.
Two caps embroidered with gold thread.
A perfume box of silver filigree work.
A pair of Indian bracelets.
A pair of gold earrings.

A kerchief embroidered by Her Highness.

A copy of *The History of Bhopál*.

A book containing a description of Mecca, written by Nawáb Sikandar Begam.

Owing to my indisposition I was unable to be present at this interview. I made the attempt, but was too weak even to reach the stairs which led to the reception-room. I was, therefore obliged to remain in a lower apartment, where the members of the Prince's staff came to see me.

NOTES

1. *Jágír*. Persian *Já*, 'a place'; *Gír*, 'occupying'. 'A tenure common under the Muhammadan Government, in which the public revenue of a given tract of land was made over to a servant of the State, together with the powers requisite to enable him to collect such revenue, and administer the general government of the district.... The assignment was either for a stated term, or, more usually, for the lifetime of the holder, lapsing, on his death, to the State, although not unusually renewed to his heir, and sometimes specified to be a hereditary assignment, without which specification it was held to be a life-tenure only' (Thomas Patrick Hughes, *A Dictionary of Islam*, London: W.H. Allen and Co., 1895).

2. *The Korán*, trans. George Sale, London, C. Ackers, 1734.

3. *Tawáf* means making the circuit of the House of the Caaba at Mecca. It is one of the principal ceremonies connected with the pilgrimage, and is often repeated many times. 'And let them pay their vows; and compass the ancient house' (Sale's Translation of the Korán, ch. xxii.).

4. Sáhibzádi Sulaiman Jahán Begam was born on the 12th of Jamádi-ul-awwal, about three years after my own birth. In spite of her having been vaccinated, she was attacked by small-pox. The physician who treated her, Hakím Ján Sáhib, mistook the nature of the disease from which she was suffering, and administered the wrong medicine, which did her great harm. She died on the 13th of Muharram, 1282 A.H.

5. The Persian word *parwánah* signifies, literally, a written order. It is a common term for any vernacular letter addressed to a subordinate officer.

6. The communication of the Secretary of State to the Government of India was as follows:

From the Secretary to the Government of India, to the Agent to the Governor-General for Central India, dated August 5th, 1875 (3rd Rajab, 1291 A.H.), No. 2179.

1. It is the desire of His Excellency the Governor-General in Council that the following directions should be communicated to you, concerning the presentation of *nazarána,* and the receiving of *khiláts* by Ruling Chiefs when paying visits to His Royal Highness the Prince of Wales.

2. His Excellency desires that the Chiefs who visit His Royal Highness at Bombay,

or Calcutta, or at any other place, should not be put to more expense than is necessary. His Excellency does not intend to hold State Durbars, and the presentation of *nazarána* and *khiláts*, which is usual at such times, will not take place. He will, however, receive visits from the Chiefs, and pay visits in return, on which occasions all the customary formalities will be observed.

3. The same procedure will be followed in regard to visits paid to, and received from, His Royal Highness the Prince of Wales.

4. It is probable that the Rulers of State may wish to present to His Royal Highness specimens of the products or manufactures of their own territories.

5. His Excellency the Governor-General sees no objection to such a procedure, provided the articles presented are not of great value or of large size.

6. Chiefs availing themselves of this privilege should furnish His Excellency, through Political Agents or other official channels, with a list describing, and giving the approximate values of, such articles as they may wish to present, so that the consent of His Royal Highness may be obtained. No presents offered under conditions other than those stated in the foregoing clauses will be accepted by His Royal Highness.

7. These presents will be placed in the Royal Museum, and they should therefore consist of such articles as may serve as mementoes of His Royal Highness's visit to India.

7. *Tosha-khána,* lit. a wardrobe, or storeroom. 'Each Native State and the Foreign Office of the Government of India has a *tosha-khána,* where stores of costly robes, jewellery, trappings, and housings are kept. It is from such stores that *khiláts* are given, and State processions are provided by Native States' *(Taj-ul-Ikbál,* p. 126, n.)

Sunity Devee Maharanee of Cooch Behar

The Autobiography of an Indian Princess contains interesting accounts of Sunity Devee's father, the reformer Keshub Chunder Sen, and, her mother's brave decision to join Keshub when he became a Brahmo and had to leave his ancestral home. Sunity Devee's marriage to the Maharajah of Cooch Behar split the Brahmo Samaj as she was not quite of age. As with some other Maharanis, Sunity Devee (b. 1864) seems to have observed purdah in her palace at Cooch Behar, but not in Calcutta.

Sunity Devee also wrote a book of stories and anecdotes, *Bengal Dacoits and Tigers* (1916) and *The Beautiful Mogul Princess* (1918).

The Autobiography of an Indian Princess

MY CHILDHOOD

I was born in 1864 at the old house known as Sen's House which my great-grandfather built in Coolootola, a part of Calcutta where many of our family lived. My birth was always remembered in connection with a storm which occured when I was six days old, a most important time to a Hindu, for then the Creator is supposed to visit the home and write upon its forehead the little one's fate. Perhaps people will think the stormy weather as the beginning signified a stormy future for me.

No girl could have been more fortunate in her parents than I. My father, the great Keshub Chunder Sen, is considered one of the most remarkable men India has ever produced, and my dear mother belonged to the best type of Hindu woman. Gentle, loving, and self-denying, her whole life was beautiful in its goodness and its simplicity.

The story of a great religious movement is not one which can be told

Sunity Devee Maharanee of Cooch Behar, *The Autobiography of an Indian Princess*, London: John Murray, 1921.

at length in a book of memories. The religion for which my father suffered and which will be for ever connected with his name is the Brahman or Religion of the New Dispensation, a religion of tolerance and charity. To quote my father's words, 'The New Dispensation in India neither shuts out God's light from the rest of the world, nor does it run counter to any of those marvellous dispensations of His mercy which were made manifest in ancient times. It simply shows a new interpretation of His eternal goodness, an Indian version and application of His universal love.'

My readers do not perhaps quite know the meaning of Brahmo. A Brahmo is a person who believes in Brahmoe (One God). There is a Hindu god called Brahmuna, with four heads—Brahmoe is not that god. Some Western people may think Brahmins are the same as Brahmos. Once I remember a English lady saying to me: 'I met some Brahmo ladies....' I asked, 'How did you know they were Brahmos?' 'Because they wore lace on their heads.' Others have an idea that all advanced Indian ladies must be Brahmos.

If my readers by some good fortune have read ancient Indian history they will know what the real Indian religion was. There was one God and no belief in caste, in fact there was no such thing as caste. Caste meant a different thing in those days. It referred to character and life. A Brahmin lived a pure and holy life, and preached religion. Next to the Brahmins were the Katnyas; they were rulers, fighting people; they guarded their families, states and countries. Then came the Sudhras, who served the others. But now there are hundreds of different castes, which makes people rather narrow-minded, for if one believes in caste one can never believe in universal brotherhood.

From the days of his youth my father was earnest and devout. He must have gone through much trouble of mind before he decided to fly in the face of family tradition and take a step which meant partial separation from his nearest and dearest. My mother was a member of a strict Hindu family, and their marriage had been solemnised with Hindu rites; but she did not fail him in the hour of trial. I have often heard my mother talk of the difficulties of those days, before she left Coolootola with my father. When he announced his approaching conversion, the 'Sen House' was plunged into a state of agitation, and my mother was by turns entreated and threatened by angry and dismayed relatives. 'Do not go against our customs', urged the purdah ladies 'You are one of us. Your place is here. You must not renounce your caste. Imagine the results of such a dreadful sin.' When thus reproached, the young girl dreaded the horrors of the unknown. It may be that she wavered; but if so, it was not for long; and it was arranged that she should go with my father to be converted by the Maharshi D. Tagore. On the day fixed for their departure a note came. My father had written simply, 'I am waiting.' Then my mother knew she must decide her future for good and all. All the relations were screaming, crying, and threatening my mother, saying that she would bring disgrace on the family by leaving the house, and thus losing her caste. But it did not hinder her, because of those three simple words— 'I am waiting'— the call of Love. When she realised their meaning, she threw off the fetters of the past and went forth to meet her destiny. There was a round staircase used by the purdah ladies where she knew my father awaited her. The trembling girl hurriedly traversed corridors and verandahs until she reached it. Fearfully she descended the dark steps, her heart beating with fright, until at last she saw my father. He said quietly: 'I want you to realise your position fully. If you come with me, you give up caste, rank, money, and jewels. The relations who love you will become estranged from you. The bread of bitterness will be your portion. You will lose all except me. Am I worth the sacrifice?'

My mother had had a most beautiful and wonderful vision, which is too sacred for me to relate. This gave her strength and courage, she did not hesitate but descended the steps and joined my father. It was a moment too wonderful for words. They looked into each other's eyes. He read perfect faith and courage in hers. She saw in his a love which gave her confidence to face the future. They passed down the corridor and found themselves in the first courtyard opposite the great entrance, where the durwans (gatekeepers) were standing on guard.

Twice my father ordered the durwans to open the door, but they did not move. It was very still in the courtyard. My mother was frightened. This was a strange adventure, and hitherto she had hardly seen a man except her husband. A trembling, slim girl, she stood near my father with her head-dress pulled quite low. Across the door there was a huge iron bar, which was too heavy for one man to lift. My father, seeing that the durwans would not open the door, went to lift the bar and did so quite easily. Then a voice was heard speaking from the upper floor. It was my father's eldest brother. He had watched all that had happened, and, seeing that my parents were determined, he decided to let them go. 'Let them pass, and open the gate', he called out to the durwans. 'The wondering durwans threw open the door, and my parents passed from the shadows into the sunlight.

My father took my mother to the beautiful house of Maharshi Debendra Nath Tagore. The household were all waiting to welcome them, though they had great doubts whether my father would be able to bring my mother away from such a strict Hindu family. The Maharshi introduced my mother to his daughters as if she had been his own child. Although a rich man's daughter-in-law and a rich youth's wife, my mother was wearing a simple sari with hardly any jewels. She always spoke of the great kindness and affection she received from this family, and she deeply revered the old Maharshi. We have always felt that there is a great bond between our two families.

My parents remained away for some time during which my father's formal conversion took place. After some months my grandmother and uncle begged him to return, and gave him a small house near the big house. There my parents lived until my father fell seriously ill, and his eldest brother declared that, in spite of all difficulties, he must come back to the old home. He came back and after long suffering and much careful nursing grew well again. My dear old grandmother and all my aunts and uncles were very glad to have my father and mother back among them. A few months later my eldest brother was born, and the Maharshi Debendra Nath Tagore gave him the name Karuna.

The new arrangement was not without its trials. Our branch of the family had lost caste, and we underwent all kinds of vexations in consequence. One great trouble was with the servants. No, Hindu would wait upon us, and a procession of cooks who objected to 'Christians' (any one who was not a Hindu in those days was called a Christian) came and went. My father's happy nature enabled him, however, to rise above such discomforts, and, as he was cheerfully seconded by my mother, caste soon had no terrors for us.

Our days were full of interest, and some of my earliest recollections are connected with the female education movement which my father started. There was an establishment called the Asram where his followers from all different classes lived in happy disregard of caste and class. This house was quite close to Coolootola, and there I spent many happy days with my sister-in-law, then Miss Kastogir, the ideal of my girlhood.

I remember another delightful house which a friend lent to my father for his people. It was a beautiful place with two big buildings in its grounds. In these houses the Asram people came and lived for months, and we stayed there too. I have the happiest memories of this Belghuria garden-house; it always seemed to me a Paradise on earth. I was a little girl when I first went there, but I never smell a rose without recalling the vanished perfume of the roses in that wonderful garden. There were roses everywhere. They scattered my path with scented softness, and turned their flushed or sweetly pale faces to meet my wondering eyes. Roses of youth...the fairest: Are any others over so treasured?

We were not allowed to pluck the fruit or flowers in the Belghuria garden, and I remember seeing cards in my father's clear handwriting fixed on the trees, which forbade to hurt the growing loveliness.

...

The afternoon was the most delightful time of the day, for then we bathed, dressed our hair, and arrayed ourselves in dainty muslin saris preparatory to going on the roof. I loved that hour, and the memory of it often comes back to me. I close my eyes and dream I am a child again sitting in the midst of that happy group, and can almost feel the welcome breeze once more fanning my face. As we sat and told stories we sometimes caught glimpses of a splash of colour on the roof of distant houses and knew that other girls were also enjoying the cool of the day.

I used always to associate perfume and soap with my married cousins; in fact, I believed that some people married on purpose to get unlimited supplies of soap and scent. 'You won't get married, Sunity', the cousins would laugh. 'Oh yes, I will', I would reply. 'Then I shall have lovely perfumes, and as much soap as I want.'

The young wives were never allowed to see their husbands during the day; but often when I played in the front courtyard I heard my name called softly and would be asked to convey love-letters between the temporarily separated couples, who found time long without each other in the first days of wedlock.

I also remember the open air operas (jatras) which were performed in the field close to the house. The advent of the players was always the signal for my father's youngest brother to nail down the shutters on that side of the house if he thought the acting of the jatras not quite proper for the ladies to hear.

One of our customs is for young girls to make vows as they worship before symbolic figures made of flour, or painted on the ground. 'May I have a good husband', prays one. 'May I be rich', sighs her worldly-minded sister. Marriage and wealth are as important in the East as in Mayfair. My vows, ordered by my father, were planned on different lines, and usually excited pity or amusement. I promised to give money to the poor, never to tell a lie, to feed animals and birds, and to give people cool beverages during the hot weather.

Oh happy days: I can still smell the incense which burnt before the idol at twilight when the elder ladies made their devotions. From across the gulf of time I can hear the faint tinkle of the bells, and the peace of the past pervades my soul. It was a heavenly feeling when Arati (evening prayer) time came and the elderly ladies, among whom the most prominent figure was that of my dear old grandmother, bowed themselves in homage to their god in the sanctuary. The conch shells and the bells sounded, the flowers and the incense gave out their delicious perfume, and family life seemed to me heavenly and pure.

Bipin Chandra Pal

In the foreword to his book, Bipin Chandra Pal (b. 1858) writes, 'The value of the life-story of any individual consists...not in itself....but only as a revelation, an explanation and interpretation of the hidden currents of social history and evolution....' The book covers the years 1860 to 1932, years that covered, as Pal says, violent religious, social, and political events, and he was in various ways a part of them. Of particular interest is the glimpses he gives us of rural Bengal, and what seems to have been an almost idyllic existence in which religious communities and castes mixed, purdah was flexible, and 'menials' (including the occasional slave) were treated as younger members of the family.

Pal initially detested the Brahmo Samaj but gradually became interested, though he ultimately joined a group that broke away from Keshub Chandra Sen's group.

In the Days of My Youth

...

The community in our village was, as has already been said, a very mixed one. We had almost every important Hindu caste, a fairly large Mahomedan population also. And the intercourse between the Hindus and Mahomedans was almost as free and friendly as that among the different Hindu castes themselves. In my father's house we used to invite our Mahomedan neighbour, the zamindar, to all our domestic functions, except the Pujas, which they could not attend, though there was regular exchange of presents between us during the Mahomedan festival of Id as well as on occasions of marriage or death. This Mahomedan neighbour, I still remember, used to send a piece of cloth and a couple of rupees whenever there was any *shradh* or after death ceremony in our house; and we used to return these to them on similar occasions. We were

Bipin Chandra Pal, *Memories of My Life and Times*, Calcutta: Modern Book Agency, 1932.

permitted to catch fish from their tanks on every festive occasion in our house as they were permitted to freely use our fish preserve on festive occasions in their own house. In these matters no manner of distinction was made between our Hindu and Mahomedan neighbours. And the general Moslem population of the village were treated similarly and practically on the same footing of social equality, within the limitations that caste and religion imposed, as the Hindu peasantry used to be treated. Our differences in religious faiths and practices made not the slightest difference in these social amenities and relations. There was perfect toleration of one another among members of both the communities.

There were neither carriages nor even bullock carts in our parts in my school-days. Everybody, including the ladies, therefore had generally to walk from house to house on festive occasions, whether religious or social, unless occasionally palanquins or the lighter *doolies* were requisitioned for going from one part of the village to another somewhat distant part. Boat was used for this purpose in our village during the rains when the country was under water. But in our own *para* my mother and other ladies of our family and class used to go about freely, just standing by the roadside with their back turned to any stranger who might by chance be met on the road, to let him pass. And though there was some sort of zenana seclusion, it did not materially affect the freedom of movement or social intercourse between the sexes.

...

Kripa was still unmarried when I attained my fifteenth year. She was over twelve then. That was a rather rare age for girls of respectable families among us to remain unmarried. But my father held somewhat liberal views in these matters; and he was evidently not anxious to secure a place for himself in heaven by giving his daughter in marriage at the age of eight or even ten, according to the law of Parasara; nor did he refuse to give her some little literary education either. My mother never knew to read or write. It was considered an evil thing in those days for respectable ladies to learn to read or write. It was not because the men were jealous of their women and did not wish them to be as educated and cultured as they themselves were, but because education had then no intrinsic value in itself, except in the case of the high caste Brahmins, who had to read the Law to be able to interpret it to their *yajmanas;* and by whom, therefore, the study of these holy books was regarded as of some intrinsic virtue and value. But Sanskrit was a very difficult language to learn and it took quite a long time to master. Those whose professional duties did not require a knowledge of this sacred and difficult language, therefore, rarely or never cared to waste so much time over it. Even the

Brahmins themselves rarely studied Sanskrit seriously; most of them, even among those who officiated at sacred rituals, wherein holy texts had to be recited, hardly understood the meaning of their own *mantrams* or of the texts they recited during their daily prayers. Persian was the language of the court; and those who wanted to enter the service of the Government learnt Persian just as the present generation of office-hunters learn English. Our vernacular was in a most neglected condition, and few people had any serious call to learn it. Under these circumstances, it was nothing strange that our ladies did not, in those days, receive any literary education.

But all the same, it will be a great mistake to think that Bengalee Hindu ladies did not know to read or write before the British came to our country. One Mr. Lushington was deputed by the Government of the East India Company in the early years of the last century to make a survey of the indigenous education of the people of Bengal, and he found that there were two classes of Bengalee women who knew very well their own language and literature—who were very well educated in the vernacular of their country. These were women of the Vaishnava denomination, who considered it a religious duty to read the scriptures of their sect; and as all, or almost all, the sacred books of the followers of Shree Chaitanya Mahaprabhu were in Bengalee, every devout Vaishnava of this denomination, male or female, had to learn to read their own vernacular as part of their religious duty. Thus it was that Vaishnava ladies, as a rule, were all literate as far back as the beginning of the last century; and they must have been literate from generation to generation, almost ever since the days of the Mahaprabhu, to be able to furnish such a large class of literate women during Mr. Lushington's investigations. I had it from Pandit Bijoy Krishna Goswami that he himself saw about the seventies of the last century learned Vaishnava women in Brindaban, and he noticed one in particular, who was a recognised and popular interpreter of the Bhagabata lore, and who used to draw large audiences to her exposition of this sacred book. She was a Bengalee lady. And she must have got her education both in Bengalee and Sanskrit long before girls' schools were started in Bengal under British auspices.

There was another class of Bengalee ladies, whom also Mr. Lushington found in his survey, who were fairly well educated. These ladies were found among the higher classes of Hindus of North Bengal. And unlike the Vaishnava ladies these ladies were prompted to educate themselves or be educated by their parents and guardians by secular motives. These families were generally connected with the big zemindar families of North Bengal; and the girls of those castes and families, who could be married to these zemindar families were taught to read and write and understand accounts as a provision against the unhappy contingency of their premature widowhood, that would leave charge of big estates in their hands, and in that case it would be of very great help to them, in discharging the heavy responsibilities of their position, if they knew how to read, write and cast accounts. This is how among the Brahmins and Kayesthas of North Bengal there grew up a class of ladies who were literate and who were systematically taught the three R's by their parents.

And as this education was given to meet the unfortunate exigencies of widowhood, it seems that the idea got abroad and took possession of the popular mind that if a girl learnt to read and write she called down the miseries of premature widowhood upon her. This prejudice was very strong in our community in my young days. I am not sure that my mother was herself absolutely free from it. But my father was a confirmed fatalist, like most people of his time and class; and his one incontrovertible argument was that if it was fated that his daughter should be cursed with early widowhood, nothing could prevent it; nor could her learning to read and write any way be instrumental in bringing about that calamity. Besides, my father's Islamic education must have proved the fallacy of the popular notion in this matter, because his Persian studies must have acquainted him with the stories of Moslem ladies of the higher classes, who were not only literate but some of them highly educated in Persian and Arabic. My father, therefore, did not at all object to my sister's receiving some literary education. And Babu Nava Kishore Sen, my father's friend and co-lodger, took upon himself the work of teaching my sister. He had already taught his young wife to read and write; and he now most willingly took up the duty of teacher to my sister. Indeed, but for him and if he were not our neighbour and had not such great influence over my father, I doubt it very much if she would have received even the little education which she did.

...

Our new dramas were, however, of a very different class. The Bengalee stage was organised in the early seventies of the last century with the opening of two theatres in northern Calcutta—the Bengal Theatre and the National Theatre. In the earlier stages female parts were represented by males as in our *yatras*. Gradually, however, actresses were introduced. There was, of course, considerable opposition to this new development at first on moral grounds. This opposition came almost exclusively from the Brahmo Samaj, which represented a powerful puritan movement in those days. But its numerous defects notwithstanding, the Bengalee stage helped very materially to prepare the ground for Surendra

Nath's political propaganda. In the early years of the seventies of the last century before Surendra Nath and Ananda Mohan had organised their new platform, it was the Bengalee stage which had found expression to the new spirit of patriotism among our rising generation of educated intellectuals. It was this stage that first proclaimed the gospel of the religion of the motherland in an opera, now completely forotten, called 'Bharata-Mata' or 'Mother India'. I forget the details of the play, but the name indicates the nature of the theme and the religious idealisation which must have inspired it. Those were the days when a new passion for freedom, personal, social and political, had possessed the educated Bengalee mind. Our youthful intellectuals were not only anxious to acquire political freedom, but also equally, if not more, anxious to break through every shackle that interfered with their freedom of thought and action. Social reform was even more popular than political reform. The desire for freedom is universally born of the sense of bondage. And in those early days consciousness of sacerdotal and social bondage was far keener than the consciousness of political bondage. The conflict between us and our foreign political masters had not as yet come out into the open. And therefore our earlier dramas were all social dramas written in support of widow re-marriage and in condemnation of polygamy by the higher classes of Bengalee Hindus, particularly the Brahmins.

But political dramas were not long in coming. Already Hem Chandra Banerjee had voiced in his national lyrics the sense of impotence of his people to assert their legitimate rights and self-respect against their British masters. Gradually this political spirit became directly vocal, though it had long been expressed indirectly through the new Bengalee poetry and fiction. 'Neela-Darpana' was the first political drama in Bengal. It presented the story of the indigo riots in Nadia and the unspeakable tyrannies on the peasants by the English indigo factors. It opened with a rustic song which lamented the untimely death of Harish Chandra Mukherjee, the Editor of the 'Hindoo Patriot' who had courageously espoused the cause of the oppressed tenants, and the imprisonment of the Rev. Mr Long for publishing the story of these tyrannies in the press. And the refrain was, 'It is difficult for the peasant to live.' When it was put upon the board of new Bengalee theatres, the audience got wild with passion against the White planters; and sometimes they so far forgot themselves that they threw their shoes at the poor actor on the stage. The next political dramas were the two productions of the late Babu Upendra Nath Das, the eldest son of Babu Sri Nath Das, who was at that time one of the leaders at the Calcutta High Court Bar—'Sarat-Sarojini' and 'Surendra-Binodinee.' In 1876 the then Prince of Wales,

Albert Edward, came on a visit to India. In Calcutta Babu Jagadananda Mukherjee of the High Court Bar, who was at that time the Government Pleader, organised a '*purdah* party' to welcome the royal visitor. It convulsed Hindu society to its very foundations. The *purdah* was still an almost religious institution. Hindu women of the upper classes never appeared before strangers, not even when they were male friends of their own families, unless they were closely related to them either by blood or by marriage. To bring these ladies to meet the Prince of Wales was incredible. Nobody believed that the ladies who met the Prince of Wales could have been drawn from the Hindu aristocracy of Calcutta. Hindu society rose up in arms against what they believed to be a wanton outrage on the sanctity of their womanhood. The incident found material for a farce, which was put on the stage of the Bengal Theatre. The Government of the day, already irritated by what it believed to be the excesses of the Bengalee press, could not tolerate this open libel against the royal visitor, and an Ordinance was immediately issued against the authorities of the stage prohibiting a repetition of its performance, and generally establishing police censorship over our new stage.

From the birth of our new literature, inspired by the ideal which we had imbibed from our new education and contact with European thought and culture, particularly that which was the creation itself of the French Revolution, Bengalee poetry and drama had been finding expression to our new love of freedom, though these expressions were somewhat veiled by fanciful allusions to the conflicts of the Hindu with their erstwhile Moslem political masters. Some referred to Rajput history depicting their conflict with the Moslem invaders. The poems of Rangalal Mukherjee, his story of Padmini, were admittedly based upon the history of the sack of Chitore by Alauddin. There were others, however, which were pure fancy pictures presenting the spoliation of the country by alien rulers.

...

When I met my father he asked me to bring my family home, saying that his health was waning, and he was not able to look after what little property he had, and if I wanted to get anything out of these after he passed away, I must come home and take charge of these. I replied, I was willing to do so not in the hope of getting anything but only if he thought that it would be some relief to him. At this my father asked me to return immediately to Calcutta and come back home as soon as possible with my wife and children. And he paid for their passage, saying that after I had come home with them he would arrange for the settlement of my affairs in Calcutta. Here again Babu Durga Mohan Das, who had taken a fatherly interest in me ever since he came to know me, once more came to my help, by undertaking to pay all my debts in Calcutta, pending the redemption of my father's words to meet these himself. So towards Christmas 1885, I left Calcutta for home with my wife, two daughters and a boy, the youngest of our children, whose advent had, perhaps more than any other thing, brought about this reconciliation between father and son.

My wife also had very materially prepared for this reconciliation. She came of a highly respectable Brahmin family. She had by her character and conduct won universal admiration and love before her marriage when she was living with Pandit Shivanath Shastri. She was not educated in the modern sense of the term. Of course, she was literate, but her literary culture was of the most meagre character. She hardly knew English. In fact, neither in her brother's home at Allahabad or elsewhere nor when she was brought to the Brahmo Samaj, did she go to any public school. All her education was only home education. But she proved in her mind and manners how a very high order of mental and moral development is not only possible but indeed, quite easy to acquire, through hereditary and domestic and social training, even without any literary education. This was really the case with my mother who was not at all literate, and her's was not a rare instance in those days. The same also was the case with my first wife, Nritya Kali. Her innate goodness and particularly her quiet strength of character, her spirit of service and natural dignity of bearing, compelled respect from all those who came in contact with her. My sister had met her in Calcutta only once and must have communicated to my father her impression of my wife. Other friends and relations had also met her and been profoundly impressed by her personality. All these had created a general pre disposition in my father towards my wife. And it was very largely this good repute of my wife which must have slowly and silently worked upon my father to lead him to wish to receive me back and see his daughter-in-law and her family.

Thus it was that at the beginning of 1886, I found myself once more in my old home at Poil, sanctified by so many memories of my mother and my early life. In asking me to go back to it, my father made almost as large a sacrifice as any man could make under those circumstances. I had deliberately put myself out of caste. To Hindu orthodoxy of those days, I and my family were as much untouchables as Mahomedans. After asking me to come back home with my wife and children my father resolved to build a new home for himself, while the old family dwelling would be left to me and my family.

...

It was a new movement which combined the religious and ethical idealism of the Brahmo Samaj under the ministrations of Keshub Chunder Sen with the new political ideal of which in a special degree Surendra Nath was undoubtedly the greatest apostle. There were Brahmo idealists who were left absolutely cold by the new political inspiration of our educated intellectuals. There were ardent politicians—and their number was very large—who were eagerly desiring the removal of British subjection from their national State and Administration, but who were untouched by the spiritual and ethical idealism of the Brahmo Samaj. To Shivanath belongs, in a special measure, the credit of realising the impossibility of attaining the moral and spiritual objective of the Brahmo Samaj without a radical reconstruction of our social life and political government as well as the impossibility of reaching the political goal of democratic self-government unless our national politics was wedded to the ideals of spiritual and social freedom for which the Brahmo Samaj openly stood.

I forget the date, but it was sometime in the autumn of 1877, that we took our oath of initiation as members of this group. Shivanath was then employed as the senior Sanskrit teacher in the Hare School. He used to sleep in one of the rooms of the first floor of the school building. One night, or more accurately, in the small hours of one morning, we assembled in one of the rooms of the first floor of the Hare School for our initiation. The poet in Shivanath could not rise above the spectacular value of all sacraments. He could not ignore the place and importance of symbolism in all cults and cultures, however rational these be. Through these symbolisms religion universally appeals to our emotions and helps in the cultivation of the consciousness of the Unseen. So he did not hesitate, his uncompromising rationalism notwithstanding, to have recourse to an imitation of ancient Hindu ritualism in our initiation ceremony. We made a fairly big fire, collected some green banyan leaves, wrote on these leaves words indicating our different passions and appetites, such as lust, anger, envy etc., as well as those which stood for the more glaring social evils about us like, for instance, caste, *zenana* seclusion and the meaningless ceremonialism of popular Hinduism. Dipping these in pure clarified butter we went round this fire, and chanting a hymn specially composed by Shivanath for this occasion, we threw these leaves into this fire, and then, after offering a fervent prayer to the Lord to lead us to our ideal, we signed this pledge.

Mohamed Ali

Mohamed Ali (1878–1931) and his brother Shaukat were key leaders in the post World War I Khilafat Movement, a pan-Islamic movement which attempted to unite Indian Muslims in a defence of the Caliph of the Ottoman Empire against the attacks of the British. For a brief time, the supporters of the Khilafat Movement in India were closely associated with the Indian National Congress (1920–3). 'During this brief period, for the first and last time the Congress was fully representative of Muslim intelligentsia and masses', it is said. But Mohamed Ali became disillusioned with Mahatma Gandhi and the Congress, and Mustafa Kemal Ataturk's abolition of the caliphan caliphate rendered the movement superfluous. Towards the end of his life, Mohamed Ali began to be a separatist at the same time that he continued to believe in the fight for freedom against British rule.

Educated at Aligarh (he was there during the last years of Sir Syed's life) and at Oxford, Mohamed Ali edited and wrote for *Comrade,* a magazine in English , and in Urdu for *Hamdard.* He was interned by the British, in 1915, for his pro-Caliphate views, an event he describes in *My Life A Fragment.* The extract chosen focuses on Mohamed Ali's mother Abadi Banu Begam (1852–1924) , called Bi Amman, who taught herself to read Urdu, though she did not learn to write. She was determined to educate her sons, even though she had to pawn her ornaments to be able to afford the education.

An 'Alim's Religious Studies

Had I belonged to one of the families that specialize in religious learning, I would, no doubt, have spent half a life-time in the study of the Qur'an and its *Tafseer* or exegesis, of *Hadeeth* or the Traditions of the Prophet, of *Fiqh* or Muslim jurisprudence, (including not only Law, as understood in European countries, but also ordinances regarding prayers, fasts,

Mohamed Ali, *My Life: A Fragment,* Afzal Iqbal (ed.), Lahore: S. Ashraf, 1966, (1942 rprt).

alms-giving and pilgrimage, and in fact, every religious duty prescribed for a Muslim) and of *Aqaid* and *Kalam* or Dogmatics and Dialectics, which form the scholastic Philosophy of the Musalmans regarding their creed, in other words 'Theology' in the narrower sense, together with logic which forms the substratum of this branch of religious studies.

As a necessary preliminary to these religious studies, I would have had to receive instruction for a number of years in Arabic Grammar, and along with it in some secular Arabic literature, and after having finished at any age from twenty to thirty, the entire syllabus of studies followed in the Arabic schools dotted all over Northern and Eastern India, I would have set up as an *'Alim* and teacher, giving instruction, in my turn, in the same text-books to younger men similarly inclined or situated.

An Average Muslim's Studies

But, as I did not belong to such a family, all that I had to do was to read with my old red-bearded pedagogue, who was innocent of all knowledge of Mathematics, History and Geography, not to mention Natural Science, half a dozen or more text-books in Persian, like the *Gulistan* and *Bostan* of Sa'di; the letters of Aurangzeb, Nizami's *Sikandarnama* or Epic about Alexander's conquest of Persia; Firdausi's more famous *Shahnama*; and some prose works composed in less intelligible and more ornate though not more graceful Persian than Sa'di's, such as Zahuri's *Sih-nasr* or that delightful but malicious lampoon of Ni'mat Khan-i-'Ali on Aurangzeb and his conquest of the Shia kingdoms of the Deccan. But these were purely cultural and literary, not religious studies. It is true one learnt a great deal of the ideals of Muslim life and even of Muslim religion in the text-books in Persian in use in these *Maktabs* (private schools) and *Madrassahs* (public schools) and particularly from books on *Akhlaq* or good morals and manners. But they did not directly aim at religious instruction, and in fact, one or two of the books so often taught as good literature in those days, were, on account of their unusually erotic nature, by no means fit for the instruction of youth.

Third 'Infidel' in a Family

As it was, hardly before I had finished a couple of these Persian text-books, I was sent to a school recently founded at Rampur and subsequently to another at Bareilly, some forty miles from my home, to learn English, and of course, along with it, the usual school subjects of Arithmetic, History and Geography. For unlike most of our cousins whose parents were averse to endangering their salvation by subjecting them to 'the Godless influence of English education', two of my brothers had already been sent to the school at Bareilly by our mother. She had become a widow at the age of 27, when cholera had suddenly cut short of our young father's life after a few hours' illness. She refused to remarry, and hiding the anguish of her heart under a light bantering tone, told those who advised her to do so, that she had had a husband to look after her long enough and now she had herself five husbands and a wife to look after, referring, of course to her five boys and one girl, the eldest of whom was only thirteen and an invalid, and the youngest of whom, the present writer, was not yet two. Women are generally more religious, or at least more superstitious than men; but our mother, who brought us up without any other assistance, although intensely religious, was remarkably free from prejudice and superstition. When the younger of these two brothers of mine, Shaukat, was selected by her for a course of English education, the uncle who was managing our property refused to sanction an allowance for his school expenses, remarking, in all sincerity, but also with all the bitterness characteristic of the times and more specially of the place, that one 'infidel' was bad enough in a family! But our mother was determined and secretly pawned some personal jewellery of her own with the help of the maid-servant of a Hindu neighbour, who was a banker, and packed off the second would-be 'infidel' of the family also to Bareilly, with the assurance that she had enough money in her own hands now to pay for Shaukat's schooling at least for sometime to come. When our uncle had been thus outwitted by a resolute woman whose self-reliance throughout a long life of hardships and difficulties had only been equalled by her implicit trust in the bountiful providence of God, he got her trinkets released from pawn and paid for the schooling of both his nephews from the proceeds of our property. And so, when yet another 'infidel' sought perdition, he accepted the inevitable, and I proceeded to Bareilly without any clandestine negotiations of my mother with a pawnbroker's maid. As in so many other things in my life, Shaukat had thus paved the way for me and made it smooth.

PREJUDICE AGAINST ENGLISH CULTURE AND EDUCATION

Here I may remark that the prejudice against English education was still very strong in Upper India. It had been the centre of Muslim political life for eight centuries and even when the rule of India passed away from Muslim hands by slow and hardly perceptible degrees in the century between the Battle of Plassey and the Indian Mutiny, Musalmans of

Upper India did not cease to regard the new rulers of India as something very inferior to themselves in civilisation and culture. This storm of ill-will and disdain had been gathering for a whole century and was precipitated among other things by the aggressive activity of Christian Missionaries. The Mutiny began as an affair of the Sepoys of the Indian Army; but in the storm-centre of my province where it had to be fought out if English rule was to continue in India, it soon attracted to itself many forms of discontent which had been gathering force and volume for more than a generation, and religion was inextricably mixed up with politics. Although so many Musalmans had at enormous risks assisted the English at a time when hardly any could have predicted their eventual success with any degree of assurance, it was the Muslim aristocracy in that Province that suffered most in the terrible aftermath of the Mutiny. In fact, in its permanent results even more than in some of its terrors it could, without any considerable exaggeration be compared to the social upheaval that the French Revolution meant to the old nobility of France. The remnants of Muslim aristocracy, deprived of all influence and many of their possessions, certainly did not expect the return of the Muslim rule. Nevertheless, a whole generation kept sullenly aloof from all contact with the culture of the new rulers of India, which in their heart of hearts they still despised, and Musalmans of these regions were in no mood to take advantage of the education provided by the Universities of Calcutta, Bombay and Madras founded in the very year in which the Mutiny convulsed these provinces. The Punjab had to be without a University for another quarter of a century, and even then it had to interlard English education with a great display of the encouragement of Oriental lore. My own province had to wait for some years longer, and then, too, it was not the University established by Government that induced the bulk of Musalmans to throw off their old prejudices against English education but one projected by a Musalman of Delhi who strenuously protested against the complete divorce of religious from secular learning. Few indeed can realise to-day the feelings of those Upper India Muslims who sulked in their tents for so long, or the difficulties of the pioneers of English Education among them like Syed Ahmad Khan, who founded within two decades of the Mutiny the Aligarh College which is now the first Chartered Muslim University in India. One of his aunts, it is said, maintained throughout the rest of her life her refusal to see him only on account of his taking too kindly to the culture of the foreigner and the infidel, though her nephew, despite the heterodoxy of his somewhat aggressive rationalism in interpreting the Qur'an and his militant opposition to superstitions and shackling customs unauthorised by Islam, was a zealous and even stern Muslim in his polemics in defence of his creed against European and Christian critics and an unbending conservative Indian in social matters such as the seclusion of women.

THE 'OASIS' IN 'BRITISH' INDIA

This attitude of the Indian Musalmans towards English culture and education took an even more hostile form in our own State of Rampur. It was the only tract in the province still under Indian and a Muslim ruler, and was on that account a veritable oasis in the surrounding 'British' India. The principal inhabitants of Rampur were, like those of the rest of the British Division of Rohilkhand, descendants of Rohillas that had come from Afghanistan. Warren Hastings had fought against the Rohillas one of the most unpopular wars for a purely mercenary reason, when British forces were, so to speak, hired by the ruler of Oudh; and the State of Rampur was the remnant of their independent territory which had extended *az sang ta Gang* (*i.e.,* from the Himalayas to the Ganges). They could not bear much love for the English whose services had been obtained against them in exchange for hard cash. When the Mutiny broke out and raged in all its fury at Meerut and Delhi, both within a hundred miles of Rampur, it soon spread to the surrounding Rohilla country. Nevertheless, the Ruler of Rampur actually rendered invaluable assistance to the hard-pressed British from that isolated centre in spite of the unpopularity of the British cause among the Rohillas. This unpopularity before long involved the ruler himself who had otherwise been very popular and deserved to be loved by his subjects for his great generosity. In fact it is related that his own soldiers when changing guard outside his sleeping apartment, and pointing out the various articles of value in their charge to the relieving soldiers would mention his gold bed and conclude the list with the bitter aside; 'And the infidel that sleeps in that gold bed!'

After the Mutiny, when neither the Court of Delhi, nor even that of Lucknow was left to attract the remnant of Muslim learning, Rampur could still offer it a refuge and an asylum. The next ruler, who has left to his successors as legacy many of the most valuable Arabic and Persian manuscripts which they greatly cherish, and which make, with the many additions made by them, the finest collection in all India, was himself no mean scholar. This emphasised the cultural conservatism of Rampur all the more, and marked it off from the rest of the province, even though, as we have seen, it bore little love for the new learning. Its antagonism to

English education may well be judged from an amusing incident that occurred towards the end of the last century. In course of time even that little bit of old unadulterated *Indian* India came to be connected with the rest of the world by telegraph wires, and one day a Rampur Pathan had the surprise of his life in getting a telegram. It was, of course, in English and when he and his friends had recovered from the first shock of surprise, they found that they had now to face the inevitable problem, who was to decipher this strange message from a heathen world? At last, somebody happened to remember that some of the boys of our family had been sent away to learn English, and mentioned this to the perplexed recipient of the telegraphic message. The moment he offered this solution of his difficulty the rest of the company expressed their pious disbelief in the information, and one of them burst out: '*Astaghfirullah* (God forgive!). What do you say? My dear man, they are gentlemen!'

EDUCATION WITHOUT TEACHER AND TEXT-BOOK

Well, 'gentlemen' though we believed ourselves to be, we had nevertheless been impious enough to study English even though we had to leave Rampur for the sake of our education. As for myself, in one of their vacations, my brothers Zulfiqar and Shaukat had constituted themselves my pedagogues in English and before long the progressive administrator on whose advice mother had sent my brothers to the Bareilly school had founded a similar school in Rampur itself. I had studied there for some months, and when I was about to enter my twelfth year, I was permitted to accompany my elder brothers to Bareilly. This departure from the code of Rampur gentility, even if not an approach to 'infidelity' as our uncle had put it, had no doubt an adverse effect on us so far as religious education was concerned. I have already explained in some detail, what poor chance there was for a youth who did not belong to a family that specialized in religious learning of receiving any but the most elementary religious education; and had the curriculum of our *maktabs* provided *all* the knowledge of his religion that such a Muslim youth could acquire, his religious equipment would have indeed been scandalously small, particularly for the inhabitant of a place that prided itself on being the latter-day centre of Muslim learning. But not all education is to be had in schools and out of text-books even in the West; and those who have such notions of education will certainly find the East a puzzle to them. Some of the wisest and greatest men of the East have been, like our Prophet himself (on whom be Allah's benedictions and peace), wholly illiterate, owing nothing to teacher or text-book.

THE MOSQUE AS A CLUB, AND THE HOME AS A SCHOOL

But apart from such exceptional cases, there is this general consideration to be kept in mind, that so much depends on the general condition and atmosphere of society. Take the case of a large University town like Oxford even to-day. How much can a man not learn, say, from the shop-windows of its booksellers? But so far as religion and the East are concerned, for all but a small minority, far the larger portion of the people's stock of religious knowledge comes from breathing in the air of the place in which they live, and the circle in which they move. To take a parallel case, whence does the average man in Europe get his knowledge of politics? Not certainly from books and political philosophers, and not always from newspapers either. To many men their club, their favourite cafe and their public-house supply most of their political wisdom—or unwisdom. And what politics is to the West to-day, religion is still to the East. Where a few men gather together, and they are not preternaturally lacking in gravity, the conversation is sure, before long, to take a religious or spiritual turn, even though their theology may not be sufficiently edifying for schoolmen. An English writer[1] intimately acquainted with Indian Muslim Society remarks of Musalmans that 'they are ready to speak in season and out of season' of their faith and quotes in support Doughty's observation about the Arabs that 'their talk is continually (without hypocrisy) of religion which is of genial devout remembrance to them'.[2] And what could serve as better meeting-place than a mosque? Unlike a Church a mosque is not a silent place with a dim religious light, deserted for the greater part of the week; but on the contrary, a very airy and well-lit place, a fairly busy haunt of men. It is a humming hive of the Muslims, the more devout of whom at least gather there oftener and with greater regularity than do the habitues of Clubs and Cafes in their customary haunts. And then, of course, there is the home. When the conversation of the secluded half of humanity in the East is not about children and the cares and duties of the household, at least in three cases out of four it is about religion. But it must be admitted that it is not dogmatic theology and the little differences of form and ritual which obsess the schoolman and which the better educated menfolk discuss only too often, that forms the chief topic of our women's conversation when it turns on religion. It is rather about the spirit and the substance of faith, the Ethics of Islam, that has been transmitted down the ages, very often in the form of legends and folklore which would not stand the severe test of the Traditionists.

Our Home Circle

If my father had been alive, or if my brothers had been older or had all remained at home, I would have had the advantage of getting better acquainted even with Muslim dogmatics, dialectics and of course that portion at least of Muslim Jurisprudence which deals with the ritual of worship. A Muslim home has two distinct divisions, the *Mardana* and the *Zanana,* or as the Turks call it the *Selamlik* and the *Haremlik,* that is to say, apartments where the male members of the family usually pass the day and receive their male visitors, and those where ladies live and where only those male members of the family can come before whom these ladies can appear without a veil. When our father died, our mother shut up the adjoining new house that father had recently built to receive his friends, for none of us was old enough to need a separate *mardana* and some years later she herself moved into it lending the old *zanana* house to her brother and his family. And although a house with us five brothers and two cousins living in the adjoining old *zanana* house which they had so long shared with us, was bound to be a noisy place and our boisterousness no doubt made us a tremendous nuisance; still mother preferred that we should be for the greater part of the day under her own eyes. So, instead of allowing us to play with our numerous cousins in their houses, all close to our own, and of course in the street which was practically monopolised by us, though legally still a public thoroughfare of the less frequented sort, she should let us invite a whole heap of these cousins to our house and romp all over the place, even though we ruined the terraces and cost mother no end of money in repairing the leaky roofs in the heavy monsoon rains. Nevertheless there was one place where we could elude her vigilance and yet still be within the bounds. That was the *mardana* house of our eldest uncle and the fear that he inspired in all of us was enough to procure us freedom to cross the street and go there whenever we cared. Here there was an endless succession of visitors belonging to all strata of Rampur society. Ours was one of the principal families engaged in administration, and apart from visitors of equal status who came to pay a social call, many others also came in who had any petition to make to the ruler of the State and sought our uncle's intercession or perhaps a favour to ask directly from himself. Everyone had an easy access and I cannot think of any place where such a variety of people congregated daily as at my uncle's, specially on Friday mornings, it became all I the more 'democratic'—and, I fear, not a little less noisy—on account of my uncle's hobby of quail-fighting which attracted quail-trainers or *bater-bazes* of the whole State. Here could be seen in the freest intercourse men in the very humblest rank of society, as well as the haughtiest members of the Rampur nobility and Court. But not being Rohillas, whose tastes were as a rule more martial than literary, Our uncles used to receive for Rampuris quite an unusual number of visitors from among the scholars and literary men that had found the Nawab's Court their last harbour of refuge when the political storms had destroyed the Courts of Delhi and Lucknow. It is true that much of their erudite conversation was above the understanding of boys of our age; but it could not fail to rouse a literary curiosity which was stimulated, and to some extent satisfied, in the company of our grown up cousins. As I was the youngest son of the youngest son of my grandfather, some of these cousins were only a few years younger than my own parents. They had their own separate apartments, on the ground floor of their father's *mardana,* where there used to be a similar endless succession of visitors everyday. Youth's code of decorum was not so rigorous and the conversation here was more lively than on the upper storey, even if it was not so erudite. When free from our *maktab* and its red-bearded pedagogue, and fatigued with fairly long intervals of play, we used to drop in and listen with great interest to the animated discussions of our cousins and their friends and visitors, and I must confess this experience of my childhood was a liberal education in itself.

OUR MOTHER

And then there was the religious schooling we unconsciously received from our mother.[3] I must rigorously restrain myself, otherwise there is no knowing to what lengths I may not digress when I am on that ever congenial topic—our mother. Suffice it to say that although she was practically illiterate, as I shall presently explain, I have, in all my experience of men of all sorts of types, come across none that I could call wiser and certainly none that was more truly godly and spiritual than our mother. Muslim society in India in the days of its decadence had sinned against the light in nothing so much as in condemning womanhood to all but universal ignorance. What used to be the general rule in the best days of Islam had, about this time, been whittled down to a few rare exceptions—women who could have intelligently followed the learned conversation of the most erudite scholars and who could partake, after their daily round of domestic duties, joys of literature not unoften in more than one language. They were still taught to read the Qur'an in the original Arabic which they could, of course, understand no more than the majority of men themselves. Some could read Urdu, which was their vernacular, and were thus enabled to read a few religious 'tracts'—for the most part metrical compositions, more legend than literature, supposed to impart good moral instruction. This additional accomplishment, however, was not a part of my mother's literary equipment. But she possessed enough intellectual curiosity not to be satisfied with what little she knew and she possessed a memory that is nothing short of a marvel. My father would often bring into the *zenana* the book he might be reading and one of these books evidently proved so attractive that he would read it in bed far into the night. It so happened that occasionally he forgot to take it along with him when he went to the *mardana* next day and that is how mother was enabled to have her innings. A cousin of ours, who was the favourite of both of my parents, and who subsequently became my father-in-law,[4] used to be very often with my father and was very frequently coming to my mother with messages from him in the course of the day, when father was himself too busy to come, besides paying visits to my mother on his own account. The attractions of the book that so often formed my father's nocturnal literature impelled my mother to ask this nephew what it was and since it turned out to be a remarkably good romance, mother eagerly asked him to read it to her whenever she could get an opportunity to taste this 'forbidden fruit'. And so astonishingly good was her memory that although she had heard these portions of the book read out to her only once, and that too fairly rapidly, she could gradually make out the words when she began to glance at the book herself, on account of the similarity of the *Nastaliq* script, in which Urdu and Persian are written, with the *Naskh* script in which Arabic and of course the Qur'an, which she could read, are written. And it was in this manner that our mother learnt to read Urdu, though she cannot write it to this day. She tells us how the attractions of the book and her own memory very nearly betrayed her secret to father, for once she repeated whole passages out of the book in her sleep to his great astonishment. And well he may have felt astonished, for we cannot help wondering even now how she can repeat to the eager circle of her grandchildren, in love with Bee Amman's stories, whole volumes of romances, including translations of English works of fiction which she had read only once. All that we could ourselves repeat even of our favourite novel would be scarcely better than the proverbial silent man's retailing of the story of Jacob and Joseph: 'Was a Prophet; had lost a son; and found him again!'

AT THE MOTHER'S KNEE

However, it was not merely for reading fiction that our mother utilized her ability to read Urdu acquired in this novel manner. Musalmans have always had a horror of translations of their Holy Writ, for fear of people forming the habit of relying upon man's words rather than on those of God; and I believe the Turks, who are perhaps the most rigidly orthodox nation among the Musalmans, have to this day no translation of the Qur'an in Turkish.[5] In India the first translation into Urdu was smuggled into general acceptance and favour under the garb of the briefest of brief *Tafseers* or Commentaries, and not long afterwards the Qur'an was printed together with a Persian translation and this Urdu 'Commentary', which was really a very *literal,* though somewhat expanded translation, both being the work of members of the same great family of divines of Delhi whose piety and learning were universally acknowledged in the country.[6] These two translations were printed along with the Qur'an in the interlinear style which has grown customary, and allusions to historical events were explained, and other useful information supplied in fairly frequent marginal notes. In these days such copies of the Qur'an are to be found in many households and yet I have only too often come across men who could read the Urdu translation with far greater ease than the Arabic original, which of course, they did not understand and who would yet be content with their unintelligent reading of the Arabic original without any desire to comprehend its meaning by reading the interlinear translation in their own vernacular. But this has never been the case with our mother. On her busiest day she would not neglect to read her Urdu translation along with the word of God in Arabic, though her sight is now very weak, and even her glasses cannot magnify the smaller Urdu print in her old copy of the Qur'an to make them half as legible to her as the larger Arabic print. She has all her life been in great demand on account of the capital way she has of retailing stories, and it is not only children that gather round her; for few 'grown-ups' can resist the temptation of spending an evening in this fashion in her company. She has a large repertiore to choose from; and it includes many a story of ancient Prophets partly culled from the Qur'an and partly from the legends and folk-lore of Jews and Arabs which, for all their apocryphal character, serve admirably to point a moral. When as children we used to sit round her forming an eager circle of listeners taking in every word of these old-world tales so faith fully and charmingly repeated, she would amplify them with comments of her own in short moral discourses that have lingered in our memories more than the vast majority of lectures of *savants* and sermons of preachers. But far the more important lesson for her children was contained in the rigorously ascetic character of life which she maintained ever since her widowhood at that early age, but which at the same time never robbed her of the least iota of her geniality and the joy of living so that except for her very simple fare and her still simpler dress and her occupying herself needlessly with the drudgeries less than with the superintendence of her large household, one would have thought that she was the merriest of merry widows. These lessons were of inestimable value to us later on in the battle of life, which the circumstances of our family had made more than ordinarily hard to wage. For not only had our father died so young, but he had left his inexperienced widow to maintain and educate half a dozen children out of the proceeds of an estate that his generous, not to say lavish, way of life had left sadly encumbered with debts. Nevertheless, it must be confessed that all this moral and spiritual training that we received from our mother, however high its practical value, left us still very ignorant about the details of Islamic faith and its history. And then on top of all this came the migration to a school where we were to receive the new godless education of the West without so much as a mention of Allah and His Prophet, and His Holy Book.

GODLESS EDUCATION AT THE SCHOOL

The British Government professed a complete religious neutrality, and carried it into practice by a rigorous exclusion of all religious, and even moral teaching, except such as the boys were left to find for themselves in the literature provided in the 'Readers' in English and Oriental languages. On the other hand the entire outlook of the education which the Government did provide for the youth of India was 'Modern' in its destructiveness. It tended to breed in the student an arrogant omni-science, and to destroy along with age-old blind beliefs in superstition all respect for Tradition and Authority. No doubt in course of time it led to the awakening of a genuine spirit of Inquiry and a search for Truth. But in its first onset it was mainly destructive, and what little it substituted in the place of the superstitions it destroyed, was itself based on blind beliefs and superstitions, albeit 'modern'. However, since it was so clearly revolutionary, there was no lack of liveliness in our schools and colleges. If at home our cousins had held animated discussions about Religion and Dogma which we could no longer attend, we had here in the 'Boarding House' of our school still more animated discussions that centred round Natural Science and Philosophy, even if our pretentious scientists and philosophers had only the most elementary and superficial ideas on the subjects in debate. In this particular school, however, the Musalmans were in a minority; but it was an assertive, not to say aggressive minority, with the result that in spite of all the destruction wrought in old-world ideas by this onset of our western education, we were unconsciously impelled to maintain the old pride of faith for all our pleasant relations with the majority of our school-fellows who were Hindus.

ALIGARH AND ITS RAISON D'ETRE

...

One of our greatest troubles on this occasion concerned Mother's insistence on accompanying us, and it was with the greatest difficulty that we had succeeded at last in sending her to Delhi after convincing her of the futility of further stay with us when the Police officer who had brought the orders intimating our transfer could give her no assurance that the police escort would permit her to accompany us on our mysterious journey. Great indeed was our surprise when just as our motor car began to move to find another car puffing and snorting and tearing towards us at a pace that seemed impossible and was certainly very risky for a ramshackle thing like it. It stopped near our car and out of it came mother who had on reaching Delhi managed to send a friend of ours who was our legal adviser to the Chief Commissioner to press him not to withhold his consent to her accompanying us. The Chief Commissioner had said that he had received no instructions on the subject, and could not prevent her following us; but, as for her accompanying us, he pointed out the obvious difficulty of making any arrangements for a Purdah lady in the only car he had available which the Police escort must of course share with us. Perhaps he believed that this would be an insurmountable difficulty, and had not specified any other objection. But evidently he had reckoned without a woman who was as resolute as she was resourceful, and Mother brushed aside his objection by saying that if the police did not mind her, she certainly would not mind them, most of whom would be younger than her own sons, and some perhaps young enough to be her grand-children. The Chief Commissioner consented, but the odds were that she could not go more than a mile or two in the fastest of carriages before we were whisked off in the police car. The local car repairer had, however, this ramshackle affair in his shop and agreed to hire it out, but guaranteed nothing beyond that. In fact he seemed to be inclined to guarantee a breakdown or two before they had left Delhi half a dozen miles behind. Fortune, however, favours the brave, and Mother won the esteem of our escort in reaching us just in the nick of time with the requisite permission from the Chief Commissioner which they found to be in order. Contrary to our expectation we were taken through Delhi itself to a small wayside station on the opposite bank of the river and there took the train which brought hundreds of Delhi men who had seen our car rush through Delhi and took the next train on the off chance of being able to see us. As soon as we had left the limits of the Imperial Enclave, the escorting officer served on us fresh orders which informed us that we were to proceed to Lansdowne, a small hill station not far from Mussoorie which had no civil population but quartered a garrison of 8th Gurkhas and 39th Garhwal Rifles. Additional restrictions were imposed on our freedom such as a censorship over our correspondence and stoppage of all writing for the press.

Censorship and the End of Journalism

As a matter of fact about the same time the poor inoffensive *Hamdard* of the tone of which the Chief Commissioner himself had expressed warm approval some time ago, and which had never offended against the Press Act, was singled out for a unique pre-censorship. A highly paid Indian official, who was however entirely innocent of all knowledge of Journalism, had been brought over from the Punjab to act as Censor and he had commenced his new career by rejecting such a large proportion of 'Copy' that for two or three days no issue of the *Hamdard* could appear at all, and even after that when the Chief Commissioner had been appealed to by the sub-editors in charge, the daily issues contained several columns of blank space, in spite of the fact that much more 'copy' used to be submitted for approval every day than what would have sufficed for a single issue. Partly out of the chagrin and partly no doubt as a test, a rather smart leader-writer dished up an old nursery tale with some queer garniture and submitted it as the next day's leader. When he laughingly pointed out to the Censor that it was the old nursery story with which he must have been familiar from his childhood, the poor man said, 'Yes, I know, but my dear man, I don't know what subtle poison you fellows may have squirted into it, and nursery tales or no nursery tales, I cannot afford to take any risks.' After this naive confession they knew that it was a hopeless task and they confessed to me subsequently that they had never felt so miserable as during the period of that censorship, when an hour's hard squeezing of unresponding brains would not yield a single 'per'. As I have stated once the unfamiliar script was no longer there to act as a damper, the people's enthusiasm for the *Hamdard* began to express itself daily in large increases of circulation and the three machines we had purchased for lithographing it, could with difficulty suffice even when worked constantly. That difficulty increased when after the forfeiture of security of the old press, a new press had to be set up and we had a smaller number of machines to work with, though of a larger size. But we had turned round the corner financially, and could afford to purchase more machines, and I was enabled to recoup some of my losses of the terrible days of typography and hoped in another year or two to see a balance sheet that would not send shudders through my frame, but produce quite a different sensation. However that was not to be and after reducing the profits on the monthly sales to zero, and then fast approaching the figure of earlier losses, I decided to 'Shut up shop'. After all the earlier losses were incurred, we offered to the readers, even though several thousand less, something worth reading. But now there was little worth reading in the *Hamdard,* and in fact little to read at all.

'INTERNMENT FINANCE'

Unlike Regulation III of 1918 which made it a statutory requirement to pay to a person on whose liberty restrictions were imposed by the Executive an allowance for himself and his family suitable for a man of his rank and position, the Defence of India Act had left the detenus entirely unprovided for and both my brother and I had asked for the grant of internment allowance when we were first interned, because on prin- ciple we thought it unfair to restrict a man's liberty for any reason short of a proved crime, and not compensate him for any consequent loss of income and at any rate a loss of the means of subsistence as had actually occurred in some cases within our knowledge, when we ourselves offered to relieve some of these fellow-sufferers. But our requests were repeatedly 'turned down' and we had finally given up asking for it. Now, however, the Government came forward, presumably knowing what was soon to follow, with the offer of allowances, which nevertheless were so meagre that the amount fixed for the subsistence of us two and of our families hardly exceeded half the salary of the Censor imported from the Punjab. We were each allowed Rs. 250 a month which comes to less than £4 a week that I used to pay to my London typist. As my brother had been anxious to retire from the public service on any condition, he had readily accepted the small pension offered to him by the Secretary of State as a special case because it was too early yet for him to retire and in fact no pension could be granted under the existing rules. However, since the department was being subjected to sweeping reductions, on account of the agreement with China in 1910 which had doomed the Opium Revenue, and the senior most men were being compulsorily retired on pensions, the Secretary of State had jumped at the offer of a comparatively junior man to retire voluntarily and had driven a good bargain with him. The amount of that pension, meagre as it was, was now deducted from the meagre subsistence allowance, and my brother was granted the magnificent sum of £1-10-0 a week for himself and his family. My brother on retirement from office had established a cotton ginning factory and press at Rampur at the cost of some 1,50,000 rupees, selecting this form of enterprise purposely as it needed his attention only during the cotton season, and let the greater part of the year to him to do his public work as the Secretary and moving spirit of the Servants of Ka'ba Society. As for myself the *Hamdard* was enough to provide for my needs and for those of my family. The refusal of Government at first to give any allowance and now their meagreness had no terrors for us at the time. But soon after the *Hamdard* had to close its doors. And my brother also found that unless he could buy and sell cotton himself at and near Rampur it was not possible to establish a new market for that commodity and give a start to a new factory, and this he could not do unless he was free to move about and finance such operations and in fact be on the spot. Consequently before many months were over we had to depend upon such subsistence allowances as Government had granted and it was just as well that my brother had not refused the hundred rupees a month that he had got as the price of his liberty, though in any case we could not make the two ends meet without other resources. Bit by bit we sold off all our landed property of which our mother would not sell an acre during our minority, and we now recalled the grim humour of the contrast that the property earned by the grand-father for assisting the British during the disastrous days of the Mutiny was lost by the grandsons sixty years later, when they were made 'prisoners of peace', presumably to prevent their assisting the enemies of British.

PEACE AT LAST

But in spite of the turmoil of war with which the rest of the world was resounding, we found in our deserted hill where a garrison used to be quartered, a 'peace that passes understanding', and we were content with our losses whether of liberty or otherwise, because they brought us the leisure that we needed for a study of our faith. When war that brought all the trouble on us was about to be declared on Turkey, my wife had suddenly been taken ill and an unsuspected heart trouble made her condition so critical that from the very first moment that medical aid had been called, it was not considered possible to leave her for a minute

without a doctor in attendance. For three whole nights and the intervening days she had been unconscious and her life hung from a slender
thread. But as she had not shown the slightest symptom of improvement,
despair had begun to settle down on all, and noticing my own condition
the doctors on the third night had insisted on my entire exclusion from
the sick chamber to offer me a little change from my restless condition.
As the night wore away and the dawn began to streak the East with the
first faint glimmer, my mother who had sat up with the doctor and the
nurses asked the doctor if I could not now be asked to come down, to
have a last look at my dying wife, and realising the hopelessness of the
situation he consented. Curiously enough before I had been many minutes in the sick room she stirred and was helped by the doctor to sit up in
the bed to ease her breathing, when she began to regain consciousness
and for the first time since she had had the attack, recognised my friend
the doctor and blushingly expressed her astonishment in finding herself
in his arms. Her recovery was a very slow affair, but thank God, the crisis
was over and had passed away as unexpectedly as it had come and her
life was thenceforward no longer in danger. An hour or two later I was
rung up by a Member of the Government of India with whom I had for
years had the most intimate relations and he asked me about the condition of my wife. When I communicated my happy news to him, he said
he had some painful news to communicate, which, however, he had
obtained the Viceroy's consent to withhold for a day or two if things did
not improve with regard to the health of my wife. And he told me that the
security of my press was to be declared forfeited, which he knew meant
the closure of my press and perhaps the end of my career as a journalist
altogether. In all conscience his news was bad enough, but with the glad
tidings that my eyes had communicated to me when my wife woke up to
receive a shock to her modesty in finding herself in the arms of my friend
the doctor, who cared for the Press Act and its forfeiture of securities, for
the closure of printing presses and the end of journalistic careers. All that
I knew at the time was that I had found a wife that I had all but lost. And
now when some eight months later I found myself in a deserted garrison
station on a remote hill without friends and companions, without the
daily work of my profession, and the wages that it brought me, with my
letters to my wife and her letters to me passing through the hands of a
stranger and a foreigner and undergoing his scrutiny, I could after
reading the Qur'an in the undisturbed calm of my sequestered retreat,
truly say that a compensating Providence had seen to it that in losing
almost all else I should at long last find life rich in content and purposeful,
the real thing for the first time and no sham or simulacrum.

OUR NEW FRIENDS

Lansdowne was not only off the beaten track, inaccessible like most hill-stations by railway and connected with a small branch line which terminated some 25 miles away from it at the foot of the hills, but had no civil population at all. And when we were removed to it, even the military were conspicuous by their absence in Europe. Only skeleton depots were kept for purposes of receiving back the wholly disabled from the war, and arranging for the pensions, and enlisting fresh recruits to fill the terrible gaps, and hurriedly training them to become cannon fodder, in their turn. The officers' bungalows were with the exception of ten or a dozen all untenanted and one of these just above the mess of the 2/8th Gurkhas and the Brigade Office had been rented for us by Government, from the widow of a Captain, who had gone back to England. In the barracks of the soldiers were to be found the remnants of these brave battalions of Gurkhas and Garhwalis that had been so mercilessly mown down by the German guns in Flanders and France. Battered and broken men that had once been so agile and were the best of hill climbers crawled round on the roads. Their ranks were from time to time strengthened by the arrival of fresh apple-cheeked boys enlisted from their homes in far off Nepal, innocent of all clothing except a blanket wrapped round their sturdy young limbs and gaily chattering away like monkeys unconscious perhaps of the doom that awaited them within the next half year. The enlistment in the Garhwal regiment being local was more gradual and not so noticeable. This was, so to speak, a migratory population; but there was besides it another that was almost permanent. These were the women in the married quarters wistfully and often alas vainly looking forward to meeting their husbands and sons on their return. All, indeed were not grass-widows, for in a very large number of cases these women had nothing to look forward to, except their repatriation in Nepal as the widows of their brave sons who had died in a foreign land, fighting for a foreigner. Autocratic as the East may often be in its governance, it is wonderfully democratic in its social life, and even more so among women than among men. Morning and evening our Mother would go out with us in her *burqa* or veiled cloak walking astonishingly long distances for one of her age, and more than age, her sorrows. The strange sight of two men and a boy—my brother's eldest son—not obviously 'Sahibs' and yet very different from the only Indians whom they used to see, the 'Babus' or clerks in the Military offices, the Sahib's servants and the few shop-keepers, men with their own complexions but dressed like 'Sahibs' and carrying themselves every whit as if they were

'Sahibs', and that strange apparition of a person in snow white cloak, thickly veiled and slightly bent soon attracted notice. And when Mother occasionally lifted her veil when there was no man to be seen on the road and past the men's barracks, and the Gurkha women saw that it was one of their own sex, they were not in the least bit shy, and in spite of an almost complete ignorance of any Indian vernacular they insisted on being visited by her and would clap their hands and beckon to her. How they managed to communicate with her is still a mystery to us; but this much is certain that before we had been a week, intimate social relations had been established between Mother and these Gurkha ladies. And when a month or two later my wife and daughters paid us a flying visit, the little ones attracted to our house quite a host of Gurkha girls who would come and dance and sing so beautifully. The local bazaar did not provide a great variety of things with which we could refresh these vigorous little dancers, but wall-nuts which grew in the hills in abundance were to be had at eight for a pice (or farthing), we could well afford to keep all our coat pockets well filled with them for free distribution during our walks among our numerous little friends in Lansdowne. We did not visit the soldiers, the strange combination of disabled veterans and raw recruits, in the barracks, and an occasional chat with a half-crippled warrior on the road about his wounds and the nature of the fighting in France and Belgium was the limit of our intercourse with them. But we had not long to wait to discover that they were attracted to us and felt a sympathy for us, even though their knowledge of our troubles could not exactly be said to be accurate. For very early after our arrival at Lansdowne, and perhaps the very next day, when out walking in the evening, we were overtaken by a dense mist which began to blot out the outlines of the surrounding hills and made our return to the house we occupied not without some risk for our Mother. A Gurkha with a lantern happening to come on the scene, we asked him which way he was going, in the hope that perhaps he may not be greatly inconvenienced if he consented to show us the way. Our astonishment was great when he cheerfully replied that it was all right as he was going to a place very near our house and would see us home. We asked him how he knew where we lived, in answer to which he astonished us all the more by telling us that he knew we occupied 'Kaptan Ishtack's', bungalow and that he was well aware we were Princes ruling over a State from which the English had removed us and hopefully added: 'But, it will soon be all right. You will soon be victorious and get back your raj'! After this if we had extended our friendships from the little Gurkha children to their fathers as well, we would have been perhaps suspected of seducing the soldiers from their allegiance. However our intercourse with them did not go beyond an occasional roadside meeting, and their inviting us and our own children along with their British Depot Officers, when they celebrated the Dasehra festival.

FROM GARHWAL TO GONDWANA

But there was a class of people whom we were actually suspected of corrupting, and these were the Musalman servants of the few remaining officers. They used to see us every Friday at the Service in the mosque and had evidently come to know all about us before we had been a fortnight at Lansdowne. Learning that we were among the founders of the Servants of Ka'ba Society and that my brother was its Secretary, they began to come to us for enlistment as members, and although my brother had never dreamed of conducting any propaganda in such a place he could not, of course, refuse to enlist such men as came of their own accord to be enrolled as Servants of Ka'ba and to obtain the familiar little badge of the 'Servants', which they openly wore on all occasions. Lord Meston seemed to have been greatly perturbed at this and had orders served on us to desist from such conduct; but my brother wrote back that although he had not made any efforts to enlist such Musalmans as there were in the place, he could not refuse those who offered themselves for enlistment, and since it was a purely religious matter he could not even give an assurance that he would not conduct a propaganda for the purpose if he felt inclined to do so. There was no further development, for this was just towards the end of our stay at this beautiful quiet hill-station, the approach of winter making it necessary for Government to transfer us to the plains, the warmer provinces. 'The world was all before them where to choose our place of rest', and this time they hit upon Chhindwara in the Central Provinces. Being situated on the Satpura Plateau, 2300 feet above the sea level and surrounded by large forest tracts, it had an excellent climate all round the year and was an ideal place from the point of view of the Government as well. It was, before we came, a dead-and-alive little place without any taint of politics and free from all religious fervour, and though served by a small metre-gauge branch line, was so remote from every place, and sequestered in such a backwood of Gondwana—the country of the aboriginal Gonds—that few visitors from the outside too could be expected, specially as now additional restrictions were imposed on our freedom even in the matter of receiving visitors. But whether it did or did not suit an over-anxious Government, or furtive political propagandists whose heart[s] were set on lighting a fiery cross in India, it was, like Lansdowne, the exact spot on earth to which two men anxious to explore the mysteries of their faith and in search of a sylvan solitude could have if they had the freest of free choices betaken themselves. Both at Lansdowne where we stayed only five months of the summer and autumn, and at Chhindwara where we passed three and a half years we had enough leisure and undisturbed peace and quiet to read the Qur'an and thoroughly soak ourselves in that perennial fountain of Truth that the gathering lust of thirteen centuries has not been able to choke or dry.

NOTES

1. Sir T.W. Arnold, *Preaching of Islam*, New York: C. Scribner's Sons, 1913, p. 413.

2. C.M. Doughty's *Travels in Arabia Deserta*, Vol. II, Cambridge: Cambridge University Press, p. 39.

3. Abadi Bano Sahiba, popularly known as 'Bee Amman' will ever be remembered as an indefatigable worker for the cause of the Khilafat. On her death in 1924, Mohamed Ali wrote three articles in *The Comrade*: 'In Mother's Memory'. All of them will figure in his 'Writings and Speeches.'—Ed.

4. Azmat Ali Khan, Azmat.

5. The Turks now possess several translations of the Qur'an in their language.—Ed.

6. The family of Shah Wali Ullah Dihlavi.—Ed.

Shaista Suhrawardy Ikramullah

In her book *From Purdah to Parliament* Shaista Suhrawardy Ikramullah
(b. 1915) discusses, among other things, the balancing act she had to achieve
between her liberal upbringing at home and the more orthodox norms of her
husband's family with regard to purdah. It was her husband who persuaded
her to give up purdah, but she was initially disappointed at the results. She had
hoped mixed society would be more interesting than purdah society, but found,
at least in Delhi, the level of conversation banal.

Influenced by Jinnah and his sister, Begum Ikramullah joined the Muslim
League, and later migrated to Pakistan.

Chapter VII

ADJUSTMENT

The greatest change that marriage brings into the life of a girl in our
society is that she has to adjust herself to the way of life of a completely
new family. In some ways, her position is similar to that of an English
girl going for the first time to a boarding school; only her ordeal is
greater.

As I have said before, in my country a girl is trained from her
childhood towards this end. She is prepared for it as for an examination.
Her manners, her behaviour, her conduct in every respect are made to
conform to the pattern which will be expected of her by her in-laws. Any
sign of self-assertiveness is curbed with the remark: 'You will not be
able -to get your own way in *susral.*'

And it is true that one could not be very self-assertive and, therefore,
it was wise to train girls to the sort of life that lay before them. It was a
life which required above all things tact and ability to give and take, a

Shaista S. Ikramullah, *From Purdah to Parliament*, London: The Cresset Press, 1963.

power to endure and to be able to put the interest of others before oneself. It puts a premium on virtues such as obedience and self-sacrifice. Mothers laid the foundation of these qualities in a girl's character and mothers-in-law built on them, so that they could grow into wives and mothers possessed of these virtues which had been the hallmark of well-bred women in our society.

At first I found adjustment comparatively easy. My in-laws had expected me to be much worse, that is to say much more modern than I was. They knew that I had been to an English school and college and this had branded me as completely *outrée* in their eyes. They had asked for my hand in marriage because their English-educated son wanted an educated wife, but they were prepared for this wife to be an absolute *kranti,* as the few girls who did go to English schools were usually completely Westernized.

What they did not know was that I had a one hundred per cent orthodox mother who was not relegated to the background as some Westernized men relegated their orthodox wives but who had as much say and influence on my education as my father, and whose personality was so strong as to dominate and subjugate the otherwise Westernized household. So, 'English-school educated' though I was, I had been drilled most rigidly to conform to the expected pattern of behaviour of a young bride at her in-laws. I kept my head down, my eyes shut and the veil well over my face. I did not move at all of my own accord but was taken from one place to another and on such occasions behaved more or less like a limp rag doll. I ate very little and that after a great deal of persuasion. This by the way, was not out of modesty but, being an active person and used to moving about a great deal in my home, I had lost my appetite completely now that I was confined to sitting in one place for hours. Though this was not intentional, it helped me to get another good mark, for it seemed that nicely brought up girls were never ravenously hungry.

In fact, I got good marks all round for I dressed in the orthodox bridal style, or rather I did not protest when I was so dressed up. I had *mehndi* on my hands, *kajal* on my eyes, *ifshans* (gold dust) and *chamki* (sequins) on my hair, the traditional cosmetic for brides, and *ittar* on my clothes, which, by the way, were always of very bright hues and richly embroidered, and I remained loaded with jewellery. I was absolutely the traditional bride.

It delighted my mother-in-law and all her family that they had found an 'English-educated' girl who was at the same time absolutely old-fashioned. That I was not so, at least not entirely, that my character would eventually reveal some unmistakable sign of Western influence, they were to discover later. But, all went well for the present.

My conforming to the traditional behaviour was not play acting. My mother had succeeded in persuading me that it was the only correct behaviour of well-brought-up girls and those who did not conform to it were ill bred. I had come to believe this and, therefore, conformed willingly. To this day I still believe in the traditional observances in a wedding, although perhaps not in all their rigidity; but I do believe that they should be observed for they are colourful and are characteristic of our way of life. Even if I had not believed in it, I would have conformed for I was not only fond of my mother but held her in great respect and, if I had not behaved according to tradition, it would have meant her losing face. This would have hurt her very much and I would not have dreamt of doing so. Anyway, had I attempted any deviation, I do not think I would have got away with it for amongst the maids who had come to look after me was Muna Buwa and I have described earlier what a stickler she was for discipline in tradition. She therefore accompanied every girl of the family on her first visit to her in-laws. My mother had borrowed her from aunt. She was taking no chances with me.

My in-laws lived in Nagpur where my father-in-law had retired and settled, but their family came from Bhopal, a Muslim Princely State which had originally belonged to the United Provinces, that centre and cradle of Muslim culture. So, though they now lived in a predominantly Hindu province, they and a few more families like them maintained an enclave of Muslim culture in the same way as my family did in Bengal. There was no difference of background to overcome except that in some ways life at my in-laws was even more orthodox than at home. My father-in-law was less Westernized than my father. He had not been to England and he had not spent years of his service living in anglicized areas of Indian towns.

The house in which we lived in Nagpur was originally a bungalow but it had been modified and built on till it had taken on the look of the traditional Muslim house with the large enclosed courtyard and a verandah running the entire length of the house. On the verandah there was the usual large *takhat* with the inevitable *pan-tan.* Alongside the wall, *charpoys* were stacked, which were taken out in the evening into the courtyard for sleeping. There were the *surhais* for drinking water and the samovar on one side for washing. All the living in the East is done on verandahs and, though we now build dining- and drawing-rooms in imitation of the West and have even taken to building suffocating little flats, we still go on living on verandahs and verandahs always have *takhats* which can be said to be the stage of all our activities. Though houses are now furnished with sofas and chairs and all modern European furniture, the *takhat* still holds its own as the most used piece of furniture in our households. It did not take me very long to feel quite at home on the large *takhat* on the verandah at Nagpur.

I have said that I found settling down in my new home easy because my in-laws were pleasantly surprised by my orthodoxy. It was also made easy by the fact that my mother-in-law was a most kindly person. She, like my mother, was in poor health and was soon to become a complete invalid, though she lived for some years after my marriage. Even the few weeks in which I saw her before she was struck down by illness, have left in my mind a great impression of her kind and mellow wisdom. She, like my mother, had a great influence over her whole household. Actually women in Muslim households invariably had great influence and a much greater say in household affairs than their menfolk. The fact that they observed purdah did not mean they were nonentities, though I know this is the general impression in the West and, like many other impressions, it is an erroneous one.

The relationship between father-in-law and daughter-in-law in our society is one of great formality. A daughter-in-law is never supposed to be seen by her father-in-law with her head uncovered or rushing round or speaking loudly, much less reclining or even sitting in a negligent manner. She is never supposed to speak to her husband before her father-in-law. During the seventeen years that my father-in-law lived after my marriage, I never once spoke to my husband in his presence, for it was not done. Despite this formality there generally is a great affection between father-in-law and daughter-in-law. As opposed to the mothers-in-law, whose attitude was traditionally critical, the fathers-in-law had an affectionate tenderness towards the young girls separated from their homes and brought under their roof. My father-in-law was wise and kind and loved his children deeply but unpossessively. He was happy if they did what he wanted them to do, but his love for them did not waver if they did not—a rare quality in a parent anywhere and still more rare in our country. His loving kindness to me throughout the years is amongst my most treasured memories.

But the person with whom I had most to do was my sister-in-law, my husband's widowed sister. Though she was only two years older than he, because she was a widow and because of my mother-in-law's frail health, she had been put more and more in charge of things and she had come to have a much greater importance in the house than her age warranted. In fact, after my mother-in-law's death, she has been virtually in the place of a mother to her brothers and a mother-in-law to all her brothers' wives.

Apa, as we all call her, is a typical product of purdah. She has all the good and bad points of the milieu she was brought up in and to this day rules over her household, consisting of a son and daughter-in-law, several grandchildren and twenty-two servants, not to say their families, in a truly matriarchal fashion. She is kind but firm with them, the firmness being more apparent than the kindness, though if one looks closely one would see that there is a lot of genuine kindness in her also. Her servants are those who have been with the family for years and she knows all about them, the exact number and the age of the youngest grandchildren of the *mali* and the latest development in the quarrel between the cook and her daughter-in-law. But she stands no nonsense from them and does not hold with the modern nonsense about everybody being equal. Even the school-going children of the servants, who entertain such ideas, show her a feudal deference, for she will have no less. She is a remarkably intelligent person and her comments on current affairs are scathingly funny, though her outlook in many ways is narrow and she is not interested in anything that does not affect her small world.

Her rapier-sharp wit and sense of humour make her an excellent raconteuse and I fell under her spell from the beginning and, not having had a sister myself, lavished on her all my affections with the unsophisticated abandon of a schoolgirl. She, on the other hand, never forgot that I was a sister-in-law and there were set rules by which a sister-in-law's conduct should be judged and, measured by these standards, I fell very short in certain matters. A warm heart was, according to her way of thinking, no substitute for being ignorant about cooking and sewing and other household arts and crafts.

Besides this, when she came to know me better, she found in me what she regarded as some alarming tendencies towards modernity which, because of my conservative behaviour as a bride, she was not prepared for. My attitude regarding the furniture and furnishing of my first home shocked her very much, for I rejected, lock, stock, and barrel, all the things my husband had accumulated in the six years of his service, saying that they were 'awful' and so they were, for they were the typical furnishings of a district officer's bungalow, a hybrid mixture of the worst styles of the East and the West and whatever I may or may not have known about running a household, I did know something about furniture. But to give one's opinion so freely and to be so critical was not expected of a new bride and it was also considered extremely extravagant to get everything new. All this bordered on self assertion and that is a quality which is not encouraged in the young in our society, particularly not in daughters-in-law. I began to feel an undercurrent of criticism where so far there had been nothing but approval and there was more to come.

My sister-in-law was very orthodox but I was only partly so and the unorthodox side of me was to come in conflict over and over again with orthodoxy. Paradoxically, it was only because part of me was orthodox that the difficulty arose. Otherwise I could have ignored the tacit criticisms and implied disapproval and gone my own way as my other sisters-in-law did later on. But the traditional training that I had ingrained into me could not ignore the disapproval of the *susral,* while the modern in me could not refrain many times from doing what was disapproved of.

While I was struggling to come to terms with this new world which from now on was to be my home, my world, my own familiar world of childhood came to an end with a suddenness that left me benumbed with shock. For my mother died at the time I needed her most. When her advice and guidance would have been of the utmost value to me, I found myself without it, alone amongst strangers. To heighten the tragedy of it, I had been away in Nagpur at the time of her death, for, true to her traditions, to the last she had refused to send for me, refused even to let me know that she was ill. And when, having heard of it by accident, I had rushed down to Calcutta, she had sent me back after a few days for, according to her, a married daughter's place was with her in-laws, particularly in the first few months after her marriage.

Such utter unselfishness and complete adherence to tradition would not have been possible to an ordinary woman even in the East, but my mother was not an ordinary woman. She was a rare person, even amongst her generation and now we will not see any women of her calibre and personality, for the very mould that fashioned her is broken.

Chapter VIII

TWILIGHT OF AN EMPIRE (1933–1936)

My husband belonged to the Indian Civil Service, commonly known as the I.C.S. This had acquired a prestige and a glamour which is not generally associated with the civil service in any other country. Its tradition of exclusiveness had made it into a caste and exposed its members to both criticism and envy. They were accused of narrow-mindedness and rigidity of outlook, but it was reluctantly conceded that their reputation for integrity and efficiency was justified. It was, at first, manned entirely by the British but at this time more and more Indians were being admitted to its charmed circle. The Indians conformed rigidly to the pattern of behaviour that had evolved over the years. This service was the backbone of the Indian Empire, the steel frame that held it up, and it was the administrative ability of the members of this service that helped the two new countries to tide over their first unusually difficult years.

Soon after we were married my husband was posted as Under Secretary to the Industries Department of the Government of India, and so I came to live in New Delhi. That was in 1933 and New Delhi was then the seat of the Empire, the Imperial Secretariat and the Central Assembly. But so much has happened since, so completely has the picture changed, had already changed even by March, 1947, when I left, that it is difficult to believe that all this was so recent.

It was a wholly official city, and an English official city at that. For, though in less than fourteen years, power was to be transferred entirely to Indian hands, the number of Indian officials in New Delhi at this time was negligible, and in the dress, manner and speech of these few men there was nothing Indian at all. They might, or rather they must, have come from Indian homes but, in their New Delhi drawing-rooms there was nothing to tell you so.

While the men were more or less of a type, the veneer of Westernization covering up differences of province, caste and class, in the case of the wives this was not so. Though they too tried to be as Westernized as their husbands and followed the code of official etiquette with meticulous care, they could not succeed in camouflaging the background from which they came. They all paid and returned calls with due formality, gave correct but dull little parties, knew the use of the right knives and forks and registered the same degree of disapproval as an English 'Memsahib' if an unfortunate bearer made the slightest mistake in serving meals or announcing callers. This spectacle of their laboured Westernization was rather pathetic and ridiculous, as was their effort to give themselves the airs of 'grandes dames'.

Simple Indian women, mostly from villages, who had not been able to shed their orthodoxy to the extent of being able to eat meat and food cooked by a non-Brahman, had yet learnt the official snobbery well enough not to notice anybody below a Joint Secretary's wife. As I was on the lowest rung of official life, being the wife of an Under Secretary, I never came to know these, for by the time I had reached a sufficiently high status to be taken notice of, I had found myself much more interesting things to do. But these were in a minority; in most their little affectations did not take away from their warm and kindly natures. They adopted the traditional Indian attitude of the older woman towards the young; that is an attitude of motherly affection. All these women were Hindus, for if the Indian officers in the Government were few, the Muslims were still fewer; in fact my husband was the only Muslim member of the I.C.S. in Delhi. But in 1933 this did not matter and the happy relationship established then has continued in most cases despite the bitterness of partition.

The English women could be similarly divided into two types. There were those whose efforts to assume Mayfair airs did not hide the fact of their suburban origin and others who had that graciousness without patronage which characterizes the best type of English woman in the East. Amongst these I made many friends and without making it obvious they gave me much valuable advice which was of great help. Even spending a morning knitting in their beautiful gardens helped me to sort out many of my problems. Friendships thus formed have endured throughout the years: have survived my participation in the struggle directed against the British, and are now being carried on into the second generation.

Though individually satisfying relationships were possible, the social pattern was a very rigid and dull one. The 'season', as it was called, started around November and went on till the end of March. The months before and after this period were taken up by the exodus from and to Simla. Its highlights were the Viceregal Ball, the Viceregal Garden Party, the Horse Show and polo. Next in importance to these came the garden parties given by Executive Counsellors. Each gave one in the season and innumerable little dinner parties. Strict precedence was observed and everything went according to established rules. One could not ask or be asked to dinner by anyone above or below a certain rank. Needless to say, I found these restrictions both boring and irksome.

It was at the garden party of one of the Executive Counsellors that I made by debut. I was till then officially still in purdah though since my marriage its rigidity had been much relaxed.

I did not enjoy my first experience of being out of purdah at all. I felt embarrassed at being looked at by hundreds of men decked up all in my best and my enjoyment of the party was further spoiled by my having to spend the entire evening trying to avoid being seen by my uncle, who very strongly disapproved of my coming out of purdah.

My subsequent sallies into mixed society I found no more interesting than the first one. I had imagined that mixed society would be composed of intelligent people, who would talk of more interesting things than were talked of in the women's world to which I had so far been confined, but to my disappointment I found that this was not so, and all that they talked was a meaningless sort of official jargon.

What I enjoyed, however, because of their spectacular quality, were the functions at the Viceregal Lodge, where I had already attended the Investiture at which my father and uncle were knighted. It had an unreal fairy-like quality even then, and the memory of it has stayed with me as of something seen in a dream. I was still in purdah and my excursion from behind the veil into this dazzling spectacle was rather like Cinderella going to the ball.

That morning I had spent seeing the tombs of Humayun and Safdar Jung, one an example of early and one of late Mogul architecture. Humayun's tomb could be compared with Westminster Abbey. It is associated with the last scene of the tragic drama of the fall of the Mogul Empire, for it was here that Bahadur Shah, the last Mogul emperor, was taken prisoner by the notorious Captain Hudson, and it was here that the two princes, sons of Bahadur Shah, were also taken prisoner and later shot by Hudson at the *Khuni Darwaza*. And that day, exactly seventy-five years after that tragedy, in the same city of Delhi was being held an Investiture by the power that had succeeded the Moguls. A few years only were to go by before this power itself was to disappear and the Empire, on which the sun never set, was to become a thing of the past.

But this did not seem possible that evening in March, 1932, when our car drove up to the Viceregal Lodge. I shall always remember that evening. My father looking magnificent in his colonel's uniform; my uncle very dignified in a Janawar Choga.

As I was in purdah I could not go up with my father and uncle and sit near them. But, as my father was a member of the Viceregal staff, being the Honorary Surgeon to the Viceroy, he knew everybody and had arranged for me to be taken up separately and put in a seat not too far from him. All along the stairs and passages stood, as if carved in stone, the Viceroy's personal bodyguards, all of them at least six feet six inches in height, all wearing brilliant uniforms with black and gold turbans, holding their lances. They struck awe in my heart.

The Investiture was being held in the Mogul Drawing-room of the Viceregal Lodge. This room has a magnificently painted ceiling and beautiful marble columns. It was ablaze with lights. At one end of the room was a raised dais upon which stood two thrones. In the seats facing it sat men in dazzling uniforms with medals and women in gorgeous evening gowns and jewels. Suddenly there was a sort of clinking noise and then my eyes saw a spectacle I have never forgotten. In a box at the side of the dais appeared the Indian princes, resplendent in the brocaded *sherwanis* and Benarasi turbans with jewels scintillating on their chests and swords strapped to their waists. They came, about ten or twelve of them, all at once and stood for a minute before taking their seats. It looked as if all the colour, the pageantry and chivalry that was India was symbolized in them. Barely a few minutes had passed when the Viceroy and Lady Willingdon came slowly up to the dais. Lord Willingdon was an extremely distinguished looking man and looked very elegant in Court Dress; many medals blazed on his chest and from his shoulders hung a blue cape, each corner held by two little page-boys. Lady Willingdon had on a magnificent evening gown and she too wore many medals. She had a diamond tiara on her head and ropes of pearls round her throat. Her cape was also held by two little page-boys, dressed in blue and white. A.D.C.s, Military Secretaries and other members of the Viceregal staff led the procession, which slowly reached the dais. The Viceroy and Vicereine sat down. It all looked like a tableau.

Soon the Viceroy was standing up. The Investiture had begun. Men were going up to receive their honours from the representative of the King. The G.C.S.I.s, the K.C.S.I.s, the G.C.I.E.s and the K.C.I.E.s came first. The recipients of these were members of the princely order. Then came the G.B.E.s, and K.B.E.s and, after them, the knights. My heart filled with pride as I saw, first my uncle and then my father go up to the dais and kneel on a velvet footstool. I watched the Viceroy touch their shoulders with his sword bidding them rise. After the knights came the Nawabs, the C.S.I.s, and the C.I.E.s, the M.B.E.s, the O.B.E.s, the Kaisar-i-Hinds and many other titles that I do not remember.

At last it was all over. Everybody was leaving. I again found myself being discreetly escorted out by an A.D.C.

Later on many of these titles were returned at the command of the Muslim League. When my father returned his knighthood, it was on a gloomy evening in Calcutta, with the dreadful scenes of the terrible riots still before our eyes and its echoes still ringing in our ears. My mind went back to this night of dazzling splendour. But all this was many years away and meanwhile I had to contend with the dull routine of society life in New Delhi. Fortunately, alongside New Delhi's narrow confines lay the wondrous historic city of Old Delhi, and soon I was to reach out to gather its richness. Delhi is one of those cities that is steeped in 'history, legend, tune and song', for it has been the heart of Indo-Muslim culture for two thousand years.

There have been eight Delhis in all, eight different dynasties have chosen it for their capital. Seven cities lie in ruin around it. In 1932, the eighth Delhi, which was called New Delhi, stood in radiant splendour encircled by the seven other cities, each one once the proud capital of an empire and still containing within its walls monuments of its past glory. Besides history Delhi is associated with our best poets and writers and in 1933, there still lived there men and women who were typical of its great culture. Mr. Asaf Ali was one of them, Khwaja Hasan Nizami was another. Nawab Sirjuddin Khan Sael was still alive and so was Rashid-ul-Khairi. I had the privilege of meeting them and of listening to their talk. It was indeed a 'liberal education'.

Mr. Asaf Ali, was not only one of the most prominent figures of the Indian National Movement but one of its most charming also. He belonged to Delhi, not only in the sense that he came from one of its oldest families, but because he was the quintessence of its culture. He had the courtesy and the charm, the grace, the elegance and the manner, that undefinable air of breeding which only those nurtured in the best tradition of our culture possess. I have never heard and never shall hear again Urdu spoken as Asaf Ali spoke it. Urdu is essentially a court language; it was born and bred in the court of the Mogul kings. It is capable of extremely subtle nuances. Stressing a single syllable the juxtaposition of a single word, can convey a world of meaning; only a few today know how to do this. Asaf Ali did. He was probably one of the last who knew how to use the language as if it were a musical instrument. It was becoming rare, even in my generation, to hear Urdu spoken in this manner. It makes me sad to think that my children have not even heard the full range of its musical cadence. I was indeed fortunate to have heard it, fortunate to have known persons of such rare quality as Asaf Ali and his young wife, Aruna.

When I met Aruna, even then she had a burning transparent sincerity and I have not been surprised at her subsequent revolutionary career. But I know that she is not the hard-headed revolutionary people imagine her to be but a woman with great sweetness and gentleness of character, capable of tender and deep affection. That is how she was when I met her and that woman I know is still there.

As Asaf Ali was a great friend of my uncle, Syud Hussain, it did not take me long to come to know him and his wife very well. I was soon to be seen very frequently at Asaf Ali's house in Kuchai Chilan, meeting other interesting people and listening avidly to their conversation. Asaf Ali knew the history of every nook and corner, every inch and stone of Delhi, and I would listen spellbound as he told me about it. He knew so many forgotten anecdotes which made the stones live and speak again.

Bhabi, as we all called Mrs Asaf Ali, gave me my first taste of social service. She got me to become a member of the Delhi Women's League. I did not do anything very much, except attend various lectures given by well-known visitors. The most interesting amongst them and the one I remember the most clearly was by the famous Turkish writer, speaker and politician, Khalida Adeeb Khanam. It seems strange, when I look back on it all, to think that I, who eventually became such an ardent Muslim Leaguer, should have begun my apprenticeship under Aruna Asaf Ali. Little did she suspect the lines on which I would develop later. Little did I know myself.

I also saw a good deal of Mrs Sarjoni Naidu. She was, without exaggeration, the most interesting, the most vivacious and the most charming person in India. She had a radiant personality which made even the staid and official drawing-rooms of Delhi pulsate with life. She was the most marvellous and interesting conversationalist that I have ever met. She had a fund of anecdotes which she told in her own inimitable manner. They all had more than a little soupçon of malice but her manner of telling them was such that one did not mind the malice, one only enjoyed the fun. She held court—no other word can describe it—at the house of Sir Sri Ram where she usually stayed when she was in Delhi. There would be anything up to thirty or forty people in the room every evening. She would be talking to all of them almost at the same time, calling them all by their first names and managing to make every- one feel absolutely and completely at home. Her memory was phenom- enal; she knew almost everybody and she never forgot a face or a name. She was a great friend of my aunt as well as all the members of my family, but had seen me only when I was ten years old. So, I had not expected her even to remember me, but she did not only that, when she met me the first time, she remembered that she had heard I had recently married and called out to my husband to come and sit next to her and get properly introduced.

She used to come to Delhi more or less every cold weather and everyone looked forward to her visit. She would ring me up directly she had arrived, fix a date when she would come to dinner with me and order the menu herself. This she did with all her special friends. She liked food as she liked all good things of life, and to any admonition to be careful, as her health was none too good and rich food was bad for her, she would reply, 'Oh, be quiet! All the doctors that gave me six months have been dead for years.'

And so, before I realized it, our three years in Delhi were over and we were due for a transfer. We should ordinarily have gone back to the Central Province, but we were fortunate to get posted to London, one of the few foreign postings available to Indians at that time.

I had already been to England with my father the year before and had loved it. So I was delighted at the prospect of spending three years there. Though I did not realize it then, these were to be the last years of my life untouched by the stress and strain of politics.

Ismat Chugtai

Both in her life and in her writing, Ismat Chugtai (1911–91) was a courageous woman, merciless in her exposure of the hypocrisy and obscurantism (as she saw them) of the Muslim middle-class of North India which was her milieu. In this she was helped by the publication of the revolutionary anthology *Angare* in 1932, which contained eight stories by Rasheed Jahan, who was to prove an important influence on Chugtai, and also stories by Sajjad Zaheer, Ahmed Ali and Mahmuduzzafar. A mullah apparently took it upon himself to start a smear campaign against the writers of the anthology, but Chugtai called upon her fellow college students to defend the book. The article she wrote in defence was published in *The Aligarh Gazette*, and the students who read it are said to have beaten up the mullah. Chugtai published eleven novels and novellas, nine books of short stories and a play. Chugtai is represented here by a short but feisty excerpt from her autobiography.

More from the Autobiography

Ismat and Purdah!

It was the first time that I was forced to wear a burqa, and I cannot begin to express the humiliation I felt—I wanted to kill myself. I was extremely agitated. Azeem Bhai had only recently created an uproar with his articles 'Quran and the Veil' and 'Hadith and the Veil'. Voices were raised in passion for and against the veil. In Bombay, Begum Atiya Faizi, Zohra Faizi, Begum Humayun Mirza and a handful of intrepid ladies created a stir by storming into a conference session where ladies were not allowed. Even though they wore burqas, the Muslims felt greatly disgraced. Had they not belonged to influential, educated and affluent sections of society, they would have been torn apart. These ladies had

Ismat Chugtai, *Kaghazi hai Pairahan*, Rashmi Govind (trans.), Lahore, 1981. Quoted in Sukrita Paul Kumar and Sadique (eds), *Ismat: Her Life, Her Times*, Delhi: Katha, 2000.

demolished the very idea of the burqa for countless immature minds. Azeem Bhai was a strict opponent of the veil. He wanted his wife to discard the veil, but the entire family sided with his wife and he was helpless.

'Why did you break the tradition of the veil?'

'Who are you talking about?'

'I am talking about Dulhan.'

'Dulhan is my wife, and I have the right to either keep or break the tradition of the veil....'

Since Dulhan Bhabhi's brothers threatened to cut off the heads of both their sister and her husband if she was made to discard the veil and parade about in the marketplace, Azeem Bhai became subdued. When he saw me in the third class compartment, livid with anger and helplessness, he realized that it was all because of the burqa. When I put on the burqa, my depraved brothers had roared so much with laughter that I came to blows with them, and instead of taking them to task, Amma had smacked me....

'You wicked, accursed creature!' Blows started raining on me from all sides. 'You stuffed the burqa in the bag deliberately, didn't you?' I accepted the blows as if they were sweets. I knew very well that it was just not possible to open the well-trussed bedding in half an hour. I was made to wrap a chadar around me and I stepped on the platform like a bold victor. My eyes met Azeem Bhai's. He laughed so loudly that he had a coughing fit. I, too, quickly disguised my laughter into a pretence of coughing. The chadar kept slipping off and whenever this happened, a shower of cuffs and pinches fell on me.

Only he, who has drunk from the fountain of victory, can experience the sweet moment I was savouring that day on the platform with my face uncovered. Very soon people started suspecting it was Azeem Bhai who had fanned the embers of this stubbornness, who had, in fact, lit the spark. The wireless message that passed between our eyes had been intercepted.

...

ON PURDAH AGAIN

...

As a matter of fact, the tradition of the veil, which had been an obstruction between the two sexes, embodied many dreams, which have disappeared now. Girls don't get worked up now when they see boys. They consider boys only as students, just like themselves. Not that the removal of the tradition of the veil spells the death of romance. Love affairs must still be flourishing and marriages still taking place.

Of course when the veil is abolished, a number of childish and superficial emotions, which flourish only on the basis of the imagination and which are the causes of many psychological complications, get sorted out. Reality becomes more comprehensible. Boys and girls consider each other fellow human beings, rather than members of the opposite sex. It is much simpler. The possibility of blind love affairs lessens. Life builds itself on comparatively more stable foundations.

There was no arrangement in Aligarh for doing BA after FA. I had obtained Abba Mian's permission to take admission in IT College, Lucknow; Jugnu had to work for two years at Habib Hospital, Bombay—that was the condition on which he had been given the scholarship.

The two years I spent at Lucknow proved very important for me. New avenues and new doors opened out for my mind.

The burqa disappeared at some point of time. Following the custom of Hindu women, all the ladies of respectable families wrapped a chadar around themselves. The women wore a ghunghat. Some wore a pishwaz over kurtas and tight pajamas. The elderly ladies did not wear ghunghats. Wrapping a dupatta around their breast constricted their hands, so in spite of the ghunghat the dupatta dangled on their backs. One corner was tucked in at the waistband to prevent the dupatta from trailing on the ground. Even with a lahanga-choli, the dupatta dangled on the back. The Marwari ladies wore dresses that were brilliant in color. The colour remained bright for months. They changed their dress only when it became threadbare. The women would take off their clothes at the pond, wash them and spread them on the sand to dry. The men who passed by did not even turn to look, and the women, too, were unconcerned.

AT JAVARE
...

I caused quite a sensation as soon as I reached Javare. A graduate, and that too a Muslim girl. Such a specimen had never before been sighted in the state. Nawab Sahab promptly appointed me headmistress of a Girls' School at a salary of a hundred rupees. Desks and benches were requisitioned from the Boys' School and put in an old palace-like bungalow. A blackboard and an old map of Hindustan were made available.

The day after tomorrow, that is, on the auspicious day of Friday, we shall leave, this dilapidated bungalow and move to the palace. How comfortably we shall sleep behind silken and velvet curtains, under gold and silver nets, on soft mattresses! I had never spat in a golden spittoon. As soon as I reach, I'll order the slaves:

'Get me the golden spittoon.' And when it is brought, I shall spit in it immediately.

What then? What shall I do then?

I could feel the discomfort of 'What then?' like the pea under a thousand mattresses.

Then, the marriage procession will arrive with great fanfare.

I'll be decked out as a bride.

My heart will beat faster when I hear the bridegroom's footfall.

And when the bridegroom raises the ghunghat...

Uff! My mind boggled at the thought. I hadn't read a book on sex education. I had devoured books on Politics, Economics, History, Geography, novels, drama, but our college didn't have a single book on practical sex education. Neither had my conversations with others drawn a very attractive picture of sex in my mind.

Mangiya, the coachman's daughter, had told me that marriage was a very offensive thing. The husband did wicked things to you and continued doing so for the rest of your life. Once Azeem Bhai had gone to Bombay in search of job opportunities. Dulhan Bhabhi would make use of me or Nayyer to read those letters, since Badi Apa, who was her confidante, had been married off. She would understand the meaning of certain sentences in those letters and turn red. If we asked, she would tell us to just go on reading. Sometimes we would hear whispered conversations, one wife saying to another, 'He is not interested in anything except lewdness. He is after me all the time.' She was talking about her respectable husband.

All of a sudden, the walls of the royal palace began to suffocate me. These nawabs do not believe in divorce; if a woman made too much noise, she was poisoned. As for me, I would not have got along with anyone even for a moment. How could I regard anyone as God-on-earth! I had stopped offering namaz years ago.

Sahibzada Ata Muhamed Khan

Sahibzada Ata Muhamed Khan remembers how in the 1930s he accompanied his uncle, the Nawab of Palanpur, to a town just on the borders of the state, where the wives of the local jagirdars expressed a wish to look upon the princes of Palanpur: 'We were sitting like idiots on these chairs wondering how these women in purdah were going to see us, when suddenly we saw this big stranji (carpet) with holes in it coming towards us. The carpet stopped six feet away from us and we could see eyes at all those holes! We didn't know where to look! Then after ten minutes or so the carpet went back.'

A reminiscence quoted in Charles Allen and Sharada Dwivedi, *Lives of the Princes*, London: Century Publishing Co., 1984, p. 189.

Literary Evocations

Ardeshir F.J. Chinoy and Mrs Dinbai A.F. Chinoy

A novel of manners set in Bombay circa 1896, which gives us an insight into the way purdah ladies were regarded. It also gives us an insight into the partial veiling of Parsee ladies of a certain generation (who were secluded at certain times, for instance during menstruation, though the novel does not deal with this practice here). No information is available about the authors.

Chapter V

SIR MADHAVDASS' PARTY

Scarcely had the clock struck the hour of eight when the guests began to pour in, and were received by the host and his son Narotam, assisted by the latter's aunt, who played the part of the hostess since the death of Lady Madhavdass. A few minutes more and the spacious hall became animated with the presence of the cream of the Bombay society. Soon the guests formed themselves into small knots, in one of which were to be seen Lilawati and Pootli with their friends Mehra and Shera. Lilawati was, of course, dressed in rich but plain and sombre-coloured garments, while Mehra and Shera were yet novices in the school of Dame Fashion to claim any attention But it was otherwise with Pootli, the devoted votary of that fickle and exacting goddess. She had spent much time and thought over her toilet, and the effect was simply fascinating. Her sari of a sky-blue colour was of a soft, gauzy texture, and so artistically arranged that its folds trailed behind her like the draperies of a Grecian damsel. She looked very smart in her low-cut, close-fitting, short-sleeved blouse,

Ardeshir F.J. Chinoy and Mrs Dinbai A.F. Chinoy, *Pootli: A Story of Life in Bombay*, London: T. Werner Laurie, n.d.

and a single string of pearls, with a diamond pendant, adorned her shapely neck.

In short she looked a perfect picture of what art and taste could do towards enhancing the natural beauty of her person, and even if her grandmother had revisited the earth, it would have cost her some efforts to recognise in the gaily dressed belle her own granddaughter. Though the chief garment—the sari—remained the same, its former plain and thick, though durable material, mostly of gaudy colours, was now replaced by soft Parisian chiffon or fine Japanese crape, smart and showy in appearance, but not lasting.

Then, too, the stylish mode in which it was worn over a skirt-fashioned silk petticoat—formerly an unknown article even in the richest lady's wardrobe—would astonish and puzzle her. The modern blouse with its hangings and trimmings, the corset and the belt, the highheeled shoes, and even the stockings would all be new to her. She was supremely innocent of each of them; for a simple, plain bodice of white linen or silk was all that she had worn over her indispensable religious garment—the sadra. Finally the old lady would search and search in vain for her favourite headgear, which was in fact a plain piece of white linen—a yard square—with which all the women of her days carefully tied, and scrupulously concealed their tresses, exposing only a narrow sulp of hair just above the forehead; and the poor girl who through carelessness or prompted by a desire to look attractive, failed to keep any of her rebellious ringlets under the close confinement of her ugly looking headdress, was looked down upon as fast and immodest. But good taste and better sense have prevailed over false and exaggerated notions of modesty, and the meaningless head-gear has by degrees been losing its hold on the minds of the Parsi ladies, many of whom, like our Pootli, have boldly dispensed with it altogether, while others have relegated it to their chignon.

With feminine inquisitiveness they were all busy in noting and criticising the dresses of some of their acquaintances, when Pootli, somewhat fatigued by the heat of the room, proposed to move on to the terrace at the rear of the house, which afforded one of the most charming and extensive prospects for which Bombay is so well known. It was a fine, cloudless night, and the full moon, shining in all her glory and brilliancy, clothed the whole city in a robe of silvery white. On the right, as far as the eye could reach, was the smooth expanse of the Arabian Sea, whose waters, rolling down in small billows, sparkled under its soft, mellow rays; on the left were the roofs of innumerable houses peeping through clusters of cocoa-nut and mango trees, while still farther away in the rear stood a forest of tall chimneys of cotton mills and other factories. To Pootli and Lilawati the scene was pretty well familiar, but it was otherwise with their young friends. They were bewitched by the exquisite beauty and charm of the whole scene, which they had witnessed that night for the first time, and overwhelmed their friends with questions upon questions as to the topography and situations of the different parts of the city. While they were thus engaged, a familiar voice from another group attracted Pootli's attention, and on turning round whom should she see but her lover Jal standing in the company of Miss Brown and her cousin Tom. Jal was, of course, unconscious of Pootli's presence on the terrace, and stood there with one arm round Lizzie's slender waist while the other was raised in the attitude of pointing out to her some interesting object in that lovely scene that lay stretched before their eyes.

Pootli turned ashy pale, and failing to conceal her agitation from her friends, she was forced to invent an excuse to ward off impertinent questions regarding so sudden a change in her appearance. The cold night air, she said, did not agree with her, and she entreated her companions to allow her to return to the warmth of the drawing room where she buried herself in a chair in a lonely corner, a prey to the most poignant feelings of anguish.

Her long-felt suspicion regarding Jal's growing coldness towards her was now fully confirmed by his familiar behaviour with Miss Brown. It was not difficult for her to conclude that the foolish and fickle-minded Jal had allowed himself to be easily beguiled into the snares cunningly spread by her. And unfortunately Pootli's surmise was well-founded. His vanity was tickled by the mere idea of being admired and loved by an Anglo-Indian beauty, and all his professions of love for Pootli, and even the sacred troth he had plighted to her in secret, evaporated before her alluring charms.

Pootli's disappointment was no doubt very keen, but, fortunately for her, she possessed a larger share of sound common sense than is generally found in most of the girls of her age and position, and was also free from much of the sentimentalism of her sex.

After she was able to collect her scattered thoughts a little, she began to take a rapid mental survey of her past conduct and her present position. She at once recognised the folly of keeping her engagement with Jal a secret from her father. Had it not been so, Jal would have considered twice before thus imposing upon an innocent and confiding girl. At the same time she was not sorry for her own sake, and sincerely thanked Providence for so miraculous an escape from the life-long yoke of a base and perfidious youth whose edifice of love and affection was based on a very insecure, sandy foundation, liable to give way by every gust of caprice and passion.

This train of reasoning so far restored the lost equanimity of her mind, that soon colour returned to her faded cheeks, and she was once more in a position to mix in the brilliant company assembled under that roof; and when a few moments later her three companions approached her, she came out from her secluded corner and joined them without any appreciable sign on her face of the great storm that so lately agitated her mind.

It was now time for the guests to assemble round the hospitable board, and the Europeans, Parsis, Mohammedans, and a few Hindus who appeared to be free from caste prejudices and restrictions, sat round it to do justice to a sumptuous dinner which the hospitality of Sir Madhavdass had provided for them. The European and Parsi ladies sat at the same table with the gentlemen, while the still bashful Hindu dames had to be served in another room all by themselves. The Mohammedan ladies were, of course, conspicuous by their absence, as the healthy rays of civilisation and progress have not yet sufficiently penetrated the thick veil of the harem to induce its inmates to leave its guarded precincts and face the world like their more refined European or Parsi sisters. The conversation that went round the dinner-table was sprightly and interesting, and related to the principal topics of the day; while amongst those who had witnessed Jal's too familiar behaviour with Miss Lizzie on the terrace, the most engrossing topic centred round them.

Rumour soon spread that Jal had proposed and Miss Brown accepted his offer of marriage. Some shook their heads in doubt and displeasure at his rashness and folly, while others, though secretly envying him for his good fortune in thus winning over the love and admiration of that lovely girl, considered it smart to applaud his bold selection, declared that their prospective marriage would serve to narrow the wide gulf that now stands not only between the rulers and the ruled, but also between the innumerable Indian races, and enlarged on the untold good that would result from such mixed marriages to the future of the race.

Rabindranath Tagore

Tagore's *Ghaire Baire* (The Home and the World) is among his most moving novels. A liberal zeminadar allows his wife to come out of purdah, with results that prove fatal to him in the end.

Poet, novelist, short-story writer, painter, and educationist, Tagore (1861–1941) was awarded the Nobel Prize in 1913. He wrote his first poem when he was about seven, and published his first book of poems when he was seventeen. He was sent to England to study but found formal education tedious, though he later lectured extensively abroad, and exhibited his paintings in the West. He and Gandhi had many disagreements—Gandhi was impatient of Tagore's lyricism because so many people were hungry and homeless. Tagore replied that he preferred to 'spin yarns' rather than yarn. Tagore was against child marriage, but inevitably, as with any human endeavour, there were contradictions. His own daughters were married when they were thirteen and ten and a half.

He taught his wife Mrinalini Devi Bengali and Sanskrit. Between 1902 and 1907 he lost his wife, his daughter, and his son.

Bimala's Story

I

Mother, to-day there comes back to my mind the vermilion mark[1] at the parting or vour hair, the *sari*[2] which you used to wear, with its wide red border, and those wonderful eyes of yours, full of depth and peace. They came at the start of my life's journey, like the first streak of dawn, giving me golden provision to carry me on my way.

The sky which gives light is blue, and my mother's face was dark, but she had the radiance of holiness, and her beauty would put to shame all the vanity of the beautiful.

Rabindranath Tagore, *The Home and the World*, Surendranath Tagore (trans.), and the translation revised by the author, London: Macmillan, 1948, 1st edn 1919.

Every one says that I resemble my mother. In my childhood I used to resent this. It made me angry with my mirror. I thought that it was God's unfairness which was wrapped round my limbs—that my dark features were not my due, but had come to me by some misunderstanding. All that remained for me to ask of my God in reparation was, that I might grow up to be a model of what woman should be, as one reads it in some epic poem.

When the proposal came for my marriage, an astrologer was sent, who consulted my palm and said, 'This girl has good signs. She will become an ideal wife.'

And all the women who heard it said: 'No wonder, for she resembles her mother.'

I was married into a Rajah's house. When I was a child, I was quite familiar with the description of the Prince of the fairy story. But my husband's face was not of a kind that one's imagination would place in fairyland. It was dark, even as mine was. The feeling of shrinking, which I had about my own lack of physical beauty, was lifted a little; at the same time a touch of regret was left lingering in my heart.

But when the physical appearance evades the scrutiny of our senses and enters the sanctuary of our hearts, then it can forget itself. I know, from my childhood's experience, how devotion is beauty itself, in its inner aspect. When my mother arranged the different fruits, carefully peeled by her own loving hands, on the white stone plate, and gently waved her fan to drive away the flies while my father sat down to his meals, her service would lose itself in a beauty which passed beyond outward forms. Even in my infancy I could feel its power. It transcended all debates, or doubts, or calculations: it was pure music.

I distinctly remember after my marriage, when, early in the morning, I would cautiously and silently get up and take the dust[3] of my husband's feet without waking him, how at such moments I could feel the vermilion mark upon my forehead shining out like the morning star.

One day, he happened to awake, and smiled as he asked me: 'What is that, Bimala? What *are* you doing?'

I can never forget the shame of being detected by him. He might possibly have thought that I was trying to earn merit secretly. But no, no! That had nothing to do with merit. It was my woman's' heart, which must worship in order to love.

My father-in-law's house was old in dignity from the days of the *Badshahs*. Some of its manners were of the Moguls and Pathans, some of its customs of Manu and Parashar. But my husband was absolutely modern. He was the first of the house to go through a college course and take his M.A. degree. His elder brother had died young, of drink, and had left no children. My husband did not drink and was not given to dissipation. So foreign to the family was this abstinence, that to many it hardly seemed decent! Purity, they imagined, was only becoming in those on whom fortune had not smiled. It is the moon which has room for stains, not the stars.

My husband's parents had died long ago, and his old grandmother was mistress of the house. My husband was the apple of her eye, the jewel on her bosom. And so he never met with much difficulty in overstepping any of the ancient usages. When he brought in Miss Gilby, to teach me and be my companion, he stuck to his resolve in spite of the poison secreted by all the wagging tongues at home and outside.

My husband had then just got through his B.A. examination and was reading for his M.A. degree; so he had to stay in Calcutta to attend college. He used to write to me almost every day a few lines only, and simple words, but his bold, round handwriting would look up into my face, oh, so tenderly! I kept his letters in a sandalwood box and covered them every day with the flowers I gathered in the garden.

At that time the Prince of the fairy tale had faded like the moon in the morning light. I had the Prince of my real world enthroned in my heart. I was his queen. I had my seat by his side. But my real joy was, that my true place was at his feet.

Since then, I have been educated, and introduced to the modern age in its own language, and therefore these words that I write seem to blush with shame in their prose setting. Except for my acquaintance with this modern standard of life, I should know, quite naturally, that just as my being born a woman was not in my own hands, so the element of devotion in woman's love is not like a hackneyed passage quoted from a romantic poem to be piously written down in round hand in a schoolgirl's copy-book.

But my husband would not give me any opportunity for worship. That was his greatness. They are cowards who claim absolute devotion from their wives as their right; that is a humiliation for both.

His love for me seemed to overflow my limits by its flood of wealth and service. But my necessity was more for giving than for receiving; for love is a vagabond, who can make his flowers bloom in the wayside dust, better than in the crystal jars kept in the drawing-room.

My husband could not break completely with the old-time traditions which prevailed in our family. It was difficult therefore, for us to meet at any hour of the day we pleased.[4] I knew exactly the time that he could come to me, and therefore our meeting had all the care of loving preparation. It was like the rhyming of a poem; it had to come through the path of the metre.

After finishing the day's work and taking my afternoon bath, I would do up my hair and renew my vermilion mark and put On my *sari*, carefully crinkled; and then, bringing back my body and mind from all distractions of household duties, I would dedicate it at this special hour, with special ceremonies, to one individual. That time, each day, with him was short; but it was infinite.

My husband used to say, that man and wife are equal in love because of their equal claim on each other. I never argued the point with him, but my heart said that devotion never stands in the way of true equality; it only raises the level of the ground of meeting. Therefore the joy of the higher equality remains permanent; it never slides down to the vulgar level of triviality.

My beloved, it was worthy of you that you never expected worship from me. But if you had accepted it, you would have done me a real service. You showed your love by decorating me, by educating me, by giving me what I asked for, and what I did not. I have seen what depth of love there was in your eyes when you gazed at me. I have known the secret sigh of pain you suppressed in your love for me. You loved my body as if it were a flower of paradise. You loved my whole nature as if it had been given you by some rare providence.

Such lavish devotion made me proud to think that the wealth was all my own which drove you to my gate. But vanity such as this only checks the flow of free surrender in a woman's love. When I sit on the queen's throne and claim homage, then the claim only goes on magnifying itself; it is never satisfied. Can there be any real happiness for a woman in merely feeling that she has power over a man? To surrender one's pride in devotion is woman's only salvation.

It comes back to me to-day how, in the days of our happiness, the fires of envy sprung up all around us. That was only natural for had I not stept into by good fortune by a mere chance, and without deserving it? But providence does not allow a run of luck to last for ever, unless its debt of honour be fully paid, day by day, through many a long day, and thus made secure. God may grant us gifts, but the merit of being able to take and hold them must be our own. Alas for the boons that slip through unworthy hands!

My husband's grandmother and mother were both renowned for their beauty. And my widowed sister-in-law was also of a beauty rarely to be seen. When, in turn, fate left them desolate, the grandmother vowed she would not insist on having beauty for her remaining grandson when he married. Only the auspicious marks with which I was endowed gained me an entry into this family—otherwise, I had no claim to be here.

In this house of luxury but few of its ladies had received their meed of respect. They had, however, got used to the ways of the family and managed to keep their heads above water, buoyed up by their dignity as *Ranis* of an ancient house, in spite of their daily tears being drowned in the foam of wine, and by the tinkle of the dancing girls' anklets. Was the credit due to me that my husband did not touch liquor, nor squander his manhood in the markets of woman's flesh? What charm did I know to soothe the wild and wandering mind of men? It was my good luck, nothing else. For fate proved utterly callous to my sister-in-law. Her festivity died out, while yet the evening was early, leaving the light of her beauty shining in vain over empty halls—burning and burning, with no accompanying music!

His sister-in-law affected a contempt for my husband's modern notions. How absurd to keep the family ship, laden with all the weight of its time-honoured glory, sailing under the colours of his slip of a girl-wife alone! Often have I felt the lash of scorn. 'A thief who had stolen a husband's love! 'A sham hidden in the shamelessness of her new-fangled finery!' The many-coloured garments of modern fashion with which my husband loved to adorn me roused jealous wrath. 'Is not she ashamed to make a show-window of herself—and with her looks, too!'

My husband was aware of all this, but his gentleness knew no bounds. He used to implore me to forgive her.

I remember I once told him: 'Women's minds are so petty, so crooked!' 'Like the feet of Chinese women', he replied. 'Has not the pressure of society cramped them into pettiness and crookedness? They are but pawns of the fate which gambles with them. What responsibility have they of their own?'

My sister-in-law never failed to get from my husband whatever she wanted. He did not stop to consider whether her requests were right or reasonable. But what exasperated me most was that she was not grateful for this. I had promised my husband that I would not talk back at her, but this set me raging all the more, inwardly. I used to feel that goodness has a limit, which, if passed, somehow seems to make men cowardly. Shall I tell the whole truth? I have often wished that my husband had the manliness to be a little less good.

My sister-in-law the Bara Rani,[5] was still young and had no pretensions to saintliness. Rather, her talk and jest and laugh inclined to be forward.

The young maids with whom she surrounded herself were also impudent to a degree. But there was none to gainsay her—for was not this the custom of the house? It seemed to me that my good fortune in having a stainless husband was a special eyesore to her. He, however, felt more the sorrow of her lot than the defects of her character.

II

My husband was very eager to take me out of *purdah*.[6]

One day I said to him: 'What do I want with the outside world?'

'The outside world may want you', he replied.

'If the outside world has got on so long without me, it may go on for some time longer. It need not pine to death for want of me.'

'Let it perish, for all I care! That is not troubling me. I am thinking about myself.'

'Oh, indeed. Tell me, what about yourself?'

My husband was silent, with a smile.

I knew his way, and protested at once: 'No, no, you are not going to run away from me like that! I want to have this out with you.'

'Can one ever finish a subject with words?'

'Do stop speaking in riddles. Tell me...'

'What I want is, that I should have you, and you should have me, more fully in the outside world. That is where we are still in debt to each other.'

'Is anything wanting, then, in the love we have here at home?'

'Here you are wrapped up in me. You know neither what you have nor what you want.'

'I cannot bear to hear you talk like this.'

'I would have you come into the heart of the outer world and meet reality. Merely going on with your household duties, living all your life in the world of household conventions and the drudgery of household tasks—you were not made for that! If we meet, and recognise each other, in the real world, then only will our love be true.'

'If there be any drawback here to our full recognition of each other, then I have nothing to say. But as for myself, I feel no want.'

'Well, even if the drawback is only on my side, why shouldn't you help to remove it?'

Such discussions repeatedly occurred. One day he said: 'The greedy man who is fond of his fish stew has no compunction in cutting up the fish according to his need. But the man who loves the fish wants to enjoy it in the water; and if that is impossible he waits on the bank; and even if he comes back home without a sight of it he has the consolation of knowing that the fish is all right. Perfect gain is the best of all; but if that is impossible, then the next best gain is perfect losing'.

I never liked the way my husband had of talking on this subject, but that is not the reason why I refused to leave the zenana. His grandmother was still alive. My husband had filled more than a hundred and twenty per cent of the house with the twentieth century, against her taste; but she had borne it uncomplaining. She would have borne it, likewise, if the daughter-in-law[7] of the Rajah's house had left its seclusion.

She was even prepared for this happening. But I did not consider it important enough to give her the pain of it. I have read in books that we are called 'caged birds'. I cannot speak for others, but I had so much in this cage of mine that there was not room for it in the universe—at least that is what I then felt.

The grandmother, in her old age, was very fond of me. At the bottom of her fondness was the thought that, with the conspiracy of favourable stars which attended me, I had been able to attract my husband's love. Were not men naturally inclined to plunge downwards? None of the others, for all their beauty, had been able to prevent their husbands going headlong into the burning depths which consumed and destroyed them. She believed that I had been the means of extinguishing this fire, so deadly to the men of the family. So she kept me in the shelter of her bosom and trembled if I was in the least bit unwell.

His grandmother did not like the dresses and ornaments my husband brought from European shops to deck me with. But she reflected: 'Men will have some absurd hobby or other which is sure to be expensive. It is no use trying to check their extravagance; one is glad enough if they stop short of ruin. If my Nikhil had not been busy dressing up his wife there is no knowing whom else he might have spent his money on!' So whenever any new dress of mine arrived she used to send for my husband and make merry over it.

Thus it came about that it was her taste which changed. The influence of the modern age fell so strongly upon her, that her evenings refused to pass if I did not tell her stories out of English books.

After his grandmother's death, my husband wanted me to go and live with him in Calcutta. But I could not bring myself to do that. Was not this our House, which she had kept under her sheltering care through all her trials and troubles? Would not a curse come upon me if I deserted it and went off to town? This was the thought that kept me back as her empty seat reproachfully looked up at me. That noble lady had come into this house at the age of eight, and had died in her seventy-ninth year. She had not spent a happy life. Fate had hurled shaft after shaft at her breast, only to draw out more and more the imperishable spirit within. This great house was hallowed with her tears. What should I do in the dust of Calcutta, away from it?

My husband's idea was that this would be a good opportunity for leaving to my sister-in-law the consolation of ruling over the household, giving our life, at the same time, more room to branch out in Calcutta. That is just where my difficulty came in. She had worried my life out, she ill brooked my husband's happiness, and for this she was to be rewarded! And what of the day when we should have to come back here? Should I then get back my seat at the head?

'What do you want with that seat?' my husband would say. 'Are there not more precious things in life?'

Men never understand these things. They have their nests in the outside world; they little know the whole of what the household stands for. In these matters they ought to follow womanly guidance.—Such were my thoughts at that time.

I felt the real point was, that one ought to stand up for one's rights. To go away, and leave everything in the hands of the enemy, would be nothing short of owning defeat.

But why did not my husband compel me to go with him to Calcutta? I know the reason. He did not use his power, just because he had it.

III

If one had to fill in, little by little, the gap between day and night, it would take an eternity to do it. But the sun rises and the darkness is dispelled—a moment is sufficient to overcome an infinite distance.

One day there came the new era of *Swadeshi*[8] in Bengal; but as to how it happened, we had no distinct vision. There was no gradual slope connecting the past with the present. For that reason, I imagine, the new epoch came in like a flood, breaking down the dykes and sweeping all our prudence and fear before it. We had no time even to think about, or understand, what had happened, or what was about to happen.

My sight and my mind, my hopes and my desires, became red with the passion of this new age. Though, up to this time, the walls of the home—which was the ultimate world to my mind—remained unbroken, yet I stood looking over into the distance, and I heard a voice from the far horizon, whose meaning was not perfectly clear to me, but whose call went straight to my heart.

From the time my husband had been a college student he had been trying to get the things required by our people produced in our own country. There are plenty of date trees in our district. He tried to invent an apparatus for extracting the juice and boiling it into sugar treacle. I heard that it was a great success, only it extracted more money than juice. After a while he came to the conclusion that our attempts at reviving our industries were not succeeding for want of a bank of our own. He was, at the time, trying to teach me political economy. This alone would not have done much harm, but he also took it into his head to teach his countrymen ideas of thrift, so as to pave the way for a bank; and then he actually started a small bank. Its high rate of interest, which made the villagers flock so enthusiastically to put in their money, ended by swamping the bank altogether.

The old officers of the estate felt troubled and frightened. There was jubilation in the enemy's camp. Of all the family, only my husband's grandmother remained unmoved. She would scold me, saying: 'Why are you all plaguing him so? Is it the fate of the estate that is worrying you? How many times have I seen this estate in the hands of the court receiver! Are men like women? Men are born spendthrifts and only know how to waste. Look here, child, count yourself fortunate that your husband is not wasting himself as well!'

My husband's list of charities was a long one. He would assist to the bitter end of utter failure any one who wanted to invent a new loom or rice-husking machine. But what annoyed me most was the way that Sandip Babu used to fleece him on the pretext of *Swadeshi* work. Whenever he wanted to start a newspaper, or travel about preaching the Cause, or take a change of air by the advice of his doctor, my husband would unquestioningly supply him with the money. This was over and above the regular living allowance which Sandip Babu also received from him. The strangest part of it was that my husband and Sandip Babu did not agree in their opionions.

As soon as the *Swadeshi* storm reached my blood, I said to my husband: 'I must burn all my foreign clothes.'

'Why burn them?' said he. 'You need not wear them as long as you please.'

'As long as I please! Not in this life...'

'Very well, do not wear them for the rest of your life, then. But why this bonfire business?'

'Would you thwart me in my resolve?'

'What I want to say is this: Why not try to build up something?' You should not waste even a tenth part of your energies in this destructive excitement.'

'Such excitement will give us the energy to build.'

'That is as much as to say, that you cannot light the house unless you set fire to it.'

Then there came another trouble. When Miss Gilby first came to our house there was a great flutter, which afterwards calmed down when they got used to her. Now the whole thing was stirred up afresh. I had never bothered myself before as to whether Miss Gilby was European or Indian, but I began to do so now. I said to my husband:

'We must get rid of Miss Gilby.'

He kept silent.

I talked to him wildly, and he went away sad at heart.

After a fit of weeping, I felt in a more reasonable mood when we met at night. 'I cannot', my husband said, 'look upon Miss Gilby through a mist of abstraction, just because she is English. Cannot you get over the barrier of her name after such a long acquaintance? Cannot you realise that she loves you?'

I felt a little ashamed and replied with some sharpness: 'Let her remain. I am not over anxious to send her away.'

And Miss Gilby remained.

But one day I was told that she had been insulted by a young fellow on her way to church. This was a boy whom we were supporting. My husband turned him out of the house. There was not a single soul, that day, who could forgive my husband for that act—not even I. This time Miss Gilby left of her own accord. She shed tears when she came to say good-bye, but my mood would not melt. To slander the poor boy so— and such a fine boy, too, who would forget his daily bath and food in his enthusiasm for *Swadeshi.*

My husband escorted Miss Gilby to the railway station in his own carriage. I was sure he was going too far. When exaggerated accounts of the incident gave rise to a public scandal, which found its way to the newspapers, I felt he had been rightly served.

I had often become anxious at my husband's doings, but had never before been ashamed; yet now I had to blush for him! I did not know exactly, nor did I care, what wrong poor Noren might, or might not, have done to Miss Gilby, but the idea of sitting in judgment on such a matter at such a time! I should have refused to damp the spirit which prompted young Noren to defy the Englishwoman. I could not but look upon it as a sign of cowardice in my husband, that he should fail to understand this simple thing. And so I blushed for him.

And yet it was not that my husband refused to support *Swadeshi,* or was in any way against the Cause. Only he had not been able whole-heartedly to accept the spirit of *Bande Mataram.*[9]

'I am willing', he said , 'to serve my country; but my worship I reserve for Right which is far greater than my country. To worship my country as a god is to bring a curse upon it.'

NOTES

1. The mark of Hindu wifehood and the symbol of all the devotion that it implies.

2. The *sari* is the dress of the Hindu woman.

3. Taking the dust of the feet is a formal offering of reverence and is done by lightly touching the feet of the revered one and then one's own head with the same hand. The wife does not ordinarily do this to the husband.

4. It would not be reckoned good form for the husband to be continually going into the zenana, except at particular hours for meals or rest.

5. *Bara* = Senior; *Chota* = Junior. In joint families of rank, though the widows remain entitled only to a life-interest in their husbands' share, their rank remains to them according to seniority, and the titles 'Senior' and 'Junior' continue to distinguish the elder and younger branches, even though the junior branch be the one in power.

6. The seclusion of the zenana, and all the customs peculiar to it, are designated by the general term 'Purdah', which means Screen.

7. The prestige of the daughter-in-law is of the first importance in a Hindu household of rank.—Tr.

8. The Nationaliat movement, which began more as an economic than a political one, having as its main object the encouragement of indigenous industries.—Tr.

9. Lit. Hail Mother; the opening words of a song by Bankim Chatterjee, the famous Bengali novelist. The song has now become the national anthem, and *Bande Mataram* the national cry since the days of the *Swadeshi* movement.—Tr.

Romesh Chunder Dutt

A member of the I.C.S., later President of the Indian National Congress, and then Dewan of Baroda, Romesh Chunder Dutt (1848–1909) was a cousin of Toru Dutt's and a writer and translator. He wrote *The Lake of Palms* (1902) and *The Slave Girl of Agra* (1909) in Bengali and translated them himself into English (three others were translated by his son). He published a Bengali version of the Rig Veda and wrote condensed versions of the Ramayana and the Mahabharata in English verse. He also wrote a number of historical surveys including *A History of Civilisation in Ancient India*, *The Economic History of British India*, and *A Brief History of Ancient and Modern Bengal*.

The Lake of Palms (abridged by P. V. Kulkarni in the extract used) is described as a story of Hindu domestic life in Bengal. It is a story of a Hindu widow and the possibility of remarriage, which shocks the local community. Some of the chapters also refer to the tensions of change. Uma, married to a wealthy man, 'heard with some degree of pity of the more orthodox arrangements of Kalee's family, where scores of members lived and fed under a common roof and acknowledged a common head'. The novel originally appeared in Bengali in 1885 under the title *Sansar*.

What the Women-Folk Said

As Sarat left the house a woman-servant from Debi Prosonno's entered with sweets for Bindu from the Puja offerings.

Bindu asked her to leave them on the plate. The woman did as she was told and then drawing the cloth over her head, turned her face a little and smiled a significant smile. She had apparently overheard what passed between Bindu and Sarat and had observed the latter when he left the house; but, feigning ignorance, she asked Bindu who the young man was, why he was there at an unwonted hour, and then began to indulge in vague insinuations. Bindu resented her impertinent malice, but thought that she might make the case worse by losing her temper. She therefore tried to allay her suspicion by telling her that Sarat, who had almost lost his wits with his solitary life and hard studies, had come to inform her that he wanted to marry a pretty girl. The mischievous woman then demanded the name of that pretty girl. Bindu replied that she would know it when the match was arranged. Fully conscious of her vantage-ground, the woman then retorted. 'What need of conceal-ment, mother, as if we had neither eyes nor ears! We are not so old as all that yet! Did I not hear him crying for Sudha as if his heart would break? Ay, ay, conceal it; will people ever reveal such scandal? Marriage of a widow! If such a proposal were made in a poor man's house, he would be put out of his caste.'

For the first time, Bindu was alarmed. So long as this ill-mannered woman was speaking of Sarat's rude behaviour towards herself she did not mind. Her virtuous life was too well-known to fear any stain from the talk of an insolent woman. But Sudha was a young widow, and the slightest breath of scandal might stain her fair name forever. Bindu knew in her heart that Sarat's proposal was madness, and the marriage could never take place; but the faintest rumour connecting their names would spread like wildfire, and would ruin the innocent girl and her reputation.

A moment of the acutest pain passed silently by. Never losing her presence of mind, Bindu opened her box and took out a coin. It is customary to pay to a servant who brings presents a trifling sum equal to two or three pence. To-night Bindu placed a silver rupee in the woman's hand. 'You are an old servant of Debi Prosonno's house, and served them long and faithfully. Accept this rupee from me on this Puja night, and buy a new cloth for yourself. And what you have seen of Sarat you will not repeat. Wise women do not heed twice a madman's wayward talk; and the thing could never come to happen. Who has heard of a widow being married? We have a name and station among our caste-people; my husband is respected by friends and neighbours; Sarat's mother is honoured for her saintly life in Benares; Sarat's sister is married to a family known for its orthodox purity. Is it possible that we should break through all duty and decorum, and permit such an alliance?'

The servant-woman looked at the bright silver rupee and was appeased. She replied with every sign of respect and courtesy: 'You speak truly, mother; whoever minds the words of a wild young man?'

'The times are bad, mother, and the young forget their duty and go astray. Why should I blame Master Sarat, and why should I tell tales about this behaviour? Trust me mother, and have no anxiety in your mind!'

She left the house much gratified, but as restless with her secret as a hen about to lay its egg. Bindu might have known better and saved her rupee; for to trust a secret to a woman-servant is the safest way to ensure its publication.

Debi Prosonno's wife sat on her mattress the next morning talking to two elderly widows, and the scandal, dear to her woman's soul, was the theme of unending comment and conversation.

'It was only what I expected, sister; I knew this was coming! For where is the distinction in these days between the well-born and the low? Anyone comes from a village and calls herself a Kayest, and forthwith mixes with the Kayest community. Are these people respectable Kayests? Have they within fourteen generations ever formed alliances with respectable Kayests? And to mix with such people! Fie upon it! Only wait till my husband comes back from his office this evening, he will hear of it from me. Why sister, does he not know his own station his rank and position in life, his connections and his reputation, that he must needs go and keep company with such people as these? Ay, ay, I knew this thing would happen! When they came to live in Bhowanipur, and have no time to call on us, I knew what manner of Kayests they were. And do you know, my dears, that young widow puts on a bordered saree and dresses like a married wife! Ay, ay, I knew all this was coming, for manners are not learnt, my sisters, but come with birth.'

'To be sure, sister, to be sure', replied Syami's mother. 'Why, that young widow never fasts on the eleventh day of the moon, as all true and honest widows should. And she takes fish too, my dear, like married women! For shame! This is the eleventh day of the moon, sister, and can any one say that we touch food or water for thirty-six hours, from one night to the next, on this day of the moon?'

'And do you know', said Bami's mother, 'they take that young widow for drives in carriages; they actually took her to see the Museum and the Zoological Gardens! It is shame and scandal!'

Pleased with this zealous assent, Debi Prosonno's lady burst forth again: 'Shame indeed—shame to the girl and to the mother who bore her! Why, that giddy girl actually talks to Hem with her head uncovered— ay, prepares dishes and sends sweet drinks for Sarat! How can we blame Sarat, my sisters? He is but a man, and he is yet unmarried, and when two scheming sisters go after him like this, is it a wonder that the poor youth should be caught in their meshes?'

The scandal ran its course from the well-side to the servants' quarters, and they were like a hive of disturbed bees, humming and whispering and restless. The news travelled to poor Uma's mother, who was still in the Lake of Palms. And Uma's mother wept many tears in silence, and wrote to her niece Bindu not to perpetrate a deed of shame, and stain the fair fame of the Mullik family.

Kalee was much distressed to hear that her brother Sarat was going to bring disgrace to their pure and unstained family. She wrote to Bindu, imploring her not to consent to a deed of shame and permit the marriage of a widow.

Bindu showed these letters to her husband and wept in silence. Rumour, trumpet-tongued, had spread and exaggerated the secret which Bindu had wished to conceal—the name of her poor innocent sister was spoken in scorn!

Meanwhile, every possible care was taken by Hem and his wife to keep Sarat's proposal secret from Sudha until the matter should be settled one way or another.

For a time they succeeded in their endeavours. But it was impossible to conceal from her altogether, simple and unsuspecting as she was, that some difficulty had arisen, that some grave question occupied their minds. Sudha marked the thoughtful face and the silent demeanour of her sister, and did not venture to ask the cause. She saw Hem receiving numerous visits from friends, writing letters in the morning, and sitting up with Bindu late at night. She saw the milk-woman whispering for a good half-hour to the servant of the house, and fancied she heard her own name and that of Sarat frequently mentioned. Sudha could not conceive such a thing. She had never given offence to any one, and no one had ever been rude to the poor and inoffensive girl. What then was the significance of these remarks?

It is hard to guess if Sudha suspected the real truth, but the most unsuspecting of women sees farther and more clearly into such matters than we generally suppose.

Though the whole story never revealed itself to her, it would be hard to say that her woman's wit, struggling against the veil of darkness, did not catch a ray of light. She listened more attentively to casual words heedlessly uttered, and noted more closely slight tokens which would not ordinarily arrest attention. And her woman's soul struggled against the dark mystery which seemed to conceal her fate and her future! She asked no questions and sought for no information, but her pale face and the light in her eyes spoke of a silent thought and an anxious doubt within her bosom.

At last the whole truth flashed upon her. One evening, as she was retiring to bed, she saw a crumpled piece of paper on the floor. She picked it up, and found it was in her aunt's handwriting. Suspecting no secret, and anxious to know what her aunt had written to her sister, she took that letter near the oil-lamp. It was a letter which was written to Bindu, and which Bindu had carelessly thrown aside. Sudha's hand trembled and her heart beat violently as she read its contents. The paper dropped from her hand, and she staggered back to her bed, dazed and bewildered.

Her first emotions were the shame and the agony of a Hindu widow. Why had Sarat, so good and generous, so wise and learned, proposed such a deed of shame? Why had he asked for her as his wife, and disgraced her in the eyes of the world? Her aunt knew of it; and Sarat's sister knew of it; and all the world knew of it; how could she show her face again to her friends and relations? A deep sense of shame, a consciousness of something unholy and impure, overwhelmed the girl. She hid her face in the pillow and wept unseen tears.

The struggle of painful thoughts tore the poor child's heart as she lay sleepless and restless through the dark, silent night

Hours passed, and the gloom of the midnight softened into the faint light of the early dawn, but no relief came. How could she show her face when the morning dawned even to her nearest and dearest friends, even to her sister?

The grey light of the morning saw her steal noiselessly from her bed, as if afraid to look her sister in the face, and speed down the steps to her domestic work. She scoured and cleaned the utensils, swept the court-yard, drew water from the well, and busied herself as if to forget. She trembled when the door opened and the servant entered the house; she ran into the kitchen to light the fire when the milk-woman came with the daily supply of milk.

Days passed in silent agitation. A deep feeling of shame oppressed her, and there was a burden on her young bosom. But Sudha was no true woman if a secret gleam of hope did not mingle in her bewilderment and confusion. The brave young Sarat, disregarding the opinion of the world, had cherished the love of her in his generous heart, had thought of her while he kept away from the house, had dared to ask for her as his wife! She trembled with a secret joy as these thoughts stole upon her. She felt it was an impure and unholy joy; but she would have been less or more than a woman if it had not flooded with a glow of sunshine the darkest recesses of her young and expanding heart.

One afternoon Bindu came into the bedroom and found Sudha sitting by the window with a book in her hand. Sudha closed the book as soon as she saw her sister.

'What is that book, sister, that you are reading?' asked Bindu, with some curiosity.

'It is a book by Bankim Chandra', said Sudha, bashfully dropping her eyes.

'And what is the name of the book?'

'It is called "The Poison Tree".'

Bindu looked grave, and she said a little sternly: 'Let me have that book, sister; don't read it.'

Sudha placed the book in her sister's band, and softly enquired: 'Is it a bad book, sister?'

'No, Sudha; it is the best novel in the Bengali language. But you are young, my sister, and need not read it yet.'

'Tell me the story then, sister. I long to know how it ends.'

'The story is short', said Bindu. 'A young widow marries the hero of the novel, but is unhappy in her marriage, and at last dies by poison.'

Sudha's face was bloodless as she silently left the room.

Rashid Jahan

One of the contributors to the revolutionary Urdu anthology *Angare*
(1932), and an important influence on Ismat Chugtai, Rashid Jahan
(1905–52) was the daughter of Shaikh Abdullah and Wahid Jahan Begum
of Aligarh, pioneers in the education of Muslim girls from upperclass
families. Herself a doctor, while her sisters were principals of girls'
colleges, Rashid Jahan wrote short stories and plays with social themes,
particularly concerned with women, social inequality, and oppression of
various kinds.

The UP government banned *Angare*, and, we are told, the book was
almost impossible to obtain until recently. In 1934, Rashid Jahan married
Sahibzada Mahmuduzzafar, one of the politically progressive writers she
met in Lucknow, and part of the Urdu Progressive Writers Movement.

Behind the Veil

a one-act play

*Translator's note: Western readers would perhaps regard this as a play only
in the sense that it is dialogue, with an occasional stage direction. For
Urdu readers the dramatic impact would derive from the fact that here is a
writer who makes public the kind of conversation that married women in
purdah would commonly engage in in private but would die rather than
have it made public. Its authenticity is not in doubt. Rashid Jahan was
herself a Muslim and a doctor who got to know such women intimately in
the course of her practice.*

*Its very authenticity poses more problems for the English reader than
do then pieces in this section, and a good deal of annotation is unavoidable.*

Rashid Jahan, 'Behind the Veil', in Ralph Russell (selection and trans.), *Hidden in the
Lute: An Anthology of Two Centuries of Urdu Literature*, Delhi: Viking, 1995. Urdu
original in *Angare*, 1932.

The description of the room, where the conversation takes place would at once tell the Urdu speaking reader what kind of women the participants are. They belong to the traditional, respectable Muslim population of Old Delhi. Their houses are enclosed on all sides, with separate parts for the men and the women so that purdah can be observed, and one, or more than one, small courtyard. The living room floors are carpeted, and over the carpets, lighter carpets, often embroidered, are laid which keep the heavier carpet clean. There are no chairs and tables. People sit on the floor, and will lean on a rather hard bolster There will be one or more beds in the room, so that people can lie down when they want to. Both men and women habitually chew paan—betel leaf, wrapped round other ingredients including often betel nut and tobacco. Spittoons will be at hand because the liquor from the paan is not swallowed but spat out. There will be earthenware pitchers of water, each covered with a lid and with a drinking bowl on top of it. Shelves are not common; small arch-shaped recesses in the wall serve the same purpose. Old fashioned houses have no electric fans. The fan is a long piece of heavy cloth, often with a fringe, fastened to a long piece of wood, hung from the ceiling and pulled to and fro by a rope. One of the servants will be there to pull the rope when needed. Such families pride themselves on being sharif—'of good family', and on maintaining the old fashioned standards. They will have several servants attending them. The play begins with a stage direction describing the setting in rather less detail than I have done, and continues:

> *A lady (Muhammadi Begam)[1] tired and depressed. An older lady [Aftab Begam], about forty years of age, is sitting facing her, slicing betel nut into a small draw-string bag. At one side of her is a small box and on the other side a spittoon. There are doors in front, and niches and shelves with pans and lids arranged on them on the other walls. In the middle of the room a fan with a pink fringe hangs from the ceiling. In one corner of the room is a bed with a bedspread on it. On the other side of the room is a small embroidered carpet, and a bolster and a spittoon.*

Muhammadi: Oh sister.[2] I've nothing left to live for. Much of my life has passed, and God will get me through the rest somehow. I'm so tired of life that if it weren't for the little ones, I swear by God I'd have taken poison.

Aftab: Have you gone mad? You're no age yet. Why talk of taking poison? These are the best days of your life. The children, bless them, are growing up, and now you want to take poison! Look at me...

Muhammadi: Why should I look at you? It's not a question of age. Is it only old people that get tired of life? I've seen more zest for life in old people than in young ones. Everyone's dying. Why don't I die? And children soon forget; after a few days everything's all right again.

Aftab: Come to your senses, girl, come to your senses. You're no age at all and here you are wanting to die. You're ten to twelve years younger than me. The year you were born they were talking about getting me married. That was the year that the queen [Victoria] died. I remember it well. Aunty,[3] God bless her—as pleased as if you'd been a boy. It was all of thirty years after she was married that you were born. A feast, and dancing to watch, and *domnis*.[4] And how happy she was when you were married! How she'd longed for that day! All Delhi welcomed it! No one can match your luck. And look at *me*, how unlucky *I* am. You, God keep you, have everything—husband, children, home, every-thing…

Muhammadi: You're right; husband, children, home, everything. But young? Who would think me young? I look like an old woman of seventy—always ill, always under the *hakim*[5] or the doctor, and every year a baby. Yes, no one can match *my* luck!

> (*Her eyes fill with tears. She wipes them with her handkerchief, spits into the spittoon, and goes on.*)

It's only two months ago—I'm talking of the time before my last miscarriage—that they decided to send for the lady doctor. Dr Ghiyas too had said that there might be something wrong inside that made me run a temperature so often, and that the lady doctor ought to look at my insides. I'll tell you what she said about my age. She asked me how old I was. I said, 'Thirty-two.' She smiled as if she didn't believe me. I said to her, 'Miss, what are you smiling at? Let me tell you I was married when I was eighteen, and I've had a baby every year since then— except for one year when my husband was in England for a year, and another year when we'd quarrelled. And these missing teeth that you can see—Dr Ghiyas pulled them out. Paria [pyorrhea] or something—I don't know what it was called. It was all because when my husband came back from England he said my breath smelt'. Poor woman, she had a good laugh at that.

Aftab: When you talk like that who can help laughing?

Muhammadi: Anyway the poor woman looked at my chest, and looked at my belly; and when she looked inside me she was alarmed and said, 'Begam Sahib.[6] it looks as though you're two months pregnant.' My heart sank, and I thought, 'More trouble.'

> (*At this point the sound of children crying, and of shouting and bawl-ing comes from the other room. Muhammadi gets up and shouts:*)

You wretches! You don't give me a chance to rest and sleep, or any time to talk. A houseful of maidservants, and *still* there's the children making a din. Better if God strike me dead. I'd be rid of all the troubles of this world.

(The door opens, and two wetnurses come in in clean dress—striped paijama,[7] muslin shirts and dupattas.[8] They bring in with them two children, who are crying. Other children, older than these two, can be seen standing in the doorway. All of them are thin, and pale, and weak. Beyond the door the courtyard can be seen.)

A wet nurse: Begam Sahib, the little master won't do as he's told. He comes into the room and teases the little ones and won't let them play. He's run off with Miss Nanni's doll and the little boy's ball, and gone straight into the men's quarters.

Muhammadi: (Furiously) Blast him! He doesn't give any of us a moment's peace. Takes after his father.

(She picks up the child and cuddles him, takes something out of the box and gives it to the two children to eat, and sends the wetnurse away again.)

Go! for God's sake go. Shouting and bawling from morning to night...

(She pauses when the servants leave the door open.)

Hey! Shut the door! I've told you several times this morning already to shut the door when you go out.

Aftab: Sister, in your house, God bless you, there's always some wretched doctor there. But look at your children—poor wretches they look thin and pale and miserable and half-starved.

Muhammadi: They're bound to be when they've not had their mother's milk. We take on any wetnurse that's going—fat, thin, pock-marked, one-eyed—anyone. Husband's orders. 'When God has given us money why should *you* be troubled?' he says. But it's his own pleasure he's thinking about. If the baby was with me *he'd* be inconvenienced. Doesn't matter whether it's day or night, he wants his wife. And not only his wife. He goes the rounds to other women too.[9]

Aftab: Muhmmadi Begam, you blame your husband for everything, poor man. If he gets you a wetnurse, that's wrong. And if he hadn't, that would've been wrong. Sister, remember what God commands you!

Muhammadi: Oh dear, sister. You weren't here when Nasir died. Poor little chap, he was only four months old. I wouldn't wish on my worst enemy all that he had to suffer. Even strangers couldn't bear to look at him. His wetnurse was quite a strapping girl. She looked quite healthy. But she had V.D., and no one had the least suspicion of it. The baby caught it. He got huge blisters all over his body, and when they burst the flesh was all raw and there was pus oozing from everywhere. The same doctor, Dr Ghiyas, used to draw off whole basinfuls of it. I used to watch him from behind the curtain. They say, 'Don't complain; give thanks to God.' Anyway he rotted away for two months and then died. After him I've had three more babies. I've said again and again, 'I'll breast feed them', but he takes no notice of me. And he threatens that if I breast feed he'll take another wife. 'I need a woman all the time', he says. 'I'm not going to stand for you spending your time fussing around children.'

Aftab: Oh, *so that's it!* I never knew. God save us from men like that. Even animals shrink from that. They're worse than animals. God save a woman from falling into the clutches of men like that. Things used not to be like that. But now every wretched man you hear about is like it. Now my husband—well, he's an old man now, but even when he was young he never went too far. (Smiling) By God, I used to keep him on tenterhooks for hours...!

Muhammadi: (sighing) We all have our own fate. What you've just said reminds me I didn't finish telling you about the lady doctor. We went off onto other things. When she said I was two months pregnant, she looked at me in astonishment and said, 'Begam Sahib, you were telling me that you've been confined to bed for the last four months, and getting a temperature every evening. And Dr Ghiyas was telling me the same thing—that you've been running a temperature of 100 to 101 every evening. And you mean to tell me that in spite of that your husband...?' I said, 'Oh, miss *you're* all right. You earn your living; you eat well and sleep soundly. It's not like that with us. These fellows don't care whether they go to heaven or to hell when they die. They know what they want here. They don't care whether their wives, poor wretches, live or die. Men want their satisfaction.' The poor woman had nothing to say to that. She said, 'You're seriously ill....' Poor woman—and don't *all* the doctors say this?—How can your children be strong and healthy when, for one thing, you're so weak, and then you have children so quickly—one after another.' What can we do? We'd have been better off if we'd been Christians.

Aftab: Don't! Don't say such wicked things! May God destroy these unbelievers! I've only one son and he's gone and married a Christian. I can't tell you how I was looking forward to arranging his marriage. I'd wanted to marry him to my brother's daughter Vahida. I'd planned their marriage when they were children.[10] And now my brother has got fed up and he's got Vahida engaged. It's agony to think that my son's married a stranger. Better he'd never been born. As far as I'm concerned he's dead already.

Muhammadi: How can you have the heart to curse him like that? He's the one who'll support you when you're old. He'll come round and be all right one day.

Aftab: Oh no he won't. It's two years now, and I haven't set eyes on him. I long to see him. He lives here in the city and he never even comes my way. I hear now that he's getting 150 a month. I thank God that at any rate there are no children yet. My one prayer to God is that even if there is no one to light a lamp on my grave when I'm dead,[11] He'll see to it that this bastard Christian woman may she die young!—never bears him a child. Anyway, sister, what's the point of telling people your troubles? Everyone's got troubles of their own.... And, Muhammadi Begam, have you heard? Mirza[12] Maqbul Ali Shah has married again. Two of his wives have died. He's even got grandchildren who have children of their own. And this new wife —how innocent she looks!— is quite a young woman, quite young; not more than twenty at the most. What rotten luck for her! But the poor girl still has six sisters not yet married. That's why her parents, poor people....

(At this point a boy of about twelve, his paijama bottoms caked with mud, bursts open the door and runs into the room. He has a cotton reel in one hand and scissors in the other. A sturdy-looking young girl [the boy's elder sister Sabira] in tight paijama and grubby clothes and trailing dupatta runs in after him.)[13]

Sabira: Mummy, Mirza[14] won't let me alone. Look (she raises her *kurta*),[15] he's cut my new paijama. I wasn't even saying anything to him. I was sitting there quietly sewing the buttons on daddy's *achkan.*[16] And look, he's torn the end of my dupatta.

(She turns her face to the wall and starts crying with frustration.)

Mirza: (Mimicking his sister) Boo hoo! You don't tell her what you were doing. Sewing, were you? Shall I tell mummy you were reading trashy books? *The Loving Friend,* or *The Lively Lad.* I didn't see properly what it was.

Sabira: (Turning quickly towards him) For God's sake don't tell such big lies. Mummy, I swear by God I was reading Maulvi Ashraf Ali Thanavi's *Bahishti Zewar.*[17] He pestered me to show him, and I wouldn't so he cut my paijama. You never say anything to *him.*[18]

Muhammadi: (Beating her forehead in exasperation, and speaking sarcastically) Well done. Daughter, well done! It's all the same to you whether your mother lives or dies. Let alone helping her, you quarrel with your young brothers and sisters. (Turning to the boy) And this pest is pestering one or other of them all day long. Get out if here!

Aftab: Give the scissors to me, son. Look at you, pestering your big sister. How much longer will she be here with you? In a year or two she'll be married and off to her in-laws. Then you'll be longing to see her.

> (*Sabira feels shy and bows her head at this and quietly creeps away. Mirza makes a horse out of his mother's bolster, sits astride it a few minutes and then begins to jump about on it.*)

Mirza: Well, why wouldn't she show me the book, then?

Muhammadi: For God's sake Mirza have mercy on me and don't shake me up like this. You're making my whole body shake. My heart's beating fast. For God's sake go out. Go to your dad. And the *maulvi* sahib[19] will be coming. Have you learnt the lesson he set you?

Aftab: You've got too many children. Bless you, the house is full of them. But all this noise wears you out. And me, I sit in the house all day like someone hired to scare the crows. He comes home to say his prayers, sits with me a few minutes and goes off to the sitting room. God shouldn't make anyone so lonely. And all the hopes I had....

> (*The door opens and a maidservant comes in carrying a dish.*)

Servant: Salaam, begam sahib. (Turning to Aftab) Salaam: I was just on my way to your house with your share. (Turning again to Muhammadi) How are you, begam sahib? And the children, God keep them, how are they?

Muhammadi: Oh, just as usual. Is your mistress well? Are all the children well? Congratulations on the birth of the grandchild.[20] That'll be *panjeri.*[21] (Turning to her own maidservant) Here, Rahiman, take the dish and empty it. (She opens a box) Sister [Aftab], give her[22] a paan.

Aftab: Rahiman, I'll take my share here too. (She begins to make up a paan. Muhammadi gives two annas to the servant who has brought the dish.)

Muhammadi: My best greetings and best wishes to everyone. One day if I feel well enough I'll come. I'm longing to see you all again. I very much want to see the children. And tell your mistress from me, 'It seems you've sworn not to come and see me.'

> (*Aftab gives her a paan and takes two annas from her waistband to give her.*)

Servant: Begam Sahib, my mistress too often thinks of you. She just doesn't have time to come and see you. And these days, of course, the house is full of people. Everyone has come.[23]

Aftab: Give my blessing to Sultan Dulhan, and my congratulations on the birth of her grandson. God willing, I'll come on Friday.

(The servant takes both the dishes and leaves.)

Muhammadi: Sultan is a really good manager. Her husband's never earned more than forty rupees a month, but, God bless her, she manages so well that she's done everything necessary—arranged the marriage of her sons, and her daughters. And now her son's got a good job—about a hundred and twenty rupees. And prospects of promotion too.

Aftab: Yes: he's got a good wife too. (Sighing deeply) We all have what's coming to us. Here's me. Well, never mind about that now. Tell me, is there any news of your cousin Razia? Your uncle[24] was in such a hurry to get her first engaged and then married that he didn't even invite anyone.

Muhammadi: No, he didn't, but what of it? He had double and triple portions of food sent to every house. And the poor girl was married like that in a hurry, because he was afraid for his family's good name. And God bless him for it!

Aftab: Oh, so *that* was it. I'd no idea. What happened, then?

Muhammadi: You don't know? Well, everyone knows now. The poor girl's no age at all—only two and a bit years older than my Sabira. It was after I was married that she was born, when my younger uncle[25] came back from Calcutta. He'd been there years. We were all there to welcome him back. Granny, poor woman—she had the palsy—was happier than any of us. When Razia was born I took her home with me for a while. Her mother went off to her parents and Razia stayed on with me three or four months. And after that too she often stayed for long periods in my house. She loved us—her father's people—and didn't like her mother's people at all. And it was quite natural that she should stay on. I was like an elder sister to her. I had no idea it would lead to any trouble.

Well, eventually she went back to her mother's house. Then one day, not long ago. she sent me a note begging me to come quickly. I don't know how to tell you what happened next. When I got there her grandmother[26]—you've seen her; you know what she's like, how big she talks. Well, she gave me a grand welcome. Razia gave me a note when she wasn't looking, and said quietly 'Uncle[27] comes to see us every day and mummy makes a great fuss of him and talks secretly with him.' She's a young, unmarried girl. How could she say more than that? Poor girl, it took courage to say even that much. When I looked at the note it was one from my husband to Razia—a more passionate love letter than the ones you read in novels. I was furious. I warned her not to say anything to anyone and said I wouldn't mention her name to anyone. I got home burning with rage. I spoke to him about it. Sister, I swear to you he looked me straight in the eye and said, 'What's wrong with it? And I'm going to marry Razia even if I have to divorce you. I said. 'Are you in your right mind? Or have you completely lost your senses? She comes from a respectable family. If you so much as mention her name her father and his brother will make mincemeat of you. Don't even think of it![28]

Aftab: That means her mother must have fixed it all up secretly. That's why he came out with it so boldly.

Muhammadi: Of course! God forgive her, she's always hated mummy and me. Even when mummy was ill she'd tell her to her face, and swear to it, that she wouldn't rest until she'd ruined me. And it wasn't only us. She had the same grudge against mummy's elder brother. And since Razia's engagement had been fixed with a boy in her father's family—our side of the family—there were quarrels every day, with her mother insisting that she wouldn't marry her daughter to anyone in her enemies' family.

Aftab (Laughing): And, sister, what makes your husband such a wonderful catch? He's got a wife and children. Granted, he has money. But the family she was to be married into isn't badly off either. Have respectable families ever done this? Those wretched Panjabis will marry off two of their daughters—two sisters—to the same man,[29] but we never do that. Well, in these days *anything* can happen....Well, what happened then?

Muhammadi: When I got angry and swore at him he began to implore me. 'I've fallen in love with her. For God's sake help me. It's your duty to help me. He'd sit down and open the Holy Quran and read out verses telling me all that would happen to me in the next world if I didn't help him. But could hell fire be any worse than this fire that I burn in all the time? Well, he kept telling me all the time that he'd go mad. He'd shut himself in his room and lie face down and cry 'Razia! Razia!' And I'd sit there listening to it all. By God. I was in such a state that I thought. 'All this money is a curse. I wish we had only dry bread, and happiness.' Sister, give me a paan. All this talking's made my mouth dry.

(She pours water from the pitcher and drinks it. Aftab eats a paan and gives Muhammadi one.)

Anyway, things went on like this, with him using lover's language about that poor innocent girl and me listening to it all and feeling all choked by it. And the girl's mother's still making the same fuss of him. 'Razia, your uncle has come to see you. Give him a paan. Give him some cardamoms.'

Aftab: So all this was her doing.

Muhammadi: Of course. The girl would cry for hours together, and if I chanced to see her she'd pour out her heart to me. For a month I said nothing. Then one day both my uncles[30] came to see me and I said, 'Well uncle, has Razia's engagement fallen through?' They both panicked. I'd restrained myself all this time and now I told them the whole story. They must have talked to each other about it, because three days later Razia was married.

Aftab: My God!

Muhammadi: But for six months after that he[31] never came near me—was off in Chavari[32] all the time. That suited me fine. As God's my witness, the day he goes off somewhere I sleep soundly at night. But every day it's, 'You're always ill. How long am I to put up with it? I'm going to marry again.' And on top of that. 'You must arrange a marriage for me. The *shariat*[33] allows a man four wives; so why shouldn't I marry again?' I told him, 'Go ahead. Sabira's due to be married in a year's time. You can get married at the same time. You'll be able to take your grandchild and your new wife's baby on your knee at the same time.' Then he starts to row with me. 'What do women know about it? God didn't give them feeling.' I said, 'And it seems to me that He gave you the feelings of all men put together for your share.'

Aftab: (Flaring up) Muhammadi Begam, wherever you look these days you see this going on everywhere. The men win either way, every time. It's too much! He not only wants to marry again: on top of that his wife, poor wretch, is to arrange it for him.

Muhammadi: And that's what burns me up and makes me pray for death. I'm ill all the time. Then the children are always falling ill. Well the eldest boy, bless him, is quite strong; but the little ones are always ailing. And all this means that there's no longer any joy in living. And I know that he'll marry again. No doubt about it. And I live in fear all the time. God take me away before I have to see the face of a co-wife. And I can't tell you all the things I've done from fear of that. I've had myself operated on twice.

Aftab: Yes. I'd heard that you'd had something done so that you couldn't have any more children.

Muhammadi: Who told you that? It wasn't that at all. My womb and all my lower parts had fallen. I got it put right so that he could get the same pleasure again as he'd got from a newly-married wife. But when a woman has a baby every year how *can* she stay in good shape? It slipped down again. And then he went on at me and threatened me until he got me butchered again. And even then he wasn't satisfied.

(The call to prayer is heard from the mosque nearby.)

Aftab: Good heavens, it's time now for the *zuhr*[34] prayer. I was so busy talking that I forgot everything else. (She closes the draw-string bag.) Now I'll have to say the prayer here before I go. My husband will be expecting me, poor man.

Muhammadi: Well sister, because of you coming I've got a lot of things off my chest. You must come a bit more often. *I'm* ill, I can't get about any more.

(Calling her servants.)

Rahiman! Rahiman! Gulshabo!

(Rahiman enters.)

Go and see to Bari Begam's ablutions.[35] And put down the prayer mat in the little room.

Notes

1. Begam: 'lady'. The usual word used in addressing, or speaking of, a lady of good family, even when one is on quite informal terms with her.

2. She is not really her sister, but a friend will commonly be so addressed.

3. She means Muhammadi's mother.

4. *domnian* A low caste of singers and dancers who regularly provide entertainment on festive occasions

5. *hakim:* A practitioner of the traditional Greek medicine, transmitted by the Arabs to the rest of the world and still current amongst the Muslims in South Asia. People will commonly have resort to this as well as to modern medicine.

6. *Begam Sahib;* The standard way of addressing a lady.

7. *paijama:* The word from which English 'pyjamas' is derived. But *paijama* (which means literally 'leg gament') is something different, corresponding to pyjama trousers, but not open at the front. Paijamas come in different styles, some have wide legs, and some fit tightly from the knee downwards. They are not, as in English usage, specifically night clothes. In Western society people customarily change clothes when they get up in the morning: in South Asia they change when they are about to go out.

8. *dupatta:* note in Russell trans., op. cit., p. 466.

9. She means prostitutes.

10. This was, and is, commonly done. Parents of cousins will plan their marriage while they are still children.

11. That is, after my death my son, and after him *his* son should keep a lamp burning on my grave. But I hope he never has a son.

12. Mirza is the form of address (or reference) to a person of Turkish

Mughal descent. It is used not only in formal contexts but in quite informal ones too, where English usage would be to use the person's name.

13. Apart from the dupatta, men's and women's clothing is more or less identical.

14. See p. 39 in Russell trans., op. cit., p. 466.

15. *kurta*: see note p. 24 in ibid.

16. *achkan*: A long coat that buttons up the front to the neck.

17. A famous book written about 1901–3 to teach Muslim women their religious duties. It is still very widely read.

18. In South Asian families it is accepted as a matter of course that sons receive favored treatment—which does not mean that daughters never complain about this!

19. *maulvi*: A Muslim divine, one of whose regular employments is to teach children to read the Quran—'read' in the sense of pronouncing the words correctly. The child does not lean what the words mean. Those who can afford it have the maulvi come to the child's home to do this.

20. Son's son.

21. *panjeri*: A sweetmeat made of five ingredients. When anyone has good news to impart to relations and friends the custom is to send sweets to them.

22. The other lady's servant, who has brought the panjeri.

23. To celebrate the birth of the grandchild.

24. That is, Razia's father. At this point it becomes difficult to follow the narrative unless one knows something of South Asian Muslim family relationships and marriages. When cousins marry, as they frequently do, the spouses' in-laws, obviously, are also related to them both. It is not considered proper to speak to, or of, one's elder relatives by name, and this creates difficulties for the translator into English because (e.g.) English 'uncle' covers a whole range of people each of whom in Urdu, has a different term to describe him. Thus, e.g. one's father's younger brother is one's *chacha* while one's mother's brother is one's *mamun*. Terms such as these recur in the dialogue that follows, and in English one has to find other means of making clear who is who. It must further be explained that family ties are far more binding than they are in Western society, and a whole hierarchy of relationships is carefully observed. In traditional families who can afford it you will find, living under a roof, a father and mother, *all* their sons, their daughters until they are married and go off to their husband's families, and the wives and children of the grown up sons. Cousins growing up in such a household are virtually brothers and sisters to one another, and are so regarded, so that when a South Asian Muslim tells you (e.g.) 'He is my brother' he may well be speaking of his cousins, and not of one, who, if he wishes to distinguish him from his cousin, he will call his 'real brother' as distinct from his 'cousin brother'.

25. Mother's brother, and Razia's father.

26. Mother's mother.

27. Muhammadi's husband.

28. Several common attitudes are involved here. Though a Muslim man may have up to four wives at any one time, and though he is permitted to divorce a wife simply by repeating the appropriate words three times in front of witnesses, public opinion strongly disapproves both of divorce and of the taking of a second wife unless (as sometimes happens) the first willingly agrees to this. Marriage of an older man to a much younger woman is also frowned upon. Finally, as subsequent dialogue shows, the fact that Muhammadi and Razia were virtually sisters would, in most people's eyes, have ruled out marriage altogether.

29. This, I am told, is a baseless slander against Panjabis. The Quran forbids this, and no Muslim violates this prohibition. Prejudice against Panjabis was (and still is) common in old Delhi Urdu-speaking families.

30. Razia's father and his brother.

31. She means her husband.

32. Delhi's red light district.

33. *shariat*: Muslim law.

34. *zuhr*: One of the five daily prayers prescribed by Islam; *zuhr* is said just after midday.

35. *Bari Begam*: 'The elder lady'—a polite way of referring to Aftab. Ablutions a ceremonial washing before prayer.

Yashpal

A take on purdah by the Marxist writer Yashpal (1903–76), 'The Curtain' tells us about the desperate respectability of a family that is sliding down to destitution. The author of over forty-two books, Yashpal is best known for his novel about the results of partition, *Jhutha Sach* (The False Truth), published in 1958.

The Curtain

Chaudhri Peerbuksh's grandfather had been an Inspector in the Octroi Department. A man of some means, he had built a small house and had his sons educated. The elder, Fazal Qurban, after passing the Matriculation Examination, secured a clerk's post in the railways. The younger, Ilahi Buksh, got a job in the Postal Department. Chaudhri Saheb had the satisfaction of seeing his sons married and of becoming a grandfather. His only regret was that his sons did not advance in life; they remained in the grades of Rs 30 and 40 a month.

Chaudhri Saheb would often recall his own times. 'Those were the days', he would say. 'Boys who passed the middle school examination became district officers. What have the times come to! Even matriculates, good in English, rot all their lives in forty rupee clerical jobs.' The old man died, without his hopes fulfilled.

But Allah is great! The sons, by increasing the number of their progeny, more than made up for their miserable jobs. Fazal Qurban was blessed with four sons and three daughters. Ilahi Buksh had four sons and two daughters.

The Chaudhris called their modest house a *haveli*—mansion. It consisted of just two rooms, the inner called the harem which was for

Yashpal, 'The Curtain', in Rajendra Awasthy (ed.), *Hindi Short Stories*, Delhi: Vikas, 1981.

the ladies and the outer where old Peerbuksh had smoked his hookah. After his death, as the family increased, the sitting-room too had to be surrendered to give them privacy. Appearances had to be kept up. The curtain had to be of right material. Old carpets came in quite handy.

A third generation of Chaudhris entered the scene. One marriage followed another. The house became too small and many were compelled to seek places elsewhere. Ilahi Buksh's eldest son passed the Matriculation examination and got a job in the Postal Department at twenty rupees a month. The second son became a compounder in a hospital. The third, a promising lad, won a scholarship and, after passing the middle standard examination, became a teacher in a village school.

The youngest son, Peerbuksh, could not go beyond the primary standard. School fees, books, stationery—proved too much for the father. Nevertheless, Peerbuksh was married at the customary age. And, with God's grace, it did not take long for him to become a father. Conscious of the family's prestige he disdained soiling his hands with manual work and instead took a job as a clerk in a small oil press.

One cannot go far on twelve rupees a month. Peerbuksh had to rent a house at two rupees a month in the slums. The neighbourhood was inhabited by menials. At one end of the unpaved lane was the municipal tap which dripped and turned the lane into a sewer where flies and mosquitoes swarmed. In front of his house was Ramzani dhobi's oven with the acrid smell of caustic soda oozing from the cauldron of soiled washings. To his right were houses of cobblers who worked on raw hides and to his left lived a gang of coolies, employed in the local workshop.

In the entire locality, Chaudhri Peerbuksh was the only man who could read and write and boast of a shirt on his back. And his was the only house that had the distinction of having a curtain across its door. People addressed Peerbuksh as Munshiji and talked to him respectfully. No one had seen the women of the house ever stepping into the lane. God willed that only daughters would be born to Chaudhri's wife. Till the age of six or seven, the girls came out into the lane to play or to fetch water but as they grew up they were confined to seclusion. Morning and evening, Peerbuksh would himself fill pitchers of water from the municipal tap and carry them home.

After fifteen years' service, Peerbuksh's salary increased from twelve to twenty rupees. God's blessing takes many forms. In fifteen years, he brought five children into the world—three daughters followed by two sons. A large family has many hardships. Sometimes a child is taken ill, sometimes its mother. Doctors and medicines cost money.

At the oil factory, employees were paid on the seventh of each month. To ask for an advance was to invite the owner's wrath. When hard-pressed for money, Chaudhri would take some household articles to the pawn shop. The broker would drive a hard bargain, paying him half a rupee for an article worth a rupee. And by adding interest, the loan of half a rupee would swell to more than one rupee. What went out of the house never came back.

Chaudhri Peerbuksh was respected because of the curtain that hung across his door. Although tattered, it hung as a symbol of respectability. When it threatened to fall apart, feminine hands from behind the curtain would put it together.

In course of time, panels of the door grew rotten. Suraj Pande, the owner of the house, did not care. When Chaudhri complained, he said sarcastically, 'Do I charge you very much? Only two rupees a month. And that remains unpaid for months. If you don't like the house, quit.'

At last the doors fell off their hinges and at night, Chaudhri had to push them back into their frames. Fear of thieves kept him up all night. More than theft, Chaudhri worried about his prestige and the respect of the ladies of the family. The doorless curtain was the last bulwark of his prestige. One night, a storm reduced the already threadbare curtain to shreds. Next morning, another cotton carpet, the last of his inheritance, took its place.

'Chaudhri Saheb, these are hard times. Why waste a carpet', his neighbours said. 'Go to the bazar and get a piece of tarpaulin or sack cloth.' Chaudhri Peerbuksh had often enquired the price of old tarpaulin. But he could not afford to throw away half a rupee on two yards of old tarpaulin. 'I don't care', he would laugh. 'In our family we always used to hang a carpet outside our mansion.'

The clothes of the ladies of the house also became tattered. On his salary, Chaudhri could barely afford flour for one meal a day; and buying new clothes was out of the question. His own shirt and pyjamas had so many patches that they defied further patching.

Peerbuksh's mother came to stay with him to look after her daughter-in-law when she was expecting her second child. None of her other sons came to fetch the old woman, and there she was for the rest of her life.

When a poor man has nothing, a Pathan money-lender is his only refuge. At the birth of his son Barkat, Chaudhri was forced to take a loan of four rupees from Babbarali Khan.

Babbarali Khan did good business in the locality. Cobblers and coolies from the workshops and, occasionally, the Ramzani dhobi took loans from him. Chaudhari had seen the Pathan hammering at the doors of his debtors with his staff. He regarded the Pathan as the devil himself, but being reduced to penury he had to take recourse to him. He borrowed four rupees at 25 per cent interest. Out of deference for Chaudhri, the money-lender agreed to the repayment in eight instalments of one rupee per month.

For seven months Chaudhri somehow managed to keep to the schedule. But in the eighth month, the price of millets shot up and it became impossible for Chaudhri to pay off his debt. The Pathan knocked at his door. Peerbuksh cringed before him and, touching his beard, swore by Allah that he would pay off the final instalment by the next month and, to make up for the delay, throw in an additional quarter rupee, for good measure. The Pathan relented.

The following month proved to be worse. Chaudhri's wife's health deteriorated. She had to be put on a diet of wheat chapatis. Wheat was not easy to come by and, when available, it sold at one and three quarter kilo per rupee. Chaudhri got an extra four rupees by way of dearness allowance. But he had already taken an advance on many occasions. On pay day, after deductions, he got only four rupees.

For one week his family had lived on the verge of starvation. Sometimes he fed his children on two pice worth of spinach and at others they managed with a bowlful of thin millet gruel. Chaudhri could not bring himself to part with a rupee and a quarter and pay it to the Pathan.

On his way back from the factory he went to the grain market. After two hours, when he felt sure that the Pathan would be gone from his door, he bought some grain and hurried homewards. He dragged his feet, thinking of his four starving children and the babe who had become thin as a reed for lack of milk in the mother's breasts. The haggard face of his own senile mother who constantly blubbered for food, danced before his eyes. His heart pounded with fear. 'Allah knows my plight. I'm in his hands!'

Having failed to meet Chaudhri the previous night, the Pathan came early next morning. Chaudhri had kept awake all night trying to invent excuses by which he could put off the money-lender.

'The factory owner is out of town for four days', he said. 'No salaries can be paid without his signature. I'll pay you the moment I receive my salary.'

It sounded plausible. But the Pathan kept growling. 'Do you think

I've come all the way from my country to dole out money in charity?'
he barked. 'I have also to think of my family. If you do not pay up in
four days, there is going to be serious trouble.'

Chaudhri had no money on the fifth day. The sixth day, as luck would
have it, happened to be a Sunday. Although it was holiday, Chaudhri
slipped away from his house early in the morning. He called on many
friends. After exchanging some trivialities, he made a casual request for
a small loan. 'By the way, could you spare me twenty annas just for a
day? I've to meet some unforeseen expenses.' He was out of luck. All
he got was the same answer. 'One must be lucky indeed to have spare
money these days.'

It was afternoon now. Chaudhri mustered courage to return home.
He was told that, true to his word, the Pathan had called. He had waited
outside the door for an hour, shouting abuses and lashing at the curtain
with his staff, when, from the other side of the curtain, Chaudhri's old
mother explained that her son had gone out to arrange for some money.
The man had become all the more abusive. 'I know that bastard!' he
shouted. 'He is hiding inside the house. I'll come back in four hours. If
he doesn't pay up I'll flay him and sell his skin in the bazar!'

Four hours later, the Pathan was at Chaudhri's door. 'Chaudhri!' he
called in a menacing voice as he beat at the curtain with his rod.
Although life seemed to have drained out of his body, Chaudhri dragged
himself on his feet and went to the door. 'You rogue! Trying to hide
from me?' Foul abuses tumbled from his mouth.

Chaudhri touched the Pathan's knees, expostulated with him, explaining his helplessness. The Pathan's temper grew. The coolies and
cobblers from the neighbourhood collected at Chaudhri's door.

'Why did you take the money if you can't repay it?' he thundered, as
he stamped his rod on the ground. 'Where is your salary, you son of a
pig? How dare you swallow my money? I'll flay you. If you are a
pauper, why this pretence of respectability?' He pounded at the curtain
with his staff. 'You better bring out your wife's jewellery, give me your
utensils, give me anything. I'll not budge till I have my money.'

Chaudhri Peerbuksh raised his hands towards the sky and invoking
Allah's blessings for the Pathan he told him in a tone of abject surrender
that he had neither money nor utensils nor any clothes to give. If the
Pathan so desired he could pull off the skin from his body and sell it in
the bazar. Then he whined for mercy in Allah's name.

The Pathan flared up. 'What good are Allah's blessings to me?' he
shouted. 'And what use is your skin to me? I won't even make a pair of
shoes. This curtain is more useful than your skin.'

With a violent tug he pulled down the curtain from the door. As the curtain fell on the ground Chaudhri felt that his life had snapped with it. His legs shook and he collapsed on the ground.

Chaudhri's mother, wife and daughters assembled in the courtyard. As the curtain was suddenly whisked away from the door, they shrank back as if someone had ripped their clothes and denuded them. The curtain was the only thing which stood between their nakedness and the outside world.

The by-standers averted their faces.

'Oh God! What a cursed sight!' The Pathan spat disgust and flung the curtain back into the courtyard.

The crowd melted away. When Chaudhri came to himself he found the curtain lying in the courtyard. But he had no heart to put it up on the door. Perhaps it was no longer necessary.

Rajinder Singh Bedi

Rajinder Singh Bedi (1915–84) was one of the major voices of the Progressive Writers Association. Of 'Lajwanti', a story placed in the period after Partition, Ralph Russell writes, 'Bedi's primary intention in the story is to highlight the plight of women in a society in which men are obsessed by concern for their own honour and the women's deepest feelings and needs are felt to be irrelevant to this. But, typically, he is also concerned to show how complex are people's emotional needs and complexities.'

Rajinder Singh Bedi started his wring career in Lahore where he worked for All India Radio. He wrote short stories and novels, and his novel *Ek Chader Maili Si* (A Torn and Dirty Sheet) won the Sahitya Akademi Award in 1972. He also wrote the dialogue for films such as *Mirza Ghalib,* Bimal Roy's *Devdas* and others.

Lajwanti

> *The Lajwanti leaves droop at the mere touch.*
> (A Punjabi folk song)

After the blood-bath of the Partition, the wounded whose number was legion, wiped the blood from their bodies and rising to their feet, turned their attention to those who though looking unharmed had their hearts full of anguish.

Rehabilitation Committees were being set up in every lane and by-lane of the city which with great fervour tried to rehabilitate the uprooted people in business, on the land and in homes. But there was one aspect of rehabilitation to which they had paid scant attention—the task of rehabilitating abducted women. However, this programme also soon got under way, its slogan being, 'Give them a place in your hearts'.

Rajinder Singh Bedi, 'Lajwanti', in Jai Ratan (trans.), *Selected Short Stories*, New Delhi: Sahitya Academy, 1989.

The Committee set up for this purpose met with great opposition, specially from the orthodox people living around Narain Bawa's temple.

To give this programme a tangible shape the residents of Mohalla Shakoor had taken the lead, Babu Sunderlal being the Secretary of the newly formed Committee. He had been elected to this office with a majority of eleven votes. A prominent local lawyer was elected its President. In the opinion of the old petition writer of Chowki Kalan and other influential residents of the place they couldn't have selected a better man than Babu Sunderlal for the Secretary's post. His own wife having been abducted he would put his heart and soul in the work. She had still to be traced and restored to her husband. And coincidentally, her name was Lajo—Lajwanti.

Early in the morning the members of the Rehabilitation Committee would lead a singing party which went round singing, 'The Lajwanti leaves droop at the mere touch'. Sunderlal's friends, Neki Ram and Rasalu would sing lustily but Babu Sunderlal's voice would falter and trait into silence. He would walk in silence thinking of Lajwanti. Where was Lajwanti now? In what condition? Did she still think of him? Would she ever come back? Sunderlal's feet would shake as he walked along the hard, cobbled road.

A time came when he stopped thinking of Lajwanti. He had abandoned all hope of retrieving her, his own personal loss having become a part of the undefined loss of the people in general. To drown his sorrows he had taken to social service. Even so, when he raised his voice to sing in unison with others he could not help reflecting on the frailty of the human heart. It could get hurt so easily, like the *lajwanti* plant whose leaves curled up at the mere touch of a finger .

Sunderlal had been very harsh with his wife, Lajwanti. He would keep an eye on her all the time, watching her where she sat, where she went and what she ate. He would beat her up at the slightest pretext.

And his poor Lajo! A simple country girl, she was delicate and slender like a branch of the mulberry tree. Her complexion had turned swarthy by remaining too much in the sun and life in the open had filled her with animal spirits. She ran about with uninhibited grace in her village like dew drops on a leaf. Her slimness was not the result of ill-health but bespoke of her inherent strength. When the heavily-built Sunderlal first set his eyes upon her, his mind wavered. But later when he saw that she could easily carry heavy loads without a scowl on her face and even put up with his beating without wincing he felt greatly reassured. It made him harsher still and he increased the doze of beatings, never caring for a moment to consider that anything carried beyond certain limits undermined one's patience and endurance, Lajwanti herself played a part in blurring these limits. She would not give herself up to despondency for long. After a beating Sunderlal had only to throw a smile in her direction. A big smile would appear on her face and she would come bounding towards him. 'Beat me again and see what happens!' she would say in mock anger. It was clear that she had already forgiven him for his beating. Like the other girls of her village she knew that all husbands beat their wives as a matter of course. If a woman rebelled, the other women would put their fingers on their noses and say, 'Call him a man do you? He can't even keep a woman on leash!'

This beating was even cannonised in songs. Sometimes even Lajo sang:

> No city boy for me
> He wears heavy boots
> And I have such a slender waist!

And the irony of it, she took a liking for a city boy the first time she saw him and ended up by marrying him. The city boy was no other than Sunderlal.

He had come to Lajwanti's village as a member of a friend's wedding party. He had whispered in the bridegroom's ear, 'Your younger sister-in-law is a peach—very coy, very juicy. And so must be your bride. Sour-sweet to make your mouth tingle!' These words had fallen on Lajo's ears and she had immediately taken a fancy for Sunderlal, forgetting that he was wearing such heavy boots and her own waist was so slim.

Such were the thoughts occupying Sunderlal's mind as he went round with the morning singing party. If only he could find Lajo again! He would nestle her in his heart like a devoted husband and impress upon the people that these hapless women were not to be blamed. They had fallen into the hands of those lechers and rioters to become their playthings. They were the victims of circumstances and a society that refused to take them back was rotten to its core and deserved to be wiped out of existence. Bearing in mind all those hypothetical cases he would come up with a strong plea to rehabilitate these women and accord them a status as is normally due to a mother, a wife, a sister in every home. He would further urge upon the people not to remind these women even by a hint about the sordid time they had passed through. He reminded them that they were sensitive like the *lajwanti* plant which withered at the touch of a finger.

In order to propagate the idea of 'Give them a place in your hearts' the Mohalla Shakoor Committee took out singing parties, morning after morning. They would start at four in the morning, considered to be the ideal time for the purpose when it was so peaceful and quiet and people were receptive to suggestions. Even the street dogs who stayed awake all night acting as self-styled night watchmen had retired to seek the dying warmth of *tandoors* (ovens). Men whose bodies were lapping up cosy warmth of winter beds would mutter on hearing the singing party passing in the street below, 'Oh, the same people again!' And then they would unwillingly lend their ears to Babu Sunderlal's harangue. Women who had managed to come across the border from Pakistan would lie sprawled in their beds like disintegrating cauliflowers while their stalk-like stiff husbands who lay by their sides would grunt expressing their pique. Children who woke up momentarily would mimic the words of the songs and slide back into sleep again.

The words heard at dawn leave their impression on the mind and keep buzzing in the ears throughout the day. Often a man keeps humming them without understanding their meaning.

It was the cumulative effect of these slogans and harangues that when Miss Mridula Sarabhai arranged for the exchange of abducted women between India and Pakistan some men of Mohalla Shakoor tacitly agreed to take their women back. The relatives of these rescued women assembled at the outpost of Chowki Kalan to receive them. For sometime the abducted women and their menfolk eyed each other in awkward silence. Then with a nod of their heads the men signified their acceptance and walked off with bowed heads, their women following them. A new chapter had begun in their lives to re-build their homes. Rasalu, Neki Ram and Sunderlal shouted 'Mohinder Singh Zindabad! Sohan Lal Zindabad!' thus lauding the men whose women had joined them.

There were many among the abducted women whom their husbands, parents, brothers or sisters had even refused to recognise. Why couldn't they have killed themselves? these people asked. To save their honour they could have taken poison or jumped into a well. They were indeed cowards to have clung to their lives when there were examples of thousands of women who had taken their own lives before giving the ravishers a chance to dishonour them. But while censuring these women they forgot that even to live required great courage. What mental tortures they would have gone through, with what dazed eyes they would have struggled against death to live in this hostile world where one day even their husbands would refuse to own them. These women would silently repeat their names to themselves—*Sohagwanti*, one who had the dignity of marital status. Once their names had a great meaning for them but now the same names had become a rebuke.

Locating her brother in the crowd, Sohagwanti said, 'Bihari, my brother, so you also refuse to recognize me? Don't you remember I had carried you in my arms when you were a little child?' But Bihari tried to slip away. While doing so his gaze fell upon his parents who had steeled their hearts and were helplessly looking at Narain Bawa while Narain Bawa was looking up at the heaven—the heaven that had no reality. Which was merely an illusion, a myth, a boundary line beyond which stretched a great void where there was nothing to see.

Miss Sarabhai had brought a truckload of Hindu women from Pakistan in exchange for Muslim women. Lajwanti was not among them. Sunderlal watched with great expectancy till the last woman had got down from the truck. Sorely disappointed, he re-dedicated himself to Committee work with redoubled zeal. Now he took out singing parties both in the morning and evening. Periodically, he would also organise street corner meetings. The venerable lawyer Sufi Kalka Prasad addressed these meetings in his halting wheezy voice while Rasalu stood by holding a spittoon. Strange noises burst forth from the microphone till the lawyer's speech lasted. Then Neki Ram, the petition writer would take over. He would go on and on quoting from the Scriptures and the *shastras* to lend weight to the points he made. But with every sentence he drifted away from what he really purported to say. Seeing that the real purpose of the meeting was getting confused and he was fast losing ground, Sunderlal would bravely rise to stem the rot but would sit down after spewing out a sentence or two, his voice having choked and his eyes brimming with tears. A hush would fall over the audience. But his two sentences which came from the depth of his anguished heart had more impact than the meandering speech of the aged lawyer, Kalka Prasad. The emotions of the audience drained out with the end of the speeches and they returned home empty-headed.

One day the Committee people came out in the afternoon a little in advance of their usual time and made an inroad into the temple zone considered to be the stronghold of fossilized orthodoxy.

Outside the temple precincts some people were sitting on a cement platform under a Peepul tree listening to a discourse on the *Ramayana*. Narain Bawa was narrating an episode from the great epic where a washerman had turned out his wife from his house saying that he was not Raja Ram Chander who took back Sita after she had lived for many years under Ravana's tutelage. The rebuke had recoiled against Lord

Rama and he had turned out Sita, the embodiment of purity, from his palace although at that time she was far gone with child

'Could one find a better example of purity of mind, an example of *Ram Rajya?*' Narain Bawa asked his audience. 'See, here even the voice of an insignificant washerman counted. This was real *Ram Rajya,* the realm of God on earth.'

The Committee procession had stopped near the temple and some of the processionists were listening to the discourse.

As Narain Bawa finished speaking, Sunderlal blurted out, 'No such *Ram Rajya* for us. We have nothing to do with it.'

'Be quiet! Who are you to interfere? Silence!' A medley of voices came from the audience.

'Nobody can stop me from speaking', Sunderlal said, breaking away from the procession.

There was a chorus of protests. 'Silence! No, we won't allow him to speak!' And then a voice came floating from a corner. 'We shall kill him!'

Narain Bawa said in a placatory tone, 'Sunderlal, you don't understand the sanctity of the holy Scriptures.'

I understand only one thing', Sunderlal retorted. 'In *Ram Rajya* they listened to a *dhobi's* voice but in the present *Ram Rajya* they refuse to listen to Sunderlal.'

The people who were going to rough up Sunderlal quickly cleared some place under the Peepul tree by sweeping away the Peepul berries. 'Give him a chance to speak', they said, sitting down.

Rasalu and Neki Ram nudged Sunderlal to speak. He said, 'Shri Ram was an exalted soul, an examplar for us. But how is it that he took a washerman's words for truth but refused to believe a great Maharani?'

Narain Bawa scratched his beard thoughtfully. 'Sunderlal, it's because Sita was his own wife. You have missed the whole point.'

'Yes, Bawa, there are many things which are beyond my comprehension', Sunderlal said. 'But I regard *Ram Rajya* as a State where a man does not suffer himself nor allows others to suffer. To be inequitable to others is as great a sin as being inequitable to one's own self. Even today Bhagwan Ram has turned out Sita because she has been forced to live with Ravana. Is she to blame for it? Like so many of our sisters and mothers, wasn't she the victim of an evil design? Was it a question of right and wrong on Sita's part or it was Ravana's palpable wickedness? Ravana, who had ten human heads and one big donkey's head. Today our own innocent Sita's have been thrown out of their homes. Sita... Lajwanti.'

Sunderlal broke down and started crying. Rasalu and Neki Ram held aloft the banner on which school children had freshly pasted paper cutouts bearing slogans. 'Sunderlal Babu Zindabad!' they shouted. 'Mahasati Sita Zindabad!' From a corner rose a solitary voice '...And Shri Ram Chander!'

There were voices from all sides, 'Silence! Silence!'

Narain Bawa's discourse which bad been going on for the past many days had suddenly come to naught. Many people rose from their seats and joined the procession which was headed by lawyer Kalka Prasad and the petition writer, Hukam Singh. They marched of triumphantly towards Chowki Kalan, tapping their old walking sticks on the ground. There were still tears in Sunderlal's eyes who was lost somewhere in the crowd. Today he had realised his plight as never before. The processionists sang with gusto as they marched: 'The Lajwanti leaves droop at the mere touch.'

The sound of the song was still echoing in the people's ears. The morning had not arrived and Mohalla Shakoor was still lost in the morning haze. The widow living in House No. 414 indolently stretched her arms in a yawn and finding that morning had not dawned again went back to sleep. Sunderlal's old village mate Lal Chand for whom Sunderlal and Kalka Prasad had obtained a ration shop through their influence came tearing through the morning darkness.

'Congratulations!' he cried sticking out his arms from under his thick cotton *chaddar*.

'Congratulations for what, Lal Chand', Sunderlal said, fixing a small piece of *gur* in his *chillum*.

'I've seen Lajo Bhabi.'

The *chillum* fell from Sunderlal's hands, scattering the tobacco laced with *gur* on the floor.

' Where?' he asked holding Lal Chand's shoulders and shaking them when a quick reply did not come.

'On the border at Wagah.'

Sunderlal let go of Lal Chand's shoulders. 'It must have been someone else', he said.

'No, Bhaiyya, it was Lajo. I'm sure of it. Lajo.'

'You recognise her?' Sunderlal asked. He picked up bits of tobacco from the floor and rubbed them on his palm. He picked the *chillum* from Rasalu's *hookah*. 'Tell me, how did you identify her?' he asked. 'Any distinguishing marks?'

'She has a tattoo mark on her chin, another on her cheek.' 'Yes, yes.' Sunderlal himself excitedly completed the description, 'and a third on her forehead.' He didn't want to be left in any doubt. He recalled all the marks Lajwanti had got tattooed on her body in childhood. He was so familiar with her body—as familiar as with green spots on a *lajwanti* leaf which fade out as the leaf droops. Lajwanti would feel embarrassed on being reminded of those marks as if all her precious secrets had been laid bare, rendering her naked. Sunderlal's body shook with an unknown fear and a wave of love surged through his heart.

'How did Lajo manage to reach the border?' he asked, gripping Lal Chand's arm.

'She came in exchange of abducted women between India and Pakistan.'

'What happened after that?' Sunderlal asked sitting stiffly on his haunches. 'Yes, what happened next?'

Rasalu sat up in his cot, coughing the rasping cough—peculiar to a tobacco smoker. 'Has Lajo really returned?' he asked.

Continuing, Lal Chand said, 'It was a fair exchange right on the Wagah border. Pakistan counted out sixteen abducted women and counted in the same number—sixteen on both sides. But there was a rumpus. Our volunteers complained that the women they were handing over to us were middle-aged and old. People gathered on both sides of the border and it appeared they were heading for a fight. Then one of their volunteers pushed Lajo forward. "Call her old, do you?" he asked. "Have a good look at her. Is any of the women you have passed on to us comparable to her!" And Lajo Bhabi stood there trying to hide her tattoo marks. The discussion became heated so that both sides threatened to take back their "goods". I cried out, 'Lajo! Lajo Bhabi!' But before I could approach her our police fell upon us and chased us away.'

Lal Chand bared his elbow to show where he had been hit by a lathi. Rasalu and Neki Ram sat silent while Sunderlal kept looking into the distance. Perhaps he was thinking of Lajo who was so near him and yet seemed to be deluding him. From his expression it appeared as if he had drearily trekked across the desert of Bikaner and had sat down to rest under a tree with his tongue hanging out and with no strength left even to say, 'Please give me some water.' He felt as if the violence which had marked the pre- and post-Partition days had not abated. Only its face had changed. Now people had become outspoken. If someone asked, 'You know there was one Lehna Singh living in Sambharwala. There was also his Bhabi Banto.' Pat would come the reply. 'Killed!' And the man would walk away without caring to note the implication of what he had said.

People had now openly started buying and selling human flesh. They would publicly examine a woman, mark her complexion, the secret contours of her body, put fingers on her tattoo marks and watch the hollows their prodding fingers made in her flesh, the paleness merging into the redness of the coursing blood. The buyer would pass on while the rejected woman, holding her *salwar* string with one hand tried to hide her face with the other and sobbed to express her humiliation.

Sunderlal was planning to leave for Amritsar on some business when he got the news of Lajo's return. The unexpected news almost swept him off his feet. He was in a quandary [sic]. Should he go to the border at Wagah to receive her there or wait at home for her arrival? He took one step towards the door and then retraced his step. He wanted to run out of the house, gather all the banners and placards he carried every day at the head of the procession and spreading them on the floor, sit in their midst and cry his heart out. But being charry [sic] of displaying his feelings so openly, he suppressed the tug-of-war that was going in his mind and proceeded towards the Chowki Kalan police station, the place where the abducted women were scheduled to be delivered.

Suddenly he found Lajo standing in front of him, shaking with some unknown fear. She knew Sunderlal and he was the only one who could identify her. He used to treat her unkindly and now as she stood there she wondered what kind of fate awaited her when she was returning after living with another man.

Sunderlal looked up at Lajo. She was carrying a red *dupatta* commonly worn by Muslim women and flung over her left shoulder in Muslim style. Her mind was so preoccupied with Sunderlal's thoughts that she had even forgotten to change her dress or not to wear it in Muslim style. She was now standing there anxiously watching Sunderlal.

Her appearance gave Sunderlal a jolt. She looked fairer and healthier than before and had put on weight. All his conjectures about Lajo had proved wrong. He had thought she would miss him so much that she would be reduced to a bundle of bones. She would have become so weak and emaciated that she would not even be able to speak. It seemed to him that she had been quite happy in Pakistan. The thought made him sad but he decided not to reveal his mind to her. But if she was so happy there why had she returned to India? Had she come against her wishes under pressure of the government? But he could not understand why there was a touch of pallor on her face and her body had become slightly flabby as if the flesh had refused to tightly cling to her bones.

The first glance at the abducted women could lead to unpredictable results. There were some men at the police station who had outright spurned their women. 'We won't have the Muslims' left-overs!' they said. But Sunderlal faced the situation boldly. Overcoming his revulsion he quietly accepted Lajwanti.

The discordant notes of those who had refused to accept their women were lost in the jubilant voices of Rasalu, the old petition writer of Chowki Kalan, Neki Ram and others, Kalka Prasad's raucous voice sounding apart from others. Greeted by these medley of sounds Sunderlal and Lajo proceeded to their home. The scene was reminiscent of what had happened thousands of years ago when Shri Ram Chander and Sita returned to Ayodhya after their self-imposed exile. People had lit lamps to celebrate their return among whom there were many who looked downncast and repentant at the privations and hardships the royal couple had suffered for no fault of theirs.

After Lajwanti's return Sunderlal did not relax his efforts in propagating the objective of 'Finding a place in our hearts'. Rather he intensified his efforts in the same spirit in which he had started them. Those who had till now considered him to be merely a bundle of emotions were impressed by his earnestness. Most of the people were pleased at this happy turn of events in Sunderlal and Lajwanti's lives. But there were others who scoffed at the couple at being united again. The widow living in House No. 414 turned her face against Lajwanti and refused to visit her.

Not that Sunderlal was worried at their inimical attitude. The queen of his heart had been restored to him; the void in his heart had been filled for he had installed Lajo's image like a golden idol in the temple of his heart and sat outside zealously guarding it. Lajo who was in the beginning afraid of Sunderlal's unpredictable behaviour gradually opened out on noticing his change of heart.

Sunderlal now did not call Lajo by her name. He called her Devi—a goddess. She would feel so pleased, almost going into raptures over it. She felt like telling Sunderlal about her experience in Pakistan and by making a clean breast of it wash away her past sins with her tears. But Sunderlal was never in a mood to listen to her. Though communicative, Lajo would still feel inhibited. At night when Sunderlal fell asleep she would lie there staring at his face. When caught doing so she would mumble out some incoherent explanation which meant she was doing it just like that. Sunderlal who was tired after the day's work would fall asleep again.

Only once soon after her arrival Sunderlal had tried to draw out Lajo about her 'black days'.

'Who was he?' he had asked her.

Lajwanti had lowered her eyes and replied, 'Jumma.' Then she had raised her eyes and scrutinized Sunderlal's face, trying to decide what more to tell. But she had felt discouraged for Sunderlal had given her a queer look. Caressing her hair, he asked her, 'Was he good to you?'

'Yes.'

'He didn't beat you, did he?'

Sliding forward Lajwanti rested her head on Sunderlal's chest. 'No, he didn't beat me but I was always scared of him. You used to beat me but I was never afraid of you. You won't beat me again, will you?'

Sunderlal's eyes filled with tears. In a voice full of remorse he said, 'No, Devi, I shall never beat you again.'

Devi! Had he said Devi? Had he raised her to the level of a goddess? She began to sob.

She wanted to tell him everything but he wouldn't let her.

'Let's forget the past', he said. 'You did not commit any sin. It's our society to blame which refuses to give women like you their honoured place. Thereby our society stultifies itself, not you.'

Lajwanti's secret remained locked in her heart. She had told Sunderlal things only in hints. She looked at her body which after the Partition had become the embodiment of a goddess. She was happy, very happy. But a happiness which was marred by a doubt. She would suddenly sit up in bed as if in her blissful moments someone had distracted her mind, taking away her happiness.

Many days passed in this way. Doubt slowly edged out her happiness. Not because Sunderlal had again started maltreating her but because he was so kind and considerate to her, which she thought was against his grain. She wanted to be the same old Lajo to him who fell out with him at the offer of a radish and patched up with him the next moment when bribed with a carrot. But Sunderlal gave her no chance to have a row with him but he always made her feel that she was fragile like glass which would crack at the touch of a feather. She would look at her reflection in the mirror and ultimately came to believe that the Lajo she had known no longer existed. Sunderlal had given her shelter under his roof but had he accepted her? She was living and yet rootless. Sunderlal had no eyes to see her tears nor ears to hear her sighs. Every morning the singing party still wended its way through the streets. The reformer of Mohalla Mulla Shakoor still sang with Rasalu and Neki Ram:

The Lajwanti leaves droop at the mere touch.

S.J. Joshi

S.J. Joshi (1915–89), who wrote in Marathi, was a popular writer, and a prolific one. He published twenty-six collections of short stories, five collections of articles, and ten novels. His stories were generally about lower middle class breadwinners, such as clerks, their modest aspirations, and their successes and failures.

One of his most popular novels was the one based on the life of Anandi Joshi who, at the end of the nineteenth century went alone, at the urging of her husband, to study medicine. She died a year after her return. The novel is based on a biography of Anandi Joshi, and is particularly interesting for its complex portrayal of Anandi's husband who urged her to study but also felt threatened by her achievements. The extract included is from the version translated and condensed by Asha Damle.

Chapter 7

The next day when Gopalrao came back from Bombay, he brought with him two books, hiding them under his scarf. He had decided to stay on in Kalyan. He was allotted a room for himself. He wanted to teach Anandi. He wanted to try out his ideas. Ganpatrao was happy that his son-in-law was back. He also felt that there was no further risk of his conversion to Christianity. After the evening meal Gopalrao was sitting with Ganpatrao on the platform swing, chatting away. The entire conversation was so trivial: When is the fourth day in the first quarter of the lunar month, for that was the day for fasting? What would they like to do on the eleventh day of the lunar calendar, for that was another fasting day? The crop was not good these days. The prices were rising, the tenants who cultivated the land on lease were getting powerful. It

S.J. Joshi, *Anandi Gopal*, Girgaon, Mumbai: K.V. Kothvale, Majestic Book Stall, 1968. Trans. from Marathi and abridged by Asha Damle, Calcutta: Stree, 1992.

was very difficult for the Brahmins, who were landlords, to earn their living.

Bored, Gopalrao got up and went upstairs to his room. The oil lamp was lit, the bed was made. He took off his shirt and sat down. He could see the backyard from his window. It was all dark. He looked at the house, the walls were thick, the main gate was huge. It was there in the same state for the last two or three generations. It wore the expression of the old dying man. On the loft above his room were stacks of old pots and pans, too heavy for lifting, tarnished with disease and age. How long would he stay awake? What else could he do? Sleep? Sleep ruled the place. Everyone slept—nights, afternoons, even during the day they looked sleepy.

Anandi had not come up yet. It was getting impossible to teach her. The women had not eaten yet. There would be cleaning up, washing up, cleaning the floor before she could come up. He had to wait till then.

With his scarf as a cover he lay on his bed. His mind was in a stupor. He thought of the previous night, and a sudden sense of disgust came over him. It was all so wrong! Would it always be like this? A physical act with a twenty-nine-year old man and a young girl of twelve as partners. He was upset. Anandi had cried profusely last night. Did she understand this relationship? Was she capable of enjoying making love yet? She was not capable of anything. She was just a mound of flesh and bones. He was disgusted and unhappy with himself, with Anandi, with the whole society of Kalyan and its stuffy ambience. When he came to and looked around, he noticed Anandi standing at the foot of his bed without saying anything, without raising her head. He asked her when she had come and why she had not woken him. She replied that she had been here quite a while and had not woken him because he was fast asleep.

All his anger for her surged up and he shouted that she should have woken him. When she remained silent with her head bent low, he yelled at her again and said he must know why she had not woken him. She said simply she was scared.

Gopalrao got up. His mind seethed with total contempt for his wife. He went near her. He said in a hoarse voice, 'What makes you so scared?' He took her hand and made her sit on the bed. 'Sit here.' She sat uncomfortably.

'Don't sit.' He screamed, 'Lie down.'

He blew out the oil lamp, and he entered her. He got up in a short while. He was sweating, his body complaining, his desire was not fulfilled. He had tried to snatch and grab whatever pleasure he could.

Now he felt nauseous. He lit the lamp. There was a soft light in the room. Anandi sat up on the bed. She was tying her blouse. She looked sad and low. Gopalrao went near her and petted her. She shuddered and stood up. He took her hand and made her sit down. He asked whether she had learnt her lesson and could write the alphabet now. She said she knew how to write already.

'Let me see how you can.' He took the book of the alphabet and the book of numbers from under the bed and said, 'Will you show me how you write?'

'Write the first letter.' She smiled, but only out of politeness. 'Where?' she asked. 'I haven't got a slate. I left it in the kitchen and Grandma broke it.'

'I see! She still bears a grudge.' Gopalrao said angrily.

In the niche in the wall opposite to them, there were big tins full of grain. He had an idea. 'I will make you a slate.'

There was a tray beside the tins and he poured some rice into it. He placed the tray in front of her saying, 'Here you are!'

Anandi wanted to laugh but dared not. He smoothed the rice in the tray and said, 'Come on, write.'

She tried to draw a line across with her finger, but it came out all crooked. She smoothed the rice, and tried again, but the line was crooked.

Gopalrao shouted at her. He smoothed the rice and then drew a straight line with his forefinger. Then he said, 'Now, draw the first letter.'

Her hand was shaking. The tears welled up in her eyes. Gopalrao's hand was right behind her back. If she went wrong she knew he would hit her. She tried very hard for ten minutes, sweat was streaming down her face but she managed somehow.

'That's not quite right, the curve here is not correct and the line at the end should be accented.'

He pulled the tray towards him and drew the first letter of the alphabet very neatly and beautifully. Then he pushed the tray towards her and said, 'That's the way. Now go over it again and again, ten times at least.'

She went over it twice. She was very sleepy, and she dozed off. When Gopalrao said she was falling asleep, she sat up with a sudden jerk and said she was going over the letter.

Gopalrao's face lit up with a smile. Lovingly he put his hand over her back and said, 'Are you really sleepy? Why didn't you come up earlier?' Then he took pity on her. Taking the tray off her hands, he said, 'Go to sleep now, we will continue tomorrow.'

Anandi found that he really meant it. Tremendously relieved, her face perked up. He tousled her hair. 'You are so tired. Come on, sleep now.'

She did not hear his last words. There was a rug on the floor. She crouched there drawing her limbs in and went to sleep in a second. He kept on rubbing her back. He looked at the sleeping little girl. He laughed. Her face was so innocent, so tender, her limbs were like the fresh leaves of a banyan tree, tiny and soft. He looked at her crumpled body. She was not really a woman but only a little child. Lovingly he passed his hand over her body and then put his arm under her neck and picked her up. She muttered something in her sleep but went back to sleep. He put her on the bed, covered her with a sheet lightly. He lay beside her but could not sleep till late.

The next day on his way back he brought her a new slate and some pencils. It was dark by the time he reached home. But the lights were not lit yet. Ganpatrao who was on the swing was coughing badly. Gopalrao took out the slate and the pencils, which he was hiding under his scarf, and put them down on the swing with a thump. 'I brought these', he said.

Pale because of his coughing fit, Ganpatrao pressed both his hands against his chest. When he found his breath, he asked, 'What is it?'

'I have brought this slate.'

Ganpatrao did not understand and asked what it was for.

'To teach Yamu.'

Realizing what was afoot, he said, 'You still have the same obsession.'

'This is no obsession!'

'What else can it be, then? A husband brings a slate to teach his wife! Never heard of such a thing!'

'You have heard of it now.'

'Should women be educated, do you think? And then spend the rest of their lives in reading with their glasses on? Who will do the house-work then—all the husbands, you mean?'

Gopalrao managed to restrain himself.

'People do have obsessions about something or the other but they don't usually last so long. After a while a person settles down, but you are mad!'

Gopalrao started at his father-in-law. It was getting darker. The oil lamp in the kitchen was lit. A strip of light came through the door and cut across the slow rocking movement of the swing.

Gopalrao scowled and said, 'I am not mad. This is what I insist on.'

Dinner was ready. Both of them went in and changed their dhoties, and started the evening prayers. When they were seated for the meal and were giving the offerings to the deities, Gopalrao made a remark. 'I brought a slate once before, and it got broken in this house.'

Grandma came out of the kitchen to serve them. His remark was meant for her. 'That won't do anymore.'

Grandma made a mental note of it. Gopalrao expected an angry response from her but she did not say anything. 'Please tell them, such things will not be tolerated any more. I don't want anybody interfering with my wife's education.'

Troubled with coughing spasms, Ganpatrao could not eat properly.

'I want to make things very clear. I want certain things to happen the way I want. If that's not done I will go my way.'

The night was jet black. A kind of ominous shadow hung over the house. Ganpatrao was anxious about so many other things as well. He could not repay the loan he had taken. The next day was the last day for repayment. He was sure that the verdict of the court would be in the favour of his opponents. The whole household was but a leaking pot. There was no income, the expenses kept on mounting up beyond limits. His title, though a namesake now, was in jeopardy. And the madness of his son-in-law was getting worse. Gopalrao had not stopped talking. The women were serving the last course of rice but Ganpatrao left his seat. In a shaky voice he said, 'Then say no more. Nobody will dare break that slate, I will see to that.' Then he tried to make an announcement. 'Listen, everybody.'

The house was quiet. The ladies in the kitchen knew that something ominous was happening. Through the little window in the wall that divided the kitchen and the dining area, Yamu's mother was watching everyone.

Ganpatrao made another effort. 'Let everyone remember. Yamu's books, her slate and her pencils, everything must be left alone. No one should touch anything.' He got up from his seat. Another fit of coughing seized him as he went to wash his hands. He dried them and wiped his mouth with the end of his dhoti. 'She is going to be a big government officer—a Revenue Collector. She is going to earn a name for herself. Don't you come in her way.'

The night was getting still darker. Gopalrao went to his room upstairs and stood at the window. Down below women were chattering as they were eating their meal. He paced up and down in the room, impatiently waiting for Anandi. An hour and a half after that, she came with the usual jug of water and a cup in her hand, her head bent politely. She stood at the door awkwardly. Gopalrao ignored her and kept pacing to and fro in the room.

He held the bar of the window. His eyes glowed with anger in the dark. He began to shout at Anandi. Why was she standing? Why did she not go to sleep? All she did was sleep. Why was she so late coming up? He went up to her and pinched her ear hard, asking, 'Why were you so late corning up?'

She started crying, her sobs growing louder. He hit her and asked again why she was so late. She managed to say that she had many chores to do, and her mother would not let her come up. Gopalrao grew more furious. He shouted that Anandi must obey him. Had she written the alphabet today? Still crying, Anandi said hesitantly that her mother had taken the books away. Gopalrao gave up in frustration. He told Anandi brusquely to go to sleep since that was all she wanted to do. Anandi stood there not knowing what to do. She wanted to sleep desperately. Gopalrao covered his face with the scarf and lay on the bed. She went near the bed and stood there. Then she said in a low voice, 'I am sorry.'

Gopalrao was disarmed. His heart was filled with pity for that twelve-year-old child. But he did not say anything and remained still. She touched his feet and shook them slightly, saying, 'I won't do this again.'

Gopalrao laughed. He pretended that she had woken him up.

'Why are you awake still? Come on, sleep.'

Still trembling with fear she stood at the end of the bed. He took her hand and pulled her on to the bed and told her to sleep. Like an obedient girl she lay on her bed. Her eyelids were closing involuntarily but she was trying hard to keep awake.

'Why aren't you sleeping, then?' He wondered.

'You haven't finished with me yet.'

'What, what do you mean?'

'The usual thing, the thing you do with me every night.'

Shaken, he realized what she was hinting at. In the dark he stared at her wildly. She lay on her back and her eyes were closed. The two tiny legs were drawn close to her belly...her legs were open....He was filled with disgust. He took his hand off her body with a jerk. His body became tense, his voice hoarse, and bereft of all emotions he muttered, 'Sleep now.'

Relieved like a child let off from a working day in school, she was happy. She straightened her legs and asked him if she could really go to sleep. When he reassured her, all the tension she felt was suddenly released. She slept like a child sleeping in her mother's arms. But Gopalrao could not sleep for a long time, feeling tense and restless.

Early at dawn, she woke up. Gopalrao's hand lay across her body.

His earlier gentleness towards her had disappeared. Suddenly she felt something. Startled, with her eyes half-open she saw Gopalrao was bent over her. Repelled, she murmured, 'Please don't.'

Furious, Gopalrao ordered her to be quiet or he would slap her. Who was she to say no? Like a child watching something dreadful happening right in front of her eyes, she kept looking at him mesmerized while he continued to force his way into her.

When the act was over, he started pacing up and down in the room. He was sweating even in the fresh morning air. After some time he ordered her to get up and study. He was tired of hearing her say she was sorry. Did she think she could get away with anything as long as she said sorry? He threatened that if she did not study he would leave her and become a Christian. She did not know what it meant to be a Christian but she knew it was something dreadful. Crying she said, 'I will study, please don't say anything horrible.'

'Well then', he looked into her eyes, 'it is dawn now, go downstairs, have a wash and come up.'

Bewildered she added, 'What for?'

'To kill me and make yourself a widow.' He flared up.

She didn't know where she went wrong. She had lived in his company only for the last two days. During those few hours she saw all his different moods. They met only at night. During those few hours she saw all the different facets of his character, one talking gruffly, the other like a wild animal using her body, one with a tender loving care, teaching her, shouting at her, saying such dreadful things that made her worried and tense.

'I am sorry.'

'I don't like anybody asking me questions. I want you to do as I tell you. Go downstairs, wash and change, then come up.'

She still did not understand why he was asking her to come upstairs again. But she dared not ask. There would be such an uproar. How could she be in her husband's room during daytime? The very idea made her tremble. Everybody in the town would know. Everybody would point a finger at her, and say that is the girl who went to her husband's room during daytime.

When she went down, she found her mother was up. They were milking the cows in the cowshed. Mother was busy helping. Grandma was sitting in front of the family icons telling her beads. Ganpatrao had not come down yet, but you could hear him coughing. She finished her morning toilet and looked around. She took a comb and started combing her hair in the ladies' room. She was in such anguish she did not know what to do. Mother came in with a heavy can of milk. She gave Yamu an intense look of dislike. 'Don't you just sit there like a lump.'

Yamu didn't say anything. Recently mother had always been talking to her like this. She dumped the heavy can on the floor and shouted again. 'Take that pot and fetch some water from the well.' The stove was burning fiercely, she pulled out some firewood, muttering to herself. 'She needs to be told every time, doesn't do anything of her own accord, just sits there lazily combing away her hair, as if we all are her servants fetching water and doing all the odd jobs.'

Somebody called from the backyard, she went in a rush to see who it was. Yamu finished doing her hair. She looked around. In the kitchen, the pot was waiting to be filled up. No one was there. There was somebody near the well. The waterwheel was in motion, and the screeching noise of the wheel could be heard in the kitchen. What should she do? She must fetch water. The empty pot was waiting. But then how could she go upstairs as her husband asked? Oh no! the whole universe would fall apart. The angry glowering face of Gopalrao was glaring at her. She saw the sparks flying from his reddened eyes. He wanted to burn her alive. She shuddered. She must go upstairs. She would have to face him at night. That scared the life out of her. She got up and like a person possessed climbed the stairs noiselessly like a cat. She feared that somebody might see her. The shame and the fear of it filled her heart. How she wished she were invisible! Still shaking and puffing she went up. Gopalrao had wrapped his shirtless body with his cotton scarf. He shouted, 'Why did you take so long?'

She didn't answer. With her head low, she stood in front of him. He gave her an angry look and told her to sit down. There was a slate in the niche. Gopalrao placed it in front of her. He took a few pencils from the inner pocket of his jacket and handed them over to her. 'You must sit properly. While writing, you should always fold one leg underneath the other and hold the slate on your knees.'

She could not sit as he suggested, but now he was filled with love for the child. He showed her how to bend one knee and get it under the other leg. She could not get it right. He moved towards her, held her right knee, telling her to bend it. Anandi recoiled. In broad daylight, her husband was touching her knees; a daring act that was unheard of in those households! She said hastily that she could do it alone, that he must not touch her. She managed to sit somehow. Then she kept the slate on her left knee and holding the pencil in her hand, said she was ready.

Gopalrao opened the book of the alphabet, and she started drawing a line nervously. He helped her by drawing a straight line for her and told her to write what she knew. She wrote the first letter with great effort and looked at him. He was pleased and patted her back. She sprang back, and when Gopalrao asked her what was wrong, she told him not to touch her. What if anybody saw them? He laughed and said he would not touch her. He would stand near the window.

He wrapped his scarf around himself and stood near the window. He looked below. Anandi's mother was standing near the well. There were two other women from the neighbourhood. A maidservant was cleaning the pots and the pans. Ganpatrao was sitting on the mud platform near the cowshed. All of them looked very serious and anxious about something. They were looking at the room upstairs as if something untoward was happening there. They were whispering to each other. Gopalrao suddenly understood what was worrying them and wanted to shock them even more. He turned to look at his wife. She was struggling with the fifth letter. He went to her and said she had done well. What reward would she like?

Her face lit up, but before she could say anything he said, 'Do you know how the Gods reward a person who has done a task well?' She was listening intently. 'They send a chariot to take him to heaven, and wait at the gate to receive him with garlands in their hands.'

Gopalrao continued, 'You have done a good job today. May be the Gods will send a chariot for you now. Don't you forget to take me with you! Otherwise I will be left behind alone.'

He got up, went to the window again. Everybody was standing around the well anxiously. Gopalrao wanted to laugh at them but he checked himself. 'There! It's come for you. God has sent it. Oh, how wonderful! God has a garland for you in his hand.'

She got up, all excited, and with one quick step, she reached the window and looked out. Mother was there, she had a broom in her hand. She was about to sweep the backyard. The neighbouring ladies were there. They were pretending that they had come to do some chores. But they were all looking up at the window. Ganpatrao was there, his face was drawn. She had forgotten them all for the last fifteen minutes when she was writing. She had forgotten that this morning in the broad daylight she was in her husband's room. Now it came back with a flash. Hell had broken loose. It was impossible for her to escape the fury. She turned colourless and looked back.

Gopalrao was standing there laughing. Bewildered, she said, 'I am going.'

She moved restlessly. 'Are you scared?' She nodded. 'What's there to be scared of? I am there.' He looked at her, adding, 'Our religion is so great, so ancient, going on since the Vedic times, no other religion is so great!'

She did not know what he was talking about. He continued, 'Hinduism says that a wife must obey her husband. Whatever other people say, she must obey her husband.'

She started to go down.

I order you to come to this room to study, you must obey me.'

'I am going down.'

'You may go down now, but in the afternoon write down all the numbers from one to hundred. Finish your meal and come upstairs.'

'Aren't you going to your office today?'

'I have taken a day off today. I am telling you, you must come upstairs.'

She went down. Everybody had an expression on their faces as if they were mourning a death. Mother was very upset. Yamu's marriage had taken so long to arrange. And when she was wedded, she never went to live with her husband, instead they had to suffer this eccentric son-in-law. That day she was in a real temper. In the broad daylight of the morning, her daughter heedlessly goes to her husband's room and reads books! She must be punished and corrected!

When Anandi came down, mother was arranging the burning twigs in the stove. Anandi came down the steps. Mother shouted with bitter sarcasm, 'Welcome, Welcome! Have you finished your studies? That's rather too soon. Well, I expected you to come down with your husband, at lunch time. All of us are your servants and we would do all the cooking, serving, washing up.'

She got up and stood near Yamu threateningly. Ganpatrao had a fit of coughing again. His throat made a wheezing sound, he was breathless. He realized his daughter was helpless, caught between the horns of a dilemma. Pressing on to his painful chest, he tried to appease his wife. 'Forget it now!'

'Yes, I knew you would say that! Here I am, breaking my back, doing all the odd jobs!' She looked at the burning twig in her hand. Yamu was right next to her. With the other hand she pinched Yamu's ear. 'Look at you, studying!' Then she smacked her on her face. 'Aren't you ashamed? Any time, any day, you just go and sit in the arms of your husband.'

Anandi's ear was hurting. Tears started streaming down her face. In a low whine she said, 'Please don't!'

In between bouts of coughing, Ganpatrao shouted at his wife, 'Don't you start hitting her now!'

'That's right, I shouldn't hit her. No, I should congratulate her!' Her anger reached a new peak. She left her ear alone but she had a burning twig in her hand. She hit Anandi with it in such frenzy, on her legs, on her back. 'You must be taught a lesson!' she shouted.

'Watch out, the twig is burning! Stop it now, the girl will be scorched to death.'

'That's what she deserves.' She hit her again. 'In broad daylight, this girl sits with her husband's arms around her. Are we not Brahmins? Do we tolerate such a thing? She seems to me a whore or perhaps a Christian!'

Stooping low, and pressing his hand on the chest, Ganpatrao came forward and stood between the two, putting the girl behind him. He appealed to his wife to control herself.

Now the mother flopped, breathing heavily and still complaining, she retreated. She started hitting her own forehead now. 'Yes, I will stop now. I am wrong. Right in the morning the girl comes down from her room after such a great accomplishment, she must be tired. I should have tried to make her comfortable.' Her tongue bad a sting of bitter sarcasm.

Anandi was badly hurt. She was in deep pain. But when she saw her mother crying she forgot her pain. She wiped her tears and said she was sorry.

Ganpatrao was used to his wife's temper. The tempo was slowing down. The tempest was over but the weather would be unpleasant for some time. He advised his daughter, 'Don't say anything anymore.'

'Yes, You don't say anything. We aren't worth being talked to. Go, go away and talk to your husband in English!'

Ganpatrao beckoned the girl to go inside. 'Don't stand there like a stupid girl. Go inside, the curds need churning.'

'Stop it, don't you dare touch my curds. You are a Christian, You haven't had a bath, you haven't said your prayers. You do not follow our religious rites, don't you go polluting everything around me here.'

If Ganpatrao had not been ill, he would have laughed at the extremes to which his wife went but he was too unwell to think of other things. Pressing his chest, he said in a shaky voice, 'All right, go and have a bath then. Go, go anywhere, don't stay here for another second!' Wiping her tears Anandi went to the backyard.

In the afternoon Gopalrao came down for his meal. Nobody spoke. Nobody knew whether Gopalrao was aware of the morning's events. He showed no sign of it. After the meal, the house went quiet for the afternoon siesta. Ganpatrao lay on the platform swing, covering himself with his cotton scarf. The children were playing in the backyard. That afternoon, Anandi was an older girl. She did not play with the children. Her mind filled up with all kinds of thoughts. Fear made her throat dry. Should she go up? Gopalrao had asked her to come upstairs with a slate and a pencil. He had asked her to write the numbers. She remembered the bloodshot eyes of her husband and feared the night.

Anandi did not go, it was impossible. Mother was lying down for her siesta in the inner room, and the children were playing. It seemed that she did not belong anywhere. She sat leaning against the pillar in the outside room. Through the well of the stairs, she could see a corner of Gopalrao's room. He was walking up and down. He did that whenever he was angry.

The afternoon ended, and then the evening meals were over. She was getting more and more restless. Mother was on the rampage. She kept piling up chores for Yamu. As the night came, children slept, and the women finished their meals. With the usual water jug and a cup in her hand she started for the room, walking like a prisoner to the gallows. Having climbed the stairs, she put her water jug down. Gopalrao, with his scarf wrapped round his body, was pacing up and down. He saw that Anandi was shaking with fear. Pleased at the effect he had on her, he asked her angrily why she had not come up that afternoon and whether she had prepared her lesson. On learning that she had not done her lesson, he raised his hand to hit her, stopping short when he saw her blue black bruise. He asked her what had happened and she explained that her mother had beat her because she had come up in the morning. Gopalrao touched her bruise gently and asked her to show him the other places where her mother had hit her. Anandi pulled up her sari and showed him the marks on her thighs. He felt sorry for her and stroked her gently on the back. She started to cry and could not stop. Gopalrao questioned her further and found that her mother kept her so busy with chores that she could not come up earlier. She did not know when she would find the time to study. Frustrated, Gopalrao shouted that they should give up. 'Let us all sleep and sleep and sleep.' He started to pace about again and then suddenly stopped. He told her to go to sleep and went downstairs.

Anandi stood near the stairwell in the dark. She could hear the conversation from there. The grandmother was with Ganpatrao, who was coughing. He was sitting on the bed, pressing his chest with his hand.

Ganpatrao asked why Gopalrao had come down at such an odd time. Gopalrao replied that he had come to decide things once and for all.

Immediately the atmosphere became tense. Anandi's mother was in the kitchen. She came and stood in the doorway.

'I don't understand. What is it?' Ganpatrao tried to be placating.

'You decide how my wife should behave.' Anandi's mother came from the kitchen to give her clear-cut opinion. 'What's there to decide? A wife should behave like a wife and that's that.'

Gopalrao countered smartly, 'And a mother-in-law should behave like a mother-in-law. I am talking to Ganpatrao. You have no business.'

'Most certainly I have. It's not always for me to observe the norms.'

'That's yet to be decided. What are the norms?'

'I don't like this roundabout talk.'

Ganpatrao knew that his wife was surpassing her limits. 'Will you keep quiet?' he shouted.

'I knew you would shout at me! Keep quiet—Why should I? Everyone has to follow the set norms. He sits in his room in broad daylight with his wife, neighbours laugh at us.'

'That's what I will always do. I have come to tell you that.'

'Brahmins don't behave like that. May be Christians do. They may be taking their wives on their knees during the day.'

'I teach her. I want to teach her.'

'You can do that at night.'

'She is kept busy the whole day. I can't stand this. She must study. If she comes up during the day, hell doesn't break loose.'

'May be not for you! But for us it's different. We live in Kalyan. People have started spitting on us!'

'You take a decision.' Gopalrao turned to his father-in-law. 'Before marriage I made you promise that she would study one way or the other. Whenever she gets time, maybe morning, afternoon or evening. When she came upstairs toady, I found she had got a good hiding.'

'Well, she deserved that! I can't tolerate such nonsense in my house', said Anandi's mother.

'You hit her with a burning twig.'

'Count herself lucky, she is still alive.'

'I won't tolerate anybody hitting my wife. She came because I told her to.'

'She will go naked in the streets tomorrow, if you force her.'

Ganpatrao found the whole situation intolerable. He shouted at his wife. 'Don't say another word. We will apologize. Oh, God! What trouble!'

Gopalrao kept insisting that a decision be taken. Ganpatrao was flabbergasted: that a girl should go to her husband's room during the day, read books, and not do any household jobs, that was not the done thing. It was all very very strange. Between fits of coughing, he begged Gopalrao to think over it. His words echoed through the silent night in an odd manner. Thin and ailing, he was sitting on the big bed in a comer of the room. There was an oil lamp beside it. There was not much oil left in it. The wick was flickering—the last hold on life—the whole house seemed to be under a dark shadow. That shadow in the form of Ganpatrao was pleading that Gopalrao think it over. Gopalrao declared that he had taken a decision. He would not stay in their house from tomorrow. He would not have another drink of water in their house.

Anandi's mother chipped in to say that in that case he should take his wife with him. Ganpatrao tried to intervene in vain.

'I will take her.' Gopalrao took a deep breath. He was calculating the effect his suggestion would have, the mayhem it would create. 'I have already met a Christian priest. I have promised him. When I go to Thane, I will become a Christian and also baptize your daughter!' The very idea sent shivers down Ganpatrao's spine. 'Don't say such ominous things. Go upstairs. You are not in your right mind.'

Anandi's mother took a firm grip on herself. She said carefully, 'You are our son-in-law, this kind of talk doesn't befit you.' If Yamu were to die, or if someone were to throw her into the well to drown or burn her alive, she would not have minded so much. But this was a new kind of threat from her son-in-law. If the daughter and the son-in-law were both baptized then the family honour would be scarred for ever and ever.

Gopalrao sneered at her attempts to be conciliatory. He laughed and said that when he and Anandi came next they would be Christians: John and Mary.

Ganpatrao could not bear it. He covered his ears with his hands, and he could not hold back his tears. 'How can you say such things? Aren't we Brahmins? Our religion is so great! You want to get converted. The untouchables have become Christians. Are you going to join them?' Weakened by his illness he lost control, and started crying as if he had lost someone very close to him. In the wordless silence of the night his pathetic crying echoed through the walls of the dilapidated mansion. Ganpatrao started slapping his face. Then he joined his hands in obeisance and suppliance, and pleaded. 'Please have pity on me. If you don't want me to die here and now of a broken heart, please don't say anything anymore. You may go up to your room.'

Gopalrao climbed the stairs and went to his room. He could not see anything in the dark. He heard a slow whimpering from the frame of the stairs. Anandi was standing there. He had almost forgotten her. He did not speak to her. Standing near the window, he forgot the world around him. Suddenly he felt little hands touching his feet. Startled he found that Anandi was touching his feet; tears were running down her face.

He had forgotten her existence. He was beyond all common thought and emotions. He glanced at the crying girl as if she did not mean anything to him. He did not wish to speak but he had to, how long could he continue like that? He said very dryly, 'Don't cry.'

She kept on crying. The thoughts that filled his mind were hard to comprehend. He felt pity for the little girl and he was angry with her as well. Then he suddenly felt contempt for her. He felt like getting up and smacking her, throttling her, crushing her like an ant or an insect. He controlled himself and asked coolly, 'Why are you crying?' She rushed into his arms and kept on crying. Amid sobs she said, 'Please, don't leave me and please don't become a Christian.'

He laughed. He took both her arms and led her to bed. She said, 'I am so scared. Please don't get converted.'

She lay on her back on the bed like an obedient girl and brought her legs near her stomach like a puppet for him to use. Repelled, he shouted that she was stupid. He ordered her to go to sleep. In the dark that figure with uplifted feet looked so weird. Infuriated he got up and stood near the window. It was dark down below.

Iqbalunnissa Hussain

Iqbalunnissa Hussain was born in Mysore and was married when she was fifteen to an official in the service of the Mysore Government, who was sympathetic to and supportive of her desire to learn to read and write English, and to study further (she already knew Urdu and Persian). She graduated from the Maharani College in 1930 and won a gold medal, and her eldest son (she had seven children by this time) graduated two years later. She accompanied her son to England in 1933. She was Headmistress of a primary school which she turned into an Urdu Girls Middle School, instituted a school of Home Industries for Muslim women in Bangalore, formed a Teachers Association for Muslim women teachers, and a Girl Guide Movement among Muslim girls.

In 1935, Iqbalunnissa represented India at the Twelfth International Women's Congress, gave a lecture on Muslim Women's Education to the Muslim Society of Great Britain in London, and an extension lecture at Mysore University on her experiences in an English University. These speeches, and her essays and pieces she wrote for newspapers, are collected in *Changing India: A Muslim Woman Speaks*, published in Bangalore in 1940. Most of the essays are about the condition of women in India, particularly Muslim women. Two are about Mysore which she regarded as a particularly enlightened state. Her unsparingly ironic novel, *Purdah and Polygamy*, was published in 1944.

Brought up in strict purdah, Iqbalunnissa Hussain did not feel that purdah had any sanction in the tenets of the Prophet, and polygamy permitted one to help women left destitute by war. While she frequently reiterates the effects of seclusion on the body and mind of women, she advises a gradual rather than a drastic attempt at change. She states: 'The purdah in the real sense of the word is not so much physical as it is moral.'

Iqbalunnissa Hussain, *Purdah and Polygamy: Life in an Indian Muslim Household*, Bangalore: Hosali Press, 1944.

Chapter V

It is a well known fact that man is superior to woman in every respect. He is a representative of God on earth and being born with His light in him deserves the respect and obedience that he demands. He is not expected to show his gratitude or even a kind word of appreciation to a woman: it is his birthright to get everything from her. 'Might is right' is the policy of the world. To express thankfulness to such a creature as she is humiliating. She should be proud, happy and thankful to him for having accepted her services. If he is depressed she must make herself so. It should matter nothing to him if she is indisposed. On the other hand he has every right to be aggrieved if the meals are not punctual or well cooked. A woman as a wife should be subservient in everything to man's comfort and exist for him and him alone. She should have no particular liking for anything. Her work should as a matter of course begin and end with him.

His polygamous nature has an excuse: a man doing brave deeds needs every sacrifice by others. A woman who does not show the proper spirit of gulping down ready-made beliefs is condemned by the rest as douzakhi (hellish). The great fuss made over him gives him no time for introspection. He has accepted and assimilated the dogmas without analysing them. Unequal distribution of labour and regard is the social code made by man in his own interest. There are some who relinquish their birthright, but their number is not legion.

There is a miraculous change between wifehood and motherhood. A wife aspires long to achieve the position. When she does it even her husband recognises some merit in her. Motherhood is sanctified. A mother holds the highest position in the estimation of her children. Even highly educated sons obey her implicitly. They owe everything to her, their birth and their upbringing. Heaven is under her feet. The greater the obedience to her the easier is admittance to it. She is the queen of the house and rules over all her subjects with an iron hand. Her administration needs more attention when strangers unfortunately take shelter in it. Her government is not constitutional, so the laws are flexible and specially formulated in the interest of the earning member. There is no court of appeal. Everybody recognises her court of justice. The elasticity of judgment depends upon the greater application by the convict. Those with supernatural powers of cunning and flexibility of mind can get on splendidly with the legislator and executive.

Nazni, Kabeer's new wife, a girl with little tact and no knowledge of the world, fell an easy victim to the tactics of the experienced ruler of the house. Nothing but her beauty pleased her mother-in-law. But what could she do with her prettiness? She wanted a young woman to look after the house, to cook and take away her responsibility. Why do people bring daughters-in-law if not to have real and well-earned comfort? One can't keep a person for her beauty and worship her as an idol.

Three months after the marriage, when Zuhra was anxiously waiting to transfer her responsibility, Nazni fell ill on account of pregnancy. Now how could the poor mother-in-law get her rest? Her hopes of dominance which soared so high at the time of marriage came down to earth. With a person in bed her work was increased. Although nothing special was prepared for the sick daughter-in-law yet the meals had to be sent to her room. Whenever she vomitted someone had to be near her and attend to her. Nazni's mother engaged a woman for it

The presence of an extra servant was a cause of annoyance to Zuhra. A servant from Doulath Khan's house was a spy in hers.

'What a clumsy woman your wife is!' said Zuhra. `Mothers think of getting a girl married before training her to be a good and useful wife. They just think of transferring the burden from their shoulders to another's. If they thought of us they would come half way to mitigate our sufferings. She's such a shabby creature. Any china she touches exists no more.'

Kabeer did not know whose side to take. Second thoughts made him flatter his mother. 'She's frightened in a new place. Under your training she'll be all right. You have trained worse people.'

'Why is she frightened? Girls of her age undergo tortures day and night in the hands of drunken and cruel mothers-in-law. It is not fear but fearlessness and indifference. She's a spoilt child. Don't you see her munching the whole day? What does she eat and from where does she get it?'

The food sent to Nazni was returned untouched. Pregnancy is a peculiar disease which makes the very sight of food repugnant. Kabeer knowing that she starved the whole day brought fruits and sweets and put them on Nazni's window sill from outside. The servant was given instructions to wait and remove the packet quietly. Kabeer was alarmed to think his mother had come to know of the secret supply of nourishment.

'Her brothers and father keep on bringing things for her.'

'They come empty-handed. I watch them when they pass through the corridor. Perhaps they carry it in their pockets', said Zuhra.

Kabeer felt satisfied that no suspicion about him had arisen.

'It seems childish the way she behaves. She knows nothing of responsibility and the care of her husband. She spends the day either in sleep or talking and laughing when her people come. I have never heard a woman laugh so loudly. In my absence she'll never manage the house even for a day.'

'She's so quiet and grave in my presence. I can never make her cheerful. She is serious by nature.'

'She does not laugh in my presence either, but I hear her shrill voice from my room. It's not good for girls to laugh so loudly. What will people say?'

'You tell her that. Even my gentle words make her cry', said Kabeer.

'You should never feel pity or trust a crying woman. They shed crocodile tears.'

'I've often heard that but I can't understand it', said Kabeer.

'The point is that a woman's nature is not constant. Her weeping or laughter has no value. You shouldn't take her tears seriously. Your love must be in your heart. Your eyes and lips should express gravity and command. Once you become familiar and expose your weakness she'll be your ruler. You'll lose control over her for ever.'

Kabeer thought over his mother's precepts for some time and came to the conclusion that she being an experienced hand and his well-wisher her instructions should be his guide. After some time he went to his room, but seeing his wife's pale and thin but smiling face he forgot his mother's teaching. He said nothing about their talk but enquired of her health. Nevertheless he felt that something prevented him from being free with her. 'Once you become familiar she'll be your ruler and you'll lose control over her.' He couldn't say it to his wife. Already, unwittingly he had been too familiar with her.

He never allowed her to discuss his mother. Her name was sacred. Any mention of her had to be in her praise. Nazni, on the other hand had a hundred and one grievances to get redressed. But how? During the six months of her married life conveyances and escorts from her parents had been sent back at least thirty times. When permission was asked from Kabeer he told her to go to his mother. Once in every third call she permitted Nazni to go home and return the same night.

'Mother wants to send the car tomorrow for Id', said Nazni's brother.

'Why does she want to humiliate herself? They will return it', said Nazni.

'Have they not humiliated us many times? What do we care? We just want to have you with us. You can come back the same night.'

'For my wretched self my parents have to be insulted. Tell them to leave me to my fate', said Nazni with tears in her eyes. 'I can't dictate to father and mother. You just listen to what they ask you.'

'I'm not master of myself or my time and wishes. Tell mother plainly it is no use to send the car.'

'I see it is you who do not want to come.'

'I wish to heaven that they would send me there. I'd really enjoy my feast with mother.'

'I shall ask Kabeer to send you.'

'He never permits it without his mother's consent.'

'Let him take it.'

'He wouldn't do it himself, knowing her attitude.'

'Can't he do even that to please you?'

'Whenever he has asked it he has been snubbed.'

'Then you ask her.'

'I can't. Last night she was telling him to stay at home on the Id day. There's only one way to do it. Bring the car and say granny is ill', said Nazni.

Zuhra had already drawn up the menu for Id. The preparations had begun two days in advance.

'Wear your red sari and green blouse on the Id day', said Zuhra.

'Can't I wear the red blouse with the red sari?' asked Nazni.

'Do as I tell you.'

Nazni was annoyed, but knew that she was going to her mother's so she could wear anything she liked.

The car was brought on the morning of Id. The old woman who accompanied Nazni's brother entered Zuhra's room.

'Big Begum Sahib suddenly got ill this morning. I am asked to fetch Nazni Begum as she wants to see her.'

'Your Nazni is not a Hakim to cure her. Old peoples' diseases are common and they are rarely serious. Your mistress should have more sense than to send for the girl so often. That girl has no interest in this house. This is her house. In her mother's house she's only a stranger. Why does a man get married? Is it to destroy his home and live in his wife's house?'

'She's still young. Young brides before they are encumbered with the responsibility of children do have an attachment to the house where they were born and brought up. Moreover she'll be alone here. Let her enjoy her Id with her brothers and sisters.'

'You came here with the excuse of someone's illness and saying she has to do the work of Maseeha. Now the truth has come out. Our arrangements for Id will be upset. She can't go.'

Nazni's younger sister, who had been listening to the argument, ran to her: 'You are not coming with us!' Nazni seeing her dear ones could not make up her mind to stay away. She thought of the lonely room. None to speak to her cheerfully, but commands and fault-finding. In spite of herself tears began to flow. Her young brother ran to Kabeer's office in the opposite building and said,

'Apa is crying. I wouldn't leave her here.'

Kabeer thought that his interference was necessary.

'What's all this?' he asked Zuhra.

'As soon as your wife sees her relations she begins to cry.'

'God forbid!' retorted the escort. 'Why should she cry to see her brothers and sisters? They are not starving or suffering. She's crying because her grandmother is ill. She loves her dearly.'

'I have often seen her crying after their visits. She loves them more than her husband', said Zuhra.

'Send her, otherwise she will make us unhappy by her wailing.'

'She knows well she can bring you down on your knees by her tears. I told her not to go and you ask me to send her. What respect will she have for me?' said Zuhra.

Kabeer did not like Doulath Khan's people in the room when his mother was angry. He gave his mother a sign to send them all away.

'Why are you wrangling here? All of you go to her room.'

'Shall I take her?' asked the old woman.

'She wants to have her own way in everything. We are puppets in her hands. Take her and bring her back tonight. We are not beggars to be elated at the invitation to celebrate the feast in somebody's house. We have to think of our own visitors and the dead.'

Though the permission was not polite the children were pleased and ran to Nazni. Mother and son were left alone but neither felt like speaking to the other. Kabeer was coming round to her view. Nazni loved her parents more than himself.

Nazni wiped her eyes to be ready to go to her mother-in-law to pay her respects before leaving the house.

'She sent her permission. You needn't go to her. Your eyes are red like flames. She'll pick up a fresh quarrel and abuse you', said Nazni's brother.

'She won't leave me alive if I go away without her blessing. Even he wouldn't forgive me for it', said Nazni.

'Crying makes you prettier. Do cry every day to make your cheeks and nose pink', said her mischievous younger sister.

Nazni smiled and looked at herself in the mirror of the dressing table and rubbed her swollen eyelids.

'Go soon and be done with it', said her brother, who was going to the car with all the little ones. He turned to the old woman and said, 'Accompany Nazni to her mother-in-law's room and bring her to the car.'

Nazni entered Zuhra's room. She dared not look either Kabeer or his mother in the face. Bending down she touched her mother-in-law's feet, who put her hand on Nazni's head. When Zuhra was in a good mood she would say a few words by way of blessing, but now she said nothing. Nazni stood there like a penitent looking at her own feet.

'Your obstinacy has had its way after all. Try to be sensible and think of your home and husband, who cares for you more than your parents. Once you are married your parents have nothing to do with you. Their unnecessary interference in your life will only destroy it. We love you and you love others.'

Nazni standing there looked like Venus. She expected no support from her husband who was sitting there with head bent. The little ones in the car blew the horn.

'It is time for lunch. We came hours ago. Come, let us go', said the old woman from behind the door.

'These rogues spoil her. Go', said Zuhra.

'Did the convict take such a long time to be released even after the judgment was passed?' said her brother as he made room for her in the car.

'She wouldn't have come even now if the children had not blown the horn', said the old woman.

Nazni was all smiles as if nothing had happened.

'The situation is out of your control. She's proud of her people and their wealth. They'll destroy her home and life', said Zuhra. No reply came from Kabeer.

She went on: 'Did you notice her clothes? She went with those she wore at home.'

'Perhaps she forgot to change.'

'She went in them with a purpose. You don't know her. She did it to defy my orders to wear a certain sari on the Id day, and to show her parents how badly we keep her. Sincere and loving girls borrow costly clothes from others while going to their parents' just to keep up their husband's dignity.'

'She must have taken them with her to change there.'

'I hope so', said Zuhra.

In the evening the car was sent by Doulath Khan for Kabeer.

'Father wants you for dinner', said Nazni's brother.

'I'm sorry I can't come. Mother will be furious if I don't stay for dinner. I shall come there after it.'

'Shall I bring the car after some time?'

'No, I shall come in ours.'

Zuhra knew nothing of the invitation, so after dinner Kabeer said, 'They sent for me for dinner, but I said that I would go there later.'

'If you don't go there she'll feel the pinch and avoid deserting you on feast days in future.'

'I'll go there to bring her.'

'She must come herself as she went.'

Kabeer had promised his brother-in-law and was in a fix. He couldn't go there without her knowledge. That would create more trouble. It was better to touch her weak point and extract permission from her.

'If we leave her to herself she might not come for Khutba. Moreover we'll be making her more independent.'

Zuhra felt that she was loosening her iron hold which would result in Nazni's separation.

'Yes, perhaps it is better to go and bring her for to-morrow.'

Although Kabeer had definitely said that he was not going for dinner Doulath Khan and the guests were waiting for him and forced him to have it a second time. Kabeer never missed a good opportunity. He did full justice to the delicious, rich dishes.

The children wanted to go the pictures and compelled Kabeer to accompany them. He agreed after some hesitation.

'Let us take Apa', said one of the young brothers who did not know that it was objectionable for ladies to go to the cinema.

All of them welcomed the idea and shouted 'Yes, let us take her with us.'

Kabeer wondered what to do. He imagined his mother's anger.

'What's going on here?' said Nazni's brother, who was also going to celebrate Id.

'We want to take Apa with us', said the children.

'Are you afraid of your mother? There's nothing wrong in taking Nazni to a picture. Hundreds of Muslim women go these days. We shall reserve box seats and there is a purdah arrangement.'

'I...I didn't ask mother's permission. She has never been to a picture and does not have a good opinion of those who do', said Kabeer.

'These old women's world is quite different from ours. They have neither desires nor strength to take part in life's enjoyments. You shouldn't try to mould your wife's life according to your mother's', said the brother, who was annoyed by Kabeer's servile behaviour.

'We'll have to take her permission. She's both father and mother to me.'

'She won't know. Even if she does, you tell her that father took you both.'

'He's not going', said Kabeer.

Kabeer respected his father-in-taw. Being fatherless he took him for his guardian and well-wisher.

'He does not often go to late pictures, but I can make him take Nazni and you. This is her first picture. Don't stop her going. Be a sport', said the brother.

'If he takes us I shall have a good excuse.'

All the little ones danced with excitement. They often described pictures they had seen to Nazni, as she liked them. Now the trouble of description was saved.

Zuhra waited for her son's return till past ten. Then she began to worry and imagine things. She asked the cook to wake up the watchman and set him to Doulath Khan's house.

The watchman made enquiries of the servants.

'Kabeer Miyan and Doulhan Begum have gone to the pictures with the children', said the watchman, vexed at being disturbed from his sleep and having to walk the long distance. He said nothing of Doulath Khan.

Zuhra and sleep were poles apart. Kabeer had taken his wife to a cinema, and without her permission! All her teachings had no value for him. She did not know that the ladies of Doulath Khan's house were so shameless. She should never have consented to bring a girl from that house. Her blood boiled. Yet she made up her mind to postpone punishment. The morning would bring numerous visitors and they would come to know about it. To pretend innocence was the best policy.

At about two o'clock Zuhra heard the car stop. She did not stir from her bed. The young couple went to their room silently and slept. In the morning Nazni said: 'If Ammajan asks me about coming home late what shall I tell her?'

'She's bound to come to know of it. We must tell her now.'

'I've no courage to face her', said Nazni.

'I shall try to get her into a good mood, then I'll break it, putting the blame on Bavajan', said Kabeer.

'If she asks me?'

'You try to avoid her for some time.'

Khutba is a grand function in every Muslim family. Even a poor Muslim spends one or two months' income on that day and does not mind suffering on account of it for several months after. Clothes for everybody have to be made and grand dishes to be prepared and sent to relations. The more numerous the dishes the greater is the valuation of one's wealth. Presents have to be given and visitors to be fed. Because of the new relationship Zuhra's plans were elaborate. Early morning at five Zuhra got up for prayers. Soon after cooking was started she herself went to the kitchen. She believed in direct action to persuade others to follow suit.

Nazni before going for her bath forgot to ask her mother-in-law for the clothes to wear that day. She could not go after it without being properly dressed. She called the cook and told her to ask the mother-in-law for them.

'Doulhan Begum wants to know which sari she should wear', said the cook.

'Who asked you to go there? You mind your work', said Zuhra.

'She's standing in her kimono.'

'If she really wants to know let her come herself.'

The cook felt sorry for Nazni but couldn't please two mistresses. Nazni waited for the cook but didn't dare call her for a reply. She wore a sari she liked.

Kabeer returned home from Idgah and paid his respects to his mother. He looked for Nazni this side and that. She hadn't come out of her room. As he was trying to be on the good side of the mother it was better to neglect her. He sat down. Nazni knowing of Kabeer's presence went to her mother-in-law to pay the Id respects. After touching her feet she stood up.

'Was it humiliating to ask me about the clothes yourself? You sent the servant, treating me as her equal.'

Nazni's eyes were full of tears.

'Why do you cry? What have I done to you? You threaten us by y[ou]r tears. You knew that I was cooking alone. You not only failed to come to help me, but also called the servant to help you. Do you think I am your servant?'

Kabeer had asked Nazni to avoid his mother so that she should not be asked about the previous evening, but she had misunderstood him.

Nazni sobbed loudly. There was a knock on the door. Relations had already started their visits. Zuhra did not like the scene to be noticed by others.

'Go and change your clothes. Who asked you to wear them now?' Zuhra commanded the culprit.

Nazni felt a relief as the ordeal was over. She could cry to her heart's content in her room. Kabeer felt like going after his wife to console her but the barrier between him and his mother was still greater. Any regard shown for her meant that the gulf between him and his mother widened still further. The matter of going to the pictures had not yet come out. He had to be careful and gather courage.

Nazeer entered and paid his respects.

'I saw you last night at the pictures. As there were ladies I didn't like to go to you.'

Kabeer's face turned blue. He had not seen Nazeer at the pictures or he would have been prepared for the ordeal.

'I was sitting with the children and Doulath Khan. You could easily have seen me', stammered Kabeer.

'Do the ladies of his house go to the pictures? It is a surprise to me. I didn't know of that before', interrupted Zuhra.

'They followed us in a separate car. There was a strict purdah arrangement.'

'So your wife also went there?'

'Yes, her father took her.'

'Nazeer saw us last night at the pictures, and he mentioned it to mother', said Kabeer, who was so confused that he did not think of consoling her first.

'What did she say?' cried Nazni.

'Not much. Don't worry. She'll be all right. I told her Bavajan took us and I being his guest could not refuse him.'

'So it is over. The very thought of it was killing me.'

'Yes. If she asks you can repeat what I said.'

'Change your clothes before you go to her. She did not notice your Lacha. Otherwise that would have given her enough cause for anger.'

'I removed it to have my bath and forgot it.'

'Don't you keep it on when you bathe?'

'I feel sticky when it gets wet.'

Nazni was thankful to her husband because of his warning.

'Her father had no right to take a married daughter. Seeing you a coward he made a fool of you. She's your property. No one can have any interest in her without your permission. If you had any regard for your mother you would have flatly refused his suggestion.'

'It was not a suggestion. It was compulsion, and I thought of him as my father and yielded to it.'

'Since when have you given him that sacred position? You should rather die a hundred times than own it! Remember a woman going to the pictures can neither be virtuous nor an obedient wife!'

'It was her first picture and it may be her last. It was all arranged within a few minutes after dinner.'

Zuhra thought it was not an appropriate time to discuss the matter. Nazeer would let others know of their differences. She asked him to have lunch with Kabeer.

'Shall I go and change my clothes? These are so heavy and I am perspiring', said Kabeer.

'Yes, be ready for lunch.'

He found Nazni in bed lying on her face.

He really did not like his mother's ill-treatment of her.

'If you try to be a little more careful there will be no trouble at home. She will have no cause to grumble. She's our well-wisher. She's old and how long will she live? Soon you'll be the mistress of the house. She has reached that position after passing through similar days. You must strive and achieve it.'

'She sees nothing good in me. The more I am afraid of her and try to be careful the more causes she finds for grievance', said Nazni.

'Old people are always like that. If you try to be patient and obey her even if she is wrong she'll come to love you.'

Although Kabeer's talk was not very encouraging Nazni felt relieved because it was expressed gently and in her own interest. She thought that she would undergo any suffering for his sake. One must not expect a bed of roses in this life.

Chapter VI

Nazni was small, thin and delicate. When she was ten years old she had fallen victim to a severe attack of rheumatic fever and was under treatment in a ladies' hospital for months. Her mother and grandmother spared no efforts to get her treated by Hakims, Pears and even witches. At length Doulath Khan look up the matter and consulted good doctors. A special nurse was appointed for her care. The fever stopped and the swelling disappeared. She was given tonics and codliver oil for years. At last came a day when she looked healthy and blooming, but still the least exertion caused her fatigue and palpitation. Nature had taught her to rest to get relief. Sometimes she would have pain in her left shoulder. Her mother and grandmother massaged it. They said that all these small ailments would heal of themselves if she were married.

From the month of conception her health gradually declined. She had constant headache and giddiness. In her seventh month symptoms caused by her weak heart began to appear. She felt better in her mother's house. As soon as she returned home her illness reappeared.

According to custom the first child must be born in the mother's house. The pregnant daughter is usually sent for in the seventh month. Doulath Khan had her examined by a heart specialist. Unfortunately it was a man. Zuhra who had lived a healthy life could not believe her ears when she heard of the heart disease. She had refused to consult a male doctor when she was ill after her husband's death, and by good luck she recovered without it. She formed a strong belief that all those who go to doctors are either fussy or immoral.

'A man can't own a woman as his wife after she has been touched by a man. There were men in former days who used to cut off that part of the body which was touched by a stranger', said Zuhra.

'I felt a sort of repulsion when the doctor was examining her heart, lungs and back. I felt that I could not be proud of her any more', said Kabeer.

Zuhra was pleased to hear him endorse her opinion. She determined that Nazni should be punished for having gone to the pictures and having been treated by a surgeon.

Under the careful nursing of a trained nurse from the seventh month Nazni withstood the strain of delivery. A baby boy was born to the rejoicing of all. Nazni's parents spent thousands of rupees on various ceremonies. On the fortieth day hundreds of people were invited to dinner. Many expensive gold presents were made for all including Zuhra.

Nazni now had to go back home, but the very idea of going there made her cry. There was a relapse. She was put to bed and was not allowed to stir from it for three months.

Zuhra often went to see her grandson. She and Nazni's grandmother became close friends. The old lady exaggerated Nazni's sufferings to gain Zuhra's sympathy and make her leave Nazni for some months more in her mother's house.

'The doctor says it is a serious disease. She should not be allowed to get up form her bed for six months. Her heart is weak and will stop working if she exerts herself.'

Zuhra thought of her son. Another six months was terrible.

'What's that heart-trouble she's suffering from?' said she to Kabeer one day.

'Her heart has been affected from the time she was a girl.'

'So they got rid of her by putting the burden on you. No one said anything about it before the marriage. They deceived you.'

'Who will say anything about one's health except doctors? They also didn't know of it till the specialists examined her. One who has heart disease has to be cared for all her life.'

'What do you mean by cared for?'

'She shouldn't be allowed to lift heavy things and exert herself too much. She must have peace of mind and complete rest, and be kept under proper medical treatment. Then she'll live for some years.'

'If not?'

'She'll soon get worse and die. At least for six months we can't expect anything from her', said Kabeer.

'So what do you want to do?'

'What can I do? It is fate. One has to be content with it.'

'Become a Fakir and give up the world. Go to a cave and live there. Young men like you can't pass their days single. If she's suffering from an incurable disease why should you be punished for it?'

'I don't know what to do. I had a talk with the doctor about her. He is of opinion that she'll never be normal. She must be kept at home as an idol.'

'And you will worship her, I suppose.'

'That's what many people do.'

'They do it if they are not men', was the nasty reply.

'What else can be done?'

'Get yourself remarried and leave that whore in her mother's house.'

The idea did not vex Kabeer. On the contrary it roused him.

'How can I do that?'

'As if it is an impossible thing! Hundreds of men have done it. They do it on lame excuses, or none. Your need is great and is quite reasonable. It can be arranged easily. If you just open your mouth there'll be hundreds of offers.'

The optimistic expression encouraged him and he began to think seriously about it.

'Before the thing is settled the whole town will know.'

'We have to be very careful till the wedding is over. It must be done through Mustafa', said Zuhra.

'Zainab Bi could do it quicker.'

'A secret matter can never be entrusted to a woman. She's popular in Doulath Khan's house. It is not the hurry we have to think of but the secrecy.'

When Kabeer mentioned the idea Mustafa welcomed it

'I can do it in no time. I'll see that a healthy, obedient and faithful girl is brought to you. She'll make you and your mother happy and comfortable. You can't expect to live with a sickly woman', said Mustafa.

In a week's time Mustafa brought numerous proposals from rich and poor families. Kabeer repeated them all to his mother for approval. When he mentioned a rich family's name she said, 'We have had enough of them. No rich girl can be obedient and loyal to you. You'll have to adjust yourself to their whims and fancies instead of being humoured by them.'

When the name of a poor fatherless girl came up she agreed.

'What does Mustafa say about the girl?' said she.

'He's of the same opinion. He says I shall be happier with her and she'll be more useful.'

'He's a man of experience.'

'What shall I ask him to do?'

'The difficulty is that I can't go to see the girl. The whole town would talk of it. Your father-in-law will come to know of it before the matter is settled, and he'll get it broken off. Our going to a poor widow's house in a dirty locality will rouse suspicion. They will humiliate us. If we bring a girl from a decent family we risk our happiness and comfort. We should care for our interest, not for the opinion of others, as we did at the first marriage.'

'They'll call us heartless if you do it when she's ill. If she comes to know of it she'll have another relapse.'

'If you can't do it when she's ill you'll not dream of doing it when she's well. You have a good cause in her long illness.'

'We can't go to see the girl and we can ask no one else to do it. We have to depend upon Mustafa's version. We are defying her and her people by the second marriage. They will have a good cause to condemn us if something goes wrong', said he thoughtfully.

'You are a coward. We are not defying them. On the other hand we want to help her by lessening her work and responsibility. They ought to be grateful instead of condemning us. An extra healthy woman at home is no more than an extra servant.'

'If she's treated like that...'

'You can't argue. Ask Mustafa to send his sister to see the girl and settle the matter soon. You are not a saint to live with a bedridden woman. Your comfort is more important than her happiness.'

Mustafa's sister went to see the girl. They showed her a decent-looking girl from the locality. There was no need for the matter to leak out. Both parties had their secrets to keep. Kabeer was hiding it from his wife and the new girl's people had to hide the name of the man who had come to their house.

The girl's mother acted dramatically and promised an expensive garment and cash to Mustafa's sister on the success of the marriage. The sister in turn praised the girl to heaven in front of Mustafa. She was very optimistic regarding her health, sense of duty, and ability to adjust herself to any circumstances. She added that Zuhra would not see a day of discomfort. She would make her sit like a queen and would be a source of joy to Kabeer. She was a girl who would eat crumbs and work like a horse.

'Mustafa in his turn exaggerated these womanly virtues in Kabeer's presence. When Kabeer repeated them to his mother she thought that this was just the type of daughter-in-law she had always sighed for. The girl's mother was asked to keep the matter strictly secret in her own interest, and the marriage was to be a very quiet affair. The conditions were welcomed and arrangements in a modest way were made on both sides.

On the day of Nikha Zuhra went with Kabeer and Mustafa's sister. It was over very soon. As everybody was in a hurry to leave the place unseen by others Zuhra asked the girl to be brought for tying the Lacha. The bride's relations said that the girl was not yet ready to be shown. She was to be given a bath. It would take an hour more. Zuhra overruled the long-established custom of the Lacha ceremony done by the husband's people. She asked them to do it themselves and left the place with Kabeer.

The Jalva was to take place in the night at about three o'clock. The mother and son reached the bride's house safely. When the bride was brought to Kabeer her face was covered. The face of the bride is shown in a mirror which is placed between the bride and the bridegroom. When he saw her face in it he could not believe his eyes. He rubbed them and looked again. He was not wrong, the face was ugly and dark. He looked at his mother furiously. She was at a distance and had not seen the bride. She smiled her congratulations. His blood boiled. He called up before his mind's eye the fair and beautiful features of Nazni. What a contrast! Even his mother was laughing at his discomfiture. He got up from the stage without a word and went out. He stood there for some time thinking of what should do. After some time Zuhra sent for him. He would not go in. He left the house alone. Zuhra was in an awkward position. She did not know the cause of her son's anger. She looked for Mustafa's sister, who however had disappeared.

'Why did he go away like that?' said she to one of the ladies.

'Go and see the girl. All her younger sisters were married years ago but she. You have been deceived. We knew of it so we came to see the fun', said the kind spectator.

Zuhra went to the stage and asked a girl to lift the bride's head. 'I won't', said she, and ran away. Zuhra called her informative friend asked her the same service. Zuhra screamed.

'What wicked people! This is sheer deception. Where's Mustafa's sister? She has ruined my son's life!'

Who would help her? She was alone, and all of them were united. Zuhra went and saw the bride a second time. She was dark, with deep pock-marks, and her upper teeth projected prominently.

A woman of Zuhra's calibre even if she loses her temper can be serene and practical after some time. Nothing could be done as the marriage was over. If she left the girl and went home as her son had done the bride's people had every right to file a suit against him. It was she who had forced him to remarry, so she was responsible for the consequences. There would be no chance of getting him remarried soon. When people came to know of this no one would give him a girl. And why waste all that money? She decided to take the bride with her and coax Kabeer to accept her. If he refused she could take her for herself. She would be an unpaid servant entirely at her disposal.

Leaving the bride in her room Zuhra went to Kabeer. He was in bed and pretended to be asleep. But she would not leave him. Yet the pill had to be sugar-coated.

'Your first wife will be pleased to see her rival. Her sense of importance will by no means be lessened and your love for her will be increased. All your desires in your first marriage are fulfilled. This one will only be a head-servant', said she to her sleeping son.

Kabeer turned and looked aghast. 'One should feel inclined to be in the company of a woman whom one calls wife. The very sight of her is repulsive. You can't think of her as both servant and wife.'

'After your first wife you can't expect such beauty in the second. She's not very ugly. There are uglier women living happily with their husbands. When you find her more useful and obedient you'll love her. It is usefulness that matters.'

'You always have your own way. What do you want me to do after making me an object of laughter?'

'Have I to tell you that after the marriage is over?'

'I hate to touch her. I can't live with her.'

Kabeer had never been so rude and obstinate. Zuhra thought she had said enough.

'I did not mean any harm to you. If you don't want her I shall have her for my service. You do as you like.' No reply coming she began again. 'In spite of all our precautions she has come to us. It's a matter of destiny. You can't change it. No human hand can do it.' Zuhra left his room.

Kabeer began to think about his mother's words, his wife's health, his inconveniences for the last nine months with no hopes of having a healthy wife in the future. Reading always bored him and thinking gave him a headache. So he released himself from his worries by sleeping soundly.

Zuhra asked the cook to make a bed for the bride in her room.

'Whose bride is she? Where's the bridegroom?' asked the cook.

'You mind your own business. You have nothing to do with our family affairs.'

'I have seen you buying clothes and jewels. I thought they were for Doulhan Begum. You gave her no present when she gave birth to a child. Other mothers-in-law overload their daughter-in-law with gifts, especially if she gets a boy.'

'I tell you not to interfere in our home affairs. If you open your mouth again I'll sack you on the spot. Your position in the house is like that of this slipper. It must know its place and lie down there.'

However the bed was made and the bride was laid on it. Munira, the bride, listened to all that took place. She had aspired all her life for marriage with no hope of getting it. Her last desire was to call herself a married woman. She would have been happy with the title even in a poor man's house, but luck is blind. The wheel of fortune brings down the most deserving to earth and raises the vilest to the top. The one satisfaction was that she was married. Let the quarrels go on. Why should she care?

If her features were the cause of her misfortune she could change it by her tact and spirit. She would not mind the work of a menial. She would work for her husband like a Russian soldier and win him. Let him love her or not so long as they lived like husband and wife.

While these thoughts were passing in the mind of Munira, Zuhra who was sleeping on a cot opposite to hers said, 'You know what has happened to you? I did my best to plead for you but my obedient son has disobeyed me—the first time in his life. I am helpless. You have to make your way to win him. Even if he treats you like a khawas you must be thankful to him. You have neither beauty nor wealth, which are the two considerations that make a man love a woman. Your only weapons are your strength and spirit, and though they are secondary ones you can make the best use of them. Your rival is seriously ill. He has been undergoing great suffering on account of her. It is up to you to exert and acquire the wealth a woman aspires for in the world. Many women in spite of their ugliness have been loved by their husbands.'

Munira had been thinking just the same thing. She made up her mind to put her ideas into practice forthwith.

'Go to the kitchen from tomorrow and see to the cooking. If you feed the brute he will want nothing else. Serve all his meals yourself. Don't leave it to the cook. After all he is a hungry man. If you try to please him sincerely without thinking of your own interest your deficiencies will be overlooked.'

Early in the morning when Zuhra returned from her prayers she found the bride's bed empty. She went to the kitchen and saw her busy preparing chapaties. As soon as she saw Zuhra she bent down her head. Zuhra was pleased to see her obeying implicitly and went to her room to keep an eye on her movements. She saw the bride carrying in the tray with numerous dishes for breakfast. The strong and tempting smell of kichdi and fried kabab made Zuhra feel hungry.

Kabeer came to the dining room, and seeing the ugly face of his wife turned his head. He pretended not to look at her and began eating. Munira not caring for his indifference went to the kitchen and brought some more dishes. She arranged and rearranged them on the dustar-khuan. Kabeer was forced to look at the person who was interfering in the quarrel of his mouth and fingers. He looked at her as a grave master to punish her for her audacity. She gave a broad smile with closed lips, as all those with projecting teeth do. Her smile was pleasing, her eyes shone. As a bride she was sweet with flowers, amber and sandal. She was wearing new and gorgeous clothes. Even an inhuman being would respond to such a smile. Kabeer was firm and did not smile, but he felt he was acting like a hypocrite. He had made her his wife, and for no fault of hers he was ill-treating her. He had been unjust to her. As for her features she was not responsible.

After his breakfast he went to his mother, who seemed serious. She asked him when he had last seen the baby.

'For the last three days I haven't been there.'

'I sent the servant and got information of both the mother and the baby', said she.

'I might go there this evening.'

Zuhra did not like the idea of his going there so soon. She wanted him to go there when things at home were more developed and his hatred for his new wife had lessened.

'You are a bridegroom and are not expected to go out', said she. She had confidence in the new girl's tactics. She would make him yield to her in two or three days. Her own absence from home would enable them to be free.

'I shall go there now. It makes no difference', said he.

Kabeer was repenting for what he had done. He thought that his treatment of her had been horrid, and nothing but yielding to her would make things up. So he said 'As you please.'

Zuhra left the house after breakfast. Kabeer went to his room to sleep.

Munira on the pretext of giving him fruit juice, which he had never taken in his life, went to his room with a glass in her hand.

'Please taste if the sugar is all right', said she, holding it out to him with a smile.

Kabeer sat up on his bed and took the glass from her hand looking into her eyes. As his mother had said, she was not so very ugly. Youth and its charm were on her side. The rich blood running in her veins made even the dark complexion attractive.

Zuhra returned home in the afternoon and found them in his room. Her plans which had fallen to earth only the night before had been fulfilled and quicker than she had expected.

Munira running from his room helped her to carry her shawl and the pandan and asked if she wanted a hot drink as the journey might have made her tired. Zuhra was pleased with the voluntary offer of service. Before the order was given Munira ran to the kitchen and asked the cook to boil water for tea. She arranged the tray herself, carried it to her mother-in-law, put it on a chair and made two cups of tea.

'For whom is the other? Has Kabeer finished his tea?'

'Yes, but I shall give him one more hot cup. The evening is so cold, he'll feel better with it', said the new loving wife.

'Call him here. He can have it with me.'

Munira disappeared for a long time. The tea was getting cold, but it did not displease the mother. It all added to the success of her own efforts. Finishing her cup of tea she asked the cook to remove the tray.

'How is Akram?' said Kabeer paying his respects to his mother.

'He is lovely, smiles, tries to talk and goes to everyone. He is not timid or frightened of anybody. She is still the same. They say she is getting better and they will send her home next month. But I don't think she'll be well so soon. She breathes so fast one can hear the loud beating of her heart sitting near her. She's pale and anaemic. She is a sight to make a healthy person sick. I told them not to hurry and follow the doctor's advice strictly. I even said they could keep her as many months as they liked.'

'So they don't know of this?' said Kabeer.

'I don't think it has reached them; none of them behaved differently. We must congratulate ourselves on the clever way we've managed things. They are bound to know in a day or two. Our cook is enough to inform them. What a fright she gave me last night!'

'Why? What does it matter to her? Tell her not mention it.'

'I am not a coward like you to ask her. Let her talk. Who cares now? Are you funky to face her? I have heard of people called henpecked husbands but now I can see one with my own eyes.'

'Oh, no…no, I shall tell her it was done in her own interest, and to make her comfortable and to live long.'

'Better put it another way. You did it because you couldn't suffer any more. Ask her to come to her home when she is well.'

'That depends upon her parents', said Kabeer.

'If they don't like to send her let them keep her for life. No woman will take the drastic step of separating herself from her husband,' said Zuhra.

'Many have done it.'

'If you go into the details of their history you will always find something immoral. Modern girls do it but they are exceptions. What'll you lose even if she refuses to come? If she really loves you she must be pleased with all that pleases and comforts you. The presence of an extra woman at home should not displease her. She was happy with the cook and she is hand and glove with her. Your fears are baseless. You will see that both of them will be happy.'

Kabeer's point had only one side where his mother was concerned. Whatever she said was an authorised fact. None could contradict it. He himself could not see beyond it. Her arguments to him were sincere and right. After all man is man and woman is woman. Why should he not do anything he liked for his own comfort and happiness? He was not living for his wife's happiness but his own. He was not going to discard her for life. What more could she want than food and shatter? His needs would be satisfied and her children brought up. If she was faithful to him she must be contented with her life.

The cook on the pretext of stomach-ache left the house after Zuhra's return. Munira was busy with the dinner. Her experience in cooking was coming in handy. She believed not only in quantity but in quality and variation. She asked the cook indirectly how many dishes were prepared and what were the things Kabeer liked. Both Zuhra and Kabeer were pleased with her cooking, as the one liked quality and the other quantity. After her work was over Munira spent her time with her mother-in-law. Unlike her rival she either stitched her clothes or massaged her body. Old age was showing itself and she needed special attention. Till very late in the night she worked for her mother-in-law.

Chapter VII

The cook was more fond of Nazni than of Zuhra, partly because of her beauty and partly for the tips she got now and then from her. The presence of a new woman at home and her connection with the master had given her brain rich food for digestion. She went straight to Nazni and sat down panting near her bed.

'Why are you panting? What has happened to you?' asked Nazni's mother.

'I came running from Doulhan Begum's house to give her a terrible piece of news', said the cook.

'Ammajan was here the whole day. She did not say anything. How is he? What has happened to him?' interrupted Nazni anxiously.

'Has he come to see you?' said the cook proudly.

'For the last four days he hasn't been here', said Nazni.

'Why would he come here? He has been enjoying his life with his new wife', said the cook.

'What!...Who is she?...When?...How is she?...'said Nazni puzzled, excited and breathing heavily.

The mother was shocked not only by the news but also because it was broken so sharply to Nazni. She got up and giving a sign to the cook to follow moved towards the door. She wanted to know the details, but they would upset Nazni. 'Amma, don't take her away. You'll kill me! I want to hear more about it', said Nazni, breathing heavily.

'You shouldn't hear anything saddening in your present condition. He will not forgive me if your health is upset', said the mother.

'There's nothing more saddening than what I have heard already. Nothing more will happen to me if I hear the details. I get the palpitation only when I talk. I promise you not to open my mouth, or put her questions', said Nazni. The mother sat down reluctantly. After all Nazni knew the worst, and it would be better if she heard direct the treacherous ways of her husband. It would lessen her sorrow.

'When was he married?' said the mother, while Nazni stared eagerly at the cook and prayed to God to make her say it was a lie and said for a joke.

'He was married yesterday morning. Both the mother and the son left home at about eleven o'clock. I thought they had gone to Nazni Begum', said the cook.

'Didn't you suspect it before? You were there day and night', said the mother.

'If I had I would have informed you beforehand.'

'Didn't they buy jewels and clothes?'

'Yes, they did. I thought they were for Nazni Begum because she had given birth to a boy. I was hoping to get her old saries after she got them.'

'They came here like beggars empty-handed on the day of Chilla', said the mother.

'Yes, I was here that day. I thought they wanted to give her presents after her return home', said the cook.

'When did the bride came home? Was he very pleased?' interrupted Nazni.

'You promised not to speak. I shall send the woman away if you don't keep quiet', said her mother. 'Didn't you hear them talking about it at home?' She went on. She wanted to hit upon those facts that would reveal Kabeer's treachery.

'They did everything so cunningly that even when they went for the Jalva I didn't know. I was sleeping in the kitchen', said the cook.

'You must have known of it when the bride came home', said the mother.

'No, not even then. Master came alone and asked me for water to drink. I asked him about Begum Sahib but he went to his room without answering', said the cook.

'How funny. When did she come?' asked the mother.

'I slept again. I was awakened to make a bed for the bride in Begum Sahib's room', said the cook.

'Why? Why there?' cried both the mother and the daughter. The mother looked a warning at Nazni. Nazni was pleased that the bride and Kabeer were not friendly. She guessed that he had not liked to take a second wife and it was his mother who had forced her on him. So she must leave her mother's house at once to help him in his determination. She must tell him that she would give her life at his feet. She would never go back to her parents. She admired his self-control and was anxiously waiting to get the proof of her guesses.

'I was equally surprised, so I asked Begum Sahib whose bride she was and where was the bridegroom. She was furious and said if I said one word more she would sack me.'

'Then what happened?'

Nazni's hopes were still high. She was waiting for a favourable reply.

'I made the bed and laying the bride on it I went to sleep', said the cook.

'So the bride and bridegroom are at sixes and sevens', said the mother.

'I knew he would never remarry. Even when a woman is forced upon him he rejects her. He often said that the charm of my eyes had a magical effect on him and that he would never be able to look at another woman. Amma, please let me go home with the cook. It doesn't matter even if I die there.'

Her mother looked at her sternly.

'Nazni, why don't you have patience and leave the thing to me? I have more experience in such matters. Whatever I do is in your interest. Every second minute you break your promise.'

'It is not exactly that', said the cook. 'In the morning when I was lighting the fire in the kitchen the bride came. I got a shock to see her. I hadn't seen her face in the night.'

'Don't tell us what happened to you. What took place there?' said the mother.

Nazni's hopes were not yet shattered. Her only consolation was that her husband was faithful to her. The sin of getting him remarried was his mother's.

'She's dark like Amavas. She has four long teeth. They don't fall below as some have them but go up like this.'

'Oh woman, come to the point!' cried the mother.

'When I describe a person I do it fully.'

'Don't describe her but tell us what she did.'

'She has deep holes on her face.'

'What, holes! Are they due to leprosy?'

'I don't know what they are due to. Don't you know, like those the night nurse has?' said the cook, who was bent upon exaggeration and irritation.

'They are marks of smallpox. What happened then?' said the mother.

'She's fat like an elephant, and looks like this when she walks.'

The mother could not help laughing. Nazni was overjoyed. She looked at her slim body and arms, touched her thin cheeks, and noticed her fair complexion by half closing her right eye and looking at her nose. A sense of superiority over her rival took root in her mind.

'Again you have started your rubbish', said the mother.

'Amma, dear, please let her say all she wants to. I feel happier', said

Nazni with the most pathetic appealing eyes. Her mother decided not to check the cook and let Nazni have a few happy minutes.

'Come on with your narration. How does she walk?' said the mother. This revived the cook's spirits who was bent upon derision. She had tied over her bag a string with tiny bells. She removed it and tied it to her leg to imitate the silver jewels on the bride's legs. She began to walk up and down the room with exaggerated gait and gestures, jingling the bells. Each movement made Nazni burst out laughing.

'She has lots of leg-rings then?' said the mother.

'Oh yes, three different kinds on each.'

'Did she bring them from her mother?'

'Tut! She's a beggar like me, even poorer. She brought only a bundle of clothes, whereas I gave my daughter boxes, trunks, a chair and a cot. I went and examined her clothes. They are very ordinary ones like this.'

'What more did your new bride bring?'

'Peesh! my new bride! Why she's just fit to bring water for me to the lavatory. I was very fair and beautiful at her age. Even now I beat her any day. My Doulhan Begum is my dear mistress. I shall live and die for her. Why, I should have left the house long ago if she was not there', said the cook, kissing Nazni's feet.

Nazni's eyes were full of tears. At least there was one person in that house to feel sympathy for her.

'What happened after she came to the kitchen?'

'She asked me about the meals and the dishes cooked for each, especially what things master liked. I was furious and felt like pulling her hair and kicking her out of the house, but I only asked why the devil she wanted to know all that. I had more right to keep them sacred to my heart, having served there for so long. I said that she was a newcomer so she should obey me.'

'Then what did she say?'

'She said that she was not a servant but master's wife. I asked her then why didn't she come with him and why did she sleep in his mother's room?'

'What did she say? Now give us the exact words.'

'She said that master after looking at her face on the takhat left the place without a word', said the cook.

'Just because she was ugly he left her. Otherwise he would have brought her quite happily', said the mother.

'Then the mother-in-law sent her to the master but he refused to accept her.'

'Didn't I tell you, Amma? He's not a man like that', interrupted Nazni.

'Wait a minute. What happened then?' said the mother.

'What a treacherous woman your mother-in-law is! She persuaded the bride to do her best to win him. She asked her to cook and serve all his meals and see to his needs.'

'Did she do all that? Did he speak to her?' said the mother.

'She served the breakfast but came back to me with tears and said that he did not even look at her. She ran in with another tray and did not say a word after that.'

'So he still does not talk to her?' said Nazni.

'Soon after Begum Sahib left home she made orange juice and took it to him. I told her that he did not like it but she wouldn't listen to me. She disappeared till two o'clock. Then she came back all smiles. The lunch was ready. She took it for him. She gave him tea. When the mother-in-law came she ran to her and helped her and gave her tea without being asked.'

The mother and daughter looked at each other meaningly. Nazni felt a pain at her heart. She began to cry. She needed an outlet for her pain.

The cook was suddenly frightened. 'Bibi', she said 'if you give them my name for telling you about it they will sack me.'

'Not only will you lose your job but there it be no one to look after Nazni in that house. You are safe with us. We shall protect you', said the mother, and hurried out of the room to fetch medicine. She went to Doulath Khan to consult him about the medicine. She was not allowed to do anything by herself. Meanwhile one by one the whole family entered the room. The father came himself with a dose of medicine and administered it immediately.

'Why did she get it so suddenly? What did you tell her?' said the father, seeing the still trembling cook.

'That wouldn't do her any harm. It is her disease', said the cook.

Doulath Khan's presence revived Nazni. She thought that her father had come to punish the culprit and revenge her. Tears were still falling from her eyes.

'I don't want this lacha and the bangles any more', said she and pulled it from her neck.

'The bangles are ours. You have worn them from the time you were born. What's the matter?'

No one answered.

'Why don't you say what you did to her?' he said to the cook.

'I told her that master has remarried.'

'So she's killing herself for that. It's a wonder he did not do it earlier', was the calm reply.

'What! He has remarried!' screamed the grandmother.

'Leave her to me. I shall look after her. All of you go out', said he.

Some obeyed the command immediately and some hesitated to leave the place of excitement. When the cook left the room all followed her to get first-hand information from her. They took her to the dining room. She was an important personage. All of them either sat or stood round her and put similar questions. The cook repeated every item with more exaggeration. Every second or third sentence was followed by an assurance that she did hot know of it earlier or she would have informed them all about it in time. The event gave them a matter to discuss for months, and to gather information from the place through other sources. Nazni's elder brother came home. The little ones ran to him and shouted.

'Doula Bhai (Kabeer) has got another bride! Apa is crying. She was dying. Bavajan is still in her room. He sent us all out.'

He went straight to Nazni's room and knocking on the door entered it. His father was sitting on Nazni's bed. Nazni looked like a corpse. He sat on the chair.

'How do you feel now?' said he.

'I'm all right. Nothing'll happen to me even if you kill me. There are many more sufferings reserved for me', said Nazni with tears in her eyes.

'Why do you cry as if all of us were dead? I would sacrifice my life to make you happy and to serve you. Your wailing won't help you or help us. He has acted treacherously. We must punish him for it', said the brother.

'I am asking her to get herself cured first. When she is well we can decide whether to send her there or not. If she still wants to go to him let her. We are ready to help her and support her either way', said the father.

'Never think of going to that brute, a coward, a cad, a puppet in his mother's hands. He thinks of his cleverness too much but I have never met such a dunce. It's a disgrace to go to him when he stabbed you in the back. Live with us happily. We will file a suit against him and get your mahar and maintenance for both', ejaculated the brother.

Nazni liked her brother's sympathy, but she was sad because of the vulgar words he used about her husband. But on second thoughts her brother was right. She had lost him and in that loss she had found a loving and supporting brother. What more did she want than her own people?

'Going or not going there we shall leave for a later date. Let her decide when she feels stronger. Our house welcomes her under any circumstances. Nothing serious has happened to her. It's her imagination. On the other hand she will be more free from the home responsibilities', said Doulath Khan. He knew the human heart.

'She can't decide anything in her present state of health', said he again.

The brother's anger had cooled down. He listened to his father. He always admired his forethought and sound judgment, yet the sight of the weeping sister made him say, 'He is a rogue and a cad. He did it without her permission, when she's in bed.'

'Often second marriages take place without the first wife's knowledge', said Doulath Khan. 'It is neither uncommon nor a sin according to social injunctions. He has every liberty to do it. Her precarious health give him a good excuse. Men with the polygamous instinct fish for an excuse. The minute they find one even if it is not a reasonable one they interpret it in such a way that any stranger hearing it puts the whole blame in the opposite party. They know the first wife would not permit it so they do it on the sly. Some first wives go themselves and get it done.'

'He was forced by his mother to do it. Even when the woman was brought home without his permission he refused to look at her. So she asked her to make her way', said Nazni despairingly.

Doulath Khan expected his daughter to side with her husband in spite of his action. He was pleased with her careful expressions. Nazni's love for her husband was blind. A separation from him or hatred for him should be by her own decision.

'What gives me more pain is that he did it on the sly. He came here almost every day and never said even a word about it', said she again.

'You wouldn't have permitted him. He knew the futility of approaching you for it. Don't bother about it. He will tell us now when everything is over and there's no fear that we'll prevent it. It's a mistake to think that he did it without your permission. Your dignity is wounded as he didn't give you as much importance as you give to yourself. The thing has taken place without your permission and it would have taken place with it. It matters nothing.'

'Why didn't you do it with all your money, and why are many others contented with one wife?' asked the brother.

'My dear son, the number of such men is not great. Those who

develop a power of thinking impartially, and see the harmful consequences of plurality of wives, remain contented. Some remain single all
their lives because they know the responsibility and their inability to
fulfil it.'

'Knowing that he has more money than he needs, that his life is idle
and that he is not a thinker, why did you give her in marriage to him?'

'Your mother and grandmother are more responsible for this catas-
trophe. They had no peace of mind and rest till they got it done. Every
rejection of an offer by me brought on a new quarrel at home. Knowing
that I find fault with new men they decided almost everything between
themselves this time. I gave my consent to satisfy them. It was a
mistake.'

Nazni was feeling extremely tired and the philosophical discussion
between them made her feel sleepy.

The cook had gone, and the ladies, finding their excitement dimin-
ishing thought of going to Nazni to get fresh matter for discussion. The
grandmother gently open the door and entered the room. The mother
followed suit.

'Don't say anything to her', said Doulath Khan. 'You people can't
understand when to talk and what to say. He is married. You can't make
him divorce his wife by unnecessary discussion.'

'We know it. We have not grown our grey hair in the hot sun', said
grandmother emphatically.

'That's why she was bad', said the father.

'Your wife was with her all the time. I came just one minute before
you', said grandmother.

Doulath Khan looked at his wife. 'All of you sail in the same boat. Let
her be left with the nurse for some days.'

'As if the nurse is more loving than we', said grandmother.

'You don't understand what I say but take it amiss', said he, and left
the room. The son also followed him.

The grandmother sat comfortably on Nazni's bed and put her hand
over her forehead. Nazni began crying noiselessly.

'Don't cry. God ought not to have shown you these days so soon,
especially when you are bedridden. What kind of a man is he? He is a
beast. Other husbands don't think of their lives when their wife is ill',
said grandmother.

'Don't mention his name any more in this house. Let us think of him no
more. After what he has done she can't forget us for him', said mother.

'I don't want to go there. There'll be none to ask me whether I ate or
not', cried Nazni, who knew nothing more of love than that.

'The cook said both of them are very happy, so your presence there will annoy them', said grandmother.

'Don't talk of those things. Let her forget she was married', said mother.

'I am not saying anything to her. She herself says that she'll not go there', said granny.

'How can I forget, Amma? When I think of Akram my heart breaks', said Nazni.

'He can live with us as one of our children. His father has no right to take him till he is seven years old', said mother.

'After bringing him up for seven years I have to give him to be tortured by his stepmother.'

'How badly stepmothers treat their step-children! We have seen with our own eyes a woman scarring her stepdaughter's feet with burning wood', said granny.

Nazni with tears in her eyes was thinking of Akram being beaten by his father and scarred by his stepmother. The nurse entered with food and asked them all to clear away. Doulath Khan had given her strict orders.

In the night the whole family was as quiet as if someone was dead. Nazni had a restless night in spite of a sleeping dose. The report of her health was given to Doulath Khan in the morning. The day nurse was reengaged.

Kabeer did not know that the cook had already created mischief. In the morning he went to see her and his son. He intended to reveal the secret tactfully after preparing the ground for it.

'No one's allowed in the room', said the nurse to Kabeer.

'Why? What has happened? How is she?'

'She's having temperature. The condition of her heart has caused anxiety.'

'I have every right to see my wife if she's not well. No one can prevent me', said he.

'Wait a minute please. I'll ask her father's permission. I shall be held responsible if anything goes wrong.'

'Damn you and her father.'

She closed the door and disappeared.

Kabeer stood thinking. Has she come to know of it? How could she? The cook was not well; she would not have come here. She resumed her duty his morning. It might be the usual relapse. He felt like going back without seeing her, but sin makes a man a coward. He decided to stay.

The nurse went to Doulath Khan and informed him of Kabeer's arrival. He was puzzled. He could not treat him ill. It might mean lifelong suffering for his daughter.

'Don't let the patient cry', he said at length.

'She's getting crazy and cries for nothing. You keep an eye on her when he is there.'

The master's warning increased the nurse's curiosity. She opened the door, and putting a chair for Kabeer, planted herself in the next room.

'How are you? The nurse said you are worse and no one's allowed in your room', said he.

'What do you care for my health?'

Kabeer had never known her to be sarcastic. She was annoyed because he had not seen her for the last four days.

'Who wants to know of you if not I? Have I not cared for you without caring for myself? Have I not suffered alone all these months while you have been enjoying yourself in your parents' house? Am I not living the life of a *sanyasi*, thinking of you, praying for you and crying for your sufferings? I am not lucky enough even to have my own son with me, for whom I am ready to give my life.'

'Now you have someone else to care for.'

This was unexpected. It was of no use to ask her about the informant. There was no way out. He was caught. The only thing he could do was to condemn the newcomer down right.

'Phoo! What a silly person you are to think that I care for that wretched negress. I hate to see her face. I didn't know that you were so foolish.'

'But Ammajan asked her to exert her influence on you and to win you. You were with her for hours in your room', interrupted Nazni.

'That's rubbish. Who told you all that? You come to know of things about me before I know them myself. I'm the master of my mind. No one can make me change unless I want to. Why don't you allow me to tell you? Then you can ask anything you want to know', said Kabeer.

Nazni began to feel despondent. It was foolish to put questions in between. Her hesitation gave Kabeer his chance.

'Do you know I locked myself in my room? I had a quarrel with Ammajan for having brought her home. When you see her you will understand why. She's not suitable even to wash your bathroom. I am surprised that you compare yourself with her. There's no one in the whole world to take your place in my heart. How can it be? None possesses even a hundredth part of your beauty. God has specially made you with His own hand and chosen me to enjoy that boon. I don't know how I deserve it. I am a loss to know why it pleased God to grant you to me.'

Kabeer was the only man she had seen in her life. The poor girl fell an easy prey to his open flattery. She thought that she would be unjust and cruel to him if she tried to make him sad. The woman who makes her husband sorry goes to the Seventh Hell where the fire burns eternally. She is burnt alive and is recreated and burnt again. This process goes on for ever even after the Day of Judgment. Tears were generously falling from her charming eyes. She did not know whether they were in sympathy for her suffering husband or in her own interest.

'Is life with you possible for me now? I am afraid of going there', said she sadly.

'If you ask how your life is possible without me, there's some sense in it. I have answered already. I can love no one but you. She's only a head cook and your servant as well as mine.'

'You got married without telling me. I was thinking that you hide nothing from me.'

'It was again because of your health. I came to tell you how it all happened but someone has already misrepresented it.'

'You did not care to see me after it. It is five days since you came.'

'It was due to you and in your interest. I had tried to persuade mother not to bring an extra woman into the house. She said you were coming home next month and she wanted you to have complete rest. You don't know how she adores you. One servant was not enough for you and Akram. By the by, did you tell her that you were coming soon?'

'Yes, mother told Ammajan.'

'That's why she was bent upon getting her soon. She wanted to train her in advance. When you come home you'll have nothing to do.'

'If you wanted to remarry why didn't you get a decent woman?'

'Because she will demand equal rights and status with you.'

Nazni felt that all she had heard was true. His regard for her was constant.

'Did the cook come to see you? She is very fond of you. Who wouldn't be? She was wanting to come here yesterday evening.'

Nazni was in a fix. She had promised not to mention her name. Kabeer realised that she was the culprit. No answer coming he said, 'Do your people know of it?'

'Yes everyone.'

'What did your father say?'

'He said my health is more important and he leaves it to me to decide whether to go back or not.'

'He's a sensible man and your well wisher. Obey him implicitly. You will never repent it.'

'But Bhai is against my going back to you. He was very angry. I felt so sad to hear him.'

'He's a fool. What does he know of the world and my love of you? If he had loved you as I do he would have felt for my feelings. These young men after learning a few words of English think too much of themselves. Our sense of justice and our ways of love are more reliable than those of the immitators of the West. They have illegal connections with many and yet believe in their fidelity.

Nazni was admiring the philosophy of her husband. She thought that God had created him with unique talents and had bestowed this personage on her.

'Yes, he was angry at first. After hearing father his anger cooled down and he didn't open his mouth till he left the room', said she.

'What do the ladies say?'

'Granny was crying and asked why God had to show me these bad days so soon.'

'Tell her that there's nothing bad in it. You'll have one extra servant to serve you. What did you say?'

'I also cried, thinking of Akram and how he'll be ill-treated by his stepmother.'

'So you are the only person who is responsible for his birth? I have nothing to do with him. He is my first-born and is a source of pride and pleasure to me. You'll have to cry for him when I die. I'm ready to give my life for him as Babar did for Humayun.'

That was the only instance in the whole history of India he remembered. He thanked his memory.

'You'll have other children.'

'Don't you know that a throne is given only to the first son? Others work under him like servants. When are you coming back? I live a lonely and sad life. Ammajan couldn't see me unhappy. She wouldn't have brought that ugly woman if you had been at home.'

'I used to come here only for the day. This time I came because I was not well', said Nazni.

'If you were ill my mother was there to look after you. Is your mother the only person who loves you?'

'When I was ill your mother never came to see me, whereas my mother hardly leaves me'.

'My mother's love is reasonable. She supplies all your needs and keeps information of your health. What more does your mother do?'

'When you are ill her treatment is quite different'.

'So you grudge the little pleasure she gives me. You ought to be pleased with it. What does your mother do to me when I am ill?'

'She can't do it because she is Gosha in front of you. Even if she were not she wouldn't do so much as she does for you.'

'That's what I say and that's why I came here.'

Kabeer thought that the matter needed some more time and flattery, though it meant a great strain.

'You are not bad by nature. Your people spoil you and will break your home. They sent for you almost every day but you refused to go there and stayed with me. Don't listen to anybody and as soon as you can come home. This is your mother's house. Your home is longing to have you.'

'I am having fever and there are two nurses to look after me'.

'Bring them with you. We shall send them here once a month for their salary.'

He got up and was trying to go but sat down quickly. 'I can't go without seeing my son', said he. He rang the bell. The nurse came. 'Bring Akram soon.'

'Baby's nurse won't let me bring him to a sick person's room. She's having fever.'

'You are an owl. The fever is in her body not in the room.'

The nurse smiled at the ignorance of the man. 'What makes you laugh? Go bring him soon.'

The nurse left the room and returned after five minutes.

'The baby is sleeping', said she.

'He sleeps at this time. He wakes at five when they get up for prayer', said Nazni.

Kabeer got up with a sigh. 'If he were in my house I would have kissed him in his bed. I go leaving my heart here.'

'Come to-morrow to see me', said the poor wretch in bed.

All the doubts that Nazni had entertained were solved. He had been married, without her permission because of her health. She found that her husband loved Akram more than she did. Her fear of losing his love and care was baseless. He loved her more than ever and she would now have more comfort. She felt sorry that because of her love for her parents a new person had had to be brought into her home.

Kabeer on his way home was very thoughtful. He was highly gratified by his success in dealing with an awkward position. He thought over the discussion and his flat denial of having had any connection with the new wife. He made up his mind to keep his word, not to live with her and to try and get a decent woman in the future to wipe away the disgrace caused by this pariah woman.

Nazni's words 'Why didn't you get a decent woman?' rang in his ears.

Sarojini Naidu

A poet who gave up poetry for nationalist politics, and an ebullient woman whose letters reveal a strain of sadness and fatigue, Sarojini Naidu (1879–1949) was one of the most impressive women on the nationalist scene. She grew up in Hyderabad and spoke Urdu fluently. She insisted on marrying a man about ten years older than she was, a widower, of another caste, and from another part of India.

She began to publish her poems in *The Indian Ladies Magazine*, edited by Kamala Satthianadhan, and eventually published her first book, *The Golden Threshold* (1905), in which the poem 'The Pardah Nashin' was published. It begins in an exotic way, but shades off into sadness, and it is one of Sarojini's better poems.

Sarojini Naidu was wary of any haste in purdah reform. In 1908 she wrote that 'incalculably tragic results would follow a premature and total abolition of the system', and she pleaded for a 'deft and wise and almost imperceptible relaxing of its rigorous laws day by day as education increases.'

The Pardah Nashin

Her life is a revolving dream
Of languid and sequestered ease;
Her girdles and her fillets gleam
Like changing fires on sunset seas;
Her raiment is like morning mist,
Shot opal, gold and amethyst.
From thieving light of eyes impure,
From coveting sun or wind's caress,
Her days are guarded and secure

Sarojini Naidu, 'The Pardah Nahin', in *The Golden Threshold*, with an intro. by Arthur Symond, New York: The John Lane Company, London: W. Heinemann, 1916 (1905).

Behind her carven lattices:
Like jewels in a turbaned crest,
Like secrets in a lover's breast.

But though no hand unsanctioned dares
Unveil the mysteries of her grace
Time lifts the curtain unawares,
And Sorrow looks into her face...

Who shall prevent the subtle years,
Or shield a woman's eyes from tears?

B.P. Sathe

A pioneer Dogri short story writer, B.P. Sathe (1910–73) began writing in the 1940s, and his collection *Pailha Phull* (1947), is considered the first such collection to be published in Dogri. He published two collections of short stories, and translated Hindi novels into Dogri.

Face-Showing

The day Rahimbibi came to our village as the newly wedded bride, all the women of our house went to see her. Each took with her something as *masahni*, a gift customarily given to see the face of the bride. My mother gave her a pair of bangles. My aunt gave her a pair of anklets. And my elder brother's wife gave her a pair of small silver toe-rings. When they returned home, they lavished so much praise on Rahimbibi's beauty that even we, small children then, were tempted to see her.

My mother said. 'What a lovely bride! She looks like a finely chiselled marble statue.'

The aunt joined in, 'What eyes! So black and lustrouse [sic]. Besides, the bride looks fairly tall.'

My sister-in-law who was a bit vain, said, 'Only her complexion is fair, the face is full of freckles. And then how can you know when she is sitting, whether she isn't lame or hasn't some other defect?'

It was my mother who replied. 'Who says she is lame? She came out from inside the house and her gait was perfectly normal.'

The aunt added, 'Purple spots on a fair face add to the charm.'

The sentence was completed by my elder brother who had come into the room. 'That is Greek beauty for you. The ornament of some royal place. Who are you talking about?'

B.P. Sathe, 'Face-Showing', in *Echoes and Shadows: A Selection of Dogri Short Stories*, selected and trans. Shivnath, Delhi: Sahitya Akademi, 1992.

Mother said, 'The washermen have brought the bride home. We were talking about Ilamdin's bride. We had gone to his place to give *masahni*. The bride is very beautiful and as fair as light.'

My elder brother's wife had extremely beautiful eyes but her complexion was a bit dark and she was short. Showing her annoyance, she went inside saying, 'After all, she is only a washerman's bride, not a Brahmin or Rajput bride!'

The aunt immediately retorted, 'She is no doubt a washerman's bride, but don't people praise beauty even in a lower caste?'

The sister-in-law retraced her steps and shot back, 'Bring her sister for your son then.' The reference was obviously to my brother. And yet, she had not understood the meaning of 'Greek Beauty'.

Ilamdin's mother was also our aunt but to distinguish her from our own aunt we called her 'washerwoman aunt'. Sometimes when both the aunts would be seated together, we just called 'auntie' to watch the fun and both responded simultaneously. It made us burst into laughter.

Several years ago my father had brought Mehtabdin with him from Saruinsar on his way back from Jammu. He had some difficulty about accommodation there and my father had asked him to come to Ramnagar. When he came, he was given a bit of land and a house to live in. He was also recruited as a sepoy in the fort. His sons started washing clothes. When he was pensioned off, his elder son Gulabdin took his place in the fort and his younger son Ilamdin carried on the washerman's work. Gulabdin's son was my age. When Ilamdin brought washed and pressed clothes of the house, Shamsu accompanied him carrying my clothes. Shamsu's grandfather did not sit idle in the house; he took to farming, raising crops of rice and maize and cauliflowers and peas and radishes and water-melons. Often Shamsu and I stole into Mehtabdin's field and picked green peas and enjoyed eating them.

For three or four days, the new bride was pampered, but eventually she had to join in the household chores. One day the washerwoman aunt brought her daughter-in-law along with her to fetch water. The daughter-in-law had a veil over her face right down the throat, a pitcher-rest on her head and a brand new pitcher on it. She wore a green artificial silk *suthan* and silver-thread embroidered sandals in her feet. Walking behind her mother-in-law, she looked an inch and a half taller than her.

The well was near our house. People from far and near came there to fill their vessels. Before going to the well the two women came to our house and the mother-in-law made the daughter-in-law touch the feet of my mother, my aunt and my sister-in-law. All the three ladies of our

house blessed her, 'May you and your husband live to a ripe old age.'
But after they left they raised another ripple in our house.

'The bride has such a lovely gait, like that of a peacock dancing.'

Mother and aunt were well-meaning women who appreciated others
and also condemned where condemnation was called for. But my sister-
in-law was young and did not like another being praised. 'Peacocks are
dark but she is so fair. Praising her like this would amount to saying that
a swan is dancing.'

Cut to the quick, the aunt said, 'What do we lose if we call a
peacock white?'

The sister-in-law kept quiet—either she could not find a suitable
reply or she did not think it expedient to prolong the argument.

The following day, the two women came to our house again on their
way to the well and sat down for a little chat. The women of our house
enquired from the daughter-in-law about the location of her house in
Saruinsar.

The mother-in-law advised her, 'You see, she is called the younger
aunt *chachi*, and she is called the elder aunt *tai*. My sons address them
like that, you should also do likewise. And this is *bhabhi*, my elder son's
wife. Her husband and Gulabdin went to school together. I call her by
her first name but you should always address her *bhabhi*.'

The daughter-in-law began to explain the location of her parents'
house in Saruinsar, 'We live a little to the north of the shops in Saruinsar,
to the left if you go from here.'

The women made the bride say a few more sentences. When the two
women were gone, they had left behind one more subject to talk about.

'How sweetly she talks! Like a cuckoo in a mango grove.'

Bhabhi said, 'You used to say the same about me also.'

'You are not inferior in any way. Your speech is also very sweet.'

Saryu *bhabhi* was pleased to hear this and the annoyance and hurt of
the earlier days were forgotten.

After a few days the mother-in-law stopped coming with her daughter-in-law. Probably she was engaged in other domestic chores at home.
Rahimbibi came to the well twice in the morning and once in the
evening. Going to school in the morning we would see her on the way.
One day, while the other boys had gone ahead, I remained behind when
I saw her coming from the opposite direction. She had her face covered
as usual, right down to the throat. A little hesitantly I said, 'Rahimbibi,
you can show your face to me. I am so small.'

Rahimbibi kept walking and said, '*Bhauji* if you want to see my face,
you will have to give *masahni*.'

We were walking in different directions and before I could give any reply she had gone some distance.

The next day I managed to remain behind again. As I crossed her path I said, 'Rahimbibi, what would you like to have as *masahni*? I shall get it for you from mother.'

Rahimbibi replied, 'No, no, not from *chachi*. I shall show you my face only when you give *masahni* out of your own earning. Until then, I will not lift my veil.'

Rahimbibi stuck to what she said. For years, she kept her veil. In the next three years, I did my eighth class and went to Jammu for further schooling. From Jammu, I went to Srinagar and could not go to the village for another year and a half. I was now fifteen and had failed in the ninth class. When I went home during the vacation and met Rahimbibi, she asked, '*Bhauji*, in what class are you studying now?'

'Ninth.'

'Last year also you were in the ninth.'

I felt at a loss for words and couldn't bear to stand in front of her and moved away, mumbling 'Yes, yes.'

As luck would have it, I failed in the ninth a second time and did not go home for a whole year. After three years in ninth, I got promoted to the tenth and then went home. I came across Rahimbibi again and she asked, 'Now you must be in college?'

'No, *bhabhi*. I am in the tenth now. I'll pass this time and then get a job. I shall arrange for your *masahni* from my first pay.'

'No, *bhauji*. Place the first pay at the feet of *chachi*. *Chachi* has to incur a lot of expenses to make offerings to deities, she will purchase things for the *puja*. I shall wait for my *masahni* for another year.'

'Rahim *bhabhi*, I did not know that it would be so difficult to see the face of my own *bhabhi*.'

'*Bhauji*, the more you wait, the stronger will the desire grow. On crossing over to the threshold of youth, the desire to see a face does not go. One wishes one would go on gazing. You are still too young and one passes through many turns at this age when several desires drop off. But I see that you have just one desire, the desire to see my face? Why do you want to finish with it? Let it mature and grow so strong that it never goes.'

Up to this time, I had thought that seeing Rahim *Bhabhi's* face was a bit of fun, a mere play. But now this desire to see her face took on a different colour. I was determined that I would give her *masahni* out of my own earning.

Destiny dictated its own course. I joined college after passing the tenth class. I was in the college for three years and there was no opportunity to earn. I had to leave college after three years to come back to look after our family lands because there was nobody else to do so. Father had passed away and my expenses in the college were managed by others. After some years I was also married. But Rahim *Bhabhi* did not lift her veil. I could not give her her *masahni* and every now and then when I met her she repeated, '*Bhauji*, I am not going to lift the veil without having *masahni*.'

Everybody showered praises on Rahim *Bhabhi*—She is very pretty, she is fair like a swan, her figure and form is so attractive and so on. My wife also felt jealous of Rahimbibi. Her own sandals were still silver thread embroidered whereas many years had passed since Rahimbibi's silver thread sandals had worn out, followed by red lac sandals, and then plain leather sandals which she has been wearing now for several years. But her complexion and loveliness rankled in the hearts of brides in embroidered sandals.

One day my wife said, 'Why does this Rahimu talk to you with such a long veil over her face?'

'Rahim *bhabhi* will lift the veil only after she gets *masahni* from me. As for talking, she talks to me in the same way as Saryu *bhabhi* does.'

'Saryu *bhabhi* is your own *bhabhi* but Rahimu is Muslim. What is your relationship with her?'

'My dear, relations among brothers remembering God by different names do not separate them. Ilamdin is like my real elder brother.'

'You may say so but people don't.'

'Well, I do not follow what others say. I wish that others would follow what I say.'

'The whole world follows what people follow.'

'But have you ever thought who people follow?'

She could not reply to this.

The month of Ramzan came. Muslims started their fasts. I asked Rahimbibi, 'You do not keep fasts?'

'I cannot fast for many days. I fast just for one day. I feel hungry. I don't mind eating plain bread of maize but I cannot remain hungry.'

'On which day will you fast?'

'On the day that I do not come to fetch water, you can take it that I am fasting.'

'I shall bring sweets for you on that day, to break the fast with.'

'No, no, it is not proper for you to bring sweets for me. Sweets will be brought by him who is supposed to bring them.'

'Then what should I bring that will be proper?'

'For you, the only proper thing is that *masahni*. When I get it, I'll see the Id moon.'

'All right. You go on seeing the Id moon. So far as I am concerned, the Purnima moon has been covered for years by the eclipse of your veil.'

After some six months, Rahimbibi started having fever. It was Shamsu now who came to the well to fetch water and I enquired from him about Rahimbibi's health. According to reports her health was fast deteriorating. The fever turned into typhoid and then to pneumonia. More complications followed. The *hakim* gave up hope. A doctor was called but he also held out no hope.

One morning Shamsu came running to our house and said to me, 'Since last night, my aunt has been sinking and telling everybody around to go and call *bhauji*. When I said I would go, she said, tell *bhauji* that I am going and that he should come to show me his face for the last time.'

I understood the situation and set out immediately with Shamsu. Rahimbibi was lying straight on her back on the cot and her face was uncovered. A fair face on a fair frail frame, black eyes and purple spots spread on the cheeks which reminded me of a Greek statue. Slowly, she turned her gaze towards me and said in a very low voice, '*Bhauji*, I have removed my veil today to get *masahni*. You may see my face now. My life was stuck in my eyes just to see your face. You must come along up to the graveyard and place a handful of soil on my face as your *masahni*. Otherwise, I will carry my craving for your *masahni* with me to my grave...'

Bibliography

SECONDARY SOURCES

Ahmed, Naseem, *Women in Islam*, Vols I and II, Delhi: APH Publishing Corporation, 2003.

Ahmed, Aziz and G.E. Grunebaum (eds), *Muslim Self-Statement in India and Pakistan, 1875–1968*, Wiesbaden: Otto Harrassowitz, 1970.

Ahmed, Mohamad Akhlaq, *Traditional Education Among Muslims*, New Delhi: B.R. Publishing, 1985.

Amin, Sonia Nishat, *The World of Muslim Women in Colonial Bengal 1876–1939*, Leiden: E.J. Brill, 1996.

Andrews, C.F., *Zaka Ullah of Delhi*, Cambridge: W. Heffer and Sons, 1929.

Asaduddin, M., *Ismat Chugtai*, New Delhi: Sahitya Akademi, 1999.

Badran, Margot and Miriam Cooke, *Opening the Gates: A Century of Arab Feminist Writing*, London: Virago Press, 1990.

Barr, Pat, *The Memsahibs*, London: Secker and Warburg, 1976.

Chandra, Sudhir, *The Oppressive Present*, Delhi: OUP, 1992

Chatterjee, Partha, *The Nation and its Fragments*, Delhi: OUP, 1997.

Clark, T.W. *The Novel in India*, London: George Allen and Unwin, 1970.

Chintamani, C.Y. (ed.), *Indian Social Reform*, Madras: Thompson, 1901.

Cousins, James H., *The Renaissance of India*, Madras: Ganesh and Co., 1918.

Cousins, Margaret E., *Indian Womanhood Today*, Allahabad: Kitabistan, 1941.

Dyson K.K., *A Various Universe: A study of the journals and memoirs of British men and women in the Indian sub-continent 1765–1856*, New Delhi: OUP, 1978.

Engles, Dagmar, *Beyond Purdah?: Women in Bengal 1890–1930*, New Delhi: OUP, 1999.

Engineer, Asghar Ali, *Islam and Liberation Theology: Essays on liberative elements in Islam*, New Delhi: Sterling, 1990.

Everett, Jana Matson, *Women and Social Change in India*, Delhi: Heritage Publishers, 1978.

Forbes, Geraldine, *Women in Modern India*, Cambridge: Cambridge University Press, 1998.

Fuller, Mrs Marcus B., *The Wrongs of Indian Womanhood*, Edinburgh and London: Oliphant Anderson and Ferrier, 1899.

Futehally, Laeeq, *Badruddin Tyabji*, New Delhi: National Book Trust, 1994.

Fyzee, A.A.A., *A Modern Approach to Islam*, Bombay: Asia Publishing House, 1963.

Ghose, Indira (ed.), *Memsahibs Abroad: Writing by women travelers in the nineteenth century*, Delhi: OUP, 1998.

Graham, G.F.I., *The Life and Works of Sir Syed Ahmad Khan*, Karachi: OUP, 1974, first edn 1885.

Harrison, Fraser, *The Dark Angel: Aspects of Victorian Sexuality*, UK: Fontana, 1979.

Hay, Stephen, *Sources of Indian Tradition*, Vol. II, first edited by Theodore de Bary with Stephen Hay and J.H. Qureshi, Columbia: Columbia University Press, 1988, Delhi: Viking, 1998.

Holmstrom, Lakshmi (ed.), *The Inner Courtyard: Stories by Indian Women*, London: Virgo Press, 1990.

Ikramullah, Begum Shaista S., *Husayn Shaheed Suhrawardy: A Biography*, Karachi: OUP, 1991.

Ingham, Kenneth, *Reformers in India 1793–1833: An account of the work of Christian missionaries on behalf of social reform*, Cambridge: Cambridge University Press, 1956.

Jain, Jasbir and Amina Amin, *Margins of Erasure: Purdah in the subcontinental novel in English*, New Delhi: Sterling, 1995.

Jayawardena, Kumari, *Feminism and Nationalism in the Third World*, UK: Zed Books, 1986, Delhi: Kali for Women, 1986.

Jones, K.W., *Socio-Religious Reform Movements in British India*, Cambridge: Cambridge University Press, 1989.

Jung, Anees, *Night of the New Moon: Encounters with Muslim women in India*, New Delhi: Penguin, 1993.

Kasturi, Leela and Vina Mazumdar (eds), *Women and Indian Nationalism*, New Delhi: Vikas, 1994.

Kaul, H.K. (ed.), *Travellers' India: An Anthology*, Delhi: OUP, 1979.

Khan, Mazhar Ul Haq, *Purdah and Polygamy*, Delhi: Amar Prakashan, 1982.

Khan, Mohammed Shabbir, *Status of Women in Islam*, Delhi: A.P.H Publishing Corporation, 1996.

Kumar, Sukrita Paul and Sadique, *Ismat: Her Life, Her Times*, New Delhi: Katha, 2000.

Mill, John Stuart, *The Subjection of Women*, Cambridge, Mass. and London: The MIT Press, 1970; first edn London: Longmans, Green, Reader and Dyer, 1869.

Minault, Gail, *Secluded Scholars*, Delhi: OUP, 1998.

Mukhopadhyaya, Sambhu Chandra, *The Career of an Indian Princess—The late Secunder of Bhopal*, KSI, Calcutta, 1869.

Noorani, A.G., *Badruddin Tyabji*, New Delhi: Govt of India Publications Division, 1969.

Papanek, Hanna and Gail Miault (eds), *Separate Worlds*, New Delhi: Chanakya, 1982.

Ratan, Jai, *Modern Urdu Short Stories*, Delhi: Allied Pub., 1987.

Ray, Bharati (ed.), *From the Seams of History: Essays on Indian Women*, Delhi: OUP, 1995.

Ray, Bharati, *Early Feminists of Colonial India*, New Delhi: OUP, 2002.

Robinson, Catherine A., *Tradition and Liberation: The Hindu Tradition in the Indian Women's Movement*, UK: Curzon Press, 1999.

Russell, Ralph, *The Pursuit of Urdu Literature: A Select History*, Delhi: OUP, 1992.

Ruthven, Malise, *Islam in the World*, London: Penguin, 1984.

Thanvi, Ashraf Ali, *Islamic Renaissance*, trans. and ed. Abdullah Muhammad, New Delhi: Adam Pub., 1997.

Tyabji, Badruddin, *More Memoirs of an Egoist*, New Delhi: Har-Anand Pub., 1994.

Zastoupil, Lynn, *John Stuart Mill and India*, Stanford: Stanford University Press, 1994.